Homicide

David Simon's *Homicide* won an Edgar Award and became the basis for the NBC award-winning drama. Simon's second book, *The Corner: A Year in the Life of an Inner-City Neighborhood*, co-authored with Edward Burns, was made into an HBO mini-series. Simon is currently the executive producer and writer for HBO's Peabody Award-winning series *The Wire*. He lives in Baltimore.

'A frank, insightful, and meticulously detailed look at detectives and their work.' SAN FRANCISCO CHRONICLE

'From the blood on the street to the repartee in the squad room, from autopsy etiquette to office politics, Simon gives us the homicide cop's beat – monstrous, draining, bleakly fascinating – as it's never been seen before.' ENTERTAINMENT WEEKLY

'One of the most engrossing police procedural mystery books ever written, not only because the crimes and plots and personalities are real, but because Simon is a terrific writer.' NEWSDAY

'The world of urban violence has never been so well portrayed, nor has the day-to-day craft of the detective.' CHICAGO TRIBUNE

'Simon has captured the poetry of the meanest streets.'
LOS ANGELES TIMES

'*Homicide* and its cast of living, swearing, thinking investigators exalt you on one page and knock you down on the next: wonderful victories for justice and humanity, but also heartbreaking unfairness, cruelty and meaninglessness.' BALTIMORE SUN

'An amazingly frank and often hilarious tribute to homicide detectives everywhere, whose ranks, like those in Baltimore, are filled with great, good and mediocre talent . . . [Simon] has taken the art of covering cops to a new high.' WASHINGTON TIMES

'With empathy, psychological nuance, racy verbatim dialogue and razor-sharp prose, he offers a rare insider's look at the detective's tension-wracked world.' PUBLISHERS WEEKLY

Also by David Simon

The Corner: A Year in the Life of an Inner-City Neighborhood
(co-authored with Edward Burns)

HOMICIDE
A YEAR ON THE KILLING STREETS

DAVID SIMON

CANONGATE
Edinburgh · London · New York · Melbourne

This edition first published in Great Britain in 2008 by
Canongate Books Ltd, 14 High Street, Edinburgh EH1 1TE

First published in Great Britain in 1992 by Hodder & Stoughton Ltd

Originally published in hardcover in 1991 by Houghton Mifflin Company,
222 Berkeley Street, Boston, Massachusetts 02116
Originally published in paperback in 1993 by Ballantine Books,
Random House, Inc, 1745 Broadway, New York, New York 10019
Published in paperback in 2006 by Holt Paperbacks, Henry Holt and Company, LLC,
175 Fifth Avenue, New York, New York 10010

5

British Library Cataloguing-in-Publication Data
A catalogue record for this book is available on
request from the British Library

ISBN 978 1 84767 311 4

Designed by Meryl Sussman Levavi

This book is printed on FSC certified paper

Printed and bound by CPI Mackays, Chatham ME5 8TD

www.meetatthegate.com

For Linda

HOMICIDE

If a man is found slain, lying in a field in the land the Lord your God is giving you to possess, and it is not known who killed him, your elders and judges shall go out and measure the distance from the body to the neighboring towns.

Then the elders of the town nearest the body shall take a heifer that has never been worked and has never worn a yoke and lead her down to a valley that has not been plowed or planted and where there is a flowing stream.

There in the valley they are to break the heifer's neck.

The priests, the sons of Levi, shall step forward, for the Lord your God has chosen them to minister and to pronounce blessings in the name of the Lord and to decide all cases of dispute and assault.

Then all the elders of the town nearest the body shall wash their hands over the heifer whose neck was broken in the valley and they shall declare:

"Our hands did not shed this blood, nor did our eyes see it done. Accept this atonement for your people Israel, whom you have redeemed, O Lord, and do not hold your people guilty of the blood of an innocent man."

Deuteronomy 21: 1–9

In contact wounds, the muzzle of the weapon is held against the surface of the body . . . the immediate edges of the entrance are seared by hot gases and blackened by the soot. This is embedded in the seared skin and cannot be completely removed either by washing or vigorous scrubbing of the wound.

Vincent J. M. DiMaio M.D.,
Gunshot Wounds: Practical Aspects of Firearms, Ballistics and Forensic Technique

ANTE MORTEM

by

Richard Price

Jimmy Breslin once wrote of Damon Runyon, "He did what all good journalists do—he hung out." But in *Homicide*, his year-in-the-life chronicle of the Baltimore Police Department's Homicide Unit, David Simon didn't just hang out; he pitched a tent. As both a reporter and a dramatist Simon has always held the conviction that God is a first-rate novelist and to *be there* when He's strutting his stuff is not only legitimate but honorable, part and parcel of fighting the good fight. Simon is a great collector and interpreter of facts, but he's also junkie and his addiction is to bearing witness.

I say this with authority (it takes one to know one), and the addiction plays itself out like this: whatever we see out on the street—with the police, with the corner boys, with people who are just trying to survive with their families intact in a world sewn with every kind of land mine—only whets our desire to see more, to hang and to hang and to hang with whoever will have us in an endless quest for some kind of urban Ur-Truth. Our bedside prayer: Please, Lord, just one more day, one more night, let me see something, hear something that will be the key, the golden metaphor for all of it, which, as any degenerate gambler knows, is in the very next roll of the dice. Truth is right around the next corner, in the next bit of throwaway street commentary, the next radio call, the next hand-to-hand drug transaction, the next unfurling of crime scene tape, as the beast that is Baltimore, is New York, is urban America, like some insatiable Sphinx whose riddles aren't even intelligible, continues to gobble up one benighted soul after another.

Or maybe it's just our inability to meet deadlines. . . .

I first met Simon on April 29, 1992, the night of the Rodney King riots. We had both just published Big Books: Simon's was the book in your hands; mine was a novel, *Clockers*. We were brought together by our mutual editor, John Sterling. The moment was almost comical: "David this is Richard; Richard, David. You guys should be friends—you have so much in common." And so of course the first thing we did was make a beeline over the river to Jersey City, one of the hot spots that night, where we were met by Larry Mullane, a Hudson County Homicide detective and my ace Virgil for the previous three years of my writing life. David's father had grown up in JC, the Mullanes and Simons had likely crossed paths over the generations, and so it went. The JC riots themselves proved elusive, perpetually around the corner but offstage, and my main recollection of that night is Simon's compulsion to *be there*, which for me was like running into my long-lost Siamese twin.

Our second encounter was a few years later when, in the aftermath of the Susan Smith horror in South Carolina, I was on something of a Medea tour laying the groundwork for my novel *Freedomland.* There had been a vaguely similar tragedy in Baltimore: the white mother of two biracial girls had torched her rowhouse while her young daughters were asleep. Her alleged motive was to clear any obstacles from the path of true love with her new boyfriend, who she said was less than thrilled about her two kids (a suggestion he later denied).

Working the phones, David hooked me up with whatever principals were available to be interviewed—the arresting detectives, the mother's boyfriend, the thrice-bereaved grandmother, the Arab who owned the corner store across the street where the mother had fled, ostensibly to call 911. (Her first call, the store owner said, was to her mother, her second to report the fire.) Journalistically, the story was past its expiration date, but Simon, in his willingness to get *me* the story, reverted to work mode. It was the first time I ever had to keep pace with a street reporter both mentally and physically; in addition to securing all the interviews, this also involved unsuccessfully trying to jive and con our way past the uniform still guarding the crime scene; shrugging off the straight-arm and working an end run; circling around and scaling backyard fences until we found ourselves inside the blackened rowhouse; and climbing what was left of the stairs to enter the small bedroom where the two girls died of smoke inhalation. At last we were there, and it was like standing inside the gut of a translucent tiger, the two of us staring everywhere—walls, ceiling, floor—at the charred striations left by the flames. A devastating little chip of hell.

But let's go back to that first night in Jersey City. At one point during the evening there were rumors that the rioters were stringing piano wire across the streets to decapitate motorcycle cops, and Larry Mullane, an ex–motorcycle cop himself, abruptly had to leave us. We found ourselves alone in an unmarked police car (an oxymoron if there ever was one), with me behind the wheel and Simon in the passenger seat. Mullane's advice to us was, "Keep it moving—and if anybody comes up on you, just try to look pissed off and floor it." That's basically what we did, which brings me to a question that has always plagued me: Are writers like us, writers who are obsessed with chronicling in fact and fiction the minutiae of life in the urban trenches of America, writers who are dependent in large part on the noblesse of the cops to see what we have to see, are we (oh shit . . .) police buffs?

And the answer I've come to believe is: No more than we are criminal buffs or civilian buffs. But for whoever allows us to walk a mile in their shoes, on either side of the law, we do feel an unavoidable empathy—in essence we become "embedded." But it's not as sinister as it sounds as long as your Thank You mantra goes something like this: As a chronicler I will honor you with the faithful reporting of what I see and hear while a guest in the house of your life. As for how you come off, you dig your own grave or build your own monument by being who you are, so good luck and thanks for your time.

Simon writes with great thoroughness and clarity about the impossibility of the job of homicide investigator. For the murder police in the field, it's not only the body lying before them that has to be dealt with but also what they carry on their backs, which is the entire hierarchy of bosses who answer to bosses—the weight of bureaucratic self-preservation. Despite the overpopularization of *CSI*-style forensic advances, at times it must seem like the only reliable science for these investigators at the bottom of the food chain is the physics of careerism, which simply and reliably states that once a murder hits the papers or touches any kind of political nerve, the shit will always roll downhill. The best of them—those who more often than not, under great if superfluous pressure, turn the red names on the board to black—are left with an air of world-weariness and well-earned elitist pride.

Homicide is a day-in, day-out journal, an intermingling of the mundane and the biblically heinous, and Simon's eagerness and avidity to absorb, to digest, to *be there* and convey the world before his eyes to the universe beyond, runs through every page. There is a love for everything he witnesses, an implicit belief in the beauty of simply stating that whatever he sees playing itself out in real time is "The Truth" of a world—this is how it is, this is how it works, this is what people say, how they act, act out, dissociate, justify, where they come up short, transcend themselves, survive, go under.

Simon also exhibits a knack for keying in on the enormity of little things: the quality of mild surprise in the half-closed eyes of the freshly dead, the ineffable poetry of a throwaway non sequitur, the physical ballet of aimlessness on the corners, the unconscious dance of rage and boredom and joy. He documents the gestures, the rueful misnomers, the way the eyes cut, the mouth tightens. He records the unexpected civilities between adversaries, the gallows humor that allegedly saves one's sanity or humanity or whatever the excuse is for making jokes at the expense of the recently murdered, the breathtaking stupidity that propels most homicidal actions, the survival strategies adopted by people living in the most dire circumstances in order simply to make it through one more day. He captures how the streets themselves are a narcotic for the cops as well as the street soldiers (and the occasional writer), everyone jacked for the next predictable yet unexpected bit of drama that will put both sides in motion and send the innocents caught in the middle dropping for cover beneath the bedroom window or huddling in the supposedly bulletproof bathtub—the family that ducks together stays together. And time after time he hammers home the fact that there's very little Black and White out there, and a hell of a lot of Gray.

Homicide is a war story, and the theater of engagement stretches from the devastated rowhouses of East and West Baltimore to the halls of the state legislature in Annapolis. It reveals with no small irony how survival games on the streets mirror survival games in city hall, how all who engage in the drug war live and die by the numbers—kilos, ounces, grams, pills, profits for one side; crimes, arrests, solve rates, and budget cuts for the other. The book is a realpolitik examination of a municipality in the midst of a slow-motion riot, but through the steadfastness of Simon's presence *Homicide* offers us the patterns hidden within the chaos. Baltimore, in fact, is Chaos Theory incarnate.

With the success of the television adaptation of this book, Simon has been able to branch out into drama—the brilliant six-part miniseries based on his follow-up book, *The Corner* (co-written with Ed Burns), and the Russian novel of an HBO series, *The Wire.* With these later projects he gets to kick out the jams a little, to nudge and mastermind the truth into a slightly artificial shapeliness to heighten the big-ticket social issues. But even with the creative freedom of fiction, his work remains an exaltation of nuance, a continuing exploration of how the smallest external act can create the greatest internal revolution—in the life of a single marginalized person or in the spiritual and political biorhythm of a major American city.

All of which is to say that if Edith Wharton came back from the dead, developed a bent for municipal power brokers, cops, crackheads and reportage, and didn't really care what she wore to the office, she'd probably look a little something like David Simon.

The Players

Lieutenant Gary D'Addario
Shift Commander

Detective Sergeant Terrence McLarney
Squad Supervisor

Detective Donald Worden
Detective Rick James
Detective Edward Brown
Detective Donald Waltemeyer
Detective David John Brown

Detective Sergeant Roger Nolan
Squad Supervisor

Detective Harry Edgerton
Detective Richard Garvey
Detective Robert Bowman
Detective Donald Kincaid
Detective Robert McAllister

Detective Sergeant Jay Landsman
Squad Supervisor

Detective Tom Pellegrini
Detective Oscar Requer
Detective Gary Dunnigan
Detective Richard Fahlteich
Detective Fred Ceruti

HOMICIDE

ONE

TUESDAY, JANUARY 19

Pulling one hand from the warmth of a pocket, Jay Landsman squats down to grab the dead man's chin, pushing the head to one side until the wound becomes visible as a small, ovate hole, oozing red and white.

"Here's your problem," he said. "He's got a slow leak."

"A leak?" says Pellegrini, picking up on it.

"A slow one."

"You can fix those."

"Sure you can," Landsman agrees. "They got these home repair kits now . . ."

"Like with tires."

"Just like with tires," Landsman says. "Comes with a patch and everything else you need. Now a bigger wound, like from a thirty-eight, you're gonna have to get a new head. This one you could fix."

Landsman looks up, his face the very picture of earnest concern.

Sweet Jesus, thinks Tom Pellegrini, nothing like working murders with a mental case. One in the morning, heart of the ghetto, half a dozen uniforms watching their breath freeze over another dead man—what better time and place for some vintage Landsman, delivered in perfect deadpan until even the shift commander is laughing hard in the blue strobe of the emergency lights. Not that a Western District midnight shift is the world's toughest audience; you don't ride a radio car for any length of time in Sector 1 or 2 without cultivating a diseased sense of humor.

"Anyone know this guy?" asks Landsman. "Anyone get to talk to him?"

"Fuck no," says a uniform. "He was ten-seven when we got here."

Ten-seven. The police communication code for "out of service" artlessly applied to a human life. Beautiful. Pellegrini smiles, content in the knowledge that nothing in this world can come between a cop and his attitude.

"Anyone go through his pockets?" asks Landsman.

"Not yet."

"Where the fuck are his pockets?"

"He's wearing pants underneath the sweatsuit."

Pellegrini watches Landsman straddle the body, one foot on either side of the dead man's waist, and begin tugging violently at the sweat-pants. The awkward effort jerks the body a few inches across the side-walk, leaving a thin film of matted blood and brain matter where the head wound scrapes the pavement. Landsman forces a meaty hand inside a front pocket.

"Watch for needles," says a uniform.

"Hey," says Landsman. "Anyone in this crowd gets AIDS, no one's gonna believe it came from a fucking needle."

The sergeant pulls his hand from the dead man's right front pocket, causing perhaps a dollar in change to fall to the sidewalk.

"No wallet in front. I'm gonna wait and let the ME roll him. Some-body's called the ME, right?"

"Should be on the way," says a second uniform, taking notes for the top sheet of an incident report. "How many times is he hit?"

Landsman points to the head wound, then lifts a shoulder blade to re-veal a ragged hole in the upper back of the dead man's leather jacket.

"Once in the head, once in the back." Landsman pauses, and Pelle-grini watches him go deadpan once again. "It could be more."

The uniform puts pen to paper.

"There is a possibility," says Landsman, doing his best to look profes-sorial, "a good possibility, he was shot twice through the same bullethole."

"No shit," says the uniform, believing.

A mental case. They give him a gun, a badge and sergeant's stripes, and deal him out into the streets of Baltimore, a city with more than its share of violence, filth and despair. Then they surround him with a chorus of blue-jacketed straight men and let him play the role of the lone, wayward joker that somehow slipped into the deck. Jay Landsman, of the sidelong smile and pockmarked face, who tells the mothers of wanted men that all the commo-tion is nothing to be upset about, just a routine murder warrant. Landsman, who leaves empty liquor bottles in the other sergeants' desks and never fails to turn out the men's room light when a ranking officer is indisposed. Lands-man, who rides a headquarters elevator with the police commissioner and leaves complaining that some sonofabitch stole his wallet. Jay Landsman, who as a Southwestern patrolman parked his radio car at Edmondson and Hilton, then used a Quaker Oatmeal box covered in aluminum foil as a radar gun.

"I'm just giving you a warning this time," he would tell grateful motorists. "Remember, only you can prevent forest fires."

And now, but for the fact that Landsman can no longer keep a straight face, there might well be an incident report tracked to Central Records in the departmental mail, complaint number 88-7A37548, indicating that said victim appeared to be shot once in the head and twice in the back through the same bullethole.

"No, hey, I'm joking," he says finally. "We won't know anything for sure until the autopsy tomorrow."

He looks at Pellegrini.

"Hey, Phyllis, I'm gonna let the ME roll him."

Pellegrini manages a half-smile. He's been Phyllis to his squad sergeant ever since that long afternoon at Rikers Island in New York, when a jail matron refused to honor a writ and release a female prisoner into the custody of two male detectives from Baltimore; the regulations required a policewoman for the escort. After a sufficient amount of debate, Landsman grabbed Tom Pellegrini, a thick-framed Italian born to Allegheny coal miner stock, and pushed him forward.

"Meet Phyllis Pellegrini," Landsman said, signing for the prisoner. "She's my partner."

"How do you do?" Pellegrini said with no hesitation.

"You're not a woman," said the matron.

"But I used to be."

With the blue strobe glancing off his pale face, Tom Pellegrini moves a step closer to take stock of what half an hour earlier had been a twenty-six-year-old street dealer. The dead man is sprawled on his back, legs in the gutter, arms partly extended, head facing north near the side door of a corner rowhouse. Dark brown eyes are fixed under half-lids in that expression of vague recognition so common to the newly and suddenly departed. It is not a look of horror, consternation, or even distress. More often than not, the last visage of a murdered man resembles that of a flustered schoolchild to whom the logic of a simple equation has just been revealed.

"If you're okay here," says Pellegrini, "I'm gonna go across the street."

"What's up?"

"Well . . ."

Landsman moves closer and Pellegrini lowers his voice, as if the spoken suggestion that there may be a witness to this murder would be an embarrassing display of optimism.

"There's a woman who went into a house across the street. Someone told one of the first officers she was outside when the shooting started."

"She saw it?"

"Well, supposedly she told people it was three black males in dark clothes. They ran north after the shots."

It isn't much, and Pellegrini can read his sergeant's mind: three yos wearing black, a description that narrows the list to about half the fucking city. Landsman nods vaguely and Pellegrini begins making his way across Gold Street, stepping carefully around the patches of ice that cover much of the intersection. It is early morning now, half past two, and the temperature is well below freezing. A bracing wind catches the detective in the center of the street, cutting through his overcoat. On the other side of Etting, the locals have gathered to mark the event, younger men and teenagers signifying, scoping the unexpected entertainment, each one straining to catch a glimpse of the dead man's face across the street. Jokes are exchanged and stories whispered, but even the youngest knows to avert his eyes and fall silent at a first question from a uniform. There is no good reason to do otherwise, because in a half hour the dead man will be laid out on a table for one at the ME's chop shop on Penn Street, the Western men will be stirring coffee at the Monroe Street 7-Eleven and the dealers will be selling blue-topped caps again at this godforsaken crossroads of Gold and Etting. Nothing said now is going to change any of that.

The crowd watches Pellegrini cross the street, eyefucking him in a way that only the west side corner boys can as he walks to a painted stone stoop and hits a wood door with a rapid, three-beat motion. Waiting for a response, the detective watches a battered Buick roll west on Gold, idling slowly toward and then past him. Brake lights flash for a moment as the car approaches the blue strobes on the other side of the street. Pellegrini turns to watch the Buick roll a few blocks farther west to the Brunt Street corners, where a small coterie of runners and touts have resumed work, selling heroin and cocaine a respectful distance from the murder scene. The Buick shows its taillights again, and a lone figure slips from one corner and leans into the driver's window. Business is business, and the Gold Street market waits for no man, certainly not the dead dealer across the street.

Pellegrini knocks again and steps close to the door, listening for movement inside. From upstairs comes a muffled sound. The detective exhales slowly and raps again, bringing a young girl to a second-floor window in the next rowhouse.

"Hey there," Pellegrini says, "police department."

"Uh-huh."

"Do you know if Katherine Thompson lives next door?"

"Yeah, she do."

"Is she home now?"

"Guess so."

Heavy pounding on the door is answered at last by a light from upstairs, where a frame window is suddenly and violently wrenched upward. A heavyset, middle-aged woman—fully dressed, the detective notes—pushes head and shoulders across the sill and stares down at Pellegrini.

"Who the hell is knocking on my door this late?"

"Mrs. Thompson?"

"Yeah."

"Police."

"Poh-leece?"

Jesus Christ, Pellegrini thinks, what else would a white man in a trenchcoat be doing on Gold Street after midnight? He pulls the shield and holds it toward the window.

"Could I talk to you for a moment?"

"No, you can't," she says, expelling the words in a singsong, slow enough and loud enough to reach the crowd across the street. "I got nothing to say to you. People be trying to sleep and you knocking on my door this late."

"You were asleep?"

"I ain't got to say what I was."

"I need to talk with you about the shooting."

"Well, I ain't got a damn thing to say to you."

"Someone died . . ."

"I know it."

"We're investigating it."

"So?"

Tom Pellegrini suppresses an almost overwhelming desire to see this woman dragged into a police wagon and bounced over every pothole between here and headquarters. Instead, he looks hard at the woman's face and speaks his last words in a laconic tone that betrays only weariness.

"I can come back with a grand jury summons."

"Then come on back with your damn summons. You come here this time a night telling me I got to talk to you when I don't want to."

Pellegrini steps back from the front stoop and looks at the blue glow from the emergency lights. The morgue wagon, a Dodge van with blacked-out windows, has pulled to the curb, but every kid on every corner is now gazing across the street, watching this woman make it perfectly clear to a police detective that under no circumstances is she a living witness to a drug murder.

"It's your neighborhood."

"Yeah, it is," she says, slamming the window.

Pellegrini shakes his head gently, then walks back across the street, arriving in time to watch the crew of the morgue wagon roll the body. From a jacket pocket comes a wristwatch and keys. From a rear pants pocket comes an identification card. Newsome, Rudolph Michael, male, black, date of birth 3/5/61, address 2900 Allendale.

Landsman pulls the white rubber gloves from his hands, drops them in the gutter and looks at his detective.

"Anything?" he asks.

"No," says Pellegrini.

Landsman shrugs. "I'm glad it's you that got this one."

Pellegrini's chiseled face creases into a small, brief smile, accepting his sergeant's declaration of faith for the consolation prize it is. With less than two years in homicide, Tom Pellegrini is generally regarded to be the hardest worker in Sergeant Jay Landsman's squad of five detectives. And that matters now, because both men know that Baltimore's thirteenth homicide of 1988, handed to them on the second leg of a midnight shift at the corner of Gold and Etting, is an exceptionally weak sister: a drug killing with no known witnesses, no specific motive and no suspects. Perhaps the only person in Baltimore who might have managed some real interest in the case is at this moment being shoveled onto a body litter. Rudy Newsome's brother will make the identification later that morning outside a freezer door across from the autopsy room, but after that the boy's family will offer little else. The morning newspaper will print not a line about the killing. The neighborhood, or whatever is left around Gold and Etting that resembles a neighborhood, will move on. West Baltimore, home of the misdemeanor homicide.

All of which is not to say that any man in Landsman's squad wouldn't give Rudy Newsome's murder a shake or two. A police department is fueled by its own stats, and a homicide clearance—any clearance—will always earn a detective some court time and a few attaboys. But Pellegrini is playing the game for more than that: He's a detective still in the process of proving things to himself, hungry for more experience and fresh to the daily grind. Landsman has watched him build cases on murders about which nothing should have been learned. The Green case from the Lafayette Court projects. Or that shooting outside Odell's up on North Avenue, the one where Pellegrini walked up and down a bombed-out alley, kicking trash until he found a spent .38 slug that put the case down. To Landsman, the amazing thing is that Tom Pellegrini, a ten-year veteran of the force, came to homicide straight from the City Hall security detail only weeks after the mayor became the odds-on favorite for governor in a Democratic primary landslide. It was a political appointment, plain and simple, handed down from the deputy commissioner for services as if the governor himself had poured the oil on Pellegrini's head. Everyone in homicide assumed that the new man would need about three months to prove himself an absolute hump.

"Well," says Pellegrini, squeezing behind the wheel of an unmarked Chevy Cavalier, "so far so good."

Landsman laughs. "This one will go down, Tom."

Pellegrini shoots back a look that Landsman ignores. The Cavalier slips past block after block of rowhouse ghetto, rolling down Druid Hill Avenue until it crosses Martin Luther King Boulevard and the Western District gives way to the early morning emptiness of downtown. The chill is keeping them in; even the drunks are gone from the Howard Street benches. Pellegrini slows before running every light until he catches the red signal at Lexington and Calvert, a few blocks from headquarters, where a lone whore, unmistakably a transvestite, gestures furtively at the car from the doorway of a corner office. Landsman laughs. Pellegrini wonders how any prostitute in this city could fail to understand the significance of a Chevy Cavalier with a six-inch antenna on its ass.

"Look at this pretty motherfucker," says Landsman. "Let's pull over and fuck with him."

The car eases through the intersection and pulls to the curb. Landsman rolls down the passenger window. The whore's face is hard, a man's face.

"Hey, sir."

The whore looks away in cold rage.

"Hey, mister," yells Landsman.

"I ain't no mister," the whore says, walking back to the corner.

"Sir, would you have the time?"

"Go fuck yourself."

Landsman laughs malevolently. One of these days, Pellegrini knows, his sergeant will say something bizarre to someone who matters and half the squad will be writing reports for a week.

"I think you hurt his feelings."

"Well," says Landsman, still laughing, "I didn't mean to."

A few minutes later, the two men are backed into a parking space on the second tier of the headquarters garage. On the bottom of the same page recording the particulars of Rudy Newsome's death, Pellegrini writes the number of the parking space and the mileage on the odometer, then circles the two figures. Murders come and go in this town, but God forbid you should forget to write the correct mileage on your activity sheet or, worse yet, forget to note the parking space so that the next man out spends fifteen minutes walking up and down the headquarters garage, trying to figure out which Cavalier matches the ignition key in his hand.

Pellegrini follows Landsman across the garage and through a metal bulkhead door to the second-floor hallway. Landsman punches the elevator button.

"I wonder what Fahlteich got from Gatehouse Drive."

"Was that a murder?" asks Pellegrini.

"Yeah. It sounded like it on the radio."

The elevator slowly ascends, opening on another, similar corridor with waxed linoleum and hospital blue walls, and Pellegrini follows his sergeant down the long hall. From inside the aquarium—the soundproof room of metal and plate glass where witnesses sit before being interviewed—comes the sound of young girls laughing softly.

Hail Mary. Here be witnesses from Fahlteich's shooting at the city's other end—living, breathing witnesses brought forth by the gods from the scene of the new year's fourteenth homicide. What the hell, thinks Pellegrini, at least somebody in the squad had a little luck tonight.

The voices in the aquarium slip away as the two men move down the hall. Just before turning the corner into the squadroom, Pellegrini looks into the darkened aquarium's side door and glimpses the orange glow of a cigarette and the outline of the woman seated closest to the door. He sees a hard face, the deep brown features fixed like granite, the eyes offering only seasoned contempt. Helluva body, too: nice chest, good legs, yellow miniskirt. Someone probably would have said something by now if she wasn't all attitude.

Mistaking this casual assessment for genuine opportunity, the girl saunters from the aquarium to the edge of the office, then knocks lightly on the metal frame.

"Can I make a call?"

"Who do you want to talk to?"

"My ride."

"No, not now. After you're interviewed."

"What about my ride?"

"One of the uniformed officers will take you home."

"I've been here an hour," she says, crossing her legs in the doorway. The woman has the face of a teamster, but she's giving this her best shot. Pellegrini is unimpressed. He can see Landsman smiling at him wickedly from the other side of the office.

"We'll get to you as fast as we can."

Abandoning any thought of seduction, the woman walks back to join her girlfriend on the fishbowl's green vinyl couch, crosses her legs again and lights another cigarette.

The woman is here because she had the misfortune to be inside a garden apartment in the Purnell Village complex on Gatehouse Drive, where a Jamaican drug dealer named Carrington Brown played host to another Jake by the name of Roy Johnson. There was some preliminary talk, a few accusations delivered in a lilting West Indian accent, and then a considerable amount of gunfire.

Dick Fahlteich, a balding, bantam-size veteran of Landsman's squad, got the call minutes after the dispatcher sent Pellegrini and his sergeant to Gold Street. He arrived to find Roy Johnson dead in the living room with more than a dozen gunshot wounds afflicting every conceivable part of his body. His host, Carrington Brown, was on the way to the University Hospital emergency room with four chest wounds. There were bulletholes in the walls, bulletholes in the furniture, automatic .380 casings and hysterical women scattered across the apartment. Fahlteich and two crime lab techs would spend the next five hours pulling evidence out of the place.

That leaves Landsman and Pellegrini to sort through the witnesses sent downtown. Their interviews begin reasonably and orderly enough; taking turns, the detectives escort each witness into a separate office, fill out an information sheet and write out a statement of several pages for the witness to sign and date. The work is routine and repetitive; in the last year alone, Pellegrini has probably debriefed a couple hundred witnesses, most of them liars, all of them reluctant.

The process abruptly enters its second, more intensive phase a half hour later when an enraged Landsman hurls a four-page statement to the floor of a back office, slams his hand on a desk, and screams for the girl in the yellow miniskirt to get her ugly, untruthful, drug-ridden self out of his office. Well, thinks Pellegrini, listening at the other end of the hall, it isn't taking Landsman long to get down to business.

"YOU'RE A LYING BITCH," Landsman shouts, slamming the office door against its rubber stop. "DO YOU THINK I'M STUPID? DO YOU FUCKING THINK I'M STUPID?"

"What did I lie about?"

"Get the fuck out of here. You're charged."

"Charged with what?"

Landsman's face contorts into pure rage.

"YOU THINK THIS IS BULLSHIT? DO YOU?"

The girl says nothing.

"You just got a charge, you lying piece of shit."

"I didn't lie."

"Fuck you. You're charged."

The sergeant points the woman toward the small interrogation room, where she slumps into a chair and stretches her legs up over a Formica table. The miniskirt rides down toward her waist, but Landsman is in no mood to enjoy the fact that the woman wears nothing under her skirt. He leaves the door slightly ajar as he yells to Pellegrini across the squadroom.

"NEUTRON THIS BITCH," he shouts before closing the soundproof door to the small interrogation room, leaving the girl to wonder what sort of technological torture awaits. A neutron activation test requires only a painless swab of the hands to determine the presence of barium and antimony, elements deposited after a handgun is fired, but Landsman wants to leave her stewing on it, hoping she's in that box imagining that someone's about to irradiate her until she glows. The sergeant slams his open palm against the metal door one last time for proper emphasis, but the rage is gone even as he walks back into the main office. A staged performance—more vintage Landsman—delivered with gusto and sincerity for the lying bitch in the yellow miniskirt.

Pellegrini comes out of the coffee room and closes the door.

"What does yours say?"

"She didn't see it," says Pellegrini. "But she said your girl knows what happened."

"I fucking know she does."

"What do you want to do?"

"Take the statement from your girl," says Landsman, bumming a cigarette from his detective. "I'm gonna let this one sit for a while, then go back in and fuck with her."

Pellegrini returns to the coffee room and Landsman slumps into a desk chair. Cigarette smoke slips from the side of his mouth.

"Fuck this," says Jay Landsman to no one in particular. "I'm not gonna swallow two open cases in one night."

And so a graceless, nocturnal ballet resumes, with witnesses gliding past one another beneath the washed-out glare of tube lighting, each flanked by a tired, impassive detective cradling black coffee and enough blank statement forms to record the next round of half-truths. Pages are collated, initialed, and signed, Styrofoam coffee cups are refilled and cigarettes bartered until the detectives again assemble in the squadroom to compare notes and decide who's lying, who's lying more, and who's lying the most. In another hour, Fahlteich will return from the murder scene and hospital with enough details to vouch for the one honest witness brought downtown that night—a woman who happened to be walking across the parking lot and recognized one of the two gunmen as he entered the apartment. The woman knows what it means to talk about a drug murder and soon wishes she could take back everything she said to Fahlteich at the scene. Sent downtown immediately, she has been kept at a distance from the occupants of the apartment and is interviewed by Landsman and Fahlteich only after the detective returns from Gatehouse Drive. She shakes violently when the detectives bring up the subject of grand jury testimony.

"I can't do that," she says, breaking into tears.

"There's no choice."

"My children . . ."

"We're not going to let anything happen."

Landsman and Fahlteich leave the office to talk softly in the hallway.

"She's fucking terrified," says Landsman.

"No shit."

"We gotta grand jury her first thing tomorrow, before she has a chance to start backing up."

"We also got to keep her separate from the others," says Fahlteich, throwing a finger toward the witnesses in the fishbowl. "I don't want any of them to get a look at her."

By morning, they will have a nickname and general description for the missing gunman, and by the end of the week, his full name, police identification number, mug shot and the address of the North Carolina relatives who are hiding him. A week more and the kid is back in Baltimore, charged with first-degree murder and a weapons violation.

The story of Roy Johnson's murder is brutal in its simplicity, simple in its brutality. The shooter is Stanley Gwynn, an eighteen-year-old moon-faced kid who served as bodyguard to Johnson, a New York cocaine connect who had armed his true and loyal subordinate with an Ingram Mac-11 .380 machine pistol. Johnson visited the Gatehouse Drive apartment because Carrington Brown owed him money for cocaine, and when Brown wouldn't pay, Gwynn ended the negotiations with a long burst from the Ingram, a weapon capable of firing six rounds a second.

It was an impulsive, awkward performance, the sort of thing to be expected from a teenager. The attack was so clearly telegraphed that Carrington Brown was afforded more than enough time to grab Roy Johnson and use him as a shield. Before the scene in front of him registered in Stanley Gwynn's brain, he had machine-gunned the man he was supposed to protect. The intended target, Carrington Brown, lay bleeding from four bullets that had somehow found their way past the dead man, and Stanley Gwynn—who will later take a second-degree plea and twenty-five years—ran in panic from the apartment building.

When the dayshift detectives bring early relief at 6:30, the Roy Johnson murder, case H88014, is tucked neatly inside a manila folder on the administrative lieutenant's desk. An hour later, Dick Fahlteich is headed home for a quick shower before returning downtown to attend the autopsy. For his part, Landsman will be in his own bed by 8:00 A.M.

But as sunlight and the sounds of the morning rush hour seep through the sixth-floor windows, the flotsam and jetsam of H88013—the murder at Gold and Etting—are still scattered in front of Tom Pellegrini, a coffee-logged wraith who stares vacantly at the first officer's report, at supplementals, evidence submission slips, body custody and fingerprint forms for the person of Rudolph Newsome. Fifteen minutes either way and Pellegrini could have been dispatched to the Gatehouse Drive shooting, where a living victim and living witnesses were waiting to give up a murder and add one more to the list of clearances. Instead, Pellegrini went to Gold and Etting, where a twenty-six-year-old dead man stared up at him with sudden, silent comprehension. Luck of the draw.

After Landsman's departure, Pellegrini works the edges of his little disaster for another ten hours—pulling the paperwork together, calling an assistant state's attorney about a grand jury summons for the Thompson woman and submitting the victim's effects to the evidence control unit in the basement of headquarters. Later that morning, a Western District patrolman calls the homicide unit about some corner boy who got locked up for drugs by the midnight shift and claimed to know about the Gold Street shooting. Seems the kid is willing to talk if he can make a lower bail on the drug charge. Pellegrini finishes his fifth cup of coffee before going back out to the Western to take a brief statement from the boy, who claims to have seen three men running north off Gold Street after hearing shots. The kid says he knows one of the men, but only by the name Joe—a statement just specific enough to match the true scenario, just vague enough to be of no practical use to the detective. Pellegrini wonders whether the kid was even there or whether he picked up what he could about the Gold Street murder while sitting in the lockup overnight, then did his best to turn the information around and try to barter out from under the drug charge.

Back in homicide, the detective slips the notes from the interview inside the case file for H88013 and then slides the folder underneath the Roy Johnson file on the desk of the administrative lieutenant, who has come and gone on the eight-to-four shift. Good news before bad. Then Pellegrini gives a man on four-to-twelve the keys to his Cavalier and goes home. It is a little after 7:00 P.M.

Four hours later, he's back for the midnight shift, hovering like a moth around the red pilot light of the coffee machine. Pellegrini takes a full cup into the squadroom, where Landsman begins playing with him.

"Hey, Phyllis," says the sergeant.

"Hey, Sarge."

"Your case is down, isn't it?"

"My case?"

"Yeah."

"Which case would that be?"

"The new one," says Landsman. "From Gold Street."

"Well," says Pellegrini, the words rolling out slowly, "I am ready to get a warrant."

"Oh yeah?"

"Yeah."

"Hmmm," says Landsman, blowing cigarette smoke at the television screen.

"Only one problem, though."

"What's that," says the sergeant, now smiling.

"I don't know who the warrant is for."

Landsman laughs until the cigarette smoke makes him cough.

"Don't worry, Tom," he says finally. "It'll go down."

This is the job:

You sit behind a government-issue metal desk on the sixth of ten floors in a gleaming, steel-frame death trap with poor ventilation, dysfunctional air conditioning, and enough free-floating asbestos to pad the devil's own jumpsuit. You eat $2.50 pizza specials and Italian cold cuts with extra hots from Marco's on Exeter Street while watching reruns of *Hawaii Five-O* on the communal nineteen-inch set with insubordinate horizontal hold. You answer the phone on the second or third bleat because Baltimore abandoned its AT&T equipment as a cost-saving measure and the new phone system doesn't ring so much as it emits metallic, sheeplike sounds. If a police dispatcher is on the other end of the call, you write down an address, the time, and the dispatcher's unit number on a piece of scratch paper or the back of a used three-by-five pawn shop submission card.

Then you beg or barter the keys to one of a half-dozen unmarked Chevrolet Cavaliers, grab your gun, a notepad, a flashlight and a pair of white rubber gloves and drive to the correct address where, in all probability, a uniformed police officer will be standing over a cooling human body.

You look at that body. You look at that body as if it were some abstract work of art, stare at it from every conceivable point of view in search of deeper meanings and textures. Why, you ask yourself, is this body here? What did the artist leave out? What did he put in? What was the artist thinking of? What the hell is wrong with this picture?

You look for reasons. Overdose? Heart attack? Gunshot wounds? Cutting? Are those defense wounds on the left hand? Jewelry? Wallet? Pockets turned inside out? Rigor mortis? Lividity? Why is there a blood trail, with droplets spattering in a direction away from the body?

You walk around the edges of the scene looking for spent bullets, casings, blood droplets. You get a uniform to canvass the houses or businesses nearby, or if you want it done right, you go door-to-door yourself, asking questions that the uniforms might never think to ask.

Then you use everything in the arsenal in the hope that something—anything—will work. The crime lab technicians recover weapons, bullets and casings for ballistic comparisons. If you're indoors, you have the techs take prints from doors and door handles, furniture and utensils. You examine the body and its immediate surroundings for loose hairs or fibers on the off chance that the trace evidence lab might actually put down a case now and then. You look for any other signs of disturbance, anything that doesn't appear to conform to its surroundings. If something strikes you—a loose pillowcase, a discarded beer can—you have a technician take it down to evidence control as well. Then you have the techs measure key distances and photograph the entire scene from every conceivable angle. You sketch the death scene in your own notebook, using a crude stickman for the victim and marking the original location of every piece of furniture and every piece of evidence recovered.

Assuming that the uniforms, upon arriving at the scene, were sharp enough to grab anyone within sight and send them downtown, you then go back to your office and throw as much street-corner psychology as you can at the people who found the body. You do the same thing with a few others who knew the victim, who rented a room to the victim, who employed the victim, who fucked, fought or fired drugs with the victim. Are they lying? Of course they're lying. Everyone lies. Are they lying more than they ordinarily would? Probably. Why are they lying? Do their half-truths conform to what you know from the crime scene or is it complete and unequivocal bullshit? Who should you yell at first? Who should you scream at loudest? Who gets threatened with an accessory to murder charge? Who gets the speech about leaving the interrogation room as either a witness or a suspect? Who gets offered the excuse—The Out—the suggestion that this poor bastard needed to be murdered, that anyone in their circumstance would have murdered him, that they only killed the bastard because he provoked them, that they didn't mean it and the gun went off accidentally, that they only fired in self-defense?

If all goes well, you lock someone up that night. If all goes not so well, you take what you know and run with it in the most promising direction, kicking a few more facts loose in the hope that something will give. When nothing gives, you wait a few weeks for the lab work to come back with a positive on the ballistics or the fibers or the semen. When the lab reports come back negative, you wait for the phone to ring. And when the phone doesn't ring, you let a little piece of you die. Then you go back to your desk and wait for another call from the dispatcher, who sooner or later will send you out to look at another body. Because in a city with 240 murders a year, there will always be another body.

Television has given us the myth of the raging pursuit, the high-speed chase, but in truth there is no such thing; if there were, God knows the Cavalier would throw a rod after a dozen blocks and you'd be writing a Form 95 in which you respectfully submit to your commanding officer the reasons why you drove a city-owned four-cylinder wonder into an early grave. And there are no fistfights or running gun battles: The glory days of thumping someone on a domestic call or letting a round or two fly in the heat of some gas station holdup ended when you came downtown from patrol. The murder police always get there after the bodies fall and a homicide detective leaving the office has to remind himself to take his .38 out of the top right desk drawer. And, most certainly, there are no perfectly righteous moments when a detective, a scientific wizard with uncanny powers of observation, leans down to examine a patch of bloody carpet, plucks up a distinctive strand of red-brown caucasoid hair, gathers his suspects in an exquisitely furnished parlor, and then declares his case to be solved. The truth is that there are very few exquisitely furnished parlors left in Baltimore; even if there were, the best homicide detectives will admit that in ninety cases out of a hundred, the investigator's saving grace is the killer's overwhelming predisposition toward incompetence or, at the very least, gross error.

More often than not, the murderer has left behind living witnesses or even bragged to someone about the crime. In a surprising number of cases, the killer—particularly one unfamiliar with the criminal justice system—can be manipulated into a confession in the interrogation rooms. On rare occasions, a latent print taken from a drinking glass or knife hilt will match up with someone's print card on the Printrak computer, but most detectives can count on one hand the number of cases made by lab work. A good cop goes to the crime scene, gathers the available evidence, talks to the right people and with any luck discovers the murderer's most glaring mistakes. But in that alone there is talent and instinct enough.

If the pieces do fall into place, some unlucky citizen gets a pair of silver bracelets and a wagon ride to an overcrowded tier of the Baltimore City Jail. There he sits as his trial date is postponed for eight or nine months or however long it takes your witnesses to change addresses two or three times. Then an assistant state's attorney, who has every intention of maintaining a better than average conviction rate so that he can one day come to rest in a better than average criminal law firm, calls you on the telephone. He assures you that this is the weakest homicide indictment he has ever had the misfortune to prosecute, so weak that he cannot believe it to be the work of a legitimate grand jury, and could you please round up the brain-dead cattle you call witnesses and bring them down for pretrial interviews because this thing is actually going to court on Monday. Unless, of course, he can convince the defense attorney to swallow manslaughter with all but five years suspended.

If the case isn't plea-bargained, dismissed or placed on the inactive docket for an indefinite period of time, if by some perverse twist of fate it becomes a trial by jury, you will then have the opportunity of sitting on the witness stand and reciting under oath the facts of the case—a brief moment in the sun that clouds over with the appearance of the aforementioned defense attorney who, at worst, will accuse you of perjuring yourself in a gross injustice or, at best, accuse you of conducting an investigation so incredibly slipshod that the real killer has been allowed to roam free.

Once both sides have loudly argued the facts of the case, a jury of twelve men and women picked from computer lists of registered voters in one of America's most undereducated cities will go to a room and begin shouting. If these happy people manage to overcome the natural impulse to avoid any act of collective judgment, they just may find one human being guilty of murdering another. Then you can go to Cher's Pub at Lexington and Guilford, where that selfsame assistant state's attorney, if possessed of any human qualities at all, will buy you a bottle of domestic beer.

And you drink it. Because in a police department of about three thousand sworn souls, you are one of thirty-six investigators entrusted with the pursuit of that most extraordinary of crimes: the theft of a human life. You speak for the dead. You avenge those lost to the world. Your paycheck may come from fiscal services but, goddammit, after six beers you can pretty much convince yourself that you work for the Lord himself. If you are not as good as you should be, you'll be gone within a year or two, transferred to fugitive, or auto theft or check and fraud at the other end of the hall. If you are good enough, you will never do anything else as a cop that matters this much. Homicide is the major leagues, the center ring, the show. It always has been. When Cain threw a cap into Abel, you don't think the Big Guy told a couple of fresh uniforms to go down and work up the prosecution report. Hell no, he sent for a fucking detective. And it will always be that way, because the homicide unit of any urban police force has for generations been the natural habitat of that rarefied species, the thinking cop.

It goes beyond academic degrees, specialized training or book learning, because all the theory in the world means nothing if you can't read the street. But it goes beyond that, too. In every ghetto precinct house, there are aging patrolmen who know everything a homicide man knows, yet somehow they spend their careers in battered radio cars, fighting their battles in eight-hour installments and worrying about a case only until the next shift change. A good detective begins as a good patrolman, a soldier who has spent years clearing corners and making car stops, breaking in on domestics and checking the back doors of warehouses until the life of a city becomes second nature to him. And that detective is further honed as a plainclothesman, working enough years of burglary or narcotics or auto until he understands what it means to do surveillance, to use and not be used by an informant, to write a coherent search and seizure warrant. And of course there is the specialized training, the solid grounding in forensic science, in pathology, criminal law, fingerprints, fibers, blood typing, ballistics, and DNA-genetic coding. A good detective also has to fill his head with enough knowledge of the existing police information data base—arrest records, jail records, weapons registrations, motor vehicle information—to qualify for a minor in computer science. And yet, given all that, a good homicide man has something more, something as internalized and instinctive as police work itself. Inside every good detective are hidden mechanisms—compasses that bring him from a dead body to a living suspect in the shortest span of time, gyroscopes that guarantee balance in the worst storms.

A Baltimore detective handles about nine or ten homicides a year as the primary investigator and another half dozen as the secondary detective, although FBI guidelines suggest half that workload. He handles fifty to sixty serious shootings, stabbings and bludgeonings. He investigates any questionable or suspicious death not readily explained by a victim's age or medical condition. Overdoses, seizures, suicides, accidental falls, drownings, crib deaths, autoerotic strangulations—all receive the attention of the same detective who has, at any given moment, case files for three open homicides on his desk. In Baltimore, investigations of all shootings involving police officers are conducted by homicide detectives rather than internal affairs men; a sergeant and a squad of detectives are assigned to probe every such incident and present a comprehensive report to the departmental brass and the state's attorney's office the following morning. Any threat on any police officer, state's attorney or public official is channeled through the homicide unit, as is any report of an attempt to intimidate a state's witness.

And there is more. The homicide unit's proven ability to investigate any incident and then document that investigation means that it is likely to be called on to handle politically sensitive investigations: a drowning at a city swimming pool where civil liability might result, a series of harassing phone calls to the mayor's chief of staff, a lengthy probe of a state legislator's bizarre claim that he was abducted by mysterious enemies. In Baltimore, the general rule is that if something looks like a shitstorm, smells like a shitstorm and tastes like a shitstorm, it goes to homicide. The headquarters food chain demands it.

Consider:

Commanding the homicide unit's two shifts of eighteen detectives and detective sergeants are a pair of long-suffering lieutenants who answer to the captain in charge of the Crimes Against Persons section. The captain, who wishes to retire with a major's pension, does not want his name associated with anything that gives pain to the colonel in charge of the Criminal Investigation Division. That is not just because the colonel is well liked, intelligent and black, and stands a good chance of getting kicked upstairs to a deputy commissioner's post or higher in a city with a new black mayor and a majority black population that has little faith in, or regard for, its police department. The colonel is also shielded from pain because whatever may arouse his displeasure requires only a brief elevator ride before it reaches the attention of Yahweh himself, Deputy Commissioner for Operations Ronald J. Mullen, who sits like a colossus astride the Baltimore Police Department, demanding to know everything about anything five minutes after it happens.

To mid-level supervisors, the deputy is simply the Great White Mullen, a man whose consistent escalation in rank began after a brief stint in Southwestern District patrol and continued unabated until he came to rest on the eighth floor of headquarters. It is there that Mullen has made his home for nearly a decade as the department's second-in-command, secured in his post by unswerving caution, good political sense and genuine administrative gifts, yet denied the police commissioner's office because he is white in a city that is not. The result is that commissioners have come and gone, but Ronald Mullen remains to keep track of who put which skeletons in which closet. Every link in the chain, from sergeant on up, can tell you that the deputy knows much of what goes on in the department and can guess most of the rest. With one phone call, he can have what he doesn't know and can't guess reduced to a memorandum and brought upstairs before lunch. Deputy Commissioner Mullen is therefore a pain in the ass to street police everywhere and an invaluable resource to Police Commissioner Edward J. Tilghman, a veteran cop who spent three decades amassing enough political capital to warrant appointment by his mayor to a five-year term. And, in a one-party town such as Baltimore, the mayor's office at City Hall is a heaven-kissed summit, a place of unfettered political power currently occupied by one Kurt L. Schmoke, a black, Yale-educated incumbent blessed with an overwhelmingly Democratic, overwhelmingly black metropolis. Naturally, the commissioner is only permitted to breathe air after first responding to the needs of the mayor, who can better contemplate reelection when His police department causes Him no humiliation or scandal, serves Him in whatever manner He sees fit, and fights crime for the common good, in approximately that order.

Underneath this towering pyramid of authority squats the homicide detective, laboring in anonymity over some bludgeoned prostitute or shot-to-shit narcotics trafficker until one day the phone bleats twice and the body on the ground is that of an eleven-year-old girl, an all-city athlete, a retired priest, or some out-of-state tourist who wandered into the projects with a Nikon around his neck.

Red balls. Murders that matter.

In this town, a detective lives or dies on the holy-shit cases that make it clear who runs the city and what they want from their police department. Majors, colonels and deputy commissioners who never uttered a word when bodies were falling all over Lexington Terrace in the summer drug war of '86 are now leaning over the shoulder of a detective sergeant, checking the fine print. The deputy wants to be briefed. The mayor needs an update. Channel 11 is on line 2. Some asshole from the *Evening Sun* is on hold for Landsman. Who's this guy Pellegrini working the case? New guy? Do we trust him? Does he know what he's doing? Do you need more men? More overtime? You do understand that this thing is a priority, right?

In 1987, two parking attendants were murdered at 4:00 A.M. in the garage of the Hyatt Hotel at the Inner Harbor—the glittering waterfront development on which Baltimore has pinned its future—and by early afternoon the governor of Maryland was barking loudly at the police commissioner. An impatient man given to sudden, spectacular histrionics, William Donald Schaefer is generally regarded to be the most consistently annoyed governor in the nation. Elected to Maryland's highest office in no small part because of the restored harbor's symbolic appeal, Schaefer made it clear in a brief phone call that people are not to be killed at the Inner Harbor without his permission and that this crime would be solved instantly—which, in fact, it pretty much was.

A red-ball case can mean twenty-hour days and constant reports to the entire chain of command; it can become a special detail, with detectives pulled out of the regular rotation and other cases put on indefinite hold. If the effort results in an arrest, then the detective, his sergeant, and his shift lieutenant can rest easy until the next major case, knowing that their captain's ear will not be gnawed upon by the colonel, who is no longer worried about turning his back on the deputy, who at this very moment is on the phone to City Hall telling Hizzoner that all is well in the harbor town. But a red-ball case that won't go down creates the opposite momentum, with colonels kicking majors kicking captains until a detective and his squad sergeant are covering themselves with office reports, explaining why someone the colonel thinks is a suspect was never questioned further about some incoherent statement, or why a tip from this brain-dead informant was discounted, or why the technicians weren't ordered to dust their own assholes for fingerprints.

A homicide man survives by learning to read the chain of command the way a Gypsy reads tea leaves. When the brass is asking questions, he makes himself indispensable with the answers. When they're looking for a reason to reach down somebody's throat, he puts together a report so straight they'll think he sleeps with a copy of the general orders. And when they're simply asking for a piece of meat to hang on the wall, he learns how to make himself invisible. If a detective has enough moves to still be standing after the occasional red ball, the department gives him some credit for brains and leaves him alone so he can go back to answering the phone and staring at bodies.

And there is much to see, beginning with the bodies battered by two-by-fours and baseball bats, or bludgeoned with tire irons and cinder blocks. Bodies with gaping wounds from carving knives or from shotguns fired so close that the shell wadding is lodged deep in the wounds. Bodies in public housing project stairwells, with the hypodermic still in their forearm and that pathetic look of calm on their faces; bodies pulled out of the harbor with reluctant blue crabs clinging to hands and feet. Bodies in basements, bodies in alleys, bodies in beds, bodies in the trunk of a Chrysler with out-of-state tags, bodies on gurneys behind a blue curtain in the University Hospital emergency room, with tubes and catheters still poking out of the carcasses to mock medicine's best arguments. Bodies and pieces of bodies that fell from balconies, from rooftops, from marine terminal loading cranes. Bodies crushed by heavy machinery, suffocated by carbon monoxide or suspended by a pair of sweatsocks from the top of a Central District holding cell. Bodies on crib mattresses surrounded by stuffed animals, tiny bodies in the arms of grieving mothers who can't understand that there is no reason, that the baby just stopped breathing air.

In the winter, the detective stands in water and ash and smells that unmistakable odor as firefighters pry rubble off the bodies of children left behind when a bedroom space heater shorted. In the summer, he stands in a third-floor apartment with no windows and bad ventilation, watching the ME's attendants move the bloated wreck of an eighty-six-year-old retiree who died in bed and stayed there until neighbors could no longer stand the smell. He steps back when they roll the poor soul, knowing that the torso is ripe and ready to burst and knowing, too, that the stench is going to be in the fibers of his clothes and on the hairs of his nose for the rest of the day. He sees the drownings that follow the first warm spring days and the senseless bar shootings that are a rite of the first July heat wave. In early fall, when the leaves turn and the schools open their doors, he spends a few days at Southwestern, or Lake Clifton, or some other high school where seventeen-year-old prodigies come to class with loaded .357s, then end the school day by shooting off a classmate's fingers in the faculty parking lot. And on select mornings, all year long, he stands near the door of a tiled room in the basement of a state office building at Penn and Lombard, watching trained pathologists disassemble the dead.

For each body, he gives what he can afford to give and no more. He carefully measures out the required amount of energy and emotion, closes the file and moves on to the next call. And even after years of calls and bodies and crime scenes and interrogations, a good detective still answers the phone with the stubborn, unyielding belief that if he does his job, the truth is always knowable.

A homicide detective endures.

MONDAY, JANUARY 18

The Big Man sits with his back to the green metal bulkhead that separates the homicide and robbery offices, staring abstractedly at the city's skyline through the corner window. His left hand cradles a glass mug in the shape of a globe, filled to the Arctic Circle with brown bile from the very bottom of the office coffeepot. On the desk in front of him is a thick red binder with the notation H8152 stamped on the front cover. He turns away from the window and stares at the binder with malevolence. The binder stares back.

It is a four-to-twelve shift, and for Donald Worden—the Big Man, the Bear, the only surviving natural police detective in America—it is the first day back from a long weekend that did nothing to change his disposition. The rest of his squad senses this and gives him wide berth, venturing into the coffee room only on errands.

"Hey, Donald," offers Terry McLarney during one such sortie. "How was the weekend?"

Worden shrugs at his sergeant.

"Did you do anything?"

"No," says Worden.

"Okay," says McLarney. "So much for small talk."

The Monroe Street shooting did this to him, stranding him at a corner desk in the coffee room like some iron-bottom dreadnought run aground in the shallows, waiting for a tide that might never come.

Five weeks old and no closer to a resolution than the morning after the murder, the death of John Randolph Scott in an alley off West Baltimore's Monroe Street remains the police department's first priority. Reports written by Worden and his partner are copied not to his sergeant and lieutenant, as with any other investigation, but to the administrative lieutenant and the captain who commands Crimes Against Persons. From there, the reports travel down the hall to the colonel, then to Deputy Commissioner Mullen, two floors above.

The reports suggest little that can be called progress. And in every conversation with a superior, a sense of paranoia is palpable. Donald Worden can almost feel the department's chain of command rustling nervously. In Worden's mind, too, the Monroe Street case is a tinderbox, waiting only for the right community activist or storefront preacher to grab hold of it and scream racism or police brutality or cover-up loud enough and long enough for the mayor or the police commissioner to start calling for heads. Worden often finds himself wondering why it hasn't happened yet.

Looking west out the coffee room window, Worden watches the winter sky fade to dark blue as the pink-orange light of the falling sun slips behind the skyline. The detective finishes his first cup of coffee, lumbers over to the metal coat rack and pulls a cigar from the inside pocket of a beige overcoat. His brand is Backwoods, a mean, black cigar sold at fine 7-Elevens everywhere.

A thin curl of acrid smoke follows Worden as he walks back to the desk and opens the red binder.

H8152

Homicide/Police Shooting

John Randolph Scott B/M/22

3022 Garrison Boulevard, Apt. 3

CC# 87-7L-13281

"What a piece of shit this turned out to be," Worden says softly, leafing through the office reports at the front of the file. Pushing back in his chair, he props one leg on the desk and opens a second binder to a series of color photographs, stapled two to a page on a set of manila dividers.

John Randolph Scott lies on his back in the center of the alley. His face is smooth and unworn; he looks younger than his twenty-two years. Locked, empty eyes stare south toward the red brick side of a rowhouse. His clothes are those of any kid on any corner: black leather jacket, blue jeans, beige shirt, white tennis shoes. Another photo shows the victim rolled on his side, the rubber-gloved hand of a detective pointing to the small hole in the back of the leather jacket. An entrance wound, with the corresponding exit found in the left center chest. Above the young man's eye is a bloody contusion caused by his fall to the concrete.

The medical examiner later determined that the bullet that killed John Randolph Scott fully penetrated his heart at a slightly downward angle, consistent with the downward slope of the alley in which he was found. Scott died almost instantly, the pathologists agreed, shot in the back while fleeing from officers of the Baltimore Police Department.

In its earliest hours, the Scott case was regarded not as a murder but as a police-involved shooting—a bad police shooting that would require some careful writing if a cop wasn't going to be torn apart by a grand jury, but nothing that anyone was going to start calling a crime.

The victim was one of two young men in a Dodge Colt that a two-man Central District car made for stolen and chased from Martin Luther King Boulevard down I-170 and then onto Raynor Avenue, where Scott and a twenty-one-year-old companion bailed out and ran in separate directions through the alleys of the rowhouse ghetto. As the two Central uniforms jumped from the radio car to begin a foot chase, one of the officers, twenty-seven-year-old Brian Pedrick, stumbled and fired one shot from his service revolver. Pedrick later told investigators that the shot was an accident, a wayward round fired when he lost his footing while staggering from his car. Pedrick believed that his gun was pointed down and that the bullet struck the asphalt in front of him; in any event, the round seemed to have no effect on the suspect he was chasing, who disappeared into the labyrinth of back alleys. Pedrick lost sight of the kid, but by then other cars from the Central, Western and Southern districts were rolling through the nearby side streets and alleys.

Minutes later, a Central District sergeant called for an ambulance and a homicide unit as he stood over a body in an alley off Monroe Street, about three blocks from where Pedrick had fired his one round. Was this a police-involved shooting? the dispatcher asked. No, said the sergeant. But then Pedrick himself walked up to the scene and admitted letting one go. The sergeant keyed his mike again. Correction, he said, this is police-involved.

Worden and his partner, Rick James, arrived at the scene minutes later, looked over the dead man, talked with the Central District sergeant and then inspected Pedrick's service revolver. One round spent. The patrolman was relieved of the weapon and taken to the homicide unit, where he acknowledged that he had fired one shot but declined to make any other statement until he had talked with a police union lawyer. Worden knew what that meant.

A union lawyer has a standard response to a detective's request to interview a police officer as part of a criminal investigation. If ordered to do so, the officer will submit a report explaining his actions during a shooting incident; otherwise, he will make no statement. Because when such a report is written in response to a direct order, it cannot constitute a voluntary statement and therefore cannot be used in court against the officer. In this case, the state's attorney on duty that night refused to order the report and, as a consequence of the legal impasse, the investigation fixed itself on an obvious course: proving that Officer Brian Pedrick—a five-year veteran with no prior record of brutality or excessive force—had shot a fleeing man in the back with his service revolver.

For twelve hours, the Monroe Street investigation was certainty and cohesion, and it would have remained so except for one critical fact: Officer Pedrick did not shoot John Randolph Scott.

On the morning after the shooting, the medical examiner's attendants undressed Scott's body and found a spent .38 slug still lodged in the bloody clothing. That bullet was compared by the ballistics lab later that afternoon, but it could not be matched with Pedrick's revolver. In fact, the bullet that killed Scott was a 158-grain roundnose, a common type of Smith & Wesson ammunition that hadn't been used by the police department in more than a decade.

Worden and several other detectives then returned to the scene of the pursuit and in daylight carefully searched the alley where Pedrick was believed to have fired his weapon. Picking through trash in that alley off Raynor Avenue, they found a mark in the pavement that appeared to have lead residue from a bullet ricochet. The detectives followed the likely trajectory of the slug across the alley and came to an adjacent lot where, incredibly, a resident was cleaning debris on that very morning. Of all the trash-strewn lots in all the ghettos in all the world, Worden thought, this guy's gotta be cleaning ours. Just as the detectives were about to begin emptying every one of the half-dozen trash bags filled by West Baltimore's last Good Samaritan, they discovered the spent .38 slug, still partially buried in the dirt lot. Ballistics then matched that bullet to Brian Pedrick's weapon.

But if Pedrick wasn't the shooter, who was?

Worden had no taste for the obvious answer. He was a cop and he had spent his adult life in the brotherhood of cops—in station houses and radio cars, in courthouse corridors and district lockups. He didn't want to believe that someone wearing the uniform could be so stupid as to shoot someone and then run away, leaving the body in a back alley like any other murdering bastard. And yet he couldn't turn away from the fact that John Randolph Scott was killed with a .38 slug while running from men with .38 revolvers. In any other investigation, there would be no debate as to where and how a homicide detective should begin. In any other case, a detective would start with the men who had the guns.

Worden being Worden, he had done precisely that, compelling nearly two dozen police from three districts to submit their service revolvers to evidence control in exchange for replacement weapons. But for each .38 submitted, a corresponding ballistics report indicated that the fatal bullet had not come from this officer's duty weapon. Another dead end.

Was a cop carrying a secondary weapon, another .38 that had since been thrown off some Canton pier? Or maybe the kid was running from police and tried to steal another car, only to get himself shot by some irate civilian who then disappeared into the night. That was a long shot, Worden had to admit, but in this neighborhood nothing was impossible. A more likely scenario had the kid getting aced with a gun of his own, a .38 taken off him in a struggle with an arresting officer. That could explain why the spent bullet wasn't department issue, just as it could explain the torn buttons.

Worden and Rick James had recovered four of them at or near the victim's body. One button appeared to have nothing to do with the victim; three were determined to be from the dead man's shirt. Two of those buttons were found near the body and were bloodied; the third was found near the mouth of the alley. To Worden and James both, the torn buttons indicated that the victim had been grabbed in a struggle, and the presence of the button near the mouth of the alley suggested that the struggle had begun only a few feet from where the victim fell. More than a straight shooting by a civilian suspect, that scenario suggested an attempted street arrest, an effort to grab or halt the victim.

For Donald Worden, the death of John Randolph Scott had become a dirty piece of business, with each possible outcome more unsettling than the last.

If the murder remained unsolved, it would resemble a departmental cover-up. But if a cop was indicted, Worden and James would become, as the men responsible for the prosecution, pariahs to the people in patrol. Already, the police union lawyers were telling members not to talk to homicide, that the Crimes Against Persons section was synonymous with IID. How the hell would they work murders with patrol against them? But in some ways the third alternative, the slim possibility of civilian involvement—that John Randolph Scott was shot by a local while trying to break into a home or steal a second car to elude the pursuing officers—was the worst of all. Worden reasoned that if he ever came up with a civilian suspect, the brass would go out of their minds trying to sell it to the city's political leadership, not to mention the powers-that-be in the black community. Well, Mr. Mayor, we thought the white officers chasing Mr. Scott may have done it, but now we're pretty much convinced that a black guy from the 1000 block of Fulton Street is responsible.

Yeah. Sure. No problem.

Twenty-five years in the Baltimore Police Department and Donald

Worden was now being asked to put the crown on his career by solving a case that could put cops in prison. In the beginning, the notion had seemed abhorrent—Worden was as much or more of a street police than any man out there. He had gone downtown after more than a decade in the Northwest District's operations unit and then only reluctantly. And now, because of this thieving kid with the bullethole in his back, patrolmen in three districts were idling their radio cars side by side, hood to trunk, in vacant parking lots, talking in hushed tones about a man who was on the street when they were hurling spitballs in grade school. Who the fuck is this guy Worden? Is he really gonna go after a police on this Monroe Street thing? He's gonna try and fuck over another police because of some dead yo? What is he, a rat or something?

"Uh-oh, Worden be looking at that nasty file."

Worden's partner stands in the doorway of the coffee room, holding a piece of scratch paper. Rick James is ten years younger than Donald Worden and has neither his instincts nor his savvy, but then again, few people in this world do. Worden works with the younger detective because James can manage a homicide scene and write a good, coherent report, and for all his virtues, Donald Worden would rather eat his gun than sit at a typewriter for two hours. In his better moments, Worden regards James as a worthy project, an apprentice on whom to bestow the lessons of a quarter century of policing.

The Big Man looks up slowly and sees the scrap paper in the younger man's hand.

"What's that?"

"It's a call, babe."

"We're not supposed to be taking calls. We're detailed."

"Terry says we should go on it."

"What is it?"

"Shooting."

"I don't handle homicides anymore," says Worden dryly. "Just give me a fucked-up police shooting any day."

"C'mon, babe, let's go make some money."

Worden downs the last of his coffee, throws the remains of the cigar into a can, and for a second or two allows himself to believe that there may just be life after Monroe Street. He walks to the coat rack.

"Don't forget your gun, Donald."

The Big Man smiles for the first time.

"I sold my gun. Pawned it for some power tools down on Baltimore Street. Where's this here shooting?"

"Greenmount. Thirty-eight hundred block."

Detective Sergeant Terrence Patrick McLarney watches the two men prepare to leave and nods his head in satisfaction. It's been more than a month since the Monroe Street shooting and McLarney wants his two men back in the rotation, handling calls. The trick is to do it gradually, so as not to suggest to the chain of command that the Monroe Street detail is in fact on its last legs. With any luck, McLarney figures, Worden will catch a murder with this call and the admin lieutenant will get off his ass about the Scott case.

"Detail leaving, sergeant," says Worden.

Inside the elevator, Rick James fingers the car keys and stares at his blurred reflection in the metal doors. Worden watches the indicator lights.

"McLarney's happy, ain't he?"

Worden says nothing.

"You're a bear and a half today, Donald."

"You drive, bitch."

Rick James rolls his eyes and looks at his partner. He sees a six-foot-four, 240-pound polar bear masquerading as a gap-toothed forty-eight-year-old man with deep blue eyes, a rapidly receding line of white hair and rising blood pressure. Yes, he is a bear, but the best part of working with Donald Worden is easily understood: The man is a natural policeman.

"I'm just a poor, dumb white boy from Hampden, trying to make his way through this world and into the next," Worden would often say by way of introduction. And on paper, he appeared to be exactly that: Baltimore born and bred, he had a high school education, a few years of navy service, and a police service record of impressive length but with no greater rank than patrolman or detective. On the street, however, Worden was one of the most instinctive, inspired cops in the city. He had spent over a quarter of a century in the department and knew Baltimore like few others ever would. Twelve years in the Northwest District, three in escape and apprehension, another eight working in the robbery unit, and now three years in homicide.

He hadn't come to the unit without second thoughts. Time and again, squad sergeants in homicide had urged him to make the switch, but Worden was a man of the old school and loyalty counted for a lot. The same lieutenant who brought him to the robbery unit wanted to keep him, and

Worden felt beholden. And his relationship with his partner, Ron Grady—an unlikely match between a would-be hillbilly from North Baltimore's all-white enclave of Hampden and a beefy black cop from the city's west side—was another reason to stay put. They were a salt-and-pepper team of legendary proportions and Worden never hesitated to remind Rick James and everyone else in homicide that Grady was the only man he could ever truly call his partner.

But by early 1985, working robberies had become a numbing, repetitive existence. Worden had run through hundreds of investigations—banks, armored cars, downtown holdups, commercial jobs. In the old days, he would tell younger detectives, a cop could go after a better class of thieves; now a Charles Street bank job was more likely to be the impulse of some nodding addict than the work of a professional. In the end, the job itself made the decision for him: Worden can still vividly remember the morning he arrived at the office to find a report of an Eastern District incident on his desk, a liquor store robbery from Greenmount Avenue. The report was filed as robbery with a deadly weapon, which meant the incident required a follow-up by a downtown detective. Worden read the narrative and learned that a group of kids had grabbed a six-pack and run from the store. The counterman tried to chase them and got hit with a piece of a brick for his trouble. It wasn't felony robbery; hell, it wasn't anything that couldn't have been handled by a district uniform. For Worden, who had been a robbery detective for almost eight years, that incident report was the end of the line. He went to the captain the next day with the transfer request to homicide.

Worden's reputation preceded him across the hall and during the next two years he proved not only that he was ready for murders but that he was the centerpiece of McLarney's squad, no small thing in a five-man unit that included two other men with twenty-year histories. Rick James had transferred to homicide in July 1985, only three months before Worden, and James quickly sized up the situation and paired up with the Big Man, following him so closely that other detectives gave him grief about it. But Worden clearly enjoyed the role of an elder sage and James was willing to hold up his end by doing a good crime scene and writing the necessary reports. If Worden taught him half of what he knew before taking that pension, Rick James would be in homicide a long, long time.

The bad thing about working with Worden was the black moods, the sullen brooding because he was still working for a patrolman's wage when he should be taking a pension and living a life of leisure as some security consultant or home improvement contractor. Worden was strangely self-conscious that he was still out there running down ghetto murders when most of the men who came on with him were retired or working a second career; the few that remained on the force were ending their days in the districts as desk sergeants or turnkeys, or in the headquarters security booths listening to the Orioles drop a double-header on a transistor radio, waiting out another year or two for a higher pension. All around him, younger men were getting out and moving on to better things.

More often than not these days, Worden found himself talking seriously about packing it in. But a large part of him didn't even want to think about retirement; the department had been his home since 1962—his arrival in homicide marked the last curl in a long, graceful arc. For three years, Worden's work in the unit had sustained and even revived him.

The Big Man took particular delight in his ongoing effort to break in the younger detectives in his squad, Rick James and Dave Brown. James was coming along all right, but in Worden's mind Brown could go either way. Worden never hesitated to press the point, subjecting the younger detective to a training regimen best characterized as education-by-insult.

The least experienced man in the squad, Dave Brown tolerated the Big Man's bluster—in large part because he knew Worden genuinely cared whether Brown stayed a detective, in smaller part because there was no real choice in the matter. The relationship between the two men was perfectly captured in a color photograph taken by a crime lab tech at a murder in Cherry Hill. In the foreground was an earnest Dave Brown, collecting discarded beer cans near the shooting scene in the vain and excessively optimistic hope that they might have anything at all to do with the killing. In the background, sitting on the front stoop of a public housing unit, was Donald Worden, watching the younger detective with what appears to be a look of unequivocal disgust. Dave Brown liberated the photograph from the case file and took it home as a memento. It was the Big Man that Brown had come to know and love. Cantankerous, annoyed, ever critical. A last, lonely centurion who sees both his affliction and his challenge in a younger generation of menials and incompetents.

The photograph showed the Big Man at the height of his powers: abrasive, confident, the nettled conscience of every younger or less experienced detective on the shift. And, of course, the Cherry Hill case went down, with Worden getting the tip that led to the murder weapon at the home of the shooter's girlfriend. But that was when Worden still felt some delight at being a homicide detective. That was before Monroe Street.

Climbing into a Cavalier on the mezzanine level, James decides to risk conversation one more time.

"If this is a murder," he says, "I'll be the primary."

Worden looks at him. "You don't want to see if someone's been locked up first?"

"No, babe. I need the money."

"You're a whore."

"Yeah, babe."

James rolls the car down the garage ramp, over to Fayette, then north on Gay Street to Greenmount, preoccupied with the complex computations of anticipated overtime. Two hours at the scene, three hours of interrogation, another three for paperwork, four more for the autopsy; James thinks about how sweet twelve hours of time-and-a-half will look on his pay stub.

But it is not a murder on Greenmount; it isn't even a straight shooting. Both detectives know that after listening to a sixteen-year-old witness rattle through an incoherent three-minute monologue.

"Whoa, start from the beginning. Slowly."

"Derrick came running in . . ."

"Derrick who?"

"That's my brother."

"How old is he?"

"Seventeen. He come running through the front door and upstairs. My older brother went up and found him shot and called nine-one-one. Derrick said he was at the bus stop and got shot. That's all he said."

"He didn't know who shot him?"

"No, he say he just got shot."

Worden takes the flashlight from James and walks outside with a patrolman.

"Are you the first officer?"

"No," says the uniform. "That's Rodriguez."

"Where is he?"

"He went to shock-trauma with your victim."

Worden shoots the patrolman a look, then walks back toward the front door of the house and turns the flashlight on the floor of the porch. No blood trail. No blood on the door handle. The detective scans the brick front of the rowhouse with the light. No blood. No fresh damage.

One hole, but too even to be from a bullet. Probably an old drill hole for a light fixture.

Worden takes the flashlight back down the front walk toward the street. He walks back inside the house and checks the rooms upstairs. Still no blood. The detective walks back downstairs and listens to James questioning the sixteen-year-old.

"Where'd your brother run to when he came in the house?" Worden interrupts.

"Upstairs."

"There's no blood upstairs."

The kid looks at his shoes.

"What's going on here?" says Worden, pressing him.

"We cleaned it up," the kid says.

"You cleaned it up?"

"Uh-huh."

"Oh," says Worden, rolling his eyes. "Let's go back upstairs then."

The kid takes the stairs two at a time, then turns into the clutter and disarray of a teenager's room, replete with pinups of models in bikinis and posters of New York rappers in designer sweats. Without further prompting, the sixteen-year-old pulls two bloodstained sheets from a hamper.

"Where were those?"

"On the bed."

"On the bed?"

"We turned over the mattress."

Worden flips the mattress. A red-brown stain covers a good quarter of the fabric.

"What jacket was your brother wearing when he came in?"

"The gray one."

Worden picks up a gray puff jacket from a chair and checks it carefully, inside and out. No blood. He goes to the bedroom closet and checks every other winter coat, throwing each on the bed as James shakes his head slowly.

"Here's what happened," says James. "You were in here playing around with a gun and your brother got shot. Now if you start telling the truth, you're not going to get locked up. Where's the gun?"

"What gun?"

"Jesus Christ. Where's the goddamn gun?"

"Don't know about no gun."

"Your brother has a gun. Let's just get the gun out of the way."

"Derrick got shot at the bus stop."

"The fuck he did," says James, simmering. "He was fucking around in here and you or your brother or someone else shot him by accident. Where's the fucking gun?"

"Ain't no gun."

Classic, thinks Worden, looking at the kid. Truly classic. A prime example of the Rule Number One of the guidebook of death investigation, the page 1 entry in a detective's lexicon:

Everyone lies.

Murderers, stickup artists, rapists, drug dealers, drug users, half of all major-crime witnesses, politicians of all persuasions, used car salesmen, girlfriends, wives, ex-wives, line officers above the rank of lieutenant, sixteen-year-old high school students who accidentally shoot their older brother and then hide the gun—to a homicide detective, the earth spins on an axis of denial in an orbit of deceit. Hell, sometimes the police themselves are no different. For the last six weeks, Donald Worden has listened to a long series of statements by men wearing the uniform in which he has spent a lifetime, listened to them as they tried to get their stories straight and explain how they couldn't possibly have been anywhere near that alley off Monroe Street.

James begins moving toward the bedroom door. "You tell us what you want," he says bitterly. "When your brother dies, we'll be back to charge you with the murder."

The kid remains mute, and the two detectives follow the uniform out the front door. Worden holds his temper until the Cavalier is rolling back down Greenmount.

"Who the hell is this guy Rodriguez?"

"I guess you're going to have something to say to him."

"I'm gonna have a lot to say. The first officer to arrive protects the crime scene. And what do they do? They go to the hospital, they go to headquarters, they go to lunch and let the people pick the scene apart. What good he was gonna do at the hospital, I don't know."

But Rodriguez isn't at the hospital. And there is no satisfaction for Worden in a brief discussion with the victim's distracted mother, who sits with two other children in the trauma unit's waiting room, clutching a tissue.

"I don't know, honestly," she tells the detectives. "I was sitting with my other son, watching TV, and I heard a noise, like a firecracker or the sound of glass breaking. Derrick's brother James went upstairs and said

Derrick had been coming home from work and got shot. I told him not to play like that."

Worden interrupts.

"Mrs. Allen, I'm gonna be frank with you. Your son was shot in his room, more than likely by accident. Except for the bed, there was no blood anywhere, not even on the jacket he was wearing when he came in."

The woman looks at the detective blankly. Worden continues, explaining her children's effort to conceal the shooting scene and the probability that the handgun that has sent her son to surgery is still in the house.

"No one is talking about charging anyone. We're from homicide and if it's an accidental shooting, then we're wasting our time and we just need to get it straightened out."

The woman nods in vague agreement. Worden asks if she would be willing to call home and ask her children to turn over the weapon.

"They can leave it on the porch and lock the door if they want," Worden says. "We're just interested in getting the gun out of the house."

The mother abdicates.

"I'd rather you do that," she says.

Worden walks into the hall and finds Rick James, who is talking with a medical technician. Derrick Allen is critical but stable; in all probability, he will live to fight another day. And Officer Rodriguez, says James, is back at homicide, writing his report.

"I'll drop you at the office. If I go back now I'm going to jump in someone's shit," says Worden. "I'll take another trip by the house for the gun. Don't ask me why I should care whether they keep the fucking thing or not."

A half hour later, Worden is rechecking Derrick Allen's bedroom and finds a hole in a back window and a spent bullet on an outside rear porch. He shows the slug and the window to the sixteen-year-old brother.

The kid shrugs. "I guess Derrick got shot in his room."

"Where's the gun?"

"Don't know about no gun."

It is a God-given truth: Everyone lies. And this most basic of axioms has three corollaries:

A. Murderers lie because they have to.

B. Witnesses and other participants lie because they think they have to.

C. Everyone else lies for the sheer joy of it, and to uphold a general principle that under no circumstances do you provide accurate information to a cop.

Derrick's brother is living proof of the second corollary. A witness lies to protect friends and relatives, even those who have wantonly shed blood. He lies to deny his involvement in drugs. He lies to hide the fact that he has prior arrests or that he is secretly homosexual, or that he even knew the victim. Most of all, he lies to distance himself from the murder and the possibility that he may one day have to testify in court. In Baltimore, a cop asks you what you saw and the requisite reply, an involuntary motor skill bred into the urban population over generations, is delivered with a slow shake of the head and an averted stare:

"I ain't seen nothing."

"You were standing next to the guy."

"I ain't seen nothing."

Everyone lies.

Worden gives the kid one last, steady look.

"Your brother was shot in this room with a gun that he was playing with. Why don't we get that gun out of the house?"

The teenager barely misses a beat.

"I don't know about no gun."

Worden shakes his head. He could call for the crime lab and spend a couple hours tearing the place apart in a search for the damn thing; if it were a murder, he'd be doing just that. But for an accidental shooting, what's the point? Pull a gun out of this house and there'll be another in its place by the end of the week.

"Your brother's in the hospital," say Worden. "Doesn't that mean anything to you?"

The kid looks at the floor.

Fine, thinks Worden. I tried. I gave it a shot. So now keep the goddamn gun as a souvenir, and when you've shot yourself in the leg or put a round through little sister, you can call us again. Why, thinks Worden, should I waste time on your bullshit when there are people waiting in line to lie to me? Why hunt for your $20 pistol when I've got the quagmire that is Monroe Street on my desk?

Worden drives back to the office empty-handed, his mood even darker than before.

Wednesday, January 20

On the long wall of the coffee room hangs a large rectangle of white paper, running most of the room's length. It is covered by acetate and divided by black rules into six sections.

Above the three right-hand sections is a letterplate bearing the name of Lieutenant Robert Stanton, who commands the homicide unit's second shift. To the immediate left, below the name of Lieutenant Gary D'Addario, are the three remaining sections. Underneath the nameplates of the two lieutenants, affixed to the top of each section, is the name of a detective sergeant: McLarney, Landsman and Nolan for D'Addario's shift: Childs, Lamartina and Barrick for Stanton's command.

Below each sergeant's nameplate are brief listings of dead people, the first homicide victims of the year's first month. The names of victims in closed cases are written in black felt marker; the names of victims in open investigations, in red. To the left of each victim's name is a case number—88001 for the year's first murder, 88002 for the second, and so on. To the right of each victim's name is a letter or letters—A for Bowman, B for Garvey, C for McAllister—which correspond to the names of the assigned detectives listed at the bottom of each section.

A sergeant or lieutenant trying to match a homicide with its primary detective, or the reverse, can scan the sections of the white rectangle and in a matter of moments determine that Tom Pellegrini is working the murder of Rudy Newsome. He can also determine, by noting that Newsome's name is in red ink, that the case is still open. For this reason, supervisors in the homicide unit regard the white rectangle as an instrument necessary to assure accountability and clerical precision. For this reason, too, detectives in the unit regard the rectangle as an affliction, an unforgiving creation that has endured far beyond the expectations of the now-retired sergeants and long-dead lieutenants who created it. The detectives call it, simply, the board.

In the time that it takes the coffeepot to fill, shift commander Lieutenant Gary D'Addario—otherwise known to his men as Dee, LTD, or simply as His Eminence—can approach the board as a pagan priest might approach the temple of the sun god, scan the hieroglyphic scrawl of red and black below his name, and determine who among his three sergeants has kept his commandments and who has gone astray. He can further check the coded letters beside the name of each case and make the same determination about his fifteen detectives. The board reveals all: Upon its acetate is writ the story of past and present. Who has grown fat on domestic murders witnessed by half a dozen family members; who has starved on a drug assassination in a vacant rowhouse. Who has reaped the bountiful harvest of a murder-suicide complete with a posthumous note of confession; who has tasted the bitter fruit of an unidentified victim, bound and gagged in the trunk of an airport rental car.

The board that today greets the shift lieutenant is a wretched, bloody piece of work, with most of the names etched beneath D'Addario's sergeants written in red. Stanton's shift began the new year at midnight, catching five murders in the early hours of January 1. Of those cases, however, all but one were the result of drunken arguments and accidental shootings, and all but one are in the black. Then, a week later, came the shift change, with Stanton's men going to daywork and D'Addario's crew taking over on the four-to-twelve and midnight shifts and catching their first cases of the year. Nolan's squad took the first murder for the shift on January 10, a drug-related robbery in which the victim was found stabbed to death in the back seat of a Dodge. McLarney's squad picked up a whodunit the same night when a middle-aged homosexual was shotgunned as he opened his apartment door in lower Charles Village. Then Fahlteich caught the first murder of the year for Landsman's squad, a robbery beating in Rognel Heights with no suspects, after which McAllister broke up the red ink with an easy arrest on Dillon Street, where a fifteen-year-old white kid was stabbed in the heart over a $20 drug debt.

But the murders were all wide open the following week, with Eddie Brown and Waltemeyer arriving at a Walbrook Junction apartment house to find Kenny Vines stretched out on his stomach in a first-floor hallway, a red puddle of wetness where his right eye used to be. Brown didn't recognize the corpse at first, though he actually knew the forty-eight-year-old Vines from years back; hell, everyone who ever worked the west side knew Kenny Vines. The owner of a Bloomingdale Road body shop, Vines had for years been deep into numbers and stolen auto parts, but it was only when he started to move a lot of cocaine that he began making serious enemies. The Vines case was followed two nights later by Rudy Newsome and Roy Johnson, the split decision for Landsman's crew, which was followed in turn by a double murder on Luzerne Street, where a gunman broke into a stash house in a dispute over drug territory and began firing wildly, killing two and wounding two more. Naturally, the survivors didn't care to remember much.

The grand total came to nine bodies in eight cases, with only one file closed and another on the verge of a warrant, a solve rate so low that D'Addario could be fairly described as one of the police department's least satisfied lieutenants.

"I can't help but note, sir," says McLarney, following his supervisor into the coffee room, "as I'm sure you, in your infinite wisdom, have also noticed . . ."

"Go on, my good sergeant."

". . . that there is a lot of red ink on our side of the board."

"Yes, quite so," says D'Addario, encouraging this pattern of courtly, classical speech, a favored ploy that never fails to amuse his sergeants.

"A suggestion, sir?"

"You have my undivided attention, Sergeant McLarney."

"Maybe it would look better if we put the open cases in black and the closed ones in red," McLarney says. "That would fool the bosses for a while."

"That's one solution."

"Of course," adds McLarney, "we could also go out and lock some people up."

"That's also a solution."

McLarney laughs, but not too much. As a supervisor, Gary D'Addario is generally regarded by his sergeants and detectives as a prince, a benevolent autocrat who asks only competence and loyalty. In return, he provides his shift with unstinting support and sanctuary from the worst whims and fancies of the command staff. A tall man with thinning tufts of silver-gray hair and a quietly dignified manner, D'Addario is one of the last survivors of the Italian caliphate that briefly ruled the department after a long Irish dynasty. It was a respite that began with Frank Battaglia's ascension to the commissioner's post and continued until membership in the Sons of Italy was as much a prerequisite for elevation as the sergeant's test. But the Holy Roman Empire lasted less than four years; in 1985, the mayor acknowledged the city's changing demographics by dragging Battaglia into a well-paid consultant's position and giving the black community a firm lock on the upper tiers of the police department.

If the outgoing tide stranded D'Addario in homicide as a lieutenant, then the men under him owed much to affirmative action. Soft-spoken and introspective, D'Addario was a rare breed of supervisor for a paramilitary organization. He had learned long ago to suppress the first impulse of command that calls for a supervisor to intimidate his men, charting their every movement and riding them through investigations. In the districts, that sort of behavior usually resulted from a new supervisor's primitive conclusion that the best way to avoid being perceived as weak was to behave like a petty tyrant. Every district had a shift lieutenant or sector sergeant who would demand explanatory Form 95s from people ten minutes late to roll call, or scour the district's holes at 4:00 A.M. in the hope of finding some poor post officer sleeping in his radio car. Supervisors like that either grew into their jobs or their best men ducked and covered long enough to transfer to another sector.

Up in homicide, an authoritarian shift commander is even more likely to be held in contempt by his detectives—men who would not, in fact, be on the sixth floor of headquarters if they weren't eighteen of the most self-motivated cops in the department. In homicide, the laws of natural selection apply: A cop who puts down enough cases stays, a cop who doesn't is gone. Given that basic truth, there isn't much respect for the notion that a cop shrewd enough to maneuver his way into homicide and then put together forty or fifty cases somehow needs to have a shift commander's finger in his eye. Rank, of course, has it privileges, but a homicide supervisor who exercises his divine right to chew ass on every conceivable occasion will in the end create a shift of alienated sergeants and overly cautious detectives, unwilling or incapable of acting on their own instincts.

Instead, and at some cost to his own career, Gary D'Addario gave his men room to maneuver, providing a buffer against the captain and those above him in the chain of command. His method carried considerable risk, and the relationship between D'Addario and his captain had frayed around the edges during the last four years. By contrast, Bob Stanton, the other shift lieutenant, was a supervisor more to the captain's liking. A buttoned-down veteran of the narcotics unit handpicked by the captain to command the second shift, Stanton ran a tighter ship, with sergeants exerting more overt control over their men and detectives pressured to hold down the overtime and court pay that lubricates the entire system. Stanton was a good lieutenant and a sharp cop, but when compared with the alternative, his frugality and by-the-book style were such that more than a few veterans on his shift expressed an eagerness to join D'Addario's crusade at the first opportunity.

For the sergeants and detectives blessed by D'Addario's benevolence, the quid pro quo was both simple and obvious. They had to solve murders. They had to solve enough murders to produce a clearance rate that would vindicate His Eminence and his methods and thereby justify his benign and glorious rule. In homicide, the clearance rate is the litmus test, the beginning and end of all debate.

Which is reason enough for D'Addario to stare long and hard at the red ink on his side of the board. Not only does the white rectangle offer ready comparisons between detectives, it offers the same superficial comparison between shifts. In that sense, the board—and the clearance rate it represents—has divided Baltimore's homicide guard into separate units, each shift functioning independently of the other. Detectives old enough to have experienced life before the board remember the homicide unit as more of a single entity; detectives were willing to work cases that began or ended on another shift, knowing that credit for clearances would be shared by the entire unit. Created to promote cohesion and accountability, the board instead left the two shifts—and each of the six squads—to compete against each other in red and black ink for clearances, as if they were a pack of double-knit salesmen moving marked-down cars for Luby's Chevrolet.

The trend began long before Stanton's arrival, but the lieutenants' different styles helped to highlight the competition. And for the last several years, detectives from one shift had interacted with those from the other only at the half-hour shift changes or on rare occasions when a detective pulling overtime on a case needed an extra body from the working shift to witness an interrogation or help kick down a door. The competition was always understated, but soon even individual detectives found themselves contemplating the white rectangle, silently computing clearance rates for opposing squads or shifts. That, too, was ironic, because every detective in the unit was willing to concede that the board was itself a flawed measurement, as it represented only the number of homicides for the year. A squad could spend three weeks of nightwork knee deep in police shootings, questionable deaths, serious assaults, kidnappings, overdose cases and every other kind of death investigation. Yet none of that would be reflected in black and red ink.

Even with the murders themselves, much of what clears a case amounts to pure chance. The vocabulary of the homicide unit recognizes two distinct categories of homicides: whodunits and dunkers. Whodunits are genuine mysteries; dunkers are cases accompanied by ample evidence and an obvious suspect. Whodunits are best typified by crime scenes where a detective is called to some godforsaken back alley to find a body and little more. Dunkers are best typified by scenes at which the detective steps over the body to meet the unrepentant husband, who has not bothered to change his bloodied clothes and requires little prompting to admit that he stabbed the bitch and would do so again given the chance. The distinction between cases that require investigation and cases that require little more than paperwork is understood and accepted by every man in the unit, and more than one squad sergeant has accused another of rushing a detective out to a call that sounded on the radio as if it were a domestic murder or, worse yet, ducking a call that had all the markings of a well-executed drug slaying.

The board, of course, does not delineate between dunkers solved by circumstance and whodunits solved by extended investigation: The ink is as black for one as the other. As a consequence, the resulting politics of whodunits and dunkers becomes part of the mind-set, so much so that veteran detectives watching an old western on the office television will always offer the same remark when gunfighters are shot down on frontier streets crowded with God-fearing townsfolk:

"Yeah, bunk. There's a dunker."

But dunkers had lately been few and far between for D'Addario's shift, and the lieutenant's dependence on both the board and the clearance rate had become even more acute in the wake of Worden's investigation into the Monroe Street shooting of John Scott. The captain had taken the extraordinary step of removing both D'Addario and McLarney from the chain of command, ordering Worden and James to report directly to the administrative lieutenant. On one level, the decision to preempt McLarney made sense because he was close to so many of the patrolmen in the Western, some of whom were potential suspects in the murder. But D'Addario had no divided allegiances, and after nine years in homicide he had seen enough red balls to know the entire drill. The suggestion that he continue to devote his time to routine matters rather than contend with a sensitive investigation such as Monroe Street could only be taken as an insult. Inevitably, D'Addario's relations with the captain were now more strained than ever.

Gary D'Addario was by reputation a man slow to anger, but Monroe Street had clearly shortened his fuse. Earlier that week, Terry McLarney had typed a routine memo requesting that two Western officers be detailed to homicide to help with an ongoing probe; he had then forwarded the missive directly to the administrative lieutenant, bypassing D'Addario. A minor oversight in chain-of-command courtesy, but now, in the quiet of the coffee room, D'Addario brings it up, using humor and overwrought formality to make his point.

"Sergeant McLarney," he says, smiling, "while I have your attention I wonder if I might inquire as to an administrative matter."

"That's not my whiskey bottle in the top right drawer," blurts out McLarney, straight-faced. "Sergeant Landsman put it there to discredit me."

D'Addario laughs for the first time.

"And," McLarney deadpans, "I would respectfully like to point out that Sergeant Nolan's men have been using the cars without signing the vehicle book as I have properly trained my squad to do."

"This is about another matter."

"Something to do with conduct unbecoming an officer?"

"Not at all. This is purely administrative in nature."

"Oh." McLarney shrugs, sitting down. "You had me worried there for a second."

"I'm just a little concerned because a certain memo you penned was addressed to a lieutenant in this police department other than myself."

McLarney sees his mistake immediately. Monroe Street has everybody stepping light.

"I didn't think. I'm sorry."

D'Addario waves off the apology. "I just need to have your answer to one particular question."

"Sir?"

"First of all, I take it you are of the Roman Catholic faith."

"And proud of it."

"Fine. Then let me ask: Do you accept me as your true and only begotten lieutenant?"

"Yes, sir."

"And thou shalt have no other lieutenants before me?"

"No, sir."

"And thou shalt forever keep this covenant and worship no false lieutenants?"

"Yes."

"Very good, sergeant," says D'Addario, extending his right hand. "You may now kiss the ring."

McLarney leans toward the large University of Baltimore band on the lieutenant's right hand, feigning a gesture of exaggerated subservience. Both men laugh and D'Addario, satisfied, takes a cup of coffee back to his own office.

Alone in the coffee room, Terry McLarney stares at the long white rectangle, understanding that D'Addario has already forgotten and forgiven the wayward memo. But the red ink on D'Addario's side of the board—that's cause for some real concern.

Like most supervisors in the homicide unit, McLarney is a sergeant with a detective's heart, and like D'Addario, he sees his role as largely protectionist. In the districts, the lieutenants can order their sergeants and the sergeants can order their men, and it all works as the general orders manual says it should—chain of command is suited to patrol. But in homicide, where the detectives are paced as much by their own instinct and talent as by the caseload, a good supervisor rarely makes unequivocal demands. He suggests, he encourages, he prods and pleads ever so gently with men who know exactly what needs to be done on a case without having to be told. In many ways, a detective sergeant best serves his men by completing the administrative paperwork, keeping the brass at bay and letting the detectives do the job. It is a reasoned philosophy, and McLarney holds firm to it nine out of ten days. But every tenth day, something suddenly compels him to attempt a pattern of behavior consistent with the sort of sergeants they warn you about in the academy.

A heavyset Irishman with cherubic features, McLarney drapes one stubby leg over a desk corner and looks up at the white rectangle and the three red entries below his nameplate. Thomas Ward. Kenny Vines. Michael Jones. Three dead men; three open cases. Definitely not the best way for a squad to start a new year.

McLarney is still staring at the board when one of his detectives walks into the coffee room. Carrying an old case folder, Donald Waltemeyer grunts a monosyllabic greeting and walks past the sergeant to an empty desk. McLarney watches him for a few minutes, thinking of a way to begin a conversation he doesn't really want to have.

"Hey, Donald."

"Hey."

"What are you looking at?"

"Old case from Mount Vernon."

"Homosexual murder?"

"Yeah, William Leyh, from eighty-seven. The one where the guy was tied up and beat," says Waltemeyer, shuffling through the file to the five-by-seven color photos of a half-nude, blood-soaked wreck, hog-tied on an apartment floor.

"What's up with that?"

"Got a call from a state trooper in New Jersey. There's a guy in a mental institution up there who says he tied up and beat a guy in Baltimore."

"This case?"

"Dunno. Me or Dave or Donald is going to have to go up there and talk to this guy. It could all be bullshit."

McLarney shifts gears. "I always said you were the hardest-working man in my squad, Donald. I tell everybody that."

Waltemeyer looks up at his sergeant with immediate suspicion.

"No, really . . ."

"What do you want, sergeant?"

"Why do I have to want anything?"

"Hey," says Waltemeyer, leaning back in his chair, "how long have I been a policeman?"

"Can't a sergeant compliment one of his men?"

Waltemeyer rolls his eyes. "What do you want from me?"

McLarney laughs, almost embarrassed at having been so easily caught playing the role of supervisor.

"Well," he says, treading carefully, "what's up with the Vines case?"

"Not much. Ed wants to bring Eddie Carey back in and talk to him, but there isn't much else."

"Well, what about Thomas Ward?"

"Talk to Dave Brown. He's the primary."

Pedaling with his feet, McLarney rolls his chair around to the side of Waltemeyer's desk. His voice drops to a conspiratorial tone.

"Donald, we've got to make something happen with some of these fresh cases. Dee was in here looking at the board just a few minutes ago."

"What are you telling me for?"

"I'm just asking you, is there anything that we're not doing?"

"Is there anything *I'm* not doing?" says Waltemeyer, standing up and grabbing the Leyh file off the desk. "You tell me. I'm doing everything I can, but either the case is there or it isn't. What should I be doing? You tell me."

Donald Waltemeyer is losing it. McLarney can tell because Waltemeyer's eyes have begun to roll up into his forehead the way they always do when he gets steamed. McLarney worked with a guy in the Central who used to do that. Nicest guy in the world. Pretty long fuse. But let some yo with an attitude ride him too far, those eyeballs would roll up like an Atlantic City slot. It was a sure sign to every other cop that negotiations had ended and nightsticks were in order. McLarney tries to shrug off the memory; he continues to press the point with Waltemeyer.

"Donald, I'm just saying it doesn't look good to start out the year with so many cases in the red."

"So what you're saying to me, sergeant, is that the lieutenant came in here and looked at the board and gave you a little kick, so now you're gonna kick me."

The whole truth and nothing but. McLarney has to laugh. "Well, Donald, you can always go kick Dave Brown."

"Shit rolls downhill, doesn't it, sergeant?"

Fecal gravity. The chain of command defined.

"I don't know," says McLarney, backing away from the conversation as gracefully as possible. "I don't think I've ever actually seen shit on a hill."

"I understand, sergeant, I understand," says Waltemeyer, walking out of the coffee room. "I been a policeman a long time now."

McLarney leans back in his chair, resting his head against the office blackboard. He absently pulls a copy of the police department newsletter off the top of the desk and scans the front page. Grip-and-grin photographs of commissioners and deputy commissioners shaking hands with whichever cop managed to survive the last police shooting. Thank you, son, for taking a bullet for Baltimore.

The sergeant tosses the newsletter back on the desk, then gets up, giving one last glance at the board on his way out of the coffee room.

Vines, Ward and Jones. Red, red and red.

So, McLarney tells himself, it's gonna be that kind of year.

TUESDAY, JANUARY 26

Harry Edgerton begins the day right, his freshly shined loafer narrowly avoiding a piece of the dead man's ear as he pushes through the screen door of a Northeast Baltimore townhouse.

"You just missed his ear."

Edgerton looks up quizzically at a ruddy-faced patrolman leaning against a living room wall.

"What was that?"

"His ear," the uniform says, pointing down at the parquet floor. "You just missed stepping on it."

Edgerton looks down at a pale lump of flesh next to his right shoe. It's an ear, all right. Most of the lobe and a short, curled stretch of the outer ridge, resting just beyond the welcome mat. The detective glances at the dead man and the shotgun on the sofa, then moves toward the other end of the room, choosing his steps carefully.

"How does that line go," says the uniform, as if he had practiced it for a week. "Friends, Romans, countrymen . . ."

"Police are some sick fucks," laughs Edgerton, shaking his head. "Who's handling this one?"

"Straight-up suicide. She's got it."

An older patrolman points to a younger uniform sitting at the dining room table. The officer, a black woman with delicate features, is already writing out her incident report. Edgerton makes her immediately for a uniform new to the street.

"Hey there."

The woman nods.

"You found him? What's your unit number?"

"Four-two-three."

"Did you touch him or move anything around?"

The woman looks at Edgerton as if he's just dropped in from another solar system. Touch him? She doesn't even want to look at the poor bastard. The woman shakes her head, then glances over at the body. Edgerton looks over at the red-faced officer, who understands and accepts the detective's silent plea.

"We'll walk her through it," the older uniform says quietly. "She'll be okay."

The academy had been turning out policewomen for more than a decade and as far as Edgerton was concerned, the verdict was still out. Many women had joined the department with a reasonable understanding of the job and a willingness to perform; some were even good cops. But Edgerton knew there were others out on the street who were absolutely dangerous. Secretaries, the older hands called them. Secretaries with guns.

The tales became worse with each telling. Everyone in the department had heard about the girl out in the Northwest, a novice who got her gun taken from her by that mental case in a Pimlico convenience store. And there was that female officer in the Western who called in the Signal 13 while her partner was getting the shit kicked from him by a family of five in a Sector 2 rowhouse. When the radio cars came racing up the street, they found the woman standing at the curb, pointing toward the front door of the house like some kind of crossing guard. Stories like that could be heard in every district roll call room.

Even as other sections of the department became grudgingly familiar with the idea of women officers, the homicide unit remained a bastion of male law enforcement, a lewd, locker room environment where a second divorce was regarded almost as a rite of passage. Only one female detective had ever lasted for any length of time: Jenny Wehr spent three years in homicide, time enough to prove herself a good investigator and exceptional interrogator, but not long enough to begin anything that could be considered a trend.

It was only two weeks ago, in fact, that Bertina Silver had transferred into the homicide unit on Stanton's shift, making her the only female among thirty-six detectives and sergeants. In the judgment of other detectives who had worked with her in narcotics and patrol, Bert Silver was a cop: aggressive, hard, intelligent. But her arrival in homicide did little to change the prevailing political view among many detectives, who regarded the decision to give badges to women as unequivocal evidence that the barbarians were rattling the gates of Rome. For many in the homicide unit, the reality of Bertina Silver did not contradict the established theory, she was simply an exception. It was an unjustified but necessary contortion of logic that kept her out of the accepted equation: The women officers are secretaries, but Bert is Bert. Friend. Partner. Cop.

Harry Edgerton would have been the last person to complain about Bert Silver, whom he regarded as one of the unit's better recruits. This opinion held despite a continuing campaign of aggression and hegemony being waged by Bert for partial control of Edgerton's desk. After years of having a place to call his own in the homicide office, Edgerton had been told at the beginning of the year to double up with Bert because of a space shortage. He did so grudgingly and soon found himself on the defensive. Once such innocuous additions as family portraits and a gold statuette of a policewoman were granted space on the desktop, they were followed by hairbrushes and loose earrings in the upper right drawer. Then came the unending assault of the lipstick canisters and the arrival of a perfumed scarf that kept finding its way back to the bottom drawer, where Edgerton kept his suspect files from several previous drug investigations.

"That's it," said the detective, pulling the scarf out of the drawer and stuffing it into Bert's mailbox for the third time. "If I don't fight back, she'll be putting curtains up in the interrogation room."

But Edgerton didn't fight back, and eventually Bert Silver had half the desk. In his heart of hearts, Harry Edgerton knows that is as it should be. Then again, this young thing writing an incident report at the dining room table is no Bert Silver. Despite the older officer's assurance, Edgerton takes the uniform aside and speaks softly.

"If she's the first officer, she's going to have to wait for the crime lab and then do the ECU submissions."

The comment is almost an open question. More than once a medical examiner has turned a seeming suicide into a murder, and God knows it won't do to have some recent academy product tangling up chain-of-custody on every item submitted to evidence control. The uniform understands without another word spoken.

"Don't worry. We'll walk her through it," he repeats.

Edgerton nods.

"She'll be okay," the officer says, shrugging. "Hell, she's more on the ball than some we're seeing."

Edgerton opens his small steno pad and walks back into the dining room. He begins asking both uniforms the standard questions, pulling together the raw material for a death investigation.

On the first page, dated 26 Jan. in the upper right corner, the detective has already recorded the details of his own notification by a police dispatcher at 1:03 P.M.: "1303 hours/Dispatch #76/serious shooting/5511 Leith Walk." Two lines below that, Edgerton has recorded his time of arrival at the scene.

He adds the name of the young female officer, her unit number and time of arrival. He asks for the incident number, 4A53881—4 representing the Northeastern District, A signifying the month of January, the remaining digits the basic tracking number—and writes that down as well. Then he records the number of the city ambulance unit that responded and the name of the medic who pronounced the victim. He finishes off the first page with the time of the ambo crew's pronouncement.

"Okay," says Edgerton, turning to take his first interested look at the dead man. "Who do we have here?"

"Robert William Smith," says the red-faced officer. "Thirty-eight, no . . . thirty-nine years."

"He lives here?"

"He did, yeah."

Edgerton writes the name on the second page followed by M/W/39 and the address.

"Anyone here when it happened?"

The female officer speaks up. "His wife called nine-one-one. She said she was upstairs and he was down here cleaning his shotgun."

"Where is she now?"

"They took her to the hospital for shock."

"Did you talk to her before she left?"

The woman nods.

"Write what she told you in a supplemental report," Edgerton says. "Did she say why he might've killed himself?"

"She said he has a history of mental problems," says the red-faced officer, breaking in. "He just got out of Springfield Hospital on the eleventh. Here's his commitment papers."

Edgerton takes a creased green sheet of paper from the officer and reads quickly. The dead man was undergoing treatment for personality disorders and—bingo—suicidal tendencies. The detective hands the paper back and writes two more lines in his notepad.

"Where did you find that?"

"His wife had it."

"Is the crime lab on the way?"

"My sergeant called them."

"How about the medical examiner?"

"Lemme check on that," says the officer, walking outside to key his radio. Edgerton throws his notepad on the dining room table and pulls off his overcoat.

He does not move directly toward the body but instead walks around the perimeter of the living room, looking along the floor, walls and furniture. For Edgerton, it has become second nature to begin at the periphery of the crime scene, moving toward the body in a slowly shrinking circle. It is a method born of the same instinct that allows a detective to walk into a room and spend ten minutes filling a notepad with raw data before taking a serious look at the corpse. It takes a few months for every detective to learn that the body is going to be there, stationary and intact, for as long as it takes to process the crime scene. But the scene itself—whether it happens to be a street corner, automobile interior or living room—begins to deteriorate as soon as the first person finds the body. Any homicide detective with more than a year's experience has already collected one or two stories about uniformed men walking through blood trails or handling weapons found at a murder scene. And not just the uniforms: More than once a Baltimore homicide detective has arrived at a shooting scene to discover some major or colonel wandering through a fresh scene, pawing the shell casings or going through a victim's wallet in a determined effort to put prints on every conceivable bit of evidence.

Rule Number Two in the homicide lexicon: The victim is killed once, but a crime scene can be murdered a thousand times.

Edgerton marks the direction of spatter from the body, reassuring himself that the spray of blood and brain matter is consistent with a single wound to the head. The long white wall behind the sofa and to the dead man's right is marred by one red-pink arc extending upward from a half foot above the victim's head to nearly eye level at the front door frame. It is a long, curled finger of individual spatters that seems to point, in its final trajectory, toward the piece of ear near the welcome mat. A smaller arc extends across the top cushions of the sofa. In the small space between the sofa and the wall, Edgerton finds a few shards of skull and, on the floor just below the dead man's right side, much of what had once occupied the victim's head.

The detective looks closely at several of the individual spatters and satisfies himself that the blood spray is consistent with a single wound, fired upwards, into the left temple. The calculation is a matter of simple physics: A blood droplet that strikes a surface from a 90-degree angle should be symmetrical, with tentacles or fingers of equal length extending in any and every direction; a droplet that strikes a surface at an odd angle will dry with the longest tentacles pointing in a direction opposite the source of the blood. In the case at hand, a blood trail or spatter with tentacles pointing in any direction other than from the victim's head would be hard to explain.

"Okay," says the detective, pushing back the coffee table to stand directly in front of the victim. "Let's see what you're about."

The dead man is nude, his lower half wrapped in a checkered blanket. He is seated in the center of the couch, with what remains of his head resting on the back of the sofa. The left eye stares at the ceiling; gravity has pulled the other deep into its socket.

"That's his federal tax form on the table," says the red-faced uniform, pointing to the coffee table.

"Oh yeah?"

"Check it out."

Edgerton looks down at the coffee table and sees the familiar cover page of a 1040.

"Those things drive me crazy, too," says the uniform. "I guess he just lost his head."

Edgerton moans loudly. It is still too early in the day for unchecked constabulary wit.

"He musta been itemizing."

"Police," Edgerton repeats, "are sick fucks."

He looks at the shotgun between the victim's legs. The 12-gauge is resting with its stock on the floor, barrel upward, with the victim's left forearm resting on the upper barrel. The detective gives the weapon a once-over, but the crime lab will need a photograph, so he leaves the gun resting between the victim's legs. He takes the dead man's hands in his own. Still warm. Edgerton convinces himself that death was recent by manipulating the ends of the fingers. Every now and then, some irate husband or wife wins the argument by shooting the significant other and then spends three or four hours wondering what to do next. By the time they seize on the notion of staging a suicide, the victim's body temperature has dropped and rigor mortis is evident in the shorter facial and finger muscles. Edgerton has had cases where the killers caused themselves much useless aggravation by attempting to push the rigid fingers of the not so recently departed inside the trigger guard of a weapon, an effort that fairly screams foul play by giving the body the appearance of a department store mannequin with a prop glued to its ungrasping hand. But Robert William Smith is one very fresh piece of meat.

Edgerton puts pen to paper: "V. braced gun between legs . . . muzzle to right cheek . . . large GSW to right side head. Warm to touch. No rigor."

Both uniforms watch as Edgerton pulls on his overcoat and deposits the notepad in an outside pocket.

"You're not staying for the crime lab?"

"Well, I'd love to but . . ."

"We're boring you, aren't we?"

"What can I say?" says Edgerton, his voice dropping to something approximating a matinee idol baritone. "My work here is done."

The red-faced officer laughs.

"When the guy gets here, tell him I just need photos of this room, and tell him to get a good shot of the guy with the gun between his legs. We're going to want to take the gun and that green sheet."

"The discharge papers?"

"Yeah, that goes downtown. What about securing this place? Is the wife coming back?"

"She was pretty messed up when they took her out of here. I guess we'll find a way to lock the place up."

"Yeah, good."

"Is that it?"

"Yeah, thanks."

"No problem."

Edgerton looks over at the female uniform, still seated at the dining room table.

"How's your report coming?"

"It's done," she says, holding up the face sheet. "Do you want to see it?"

"No, I'm sure it's fine," says Edgerton, knowing a sector sergeant will review it. "How do you like the job so far?"

The woman looks first at the dead man, then at the detective. "It's okay."

Edgerton nods, waves to the red-faced officer and walks out, this time carefully sidestepping the ear.

Fifteen minutes later, he is at a typewriter in the homicide unit's administrative office, converting the contents of three notepad pages into a single-page 24-hour crime report, Criminal Investigation Division form 78/151. Even with Edgerton's hunt-and-peck typing skills, the details of Robert William Smith's terminus are condensed to a manageable memorandum in little more than a quarter hour. Case folders are the essential documentation for homicides, but the 24-hour reports become the paper trail for the activities of the entire Crimes Against Persons section. By checking the log containing the twenty-fours, a detective can quickly familiarize himself with every ongoing case. For each incident, there is a corresponding one- or two-page missive with a brief, declarative heading, and a detective flipping through the log can look at those headings for a complete chronological account of Baltimore's violence:

". . . shooting, shooting, questionable death, cutting, arrest/homicide, serious shooting, homicide, homicide/serious shooting, suicide, rape/cutting, questionable death/poss overdose, commercial robbery, shooting . . ."

Dead, dying or merely wounded, there is a form 78/151 for every victim in the city of Baltimore. In little more than a year in homicide, Tom Pellegrini has probably filled in the blanks on more than a hundred twenty-fours. By that same estimate, Harry Edgerton has gone through five hundred forms since transferring to homicide in February 1981. And Donald Kincaid, the senior detective in Edgerton's squad and a homicide man since 1975, has probably typed well over a thousand.

More than the board, which tallies only homicides and their clearances, the 24-hour log is the basic measure of a detective's workload. If your name is on the bottom of a twenty-four, it means you were picking up phones when the call came in or, better still, you volunteered yourself when another detective held up a green pawn shop card with an address scrawled on it and asked a question older than the headquarters building itself: "Who's up?"

Harry Edgerton didn't volunteer often and among the other members of his squad, that simple fact had turned into an open wound.

No one in the squad doubted Edgerton's abilities as an investigator and most would admit that, personally, they kind of liked the guy. But in a five-man unit where the detectives all worked one another's cases and handled every kind of call, Harry Edgerton was something of a lone wolf, a man who regularly wandered off on his own extended adventures. In a unit where most murders were won or lost in the first twenty-four hours of investigation, Edgerton would pursue a case for days or even weeks, running down witnesses or conducting surveillance on a time clock all his own. Perennially late for roll calls and shift relief on nightwork, Edgerton might just as easily be discovered putting together a case file at 3:00 A.M. when his shift had ended at midnight. For the most part, he worked his cases without a secondary detective, taking his own statements and conducting his own interrogations, oblivious of whatever storms were buffeting the rest of the squad. They regarded Edgerton as more of a finesse pitcher than a bullpen workhorse, and in an environment where quantity seemed to matter more than quality, his work ethic was a constant source of tension.

Edgerton's background only added to the isolation. The son of a respected New York jazz pianist, he was a child of Manhattan who joined the Baltimore department on a whim after glancing at an ad in the classifieds. Whereas many of those in homicide had spent their childhood on the same streets they were now policing, Edgerton's frame of reference was Upper Manhattan, tinged with memories of visits to the Metropolitan Museum after school and nightclub engagements where his mother would accompany the likes of Lena Horne or Sammy Davis, Jr. His youth was as far removed from police work as a life could conceivably be: Edgerton could claim to have seen Dylan in the early Greenwich Village years, and he later sang lead for his own rock 'n' roll group, an ensemble with the flower child name of Aphrodite.

A conversation with Harry Edgerton was apt to wander from foreign art films to jazz fusion to the relative quality of imported Greek wines—an expertise acquired through his marriage into the Brooklyn family of a Greek merchant who had brought his family to New York after several successful years of trading in the Sudan. All of which made Harry Edgerton, even at the settled age of forty, an enigma to his colleagues. On midnight shift, when the rest of his squad might be sitting together, watching Clint Eastwood fondling the largest and most powerful handgun in the world, Edgerton could be found writing out an office report in the coffee room, listening to a tape of Emmylou Harris singing Woody Guthrie.

And during the dinner hour, Edgerton was likely to disappear into the back of an East Baltimore Street carryout, where he would park in front of a bank of video games and lose himself in a fevered effort to blast apart multicolored space critters with a laser death ray. In an environment where a willingness to wear a pink necktie is held suspect, Edgerton was a certified flake. One of Jay Landsman's throwaway lines pretty much summed things up for the entire unit: "For a communist, Harry's a helluva detective."

And though Edgerton was black, his cosmopolitan background, his coffeehouse leanings, even his New York accent so completely confounded expectations that he was regarded as inauthentic by white detectives accustomed to viewing blacks through the limited prism of their own experience in the Baltimore slums. Edgerton crossed up stereotypes and blurred the unit's preconceived racial lines: Even black detectives with local roots, like Eddie Brown, would routinely suggest that while Edgerton was black, he certainly wasn't "po' and black," a distinction that Brown, who drove a Cadillac Brougham the size of a small container ship, reserved for himself. And on those occasions when white detectives needed someone to anonymously call some West Baltimore address to see if a wanted suspect happened to be at home, Edgerton would be quickly discouraged.

"Not you, Harry. We need someone who sounds like a black guy."

Edgerton's detachment from the rest of the unit was furthered by his partnership with Ed Burns, with whom he had been detailed to the Drug Enforcement Administration for an investigation that consumed two years. That probe began because Burns had learned the name of a major narcotics trafficker who had ordered the slaying of his girlfriend. Unable to prove the murder, Burns and Edgerton instead spent months on electronic and telephone surveillance, then took the dealer down for drug distribution to the tune of thirty years, no parole. To Edgerton, a case like that was a statement of a kind, an answer to an organized drug trade that could otherwise engage in contract murder with impunity.

It was a persuasive argument. Close to half of Baltimore's murders were believed to be related to the use or sale of narcotics, though the solve rate for drug murders was consistently lower than that for nearly any other motive. Yet homicide's methodology hadn't changed with the trend: Detectives worked the drug-related murders independently, as they would any other homicide. Both Burns and Edgerton had argued that much of the violence was related and could only be reduced—or, better still, prevented—by attacking the city's larger narcotics organizations. By that argument, the repetitive violence of the city's drug markets betrayed the weakness in the homicide unit, namely, that the investigations were individual, haphazard and reactive. Two years after that initial DEA case, Edgerton and Burns again proved the point with a year-long probe of a drug ring linked to a dozen murders and attempted murders in the Murphy Homes housing project. Every one of those shootings had remained open after detectives followed the traditional approach, yet as a result of the prolonged investigation, four murders were cleared and the key defendants received double life sentences.

It was precision law enforcement, but other detectives were quick to point out that those two probes consumed three years, leaving two of the unit's squads short a man for much of that time. The phone still had to be answered and with Edgerton reporting to work at the DEA field office, the other members of his squad—Kincaid and Garvey, McAllister and Bowman—would each be handling more shootings, more questionable deaths, more suicides, more murders. The fallout from Edgerton's prolonged absences had served to push him further from the other detectives.

True to form, Ed Burns is at this very moment detailed to a sprawling FBI probe of a drug organization in the Lexington Terrace projects—an investigation that will eventually consume two years. Edgerton originally went with him, but two months ago he was shipped back to the homicide unit after a nasty budget dispute between federal and local supervisors. And the fact that Harry Edgerton is now back in the standard rotation, pecking away at a 24-hour report on something as menial and undramatic as a suicide, is a source of glee to the rest of the shift.

"Harry, what're you doing at the typewriter?"

"Hey, Harry, you didn't handle a call, did you?"

"What is it, Harry, a big investigation?"

"Are you gonna get detailed again, Harry?"

Edgerton lights a cigarette and laughs. After all the special details, he knows he has this coming.

"Pretty funny," he says, still smiling. "You guys are a fucking riot."

Carrying paperwork of his own to the other admin office typewriter, Bob Bowman leans over and looks at the headings on Edgerton's twenty-four.

"A suicide? Harry, you went out on a suicide?"

"Yeah," says Edgerton, playing the game. "See what happens when you answer the phone?"

"I'll bet you're never gonna do that again."

"Not if I can help it."

"I didn't know you were allowed to do suicides. I thought you only did big investigations."

"I'm slumming."

"Hey, Rog," says Bowman as his squad sergeant walks into the office, "do you know Harry went out on a suicide?"

Roger Nolan only smiles. Edgerton could be a problem child, but Nolan knows him to be a good detective and is therefore tolerant of his idiosyncrasies. Besides, Edgerton has more than a simple suicide on his plate: He caught the first murder of the year for Nolan's squad, a particularly vicious stabbing from the Northwest that showed no sign of going down easily.

It was the first leg of a midnight shift two weeks back that Edgerton met Brenda Thompson, an overweight, sad-faced woman who finished twenty-eight years in the rear seat of a four-door Dodge found idling at a bus stop and pay phone in the 2400 block of Garrison Boulevard.

The crime scene was largely the Dodge, with the victim slumped in the back seat, her shirt and bra hiked up to display a chest and stomach marked by a dozen or more vertical stab wounds. On the floor of the back seat, the killer had dumped the contents of the victim's purse, indicating an apparent robbery. Beyond that, there was no physical evidence in the car—no fingerprints, no hairs, no fibers, no torn skin or blood beneath the victim's fingernails, no nothing. Without witnesses, Edgerton was in for a long haul.

For two weeks, he had worked backward on Brenda Thompson's last hours, learning that on the night of her murder she was picking up money from a stable of young street dealers who sold her husband's heroin along Pennsylvania Avenue. The drugs were one motive, but Edgerton couldn't discount a straight-up robbery either. Just this afternoon, in fact, he had been across the hall in CID robbery, checking knife attacks in the Northwest, looking for even the slimmest of new leads.

That Edgerton has been working a fresh murder doesn't count for much. Nor does it matter to anyone in his squad that he took the suicide call with little complaint. Edgerton's workload remains a sore point with his colleagues, Bowman and Kincaid in particular. And as their sergeant, Roger Nolan knows that it can only get worse. It's Nolan's responsibility to keep his detectives from one another's throats, and so, more than anyone in the room, the sergeant listens to the banter with the understanding that every comment has an edge.

Bowman, for one, can't leave it alone. "I don't know what we're coming to when Harry has to go out and handle a suicide."

"Don't worry," mutters Edgerton, pulling the report from the typewriter, "after this one, I'm done for the year."

At which point, even Bowman has to laugh.

TWO

THURSDAY, FEBRUARY 4

It is the illusion of tears and nothing more, the rainwater that collects in small beads and runs to the hollows of her face. The dark brown eyes are fixed wide, staring across wet pavement; jet black braids of hair surround the deep brown skin, high cheekbones and a pert, upturned nose. The lips are parted and curled in a slight, vague frown. She is beautiful, even now.

She is resting on her left hip, her head cocked to one side, her back arched, with one leg bent over the other. Her right arm rests above her head, her left arm is fully extended, with small, thin fingers reaching out across the asphalt for something, or someone, no longer there.

Her upper body is partially wrapped in a red vinyl raincoat. Her pants are a yellow print, but they are dirty and smudged. The front of her blouse and the nylon jacket beneath the raincoat are both ripped, both blotted red where the life ran out of her. A single ligature mark—the deep impression of a rope or cord—travels the entire circumference of her neck, crisscrossing just below the base of the skull. Above her right arm is a blue cloth satchel, set upright on the pavement and crammed with library books, some papers, a cheap camera and a cosmetic case containing make-up in bright reds, blues and purples—exaggerated, girlish colors that suggest amusement more than allure.

She is eleven years old.

Among the detectives and patrol officers crowded over the body of Latonya Kim Wallace there is no easy banter, no coarse exchange of cop humor or time-worn indifference. Jay Landsman offers only clinical, declarative statements as he moves through the scene. Tom Pellegrini stands mute in the light rain, sketching the surroundings on a damp notebook page. Behind them, against the rear wall of a rowhouse, leans one of the first Central District officers to arrive at the scene, one hand on his gun belt, the other absently holding his radio mike.

"Cold," he says, almost to himself.

From the moment of discovery, Latonya Wallace is never regarded as anything less than a true victim, innocent as few of those murdered in this city ever are. A child, a fifth-grader, has been used and discarded, a monstrous sacrifice to an unmistakable evil.

Worden had first crack at the call, which came in from communications as nothing more specific than a body in the alley behind the 700 block of Newington Avenue, a residential block in the Reservoir Hill section of the city's midtown. D'Addario's shift had gone to daywork the week before, and when the phone line lit up at 8:15 A.M., his detectives were still assembling for the 8:40 roll call.

Worden scrawled the particulars on the back of a pawn shop card, then showed it to Landsman. "You want me to take it?"

"Nah, my guys are all here," the sergeant said. "It's probably some smokehound laid out with his bottle."

Landsman lit a cigarette, located Pellegrini in the coffee room, then grabbed the keys to a Cavalier from a departing midnight shift detective. Ten minutes later, he was on the radio from Newington Avenue, calling for troops.

Edgerton went. Then McAllister, Bowman and Rich Garvey, the workhorse of Roger Nolan's squad. Then Dave Brown, from McLarney's crew, and Fred Ceruti, from Landsman's squad.

Pellegrini, Landsman and Edgerton all work the scene. The others fan out from the body: Brown and Bowman walking slowly in the light rain through adjacent yards and trash-filled alleys, eyes fixed on the ground for a blood trail, a knife, a piece of quarter-inch rope to match the ligature on the neck, a shred of clothing; Ceruti, and then Edgerton, crawling up a wooden ladder to the first- and second-floor tar roofs of adjacent rowhouses, checking for anything not visible from the alley itself; Garvey and McAllister splitting away from the scene to work back on the young girl's last known movements, checking first the missing persons report that had been filed two days earlier, then interviewing teachers, friends and the librarian at the Park Avenue branch, where Latonya Wallace had last been seen alive.

Just inside the rear door of 718 Newington, a few feet from the body, Pellegrini deposits the rain-soaked satchel on a kitchen table surrounded by detectives, patrolmen and lab technicians. Landsman carefully opens the top flap and peers inside at a schoolgirl's possessions.

"Mostly books," he says after a few seconds. "Let's go through it at the lab. We don't want to get into this stuff out here."

Pellegrini lifts the blue bag off the table and carefully hands it to Fasio, the lab tech. Then he returns to his notebook and reviews the raw details of a crime scene—time of call, unit numbers, times of arrival—before walking out the rear door and staring for a few more moments at the dead child.

The black Dodge morgue wagon is already parked at the end of the alley and Pellegrini watches Pervis from the ME's office make his way down the pavement and into the yard. Pervis looks briefly at the body before finding Landsman in the rear kitchen.

"Are we ready to go?"

Landsman glances over at Pellegrini, who seems to hesitate for a moment. Standing in that kitchen doorway on Newington Avenue, Tom Pellegrini feels a fleeting impulse to tell the ME to wait, to keep the body where it is—to slow the entire process and take hold of a crime scene that seems to be evaporating before his eyes. It is, after all, his murder. He had arrived first with Landsman; he is now the primary detective. And although half the shift is now snaking through the neighborhood in search of information, it will be Pellegrini alone who stands or falls with the case.

Months later, the detective will remember that morning on Reservoir Hill with both regret and frustration. He will find himself wishing that for just a few minutes he could have cleared the yard behind 718 Newington of detectives and uniforms and lab techs and ME attendants. He will sit at his desk in the annex office and imagine a still, silent tableau, with himself at the edge of the rear yard, seated in a chair, perhaps on a stool, examining the body of Latonya Wallace and its surroundings with calm, rational precision. Pellegrini will remember, too, that in those early moments he had deferred to the veteran detectives, Landsman and Edgerton, abdicating his own authority in favor of men who had been there many times before. That was understandable, but much later Pellegrini will become frustrated at the thought that he was never really in control of his case.

But in the crowded kitchen that morning, with Pervis leaning into the doorway, Pellegrini's discomfort is nothing more than a vague feeling with neither voice nor reason behind it. Pellegrini has sketched the scene in his notebook and, along with Landsman and Edgerton, has walked every inch of that yard and much of the alley as well. Fasio has his photos and is already measuring the key distances. Moreover, it is now close to nine. The neighborhood is stirring, and in the bleak light of a February morning, the presence of a child's body, eviscerated and splayed on wet pavement under a slow drizzle, seems more obscene with each passing moment. Even homicide detectives must live with the natural, unspoken impulse to bring Latonya Kim Wallace in from the rain.

"Yeah, I think we're ready," says Landsman. "What do you think, Tom?"

Pellegrini pauses.

"Tom?"

"No. We're ready."

"Let's do it."

Landsman and Pellegrini follow the morgue wagon back downtown to get a jump on the postmortem while Edgerton and Ceruti pilot separate cars to a drab pillbox of an apartment building on Druid Lake Drive, about three and a half blocks away. Both men drop cigarette butts outside the apartment door, then step quickly to the first-floor landing. Edgerton hesitates before knocking and looks at Ceruti.

"Lemme take this one."

"Hey, it's all yours, Harry."

"You'll bring her down to the ME, okay?"

Ceruti nods.

Edgerton puts his hand to the door and knocks. He pulls out his shield and then inhales deeply at the sound of footsteps inside apartment 739A. The door opens slowly to reveal a man in his late twenties or early thirties, wearing denims and a T-shirt. He acknowledges and accepts the two detectives with a slight nod even before Edgerton can identify himself. The young man steps back and the detectives follow him across the threshold. In the dining room sits a small boy, eating cold cereal and turning the pages of a coloring book. From a back bedroom comes the sound of a door opening, then footsteps. Edgerton's voice falls close to a whisper.

"Is Latonya's mother home?"

There is no chance to answer. The woman stands in a bathrobe at the edge of the dining room, beside her a young girl, just into her teens perhaps, with the same flawless features as the girl on Newington Avenue. The woman's eyes, terrified and sleepless, fix on Harry Edgerton's face.

"My daughter. You found her?"

Edgerton looks at her, shakes his head sideways, but says nothing. The woman looks past Edgerton to Ceruti, then to the empty doorway.

"Where is she? She . . . all right?"

Edgerton shakes his head again.

"Oh God."

"I'm sorry."

The young girl stifles a cry, then falls into her mother's embrace. The woman takes the child in her arms and turns toward the dining room wall. Edgerton watches the woman fight a wave of emotion, her body tensing, her eyes closing tight for a long minute.

The young man speaks. "How did . . ."

"She was found this morning," says Edgerton, his voice barely audible. "Stabbed, in an alley near here."

The mother turns back toward the detective and tries to speak, but the words are lost in a hard swallow. Edgerton watches her turn and walk toward the bedroom door, where another woman, the victim's aunt and the mother of the boy eating cereal, holds out her arms. The detective then turns to the man who opened the door, who, though dazed, still seems to understand and accept the words thrown at him.

"We'll need her to go to the medical examiner's office, for a positive identification. And then, if it's at all possible, we'd like you all to come to headquarters, downtown. We're going to need your help now."

The young man nods, then disappears into the bedroom. Edgerton and Ceruti stand alone in the dining room for several minutes, awkward and uncomfortable, until the silence is broken by an anguished wail from the back bedroom.

"I hate this," says Ceruti softly.

Edgerton walks over to a set of dining room shelves and picks up a framed photograph of two young girls seated side by side in pink bows and lace, carefully posed before a blue backdrop. Toothy, say-cheeseburger smiles. Every braid and curl in place. Edgerton holds up the photograph for Ceruti, who has slumped into a dining room chair.

"This," says Edgerton, looking over the photo, "is what this motherfucker gets off on."

The teenage girl closes the bedroom door softly and walks toward the dining room. Replacing the picture frame, Edgerton suddenly recognizes her as the older girl in the photograph.

"She's getting dressed now," the girl says.

Edgerton nods. "What's your name?"

"Rayshawn."

"And you're how old?"

"Thirteen."

The detective looks again at the picture. The girl waits a few moments for another question; when none is forthcoming, she wanders back into the bedroom. Edgerton walks softly through the dining room and living room, then into the apartment's tiny kitchen. The furnishings are spare, the furniture mismatched, and the living room sofa worn around the edges. But the place is well kept and clean—very clean, in fact. Edgerton notices that most of the shelf space is devoted to family photographs. In the kitchen, a child's painting—big house, blue sky, smiling child, smiling dog—is taped to the refrigerator door. On the wall is a mimeographed list of school events and parent association meetings. Poverty, perhaps, but not desperation. Latonya Wallace lived in a home.

The bedroom door opens and the mother, fully dressed and followed by her older daughter, steps into the hallway. She walks wearily through the dining room to the front closet.

"Ready?" Edgerton asks.

The woman nods, then pulls her coat from its hanger. Her boyfriend takes his own jacket. The thirteen-year-old hesitates at the closet door.

"Where's your coat?" her mother asks.

"In my room, I think."

"Well, go find it," she says softly. "It's cold out."

Edgerton leads the procession from the apartment, then watches as the mother, boyfriend and sister squeeze into Ceruti's Cavalier for the slow ride to Penn Street, where a silver gurney will be waiting in a tiled room.

Meanwhile, on the southwestern edge of Reservoir Hill, Rich Garvey and Bob McAllister are tracing the last movements of Latonya Wallace. A report of the child's disappearance had been filed by the family about 8:30 on the evening of February 2, two days earlier, but it read like dozens of other reports filed every month in Baltimore. The paperwork had not yet reached homicide, and any investigation had been limited to routine checks by the missing persons unit at Central District.

The two detectives head first to Latonya's school to interview the principal, several teachers, and a nine-year-old playmate of the victim as well as the playmate's mother, who had both seen Latonya on the afternoon of her disappearance. The interviews confirm the substance of the missing persons report:

On the afternoon of Tuesday, February 2, Latonya Wallace returned home from Eutaw-Marshburn Elementary School. She arrived about three o'clock and left the house less than a half hour later with her blue bookbag, telling her mother she wanted to visit the city library branch on Park Avenue, about four blocks from the family apartment. Latonya then walked to the building next door, knocking on the door of the playmate's apartment to see if she, too, wanted to go to the library. When the younger girl's mother decided to keep her daughter home, Latonya Wallace set out on her own.

Garvey and McAllister pick up the chronology at the Park Avenue library branch, where the afternoon librarian remembers the visit by the girl in the red raincoat. The librarian recalls that the child stayed only a few minutes, picking out a series of books almost at random, giving little or no thought to the titles or subjects. Thinking back, the librarian also tells the detectives that the young girl had seemed preoccupied or troubled, and had paused in thought at the library door just before leaving.

Then Latonya Wallace carried her bookbag into the daytime bustle of a Baltimore street and vanished, her passing unseen by any known witness. The child had remained hidden for a day and a half before being dumped in that back alley. Where she had been taken, where she had stayed for more than thirty-six hours—the primary crime scene—was still not known. The detectives would begin their pursuit of Latonya Wallace's killer with little more physical evidence than the body itself.

Indeed, that is where Tom Pellegrini begins. He and Jay Landsman wait in the basement autopsy room of the medical examiner's offices on Penn Street, watching the cutters extract cold, clinical data from the earthly remains of Latonya Wallace. The facts initially seem to suggest a prolonged abduction: The victim's stomach is determined to contain one fully digested meal of spaghetti and meatballs followed by a partially digested meal of hot dogs and a shredded, stringy substance believed to be sauerkraut. A detective calls the school cafeteria and is told that the lunch menu on February 2 was spaghetti, and yet Latonya Wallace did not eat anything at home before heading for the library later that afternoon. Had the murderer kept the child alive long enough to provide her with a last meal?

As the detectives stand at the edge of the autopsy room and confer with the medical examiners, Pellegrini's foreboding at the crime scene begins to take solid form: Newington Avenue had indeed been cleared too soon. At least one piece of evidence was forever lost.

Informed of the child's murder even as the detectives were finishing their work at the scene, the state's chief medical examiner, John Smialek, rushed from his office to Reservoir Hill only to arrive after the body was removed. Lost was an opportunity for Smialek to use an internal thermometer to calibrate the body temperature, which would have allowed him to narrow the time of death based on a degrees-lost-per-hour formula.

Without a time-of-death estimate based on body temperature, a medical examiner is aided only by the degree of rigor mortis (the stiffening of the muscles) and lividity (the settling and solidification of blood in the dependent parts of the body). But the rate at which any postmortem phenomenon occurs can vary widely, depending on the size, weight and build of the victim, the external temperature of the body at the time of death and the temperature or conditions of the death scene. Moreover, rigor mortis sets and then disappears, then sets again in the first hours after death; a pathologist would have to examine the body more than once—and hours apart—to assess the true status of rigor correctly. As a result, detectives seeking time-of-death estimates have become accustomed to working within a spread of six, twelve, or even eighteen hours. In cases where decomposition has begun, the ability of a pathologist to determine time of death is further impaired, although the onerous task of sizing individual maggots taken from the body can often bring the estimate to within a two- or three-day span. The truth is that medical experts can often provide no more than a rough guess as to a victim's time of death; coroners capable of telling Kojak that his victim stopped breathing between 10:30 and 10:45 P.M. are always a source of amusement for cops slumped in front of the tube on a slow nightshift.

When Pellegrini and Landsman press the pathologists for the best possible estimate, they are told that their victim appears to be coming out of first-stage rigor and has therefore been dead for at least twelve hours. Given the absence of any decomposition and the extra meal in her stomach, the detectives make their first assumption: Latonya Wallace was probably held captive for a day, killed on Wednesday night, and then dumped on Newington Avenue in the early hours of Thursday morning.

The remainder of the autopsy is unambiguous. Latonya Wallace had been strangled with a piece of cord or rope, then brutally disemboweled with a sharp instrument, probably a serrated table knife. She sustained at least six deep wounds to the chest and abdomen, suggesting a level of violence and intensity that detectives categorize as overkill. Although the victim was discovered fully clothed, a fresh vaginal tear indicates some type of molestation, but vaginal, anal and oral swabs come up negative for semen. Finally, the pathologists note that a tiny star-shaped earring is present in one earlobe but missing from the other. The family would later confirm that she wore two such earrings to school on Tuesday.

Examining the wounds in detail, Pellegrini and Landsman are convinced that the rear of Newington Avenue is not the site of the murder. There was little blood at the death scene, even though the child's wounds were severe and bleeding would have been pronounced. The first and most essential question for the detectives is clear: Where was the child murdered, if not in the back alley? Where is the primary crime scene?

As the detectives working the case gather in the homicide office late that afternoon to compare notes, Jay Landsman outlines a scenario increasingly obvious to most of the men in the room:

"She's found between the library and her house," says the sergeant, "so whoever took her is from the neighborhood, and she probably knew him if he was able to get her off the street in the middle of the day. He has to take her inside someplace. If you grabbed her off the street in a car, you'd drive her somewhere else; you wouldn't bring the body back into the neighborhood after you killed her."

Landsman also suggests, to general agreement, that the girl was probably murdered within a block or two of where she was dumped. Even in the early morning hours, he reasons, someone carrying the bloody body of a child, concealed in little more than a red raincoat, would not want to travel in the open for any great distance.

"Unless he takes her to the alley in a car," adds Pellegrini.

"But then you're back to asking yourself why the guy, if he's already got her in a car, would go and dump her in an alley where anyone could look out a window and see him," argues Landsman. "Why not just drive her out into the woods somewhere?"

"Maybe you're dealing with a goof," says Pellegrini.

"No," says Landsman. "Your crime scene is right in that fucking neighborhood. It's probably going to be someone who lives in one of the houses in that block who took her right out of his back door . . . or it's a vacant house or a garage or something like that."

The meeting, such as it is, breaks down into smaller groups of detectives, with Landsman putting men to work on small, insulated parts of the whole.

As the primary detective, Pellegrini begins reading through the key statements of relatives taken by half a dozen detectives earlier in the day, digesting pieces of the puzzle that fell to the other investigators. Q-and-A sheets from the victim's family members, from some of the child's schoolmates, from the fifty-three-year-old resident of 718 Newington who, on taking out the trash that morning, had discovered the body—Pellegrini scans each page with an eye for an unusual phrase, an inconsistency, anything out of the ordinary. He was there for some of the interviews; others took place before he returned from the autopsy. Now, he is playing catch-up, working to stay on top of a case that is expanding geometrically.

At the same time, Edgerton and Ceruti sit in the annex office, surrounded by a collection of brown paper evidence bags containing the jetsam from the morning autopsy: shoes, bloodied clothes, scrapings from the victim's fingernails for possible DNA or blood typing, samples of victim's blood and hair for possible future comparisons, and a series of hairs, both negroid and caucasoid, which were discovered on the victim and might or might not have anything to do with the crime.

The presence of foreign hairs is carefully noted, but in Baltimore at least, homicide detectives have come to regard that kind of trace evidence as the least valuable. For one thing, the crime lab can only on rare occasions—usually those involving distinctly colored caucasoid hairs—match beyond any reasonable doubt a recovered strand with a suspect. Particularly with negroid and darker caucasoid hairs, the best that forensic science can do is declare that the same class characteristics exist between a suspect's hair and the recovered strand. DNA-genetic coding, which can unambiguously link trace evidence to a single suspect by matching gene characteristics, is now becoming more widely available to law enforcement, but the process works best with blood and tissue samples. To match the DNA coding of human hair to a suspect, at least one entire hair, with its root intact, is needed. Moreover, Landsman and many other detectives have strong doubts about the integrity of trace evidence at the medical examiner's office, where the number of autopsies performed daily in cramped conditions can produce a less than pristine environment. Hairs recovered from Latonya Wallace could just as easily have come from the plastic wrap on the body litter or a towel used to clean the victim prior to the internal examination. They may be hairs from the ME's attendants and investigators, or the paramedics who pronounced the victim, or from the last body carted away on the body litter or laid out on the examination gurneys.

Edgerton begins filling in the blanks on the first of a series of lab forms: One red raincoat, bloodstained. One red waist jacket, bloodstained. One pair blue rain shoes. Request blood and trace evidence analysis. Special latent print analysis.

Other detectives collate and catalogue witness statements for the case file or work the typewriters in the admin office, pounding out one report after another on the day's activity. Still other detectives are clustered around the computer terminal in the admin office, punching up criminal records for nearly every name obtained in a preliminary canvass of the north side of Newington's 700 block—a stretch of sixteen rowhouses that back up against the alley where the body was found.

The result of the computer check is itself an education in city living, and Pellegrini, after digesting the witness statements, begins reading each printout. He soon grows weary at the repetition. More than half of the four dozen names typed into the computer generate a couple of pages of prior arrests. Armed robbery, assault with intent, rape, theft, deadly weapon—in terms of criminal endeavor, there seem to be few virgins left in Reservoir Hill. Of particular interest to Pellegrini are the half dozen males who show priors for at least one sex offense.

Also punched through the computer is one name that the victim's family gave to the police, the name of the proprietor of a fish store on Whitelock Street. Latonya Wallace occasionally worked at the store for pocket change until her mother's boyfriend—the quiet young man who opened the apartment door for Edgerton that morning—became suspicious. The Fish Man, as he has long been known in the neighborhood, is a fifty-one-year-old living alone in a second-floor apartment across the street from his store. A one-story, single-room affair near the elbow bend of Whitelock Street, Reservoir Hill's short commercial stretch, the store itself is about two blocks west of the alley where the body was dumped. The Fish Man, a grizzled, timeworn piece of work, was quite friendly with Latonya—a little too friendly, as far as the child's family was concerned. There had been some talk among the schoolchildren and their parents, and Latonya was told explicitly to avoid the Whitelock Street store.

Pellegrini finds that the Fish Man also has some history in the computer, which can scan city arrests going back to 1973. But the old man's sheet shows nothing exceptional, mostly a few arrests for assault, disorderly conduct, and the like. Pellegrini reads the sheet carefully, but he pays at least as much attention to the brief, insubstantial record for the boyfriend of the victim's mother. Homicide work offers no respite from cynical thoughts, and only with reluctance does a detective delete the nearest and dearest from his list of suspects.

The clerical work continues through the four o'clock shift change and into early evening. Six of D'Addario's detectives are working overtime for no other reason than the case itself, giving little thought to their pay stubs. The case is a classic red ball, and as such it has the attention of the entire department: Youth division has assigned two detectives to assist homicide; the tactical section has put another eight plainclothes officers into the detail; special investigations across the hall sends two men from the career criminals unit; the Central and Southern districts each add two men from their operations units. The office is crowded with the growing herd of warm bodies—some involved in specific aspects of the investigation, some drinking coffee in the annex office, all dependent on Jay Landsman, the squad sergeant and case supervisor, for guidance and purpose. The nightshift detectives offer assistance, then take stock of the growing crowd and gradually retreat to the shelter of the coffee room.

"You can tell a little girl got killed today," says Mark Tomlin, an early arrival from Stanton's shift, "because it's eight P.M. and the entire police department doesn't want to go home."

Nor do they want to stay in the office. As the core group of Pellegrini, Landsman and Edgerton continue to sort through the day's accumulated information and plan the next day's effort, other detectives and officers newly detailed to the case gradually drift toward Reservoir Hill until radio cars and unmarked Cavaliers are crisscrossing every alley and street between North Avenue and Druid Park Lake.

Tactical plainclothes officers spend much of the late evening jacking up street dealers at Whitelock and Brookfield, driving away, and then returning an hour later to jack them up again. Central District radio cars roll through every back alley, demanding identification from anyone who strays close to Newington Avenue. Foot patrolmen clear the Whitelock corners from Eutaw to Callow, questioning anybody who looks even a little out of place.

It is an impressive parade, a reassuring performance to those in the neighborhood who crave reassurance. And yet this is not a crime of cocaine dealers or heroin users or stickup artists or streetwalkers. This is an act undertaken by one man, alone, in the dark. Even as they are tossed off their corners, the Whitelock Street homeboys are willing to say as much:

"I hope you catch the cocksucker, man."

"Go get his ass."

"Lock that motherfucker up."

For one February evening the code of the street is abandoned and the dealers and dopers readily offer up to the police whatever information they have, most of it useless, some of it incoherent. In truth, the cavalry maneuvers in Reservoir Hill speak not to the investigation itself but to a territorial imperative, a showing of the colors. It announces to the inhabitants of one battered, beleaguered rowhouse slum that the death of Latonya Wallace has been marked from its earliest hours, elevated above the routine catalogue of sin and vice. The Baltimore Police Department, its homicide unit included, is going to make a stand on Newington Avenue.

And yet for all the swagger and bravado tendered on that first night after Latonya Wallace is found, there is an equal and opposing spirit in the streets and alleys of Reservoir Hill, something alien and unnatural.

Ceruti feels it first, when he walks two steps from a Cavalier on Whitelock and some fool tries to peddle him heroin. Then it touches Eddie Brown, who walks into the Korean carryout on Brookfield for cigarettes only to be confronted by a wild-eyed smokehound, half in the bag, who tries to shove the detective back out the door.

"Get the hell away from me," growls Brown, hurling the drunk onto the sidewalk. "Are you out of your damn mind?"

And a half hour later, the spirits reveal themselves again to a whole carload of detectives, who roll through the rear of Newington Avenue for one last look at the death scene. As the car creeps down the garbage-strewn alley, its headlights fix upon a rat the size of a small dog.

"Jesus," says Eddie Brown, getting out of the car. "Lookit the size of that thing."

The other detectives spill from the unmarked car for a closer look. Ceruti picks up a piece of broken brick and throws it half the length of the block, missing the rat by a few feet. The animal stares back at the Chevrolet with seeming indifference, then wanders farther down the alley, where it corners a large black and white alley cat against a cinder block wall.

Eddie Brown is incredulous. "Did you see the size of that monster?"

"Hey," says Ceruti. "I saw all I needed to."

"I been a city boy for a long time," says Brown, shaking his head, "and I never, ever seen a rat back up a cat like that."

But on that night, in that alley, behind that ragged stretch of rowhouses on Newington Avenue, the natural world has been vanquished. Rats are chasing cats, just as glassine bags of heroin are thrust upon police detectives, just as schoolchildren are used for a moment's pleasure, then torn apart and thrown away.

"Fuck this place," says Eddie Brown, climbing into the Chevrolet.

On paper, at least, the prerogatives of a Baltimore homicide detective are few in number. His expertise accords him no greater rank and, unlike counterparts in other American cities, where detective grades and gold shields offer better pay and more authority, a Baltimore detective carries a silver shield and is regarded by the chain of command as a patrolman in plainclothes, a distinction that brings only a small wardrobe allowance. Regardless of training or experience, he is governed by the same pay scale as other officers. Even granting a homicide detective's ability to earn—whether or not he so desires—a third or half of his salary again in overtime and court pay, the union scale still begins at only $29,206 after five years of service, $30,666 after fifteen, and $32,126 after a quarter century.

Departmental guidelines display a similar indifference to the special circumstances of the homicide detective. The BPD's general orders manual—to the brass, a well-reasoned treatise of authority and order; to the working cop, an ever-amended tome of woe and suffering—does little to distinguish between patrolmen and detectives. The one critical exception: A detective owns his crime scene.

Whenever and wherever a body falls in the city of Baltimore, no authority exceeds that of the primary detective on the scene; no one can tell that detective what should or shouldn't be done. Police commissioners, deputy commissioners, colonels, majors—all are under the authority of the detective within the confines of a crime scene. Of course, this is not to say that many detectives have countermanded a deputy commissioner with a dead body in the room. In truth, no one is really sure what would happen if a detective did so, and the general consensus in the homicide unit is that they'd like to meet the crazy bastard who would try. Donald Kincaid, a veteran detective on D'Addario's shift, made history ten years back by ordering a tactical commander—a mere captain—to get the hell out of a downtown motel room, an action necessitated by the commander's willingness to allow a dozen of his herd to graze unimpeded over Kincaid's yet-to-be-processed scene. The action prompted memos and administrative charges, then more memos, then letters of response, then responding letters of response until Kincaid was summoned to a meeting in the deputy commissioner's office, where he was quietly assured that he had interpreted the general orders correctly, that his authority was unequivocal and he was absolutely right to invoke it. Unswervingly right. And if he chose to fight the pending charges at a trial board, he would probably be vindicated and then transferred out of homicide to a foot post near the southern suburbs of Philadelphia. On the other hand, if he was willing to accept the loss of five vacation days as punishment, he could remain a detective. Kincaid saw the light and yielded; logic is rarely the engine that propels a police department forward.

Still, the authority granted to a detective on that small parcel of land where a body happens to fall speaks to the importance and fragility of a crime scene. Homicide men are fond of reminding one another—and anyone else who will listen—that a detective gets only one chance at a scene. You do what you do, and then the yellow plastic police-line-do-not-cross strips come down. The fire department turns a hose on the bloodstains; the lab techs move on to the next call; the neighborhood reclaims another patch of pavement.

The crime scene provides the greater share of physical evidence, the first part of a detective's Holy Trinity, which states that three things solve crimes:

Physical evidence.

Witnesses.

Confessions.

Without one of the first two elements, there is little chance that a detective will find a suspect capable of providing the third. A murder investigation, after all, is an endeavor limited by the very fact that the victim—unlike those who are robbed, raped or seriously assaulted—is no longer in a position to provide much information.

The detective's trinity ignores motivation, which matters little to most investigations. The best work of Dashiell Hammett and Agatha Christie argues that to track a murderer, the motive must first be established; in Baltimore, if not on the Orient Express, a known motive can be interesting, even helpful, yet it is often beside the point. Fuck the why, a detective will tell you; find out the how, and nine times out of ten it'll give you the who.

It's a truth that goes against the accepted grain and court juries always have a hard time when a detective takes the stand and declares he has no idea why Tater shot Pee Wee in the back five times, and frankly, he could care less. Pee Wee isn't around to discuss it, and our man Tater doesn't want to say. But, hey, here's the gun and the bullets and the ballistics report and two reluctant witnesses who saw Tater pull the trigger and then picked the ignorant, murdering bastard from a photo array. So what the hell else you want me to do, interview the goddamn butler?

Physical evidence. Witnesses. Confessions.

Physical evidence can be anything from a usable latent print on a water glass to a spent bullet pulled from the drywall. It can be something as obvious as the fact that a house has been ransacked, something as subtle as a number on the victim's telephone pager. It can be the victim's clothes, or the victim himself, when the small, dark specks of stipplin against fabric or skin show that the wound was inflicted at close range.

Or a blood trail that shows the victim was attacked first in the bathroom, then pursued into the bedroom. Or the what's-wrong-with-this-picture game, in which a witness is claiming that no one else was home, but there are four used plates on the kitchen counter. Physical evidence from a crime scene can also be measured by what is not present: the absence of any forced entry to a house; the lack of blood from a gaping neck wound, suggesting that the victim was killed elsewhere; a dead man in an alley with the trouser pockets pulled inside-out, indicating that robbery was the motive.

There are, of course, those sacred occasions when physical evidence itself identifies a suspect. A spent bullet is recovered intact and with little apparent mutilation, so that it can be matched ballistically against a recovered weapon or against same-caliber projectiles from another shooting in which a suspect has been identified; a semen sample recovered in a vaginal swab is DNA-matched to a possible assailant; a footprint found near a body in the dirt of a railroad bed is paired with a sneaker worn by a suspect into the interrogation room. Such moments offer clear evidence that the Creator has not yet shelved his master plan and that, for one fleeting moment, a homicide detective is being used as an instrument of divine will.

More often, however, the physical evidence gathered at the crime scene provides the detective with information that is less absolute, but nonetheless essential. Even if the evidence doesn't lead directly to a suspect, the raw facts provide a rough outline of the crime itself. The more information that a detective brings away from the scene, the more he knows what is possible and what is not. And in the interrogation rooms, that counts for a great deal.

In the soundproof cubicles used by the homicide unit, a witness will readily claim he was asleep in bed when the shooting started in the next room, and he will maintain the deceit up to the point when a detective confronts him with the fact that the sheets were not disturbed. He will tell the detectives that the shooting could not have been over drugs, that he knows nothing about drugs, until the detective tells him they've already found 150 caps of heroin under his mattress. He will claim that only the lone assailant was armed and there was no shootout until the detective makes it clear that .32 and 9mm casings were both recovered in the living room.

Denied the knowledge provided by physical evidence, a detective walks into the interrogation room without leverage, without any tool to pry truth from suspects or reluctant witnesses. The bastards can lie themselves blind and the detectives, disbelieving and frustrated, can scream at them for lying themselves blind. Without physical evidence, there is only stalemate.

Beyond those who don't want to talk, the physical evidence keeps honest those who willingly volunteer information. Seeking to cut deals on their own charges, inmates at the city jail routinely claim to have heard fellow prisoners boast about or confess to murders, but detectives seriously pursue only those statements that include details from the crime scene that only a perpetrator could know. Likewise, a confession obtained from a suspect that includes details of the crime known only to the killer is inherently more believable in court. For these reasons, a detective returns from every crime scene with a mental list of essential details that he plans to withhold from newspaper and television reporters who will be calling the homicide office half an hour after the body hits the ground. Typically, a detective will hold back the caliber of the weapon used, or the exact location of the wounds, or the presence of an unusual object at the scene. If the murder occurred inside a house rather than on a street where a crowd can gather, the investigator may try to withhold a description of the clothes worn by the victim or the exact location of the victim's body in the house. In the Latonya Wallace case, Landsman and Pellegrini were careful not to mention the ligature marks on the victim's neck or that a cord or rope was used in the strangulation. They also kept the evidence of sexual molestation, or at least they tried to keep it—a week after the murder, a colonel felt the need to reveal the motive for the slaying to concerned parents at a Reservoir Hill community meeting.

From a detective's point of view, no crime scene is better than a body in a house. Not only does a murder indoors mean that details can be kept from gathering crowds or prying reporters, but the house itself offers immediate questions. Who owns or rents the house? Who's living there? Who was inside at the time? Why is my victim inside this house? Does he live here? Who brought him here? Who was he visiting? And call for a wagon, because everyone in the place is going downtown.

To murder someone in a house, a killer has first got to gain entry, either at the invitation of the victim or by forcing a door or window. Either way, something is gained by the investigator. The absence of forced entry suggests that the victim and assailant were probably known to each other; forced entry allows for the possibility that the killer has left fingerprints on a windowpane or door frame. Once inside a house, the killer may well touch a variety of utensils and smooth surfaces, leaving more latent prints. If the killer sprays some bullets around, most of the stray shots will appear as holes in the walls, in the ceiling, in the furniture. If the victim struggles and the assailant is injured, blood spatter or pulled hairs will be more easily discovered in the limited confines of a living room. The same thinking applies to loose fibers and other trace evidence. A lab tech can take a vacuum to a three-bedroom house in under an hour, then turn the vacuum bag's contents over to the whitecoats for sifting in the fifth-floor labs.

But a body in the street offers less. Kill a man while he's walking to the liquor store and you can rest assured that no civil servant is going to suck the lint from the 2500 block of Division Street. Shoot a man outside and there's a good chance that most of the projectiles will not be recovered. Kill someone in the street and often the crime scene will provide a detective with little more than some blood spatter and a couple of spent casings. Not only are the opportunities for recovering physical evidence fewer, but the spatial relationship between the killer, the victim and the scene is obscured. With an indoor murder, the killer and victim can both have discernible connections to the location; out in the street, a detective can't check utility bills or rental agreements to learn the names of people associated with his crime scene. He can't collect the photographs and loose paper, telephone messages and notes scrawled on pieces of newspaper that would be waiting for him at an indoor murder.

Of course, a detective knows that a street murder carries its own advantages, notably the possibility of witnesses, the second element of the investigative triad. For this reason, one alternative has long held a special place in the catalogue of urban violence, particularly in a rowhouse city such as Baltimore, where every block has a rear promenade. Kill someone in an alley and you minimize the risks of both physical evidence and witnesses. In Baltimore, the report of a body in an alley is bound to bring groans and other guttural noises from the throat of a responding homicide detective.

Only one scenario, in fact, offers less hope than a body in an alley. When a Baltimore homicide detective is called to the woods and brambles along the far western edge of the city, it can only mean that one of the city's inhabitants has done a very bad thing and done it very, very well. For two generations, Leakin Park has been Baltimore's favored dumping ground for those who depart this vale by bullet or blade. A sprawling, thickly wooded wilderness surrounding a small stream known as the Gywnns Falls, the park has been the scene of so many unlicensed interments as to warrant consideration as a city cemetery. In New York, they use the Jersey marshes or the city's rivers; in Miami, the Everglades; in New Orleans, the bayou. In Baltimore, the odd, inconvenient corpse is often planted along the winding shoulders of Franklintown Road. Police department legend includes one story, apocryphal perhaps, in which a class of trainees searching one quadrant of the park for a missing person was reminded by a Southwestern District shift commander, with tongue planted in cheek, that they were looking for one body in particular: "If you go grabbing at every one you find, we'll be here all day."

Veteran detectives declare that even the most unremarkable crime scenes offer some information about the crime. After all, even a body in an alley leaves a detective with questions: What was the dead man doing in that alley? Where did he come from? Who was he with? But a dump job, in Leakin Park or in an alley, in a vacant house or a car trunk, offers nothing. It stands mute to the relationship between the killer, the victim and the scene itself. By definition, a dump job strips a murder of any meaningful chronology and—with the exception of whatever items are abandoned with the body—of physical evidence.

Whatever and wherever the scene, its value as the baseline of a murder investigation depends entirely on the detective—his ability to keep out the rabble and maintain the scene itself; his capacity for observation, for contemplating the scene in its totality, in its parts, and from every conceivable angle; his willingness to perform every task that could possibly yield evidence from a particular scene; his common sense in avoiding those procedures that would be meaningless or futile.

The process is subjective. Even the best investigators will admit that no matter how much evidence is pulled from a scene, a detective will invariably return to the homicide office with the discomforting knowledge that something was missed. It is a truth that veterans impress upon new detectives, a truth that emphasizes the elusive quality of the crime scene itself.

Whatever happens before the scene is secured can't be controlled and in the wake of a shooting or stabbing, no one objects to the behavior of uniformed officers, paramedics or bystanders who alter a scene in an effort to disarm the participants or administer aid to the victim. But apart from such necessary actions, the first uniform at the site of a murder is supposed to preserve the scene from being trampled, not only by the locals, but by his fellow officers as well. For the first officer and those who arrive after him, good police work also means grabbing hold of any potential witnesses who happen to be standing around.

The first officer's duties end upon the arrival of a downtown detective, who, if he knows his business, will start by slowing everything down to a crawl, making it much more difficult for anyone to express stupidity in any truly meaningful way. The more complex the scene, the slower the process, giving the detective some semblance of control over the uniforms, the civilian witnesses, the bystanders, the crime lab technicians, the ME's attendants, the secondary detectives, the shift commanders and every other human being in the vicinity. With the exception of the civilians, most of this crowd will know the drill and can be trusted to do their jobs, but as in everything else, assumption is mother and midwife to the most egregious mistakes.

Before this year is out, a detective on Stanton's shift will arrive at a scene to find that a novice team of paramedics has taken a dead person—a very dead person—for a last ride to a nearby emergency room. There they will be told that it is hospital policy to accept only those patients who are at least clinging to life. The flustered paramedics will mull this over and then decide to take the body back to the street. Upon their return to the death scene, this plan will be given tentative approval by the uniforms, who assume that the ambulance crew must know its business. No doubt the officers would then have done their best to place the cadaver in its original position had not the detective arrived to say thank you, but no thank you. Let's just say the hell with it and take the poor guy down to the autopsy room.

Likewise, Robert McAllister, a seasoned detective and a veteran of several hundred crime scenes, will soon find himself standing in a Pimlico kitchen above the blood-soaked body of an eighty-one-year-old man, stabbed forty or fifty times in a brutal housebreaking. On a dresser in a back bedroom is the bent-blade murder weapon, caked with dried blood. So preposterous is it that anyone would disturb such a glaring evidentiary item that McAllister will think it unnecessary to warn against doing so. This crime of omission ensures that a young officer, fresh to the street, will wander into the bedroom, pick up the knife by its hilt and carry it into the kitchen.

"I found this in the bedroom," she will say. "Is it important?"

Assuming that such calamities are avoided and the scene preserved, what remains for the detective is to find and extract the available evidence. This is not done by vacuuming every room, fingerprinting every flat surface, and taking every beer can, ashtray, shred of paper and photo album down to evidence control. Discretion and common sense are valued as much as diligence, and a detective unable to discern the differences among probabilities, possibilities and the weakest kind of long shots soon finds that he risks overloading the evidence recovery process.

Remember, for instance, that the overworked examiners in the ballistics lab are weeks behind on projectile comparisons. Do you want them to compare your .32 slug with other .32-caliber shootings this year, or should they go back another year? Likewise for the fingerprint examiners, who in addition to the open murders are handling latents from burglaries, robberies and half a dozen other types of crime. Do you tell the lab techs to dust surfaces in rooms that seem to be undisturbed and apart from the scene, or do you have them concentrate on objects that appear to be moved and that are close to the death scene? When an elderly woman is strangled in bed, do you vacuum every room in the house, knowing how long it will take the trace lab to go through one room's worth of dirt and lint, hair and fiber? Or, knowing that there wasn't any far-flung, room-by-room struggle, do you instead have the ME's people carefully wrap the body in the sheets, preserving any hairs or fibers that came loose during the action near the bed?

With only a few available on each shift to process evidence, the lab techs themselves are a limited resource. The tech working your scene may have been pulled off a commercial robbery to work this homicide or may be needed a half hour later to work another shooting on the opposite side of town. And your own time is equally precious. On a jumping midnight shift, the hours you could spend at one scene might be divided between two homicides and a police shooting. And even with a single murder, hours spent at a scene have to be measured against time that could be spent interviewing witnesses who are waiting downtown.

Every scene is different, and the same detective who requires twenty minutes at a street shooting may spend twelve hours to process a double stabbing inside a two-story rowhouse. A sense of balance is required at both scenes, an understanding of what has to be done and what can reasonably be done to produce evidence. Also required is the persistence to oversee the essentials, to make sure that what's being done is done correctly. On every shift, there are those lab techs who arrive at complex crime scenes and provoke sighs of relief from detectives, just as there are others who can't lift a usable print if a suspect's hand is attached to it. And if you want the photos to show the location of critical pieces of evidence, you better say as much, or the five-by-eight glossies will come back with every angle but the one you need.

These are the basic requirements. But there is something else about crime scenes, an intangible on the continuum between honed experience and pure instinct. An ordinary person, even an observant person, looks at a scene, takes in many of the details and manages a general assessment. A good detective looks at the same scene and comprehends the pieces as part of a greater whole. He somehow manages to isolate the important details, to see those items that conform to the scene, those that conflict, and those that are inexplicably absent. He who speaks of Zen and the Art of Death Investigation to a Baltimore homicide detective is handed a Miller Lite and told to stop talking communist hippie bullshit. But some of what happens at a crime scene, if not exactly antirational, is decidedly intuitive.

There is little else to explain Terry McLarney staring at the seminude body of an elderly woman, rigored in her bed with no apparent trauma, and deciding correctly—on the basis of an open window and a single stray pubic hair on the sheet—that he is working a rape-murder.

Or Donald Worden, walking down an empty East Baltimore street minutes after a fatal shooting, putting his hand on the hood of one parked car out of twenty and feeling the heat of an engine—a sure sign that the car was recently occupied by persons who fled rather than be identified as witnesses. "There was some condensation on the back window," he says later, shrugging. "And it was a little ways from the curb, like the driver parked it in a hurry."

Or Donald Steinhice, a veteran from Stanton's shift, who is entirely convinced that the woman hanging from the ceiling of her bedroom has taken her own life, but somehow can't leave the room until one last detail is settled in his mind. He sits there in the shadow of the dead woman for half an hour, staring at a pair of bedroom slippers on the floor below the body. The left slipper is below the right foot, the right below the left. Was she wearing the slippers on the wrong feet? Or did someone else, someone who staged the scene, place the slippers there?

"It was the only thing about that scene that really bothered me, and it bothered me for a good long while," he later recalls, "until I thought about how a person takes off their bedroom slippers."

Steinhice finally imagines the woman crossing her legs so as to wrap the toe of one slipper around the heel of the other, prying the slipper off from the back—a common maneuver that would leave the slippers on opposite sides.

"After that," he says, "I could leave."

FRIDAY, FEBRUARY 5

In the clear sunlight of a winter morning, the academy trainees feel no sense of foreboding in the alley behind the rowhouses on Newington Avenue. As they crawl through its recesses and kick through its clutter, they find it to be an alley like any other.

Dressed in the khaki uniforms of the Education and Training Division, the class of thirty-two trainees begins the second day of the Latonya Wallace investigation by moving slowly through the alley and the back yards of every house in the block bounded by Newington and Whitelock, Park and Callow. They search inches at a time, stepping only where they have already searched, picking up each piece of trash with great care, then setting it down with the same deliberation.

"Go slowly. Check every inch of your yard," Dave Brown tells the class. "If you find something—anything—don't move it. Just go and grab a detective."

"And don't be afraid to ask questions," adds Rich Garvey. "There's no such thing as a stupid question. Or at least for right now, we're going to pretend that there isn't."

Earlier, watching the trainees bound off a police department bus and count off for their instructor, Garvey expressed misgivings. Allowing a herd of new recruits to graze through a crime scene had all the makings of what detectives and military men like to call a clusterfuck. Visions of self-satisfied cadets trampling over blood trails and kicking tiny bits of evidence into sewer drains danced in Garvey's head. On the other hand, he reasoned, a lot of ground can be covered with thirty-two interested persons, and at this point, the Latonya Wallace probe needs all the help it can get.

Once loosed upon the alley, the trainees are, to no one's surprise, genuinely interested. Most of them attack the chore with zeal, picking through piles of garbage and dead leaves with all the fervor and devotion of the newly converted. It's quite a sight, prompting Garvey to wonder what primal force of nature could inspire thirty patrol veterans to get down on their hands and knees in a Reservoir Hill alley.

The detectives divide the recruits into pairs and assign each to a rear yard behind the 700 block of Newington Avenue as well as the yards on

Park and Callow avenues, which form the east and west boundaries of the block in which the child was found. There are no yards or open areas behind the block's northern boundary, Whitelock Street; there, a red brick warehouse backs right up to the alley. The search takes more than an hour, with the trainees recovering three steak knives, one butter knife and one kitchen carving utensil—all marred by more rust than could accumulate on a murder weapon overnight. Also harvested are a variety of hypodermic syringes, an item commonly discarded by the local citizenry and of no particular interest to the detectives, as well as combs, hair braids, assorted pieces of clothing and a child's dress shoe—none of it related to the crime. One enterprising recruit produces, from the rear yard of 704 Newington, a clear plastic bag half filled with a dull yellow liquid.

"Sir," he asks, holding the bag up to eye level, "is this important?"

"That appears to be a bag of piss," says Garvey. "You can put it down anytime you like."

The search does not produce a child's small star-shaped gold earring. Nor does it yield a blood trail, the one clue that might point to the murder scene, or at least the direction from which the body was carried to the rear of 718 Newington. Small purple blobs of coagulated blood dot the pavement where the little girl was discovered the morning before, but neither the detectives nor the trainees can locate another droplet anywhere else in the alley. The severity of the child's wounds and the fact that she was carried to the alley wrapped in nothing more constricting than her little raincoat almost assures that the killer left blood spatters, but the rain that blanketed the city from late Wednesday to Thursday morning has neatly destroyed any such evidence.

As the cadets search, Rich Garvey walks once more through the yard behind 718 Newington. The yard itself, about 12 by 50 feet, is mostly paved, and it is one of the few rear parcels in the 700 block that is enclosed by a chain-link fence. Rather than dump the child's body in the common alley or in one of the more accessible yards nearby, the murderer inexplicably took the trouble to open the rear gate and carry the body through the yard to the rear entrance of 718 Newington. The body had been found only a few feet from the kitchen door, at the foot of a metal fire stair that runs from the roof to the rear yard.

It made no sense. The killer could have dumped the little girl anywhere in the alley, so why risk taking her body inside the fenced-in yard of an occupied house? Did he want it to be found immediately? Did he want to cast suspicion on the elderly couple that lived at 718? Or did he feel, in the end, some perverse sense of remorse, some human impulse that told him to leave the body inside a fenced yard, protected from the stray dogs and alley rats that roam through Reservoir Hill?

Garvey looks toward the far end of the yard, where the back section of the fence meets the common alley, and notices something silver on the ground behind a dented trash can. He walks over and discovers a small, six-inch piece of hollow metal pipe, which he carefully lifts at one end and holds up to the light. Inside the tube is a thick mass of what appears to be coagulated blood as well as a dark strand of human hair. The pipe looks like a piece of some larger assembly, and Garvey allows himself a hard thought, wondering whether just such an item could have caused the vaginal tear. The detective carefully hands the pipe to a lab tech, who bags it.

A television cameraman, one of several hovering around Newington Avenue this morning, watches the exchange and wanders across the alley.

"What was that?"

"What?"

"That piece of metal you picked up."

"Listen," says Garvey, placing a hand on the cameraman's shoulder. "You gotta do us a favor and keep that out of your film. It might be a piece of evidence, but if you put it on the tube, it could really fuck us. Okay?"

The cameraman nods.

"Thanks. Really."

"No problem."

The presence of television cameramen on Newington Avenue that morning—one from each of the three network affiliates—is, in fact, the other reason for the trainee search of the alley. Garvey's lieutenant, Gary D'Addario, gained a good understanding of the command staff's priorities in the first hours of the investigation, when his captain ventured out of the admin offices to suggest that detectives should maintain a high profile in Reservoir Hill. Maybe, he said, something could be done for the television cameras. D'Addario had been unable to contain his aggravation. The Latonya Wallace case was only hours old and already the brass was asking his people to jump through hoops for the media.

He responded with an uncharacteristic lack of diplomacy: "I'd rather have them doing something that will solve the case."

"Of course," said the captain, with a mixture of anger and embarrassment. "That's not at all what I was saying."

The exchange, which took place in the main homicide office, was overheard by several of D'Addario's detectives, who related it to several others. Before the end of the day, many of the men on both shifts were willing to believe that D'Addario, already frustrated by his exclusion from the Monroe Street probe, had needlessly thrown down a gauntlet. Even if the call to Education & Training had been accompanied by calls to television assignment editors, the trainee search wasn't exactly the worst idea the brass had ever seized upon. More to the point, the captain was a captain and D'Addario was a lieutenant, and if this case went down in flames, the supervisors with lower rank were more likely to end up as casualties. As the immediate supervisor of all the detectives involved, D'Addario might be crucified on Latonya Wallace alone.

Isolated from the command staff, D'Addario now put his faith—and quite possibly, it seemed to some, his career—in the hands of Jay Landsman, a man who for all his profane and comic impulses was the senior and most experienced sergeant in the homicide unit.

At thirty-seven, Landsman was the last of a line: His father had retired with a lieutenant's rank as acting commander of the Northwestern District, the first Jewish officer to rise to a district command on a predominantly Irish force; his older brother, Jerry, had left the homicide unit only a year before, going out as a lieutenant after twenty-five years. Jay Landsman signed up for no less of a reason than his father, and the family tradition allowed him to come out of the academy with a veteran's knowledge of the department's inner workings. The family name was some help, but Landsman thrived in the department by proving himself to be a smart, aggressive cop. Soon there were three bronze stars, one commendation ribbon, three or four commendatory letters. Landsman was in Southwestern patrol for less than four years before coming downtown to CID; similarly, he was in homicide for only a few months before being bumped to sergeant in 1979, yet in that short time he put down every case to which he was assigned. Then they shipped him to the Central for an eleven-month tour as a sector supervisor before bringing him back to the sixth floor as a detective sergeant. When the Latonya Wallace investigation began, Landsman had been leading a homicide squad for almost seven years.

In his senior sergeant, D'Addario had a supervisor who could be expected to act like a detective, following his own instincts and pressing an investigation over days or weeks. Landsman had managed to limit the effect of gravity on his stocky, 200-pound frame, and after sixteen years of police work, his tousled black hair and mustache were just beginning to show the occasional slivers of gray. Other sergeants in the homicide unit might resemble grocers who consumed too much of the profits, but at an inch over six feet, Landsman still looked like a street police, a hard case who on any given night might take a nightstick and wander down Poplar Grove for that rendezvous with destiny. In fact, he did his best work not as a supervisor, but as a sixth detective in his squad, affixing himself to red balls, police shootings and other sensitive cases, then sharing the crime scenes, the legwork, and the interrogations with the primary detective.

Landsman's instincts were especially acute: In his time as both a detective and a sergeant, he had broken a good share of cases simply by following his own gut. More often than not, Landsman's contribution to a case would appear in retrospect to be little more than sheer impulse—a wild rant in an interrogation room, a bald accusation against a seemingly cooperative witness, a spur-of-the-moment consent search of a witness's bedroom. As police work, it often appeared random and idiosyncratic, but then again, it often worked. And with two fresh murders every three days, the Baltimore Police Department's homicide unit was not exactly the best place to hone an exacting, meticulous approach. Landsman's damn-the-torpedoes method had its share of adherents among the detectives, but even the men who worked for Landsman would admit that it wasn't always pretty. Most of those on D'Addario's shift could remember nights when Landsman had shouted his throat raw, accusing three separate suspects in three separate rooms of murdering the same man, then offering two an apology an hour later while handcuffing the third.

The Landsman blitzkrieg often succeeded simply because of its speed. Landsman worked fast and gave free rein to his impulses, and he held a firm belief in Rule Number Three in the homicide manual, which declares that the initial ten or twelve hours after a murder are the most critical to the success of an investigation. In that time, bloody clothes are being dumped or burned, stolen cars or tags ditched, weapons melted or thrown into the harbor. Accomplices are consolidating their stories, agreeing on places and times and shedding wayward and conflicting details. Coherent and reliable alibis are being established. And in the neighborhood where the murder took place, the locals are mixing rumor and fact into one thick, homogeneous gruel, until it becomes almost impossible for a detective to know whether a potential witness is expressing firsthand knowledge or barroom talk. The process begins when the body hits the pavement and continues unabated until even the best witnesses have forgotten critical details. When Landsman's squad was handling calls, however, the process of deterioration would never be far along before someone, somewhere, was locked in a soundproof cubicle and forced to endure the heat from a detective sergeant in the throes of spontaneous combustion.

But this methodology was often in conflict with an opposite truth in homicide work: Speed is a risk as well as an ally. If Landsman's tactical onslaught carried a weakness, it was its decidedly linear progression, its preference for immediate depth over widening scope. The decision to pursue a single-minded plan of attack was always a gamble and a detective charging down one corridor in a labyrinth had no assurance that he wasn't rushing toward a dead end. Nor could he be sure that other, unopened doors would still be there when he tried to retrace his steps.

Up on Reservoir Hill, the labyrinth seems to grow in size and complexity with each passing hour. Even as the trainee class is returning to its bus, other detectives and detail officers are extending the previous day's canvass to the rowhouses on Park and Callow avenues, east and west of the alley where the body was discovered. Others check the carryouts and corner stores on Whitelock and nearby North Avenue, asking about which businesses sold hot dogs with sauerkraut and whether those items had been sold to anyone on Tuesday or Wednesday. Still others are at the homes of Latonya Wallace's playmates, asking about her daily routine, her habits, her interest in boys, their interest in her—necessary questions that nonetheless seem stilted when asked about so young a child.

The lead investigators, Tom Pellegrini and Harry Edgerton, spend some of the day on the computer, feeding new names into the data base, pumping out another spate of criminal histories. Edgerton has still not solved the Brenda Thompson murder, but the case file, containing page after page of handwritten notes from his last interview with a potential suspect, has disappeared from his desk, replaced by white manila folders that divide the criminal histories of Reservoir Hill residents by street and block number. Likewise, the two-week-old Rudy Newsome case no longer plagues Tom Pellegrini; as the primary on a child murder, he isn't expected to work on anything else. Forced priorities are a truth about homicide work that every detective learns to accept. In life, Rudy Newsome was a faceless drone in Baltimore's million-dollar-a-day drug trade, a street-corner entrepreneur who proved himself entirely expendable. In death, he is again supplanted, this time by a greater tragedy, one that cries louder for vengeance.

Later that second day, Pellegrini slips out of the office to spend a few hours on Whitelock Street, talking to merchants and residents, asking background questions about the Fish Man, who remains at the top of his list of suspects. Pellegrini asks everyone he encounters about the store owner's apartment, his whereabouts earlier in the week, his seeming interest in young girls, his relationship to the victim. The plan is to bring the Fish Man downtown tomorrow, after Pellegrini and the other detectives have a chance to do some checking into his background. And with any luck at all, someone on Whitelock Street knows a little something about the old man, something that can be used as leverage in the interrogation room.

Pellegrini works the street and comes up with a little more innuendo, a little more rumor. There is a lot of talk about the Fish Man and young girls, but nothing that can be called a smoking gun, and for now, Pellegrini can only consider him the first of many suspects.

After his interviewing on the street, Pellegrini returns to the office to check in with Edgerton, who is still collating the criminal histories of residents near Newington by street and block number. Pellegrini picks up one file for the Callow Avenue addresses and shuffles through a dozen computer printouts. The sheets with sex offense arrests are marked by a red grease pencil.

"That's a lot of perverts for one city block," says Pellegrini wearily.

"Yeah," agrees Edgerton, "there must be some kinda special zoning up there."

The weakest prospects are parceled out to the detail officers, with the detectives themselves running down alibis for the more promising suspects. Edgerton takes a young addict over on Lindin; Pellegrini, in turn, checks the background on a Callow Avenue man. It is a little like trying to draw to an inside straight, but without a murder scene—a primary site where the little girl was actually killed—there is no way to limit the prospects.

And where the hell is that scene? Where the hell did this bastard keep that girl for a day and a half without anyone knowing? With every passing hour, Pellegrini tells himself, the scene is deteriorating. Pellegrini is certain that the site is somewhere up in Reservoir Hill, a veritable treasure house of physical evidence waiting for him in some bedroom or basement. Where, he wonders, haven't they looked?

By late afternoon, Jay Landsman, Eddie Brown and other detail officers are once again up in Reservoir Hill, checking the vacant houses and garages on Newington, Callow and Park for the murder site. Tactical units supposedly went through every vacant property in the area on the previous night, but Landsman wants to be sure. After one such search, the men go for a soda at a Whitelock Street carryout, where they fall into conversation with the owner, a young, light-skinned woman who waves away the detectives' pocket change.

"How's it going?" Landsman asks.

The woman smiles, but says nothing.

"Have you heard anything?"

"You all are up here about the little girl, right?"

Landsman nods. The woman seems anxious to say something, glancing at both detectives, then looking out at the street.

"What's up?"

"Well . . . I heard . . ."

"Wait a sec."

Landsman closes the front door of the carryout, then leans back across the front counter. The woman catches her breath.

"This might be nothing . . ."

"Hey, that's all right."

"There's this man lives over on Newington, across the street from where they say it happened. He drinks, you know, and he came in that same morning saying a little girl got, you know, raped and murdered."

"What time was this?"

"Had to be about nine or so."

"Nine in the morning? Are you sure?"

The woman nods.

"What did he say exactly? Did he say how the girl was murdered?"

The woman shakes her head. "He just said she got killed. I just wondered 'cause no one up here had heard about it yet and he was acting, like, strange . . ."

"Strange, like nervous?"

"Nervous, yeah."

"And this guy drinks?"

"He drinks a lot. He's old. He's always been, you know, a little strange."

"What's his name?"

The woman bites her bottom lip.

"Hey, no one's going to find out it came from you."

She gives it up in a whisper.

"Thanks. We won't mention you at all."

The woman smiles. "Please . . . I don't wanna get people up here against me."

Landsman slides back into the passenger seat of the Cavalier before writing the name—a new name—in his notebook. And when Edgerton punches it up on the computer that afternoon he does indeed find a man with that same name and a Newington Avenue address. And damned if the guy's sheet doesn't show a couple of old rape charges.

Another corridor.

MONDAY, FEBRUARY 8

They arrive in two cars—Edgerton, Pellegrini, Eddie Brown, Ceruti, Bertina Silver from Stanton's shift and two of the detail officers—an exaggerated escort for one old smokehound, but just about the right number of people to perform a plain-view search of the man's apartment.

For that they have no legal authority; their reasons for suspecting the old man fall far short of the legal requirements of probable cause, and without a search and seizure warrant signed by a judge, the detectives can't take any items or conduct a thorough search, upending mattresses or opening drawers. On the other hand, if the old man allows them to enter the apartment, they can look around at what is plainly visible. For that purpose, the more eyes, the better.

Bert Silver takes charge of their suspect as soon as the front door opens, addressing him by name and making it clear, in a single declarative sentence, that half the police department has come to request the honor of his presence at headquarters. The other detectives slide past the two and begin moving slowly through a fetid, cluttered three-room apartment.

The old man moans and shakes his head, then tries to formulate an argument from a series of seemingly unrelated syllables. It takes a few minutes for Bert Silver to get the hang of it.

"Nuh gago t'nite."

"Yeah, you do. We need to talk to you. Where are your pants? Are these your pants?"

"Dunwanna go."

"Well, we have to talk to you."

"Nuh . . . dunwanna."

"Well, that's the way it's got to be. You don't want us to have to arrest you, do you? Are these your pants?"

"Blackuns."

"You want the black ones?"

As Bertina Silver assembles their suspect, the other detectives move carefully through the rooms, looking for blood spatter, for serrated knives, for a small, star-shaped gold earring. Harry Edgerton checks the kitchen for hot dogs or sauerkraut, then returns to the bedroom, where he finds a thick red stain by the old man's bed.

"Whoa. What the fuck is this?"

Edgerton and Eddie Brown bend down. The color is purple-red, but with a high gloss. Edgerton puts his finger to the edge.

"Sticky," he says.

"Probably wine," says Brown, turning to the old man. "Hey, my man, did you drop your bottle here?"

The old man grunts.

"That ain't blood," says Brown, laughing softly. "That be Thunderbird."

Edgerton agrees, but pulls out a pocket knife and pries up a small piece of the substance, then drops it into a small glassine bag. In the front hall, the detective does the same thing with a red-brown smear that runs across the plasterboard for about four feet. If either sample comes back blood, they'll have to return with a warrant and take fresh samples for evidence, but Edgerton believes that the possibility is remote. Better to let the lab techs test a sample tonight and be done with it.

The old man looks around, suddenly aware of the crowd.

"Whaterey doin'?"

"They're waiting for you. You need a jacket? Where's your jacket?"

The old man points to a black ski jacket on a closet door. Silver grabs the garment and holds it up for the old man, who slowly negotiates his arms into the sleeves.

Brown shakes his head. "This ain't the guy," he says softly. "No way."

Fifteen minutes later, in the hall outside the sixth-floor interrogation room, Jay Landsman comes to the same conclusion. He stares through the small, wire mesh window of the door to the large room. The window is a one-way affair: Landsman's face cannot be seen from inside the eight-by-six-foot cubicle; the window itself appears to be almost metallic, something between steel plate and dull mirror.

Framed in the small window is the old man from the south side of Newington—the old man who supposedly knew about this murder before anyone else in the neighborhood. Yet here he sits, their latest suspect, a stone-cold smokehound apprehended somewhere on that well-traveled road between Thunderbird and Colt 45, his zipper down, the buttons of his soiled work shirt secured in the wrong buttonholes. Bert Silver didn't exactly waste time worrying about wardrobe.

The sergeant watches the old man rub his eyes and slump against the metal chair, then lean forward to scratch himself in buried, forbidden places that even Landsman doesn't want to think about. Though he was roused from stupor and squalor less than an hour before, the old man is now fully awake and waiting patiently in the empty cubicle, his breath wheezing at regular intervals.

This in itself is a bad sign, clearly contradicting Rule Number Four in the homicide lexicon, which states that an innocent man left alone in an interrogation room will remain fully awake, rubbing his eyes, staring at the cubicle walls and scratching himself in the dark, forbidden places. A guilty man left alone in an interrogation room goes to sleep.

Like most theories involving the interrogation room, the Sleeping Suspect Rule cannot be invoked across the board. Some novices not yet accustomed to the inherent stress of crime and punishment are prone to babbling, sweating and generally making themselves sick before and during an interrogation. But Landsman can hardly be encouraged when he sees that the old man from Newington Avenue, drunk and disheveled and hauled from his bed in the middle of the night, is still unwilling to take his present condition as an anesthetic. The sergeant shakes his head and walks back into the office.

"Geez, Tom, this guy looked a lot better before we got him down here," Landsman says. "I can't see him being anything but a smokehound."

Pellegrini agrees. The old man's appearance in the homicide unit and his almost immediate dismissal as a suspect by Landsman mark the last stage in the transformation from aging alcoholic to suspected child killer and back to harmless drunk. For the old man, it was a frenetic, three-day metamorphosis of which he had remained blissfully unaware.

From the moment that the Whitelock Street carryout owner first uttered the old man's name to Landsman and Brown, everything looked good.

First of all, he told the woman at the carryout about the child's murder at 9:00 A.M. on Thursday—even before the detectives had cleared the crime scene—and he behaved strangely while doing so. But how could he have known about the little girl's murder at that time? Although the elderly couple living at 718 Newington had told several neighbors of the discovery before calling the police, there was no indication that they had talked to the old man across the street. Moreover, the detectives had almost immediately barred onlookers from the alley behind Newington; because the old man lived on the south side of the street, he should not have been able to see the body.

Then there were the rape charges—old ones to be sure—with no indication of conviction or sentence on the sheet. But when detectives pull the reports from Central Records they find one of the victims to be a young girl. Also, the old man appears to live alone and his first-floor rowhouse apartment is in the 700 block of Newington, a short run from where the body was dumped.

A bit thin, perhaps. But Landsman and Pellegrini both know that four days have passed since the discovery of the body and at this moment, there is nothing better on the horizon. The first and seemingly best suspect developed thus far—the Fish Man—was brought downtown for an interview two days ago, but that interrogation had led them nowhere.

The Fish Man showed little interest in talking about the death of a child who had once worked in his store. Nor did he seem at all interested in accurately establishing his own whereabouts on Tuesday and Wednesday. After overcoming a general loss of memory, he came up with an alibi for the Tuesday of Latonya Wallace's disappearance—an errand across town that he had run with a friend. Checking on the alibi, Pellegrini and Edgerton found that the trip had in fact occurred on Wednesday, leaving them to wonder whether the man had lied intentionally or had simply confused the days. Moreover, in checking the alibi, the detectives learned that the Fish Man had invited two friends up to his apartment to eat chicken on Wednesday evening. That, of course, left an obvious problem: If, as the autopsy seemed to indicate, Latonya Wallace was abducted on Tuesday, killed on Wednesday night and then dumped in the early morning hours of Thursday, then what was the Fish Man doing running errands on Wednesday afternoon or cooking a chicken dinner on Wednesday night? A full statement was taken from the Fish Man at the Saturday interrogation and, given the number of unanswered questions, both Edgerton and Pellegrini considered him a suspect. Still, the problems with apparent time of death—based on the extra, partially digested meal and the lack of decomposition—had to be overcome.

But as with everything else in this case, even the time of death remained a moving target. Earlier in the evening before the raid on the old man's rowhouse, Edgerton had argued briefly against the prevailing opinion: "What if she was killed on Tuesday night? Could she have been killed late Tuesday or early Wednesday morning?"

"Can't be," said Landsman. "She's just starting to come out of rigor. And the eyes are still moist."

"She could be coming out of rigor after twenty-four hours."

"No fucking way, Harry."

"Yeah she could."

"No fucking way. It's gonna happen faster for her because she's smaller . . ."

"But it's also cold out."

"But we know the guy has her inside somewhere until he can dump her that morning."

"Yeah, but . . ."

"No, Harry, you're fucked up on this," said Landsman, producing the office medical text on death investigation and turning to the section on rigor mortis. "Eyes not dry, no decomp. Twelve to eighteen hours, Harry."

Edgerton scanned the page. "Yeah," he said finally. "Twelve to eighteen. And if she's dumped at three or four . . . that's . . ."

"Middle of the day on Wednesday."

Edgerton nodded. If she was killed on Wednesday, then the Fish Man was out and there was every reason to move Landsman's candidate, the old drunk from across the street, to the top of the list.

"Hey, fuck it," said Landsman finally. "We got no reason not to pick this guy up."

No reason save that their suspect can barely hang on to his bottle, much less lure a young girl off the street and hold her captive for a day and a half. The interrogation lasts only long enough to establish that the old drunk had only heard of the murder on that Thursday morning from a neighbor who had heard it from the woman who lived at 718 Newington. He doesn't know about the murder. He doesn't know the little girl. He can't remember much about his old charges except that whatever they were, he was innocent. He wants to go home.

A lab tech takes Edgerton's samples to a detective's desk and subjects each to a leuco malachite test, a chemical examination in which items are daubed with a cotton-tipped applicator that will turn blue if blood—animal or human—is present. Edgerton watches as each applicator turns a dull gray, an indication of dirt and nothing more.

A few hours before dawn, as the old man is returned to anonymity in a Central District radio car and the detectives collate and copy another day's reports, Pellegrini dryly offers a fresh alternative.

"Ed, you wanna break this case?"

Brown and Ceruti both look up in surprise. Other detectives glance over as well, their curiosity piqued.

"Then I'll tell you what you do."

"What's that?"

"Ed, you go prepare a statement of charges."

"Yeah?"

"And Fred, you read me my rights . . ."

The room breaks up.

"Hey," says Landsman, laughing. "What do you guys think? Is this case getting to Tom? I mean, he kinda looks like he's beginning to molt." Pellegrini laughs sheepishly; in truth, he is beginning to look a little played out. His features are almost classically Italian: dark eyes, sharp facial lines, stocky build, thick mustache, jet black hair cresting in a pompadour that on a good day seems an affront to gravity itself. But this is not a good day; his eyes are glazed, his hair a dark, unruly cascade over his pale forehead. His words come drag-ass out of his mouth in a mountain drawl slowed by lack of sleep.

Every man in the room has been there before, working 120-hour weeks as the primary investigator on a case that simply doesn't add up, a set of facts that won't solidify into a suspect no matter how long you stare at them. An open red ball is a torture tour, a ball-busting, blood-draining ordeal that always seems to shape and mark a detective more than the ones that go down. And for Pellegrini, still new to Landsman's squad, the Latonya Wallace murder is proving to be the hardest rite of passage.

Tom Pellegrini had nine years on the force when his transfer to homicide was finally approved, nine years of wondering whether police work was truly a calling or merely the latest meandering in what had become a lifetime of detours.

He was born to a coal miner in the mountains of western Pennsylvania, but his father—himself the son of a miner—left the family when Pellegrini was a boy. After that, there was nothing to bind them. Once, as an adult, he had gone to see his father for a weekend, but the connections he had been looking for simply weren't there. His father was uncomfortable, his father's second wife unwelcoming, and Pellegrini left that Sunday knowing that the visit had been a mistake. His mother offered little solace. She had never expected much of him and from time to time she actually came right out and said so. For the most part, Pellegrini was raised by a grandmother and spent summers with an aunt, who took him down to Maryland to see his cousins.

His first choices in life seemed—like his childhood—uncertain, perhaps even random. Unlike most of the men in the homicide unit, Pellegrini had no prior connection to Baltimore and little in law enforcement when he joined the department in 1979. He arrived as something close to a blank tablet, as rootless and unclaimed as a man can be. In his past, Pellegrini could count a couple of frustrating years at Youngstown College in Ohio, where a few semesters were enough to convince him that he was not at all suited for academics. There was a failed marriage as well, along with six months in a Pennsylvania coal mine—enough for Pellegrini to know that the family tradition was something to walk away from. He signed on for a couple of years as the manager of a carnival, where he worked the towns and state fairs and kept the amusement rides running. Eventually, that job led to a more permanent position as manager of an amusement park on a lakeshore island between Detroit and Windsor, Canada, where he spent most of his time trying to keep the joyrides from rusting during the northern winters. When the amusement park owners refused to pay for better, safer maintenance, Pellegrini quit, convinced that he wanted to be nowhere near the place when the Tilt-A-Whirl altered its usual orbit.

The want ads led south—first to Baltimore, where he visited the aunt who had taken him in during those childhood summers. He stayed in Maryland for a week, long enough to answer a newspaper ad encouraging applications to the Baltimore Police Department. He had once worked for a brief time at a private security firm, and though the job offered nothing even remotely resembling police work, it left him with the vague feeling that he might enjoy being a cop. In the late 1970s, however, the prospects for a law enforcement career were uncertain; most every city department was dealing with budgetary retrenchment and hiring freezes. Still, Pellegrini was intrigued enough to attend the interview for the Baltimore department. But rather than wait for a reply, he pushed on to Atlanta, where he had been led to believe that the Sun Belt's economic boom was a better guarantee of employment. He stayed overnight in Atlanta, reading the classifieds at a depressing diner in a ragged section of the city, then returning to the motel to hear from his aunt, who called to say he had been accepted by the Baltimore academy.

What the hell, he told himself. He didn't know much about Baltimore, but what he'd seen of Atlanta couldn't exactly be described as paradise. What the hell.

After graduation, he was assigned to Sector 4 of the Southern, a white enclave almost evenly divided between affluent urban homesteaders and an ethnic working class. It was hardly the most crime-ridden section of the city, and Pellegrini understood that if he stayed there ten years, he would never learn what he needed to know to rise in the department. If he was going to be any good at this, he told himself, he had to get to one of the rough-and-tumble districts like the Western or, better still, to a citywide unit. After less than two years in a radio car, his ticket out of the hinterlands came in the form of an approved transfer to the Quick Response Team, the heavily armed tactical unit responsible for handling hostage situations and barricades. Working out of headquarters, QRT was considered something of an elite unit, and the officers were divided into four-man teams that trained constantly. Day after day, Pellegrini and the rest of his squad would practice kicking in doors, fanning out across unfamiliar rooms and then mock-firing at cardboard cutouts of gunmen. There were cardboard cutouts of hostages as well, and after enough practice, a team could get to the point where, under optimal conditions, if every man did his job, they might hit a hostage no more than every fourth or fifth time.

The work was precise and demanding, but Pellegrini felt no more at ease in QRT than he had anywhere else in his life. For one thing, his relationship with the other members of his team was difficult, primarily because the unit was short one sergeant and Pellegrini was selected by the other supervisors to serve as the officer-in-charge. An OIC is accorded a little extra pay, Pellegrini learned, but little extra respect from the men under him. After all, it was one thing for the rest of his team to take orders from a sergeant with real stripes on his sleeve, it was another to have those orders coming from a temporary supervisor with no more rank than the men under him. But more important to Pellegrini than the office politics was his memory of one particular encounter in the spring of 1985, an incident that gave him his first look at the kind of police work that truly appealed to him.

For almost a week that year, the QRT took its orders directly from the CID homicide unit, hitting several dozen locations in East Baltimore in a search for a wanted man. Those raids came in the wake of a police shooting in which Vince Adolfo, an Eastern District patrolman, was murdered while trying to stop a stolen car. An east side boy was quickly identified as the shooter, but in the hours after the slaying the suspect managed to stay on the wing. As quickly as the homicide detectives identified an address as a possible hideout, the QRT was there with a maul and shield, taking down the front door. It was the first time that Pellegrini got a chance to watch the homicide unit up close, and when the Adolfo detail ended, one thing was certain in his mind: He wanted to be one of the people who live by finding the right door. Some other cop could have the job of kicking it down.

He acted on that thought by doing something extraordinary—at least by the standards of the average police department. Armed with a carefully prepared résumé and letter of introduction, he took the elevator to the sixth floor of headquarters and walked into the administrative offices next to the homicide unit, where the commander of the Crimes Against Persons section makes his home.

"Tom Pellegrini," he said, extending a hand to the captain in charge. "I'd like to be a homicide detective."

The captain, of course, looked upon Pellegrini as if he were the citizen of some other planet, and with good cause. In theory, an officer could apply for posted openings in any section; in practice, the appointment process for CID detectives was both subtle and politicized—even more so in the years since the department had abandoned standardized testing for detectives.

For older hands like Donald Worden and Eddie Brown, and even Terry McLarney, who arrived as late as 1980, there was an entrance examination for CID—a test that managed to weed out those applicants incapable of writing a respectable warrant, but also to promote a good many people who were simply good at taking tests. Moreover, the test results—though they implied a quantitative approach—had always been subject to politics: an applicant's score on his oral exam was usually only as good as his departmental connections. Then, in the early 1980s, testing was discontinued and appointment to detective became purely political. In theory, police officers were supposed to make homicide by distinguishing themselves elsewhere in the department, preferably in some other investigative unit on the sixth floor. Although most of the applicants did indeed manage that prerequisite, the final decision usually had more to do with other factors. In a decade of affirmative action, it helped to be black; it also helped to have a lieutenant colonel or deputy commissioner as a mentor.

Pellegrini and the captain had a brief and inconclusive conversation. He was a good cop with a respectable performance sheet, but he was neither black nor the disciple of any particular boss. But Jay Landsman heard about this brief meeting and was impressed with Pellegrini's approach. To walk into a commander's office with nothing more than some typewritten pages and a handshake required stones. Landsman told Pellegrini that if he made it to homicide, he'd be welcome as a member of his squad.

In the end, Pellegrini had only one card to play: a well-connected lawyer for whom he had once done a favor during his time in the Southern. If there's ever anything I can do, the guy had said. That was a few years earlier, but Pellegrini called in the marker. The lawyer agreed to do what he could, then called him back two days later. There were no openings in Crimes Against Persons, but through a connection with one of the deputy commissioners, he could get Pellegrini into William Donald Schaefer's security detail. It wasn't homicide, the lawyer said, but if you can last a year or two in the service of Mayor Annoyed, you can pretty much name your poison.

Reluctantly, Pellegrini took the transfer and thereafter spent nearly two years following Hizzoner from community meetings to fund-raisers to Preakness Parades. Schaefer was a tough man to work for, a machine-bred politician who prized loyalty and a willingness to eat shit above all other human attributes. There were several days when Pellegrini left work with mayoral insults ringing in his ears, and several more when he went home suppressing an almost overwhelming desire to cuff the city's highest elected official to a radio car bumper.

Once, at a March of Dimes event where Schaefer was serving as master of ceremonies, Pellegrini made the mistake of intervening in the mayor's performance. As Schaefer waxed prolific on everything from birth defects to Baltimore's new aquarium, an event organizer pointed out that the March of Dimes poster child, a little girl confined to her wheelchair, was not being included. Sensing disaster, Pellegrini reluctantly wheeled the child closer to the mayor, speaking in a soft stage whisper.

"Uh, Mr. Mayor."

Schaefer ignored him.

"Mr. Mayor, sir."

Schaefer waved him away.

"Mr. Mayor . . ."

When the mayor finished his speech, he wasted no time wheeling around on the plainclothes detective.

"Get the fuck away from me," said Schaefer.

Still, Pellegrini played the good soldier, knowing that in Baltimore a machine politician's word is gold. Sure enough, when Schaefer was elected Maryland's governor in 1986, the people in his entourage got their pick of the lot. Within days of each other, there were two appointments to CID homicide: Fred Ceruti, a black plainclothesman from the Eastern, and Tom Pellegrini. Both men went to Jay Landsman's squad.

Once there, Pellegrini surprised everyone, including himself, by doing the job. Handling those early calls, he could not yet rely on natural instinct or experience; the City Hall detail wasn't exactly a noted breeding ground for competent homicide detectives. But what he lacked in savvy, he made up for in a willingness to learn. He enjoyed the work, and more important, he began to feel as though there was something in this world that suited him. Landsman and Fahlteich led him through the early calls, just as Dunnigan and Requer tried to break in Ceruti by sharing their cases.

Orientation to CID homicide wasn't all that sophisticated. There was no training manual; instead, a veteran detective would hold your hand for a few calls and then, suddenly, let go to see if you could walk on your own. Nothing was more terrifying than your first time as primary, with the body stretched out on the pavement and the corner boys eyefucking you and the uniforms and ME's attendants and lab techs all wondering if you know half of what you should. For Pellegrini, the turning point was the George Green case from the projects, the one where no one else in his squad expected a suspect, much less an arrest. Ceruti and Pellegrini handled that call together, with Ceruti off for a long weekend the following day. When Ceruti returned on Monday, he asked casually if anything was new on their homicide.

"It's down," Pellegrini told him.

"What?"

"I locked up two suspects over the weekend."

Ceruti couldn't believe it. The Green case was nothing out of the ordinary, a straight drug murder with no initial witnesses or physical evidence. Given a new detective as a primary, it was precisely the kind of case that everyone expected to stay open.

Pellegrini solved it by legwork alone, by bringing in people and talking to them for hours on end. He soon found that he had the temperament for long interrogations, a patience that even the other detectives found exasperating. With his slow, laconic manner, Pellegrini could spend three minutes recounting what he had for breakfast that morning or a full five minutes telling the joke about the priest, the minister and the rabbi. While that might drive the likes of Jay Landsman to distraction, it was perfectly suited to interviewing criminals. Slowly, methodically, Pellegrini mastered more and more of the job, and he began to close a healthy majority of his cases. His success, he realized, was important to him only. His second wife, a former trauma unit nurse, had no problem with the morbidity that surrounded homicide work, but she had little interest in the intricacies of the cases. His mother expressed only general pride in her son's success; his father was lost to him entirely. In the end, Pellegrini had to accept that this victory was something that he would celebrate alone.

He thought it was a victory, at least, until Latonya Wallace showed up dead in that alley. For the first time in a long while, Pellegrini began to question his own ability, deferring to Landsman and Edgerton, allowing the more experienced investigators to chart the course.

This was understandable; after all, he had never handled a true red ball. But the blend of personalities, of individual styles, also contributed to Pellegrini's doubt. Landsman was not only loud and aggressive but supremely confident as well, and when he worked a case he tended to become its center, drawing other detectives toward him by centripetal force. Edgerton, too, was the picture of confidence, quick to put his ideas forward or argue with Landsman about one theory or another. Edgerton had the New York attitude, the inner sense that tells a city boy to speak first in a crowded room, before someone else opens his mouth and the opportunity is gone.

Pellegrini was different. He had his ideas about the case, to be sure, but his manner was so restrained, his speech so casual and slow, that in any debate the veteran detectives tended to run over him. At first, it was only moderately irritating, and how much did it matter, anyway? He really didn't disagree with either Landsman or Edgerton in his choice of direction. He had been with them when they first focused on the Fish Man as a suspect and he had been with them when Landsman offered the theory that the killer had to live in that same block of Newington. He agreed with them when they had jumped on the old drunk living across the street. It all sounded reasoned, and whatever else you could say about Jay and Harry, you had to admit that they knew their business.

It will be months before Pellegrini begins to chastise himself for being so unassertive. But eventually the same thoughts that plagued him at the crime scene—the feeling that he is not completely in control of his case—will bother him again. Latonya Wallace was a red ball, and a red ball brings the whole shift into a case for better or worse. Landsman, Edgerton, Garvey, McAllister, Eddie Brown—all of them had a hand in the pie, all of them were intent on turning over the stone that would reveal a child killer. True, they were covering a lot of ground that way, but in the end, it wouldn't have Landsman's or Edgerton's or Garvey's name on the case file.

Landsman is definitely right about one thing: Pellegrini is tired. They all are. That night, as the fifth day of the investigation ends, every one of them leaves the office at 3:00 A.M. knowing they will be back in five hours and knowing, too, that the sixteen- and twenty-hour shifts they have been working since Thursday are not going to end soon. The obvious, unspoken question is how long can they keep it up. Dark ridges have already become fixed below Pellegrini's eyes, and whatever sleep the detective does get is often punctuated by nocturnal declarations from his second son, now three months old. Never much on appearances as a plainclothesman, Landsman is now shaving every other day, and his attire has spiraled down from sport coats to wool sweaters to leather jackets and denims.

"Hey, Jaybird," McLarney tells Landsman the following morning, "you look a little beat."

"I'm okay."

"How's it going? Anything new?"

"This one'll go down," says Landsman.

But in truth, there is little cause for optimism. The red binder on Pellegrini's desk, number 88021, has grown thick with canvass reports, criminal histories, office reports, evidence submission slips and handwritten statements. The detectives have canvassed the entire block surrounding the alley and are beginning to cover adjacent blocks; most of those identified in the first canvass as having any criminal history have already been eliminated. Other detectives and detail officers are checking out every report in which an adult male so much as looks at any girl under the age of fifteen. And though several phone calls have come in with tips about possible suspects—Landsman himself spent half a day tracking one mental case mentioned by a Reservoir Hill mother—no one has come forward to say they saw the little girl walking home from the library. As for the Fish Man, he is accounted for on the critical Wednesday. And the old drunk is now, in fact, an old drunk. Worst of all, Landsman pointed out, they still haven't found their murder scene.

"That's what's killing us," Landsman tells them. "He knows more than we do."

Edgerton, for one, is aware of the long odds.

On Tuesday, the night after they jack up the old drunk, Edgerton finds himself at a red brick Baptist church on upper Park Avenue, around the corner from Newington, walking slowly through the stifling heat of a packed sanctuary. The small coffin, off-white with gold trim, is at the far end of the center aisle. The detective makes his way to the front of the church, then hesitates for a moment, touching the corner of the casket with his hand before turning to face the front row of mourners. He takes the mother's hand and bends down, his voice a whisper.

"When you pray tonight, please say a prayer for me," he tells her. "We're going to need it."

But the woman's face is broken, empty. She nods abstractedly, her eyes washing over the detective to fix again on the floral arrangement in front of her. Edgerton walks to the side of the church and stands with his back to the wall, eyes closed more from fatigue than spiritual conviction, listening to the deep, gospel tones of the young minister:

". . . though I walk through the valley of the shadow . . . and I heard a loud voice from the throne saying . . . no more death or mourning or crying or pain, for the old order of things has passed away."

Listening to the city's mayor, whose voice breaks as he stumbles through his words:

"To the family and friends . . . I, uh . . . this is a terrible tragedy, not only for your family . . . for the entire city . . . Latonya was Baltimore's child."

Listening to the U.S. Senator:

". . . the poverty, the ignorance, the greed . . . all the things that kill little girls . . . she was an angel to us all, the angel of Reservoir Hill."

Listening to small, brief details of a child's life:

". . . attended this school from age three until the present time with a perfect attendance record . . . such involvements as student council, school choir, modern dance, majorette . . . Latonya's goal was to become a great dancer."

Listening to a eulogy, to reasons that never sounded more hollow, more empty:

"She is home now . . . because we are not judged by the fleetest of foot or the strongest, but those that endure."

Edgerton follows the crowd that gathers behind the white casket as it is carried toward the front door. Already back at work, he corners a white-gloved usher to ask about obtaining a copy of the mourners' book, signed by those in attendance. From a surveillance van on the opposite side of Park Avenue, a technician begins discreetly taking photographs of the departing crowd in the hope that the killer might muster enough remorse to risk an appearance. Edgerton stands at the base of the church steps, scanning the male faces as the crowd files slowly into the street.

" 'Not the fleetest of foot or the strongest, but those that endure,' " he says, pulling out a cigarette. "I like that part . . . I hope he was talking about us."

Edgerton watches the last of the mourners leave the church before walking back to his car.

MONDAY, FEBRUARY 8

Donald Worden sits in the coffee room and scans the metro section of the paper, half listening to the roll call taking place in the outer office. Wordlessly, he sips his coffee and takes in the headline:

> LEADS ELUSIVE IN DEC. SLAYING OF FLEEING SUSPECT; FOCUS ON OFFICERS SHIFTS TO CIVILIAN.

The article itself begins with a question:

> Who killed John Randolph Scott, Jr.?
>
> Baltimore homicide detectives have asked the question hundreds of times since December 7, when Mr. Scott, 22, was shot in the back while being pursued on foot by police.
>
> For several weeks, the investigation appeared to be focusing on officers who had been in the area when the young man—fleeing from a stolen car that had been chased by police—was gunned down in the 700 block of Monroe Street.
>
> But now, investigators appear to be considering another possible suspect—a civilian who lives in that neighborhood, and whose mother, girlfriend and son have been questioned before the city grand jury, according to police sources.

Worden lets his eyes drift slowly down the entire column, then turns the page and begins reading the jump on 2D. It only gets worse:

> A police source said that a man living near Monroe Street has been extensively interrogated in connection with the death. . . . The same man—pointed out to police by another resident of the area—had told investigators that he saw a police car leaving Monroe Street the morning of the shooting at a high rate of speed, with its lights out.
>
> No evidence was found to substantiate that claim, the source said, and now investigators believe the man may somehow be responsible for the shooting—or at least know more than he has been willing to divulge.

Worden finishes his coffee and hands the newspaper to Rick James, his partner, who rolls his eyes and grabs the newspaper from the older detective.

Wonderful. For the first time in two months they catch a break in this star-crossed case, only to have Roger Fucking Twigg, the morning paper's veteran police reporter, spray it across the front page of the city section. Lovely. For two months, no one in the neighborhood around Fulton and Monroe will admit to knowing anything about the murder of John Scott. Then, a week ago, Worden finally digs out a reluctant witness—possibly an eyewitness—for the grand jury. But before prosecutors can lean on this man, pressuring him to testify under threat of a perjury charge, the *Baltimore Sun* calls him a suspect. Now it'll be hell getting this guy's story into the grand jury room, because if he reads the newspapers—if his lawyer reads the newspapers—prudence suggests that he invoke the Fifth Amendment and remain silent.

Twigg, you miserable bastard, thinks Worden, listening to D'Addario run through the day's teletypes. You did me. You really did me on this one.

That Worden has come up with any kind of witness is testament to how hard he has worked the case. Since the discovery of John Scott's body in early December, he has conducted four separate door-to-door canvasses of the area around the 800 block of Monroe Street, with the first three efforts producing little. It was only on the fourth canvass that Worden learned from a neighbor the name of a possible eyewitness, a resident of the 800 block who had parked his car on Monroe Street next to the mouth of the alley and had told several others that he had been outside when the shooting occurred. When Worden got to the man, he found a middle-aged laborer who lived with his girlfriend and elderly mother on Monroe Street. Nervous and reluctant, the man denied that he was on the street when the incident occurred, but he admitted that he heard a gunshot, then from his window saw a police car leaving the 800 block with its lights out. He then saw a second police car turn onto Monroe Street from Lafayette and stop near the mouth of the alley.

The man also told Worden that after police began gathering in the alley, he had called his son to tell him what was happening. Worden then interviewed the son, who remembered the phone call and remembered further that his father had been quite specific: He had seen a police officer shoot a man in an alley across the street from his house.

Worden went back at the witness, confronting him with his son's statement. No, said the man, I never told him that. He stood by his previous account involving the two cars.

Worden suspected that his newfound witness had seen a good deal more than the arrival and departure of the radio cars, and the detective had two possible explanations for the man's obvious reluctance. First, the witness was genuinely afraid of testifying against a police officer in a murder trial. Second, there never was a radio car that fled down Monroe Street with its headlights out. The witness had instead seen a confrontation between John Scott and another civilian, a neighbor or friend, perhaps, whom the witness was now trying to protect. For that matter, the confrontation could have involved the witness himself, who had parked his own car at the mouth of the alley a few minutes before the shooting.

Technically then, this morning's newspaper article is correct in asserting that the witness can also be considered a potential suspect. But what Roger Twigg does not know—or has not been told by his sources—is that this new witness was not discovered in a vacuum; other evidence is leading Worden back in the opposite direction, back toward the police.

It's more than the shirt buttons found at the edge of the alley. And it's more than the fact that too many of the officers involved seem to be having trouble keeping their stories straight. The most unnerving piece of evidence in Worden's case file is a copy of the Central District radio tape, which had been sent to the FBI for audio enhancement. Deciphered by the detectives and transcribed weeks after the murder, it revealed a strange sequence of radio transmissions.

At one point on the tape, a Central officer can be heard broadcasting a description of the suspect seen running from the passenger seat of the stolen car.

"It's a number one male, six foot, six-foot-one, dark jacket, blue jeans . . . last seen at Lanvale and Payson . . ."

Then, a Central District sergeant, a seven-year veteran named John Wylie, cuts in. Having followed the chase into the Western District, it is Wylie who first found the body of John Scott.

"One-thirty," Wylie says, giving his unit number. "Cancel that description at the eight-hundred block of Fulton . . . or Monroe."

One of the officers involved in the early chase breaks in, assuming that the suspect is in custody: "One twenty-four. I can ID that guy . . ."

Moments later, Wylie comes back on the radio. "One-thirty. I heard a gunshot before I found this guy."

"One-thirty, where is that, the eight-hundred block Monroe?"

"Ten-four."

Then, several moments later, Wylie can again be heard on the radio tape, acknowledging for the first time that there is a "possible shot victim in the alley."

The transmissions presented Worden with an obvious question: Why would the sergeant cancel the description for the suspect unless he believed the man was already in custody? The buttons, the radio tape—such evidence led not toward a civilian suspect but toward the pursuing officers. And yet for every officer working a post anywhere near Monroe Street, Worden and James had checked and rechecked the run sheets—required departmental paperwork that chronicles every uniform's entire tour of duty from one call to the next. But all of the radio cars in the Central, Western and Southern districts appeared to be accounted for at the time of the shooting. The officers involved in the chase of the stolen Dodge Colt and the subsequent bailout had already given an account of their movements in supplemental reports, and the two detectives reviewed those as well. The investigators had found that most of the officers had encountered one another during the incident and could confirm each other's reports.

If the shooter was another police officer who fled before Sergeant Wylie arrived, there was nothing in the paperwork that could identify him. In all, fifteen Western and Central officers had been interviewed, but they could offer little, and Wylie, for his part, insisted that he had seen nothing before or after hearing the gunshot. Several officers—including Wylie and two others who were among the first to arrive at the shooting scene—were ordered to undergo lie detector tests. The results showed no deception for all officers with the exception of Wylie and one other, whose results were deemed inconclusive.

The polygraph results, coupled with Wylie's premature broadcast canceling the description for the suspect, led both Worden and James to conclude that, at the very least, the Central District sergeant had seen something before he discovered the body. But in a two-and-a-half-hour interview with the detectives, Wylie insisted that he had heard only the single gunshot and had seen no other officers near the alley on Monroe Street. He did not know why he would have canceled the description of the suspect, nor did he recall doing so.

Wylie asked the detectives if he was a suspect.

No, he was told.

Nonetheless, it was during that interview that the detectives asked the sector sergeant to consent to a voluntary search of his house. Wylie agreed, and the detectives confiscated his uniforms, service weapon and off-duty revolver for examinations that would also prove inconclusive.

Am I a suspect? the sergeant asked again. If so, I want to be advised of my rights.

No, they told him, you are not a suspect. Not now. With the sergeant insistent that he had seen or heard nothing apart from the gunshot, what had remained for the investigators was the possibility that some other cop or a civilian had witnessed the shooting or its aftermath. Now, just as that possibility had become very real, a single column of newsprint was threatening to drive their only witness back underground.

Still, if it was a cop who killed John Scott, Worden believed that the incident probably added up to something less than intentional murder. It was, he reasoned, a fight in an alley that went bad, a tussle that ended when a patrolman—rightly or wrongly—used his weapon, or perhaps another .38 he grabbed from John Scott. A second or two later, the suspect is on the ground, a gunshot wound to the back, and the cop is spitting up adrenaline, panicking, wondering how in the hell he's going to write his way out of this one.

If that was the scenario, if a patrolman fled from that alley because he had no faith in the department's ability to protect him, then it was an inevitable act. If that was the case, then Monroe Street was the last, twisted curve on a piece of bad road on which the Baltimore department had been traveling for a long time. Donald Worden had been there for the beginning of the journey, and he had seen the full swing of the pendulum.

Only once in that long career did Worden himself fire a weapon in the line of duty. It was a wayward shot, a .38 round-nose with an almost vertical trajectory, spinning high above any conceivable target. That was twenty years earlier, on a summer day when he and his partner caught a robbery on view in Pimlico, witnessing the ever-elusive communion of a criminal with his crime. After they had duly chased the perpetrator for a greater distance than the average cop considers reasonable, Worden's partner began firing. Worden, feeling an obscure need to show solidarity, then sent his own missile into the ether.

Worden knew the man they were chasing, of course, just as the man knew Worden. For these were the halcyon days of the Big Man's twelve-year tour in the Northwest, when a rough cordiality still existed among the players and Worden was on a first-name basis with anyone in the district who was worth arresting. When the gunfire ended the foot chase and they caught up to their suspect, the man was shocked.

"Donald," he said, "I can't believe it."

"What?"

"You tried to kill me."

"No, I didn't."

"You shot at me."

"I fired over your head," Worden said, chastened. "But look, I'm sorry about it, okay?"

Worden never did manage a taste for gunplay, and the embarrassment of that one stray round never left him. For him, the real authority was a cop's shield and his reputation on the street; the gun had very little to do with it.

Still, it was entirely appropriate that Worden was the detective assigned to the murder of John Randolph Scott. In more than a quarter century on the street, he had borne witness to more than his share of police-involved shootings. Most were good, some were not so good, a few were genuinely malevolent. More often than not, the outcome was decided in seconds. Often, too, the act of compressing the trigger was precipitated by little more than instinct. Usually the suspect needed to be lit up, sometimes he didn't, and sometimes there was room for debate. Sometimes, too, the suspect should have been shot and shot repeatedly, but somehow wasn't.

The decision to use lethal force was inevitably subjective, defined not so much by empirical standards as by what an officer was willing to justify in his own mind and on paper. But regardless of the circumstances, one ethic remained constant: When a cop shoots someone, he stands by it. He picks up a radio mike and calls it. He turns in the body.

But times had changed. A quarter century ago, an American law officer could fire his weapon without worrying whether the entrance wound would be anterior or posterior. Now, the risk of civil liability and possible criminal prosecution settles on a cop every time he unholsters a weapon, and what could once be justified by an earlier generation of patrolmen is now enough to get the next generation indicted. In Baltimore, as in every American city, the rules have changed because the streets have changed, because the police department isn't what it used to be. Nor, for that matter, is the city itself.

In 1962, when Donald Worden came out of the academy, the code was understood by the players on both sides. Break bad on a police, and there was a good chance that the cop would use his gun and use it with impunity. The code was especially clear in the case of anyone foolish enough to shoot a police. Such a suspect had one chance and one chance only. If he could get to a police district, he would live. He would be beaten, but he would live. If he tried to run and was found on the street in circumstances that could be made to look good on paper, he would not.

But that was a different era, a time when a Baltimore cop could say, with conviction, that he was a member of the biggest, toughest, best-armed gang on the block. Those were the days before the heroin and cocaine trade became the predominant economy of the ghetto, before every other seventeen-year-old corner boy could be a walking sociopath with a 9mm in the waistband of his sweats, before the department began conceding to the drug trade whole tracts of the inner city. Those were also the days when Baltimore was still a segregated city, when the civil rights movement was little more than an angry whisper.

In fact, most of the police-involved shootings of that time had racial overtones, the deadliest proof of the notion that for the black, inner-city neighborhoods of Baltimore, the presence of the city's finest was for generations merely another plague to endure: poverty, ignorance, despair, police. Black Baltimoreans grew up with the understanding that two offenses—talking up to a city cop or, worse, running from one—were almost guaranteed to result in a beating at best, gunfire at worst. Even the most prominent members of the black community were made to endure slights and insults, and well before the 1960s, the contempt felt for the department was close to universal.

Things within the department weren't much better. When Worden came on the force, black officers (among them two future police commissioners) were still prohibited from riding in radio cars—legally prohibited; the Maryland legislature had yet to pass the first law allowing blacks access to public accommodations. Black officers were limited in rank, then quarantined on foot posts in the slums or used as undercovers in the fledgling narcotics unit. On the street, they endured the silence of white colleagues; in the station houses, they were insulted by racial remarks at roll calls and shift changes.

The transformation came slowly, prompted in equal part by increased activism in the black community and by the arrival of a new police commissioner in 1966, an ex-Marine named Donald Pomerleau, who took the helm with a mandate to clean house. The year before, Pomerleau had written a scathing report on the BPD, issued under the independent aegis of the International Association of Chiefs of Police. The study declared the Baltimore force to be among the nation's most antiquated and corrupt and characterized its use of force as excessive and its relations with the city's black community as nonexistent. The Watts riot that had shaken Los Angeles in 1965 was still fresh in every civic leader's mind, and with all of the nation's cities living under threat of summer violence, Maryland's governor and Baltimore's mayor took the IACP assessment seriously: They hired the man who wrote it.

Pomerleau's arrival marked the end of the Baltimore department's Paleozoic era. Almost overnight, the command staff began stressing community relations, crime prevention and modern law enforcement technology. A series of citywide tactical units was created and multichannel radios replaced the call boxes still used by most patrolmen. Shootings by police officers were for the first time investigated systematically, and those reviews made some difference; together with community pressure, they discouraged some of the most blatant brutality. But it was Pomerleau himself who successfully fought a prolonged battle against the creation of a civilian review board, assuring that in cases of alleged brutality the Baltimore department would continue to monitor itself. As a result, the men on the street in the late sixties and early seventies understood that a bad shooting could be made to look good and a good shooting could be made to look better.

In Baltimore, the drop piece became standard issue in the police districts, so much so that one particular shooting in the early 1970s has become a permanent part of department lore, a touchstone for a particular era in Maryland's largest city. It happened on one of the side streets off Pennsylvania Avenue, when a sudden spasm of violence struck as five narcotics detectives were preparing to hit a rowhouse. From the darkness of an adjacent alley someone started shouting, yelling to another cop about the man behind him, the man with a knife.

In a rush of adrenaline, one detective fired all six, though he later swore—until he checked his gun—that he pulled the trigger once. He ran into the alley to find the suspect lying on his back, surrounded by five knives.

"Here's his knife, here," said one cop.

"Man, that ain't my fuckin' knife," the wounded man declared, then pointed to another switchblade a few feet away. "That's my knife."

But the drop weapons were little more than a temporary solution, one that became less effective and more dangerous as the general public became aware of the ploy. In the end, the department could do little more than fight a rearguard action as complaints of excessive force multiplied and police brutality became a catchphrase. In Donald Worden's mind, the end of the old Baltimore Police Department could be marked with precision. On April 6, 1973, a twenty-four-year-old patrolman named Norman Buckman was shot six times in the head with his own service revolver on a Pimlico street. Two fellow officers about a block away heard the shots and raced down Quantico Avenue. They found a young suspect standing over the dead officer's body, the murder weapon on the ground beside him.

"Yeah," said the man, "I shot the motherfucker."

Instead of emptying their guns, the arresting officers merely cuffed the shooter and took him downtown. Where once on the streets of Baltimore there had been a code, now there were dead police and living cop killers.

Worden was torn. A part of him knew the old ways could not be defended or even sustained, but still, Buckman had been a friend, a young patrolman who had been busting his ass to make Worden's operations squad in the Northwest District. Called at home by his shift lieutenant, Worden dressed quickly and arrived at the station house with a dozen other officers at about the same moment that Buckman's murderer was transferred to the lockup. The official story was that the suspect complained of abdominal pains while being processed and photographed, but everyone in the city understood the source of that pain. And when Baltimore's black newspaper, the *Afro-American*, sent a photographer to Sinai Hospital in the hope of depicting the suspect's injuries, it was Worden himself who locked the man up on a trespassing charge. When the NAACP demanded an inquiry, department officials simply stonewalled, insisting that no beating had occurred.

But it was a small, pathetic victory, and in the roll call rooms and radio cars there were hard words for the two officers who, with a .38 already on the ground, had allowed Buckman's killer to surrender. The words became harder still after the trial, when the man slipped away with a second-degree verdict and a sentence that would allow parole in little more than ten years.

The Buckman murder was one milestone, but the journey was far from over. Seven years later, in an East Baltimore carryout, the department once again came to terms with its future. And once again Worden stood on the periphery, helpless, as another cop, another friend, was sacrificed in an altogether different way.

In March 1980, the victim was a seventeen-year-old kid with the unlikely monicker of Ja-Wan McGee; the shooter, a thirty-three-year-old detective named Scotty McCown. A nine-year veteran who was then working with Worden in CID robbery, McCown was off duty and in plainclothes at a sub shop on Erdman Avenue, ordering a pizza, when McGee and a companion entered and walked to the counter. McCown had already been watching the two teenagers for a few minutes, glimpsing them as they returned several times to the window, scoping the store's interior, apparently waiting for something. Only when most of the customers left did the two walk inside and make their way toward the counter. McCown had been a robbery detective for five years, and the scene he was witnessing seemed a little familiar. This is it, he thought, slipping his off-duty weapon from its holster and into his raincoat pocket.

And when the flash of silver came out of Ja-Wan McGee's coat pocket at the counter, McCown was more than ready. He fired three without warning, wounding McGee in the upper back. The detective ordered the other teenager to stay where he was, then shouted for the counterman to call for the police and an ambulance. Then he leaned over the prone victim. On the floor was a black and silver cigarette lighter.

The shooting of Ja-Wan McGee came only weeks after a similarly questionable shooting by a white officer had sparked race riots in Miami. When the picketing began in earnest outside City Hall, everyone in the department could see the writing on the wall. Everyone but Scotty McCown.

Worden had come to the robbery unit in 1977, two years after McCown, and he knew the younger man to be a good cop who was about to be destroyed by a bad shooting. Worden dug out a couple of fresh reports from the Eastern District, robberies in which the suspect had used a small pistol, a chrome .25-caliber.

"Maybe these will help," Worden offered.

"Thank you, Donald," the younger detective told him, "but I'll be okay."

But he would not be okay. The protests, the whispered threat of riots, grew louder after the state's attorney's office declined to present the case to a grand jury, citing a lack of criminal intent on the part of the detective. Three months later, a departmental trial board convened to hear testimony from McCown, who insisted that he fired his weapon because he feared for his own safety and the safety of others. The five-member panel heard from the victim's companion in the carryout, who explained that he and his friend were not casing the store, that they repeatedly looked through the window before entering because the shop was crowded and they didn't want to wait in line to buy sodas. Most important, the panel heard from Ja-Wan McGee, now paralyzed at the waist, who testified from a wheelchair that he "was walking in the door, and the guy took two steps and started firing." The trial board deliberated for an hour, then found the detective guilty of violating three departmental rules involving the use of a firearm as well as acting "in a manner which reflected discredit on the department." A week later, the police commissioner declined to consider any lesser punishment or rehabilitation for the detective. Instead, Pomerleau accepted the trial board's recommendation and fired the detective.

"Miami brought justice for us," declared the regional head of the NAACP, but to police on the street the case against Scotty McCown made it clear that a department that had once refused to discipline even the most wanton acts of brutality was now sounding a general retreat. The question was not whether the Ja-Wan McGee shooting was good or bad; every cop who ever felt the need to draw his weapon winced at the thought of a cigarette lighter on the linoleum and a seventeen-year-old crippled for life. The question was whether the department was going to sacrifice its own rather than confront one of the most unavoidable truths about police work: the institutionalized conceit that says in every given circumstance, a good cop will give you a good shooting.

A heavily armed nation prone to violence finds it only reasonable to give law officers weapons and the authority to use them. In the United States, only a cop has the right to kill as an act of personal deliberation and action. To that end, Scotty McCown and three thousand other men and women were sent out on the streets of Baltimore with .38-caliber Smith & Wessons, for which they received several weeks of academy firearms training augmented by one trip to the police firing range every year. Coupled with an individual officer's judgment, that is deemed expertise enough to make the right decision every time.

It is a lie.

It is a lie the police department tolerates because to do otherwise would shatter the myth of infallibility on which rests its authority for lethal force. And it is a lie that the public demands, because to do otherwise would expose a terrifying ambiguity. The false certainty, the myth of perfection, on which our culture feeds requires that Scotty McCown should have shouted a warning before firing three shots, that he should have identified himself as a police officer and told Ja-Wan McGee to drop what he believed was a weapon. It demands that McCown should have given the kid time to decide or, perhaps, should have used his weapon only to wound or disarm the suspect. It argues that a detective who fails to do these things is poorly trained and reckless, and if the detective is white, it allows for the argument that he is very possibly a racist capable of viewing every black teenager with a shiny lighter as an armed robbery in progress. It doesn't matter that a shouted warning concedes every advantage to the gunman, that death can come in the time it takes for a cop to identify himself or demand that a suspect relinquish a weapon. It doesn't matter that in a confrontation of little more than a second or two, a cop is lucky if he can hit center mass from a distance of twenty feet, much less target extremities or shoot a weapon from a suspect's hand. And it doesn't matter whether a cop is an honorable man, whether he truly believes he is in danger, whether the shooting of a black suspect sickens him no less than if the man were white. McCown was a good man, but he let go of a .38 round a moment or two before he should have, and in that short span both victim and shooter became entwined in the same tragedy.

For the public, and the black community in particular, the shooting of Ja-Wan McGee became a long-awaited victory over a police department that had for generations devalued black life. It was, in that sense, the inevitable consequence of too much evil justified for too long. It made no difference that Scotty McCown was neither incompetent nor racist; in Baltimore, as in other police departments nationwide, the sons would be made to pay for their fathers' crimes.

For cops on the street, white and black, the McGee shooting became proof positive that they were now alone, that the system could no longer protect them. To preserve its authority, the department would be required to destroy not only those men who used and believed in brutality, but also those who chose wrongly when confronted with a sudden, terrifying decision. If the shooting was good, you were covered, though even the most justified use of force could no longer occur in Baltimore without someone, somewhere, getting in front of a television camera to say that police murdered the man. And if the shooting was borderline, you were probably still covered, provided you knew how to write the report. But if the shooting was bad, you were expendable.

For the department, for the city itself, the consequences were predictable, inevitable. And now, every cop who knew his history could look at Monroe Street and see the bastard child of an earlier tragedy in an east side carryout. Maybe John Scott was killed by a police, and maybe it was a calculated murder, though it was hard for Worden or anyone else to imagine a cop consciously risking both his career and his freedom to ace a car thief. More likely, the death of John Scott was nothing more or less than a chase, a scuffle and a half-second of fearful deliberation in a dark alley. Perhaps the gun was leveled and the trigger squeezed by a mind haunted by memories of Norman Buckman or any other cop who hesitated and lost. Perhaps, in the echo of a gunshot, a cop wondered in panic how it could be written, how it would play. Perhaps, before driving away from Monroe Street with headlights dimmed, a Baltimore cop thought of Scotty McCown.

"Roger Twigg done put our shit out on the street," says Rick James, reading the article a second time and lapsing into west side vernacular. "Somebody 'round here been doin' some talking, yo."

Donald Worden looks at his partner but says nothing. In the main office, D'Addario is finishing up with the last items on his clipboard. Two dozen detectives—homicide, robbery, sex offense—are clustered around him, listening to another morning's allotment of teletypes, special orders and departmental memoranda. Worden listens without hearing any of it.

"That's the problem with this whole investigation," he says finally, rising for a second pass at the coffeepot. "This place leaks like a fucking sieve."

James nods, then tosses the newspaper on Waltemeyer's desk. D'Addario ends the roll call and Worden wanders out of the coffee room, looking at the faces of at least a half-dozen men who were tight with some of the Western and Central District officers now under investigation for the Scott killing. Worden allows himself a hard thought: Any of them could be a source for the newspaper story.

Hell, Worden feels some obligation to put his own sergeant on the list. Terry McLarney had no stomach for chasing other cops, particularly those he had worked with in the Western District. He had made that much clear from the moment John Scott hit the pavement, and it was for that reason that the Monroe Street probe had been taken away from him.

For McLarney, the notion that his own detectives were being used to pursue his old bunkies from the Western was obscene. McLarney had been a sector sergeant in that godforsaken district before returning to homicide in '85. He was damn near killed in that district, shot down like a dog while chasing a holdup man on Arunah Avenue, and he'd seen the same thing happen to some of his men. If you were going after cops in the Western, you were going without McLarney. His world did not allow for that much gray. The cops were good, the criminals bad; and if the cops weren't good, they were still cops.

But would McLarney leak? Worden doubts it. McLarney might bitch and moan and keep his distance from the Scott case, but Worden doesn't believe he would undercut his own detectives. In truth, it was hard to imagine any detective consciously leaking details to thwart an investigation.

No, thinks Worden, dismissing the thought. The newspaper story came from within the department, but probably not directly from a homicide detective. A more likely source would be the police union lawyers, trying hard to portray the fresh witness as a suspect so as to take the heat off any officers. That made sense, particularly since one of those lawyers was quoted by name near the end of the article.

Still, Worden and James both know that the newspaper story is largely accurate and up to date—a bit leaden in its suggestion that the new civilian witness is a suspect, but otherwise on the mark. And both men know, too, that Twigg's source is therefore close enough to the investigation to get the facts straight. Even if the union lawyers are the reporter's primary source, they're still getting inside information on the status of the investigation.

For Worden, the newspaper article is part and parcel of the larger problem with the Monroe Street probe: the investigation is taking place in a fishbowl. And no wonder. When cops investigate other cops, it's usually the work of an internal investigations unit, a squad of detectives committed to prosecuting fellow officers. An IID detective is trained for the adversarial role. He works out of a separate office on a separate floor of the building, reporting to separate supervisors who are being paid to make cases against sworn members of the department. An IID detective is unaffected by station house loyalty, by the brotherhood itself; his allegiance is with the system, the department. He is, in patrolman's parlance, a cheese-eating rat.

Because the uniforms who chased John Scott were all potential suspects, the Monroe Street probe was, for all practical purposes, an internal investigation. And yet because John Scott was murdered, the investigation could not go to IID. It was a criminal case and therefore the responsibility of the homicide unit.

Worden had to contend with his own divided loyalties as well. A quarter century was no small thing in any profession, but for Worden, the years in uniform meant everything. He carried a little bit of Norman Buckman with him, a little bit of Scotty McCown, too. Yet he was committed to the Monroe Street investigation because it was his letter up on the board, written in red next to the name of John Scott. It was a murder—his murder. And if some cop out there didn't have brains and balls enough to turn in that body, then Worden was willing to write him off.

It somehow made it easier on Worden that many of the officers involved had behaved like witnesses in any other murder. Some had willfully lied to him, some had been purposely ambiguous; all were reluctant. For Worden and James both, it hurt to sit there in an interrogation room and have men wearing the uniform piss up your leg, then tell you it's raining. Nor was there any outside cooperation coming in from the districts. The phone wasn't ringing off the hook from uniforms who feared being jammed up in another cop's shooting, who might be trying to keep out of a jackpot or cut deals for themselves. Clearly, Worden realized, the word on the street was that homicide didn't have enough to charge anyone. If a cop was responsible for this murder, no one would come forward as long as it was believed that the probe had bottomed out.

That, too, was a result of too much talk, too many connections between the homicide unit and the rest of the department. For two months, Worden and James had conducted a criminal investigation in full view of the potential suspects and witnesses, their every move telegraphed through the department grapevine. Today's newspaper account was only the most graphic example.

What the hell, thinks Worden, walking toward the men's room with a cigar clenched between his teeth. At least the bosses can't ignore the problem. When half your fucking case file is floating around in newsprint, it's time to change tactics. Already that morning, Tim Doory has called twice from the state's attorney's office to set up a morning meeting with Worden and James at the Violent Crimes Unit offices.

Still pushing pieces around in his mind, Worden walks out of the bathroom just as Dick Lanham, the colonel in command of CID, rounds the corner on his way back to his office. Lanham, too, is in high dudgeon, a copy of the newspaper rolled up tight in one fist.

"I'm sorry, Donald," says the colonel, shaking his head. "You've got your work cut out for you now."

Worden shrugs. "Just one more thing to deal with."

"Well, I'm sorry you have to deal with it," says Lanham. "I tried like hell to get Twigg to hold off on this thing and I thought he was gonna do that."

Worden listens passively as the colonel launches into an extended account of his efforts to delay the news article—an account punctuated by his assertion that Roger Twigg is the most stubborn, arrogant, pain-in-the-ass reporter he has ever known.

"I told him what it would do to us if he put that stuff in the paper," the colonel says. "I asked him to wait on it for a couple weeks, and what does he do?"

As a major, Lanham himself ran the IID and in that post had dealt with Twigg on a series of sensitive stories. So it is no surprise to Worden that the colonel and the reporter had a long conversation before the article was published. But would the colonel purposely leak this investigation? Probably not, Worden reasons. As the CID commander, Lanham doesn't want an unsolved police shooting on the books, and as a former IID man, he certainly doesn't have any problem with investigating other cops. No, Worden thinks, not the colonel. If Lanham was talking to Twigg, it was only to try to stall the story.

"Well," Worden says, "I'd sure like to know who his source is."

"Oh yeah," says Lanham, turning toward his office, "I'd like to know that myself. Whoever it is knows what he's talking about."

Three hours after digesting the newspaper article, Worden and James walk the three blocks from headquarters to the Clarence M. Mitchell Jr. Courthouse on Calvert Street, where they badge their way past sheriff's deputies and take the elevator to the third floor of the city's judicial palace.

There, they walk through a cramped labyrinth of offices which houses the Violent Crimes Unit and settle in the largest cubicle, the office of Timothy J. Doory, assistant state's attorney and the head of the VCU. On Doory's desk is, of course, a copy of the *Sun*'s metro section, folded to Roger Twigg's exclusive.

The meeting is a long one, and when the two detectives return to the homicide unit, they are carrying a list of a dozen witnesses, civilians and officers who are to be issued witness summonses.

Fine with me, thinks Worden, walking back toward headquarters. I've been lied to on this case, I've been stonewalled, I've seen my best evidence spread across a newspaper page. So what the hell, if they're gonna lie about this shooting, they may as well do it under oath. And if they're gonna be leaking the case file to reporters, they're gonna have to get their information out of the courthouse.

"Fuck it, Donald," James tells his partner, hanging his coat in the main office. "If you ask me, Doory should've done this weeks ago."

Before the Monroe Street probe is further compromised—by Twigg or anyone else—it will be brought out of the homicide unit. It will go to a grand jury.

WEDNESDAY, FEBRUARY 10

The Fish Man comes to the door, fork in hand, wearing a worn flannel shirt and corduroy pants. His unshaven face is impassive.

"Step back," says Tom Pellegrini. "We're coming in."

"Am I under arrest?"

"No. We got a warrant for your place, though."

The Fish Man grunts, then walks back into the kitchen. Landsman, Pellegrini and Edgerton lead a half-dozen others into the three-room, second-floor apartment. The place is dirty, but not unbearably so, and sparsely furnished. Even the closets are almost empty.

As each of the detectives takes a room and begins searching, the Fish Man returns to his barbecued chicken, greens and Colt 45. He uses his fork to tear the meat from a thigh, then picks up a chicken leg with his fingers.

"Can I see it?" he asks.

"See what?" says Landsman.

"Your warrant. Can I see it?"

Landsman walks back into the kitchen and drops the target copy on the table. "You can keep that one."

The Fish Man eats his chicken and reads slowly through Landsman's affidavit. The warrant offers a mechanical summary of reasons for the raid: Known to victim. Employed victim at store. Misled investigators about alibi. Unaccounted for on day of disappearance. The Fish Man reads without any suggestion of emotion. His fingers leave grease marks on a corner of each page.

Edgerton and Pellegrini meet Landsman in the back bedroom as other detectives and detail officers poke through the store owner's few possessions.

"Not much here, Jay," says Pellegrini. "Why don't we take some guys and hit Newington while you go across the street and do the store."

Landsman nods. Newington Avenue is the second of two raids planned for this night. The separate warrants for separate addresses reflect a divergence of opinion in the Latonya Wallace case. Earlier this afternoon, the lead investigators were at opposite ends of the admin office, playing at dueling typewriters—Pellegrini and Edgerton collecting their probable cause for a new set of suspects at 702 Newington; Landsman putting everything he knew about the store owner into a pair of warrants for the Fish Man's apartment and the shell of his Whitelock Street store, which had been gutted by fire shortly before the child's disappearance. It was a little bit ironic: Landsman had come back to the Fish Man even as Pellegrini and Edgerton—who a few days earlier had argued that the store owner was their best hope—had come around to the new theory.

Landsman's refusal to give up on the Fish Man was also a marked change from his earlier arguments, when his own estimates on the time of death had seemingly eliminated the store owner. But in a later consultation with the medical examiners, Landsman and Pellegrini went through the calculations one more time: body still coming out of rigor, eyes moist and no signs of decomposition; twelve to eighteen hours. Most probably, agreed the MEs, unless, of course, the killer was able to store the body in a cool place, which, given the season, could be a vacant rowhouse, a garage, an unheated basement. That might delay the post-mortem processes.

How much of a delay? Landsman asked.

Up to twenty-four hours. Maybe more.

Damned if Edgerton hadn't been right in arguing the time-of-death estimates two nights ago. With twenty-four to thirty-six hours to work with, the detectives could consider the possibility of a Tuesday abduction followed by a murder that night or early Wednesday morning. The Fish Man still had no alibi for that period of time. Assuming he had a way to keep the body cool, the new calculation left him exposed. Pellegrini's legwork dislodged the other fact that had led the detectives to assume a prolonged abduction and Wednesday night murder: the extra meal of hot dogs and sauerkraut in the child's stomach. That disappeared when Pellegrini happened to interview a Reservoir Hill local who worked in the Eutaw-Marshburn school cafeteria. Taking the opportunity to double-check the material in the case file, the detective asked the employee if the meal on February 2 was, in fact, spaghetti and meatballs. The employee checked the old menus and called Pellegrini the following day; the February 2 lunch was actually hot dogs and sauerkraut. The spaghetti was a previous night's meal. Somehow, the detectives had been misinformed; now, too, the victim's stomach contents suggested a Tuesday night murder.

To Pellegrini, it was unnerving that such basic assumptions made in the earliest hours of the case were still being questioned or knocked down by new information. It was as if they had pulled on a single thread and half the case file had unraveled. In Pellegrini's mind, the quickest way for a case to become a quagmire was for the investigators to be sure of nothing, to feel compelled to question everything. The time-of-death estimate, the stomach contents—what else was waiting in that file to turn on them?

At least, in this instance, the changing scenario allowed them to keep one of their best suspects. While it was true that the Fish Man's apartment and store were a long block and a half from Newington Avenue—contradicting Landsman's theories about the proximity of the crime scene—it was also true that the store owner had access to at least one vehicle, a pickup truck that he routinely borrowed from another Whitelock Street merchant. In checking his Wednesday alibi, the detectives learned that he was in possession of the truck on the night the body had been dumped behind Newington Avenue. So far, the working theory had been that if the killer had the body in a vehicle, he'd drive to an isolated spot rather than a nearby alley. But what if he was scared? And what if the body was covered in the back of a pickup truck, relatively exposed?

And why the hell didn't the Fish Man make any attempt in that first interrogation to account for his whereabouts on Tuesday and early Wednesday? Was he merely a marginally employed merchant unable to distinguish one day from the next? Or was he making a conscious effort to avoid a false alibi that detectives would be able to knock down? In the first interrogation, the Fish Man had mentioned the errands he ran with a friend on Wednesday as an alibi. Was that a simple failure of memory or a conscious effort to mislead investigators?

In the weeks since the murder, the rumors of the Fish Man's interest in young girls had pervaded Reservoir Hill to the point where the detectives were regularly receiving fresh allegations of past molestation attempts. The allegations were largely unsubstantiated. But when the detectives ran the store owner's name through the National Crime Index Computer they did come up with a relevant charge that predated his record in the Baltimore computer: a statutory rape charge from 1957, when the Fish Man was in his early twenties. The charge involved a fourteen-year-old girl.

Pellegrini pulled the microfilm of the police reports from storage, and the records showed a conviction and a sentence of nothing more than a year. The ancient history offered little more detail, but it gave the detectives some hope that they were dealing with a sex offender. More than that, it gave Landsman a little more meat to hang on the dry bones of his search warrants.

That afternoon, Landsman had shown his affidavits to Howard Gersh, a veteran prosecutor who had wandered into the homicide unit earlier that day. "Hey, Howard, take a look at this."

Gersh scanned the probable cause in less than a minute.

"It'll fly," he said, "but aren't you giving up a hell of a lot?"

The question was one of tactics. When the warrant was served, the Fish Man would see the affidavit and would learn what detectives believed linked him to the crime. He could also learn where his alibi was weakest. Landsman pointed out that at least the affidavit withheld the identity of those who were contradicting the suspect's initial story.

"We're not giving up any witnesses."

Gersh shrugged and handed the document back. "Good hunting."

"Thanks, Howard."

At ten that evening, Landsman had hurried the warrants to the home of the duty judge, and the detectives and detail officers gathered in the parking lot of the Park Avenue library, where Latonya Wallace had last been seen alive. The plan was to hit the Fish Man's apartment and store first, but now, after finding so little on Whitelock Street, Pellegrini and Edgerton are suddenly impatient to pursue the new theory. They leave Landsman and a detail officer to finish the search of the Fish Man's gutted store while they lead a second group a block and a half east to Newington Avenue.

Two Cavaliers and two radio cars pull in front of a three-story stone rowhouse on the north side of the street, where police tumble out and take the house in rough approximation of a Green Bay Packer sweep. Eddie Brown is through the door first with the lead block, followed by two of the Central District uniforms. Then Pellegrini and Edgerton, then Fred Ceruti and more uniforms.

A seventeen-year-old who meandered down the front hallway to answer the loud banging on the door frame is now pressed against the flaking plaster, a uniform shouting at him to shut the fuck up and keep still for the body search. A second kid in a gray sweatsuit steps through the doorway of the first floor's middle room, assesses the interlopers for what they are, then races back across the threshold.

"Poh-leece," he shouts. "Yo, man, yo, po-leeces comin' . . ."

Eddie Brown yanks Paul Revere out of the doorway and pushes him against an inside wall as Ceruti and more uniforms shove their way down the dark hall toward the light of the center room.

There are four of them in there, crowded around an aerosol cleaning product and a small box of plastic sandwich bags. Only one of them bothers to look up at the intruders and for that kid, there is a moment or two of nonrecognition before the gray ether parts and he begins shouting wildly, running for the rear door. One of the detail officers from the

Southern catches him by the shirt in the kitchen, then bends him over the sink. The other three are lost to the world and make no effort to move. The oldest expresses his indifference by pressing the plastic bag to his face and sucking down a final blast. The chemical stench is overpowering.

"I'm gonna get sick breathing this shit," says Ceruti, shoving one kid over a bureau.

"What do you think?" asks a uniform, pushing another captive into a chair. "Is Momma gonna be upset to find you been huffing on a school night?"

From the second-floor bedrooms comes the cacophony of cursing officers and screaming women, followed by more distant shouting from the third-floor rooms. In twos and threes, the occupants are roused from nearly a dozen bedrooms and marched down the wide, rotting stairwell in the center of the house—teenagers, small children, middle-aged women, grown men—until a full cast of twenty-three is assembled in the middle room.

The crowded room is strangely silent. It is almost midnight and a dozen police are parading through the rowhouse, but the beleaguered population of 702 Newington asks no questions about the raid, as if they have reached that point when police raids no longer require reasons. Slowly, the group settles in sedimentary layers throughout the room: younger children lying in the center of the floor, teenagers standing or sitting on the periphery with their backs against the walls, older men and women on the sofa, chairs and around the battered dining room table. A full five minutes pass before an older, heavyset man, wearing blue boxer shorts and bathroom slippers, asks the obvious question: "What the hell you doing in my house?"

Eddie Brown moves into the doorway, and the heavyset man gives him an appraising look. "You the man in charge?"

"I'm one of them," says Brown.

"You got no right to come into my house."

"I got every right. I got a warrant."

"What warrant? What for?"

"It's a warrant signed by a judge."

"There ain't no judge signing a warrant on me. I'll go get a judge myself about you breakin' into my home."

Brown smiles, indifferent.

"Lemme see your warrant."

The detective waves him off. "When we're done we'll leave a copy."

"You ain't got no damn warrant."

Brown shrugs and smiles again.

"Cocksuckers."

Brown jerks his head up and stares hard at the man in the blue boxer shorts, but the only thing coming back is a look of abject denial.

"Who the hell said that?" Brown demands.

The man turns his head slowly, looking across the room at a much younger occupant, the kid in the gray sweatsuit who shouted the warnings earlier. He is leaning against the inside of the open hallway door, eye-fucking Eddie Brown.

"Did I hear you say something?"

"I say what I want," the kid says sullenly.

Brown takes two steps into the room, yanks the kid off the door and drags him into the front hall. Ceruti and a Central District uniform step back to watch the show. Brown brings his face so close that there is nothing else in the kid's universe, nothing else to think about but one aggravated, 6-foot-2, 220-pound police detective.

"What do you have to say to me now?" Brown asks.

"I didn't say nothin'."

"Say it now."

"Man, I didn't . . ."

Brown's face creases into a sardonic smile as he wordlessly drags the kid back across the threshold of the room, where two of the detail officers are already at work, taking names and dates of birth.

"How long we got to sit like this?" asks the man in the blue boxer shorts.

"Until we're done," says Brown.

In a rear upstairs bedroom, Edgerton and Pellegrini are slowly, methodically, beginning to carve a path through rag piles and mildewed mattresses, paper trash and rancid food scraps, searching 702 Newington for the place where Latonya Kim Wallace was last alive.

The search and seizure raid on the glue sniffers of 702 Newington is the latest corridor in the week-old investigation, the test of a theory that Pellegrini and Edgerton have been piecing together over the past two days. The fresh scenario makes sense out of those things about the murder that seem most senseless. In particular, the theory appears to explain, for the first time, why Latonya Wallace had been dumped behind the back door of 718 Newington. The placement of the body was so illogical, so bizarre, that any argument that could justify that location was enough to bring new direction to the probe.

From the morning Latonya Wallace was found, every detective who had surveyed the death scene asked himself why the killer would risk carrying the child's body into the fenced rear yard of 718 Newington, then deposit it within sight and hearing of the back door. If the murderer had, in fact, managed to enter the rear of Newington Avenue undetected, why not leave the body in the common alley and flee? For that matter, why not leave the body in a yard closer to either end of the block—the only points at which the killer could have entered the alley? And why, above all, would the killer risk entering the fenced yard of an occupied home, then carry the body 40 feet and deposit it so close to the rear door? Other yards were more accessible and three of the rowhouses that backed up to the alley were obviously vacant shells. Why risk being seen or heard by the residents of 718 Newington when the body could just as easily be left in the yard of a house where plywood covered the windows and no occupant would ever peer out to witness the act?

Even before the old drunk from Newington Avenue had proven himself to be insufficient for murder, an answer began to take shape in the two detectives' minds, an answer that dovetailed neatly with Landsman's earliest theories.

From the first day, Landsman contended that the murder had in all likelihood occurred in a house or garage close to where the body was dumped. Then, in the early morning hours, the murderer carried the dead child into the alley, laid her at the door of 718 and fled. Most likely, Landsman had argued, the crime scene was in one of the houses on Callow, Park or Newington avenues, which backed up on the alley from three sides. And if the crime scene was not in the immediate block, then it was at most a block in any direction; the detectives could not envision a murderer, an unconcealed body in his arms, wandering across several blocks of his neighborhood when, for disposal purposes, one alley was as good as another.

There was, of course, a slim possibility that the murderer, fearful of driving very far with a dead girl's body, had used a vehicle to bring the body a short distance to the alley behind Newington—a possibility that Landsman was considering in regard to the Fish Man, who lived blocks from the scene on Whitelock and therefore contradicted the working theory. One resident in 720 Newington had, in fact, told canvassing detectives that she had a vague memory of seeing headlights shine on her rear bedroom wall at four o'clock on the morning the body was discovered. But beyond that sleepy recollection, no resident recalled seeing a strange vehicle in the rear of Newington Avenue. In fact, with the exception of one man who often parked his Lincoln Continental in the rear yard of 716 Newington, no one could remember seeing any car or truck in the cramped back alley.

The new gospel of the Latonya Wallace case—with Edgerton as its author and Pellegrini, his first convert—accepted all those earlier arguments and yet seemed to explain the strange, illogical placement of the body: The killer had not come through the alley. Nor had the child been carried through the premises of 718 Newington—the obvious alternative. The elderly couple who lived at that address and discovered the body were well accounted for and their home had been checked carefully by detectives. No one believed that they were involved, nor was it possible that the body could have been carried through the house without their knowledge.

Only after looking at the scene from a dozen different angles did Edgerton seize on a third possibility: The killer had come from above.

A week ago, when the body was discovered, several detectives had walked up and down the metal fire stair that began on the roof of 718 Newington and descended two flights to the back yard, ending a few feet from the kitchen door and the death scene itself. The detectives checked the stairs for a blood trail or other trace evidence and found nothing. Edgerton and Ceruti had even climbed up to the single-story rear landings of nearby rowhouses to check old pieces of clothesline for comparison with the ligature marks on the child's neck, but none of the men had given any systematic thought to the idea of rooftops. Only after a dozen visits to the scene did the idea begin to shape itself in Edgerton's mind and on Sunday morning, three days after the discovery of the body, the detective began putting the theory to paper.

Edgerton taped two sheets of letter paper together and divided the space into sixteen long rectangles, each representing one of the sixteen adjoining rowhouses on the north side of Newington Avenue. In the center of the diagram, behind the rectangle marked 718, Edgerton crudely drew a small stickman to mark the location of the body. Then he indicated the location of the fire stairs at 718, extending from the rear yard to a second-floor landing and then the roof, as well as other fire stairs and ladders on other properties.

Ten of the sixteen rowhouses had direct access to the roof from inside. Latonya Wallace could have been lured into one of the homes on the north side of Newington, molested and murdered, then carried out one of the second-floor windows onto the flat, tar-covered landings above the rear additions. From there, using the fire stairs, the killer could have carried the body to the third-floor roofs, walked a short distance across the common roof and then descended the metal stair into the yard of 718 Newington. That theory alone could explain why the body was dumped near the back door in the fenced yard of 718 and why the killer did not take the lesser risk of leaving the body in the common alley, or a more accessible yard. From the ground, 718 Newington made no sense. But from the roof, 718 Newington was—by virtue of its secure, metal stair—one of the most accessible yards in the block.

On that same Sunday, Edgerton, Pellegrini and Landsman explored the tops of the Newington rowhouses, looking for evidence and trying to determine which houses had direct access to the roofs. The detectives checked the roof caps of each house and found all to be either sealed with tar or otherwise secure. But from the rear second-floor rooms of ten homes, an occupant could have crawled from the window and taken a fire stair or ladder to the roof.

Edgerton marked those homes—700, 702, 708, 710, 716, 720, 722, 724, 726 and 728—on a steno pad, noting as well that 710 and 722 were vacant buildings that had already been checked by detectives. He crossed those houses off, as well as 726 Newington, which had been renovated recently into one of those skylight-and-track-lighting yuppie wonders, the block's sole concession to a decade-long campaign to attract homeowners and rebuild Reservoir Hill's slum properties. That house was being prepared for sale and was unoccupied, leaving seven viable rowhouses with access to the roof.

On Tuesday, the new theory was granted even more credibility when Rich Garvey, reviewing the color photos from the death scene, noticed the black smudges on the child's yellow print pants.

"Hey, Tom" he said, calling Pellegrini over to his desk. "Look at this black shit on her pants. Does that look like the usual kind of dirt to you?"

Pellegrini shook his head.

"Christ, whatever the hell that stuff is, the lab ought to be able to tell you something. It looks like it might be oil-based."

Roofing tar, thought Pellegrini. He walked the photograph down to the fifth-floor crime laboratory to check it against the child's clothes, which were being examined for hairs, fibers and other trace evidence. A chemical breakdown of the jet black smudges could take weeks or even months and might only yield the class characteristics of the substance. Pellegrini asked whether it could be determined if the stuff was petroleum-based or if it was at least consistent with roofing tar. Yes, he was told after a preliminary examination by the chemists, probably so, although a full analysis would take time.

Later that day, Edgerton and Pellegrini finished comparing the rooftop diagram with the results of the canvass of the 700 block of Newington, checking the seven likely rowhouses against the occupant lists and criminal histories. The detectives concentrated on those addresses where male occupants either lived alone or were not entirely accounted for on the days of the child's disappearance, along with those houses occupied by males with criminal careers. Among confirmed alibis, female residents and otherwise law-abiding citizens, the process of elimination took them quickly to 702 Newington.

Not only was it home to the block's most prolific collection of derelicts, criminals and dopers, but a review of incident reports in the sex offense unit turned up an intriguing item from October 1986, when a six-year-old girl was removed from the house by social workers following indications of sexual abuse. No charges had resulted from the report, however. As for the house itself, 702 Newington had a second-floor tar landing with a wooden ladder that extended to the third-floor roof, and detectives noted during the Sunday search that the rear second-floor windows appeared to have been pushed open recently. A metal screen had been partially cut away from its frame, allowing access to the landing. Moreover, at the rear edge of the third-floor roof, Pellegrini found what seemed to be a fresh imprint in the tar from a dull object, perhaps one covered by a fabric.

On the basis of their criminal histories, six older male occupants of 702 Newington and other residents of the block were brought to homicide on the day the body of the child was discovered—all part and parcel of the preliminary canvass. In those early interviews, the men offered nothing to arouse suspicion, but neither did they endear themselves to the homicide unit. Before being interviewed, the occupants of 702 Newington spent a full hour sitting in the fishbowl, laughing uproariously and challenging each other to perform feats of flatulence.

That performance seems almost understated now, as the detectives work their way through the rubble of 702. Once a stately Victorian home, the structure is now nothing more than a gutted shell without electricity or running water. Plates of food, piles of abandoned clothing and diapers, plastic buckets and metal pots filled with urine clutter the corners of the house. The stench of the squalor becomes more oppressive with every room, until both uniforms and detectives are going downstairs at regular intervals for a cigarette and a breath of winter air on the front steps. In every room, the occupants accommodated for the absence of running water by urinating in a communal container. And in every room, paper and plastic plates laden with food have been deposited in layers, one on top of the other, until a week's feedings can be traced in archaeologic sequence. Cockroaches and water beetles bolt in every direction when debris is moved, and despite the heat in the upper floors of the house, no detective is willing to shed an overcoat or sport jacket for fear that the garment will be overrun.

"If this is where she was killed," says Edgerton, moving through a room given over to discarded food and wet, mildewed rags, "imagine what her last hours were like."

Edgerton and Pellegrini, and then Landsman, arriving later from Whitelock Street, begin to search in the rear second-floor bedroom that belongs to the older man suspected in the earlier rape of the six-year-old. Brown, Ceruti and the others work their way through the third floor and front rooms. Behind them come the lab techs, taking photographs of each room and any items recovered, dusting for fingerprints on any surface suggested by a detective, and administering leuco malachite tests to any stain that vaguely resembles blood.

It is slow going, made worse by the incredible amount of clutter and filth. The back bedrooms alone—those with direct access to the roof—take nearly two hours to cover, with the detectives moving each item individually until the rooms are slowly emptied and the furniture overturned. In addition to bloody clothes or bedsheets and a serrated knife, they are searching for the star-shaped gold earring, nothing less than the proverbial needle in the haystack. From the rear bedroom in which the window screen had been knocked out, they take two pairs of stained denim pants and a sweatshirt that shows positive on a leuco test, as well as a sheet with similar stains. These discoveries prod them to continue through the early morning hours, turning over rotting mattresses and moving battered dressers with broken drawers, in a methodical search for a buried crime scene.

The search and seizure raid that began a little before midnight stretches to three, then four, then five o'clock, until only Pellegrini and Edgerton are left standing and even the lab techs are beginning to balk.

Dozens of latent prints have already been lifted from doorways and walls, dresser tops and banisters, in the unlikely chance that one will match those of the victim. But still Edgerton and Pellegrini are not content, and as they work their way to the third floor, they call for more items to be dusted.

At 5:30 A.M., the adult male occupants of the house are handcuffed together and herded single file into a Central District wagon. They will be taken downtown and dumped in separate rooms, where the same investigators who spent the night picking through the rowhouse will begin an unsuccessful effort to provoke each man into acknowledging a child murder. And though they have not yet been charged with any crime, the suspects from 702 Newington are treated with an almost exaggerated disdain by the detectives. Their contempt is both unspoken and unsubtle, and it has little to do with the murder of Latonya Wallace. Maybe one of the half-dozen men killed the little girl; maybe not. But what the detectives and uniforms know now, after six hours inside 702 Newington, is evidence enough for an indictment of an entirely different sort.

It isn't about poverty; every cop with a year on the street has seen plenty of poverty, and some, like Brown and Ceruti, were themselves born into hard times. And it has little to do with criminality, despite the long arrest sheets, the sexual abuse report on the six-year-old and the teenagers huffing cleaning products in the living room. Every cop at 702 Newington has dealt with criminal behavior on a daily basis, until evil men are accepted without any excess of emotion as the necessary clientele, as essential to the morality play as the lawyers and judges, the parole officers and prison guards.

The contempt shown to the men of 702 Newington comes from a deeper place, and it seems to insist on a standard, to say that some men are poor and some men are criminals, but even in the worst American slum, there are recognizable depths beyond which no one should ever have to fall. For a homicide detective in Baltimore, every other day includes a car ride to some godforsaken twelve-foot-wide pile of brick where no taxpayer will ever again breathe air. The drywall will be rotted and stained, the floorboards warped and splintered, the kitchen filled with roaches that no longer bother to run from the glow of an electric light. And yet more often than not, the deprivation is accompanied by small symbols of human endeavor, of a struggle as old as the ghetto itself: Polaroid snapshots stapled to a bedroom wall showing a young boy in his Halloween costume; a cut-and-paste valentine from a child to his mother; school lunch menus on the ancient, round-top refrigerator; photographs of a dozen grandchildren collected in a single frame; plastic slipcovers on the new living room sofa, which sits alone in a room of battered, soiled remnants; the ubiquitous poster of *The Last Supper* or Christ with a halo; or the air-brushed portrait of Martin Luther King, Jr., on posterboard, on paper, on black velvet even, his eyes uplifted, his head crowned by excerpts from the March on Washington speech. These are homes where a mother still comes downstairs to cry on the front steps when the police wagon pulls up outside, where the detectives know enough to use formal titles of address, where the uniforms ask the kid if the handcuffs are too tight and put a protective hand on his head when he negotiates his way into the back of a cage car.

But in one rowhouse on Newington Avenue, two dozen human beings have learned to leave food where it falls, to pile soiled clothes and diapers in a corner of the room, to lie strangely still when parasites crawl across the sheets, to empty a bottle of Mad Dog or T-Bird and then piss its contents into a plastic bucket at the edge of the bed, to regard a bathroom cleaning product and a plastic bag as an evening's entertainment. Historians note that when the victims of the Nazi holocaust heard that the Allied armies were within a few miles of liberating the camps, some returned to scrub and sweep the barracks and show the world that human beings lived there. But on Newington Avenue the rubicons of human existence have all been crossed. The struggle itself has been mocked, and the unconditional surrender of one generation presses hard upon the next.

For the detectives inside the rowhouse, contempt and even rage are the only natural emotions. Or so they believe until the early morning hours of the search, when a ten-year-old boy in a stained Orioles sweatshirt and denims emerges from the clutter of humanity in the middle room to tug on Eddie Brown's coat sleeve, asking permission to get something from his room.

"What is it you need?"

"My homework."

Brown hesitates, disbelieving. "Homework?"

"It's in my room."

"Which room is that?"

"It's upstairs in the front."

"What do you need? I'll bring it."

"My workbook and some papers, but I don't remember where I left it."

And so Brown follows the boy to the largest bedroom on the second floor and watches as the kid pulls a third-grade reader and workbook from the cluttered table.

"What kind of homework is it?"

"Spelling."

"Spelling?"

"Yeah."

"You a good speller?"

"I'm okay."

They walk back downstairs and the boy is gone, lost in the sweltering mass of the middle room. Eddie Brown stares through the doorway as if it were the other end of a long tunnel.

"I tell you," he says, lighting a cigarette, "I'm getting too old for this."

THREE

Wednesday, February 10

It has been 111 days since Gene Cassidy was shot down at the corner of Appleton and Mosher streets, and for 111 days Terry McLarney has been walking around with the weight of the Baltimore Police Department on his back. Never has there been an open file in the murder or wounding of a Baltimore police officer; never has there been a failed prosecution. Yet McLarney knows, as does every other cop in the department, that a day of reckoning is coming. For years, city juries have been willing to award second-degree verdicts in the shooting of police officers; the boy who shot Buckman six times in the head got second-degree and was already on parole. The doper who killed Marty Ward, shot him in the chest in a drug raid gone bad, also walked with second-degree. McLarney knows, as does every other detective, that it's only a matter of time before the unthinkable happens and one gets away. McLarney tells himself it is not going to be on him, and it is not going to be on Cassidy.

But the days are bleeding away without any fresh leads, without anything to corroborate a case that the prosecutors say is still too weak to give to a jury. The folder for the Cassidy shooting is thick with office reports, but in truth, McLarney has no more on his suspect than he did back in October. In fact, he has less. In October, at least, he was convinced that the man locked up for shooting Gene Cassidy had actually done the crime.

Now he can't be sure. Now, as the case edges closer to a May trial date, he has moments when he actually catches himself in silent prayer. The appeals are short, petitional and blunt: prayers offered on street corners or in the back of the office coffee room, prayers to a Roman Catholic God who did not hear from Terry McLarney when he himself was out there bleeding on Arunah Avenue. Now, at odd moments, McLarney finds himself muttering the kind of single-issue requests with which He is forever deluged. Dear God, help me put together a case against the man who shot Gene and, rest assured, you will not be burdened with my problems again. Respectfully submitted, Detective Sergeant T. P. McLarney, CID Homicide, Baltimore, Maryland.

The late night calls from Gene only added to the pressure. Unaccustomed to a permanent darkness, Cassidy would sometimes wake up in the middle of the night wondering if it was morning or afternoon. Then he would call the homicide unit to learn what was new, what else they had on this boy Owens. McLarney would tell him the truth, tell him that the case against Anthony Owens was still nothing more than two reluctant, underage witnesses.

"What do you want, Gene?" McLarney asked in one such conversation.

"I think," Cassidy replied, "that for every day I'm blind, he should be in prison."

"Can you live with fifty?"

Yes, said Cassidy. If I have to.

Fifty wasn't enough; both of them knew that. Fifty years meant parole before twenty. But right now McLarney couldn't even think about fifty or any other kind of plea. Right now, McLarney could look at the most important case file in his life and see nothing but a loser. Hell, if Cassidy wasn't a cop, this thing would be stetted before it ever got near a courtroom.

There could be no stet on this case, no acquittal, no half-assed plea agreement. Gene Cassidy had to walk away from this with nothing less than a first-degree verdict from a city jury. The department owes him that, and for all practical purposes McLarney is now the personification of the department. As Cassidy's friend, as the supervisor responsible for the case, as the man who has shaped and guided the investigation, it is on Terry McLarney to deliver, to set the thing right.

The pressure is further compounded by a strange, unspoken guilt. Because on that warm night in October, when the call first came to homicide, McLarney wasn't in the office. He had left the four-to-twelve shift after the midnight relief began arriving and heard of the shooting only when he called back to the office from a downtown bar.

Officer down in the Western.

Head shots.

Cassidy.

It's Cassidy.

McLarney raced back to the office. To him, it was more than a police shooting. Cassidy was a friend, an up-and-coming patrolman whom

McLarney had tutored during his brief tour as a sector sergeant in the Western. The kid was a prodigy—smart, hard, fair—the kind of cop the department wanted out on the street. Even after McLarney had transferred back to homicide, he and Gene had stayed close. And now, suddenly, Cassidy was down, maybe dying.

They had found him sitting up at the northeast corner of Appleton and Mosher. Jim Bowen, walking foot a few blocks from the district, was the first to arrive and was shocked that he couldn't immediately recognize a fellow Western man. The face was a bloody pulp, and Bowen knelt to read the breastplate on the uniform: Cassidy. Bowen also saw that Gene's gun was holstered, his nightstick inside the radio car, which was idling a few feet from the curb. Other Western men began arriving, each more shocked than the last.

"Gene, Gene . . . Oh man."

"Gene, can you hear me?"

"Gene, do you know who shot you?"

Cassidy spoke only one word.

"Yes," he said. I know.

The ambulance sped less than a mile to the shock-trauma unit at University Hospital, where doctors calculated a 4 percent chance of survival. One bullet had entered the left cheek, boring upward across the front of the skull and severing the right eye's optic nerve. The second slug smashed through the left side of the face, shattering the other eye and plunging Gene Cassidy into darkness before continuing on its path, lodging in the brain beyond reach of a surgeon's knife. That second bullet left the doctors discussing the worst possibility, that even if the twenty-seven-year-old officer survived, he might suffer severe brain damage.

A vigil began at the trauma unit when Cassidy's young wife arrived with two other Western men. Then came the parade of white hats and gold trim—colonels and deputy commissioners—followed by detectives, surgeons, a Catholic priest who offered last rites.

In its earliest hours, the investigation traveled the time-honored path of all police shootings. Enraged detectives and Western uniforms flooded the area around Mosher and Appleton, grabbing anyone and everyone hanging on the corners. Residents, street dealers, addicts, derelicts—everything that walked was jacked up, intimidated, threatened. Two bullets fired at point-blank range were a declaration of war, and whatever lines of demarcation had once existed between police and the Western locals were suddenly swept aside.

More than any other supervisor in homicide, McLarney led the charge on that first, miserable night, raging from one possible witness to the next, ranting, raving, throwing the fear of God, the devil and T. P. McLarney into the hearts of everyone and everything in his path. When a police officer gets shot, the I-ain't-seen-nuthin' routine doesn't play anymore; even so, McLarney's intensity on that first night bordered on recklessness. It was viewed by the detectives under him almost as an act of contrition, a wild-eyed attempt to compensate for the simple fact that when the call came, he had been drinking beer.

In truth, McLarney's early departure in the late hours of his shift meant nothing. Homicide work is largely flex time, with one shift blending into another as paperwork is completed and fresh troops arrive. Some men leave early, some late, some work overtime on fresh cases, some are at the bar a few minutes after the relief comes walking off the elevators. No one can anticipate the arrival of a red ball, but in McLarney's heart of hearts that kind of rationalization meant little. This was more than a red ball, and it mattered to McLarney that when Gene Cassidy got shot down in the street, he was not on post.

The sergeant's uncontrolled rage on that first night made the other detectives cautious. Several men—including Lieutenant D'Addario—tried to calm him, to tell him that he was too close to the situation, to suggest that he go home, that he leave the case to detectives who had not served with Cassidy, detectives who could work the shooting as if it were a crime—a vicious crime, but not a personal wound.

In one confrontation on the street, McLarney actually threw a punch that shattered the bones of his fist. Months later, in fact, it would become a standard joke in the unit: McLarney broke his hand in three places on the night Cassidy was shot.

In three places?

Yeah, in the 1800 block of Division Street, in the 1600 block of Laurens, in the . . .

McLarney was out of control, but he couldn't leave. Nor did anyone really expect him to. Whatever else they felt about his involvement in that first night's investigation, the men who worked with McLarney understood his rage.

At 2:00 A.M., about three hours after the shooting, an anonymous caller dialed 911 and told police to go to a North Stricker Street house, where they would find the gun used to shoot the officer. No weapon was discovered, but the detectives nonetheless grabbed a sixteen-year-old at that address and took him downtown, where he began by denying any involvement in the incident. The questioning was both prolonged and heated, especially after detectives did a leuco malachite test on the bottom of the kid's sneakers and came up positive for blood. At that point, it was all the detectives could do to keep McLarney away from the terrified, beleaguered kid who, after several hours of heated interrogation, finally gave up one Anthony T. Owens as the gunman. A second man, Clifton Frazier, was named as being present at the time of the shooting but otherwise uninvolved. The young witness put himself within a few feet of the shooting and declared that he had seen the officer wade into a crowded drug corner before being shot without provocation by the eighteen-year-old Owens, a small-time narcotics dealer.

Detectives working around the clock typed up arrest and search warrants for Owens, got them signed by the duty judge, then hit Owens's apartment in Northwest Baltimore at six-thirty that evening. The raid produced little, but before detectives left the address, another anonymous caller said that the man who shot the police was inside a Fulton Street rowhouse. Police raced to that address and failed to find Owens. They did, however, discover twenty-four-year-old Clifton Frazier, the man named as a witness. Frazier was taken downtown, where he refused to make a statement and demanded a lawyer. Wanted on a seemingly unrelated assault warrant, Frazier was taken to the city jail, but bailed out hours after his hearing with a court commissioner.

Late that evening, the younger sister of the reluctant sixteen-year-old witness showed up at the homicide unit and declared that she, too, had been on Appleton Street with several young girlfriends and had seen the police get shot when he walked onto the crowded corner. She claimed that just before the shooting, she had seen Clifton Frazier nudge Owens and say something. The girl also insisted that after the shooting, Owens fled in a black Ford Escort driven by Frazier. Based on that statement, detectives again began looking for Frazier; they found that after being released on bail, he had gone on the wing. They issued a second warrant for him and continued the search for Owens. Later that same night, as the thirteen-year-old girl was initialing the pages of her statement, Anthony Owens walked up to the deskman at the Central District.

"I'm the man they say shot the police."

He had gone to the Central for fear that he would be beaten, or even killed, if he was taken on the streets of the Western, a fear that was in no way unjustified. The other detectives managed to keep McLarney away from the suspect, but Owens was not about to make it through processing, the district lockup and the ride to the city jail without taking some licks. It was brutal, of course, but not indiscriminate, and perhaps Anthony Owens understood that it was in some way required when a police gets shot twice in the head. He took the blows that came his way and made no complaint.

For days after surgery, Gene Cassidy drifted between life and death, lying in a semicomatose state in the intensive care unit with his wife, mother and brother at his bedside. The brass had disappeared after the first night's vigil, but the family was joined by friends and officers from the Western. Each day, the doctors adjusted and readjusted the odds, but it was two full weeks before Cassidy gave them a clue, squirming restlessly as a trauma unit nurse worked with his bandages.

"Oh, Gene," said the nurse, "life's a bear."

"Yeah," said Cassidy, struggling with each word, "a . . . real . . . bear."

He was blind. The bullet in his brain had also destroyed his senses of smell and taste. Beyond that permanent damage, he would have to learn to talk again, to walk, to coordinate his every movement. Once their patient's survival was assured, the surgeons proposed a four-month hospital stay followed by months of physical therapy. But, incredibly, by the third week, Cassidy was walking with the help of an escort and relearning vocabulary in sessions with a speech therapist, and it became increasingly clear that his brain functions were intact. He was discharged from the trauma unit at the end of a month.

As Cassidy returned to the world of the living, McLarney and Gary Dunnigan, the primary on the case, were there with questions, hoping Cassidy could strengthen the case against Owens by recalling details of the shooting independently, perhaps even identifying or describing the shooter in some way. But to his great frustration, the last thing Cassidy could remember was eating a hot dog at his father-in-law's house before going to work that day. With the exception of a brief image of Jim Bowen's face leaning over him in the ambo—a scene the doctors believe he could not have witnessed—he recalled nothing.

When they told him the story about the Owens kid, about being shot without provocation as he tried to clear a drug corner, Cassidy drew a blank. Why, he asked them, would I leave my nightstick in the radio car if I'm clearing a corner? And since when was Appleton and Mosher a drug corner? Cassidy had worked that post for a year and couldn't remember anybody dealing off Appleton. To Cassidy, the story didn't mesh, but try as he might, Cassidy simply couldn't remember.

And yet there was something else Gene Cassidy couldn't recall, an incident that had occurred one night in a hospital room, when his mind was still veiled in a gray haze. Something, some hidden vein of Western District ethic, perhaps, prompted Cassidy to get up and walk on his own for the first time since Appleton Street. Slowly, he made his way to the bedside of another patient, a fifteen-year-old boy injured in an auto accident.

"Hey," said Cassidy.

The kid looked up at a terrifying apparition clothed only in a hospital smock, its eyes swollen and unseeing, its head shaved and scarred from surgery.

"What?" asked the kid.

"You're under arrest."

"What?"

"You're under arrest."

"Mister, I think you better go back to bed."

The ghost seemed to consider this for a moment before turning away. "Okay," Cassidy said.

In the weeks after the shooting, McLarney and other detectives gathered narcotics officers from CID and the Western District's drug enforcement unit and began surveillance of the drug markets near Appleton Street. The assumption was simple: If Cassidy was shot because he had tried to clear a drug corner, then every dealer in the sector would know about it. Some of those dealers would be witnesses; others would know witnesses. More than a dozen traffickers were, in fact, locked up, then interviewed from a position of strength by detectives who could demand information while offering a chance to deal with prosecutors on the drug charges. Incredibly, none had useful information.

Likewise, the night of the shooting had been brisk but not particularly cold, and there was every reason to believe that the locals would have been out on rowhouse stoops well into the evening. Yet a second canvass of Mosher and Appleton streets produced little in the way of witnesses. A lengthy search for the black Ford Escort that was supposed to be the getaway vehicle yielded nothing at all.

In late January, the case was shifted to the career criminals unit of the state's attorney's office, where two veteran prosecutors, Howard Gersh and Gary Schenker, reviewed the indictments and the witness statements.

Owens and Frazier were still being held without bail, but as a prosecution, the case was a disaster. For witnesses, they had a reluctant sixteen-year-old delinquent and his thirteen-year-old sister, whose penchant for running away from home made her unreliable and almost impossible to find. Moreover, the statements from the two children, though similar, differed on key points, and only the girl's statement implicated Frazier as an accomplice. Meanwhile, there was no weapon, no physical evidence, no motive that might placate a juror asked to consider weak evidence.

McLarney felt real fear. What if there was still a lack of evidence at the point of trial? What if they never found another witness? What if they went to court and lost this thing on the merits? What if the shooter went free? In one particularly bad moment of doubt, McLarney actually called Cassidy and, at the suggestion of prosecutors, asked about a thirty-year plea for Owens on a second-degree attempted murder. That meant parole in ten.

No, said Cassidy. Not thirty.

Good for him, thought McLarney. It was obscene even to be thinking about a plea agreement. Cassidy was blind, his career finished. And although Patti Cassidy's employers had offered to hold her position, she had given up her job as an accountant to be with Gene through the months of therapy. Two lives would never be the same—more than two, thought McLarney, correcting himself.

It was just before Christmas when Patti Cassidy's persistent ailments were properly diagnosed. Her nausea and exhaustion were not, as she had believed, the result of stress following the shooting. She was pregnant. Conceived only days before Gene was wounded, the couple's first child was a wonderful blessing, a living, breathing claim to the future. But no one needed to mention that the pregnancy, too, was bittersweet; that this was a child Gene Cassidy would never see.

Patti's pregnancy only fueled McLarney's obsession with the case. But some detectives believed that McLarney's intensity could be attributed in part to something else, something that had nothing to do with Cassidy or the baby, but something that happened in a back alley off Monroe Street, little more than two blocks from where Cassidy fell.

For McLarney, the investigation into the death of John Randolph Scott had become an obscenity. For him, the pursuit of other police officers was unthinkable. There was no way that he could reconcile a world in which Gene Cassidy is shot down in the street and less than a month later, the homicide unit—McLarney's squad, in fact—is out in the districts chasing the men who worked with Gene, putting beat cops on a polygraph, checking service revolvers and searching station house lockers.

It was absurd, and in McLarney's opinion, the John Scott case was still open because the suspects were cops. In McLarney's world, a cop would not shoot someone and leave the body in an alley, not the men he had worked with anyway. That was where Worden had gone off course. Worden was a helluva cop, a good investigator, but if he really believed a police murdered that kid then he was just wrong. Dead wrong. McLarney didn't really blame his detective directly. Worden, in his eyes, was a product of the old school, a cop who followed a superior's orders, no matter how ass-backward. The blame therefore belonged, not to Worden, but to the command staff, and especially to the admin lieutenant and the captain who had taken the Monroe Street probe out of the regular chain of command. Too early in the investigation they discarded the possibility of a civilian suspect, McLarney thought, too early they sent Worden after the cops on the street. The admin lieutenant wasn't an investigator, neither was the captain; for that reason alone McLarney believed they should never have taken the Scott case from him and D'Addario. More to the point, McLarney had been in the Western and they had not. He knew what could happen on the street and what couldn't. And he believed that Monroe Street was lost the moment everyone involved decided that a cop had done the murder.

It all made for a helluva speech, and among the detectives on his shift, no one was ready to deny that McLarney believed every word of it. Then again, he *had* to believe it. Because more than anything else in his life, what Terrence McLarney felt about the Western, about himself, could not be compromised. In McLarney's mind, anyone who wanted the truth need not look farther than Gene Cassidy bleeding at the corner of Appleton and Mosher.

That was police work in the Western District. And if everyone else in the police department couldn't see that, well, McLarney could give eloquent expression to his feelings: fuck it and fuck them. He decided he would have nothing to do with the Monroe Street case. Instead, he would do something much more productive and satisfying: He would fix the Cassidy file.

It was just after the news about Patti's pregnancy that McLarney sent a note to the captain, requesting a detail of two men from the Western District beginning February 1, telling himself that if necessary, they would work the case right up to the May trial date. There was nothing else to do; to lose a police shooting, this police shooting, was too much to contemplate.

The captain had given him the detail and the Western had sent him two of their best. They were a Mutt and Jeff pair: Gary Tuggle, a short, wiry black kid who worked in the district's plainclothes unit, and Corey Belt, a tall, thick-necked monolith with the appearance and temperament of a defensive end, attributes that appealed to the varsity lineman in McLarney's past. Both were smart, both were healthy and both were aggressive even by Western standards. Out on the street, McLarney took a certain amount of delight in the sheer spectacle of his new detail, the obvious contrast between a thickening thirty-five-year-old sergeant and the two well-proportioned carnivores in his charge.

"We pull up to a corner and I get out of the car," mused McLarney after a day's adventures on the west side. "The criminals just look at me and figure, 'No problem, I can outrun this derelict.' Then these two get out of the car and automatically everyone just turns and puts their hands against the wall."

McLarney, Belt, Tuggle—since the first of the month, the trio had spent every working day on the streets of the Western, canvassing the streets near the shooting scene, jacking up witnesses, running down even the vaguest rumor.

But now, after nine days, McLarney and his detail have nothing to show for the effort. No fresh witnesses. Still no weapon. Nothing beyond what they learned in October. There wasn't even talk on the street about a shooting now four months old.

Preparing to go back into the district again this morning, McLarney can feel his fear grow a little bit larger. Having once served as Cassidy's sergeant, having called him a friend, he can regard the case as nothing less than a crusade. Not only because of what the case means to Cassidy, but because of what it means to McLarney, a man defined and obsessed by the badge as few men are anymore, a true believer in the brotherhood of cops, as pagan a religion as an honest Irishman may find.

Terrence Patrick McLarney recognized his obsession years ago, the day he was working a Central District radio car and drew a bank alarm at Eutaw and North. Was there any greater feeling than racing up Pennsylvania Avenue with that blue strobe light show on top of the car and "Theme from Shaft" blasting from a tape player on the front seat? Was there a bigger kick than charging past stunned patrons into the bank lobby, a twenty-six-year-old centurion living by the big stick and the .38 bouncing around on his belt? Never mind that the alarm was sounded in error; it was the sheer spectacle of the thing. In a world of gray, weightless equivocation, McLarney was a good man in a city besieged by bad men. What other job could offer anything as pure as that?

In time, McLarney grew into the part in a way that few men do, becoming a street-worn, self-mocking, hard-drinking cop of almost mythic proportions. He looked, laughed, drank and swore like some retrograde Irish patrolman whose waistline was losing a rearguard action against the weighty properties of domestic beer. Before his form congealed into that of a 230-pound detective sergeant, McLarney had played college football, and only over a period of years had the muscular contours of an offensive lineman succumbed to a daily regimen of radio car, barstool and bed.

His wardrobe accelerated the suggestion of physical decline, and among his detectives there was a consensus that McLarney wouldn't come to work until the family dog had a chance to drag his shirt and sport coat across the front lawn. McLarney repeatedly claimed to have no understanding of the phenomenon, insisting that his wife had ventured into a well-kept suburban mall and emerged with acceptable menswear. Within the confines of his Howard County home and for the first few miles of Interstate 95, the garments would appear attractive and well tailored. But somewhere between the Route 175 interchange and the city line, a sort of spontaneous explosion would occur. McLarney's shirt collar would crease at an unspeakable angle, causing the knot of his tie to execute a contorted half twist. The cuffs of the sport coat would suddenly fray and jettison buttons. The jacket lining above the right hip would catch the butt of his revolver and begin tearing itself free. An ulcer would form on the bottom of one shoe.

"I can't control it," McLarney would insist, acknowledging no dereliction except on those days when he was late for work and had ironed only the front of his shirt, confident that "it's the only part that people are gonna look at anyhow."

Stout, fair-haired and possessed of a quick, chipped-tooth smile, Terry McLarney didn't look like much of a thinker or even much of a wit. Yet to those who knew him well, McLarney's appearance and behavior often seemed calculated to obscure his true character. He was a product of the middle-class suburbs of Washington, the son of a Defense Department analyst with a high GS rating. As a patrolman, McLarney had studied for a law degree out of the passenger seat of a Central District radio car, yet he had never bothered to take the Maryland bar exam. Among cops, some vague taint has always been attached to the title of lawyer, some grounded ethic that believes even the best and most devoted attorneys to be little more than well-paid monkey wrenches hurled into the criminal justice machine. Despite his legal training, McLarney adhered to that ethic: He was a cop, not a lawyer.

Yet McLarney was also one of the most intelligent, self-aware men in homicide. He was the unit's Falstaff, its true comedic chorus. Elaborate practical jokes and bizarre profanity were Jay Landsman's steady contributions, but McLarney's humor, subtle and self-effacing, often caught the peculiar camaraderie that results from police work. Generations from now, homicide detectives in Baltimore will still be telling T. P. McLarney stories. McLarney, who as a sergeant spent a single day sharing an office with Landsman before deadpanning a confidential memo to D'Addario: "Sgt. Landsman stares at me strangely. I am concerned that he views me as a sex object." McLarney, who after four beers spoke in football metaphors and would always offer his detectives the same shred of advice: "My men should go into the game with a plan. I don't want to know what it is, but they should have one." McLarney, who once drove home on a busy shift to rescue his wife and son by using his .38 to shoot a rampaging mouse in the bedroom closet. ("I cleaned it up," he explained on his return to the office. "But I thought about leaving it there as a warning to others.")

At the same time, McLarney was also a tireless investigator who worked cases with care and precision. His best moment came in 1982, as the lead investigator on the Bronstein murders, an unspeakable crime in which an elderly Jewish couple was repeatedly stabbed and left on the living room floor of their Pimlico home. The two killers, their girlfriends, even a thirteen-year-old cousin, returned to the house time and again to step over the bodies and carry off another armful of valuables. McLarney worked the case for weeks, tracing some of the stolen items to a fence in the Perkins Homes housing project, where he learned the names of two suspects who would later be sentenced to death and life without parole, respectively.

As in the Bronstein investigation, McLarney's best efforts came in those cases where a woman was the victim. It was a prejudice that endured long after he returned to homicide as a sergeant. In McLarney's squad, detectives who caught a case with a female victim were routinely prodded and henpecked by their sergeant, a cop governed by the traditional, sentimental judgment that while men might violate the law by killing each other, the murder of a woman constituted real tragedy.

"This one," he would say, staring at the scene photos and oblivious of the melodrama, "has got to be avenged."

He graduated from the academy in March 1976 and went to the Central, but even then he was thinking seriously about a law degree, maybe even a prosecutor's salary—an alternative that Catherine, his wife, readily encouraged. McLarney enrolled in the University of Baltimore law program about the same time that his sector sergeant paired him with Bob McAllister in a two-man car on the Pennsylvania Avenue post. It was a bizarre, schizophrenic existence: days spent in a freshman law class discussing torts and contracts, nights spent handling calls in the Lexington Terrace and Murphy Homes, the city's worst high-rise projects. On a post where every other incident seemed to call for nightsticks, both men learned that they could fight when fighting was the order of the day. The west side high-rises were a world unto themselves, eight towers of decay and despair that served as the city's twenty-four-hour supermarket for heroin and cocaine. And, as if the terrain wasn't bad enough, the two men were together throughout the '79 riots, an event known to BPD veterans as simply the Winter Olympics, when a snowbound Baltimore was robustly looted by its inhabitants. It was McAllister who kept them on an even keel; more often than not he was the calming influence, the voice of reason. In the early morning hours, the two would park the car in a Central hole, where McAllister would read McLarney questions from a legal text, bringing him back to earth after a long night in the projects. Quiet, sensible and self-mocking, Mac was the bridge between worlds, the only thing that stopped McLarney from getting up in a second-year law class to explain that Plaintiff A was trying to fuck over Defendant B and that Judge C should have both of them locked up if they don't cut the shit.

Both men eventually took the entrance test for the Criminal Investigations Division. McAllister was sick of the projects and wanted, more than anything else, to get to homicide, but death investigation held little appeal for McLarney. He wanted simply to be a robbery detective, for the childlike reason that even after two years on the street, he viewed armed robbery—"You're short on cash, so you go to a bank with a gun and just take it?"—as truly amazing, a comic book concept.

Both scored high on the CID exam for two years running, but when positions finally opened up, Mac had to settle for burglary while McLarney eventually landed in the homicide unit by way of the police academy, where he did a brief stint as a legal instructor. To his surprise, he immediately fell in love with homicide—the work, the people. It was an elite unit, an investigative unit—the best in the department—and McLarney had always imagined himself as an investigator. The Maryland bar exam and a legal career were both dim memories from the moment he was handed a detective's shield and assigned a desk.

Then, after two of the happiest years of his life, McLarney made what he later considered his gravest mistake: He passed the sergeant's test. The stripes on his sleeve brought a slightly better pay scale and a transfer to the Western, where they gave him Sector 2 and a squad of fresh-faced, healthy kids to fill the radio cars, twenty-three- and twenty-four-year-old specimens who made him feel like a fossil at the advanced age of thirty-one. Suddenly it was McLarney who had to be the calm, reasoned one. Every night for his two years as a sector sergeant, he would assign the cars and send his flock out into a violent, unforgiving section of the city, a district where a man trusted no one but himself and the others on his shift. Too much happened too quickly in the Western, where every uniform spent the shift alone in a one-man car, dependent on his side partners to hear his call, to get there in time, to keep control.

McLarney came to differentiate the weak from the strong, those who would fight and those who would not, those who knew the street and those who were casualties waiting to happen. Pope, a good man. Cassidy, very good. Hendrix, a fighter. But McLarney knew others shouldn't be out there, and yet the same post cars had to be filled. Every night he would spend an hour or two racing through the required paperwork, then take his own car out into the sector and roam for the rest of the shift, trying to back every call. McLarney spent those two years wondering, not whether one of his men would fall, but how it would happen. In the Western, a cop didn't have to screw up to get hurt, and McLarney wondered if that was how it would be. Or would that godawful moment involve a man who lacked the training, who couldn't control his post, who should never have been in the goddamn car. Above all, McLarney wondered whether it would be something he could live with.

The day, when it came, was beautiful, the first day of September in fact. McLarney remembered the weather because it marked the end of another Baltimore summer, and he hated wearing the Kevlar vest in higher temperatures. He heard the radio call while checking the city pumps on Calverton, several blocks farther west, and he hit the bluetop and raced across Edmondson, arriving in the neighborhood about the same time as a second call for a sighting of the suspect on Bentalou. McLarney tried the first cross street north, rolling slowly. On a shaded porch in the middle of the block, an old couple sat quietly, and when McLarney looked at them, they both turned their eyes to the ground. Maybe they just didn't want to talk to a police; then again, maybe they had seen something. McLarney got out of the car and walked to the porch, where the old man greeted him with a strange, pensive expression.

"You didn't see a man run by here, did you? The gas station got robbed."

The old man seemed to know about the gas station and mentioned almost casually that he had seen a man run down the street, fall, get up again and dart around the corner into a thick clump of bushes.

"Those bushes there?"

From the porch, McLarney couldn't see very much at all. He called for a backup; Reggie Hendrix showed first. McLarney watched his officer walk up an incline into the corner lot and yelled for him to be careful, the suspect might still be in the bushes. Both men had their revolvers out as another resident came off his front porch to ask what was going on, and McLarney turned away to order the man back inside.

"There he is," shouted Hendrix.

McLarney couldn't see. He ran up the small incline toward the other officer, figuring that the best thing to do was to stay close to Hendrix so that the suspect couldn't get between them.

Hendrix kept shouting, but McLarney saw nothing until the man was already out in the open, moving fast across the yard but still facing them. McLarney saw the gun, saw the man shooting, and began firing back. Hendrix fired as well. This is bizarre, thought McLarney, somehow detached, marveling that they seemed to be just standing there shooting each other—which was, in fact, exactly what they were doing. He felt both bullets hit, each one knocking him a bit, and at almost the same moment watched the other man flinch and stagger down the incline toward the street.

McLarney turned and tried to run back across the yard, but his leg was useless. He had fired four and was now stumbling toward the street, where he expected to let the last two go in whatever direction the gunman happened to be running. But when McLarney came down the incline, he saw the man stretched out on the sidewalk, silent, his gun on the pavement near him. McLarney staggered down to the sidewalk and lay down on his stomach a few feet away. He kept one arm outstretched, the gunsight aimed at the other man's head. Next to him on the pavement, the gunman looked over at McLarney and said nothing. Then he lifted his hand enough to manage a weak, waving motion. No more, it said. Enough.

Half the Western was standing over them by then and McLarney let go of his own gun when he saw Craig Pope's .38 in the other man's face. Then came the pain—sharp, shooting pain in his abdomen—and he began to wonder where he'd been hit. The leg was fucked up; but, he thought, what's a leg? He guessed that the second bullet had caught him in the gut, underneath the edge of the vest. Good again, thought McLarney, nothing vital down there.

He felt wetness on his back. "Mike, roll me and see if it came through the other side."

Hajek pushed up on the shoulder blade. "Yeah, it did."

Through and through. A helluva way to find out that the Kevlar vests weren't worth a shit, but McLarney was at least relieved to know the bullet was out.

Separate ambulances took both men to the same trauma unit, with McLarney telling the medics in his ambo that he felt as if he was falling, as if he was going to fall off the litter. When he felt that way, the pain seemed to let up.

"Don't go out," they began screaming at him. "Don't go out."

Oh yeah, thought McLarney. Shock.

In the surgery prep area, he could hear the man he shot making all kinds of noise on the litter beside him and could watch as the trauma team poked at his own body with IVs and catheters. Phillips, another man from his sector, went to tell Catherine, who took it the way any reasonable person would, expressing an unequivocal concern for her husband's well-being and an equally unequivocal conviction that even in a city like Baltimore, most lawyers go through life without being hit by gunfire.

This is it, she told him later. What other reason do you need? McLarney had no right to argue with her; he knew that. He was thirty-two years old, with a family, making half of what most other college graduates do and getting shot down like a dog in the street for the privilege. Boiled to its core, the truth is always a simple, solid thing, and yeah, McLarney had to admit, there was no percentage in being a cop. None at all. And yet nothing about that shooting could change his mind; things had somehow gone too far for that.

He didn't return to active duty for eight months, and for much of that time he was using a colostomy bag until his digestive system healed enough to permit the reversal surgery. After each operation, the abdominal cramps were so bad that he would get down on the floor at night, and after the reversal surgery, a bout of hepatitis prolonged the recovery. Gene Cassidy came by to visit a couple of times and once took his sergeant out to lunch. And when McLarney attempted to cut corners on his rehabilitation by ordering a proscribed beer, Cassidy chewed ass. Good man, Cassidy.

A standing tradition in the Baltimore department dictates that a man shot in the line of duty, upon returning to duty, can take any posting for which he is qualified. That summer, as McLarney was preparing to go back into uniform, Rod Brandner was taking his pension, leaving behind a reputation as one of the best sergeants the homicide unit had ever seen. Brandner had put together a good squad and he worked for D'Addario, which meant that McLarney would also be serving under a lieutenant known to be human.

He returned to the sixth floor expressing little pride at having been shot and little interest in telling and retelling the story. At times, he would express amusement at the status it accorded him. Whenever a shitstorm was breaking, McLarney would simply smile and shake his head. "They have to leave me alone," he would say. "I'm a sworn member who got shot in the line."

In time, it became a standard joke in the unit. McLarney would emerge stone-faced from a meeting in the captain's office and Landsman would play straight man.

"Captain shit on you, Terr?"

"Nah, not really."

"What'd you do? Show him your wounds?"

"Yeah."

"Fuckin'-A right. Every time the captain gets wound up, McLarney just unbuttons his shirt."

But he was not proud of those scars. And over time, he began to talk about getting shot as if it were the most irresponsible thing he had ever done. His son, Brian, had been eight years old and was told only that his father had slipped and fallen on the stairs. But a day or so later the boy heard McLarney's father talking to a family friend on the phone, then went back into his room and began throwing things around. A kid that age, McLarney would later tell friends, I had no right getting shot.

In the end, he rested his pride on a smaller, lesser point. When the bullets hit him on Arunah Avenue, Terrence McLarney did not fall. He stood there, firing his own weapon until he brought his man down.

Raeford Barry Footman, twenty-nine years old, died two days after the incident of complications from a gunshot wound to the chest. When they compared the bullet recovered at autopsy, they found that it had come from McLarney's service revolver.

Some time after the shooting, a detective brought McLarney a printout of the dead man's priors, which ran for several pages. McLarney scanned the sheet until he was satisfied, noting in particular that Footman had only recently been paroled from a felony conviction. He did not want to see an ident photo of the dead man, nor did he want to read the case folder. To McLarney, that seemed to go too far.

Friday, February 12

McLarney sits behind Dunnigan's desk in the annex office, listening to the steady rhythm of a young girl sobbing disconsolately behind the interrogation room door. The tears are real. McLarney knows that.

He leans across the desk, listening to the girl trying to collect herself as the men inside the room go through her statement one more time. Her voice is breaking, her nose running. The girl feels pain, a sense of loss even, as genuine as any felt for Gene Cassidy. And that, to McLarney, is a little obscene.

D'Addario comes out of his office, walks to the interrogation room door and stares through the mirrored window. "How's it going?"

"It's down, lieutenant."

"Already?"

"She gave up Butchie."

Butchie. Tears for Butchie Frazier.

The crying jag began a half hour before, when they finally broke through to Yolanda Marks and the truth began slipping from her in fits and starts. In the interrogation room, McLarney listened to the sobbing until the contradictions, the fractured morality, became too much. A little speech forced its way up into his throat, and then he told a young West Baltimore girl that she was doing the right thing. He told her what Butchie Frazier was, what he had done, and why it needed to end this way. He told her about Gene and Patti Cassidy and the child not yet born, about a darkness that would not go away.

"Think about those things," he told her.

There was silence after that, a minute or two when someone else's tragedy took shape in the young girl's mind. But then McLarney left the room and she was sobbing again, and the tears had nothing to do with

Gene Cassidy. The simple truth was that Yolanda Marks loved Butchie Frazier, and she had given him up.

"Is she talkin' in there?" asks Landsman, walking through the annex.

"Yeah," says McLarney, absentmindedly opening Dunnigan's top drawer. "We're getting ready to write up the statement."

"What's she saying?"

"It's down."

"Hey, way to go, Terr."

Landsman disappears into his office, and McLarney pulls a handful of paper clips from the drawer, lines them up on the desk and begins torturing the first, twisting it back and forth between stubby fingers.

The last two days had made all the difference, and this time they had it right. This time, the investigation had been temperate and clinical, precise in a way that it never could have been in the hours after the shooting. Rage and frustration had marked those first days, but those emotions had finally been sublimated by time and necessity. For McLarney, the Cassidy detail was still a crusade, but one now fueled more by deliberate reason than raw vengeance.

Yolanda Marks's journey to the interrogation room actually began more than a week ago, when McLarney and the two detail men brought their two reluctant eyewitnesses—the sixteen-year-old and his younger sister—downtown to the state's attorney's office. There, detectives and prosecutors began a series of pretrial interviews to elicit additional details about the shooting, details that might then be corroborated to strengthen the existing testimony or, better still, that might lead to additional witnesses. In particular, McLarney wanted to identify and locate the young girlfriends who were supposedly with the thirteen-year-old witness when the crime occurred.

Given the youth of their witness and the intimidating confines of the state's attorney's office, the investigators found it surprising that they had to press the young girl to reveal the names of her friends. When she finally began talking, McLarney and the others were provided with only given or street names—Lulu, Renee, Tiffany and Munchkin—all of whom supposedly lived in the Murphy Homes high-rises. McLarney, Belt and Tuggle went to the projects, finding a variety of young girls who answered to the names provided, but none knew about the shooting. Nor, for that matter, did they seem to know anything about the thirteen-year-old witness.

Once again, McLarney also sent the detail in search of the black Ford

Escort that Clifton Frazier had supposedly used to drive Owens away from the shooting scene. But no such car could be in any way connected to either Frazier or Owens, although the men spent several days watching and following several black Escorts they found near the shooting scene.

The effort to confirm the statements of their two witnesses was going nowhere. Moreover, the defense attorneys appeared to be lining up a series of alibi witnesses who were ready to testify that Anthony Owens wasn't even on Appleton Street when the shooting occurred. Something was clearly wrong and McLarney, sensing a dead end, went back to square one. Three days ago, he pulled out the case file and began reviewing the initial statements provided by neighborhood residents who had been standing in the crowd at the shooting scene and who were grabbed by uniforms and sent downtown. There were several such witnesses, all of whom had claimed that they knew nothing and had merely joined the spectators after the shooting. With nothing left to lose, McLarney decided it wouldn't hurt to begin poking through those statements a second time, so the detail began interviewing each of the witnesses again. After another day on the street, they finally came upon a twenty-year-old resident of Mosher Street named John Moore.

On the night of the shooting, Moore had been yanked off a corner by uniforms and sent downtown, where he told detectives that he had heard the shots but seen nothing. This time, after several hours of friction in the large interrogation room, however, the story changed.

In fact, Moore didn't see the shooting, but he saw everything leading up to it. He was out on his stoop on the night of October 22, watching Clifton "Butchie" Frazier and a young girl he didn't know walking west on Mosher toward Appleton. Frazier and the girl were halfway down the block when a marked police car began rolling slowly down the street. Moore saw the radio car come abreast of the couple, then roll around the corner onto Appleton. A few seconds later, Frazier and the girl rounded the corner as well.

Then came the gunshots. Three of them.

Asked whether there had been a crowd at the corner of Mosher and Appleton, Moore said that the corner was empty at the time of the shooting. He further confirmed his story by leading detectives to a nineteen-year-old friend who had been with him on the stoop.

The second witness recounted the same sequence of events as Moore, adding two more facts to the record. First, the friend remembered that when the radio car came abreast of the couple on Mosher Street, the officer behind the wheel and Butchie Frazier had eyed each other for a moment or two. Second, and more important, the girl with Frazier was named Yolanda. She lived around the corner on Monroe Street. And yeah, if he had to, he could point out the house.

Earlier this morning, McLarney and the two detail officers gathered in the vestibule of that West Baltimore rowhouse, waiting for Yolanda Marks to gather her things and walk to the waiting Cavalier. She was a sad-faced thing, seventeen years old, with deep brown eyes that began to tear as soon as they took her downtown and closed the door to the interrogation room. Yolanda was a juvenile, of course, so her mother came to the office as well, and that proved fortunate. Because after every moral appeal and veiled threat fell short of the mark, it was the mother who went into the room and told her teenage daughter to get it over with, to do the right thing.

Yolanda wiped her eyes, then cried some more, then daubed her eyes again. Then, for the first time, McLarney learned the truth about the attempted murder of Officer Eugene Cassidy.

"Butchie shot the police."

According to the girl, the whole thing happened in less than a minute. Cassidy was already out of the radio car and waiting for the couple when they turned the corner onto Appleton.

"Hey, I want to talk to you."

"What for?"

"Put your hands against the wall."

Butchie Frazier began to assume the position, then suddenly pulled a handgun from his right jacket pocket. A southpaw, Cassidy grabbed Frazier's weapon with his left hand; as a result, he was unable to pull his own revolver from the holster on his left hip. With Cassidy still grappling for the gun, Frazier compressed the trigger. The first shot went wide. Seconds later, the gun was flush against the left side of Cassidy's face and Frazier fired two more rounds.

Cassidy fell to the sidewalk a few feet from his radio car as Frazier fled with the gun through a back alley. Yolanda screamed, backed into the street, then wandered around the block to her house on Monroe Street, where she told her mother what had happened. At that point, neither mother nor child entertained thoughts about calling the police. Nor, for that matter, did John Moore, who had claimed no knowledge of the event on the night of the shooting. Moore's friend also refused to volunteer himself as a witness until detectives confronted him. And yet another couple, who had been walking on Appleton Street and witnessed the struggle between Frazier and the officer, failed to come forward and were only located after Moore and his companion began naming others who were on the street at the time of the shooting.

West Baltimore. You sit on your stoop, you drink Colt 45 from a brown paper bag and you watch the radio car roll slowly around the corner. You see the gunman, you hear the shots, you gather on the far corner to watch the paramedics load what remains of a police officer into the rear of an ambulance. Then you go back to your rowhouse, open another can, and settle in front of the television to watch the replay on the eleven o'clock news. Then you go back to the stoop.

McLarney knows the Western, knows the code. But even after all those years on the street, it still seems incredible that a cop can be shot twice in the head and get no response from an entire neighborhood. And so, when Yolanda Marks finally begins to break, McLarney stops beating up on paper clips and returns to the interrogation room like a true innocent, speaking to her about human tragedy, about lives that can never be made whole. Then he leaves, knowing that nothing he said will stop those tears.

Later that night, when McLarney calls Cassidy at home to tell him the story of Appleton Street, Cassidy suddenly realizes that he knew the man who tried to kill him. Clifton Frazier was the neighborhood badass on Cassidy's post, an arrogant dope peddler who had only a week earlier beaten an elderly man senseless. The old man lost the use of an eye in that attack, a beating inflicted because the victim had seen Frazier slapping a young woman on the street and had the temerity to tell the younger man to let the girl alone. Cassidy knew about the beating because he had been trying for days to find and arrest Frazier on the outstanding warrant.

To Cassidy, Appleton Street now made sense; more than that, it meant something. In the end, he had not been shot down because he wandered onto a crowded drug corner like some brainless academy product. He had been shot doing his job, trying—as he had tried with a fifteen-year-old in a hospital recovery room—to arrest a wanted man. He could live with that. He would have to.

Three days after her interrogation, Yolanda Marks is taken to a nearby Maryland State Police barracks, where a polygraph examiner determines that her statement is truthful. The same day, the sixteen-year-old witness who had implicated Anthony Owens as the shooter is also taken to the same barracks, but just before undergoing the test the teenager recants his earlier statement, admitting that he did not witness the shooting and that he only repeated what he heard on the street, hoping to end his own interrogation. The polygraph is then administered and the examiner concludes that in recanting his story, the teenager shows no deception. When the detectives confront his thirteen-year-old sister, she, too, acknowledges the lie, telling them that she had gone down to homicide and told her story because she was afraid her brother would be charged.

The case is down.

McLarney knows that the Cassidy detail still has weeks of work before it will be fit for trial. For one thing, the wrong man had been indicted, and his innocence will now have to be firmly established or a defense attorney could use him to wreak havoc. Likewise, the case will be bolstered immensely if investigators can find the gun or some other physical evidence to link Frazier with the crime. But it is down.

On the night that Yolanda passes the box, there is a homecoming of sorts when McLarney returns to Kavanaugh's, the city's predominant Irish cop watering hole, and stands his ground at the end of the bar. He leans against the wooden rail, centered between the pinball machine and the St. Francis Center poor box. It is a slow weekday night, with only a handful of detectives in the place, along with a few uniforms from Central and Southern and a couple guys from the tac sections. Corey Belt stops in for a little while but slips out after drinking a soda or two, leaving McLarney to wonder aloud what has become of the vaunted Western District when its best men don't even drink beer. McAllister shows up, too, and stays, bellying up on the stool next to McLarney. This in itself makes the occasion special, because Mac doesn't get out as much anymore, not since he and Sue moved from the city to a new home they built in the rural greenery of northern Baltimore County. To McLarney's distress, his old Central District partner has in recent years been spinning in a more sensible, suburban orbit.

On this February night, however, when McLarney's very universe has been righted by a rare, precious victory, when the brotherhood of cops has once again been affirmed in McLarney's mind, the arrival of McAllister at Kavanaugh's is serendipity itself. Good old Mac. Miracles have been marked on the streets of Baltimore, and Mac, a true pilgrim, has no doubt traveled many dangerous leagues to pay proper homage at this, the true shrine of Celtic sheriffry. McLarney sidles down the bar to wrap a beefy arm around his old partner's shoulder.

"Mac," says McLarney.

"T.P."

"Mac," McLarney says again.

"Yes, T.P."

"My partner."

"Your partner."

"My bunky."

McAllister nods, wondering how long this can possibly go on.

"You know, when we were working together you taught me a lot of shit."

"I did?"

"Yeah, all kinds of important stuff."

"Like what, T.P.?"

"You know, all kinds of shit."

"Oh," says McAllister, laughing. Nothing is so amusingly pathetic as when one cop tries to bond with another. Conversations descend into vague mutterings. Compliments are transformed into insults. Words of genuine affection become comically perverted.

"Really, you taught me a lot," says McLarney. "But that's not why I respect you. I respect you for one thing."

"What's that, Terry?"

"When it was time for you to fuck me," says McLarney soberly, "you were very gentle."

"Of course I was," says McAllister without hesitation.

"You could have just bent me over the hood of the car and had your way, but you were gentle with me. And very patient."

"Well, I knew it was your first time," says McAllister. "I wanted it to be special."

"And it was, Mac."

"I'm glad."

The brotherhood understands, the tribe hears the words unsaid. And when the two detectives finally let go of their deadpan and begin to laugh, all of Kavanaugh's laughs with them. Then they kill off what's left in their cans and argue briefly over the next round, each pulling his wallet and telling the other to take his money off the bar.

As old partners always should.

Thursday, February 18

On the day that marks the end of two full weeks in the Latonya Wallace probe, Jay Landsman manages to slip away from the office in late evening. He drives west into the county, where a wife and five kids are beginning to forget what a husband and father looks like.

The route is so familiar that Landsman's mind drifts free, and in the solitude of the car's dark interior he tries to pull away from the details of the case and view the entire puzzle. He thinks about the terrain on Reservoir Hill, about the alley behind Newington Avenue, about the location of the body. What, he asks himself, are we missing?

The sergeant couldn't argue with the logic behind Edgerton's rooftop theory, its explanation for the placement of the child's body. But he never believed that the warrant on 702 Newington would yield anything. For one thing, there were nearly two dozen people living in that shithole. Even if one homicidal child molester managed to lure the kid into the house, kill her and keep the body in his room for a prolonged period of time, how could he have kept eighteen other occupants from knowing about it? Landsman was certain that the murder was the work of one man, acting alone, but the house at 702 Newington looked as though it were hosting the citywide convention for Baltimore's underclass. Landsman wasn't surprised when the lab reports on the clothing and sheets from the raid came back positive for blood, but negative for the victim's blood type, just as none of the latent prints taken from the house matched those of the victim.

The outcome of the raid on 702 Newington left both Landsman and Tom Pellegrini wishing that they had spent more time searching the Fish Man's store and apartment. Their haste at the Whitelock Street addresses—like everything else with this case—was particularly upsetting to Pellegrini, who worried about what may have been missed. Edgerton's theory had been so sound, so sensible, and given the earlier child abuse report from 702 Newington, Pellegrini had been convinced. With the raid a bust, he had returned with Landsman to the old store owner.

Their interest in the Fish Man had increased since the raids, not only because of the outcome on Newington Avenue, but also because of a profile of Latonya Wallace's killer prepared by the National Center for the Analysis of Violent Crimes, the FBI's behavioral analysis unit. On the day after the raids, Rich Garvey and Bob Bowman had been dispatched to the FBI academy in Quantico, Virginia, where they provided raw data from the crime scene and autopsy to federal agents trained in psychological profiling.

The FBI's characterization of a likely suspect had considerable detail.

He would be "a nocturnal individual who will feel more comfortable at night . . . the offender will be known to young kids in the neighborhood and will be considered strange but nice to children. The offender may have already been interviewed by investigators or he may interject himself into the investigation . . . In most cases the offender will follow press accounts of the investigation and will make some effort to establish an alibi. The offender, who probably has been involved in similar crimes previously, will show no remorse over having killed the victim, but will be concerned over the possibility of being apprehended."

The analysis further noted that "offenders of this type are difficult to interview and as time goes on, the events which occurred will be altered in the offender's mind, making it difficult for him to relate to the crime. It is possible that the offender killed the victim within a short period of time of coming in contact with her . . . The victim in this instance may not have responded to the offender as he thought initially she would have responded. His difficulty in controlling her may have led to the victim's death. Possibly the victim may have initially felt safe or comfortable with the offender and gone willingly with him into a residence or building."

The profile described the probable offender as fifty years of age, probably unmarried and with a history of problems involving female relationships: "The offender most likely had earlier encounters with young girls in this neighborhood. The death of Latonya Wallace is not believed to be a stranger murder."

To Landsman and Pellegrini, the FBI profile seems to match the Fish Man. But without any substantive evidence, the only option is to hammer on the old man in another long interrogation in the hope that something new will be revealed. For this very reason, Edgerton and Pellegrini are still at the office as Landsman drives home; they plan to work late into the night preparing for a second confrontation with the Fish Man scheduled for the weekend.

But Landsman isn't optimistic about the coming interrogation either. The FBI analysis also made it clear that a violent sex offender is among the most difficult suspects to break. There was no Out to offer such people, no reasonable suggestion that the murder could be mitigated in some way. Moreover, the crime was genuinely sociopathic: An absence of remorse would probably be coupled with rationalizations in the suspect's mind. All that had to be coupled with the fact that the Fish Man had previously walked out a free man after one interrogation; he would be less intimidated by a second attempt. And still there is the missing crime scene, the absence of any physical evidence with which to link a suspect to the crime. The detectives have rumors, suspicions, and now a psychological profile. But working without a scene, they have nothing that can argue against the Fish Man's story, nothing that can be used as leverage in an interrogation.

It is a bastard of a case, and again Landsman asks himself: What are we missing? Maneuvering through the evening traffic on Liberty Road, he runs two weeks of investigation through his mind. Every day since February 4, the detectives had marched into Reservoir Hill, questioning locals, checking garages and vacant apartments in an ever-growing radius from Newington Avenue. With the consent of the occupants, detectives had managed to perform plain-view searches of every one of the thirteen occupied rowhouses on the north side of Newington, as well as many of the properties on the Callow and Park Avenue sides of the block. They had checked alibis and living quarters for every male suspect identified in the early canvassing.

The dead girl's clothes and belongings were still being checked for trace evidence; but excepting those black smudges on her pants, nothing looked especially promising. The blue satchel and its contents had been sent to the Bureau of Alcohol, Tobacco and Firearms laboratory, thirty-five miles away in Rockville, Maryland, for laser fingerprinting, an examination that yielded a few latent prints on the library texts. Those prints were now on the fifth floor of headquarters, running through a Printrak computer that electronically searches for possible matches among the fingerprint files of everyone with a previous arrest in Baltimore.

On the chance that the little girl had left something more than an earring at the crime scene, Edgerton had checked with the library for the titles of the books she checked out that Tuesday afternoon. And when the library system explained that such information could not be released without infringing on the borrower's privacy, Edgerton actually called the mayor himself; Hizzoner made it easy for the librarians to change their minds. Meanwhile, Pellegrini had gone back more than a decade in the old homicide files, looking for any unsolved murder or disappearance involving young girls. Landsman had checked the sex offense unit for any recent reports in the Reservoir Hill area. Then, with the family's permission, Pellegrini had walked through the little girl's room, read through her pink and blue diary, even developed the film in her Polaroid camera in search of a suspect. And all of the detectives and detail officers had spent hours running down the telephone tips that followed any TV broadcast that mentioned the case:

"I have the killer of Latonya Wallace in my house."

"The family was involved with drugs. The little girl was killed as a warning."

"My boyfriend killed her."

When one ninety-two-year-old woman with failing eyesight claimed to have seen a little girl in a red raincoat enter a Park Avenue church on the afternoon of February 2, Pellegrini dutifully arranged to check inside the building and interview the minister. When a detail officer asked what questions would be put to the clergyman, Pellegrini simply shrugged and offered a Landsman-like deadpan: "How about, 'Why did you kill her?' "

Like every corridor in the Latonya Wallace labyrinth, the anonymous calls and false sightings led nowhere. Landsman wonders which part of the maze has been overlooked, which portal has yet to be explored. What the hell are they missing?

The sergeant is nearly home when a fresh thought forces its way to the surface, suddenly breaking through the thick crust of detail: the car. Right next door. A cool, dry place.

The neighbor's goddamn Lincoln, the only fucking car that anyone ever saw in the alley. And it was parked just on the other side of the fence from the rear yard of 718 Newington. Hell yes.

Landsman pulls to the slow lane of Liberty Road, looking for a pay phone so that he can call and tell Pellegrini and Edgerton to stay put. He's going back in.

Twenty minutes later the sergeant storms into the annex office, still cursing himself for not seeing it earlier. "It's right there in front of us," he tells Pellegrini. "This is it. It's gonna go down."

Landsman lays it out for the two detectives: "If she's killed Tuesday, he needs to put the body in a cool, dry place or we're going to have decomp, right? So he gets the body out the back door and into the car trunk, thinking he's gonna drive it somewhere at night. But for some reason he's unable to dump the body. Or maybe when he goes out, he gets scared . . ."

"This is the guy who lives at seven-sixteen?" asks Edgerton.

"Yeah, the husband of Ollie's neighbor. What's-his-name."

"Andrew," says Pellegrini.

"Yeah, Andrew. Ollie doesn't like him a little bit."

Landsman recalls the first hours of the investigation, when Ollie's husband, the old man who lives at 718 Newington and found the child's body, was asked whether anyone parked a car in the alley. The man had mentioned his neighbor, a middle-aged man who had recently married the churchgoing woman who lived at 716 and often left his Lincoln Continental in the back yard. In fact, the car had been out back for most of the previous week.

"When he told me, he even walked to his back window and looked out, like he expected it to be there." Landsman cuts to the chase: "The motherfucker moved it. He parks back there all the time. Why all of a sudden, on that morning, is the Lincoln parked out in front of the house on Newington?"

Edgerton finds the arrest sheet for the man who lives at 716 Newington: no sex offenses, but someone who at certain points in his life would not have been mistaken for a civic asset.

"That's the other thing," says Landsman. "This guy Andrew, he don't fit. What's a guy with a record doing married to a churchgoing woman? It's fucked up."

It is closing on nine o'clock, but Landsman is now too wired to call it a night. Instead, the trio barter the keys to a Cavalier and drive back up to Newington Avenue. They check front and back, but the Lincoln isn't on the block. Landsman knocks on the front door of 718, where a sad-faced woman answers the door in a worn cotton nightgown.

"Hey, Ollie," says Landsman, "is your husband around? We just need to check a couple things."

"He's lying down."

"We just need a minute or two."

The woman shrugs and leads the way to the rear bedroom on the first floor. Stretched out on his back beneath a gray sheet, the old man who found the little girl's body in his back yard watches the parade of detectives with mild curiosity.

"He got sick this week," says the woman, retreating to the corner of the room.

"Sorry to hear that. What're you sick with?"

"Cold or somethin'," the old man says in a low mumble. "Y'know the hawk's been out."

"Yeah it has, um, hey, listen," says Landsman, shifting gears suddenly. "You remember that day you found the body and we were talking? You remember when I asked you if anyone parked in the alley and you told me about Andrew next door?"

The old man nods.

"I remember you even walked over to the kitchen window, like you were gonna show me his car, but it wasn't there that morning, remember?"

"Yeah, I thought he had it there."

"What we need to know is if Andrew had his car parked out there earlier in the week, like on Tuesday or Wednesday?"

"It's a while back now," the old man says.

"Yeah it is, but can you think on it . . ."

The old man drops his head back against a pillow and stares at the cracked ceiling. The room waits.

"Think he did, yeah."

"You think so, huh?"

"He park it back there a lot, you know," says the old man.

"Yeah, that's what I remember you telling me," says Landsman. "Listen, what do you know about Andrew?"

"Don't know nuthin', really."

"I mean what kind of a guy is he?"

The old man looks nervously at his wife. "I really don't know . . ."

Landsman looks at Ollie and catches something on her face. She has something to say she doesn't want her husband to hear.

"Well, listen, thanks a lot for helping," says Landsman, moving toward the bedroom door. "You take care of yourself now, okay?"

The old man nods and watches his wife follow the detectives out of the room. She closes the door and follows Landsman to the other end of the hall.

"Hey, Ollie," Landsman says to her, "remember what you were saying about Andrew?"

"I don't . . ."

"About how he's like a gigolo living off . . ."

"Well," says Ollie, a little embarrassed, "I know she bought that car for him and now he uses it to go out on the town. He's gone every night."

"Yeah? Do you know if he likes young girls?"

"Yeah, he likes young girls," she says, disapproving.

"I mean, real young."

"Well, that I can't really say . . ."

"Okay, that's all right," Landsman says. "Where's the car now? Do you know?"

"He say the repo man came an' took it."

Pellegrini and Edgerton look at each other. It's almost too perfect.

"It was repossessed?" asks Landsman. "He told you that?"

"She told my husband that."

"Your neighbor did? Andrew's wife?"

"Yeah," she says, wrapping her robe tight in the chill of the front hall. "She say Johnny's Cars came an' got it."

"Johnny's? Up on Harford Road?"

"I guess."

The detectives thank the woman, then head straight to Johnny's in Northeast Baltimore, where they walk the entire lot looking for the car that Andrew's wife said had been repossessed. No Lincoln. Landsman is now completely convinced.

"This motherfucker dumps the body, gets rid of his car, and when people ask him, he says it got repo'd. Fuck it, we need to talk to this motherfucker tonight."

It is after 11:00 P.M. when they return to Newington Avenue and talk their way into 716. Andrew is a short, balding man with a face that is all hard angles. He is still awake, drinking warm beer and watching the local news in the basement. Three plainclothes detectives walking down the stairs do not seem to surprise him.

"Hey, Andrew, I'm Sergeant Landsman, this is Detective Edgerton and Detective Pellegrini. We're working on the little girl's murder. How you doin' tonight?"

"Awright."

"Listen, we want to ask you a couple questions about your car."

"My car?" asks Andrew, curious.

"Yeah. The Lincoln."

"They took that away," he says, as if that should end any discussion.

"Who did?"

"The car dealer."

"Johnny's?"

"Yeah. 'Cause my wife, she didn't make the payment on it," he adds, a little put out.

Landsman steers the conversation toward the parking pad in the back alley. Andrew readily acknowledges his habit of keeping the car in the rear yard to prevent theft or vandalism, then further agrees that the car had been in the rear yard on the Tuesday night of the girl's disappearance.

"I remember it 'cause I went out to the car for something and felt like someone was out there watching me."

Landsman, startled, looks hard at the man.

"How's that again?"

"I went out to the car that night to get something and I felt real nervous, like someone was out there watching me," he repeats.

Landsman gives Pellegrini one of those did-I-hear-what-I-just-thought-I-heard stares. Three minutes into the conversation and the guy is already putting himself out in the alley on the night the child is abducted. Hell, he probably had reason to be nervous about being watched out there in the alley on Tuesday. Who the fuck wouldn't be nervous carrying a little girl's body from their back door to a car trunk?

"Why were you nervous?"

Andrew shrugs. "I just got a strange feeling, you know . . ."

Edgerton begins walking the length of the basement room, looking for red-brown stains or a child's gold earring. The basement is a poor version of a bachelor's lair, with a sofa and television in the center of the room and, against the long wall, five or six liquor bottles on top of an old dresser being used as a bar. Behind the sofa is a plastic laundry tub containing two to three inches of urine. What the hell is it about Newington Avenue that makes people piss into buckets?

"This is kind of your place down here, huh?" asks Edgerton.

"Yeah, this is where I hang."

"Your wife don't come down here much?"

"No, she leaves me be."

Landsman brings Andrew back to the night in the alley: "What did you go out to the car for?"

"I can't remember. Something in the glove compartment."

"You didn't go in the trunk?"

"The trunk? No, the glove compartment . . . I had the car doors open and I just felt like I was being watched. I was, you know, a little scared about it and said, well, damn, I'll get whatever I need to get tomorrow morning. So I went back inside."

Landsman looks at Pellegrini, then back at Andrew. "Did you know the little girl?"

"Me?" The question startles him. "The girl that got killed? I haven't been here that long, you know. I don't know most people around here."

"What do you think they should do to the guy that killed her?" asks Landsman, smiling strangely.

"Hey," says Andrew, "do what you have to do. Make sure it's the right guy and then you don't even need a trial. I have a daughter, and if it were her, I'd take care of it myself . . . I have friends who would help me take care of it."

Edgerton takes Pellegrini out of earshot to ask if the detectives and detail officers doing the consent searches on Newington Avenue have checked the basements. Pellegrini doesn't know. That was the trouble with a sprawling red ball; between five detectives and a dozen detail officers, progress is dependent on too many people.

"Andrew," says Landsman, "we're gonna need to talk to you downtown."

"Tonight?"

"Yeah. We'll bring you back up when we're done."

"I been sick. I can't really leave the house."

"We really need to talk to you. It could help us out with the little girl's murder."

"Yeah, well, I don't know nothing about that, you know. I'm sick . . ."

Landsman ignores the protestations. Short of arrest, which requires both a crime and probable cause, there is no law that can make a man go against his will to an interrogation room in the middle of the night. It's one of the small joys of American police work that few people ever argue the point.

Andrew comes to rest in the large interrogation room fifteen minutes later, with Landsman standing on the other side of the door in the sixth-floor corridor, telling Pellegrini and Edgerton to find that Lincoln.

"I'll take a long statement and keep him here," says the sergeant. "We gotta know if his car was really repo'd."

Pellegrini's call to old Johnny wakes him up. It's now the middle of the night, but the detective asks the auto dealer to go down to the sales office and dig out the paperwork. Johnny and Mrs. Johnny are already there when the two detectives get to Harford Road. The dealer finds a record of the sale and the payment schedule, but nothing to indicate a repossession order. Maybe, he suggests, the paperwork hasn't yet come from the finance company.

"If it was repossessed, where would they tow it?"

"They got one lot over on Belair Road."

"Can you show us?"

Johnny and Mrs. Johnny pile back into their Cadillac Brougham and pull out of the lot. The detectives follow them to a fenced impound lot near the city's northeastern edge. The car isn't there. Nor is it at a second lot out in Rosedale, in eastern Baltimore County. And at 3:00 A.M., when the two detectives learn of a third lot in the northeast county near the Parkville police precinct, they head north with growing confidence that no one has towed Andrew's shit-brown Lincoln Continental anywhere, that the lying bastard ditched the car somewhere on his own.

The third impound lot is protected by a ten-foot chain-link fence.

Pellegrini walks up to one corner and stares through the metal mesh at a row of cars parked along the far end, hopeful that Andrew's car isn't among them. But the next to the last car in the row is a Lincoln Continental.

"There it is," he says, his voice flat with disappointment.

"Where?" asks Edgerton.

"Near the end there. The brown one."

"Is that it?"

"Well, it's a brown Lincoln."

Pellegrini scans the lot for any sign of life. They do not need a warrant for the car; Andrew no longer has any claim to ownership. But the front gate is chained and padlocked.

"Well," says Pellegrini, "here goes nothing." The detective digs the tip of one black Florsheim into the metal links and begins pushing himself up the front of the fence. Two large Dobermans race the length of the impound lot, yelping and growling and baring their teeth. Pellegrini jumps down.

"Go on, Tom," says Edgerton, laughing. "You can take 'em."

"No, that's all right."

"They're just animals. You're a man with a gun."

Pellegrini smiles.

"Go on. Show 'em your badge."

"I think we can wait," says Pellegrini, walking back to the car.

Four hours later, Pellegrini is headed back toward the lot with Landsman, who finished taking Andrew's statement a little before 6:00 A.M. Although neither detective has slept in twenty-eight hours, there is little sign of fatigue when they roll out Perring Parkway toward the county, or when they follow a bored attendant across the dirt lot to the Lincoln. So it really was repo'd, thinks Pellegrini, so what. Maybe Andrew gave up the car figuring that it was clean, that there was nothing to link him to the murder.

"This the one?"

"Yeah. Thanks."

The two detectives check the car's interior first, searching the upholstery and carpeting for red-brown stains, hairs or fibers. Landsman finds a piece of imitation gold chain, a woman's bracelet, above the dashboard. Pellegrini points to a small dark brown stain on the passenger seat.

"Blood?"

"Nah. I don't think so."

Landsman pulls a leuco malachite kit from his pocket, treats a cotton swab with chemical and runs it across the stain. Dull gray.

Pellegrini finishes checking the back seat, then both men walk around to the trunk. Landsman turns the key, but hesitates for just a moment before opening the top.

"C'mon, you mother," he says, coming as close to genuine prayer as Jay Landsman ever does.

The trunk is clean. He treats seven or eight leuco swabs with chemical and drags them into every one of the trunk's indentations and crevices. Dull gray.

Pellegrini exhales slowly, his breath clouding in the frigid air. Then he walks to the Cavalier and sits in the driver's seat. He holds up the bracelet and looks carefully at the gold strand, sensing that it, too, leads nowhere, that within a day or two the family of Latonya Wallace will answer no, they have never seen the chain before. Pellegrini waits silently as Landsman scrapes two more swabs along the interior before closing the trunk, sticking his hands deep into his jacket pockets and walking back to the Chevrolet.

"Let's go."

Suddenly, the exhaustion is overpowering, and both detectives are squinting in the morning light as the car rolls south on Harford Road and then west on Northern Parkway. For fifteen solid days, they have worked sixteen- and twenty-hour shifts, living on a roller-coaster ride from one suspect to another, bouncing wildly between moments of elation and hours of despair.

"I'll tell you what I think," says Landsman.

"What?"

"I think we need a day off. We gotta get some sleep, wake up and think on it."

Pellegrini nods.

Somewhere near the Jones Falls interchange, Landsman speaks again.

"Don't worry, Tom," he says, "it'll go down."

But Pellegrini is awash in fatigue and doubt, and he says nothing.

In Jay Landsman's office, the Latonya Wallace probe is spreading like a cancer. Crime scene photos, lab reports, diagrams, office reports, aerial photographs of Reservoir Hill taken from the police helicopter—the paper pours out of the case folder and marches across the sergeant's desk and file cabinets. A second column of documents begins a flanking maneuver, attacking Pellegrini's work area in the annex office, then overwhelming a cardboard box behind the detective's chair. The case has become a world unto itself, spinning in an orbit of its own.

But for the rest of the homicide unit, it's business as usual. For much of the decade, homicide detectives in Baltimore have believed that the law of averages will guarantee somewhere between 200 and 250 murders a year, a total that shakes out to about two homicides every three days. The unit's institutional memory includes a few 300-plus years in the early 1970s, but the rate declined abruptly when the state's shock-trauma medical system came on line and the emergency rooms at Hopkins and University started saving some of the bleeders. For the last two years, the body count has edged slightly higher, cresting at 226 in 1987, but the trend is nothing that makes the act of murder in Baltimore seem like anything more than a point on the probability curve. On Friday afternoons, the nightshift detectives can watch Kim and Linda, the admin secretaries, stamp case numbers on empty red binders—88041, 88042, 88043—and know with fat, happy confidence that somewhere on the streets of the city, several victims-to-be are stumbling toward oblivion. The veteran detectives will joke about it: Hell, the case numbers are probably tattooed on the backsides of doomed men in ultraviolet ink. If you put one through a postage meter, if you showed him the 88041 stenciled on his right cheek and told him what it meant, the poor fuck would change his name, lock himself in his basement, or jump the first Greyhound to Akron or Oklahoma City or any other spot a thousand miles away. But they never do; the math remains absolute.

Of course, within the confines of the established rate, statistical fluctuation permits the slow weekend due to rain, snow or a pennant race in the American League East. Also permitted is the aberrant full-moon midnight shift, when every other right-thinking Baltimorean reaches for a revolver, or those occasional and unexplained homicidal binges in which the city seems hell-bent on depopulating itself in the briefest time span possible. In late February, as the Latonya Wallace detail stretches into its third week, the homicide unit begins one such period when detectives on both shifts are hit with fourteen murders in thirteen days.

It is two weeks of mayhem, with bodies stacked like firewood in the ME's freezer and detectives arguing over the office typewriters. On one particularly bad night, two men from McLarney's squad find themselves acting out a scene that could only occur in the emergency room of an urban American hospital. The green-smocked vanguard of medical science is at stage right, struggling to repair a man with holes in his body. At stage left is Donald Waltemeyer, playing the role of First Detective. Enter Dave Brown, the Second Detective, who has come to assist his partner in the investigation of a Crime of Violence.

"Yo, Donald."

"David."

"Yo, brother, what's up? Is this our boy here?"

"This is the shooting."

"That's what we've got, right?"

"You got the stabbing, right?"

"I came up here looking for you. McLarney thought you might want help."

"Well, I got the shooting."

"Okay. Great."

"Well, who's gonna take the stabbing?"

"Whoa. The shooting and stabbing are separate?"

"Yeah. I got the shooting."

"So where's the stabbing?"

"Next room over, I think."

The Second Detective moves stage right, where another team of green-smocked technicians is now visible, struggling to repair another man with even larger holes.

"Okay, bunk," says the Second Detective impassively. "I'll take it."

A night after Waltemeyer and Dave Brown trade bleeders at the Hopkins trauma unit, Donald Worden and Rick James catch their first fresh murder since Monroe Street, a picture-perfect domestic from the kitchen of a South Baltimore townhouse: a thirty-two-year-old husband is stretched across the linoleum, blood leaking from .22-caliber holes in his chest, undigested rum and cola leaking from his open mouth. It started with an argument that progressed to a point where the wife called police just after midnight, and the responding uniform graciously drove the very drunk husband to his mother's house and told him to sleep it off. This meddlesome action, of course, violates the inalienable right of every drunken South Baltimore redneck to beat his estranged wife at one in the morning, and the husband responds by shaking off his stupor, calling a taxi and kicking down the kitchen door, whereupon he is shot dead by his sixteen-year-old stepson. Called at home that morning, the state's attorney on duty asks for manslaughter charges in juvenile court.

Two days later, Dave Brown picks up a drug murder from the open-air market at North and Longwood, and when it shakes out three days later, Roddy Milligan is credited with another notch on his gun. At the tender age of nineteen, Roderick James Milligan has become something of a pest to the homicide unit, what with his penchant for shooting every competing street dealer in the Southwestern. A small, elfin thing, Milligan had previously been sought on two 1987 murder warrants and was a suspect in a fourth slaying. His whereabouts unknown, young Roderick was beginning to irritate the detectives; Terry McLarney, in particular, takes as an insult the youthful offender's decision to shoot more people rather than surrender.

"Can you believe a little shithead like this is able to stay on the run for so long?" McLarney declares, returning from yet another unsuccessful turn-up of a Milligan hideout. "You shoot a guy, hey," the sergeant adds with a shrug. "You shoot another guy—well, okay, this is Baltimore. You shoot three guys, it's time to admit you have a problem."

Although Milligan has taken a line from Cagney, telling relatives he'll never be taken alive, he's eventually picked up in a raid a month later, caught dirty at a girlfriend's house with heroin still in his pocket. His reputation suffers when it later gets out that after being tossed into an interrogation room, he cries uncontrollably.

For Stanton's shift, there is the thirty-nine-year-old Highlandtown native who goes with a friend to buy PCP in a blighted section of Southeast Washington, where he is instead robbed and shot in the head by a street dealer. The friend then takes the wheel of the car and drives the thirty-five miles back up the Baltimore-Washington Expressway with the victim a bloody, dying wreck in the passenger seat. He takes the corpse to an east side hospital, claiming to have been attacked and robbed by a hitchhiker on nearby Dundalk Avenue.

There is the argument at a West Baltimore bar that begins with words, then escalates to fists and baseball bats until a thirty-eight-year-old man is lingering in a hospital bed, where three weeks later he rolls the Big Seven. The argument is between two Vietnam veterans, one declaring that the 1st Air Cavalry was the war's premier fighting unit, the other advocating for the 1st Marine Division. In this particular instance, the Air Cav carries the day.

And there can be no forgetting the Westport mother who shoots her boyfriend, then tells her teenage daughter to confess to the crime, arguing that she would be charged only as a juvenile. And the young drug dealer from the Lafayette Courts projects who is abducted and shot by a competitor, then dumped in a Pimlico gutter, where he is mistaken for a dead dog by passersby. And the twenty-five-year-old East Baltimore entrepreneur who is shot in the back of the head as he weighs and dilutes heroin at a kitchen table. And the is-this-a-great-city-or-what homicide that

Fred Ceruti handles in a Cathedral Street apartment, where one prostitute plunges a knife into the chest of another for a $10 cap of heroin, then fires the drugs before the police arrive. The key witness to the crime, a businessman from the Washington suburbs who fled to his wife and children at the first sign of blood, is chagrined to be called at 4:00 A.M. by a detective who learns his identity from credit card slips left behind on Baltimore's Block, the downtown erogenous zone where he met the whores.

"Is Frank home?"

"Yes," says a woman's voice, "who is this?"

"Tell him it's his friend Fred," says Ceruti with genuine charity, adding, a few seconds later, "Frank, this is Detective Ceruti from the Baltimore Police Department's homicide unit. We have a problem here, don't we?"

In contrast, there is a rare, refreshing moment of civic responsibility displayed by one James M. Baskerville, who flees after shooting his young girlfriend in her Northwest Baltimore home, then calls the crime scene an hour later and asks to talk with the detective.

"Who am I talking to?"

"This is Detective Tomlin."

"Detective Tomlin?"

"Yeah, who's this?"

"This is James Baskerville. I'm calling to surrender to you for killing Lucille."

"Goddammit Constantine, you bald-headed motherfucker, I'm up here trying to do a crime scene and all you can find to do is fuck with me. Either come up here and help or—"

Click. Mark Tomlin listens to a dead phone line for a moment, then turns to a family member. "What did you say was the name of Lucille's boyfriend?"

"Baskerville. James Baskerville."

When the second call comes, Tomlin catches it on the first ring. "Mr. Baskerville, listen, I'm real sorry about that. I thought you were someone else . . . Where are you now?"

Later that night, in the large interrogation room, James Baskerville—who would later agree to life plus twenty years at his arraignment—offers no excuses and readily initials each page of his statement of confession. "I've committed a serious crime and I should be punished," he says.

"Mr. Baskerville," asks Tomlin, "are there any more like you at home?"

And like Latonya Wallace, there are those rare victims for whom death is not the inevitable consequence of a long-running domestic feud or a stunted pharmaceutical career. Poor souls like Henry Coleman, a forty-year-old cab driver who picks up the wrong fare at Broadway and Chase; and Mary Irons, age nineteen, who leaves a downtown dance club with the wrong escort and is found cut up behind an elementary school; and Edgar Henson, thirty-seven, who is leaving an east side 7-Eleven when a group of teenagers announce a robbery and then, without warning, begin blasting away. The gang takes two dollars in food stamps, leaving behind a quart of milk and a can of Dinty Moore stew.

And Charles Frederick Lehman, fifty-one, a Church Home hospital employee whose last moments on earth are consumed by the carry-out purchase of a two-piece extra crispy dinner from the Kentucky Fried outlet on Fayette Street. Lehman doesn't make the twenty feet between the restaurant door and his Plymouth; he is found spread-eagled on the rain-soaked parking lot, his wallet gone, the contents of one pocket spread across the asphalt, the chicken dinner lying in a puddle near his head. From inside the restaurant, another customer watched the brief struggle with three teenagers, heard the gunshot and saw the victim fall. He stared as one kid leaned over the stricken man, methodically rifled his pants pockets, then raced his two companions across Fayette Street into the Douglass Homes project. But the sixty-seven-year-old witness is nearsighted, and he can provide no description better than three black males. The dead man's car is towed to headquarters for processing in the hope that one of the three kids touched the car and left a clear print. When that fails, there is only the anonymous caller with a white male's voice who tells Donald Kincaid that a black co-worker had talked about watching three kids—one of whom he knew by name—running through the Douglass Homes after the shooting. But the co-worker doesn't want to be a witness. Neither, for that matter, does the caller.

"He doesn't have to give his name. He can just talk to me like you're talking to me now," pleads Kincaid. "You got to get him to call because I'll tell you the truth, this is the only clue I got." The voice on the other end promises to try, but Kincaid has been in homicide for a dozen years, and he drops the receiver into its cradle knowing that in all probability, he is waiting for a call that will never come.

Sunday, February 21

They take a page from the book written by the FBI's psychological analysts, with Pellegrini and Landsman bringing the Fish Man down to the homicide office in the early morning—a time when a supposedly nocturnal suspect would be least comfortable. Then they do everything conceivable to make him believe that he is not in control, that their precision, their persistence, the sheer weight of their technologies, are certain to wear him down.

On the way upstairs to the interrogation, they walk him past the trace evidence lab. Normally locked on a Sunday morning, the fifth-floor laboratory has been opened and the equipment turned on by the detectives themselves. An elaborate show has been prepared to intimidate the suspect, to break him down before he even reaches the interrogation room. On one counter, the little girl's bloodied clothes have been carefully laid out in a graphic display; on another table, her school books and satchel.

Hovering over the dead girl's clothes, Terry McLarney and Dave Brown are dressed in white lab coats, their faces bathed in studious, professorial intensity. They seem to be amassing a collection of microscopic clues as they putter back and forth between the clothing and the lab equipment.

As Pellegrini marches the suspect past the lab windows, he watches the Fish Man intently. The old man seems to be taking it all in, but he offers no reaction. The detective ushers the suspect into the back stairwell and up one flight to the homicide office, through the aquarium and into the greater authority of the captain's office. With its expansive desk and high-backed chair, its sweeping view of the Baltimore skyline, the office seems to add even more prestige to the process. Before beginning with the Miranda, Pellegrini and Edgerton make sure the Fish Man gets a good long look at the maps and the aerial photos and the impersonal, black-and-white shots of the dead girl's face, taken by the overhead camera at the ME's office—all of it arrayed on the bulletin boards and blackboards that clutter the room. They let him see his own face, an ident photograph, affixed to the same board as the child's picture. They do every conceivable thing to make this, their best suspect in the death of Latonya Wallace, believe that they have or will soon have the physical evidence, that they are dealing from a position of strength, that exposure and punishment are inevitable.

Then they go at him. First Pellegrini, then Edgerton. Talking loud and fast, then whispering, then droning on laconically, then shouting, then asking questions, then asking the same questions again. Just outside the door, Landsman and the others listen to the assault, waiting for something to provoke the grizzled old man, something that will strike a chord and bring the beginning of the story up out of the Fish Man's throat. One at a time the detectives leave the room, return, leave again, then come back again, each time bringing new questions, new tactics, suggested by those listening in silence just outside.

The confrontation is perfectly choreographed, so much so that many of the detectives allow themselves to believe that for once, the entire shift has pulled together around a single red ball, doing everything humanly and legally possible to squeeze a murder confession from a suspect. Yet the old man in the captain's office remains unimpressed. He is a stone, a solid, stoic mass without fear, without any sense of distress, without any rage at being made a suspect in the molestation and murder of a child. He meets every argument with only abject denial and provides nothing more than the vague outline of his earlier statements. He will give no alibi for Tuesday. He will admit nothing.

In the early hours of the interrogation, Pellegrini defers once again to Edgerton, who has done this so many times before. With a certain unease, he listens to Edgerton lay everything they have in front of their suspect. Trying to convince him of their omniscience, Edgerton tells the Fish Man that they know about the little girls, that they told us how you could be fresh. We know about the old rape charge, Edgerton assures him. We know why you still don't have an alibi.

Pellegrini listens to the veteran detective shovel his best stuff onto the old man's lap with little effect and realizes, too late, that it isn't enough. Hour after hour, Edgerton is spitting out words and phrases in that double-time New York cadence, but Pellegrini can almost feel the old man's indifference growing. The detectives have their suspicions, they have probabilities, they have the mere beginnings of a circumstantial case. What they do not have is evidence: raw evidence, real evidence. The kind that breaks a man down to his smallest parts and makes him admit to that which no man will ever willingly admit. They're in the room, firing their guns, and they don't have it.

If they are right—if the Fish Man molested and killed Latonya Wallace—then they have only one or two chances to break him, one or two sessions to bring the man to a confession. Last Saturday was the first bite of the apple and now, with nothing else on their plate, they are wasting the rest of the meal.

As Edgerton begins to tire, Pellegrini picks up what few threads remain untouched. He asks the old man open-ended questions, hoping to arouse something other than monosyllabic answers. He tries to probe the old man's feelings for the dead girl. But they are random questions, a few shots in the dark delivered independent of any plan or science. Pellegrini watches the old man's unchanging face and curses himself. He is locked in this room with his best, most enduring suspect, and yet he has no trump card, no tool with which to pry into the man's soul.

Once again, Pellegrini feels that insistent regret, that same unnerving notion that his case is running away from him. When it came to this, the investigation's most critical confrontation thus far, he had given the helm to Edgerton. But Edgerton had no plan; hell, none of them did.

Everything had rested on the forlorn hope that the Fish Man would fear their expertise, their knowledge and their authority—fear all of it enough to give up his darkest secrets. Pellegrini wonders whether their suspect even understands enough to feel that kind of fear. The walk by the lab didn't even faze him; neither had the morgue photos. The Fish Man was either a true innocent or a true sociopath.

After eight hours, they call for a Central District radio car as first Pellegrini, then Edgerton, surrenders to both frustration and exhaustion. The store owner waits quietly on the green vinyl sofa in the aquarium until a uniform arrives to shuttle him back to Whitelock Street. Then the Fish Man collects himself slowly and shuffles down the sixth-floor corridor, once again a free man.

Two nights later, Pellegrini shows up for a midnight shift, checks the roll book, and learns he's the only detective on active duty. Fahlteich's on vacation, Dunnigan and Ceruti are off, and Rick Requer, just off medical from a broken arm, is still working light duty.

"You all can head out," he tells Kincaid and the others on the four-to-twelve crew after getting a cup of coffee.

"Where's the rest of the relief?" asks Kincaid.

"I'm it."

"Just you?"

"Hey," says Pellegrini. "One city, one detective."

"Shit, Tom," says Kincaid. "I sure hope that fuckin' phone don't ring."

But ring it does. And at 5:00 A.M., Pellegrini finds himself standing in the piss stench of a small, dark passageway between two downtown buildings on Clay Street, looking at the earthly remains of a street person, a homeless derelict with his head crushed and his pants pulled below his knees. He wanted nothing more than a warm place to defecate and got beaten to death for that simple ambition. A more meaningless murder cannot be committed.

Later that morning, the admin lieutenant makes it clear to Pellegrini that he's the primary investigator on Latonya Wallace and orders him to dump 88033, the murder of Barney Erely, age forty-five, of no fixed address, on Roger Nolan's squad. This decision somehow fails to make Nolan the most contented sergeant in homicide.

Transferring the case solves nothing. This is a world with more murders than detectives, a city in which time will not stand still, not even for Latonya Wallace. One week later, Pellegrini and Gary Dunnigan are alone in the office on a midnight shift when the phone rings with a fatal stabbing from the Southeast.

And Pellegrini goes back in the rotation.

FOUR

Monday, February 22

No witnesses, no motive, and a forty-year-old woman stabbed, stabbed some more, and then, it would seem, shot once in the head at close range. At least, Rich Garvey tells himself, she's dead in a house.

Wilson, the lab tech, stops flashing pictures long enough to reload his camera and Garvey uses the respite to walk through the bedroom one more time, running through mental lists. You can almost hear file cards turning inside his head.

"Hey, where's your buddy?" Wilson asks.

The detective looks up, distracted. "Who's my buddy?"

"You know, your partner, McAllister."

"He's off tonight."

"Left you all alone, huh?"

"That's right, stick ol' Garvo with the tough ones . . . You got a shot of the clothes, right here by the door?"

"I took a few."

Garvey nods.

Charlene Lucas was found by a neighbor, a middle-aged man who lives in the upstairs apartment. On leaving for work at 5:00 a.m., he noticed that the door to her apartment was ajar, and when he came back from work, just after 4:00 p.m., the door to the second-floor apartment was still open. Calling his neighbor's name, he wandered far enough into the back bedroom to see the woman's legs stretched across the floor.

The paramedics pronounced her at 4:40 p.m. and Garvey pulled up on Gilmor Street fifteen minutes later. The scene was secure, with the Western uniforms keeping everyone but the other residents outside the red brick building. The three-story rowhouse had been recently renovated into a cluster of small, one-bedroom apartments and, from all appearances, the contractor had done a respectable job. Nestled in one of the more ragged west side sections, the building in which Lena Lucas lived could only be called a credit to the neighborhood. Fully rehabbed, the apartments were each equipped with burglar alarms and dead-bolt locks as well as intercoms connected to the front door buzzer.

Making his way into the building and up to the second-floor landing, Garvey notes right away that there is no sign of forced entry, either at the front door or at the door of the victim's apartment. In both the living room and back bedroom, the windows are secure.

Lena Lucas is on her back, centered in a pool of coagulated blood that has stained the beige carpeting in a wide circle. Her eyes are closed, her mouth is parted slightly and, except for a pair of white panties, she is nude. The blood pool suggests that there are serious wounds to the back, but Garvey also notices matted blood around the left ear, a possible gunshot wound. The woman's neck and jaw are further marred by perhaps a dozen shallow cuts—some of them little more than scratches.

Head north, feet south, the body rests just beside a double bed in the cramped rear room. On the floor near the bedroom door are the rest of the victim's clothes; Garvey notes that they are nested in a small pile, as if she had undressed from a standing position, leaving the garments at her feet. Lena Lucas had no problem taking her clothes off in front of her killer, Garvey reasons. And if she had undressed prior to the murderer's arrival, she had apparently opened her apartment door without bothering to put anything on.

The bedroom itself, as well as the rest of the apartment, is largely intact. Only a metal dressing locker has been ransacked, its doors flung wide and a handful of garments and purses dumped on the floor. In one corner of the room, a bag of uncooked rice has been broken and strewn across the carpet; near the rice lies a small amount of white powder, probably cocaine, and about a hundred empty gelatin capsules. This makes sense to Garvey; rice retains moisture and is often packed with cocaine to prevent the powder from crystallizing.

Garvey examines the wooden headboard of the bed. Near the corner closest to the victim's head is a series of vertical, jagged scratches, fresh damage that is consistent with the downward thrusts of a sharp edge. There is also a small amount of blood spatter near that corner of the sheet, and on the floor near the bed is a kitchen knife with a broken blade.

Theory: The woman was lying on her back in bed, head north, when the knife attack began. The killer struck at her from directly above, his wayward thrusts damaging the headboard. Either from the force of the attack or from her own efforts to escape, the victim rolled off the side of the bed and onto the floor.

Near the dead woman's head are a pillow and pillowcase blackened with what looks like gunpowder residue. But it isn't until the ME's people arrive to roll the body that Garvey finds the small, irregular lump of dull gray metal, surrounded on the carpet by a small amount of blood spatter where the victim's head came to rest. The coup de grâce was no doubt delivered with the victim prone on the bedroom floor and with the pillow wrapped around the gun to muffle the shot.

The bullet itself is a strange piece of work. Garvey looks at it closely: medium-caliber, probably a .32 or .38, but it's some ass-backwards type of semi-wadcutter design he hasn't seen before. The projectile is pretty much intact, with little evidence of splintering or mutilation, and therefore suitable for ballistics comparisons. Garvey drops the slug into a manila evidence envelope and hands it over to Wilson. In the kitchen, the utensil drawer containing the knives is pulled partly open. Otherwise, little outside the bedroom is disturbed. The living room and the bathroom appear untouched.

Garvey has the lab tech concentrate on lifting latent prints from the rear bedroom, as well as the apartment and bedroom doors. The tech also spreads the sooty print dust along the kitchen counters and the open utensil drawer, then across the sink tops in the kitchen and bathroom, on the chance that the killer touched something while trying to wash his hands. Whenever the black dust reveals the outline of a usable print, the tech presses an ordinary piece of transparent tape against the print and backs the tape against a white 3-by-5 card. The collection of lift cards begins to grow as the tech moves from the bedroom to the kitchen. After finishing the counters, he gestures to the other end of the hallway.

"You want me to do anything with the front room?"

"I don't think so. It looks like he left that alone."

"I don't mind . . ."

"Nah, fuck it," says Garvey. "If it's somebody who has access to the apartment, the prints aren't going to mean much to us anyway."

In his mind, the detective catalogues the evidence that needs to go downtown: The bullet. The knife. The nested pile of clothes. The dope. The gelatin capsules. A small purse, now marred by print dust, that probably held the cocaine, the rice and the capsules. The pillow and pillowcase, stained with gunpowder residue. The bedsheet, lifted carefully off the mattress and folded slowly so as to keep any loose hairs or fibers intact. And, of course, the photos of the apartment rooms, of the death scene, of the bed with the damage to the headboard, of each piece of evidence in its original location.

News travels fast in a city neighborhood and the dead woman's family—mother, brother, uncle, young daughters—shows up on Gilmor Street even before the ME's attendants load the body litter into the black van. Garvey sends the crowd down to homicide in radio cars; other detectives will compile the necessary background information.

Two hours later, some of Lena Lucas's family begin drifting back to the murder scene. Nearly finished there, Garvey walks downstairs to find the dead woman's younger daughter leaning against a radio car. She is a thin, wiry thing, not yet twenty-three, but level-headed and shrewd. Experience teaches a homicide detective that there is always one member of the victim's family who can be trusted to keep calm, to listen, to answer questions correctly, to deal with the raw details of a murder when everyone else is wailing with grief or arguing over who should get the victim's ten-speed blender. Garvey had talked with Jackie Lucas before sending the family downtown and that brief conversation marked the young woman as the detective's best and brightest family contact.

"Hey, Jackie," says Garvey, motioning for her to follow him down the sidewalk a respectable distance from the crowd outside the apartment house.

Jackie Lucas catches up to the detective, who then walks a few more yards down the pavement.

The conversation begins where such conversations always do, with the dead woman's boyfriend, habits and vices. Garvey has already learned some things about his victim and the people in her life from earlier conversations with family members; the details from the crime scene—the absence of forced entry, the pile of clothes, the rice and gelatin caps—add to the knowledge. As he begins asking questions, Garvey touches the young woman's elbow lightly, as if to emphasize that only the truth should pass between them.

"Your mother's boyfriend, this boy Frazier, he's selling drugs . . ."

Jackie Lucas hesitates.

"Did your mom deal for Frazier?"

"I don't . . ."

"Listen, nobody cares about that now. I just need to know this if I'm going to find out who killed her."

"She just held the drugs for him," she says. "She didn't sell none, not that I know about anyway."

"Did she use?"

"Marijuana. Now and then."

"Cocaine?"

"Not really. Not that I know of."

"Does Frazier use?"

"Yeah, he do."

"You think Frazier could have killed your mother?"

Jackie Lucas pauses, focusing the image in her mind. Slowly, she shakes her head sideways.

"I don't think he did it," she says. "He always treated her nice, you know, never beat her or anything."

"Jackie, I have to ask this . . ."

The daughter says nothing.

"Was your mother, you know, kind of loose about men?"

"No, she wasn't."

"I mean, did she have a lot of boyfriends?"

"Jus' Frazier."

"Just Frazier?"

"Jus' him," she says, insistent. "She was seeing another man a while back, but only Frazier for a long time since."

Garvey nods, lost for a moment in thought.

Jackie breaks the silence. "The policeman downtown say we shouldn't say nothing to Frazier, 'cause if we do he might run."

Garvey smiles. "If he runs, then at least I know who did it, right?"

The young woman takes in the logic.

"I don't think he's your man," she says finally.

Garvey tries a different tack. "Did your mom let anyone else up into her apartment? If she was alone, would she let anyone besides Frazier come up?"

"Only this boy named Vincent," she says. "He works for Frazier, and he been up there before for the drugs."

Garvey lowers his voice. "You think she would fool around with this Vincent?"

"No, she wouldn't. I don't think Vincent ever been up there without Frazier being there, too. I don't think she would let him in," she adds, changing her mind.

"You know Vincent's name?"

"Booker, I think."

"Jackie," says Garvey, turning to one last detail. "You told me before about Frazier keeping a gun in the bedroom."

The daughter nods. "She has a twenty-five, and sometimes Frazier keeps a thirty-eight there."

"We can't find them."

"She keeps them in that cabinet," the daughter says. "Up on the back of the shelf."

"Listen," says Garvey, "if I let you go up there and look for the guns, do you think you'll be able to find them?"

Jackie nods, then falls in behind him.

"Is it bad?" she asks on the way upstairs.

"Is what bad?"

"The room . . ."

"Oh," says Garvey. "Well, she's gone . . . but there's some blood."

The detective leads the young woman into the rear bedroom. Jackie looks briefly at the red stain, then walks to the metal dressing cabinet and pulls the .25 from the rear of the top shelf.

"The other one ain't here."

From a shelf in the closet directly behind the bed, she also produces a case containing a little more than $1,200 in cash, money that her mother had collected from a recent insurance settlement.

"Did Frazier know she had that money?"

"Yeah he did."

"Did he know where it was?"

"Yeah."

Garvey nods, giving this fact a moment of thought. Then a Western uniform bounds up the stairwell and into the hall of the apartment, looking for the detective.

"What's up?" asks Garvey.

"The rest of the family wants to come up."

Garvey looks at the lab tech. "You have everything you need?"

"Yeah, I'm just packing my stuff."

"Yeah, go 'head," says Garvey to the uniform, who goes downstairs to open the front door of the building. Seconds later, half a dozen relatives, including the victim's mother and older daughter, move quickly into the apartment, creating instant pandemonium.

The older family members busy themselves with taking stock of the kitchen appliances, the color television, the stereo system. For places like Gilmor Street, the reclamation of a victim's valuables is a postmortem imperative, less from greed than from the certain knowledge that as soon as word of the murder hits the street, any number of break-in artists will plan to acquire the worldly wealth of the newly departed, providing they can get into the place after the police leave and before the family has a chance to think. Grief may come later, but tonight the victim's mother has no intention of leaving to the wolves that multichannel home entertainment center.

The rest of the family is curious in a morbid way. A cousin points to the coagulated red pool on the bedroom carpet. "That Lena's blood?"

A Western uniform nods, and the cousin turns to the victim's older daughter.

"Lena's blood," he says again. Bad thought. Because now Jackie's older sister is wailing for all she's worth, making a bee-line for the red stain, her arms extended, palms open wide.

"MOMMY, MOMMY, I SEE MOMMY." The kid is rubbing her hands through the pool, gathering up as much of the wetness as she can. "MOMMY. I SEE MOMMY . . ."

Garvey watches as the cousin and another relative grab the older daughter and lift her away from the blood.

". . . MOMMY, DON'T GO, MOMMY . . ."

The girl comes up screaming with her forearms extended, both palms covered with blood. Sensing an ugly dry cleaning bill, Garvey steps back, then moves toward the door.

"All right, Jackie," he says. "Thank you, honey. You've got my phone number, right?"

Jackie Lucas nods, then turns away to comfort her sister. As the screaming reaches a still higher pitch, Garvey makes his escape, following the lab tech down the steps and crawling into the cold interior of the Cavalier. He has spent a little less than four hours working the scene.

Before returning to the homicide office, Garvey makes a point of driving another twelve blocks north to see if an extra hand is needed on a suspicious death call that came in three hours after the call for Gilmor. Earlier, Garvey telephoned the office and heard from Dave Brown that the second call might also be a murder and might in some way be related to Gilmor Street. Garvey arrives on the second floor of a Lafayette Avenue rowhouse to find Rick James and Dave Brown working the murder of a fifty-year-old man.

Like Lena Lucas, the Lafayette Avenue victim has been shot in the head and stabbed repeatedly, this time in the chest. And like Lena Lucas, there is a pillow near the victim's head, marred by a large amount of gunshot residue. Moreover, the face of this victim is also covered by the same series of shallow cuts—more than twenty this time. Obviously dead for some time, the victim was found by several family members who had become concerned and entered through an unlocked rear door. Here, too, there was no sign of forced entry, but this time the room where the victim was found had been ransacked.

The two cases become unequivocally joined when Garvey learns that the dead man is Purnell Hampton Booker, the father of one Vincent Booker, who is the same entrepreneurial lad who works for Robert Frazier, who sells dope and sleeps with Lena Lucas. Standing in the dead man's bedroom, Garvey knows that the same hand almost certainly took both lives.

Leaving Brown and James to work their scene, Garvey returns to the homicide office and buries himself in paperwork at a back desk. He's still there when the detectives return from Lafayette Avenue.

As if the immediate similarities between both crime scenes aren't enough to link the killings, the spent bullet pulled from Purnell Booker's brain at the next morning's autopsy is a .38 ass-backward wadcutter. Later that evening, Dave Brown, the primary on Lafayette Avenue, saunters over to Garvey's desk with an ident photo of young Vincent Booker.

"Yo bunk, looks like we be working together."

"Looks like."

As it happens, already that afternoon Garvey has heard from an anonymous tipster, a woman who called the homicide office to say she heard talk at a West Pratt Street bar. One man was telling another that the same gun was used to kill Lena Lucas and the old man on Lafayette.

Interesting rumor. A day later, ballistics says the same thing.

Monday, February 29

A week has passed since Lena Lucas and Purnell Booker were found dead on the same night, yet the two cases are still moving slowly, inexorably, forward. Fresh reports clutter both files, and in the Baltimore homicide unit, where one day's violence is overwhelmed by that of the next, a thick file is regarded as a healthy sign. Time itself mocks the most careful investigations, and a detective—conscious of that fact—spends his precious hours working the best angles, bringing the likely witnesses and suspects downtown, hoping that something will fall. For he knows that well before he has a chance to play long shots or, better still, to embark on a prolonged, detailed investigation, another case folder will arrive on his desk.

But somehow, in some special way, the law of diminishing returns has never applied to Rich Garvey.

"He's like a dog with a bone," Roger Nolan once told another sergeant with pride. "If he gets a case and there's anything there at all, he won't let go of it."

Of course, Nolan only says that to other sergeants; to Garvey he says nothing of the sort, cleaving instead to the fiction that it's normal for a detective to drop a case only when there's nothing left to give up on. It is, in truth, anything but normal. Because after fifty or sixty or seventy homicides, the reality is that the dead-yo-in-the-alley scenario begins to wear thin. And nothing deflates a detective more than going back to the office, punching a victim's name into the admin office terminal and pulling out five or six computer pages of misbehavior, a criminal history that reaches from eye level to the office floor. Burnout is more than an occupational hazard in the homicide unit, it is a psychological certainty. A contagion that spreads from one detective to his partner to a whole squad, the who-really-gives-a-shit attitude threatens not those investigations involving genuine victims—such cases are, more often than not, the cure for burnout—but rather those murders in which the dead man is indistinguishable from his killer. An American detective's philosophical cul-de-sac: If a drug dealer falls in West Baltimore and no one is there to hear him, does he make a sound?

After four years in homicide and thirteen on the force, Garvey is one of the few residents of the unit still unafflicted with the virus. It is telling that while most detectives can't keep the cases straight in their minds after a few years in the trenches, Garvey can immediately tell you that out of twenty-five or twenty-six cases in which he was the primary, the number of open files can be counted on one hand.

"How many exactly?"

"Four, I think. No, five."

Vanity isn't what prompts Garvey to keep such a statistic in his head; it's simply his central frame of reference. Determined, aggressive, persistent to a fault, Garvey likes working murders; more than that, he still takes an open murder or a weak plea bargain personally. That alone is enough to make him seem like a relic, a surviving piece of shrapnel from an ethic that crashed and burned a generation or two back, when the "if at first you don't succeed" platitude was replaced in all Baltimore municipal offices by the more succinct "that's not my job," then, later, by the more definitive "shit happens."

Rich Garvey is an anachronism, a product of a Middle American childhood in which the Little Engine That Could was taken seriously. It's Garvey who will readily abandon decorum and diplomacy to jump in a prosecutor's shit when second-degree and twenty just isn't good enough, telling an assistant state's attorney that any lawyer with hair on his ass wouldn't take anything less than first-degree and fifty. It's Garvey who shows up for work with a raging flu, then works a Pigtown bludgeoning because, what the hell, if he's on the clock he may as well handle a call. And it's Garvey who photocopies the "Remember, we work for God" quote by Vernon Geberth, the New York police commander and homicide expert, then posts one above his desk and distributes the rest around the office. Blessed with an acute sense of humor, Garvey is aware that as credos go, Geberth's is both maudlin and pompous. He can't help it; in fact, that makes him like it all the more.

He was born in an Irish, working-class neighborhood of Chicago, the only son of a sales executive for the Spiegel catalogue retailing company. At least until the end of his career, when the company judged his position to be expendable, Garvey's father had prospered, and his family had enough to escape to the suburbs when the old neighborhood began going bad in the late 1950s. The elder Garvey applied his own ambition to his son, whom he liked to imagine as a future sales executive, maybe even for Spiegel; Garvey thought otherwise.

He spent a couple of years at a small Iowa college, then finished up with a degree in criminology at Kent State. In 1970, when National Guardsmen fired their lethal volley into a crowd of Vietnam protestors on the Ohio campus, Garvey was walking away from the disturbances. Like many students, he had doubts about the war, but he also happened to have a class that day and, if the shootings hadn't closed the campus, Garvey would have been front and center, taking notes. A young man out of step with his times, he was looking to a police career in an era when law enforcement did not exactly stir the imagination of America's young. Garvey had his own way of looking at things. Police work would always be interesting, he believed. And even in the worst economic recession, there would always be a job for a cop.

Upon graduation, however, that last bit of logic was not so easily demonstrated. Open positions were hard to come by in the mid-1970s, with many urban police departments retrenching in an inflationary economy. Newly married to his college sweetheart, Garvey fell into a security job with Montgomery Ward. It was nearly a year later, in 1975, when he heard that the Baltimore department was hiring patrolmen, offering pay and benefit incentives for college graduates. He and his wife drove down to Maryland, then toured the city and surrounding counties. Driving through the gentle, contoured valleys and sprawling horse farms in northern Baltimore County, they fell in love with the Chesapeake region. It was, they reasoned, a fine place to raise a family. Then Garvey took his own tour of the city's slums—east side, west side, lower Park Heights—scouting the places in which he would earn a living.

He went from the academy to the Central District, where he drew the post at Brookfield and Whitelock. Business was brisk; Reservoir Hill in the late 1970s was as ragged a neighborhood as when Latonya Wallace turned up in an alley there a decade later. McLarney, for one, could remember Garvey from the years when both men were in the Central; he could remember, too, that Garvey was without doubt the best man in his squad. "He answered calls and he would fight," McLarney would say, commending the two qualities that truly matter in a radio car.

Given his hunger for work, Garvey's career ran a steady course: six years in the Central, then another four as one of the most reliable burglary detectives in CID's property crimes section, then the transfer to homicide. Arriving in June 1985, Garvey soon became the centerpiece of Roger Nolan's squad. Kincaid was the veteran, Edgerton the artful loner, but it was Garvey who worked the lion's share of the calls, readily teaming himself with McAllister, Kincaid, Bowman or any other warm body that happened on a fresh murder. Tellingly, when other detectives in the squad began ranting about Edgerton's workload, Garvey would often remind everyone, without any sarcasm, that he had no complaint.

"Harry's going to do what he's going to do," Garvey would offer, as if murder had somehow become a precious commodity in Baltimore. "That just means there's more for me."

Garvey genuinely loved being a murder police. He loved the scenes, he loved the feeling of pursuit, the adolescent rush of hearing handcuffs click. He even loved the sound of the word itself; that much was evident every time he returned from a scene.

"What'd you have out there?" Nolan would ask.

"Murder, mister."

Give the man a fresh one every three weeks and he's content. Give him more than that, he's downright pleased. During one midnight tour in the summer of 1987, Garvey and Donald Worden worked five murders in five days, three of them on a single night. It was the sort of midnight shift when a detective has trouble remembering which witnesses came downtown from which homicide. ("Okay now, everyone who's here from Etting Street raise your right hand.") Still, four of the five went down, and both Garvey and the Big Man relished that week as a pleasant memory.

Yet ask other detectives to name the best men at a crime scene and they'll mention Terry McLarney, Eddie Brown, Kevin Davis from Stanton's shift, and Garvey's partner, Bob McAllister. Ask about the best interrogators and the list will include Donald Kincaid, Kevin Davis, Jay Landsman and maybe Harry Edgerton if his co-workers are feeling generous enough to include known subversives in the balloting. The best men to testify in open court? Landsman, Worden, McAllister and Edgerton are the usual nominees. The best man out on the street? Worden, hands down, with Edgerton a close second.

So what about Garvey?

"Oh Christ, yeah," his colleagues will say, suddenly reminded. "He's a helluva detective."

Why?

"He stays with them."

For a homicide detective, staying with them is half the battle, and tonight, with the arrival of Robert Frazier in the homicide office, the battle over Lena Lucas and Purnell Booker is yet another step closer to being won.

Frazier is tall and thin, dark complected, with deep-set brown eyes beneath a high, sloping forehead, above which a layer of close-cropped hair is just beginning to recede. He moves like a man who has spent his years on street corners, gliding down the sixth-floor corridor toward the interrogation rooms in a practiced pimp roll, shoulders and hips pushing the body forward in a slow, locomotive fashion. Frazier's face rarely breaks from an unsettling stare, a gaze all the more unnerving because he rarely blinks his eyes. His voice is a deep monotone, and his sentences are braced by an economy of language that suggests words being chosen with care or, perhaps, few words from which to choose. At thirty-six, Robert Frazier is a part-time steelworker and state parolee who can look upon his shoestring cocaine enterprise as a second career of sorts; a previous apprenticeship at armed robbery was curtailed abruptly by a six-year sentence.

The total package pleases Garvey immensely, for the simple reason that Robert Frazier looks exactly like a murderer.

It is a small satisfaction, but one that always makes the chase seem a little more worthwhile. By and large, what sits at the defendant's table in a Baltimore circuit court rarely seems at first glance to be sufficient to the wanton destruction of human life, and even after forty or fifty cases, there is still something in the heart of every detective that registers disappointment when the person responsible for an extraordinary act of evil turns out to resemble nothing more sinister than the counterman at a midtown 7-Eleven. Alcoholics, dopers, welfare mothers, borderline mental cases, adolescent yos and yoettes in designer sweatsuits—with only a handful of exceptions, those who claim a place on Baltimore's murderers row aren't the most visually threatening crew ever assembled. But with a low rumble to his voice and that thousand-yard stare, Frazier adds a little something to the melodrama. Here is a man for whom large-caliber handguns were created.

All of which seems to go to waste the minute he hits the interrogation room door. Because once Frazier comes to rest across the table from Garvey, he shows a complete willingness to discuss his girlfriend's violent death. More to the point, he is now able to provide a suspect more plausible than himself.

Of course, Frazier was only convinced of the need for a voluntary appearance in the homicide office after a week's legwork by both Garvey and Donald Kincaid, who signed on as a secondary when Dave Brown was himself tied up with an unrelated murder. Looking for a little leverage, the two detectives put Frazier's dirty laundry out on the street, visiting the man's home on Fayette Street and asking his wife a series of questions about her husband's work hours, habits and drug involvement before dropping the Big One.

"Did you know he had a thing going with Lena?"

Whether the news affected the woman to any great degree was uncertain; she conceded that the marriage had seen rough times recently. Either way, she made no effort to alibi her husband on the night of the murder. And the next day, plant officials at Sparrows Point told the detectives that Frazier had not been on his shift for the two days before the killing.

Then, last night, Frazier telephoned Garvey at the homicide office, declaring that he had information about Lena's murder and wanted to meet with detectives right away. But by midnight he had failed to post and Garvey headed home. An hour later, Frazier wandered up to the garage security booth and asked to speak with detectives. Rick Requer talked to him, long enough to determine that Frazier was wired tight, and judging from his pupils, which were dancing a mad Bolivian samba, the wire of choice was probably cocaine. Requer called Garvey at home and the two men agreed to abort the interview and tell Frazier to come back clean.

Before leaving the floor, however, Frazier asked a question that Requer found curious: "Do you know if she was shot and stabbed?"

Maybe he picked it up on the street. Maybe not. Requer wrote a report for Garvey that included the statement.

Now, on his return visit to headquarters, Frazier seems not only cognizant of his surroundings but genuinely curious about his girlfriend's death. Over the hour-and-a-half interview with Garvey and Kincaid, he asks as many questions as he answers and volunteers a good bit of information on his own. Leaning back in his chair, tipping it slightly with every stretch of his legs, Frazier tells the detectives that although he has a wife and a second girlfriend, who lives in the Poe Homes, he had been seeing Lena Lucas for some time. He also claims they rarely fought and says that he, as much as the police, would like to know who killed Lena and stole his cocaine from the bedroom dresser.

Yeah, he admits, Lena often kept cocaine for him in the Gilmor Street apartment. Kept it in that stand-up dresser, in a purse in a bag of rice. He had already heard from the family that whoever killed Lena took what she was holding at the time.

Yeah, he dealt cocaine and a little heroin, too, when he wasn't working down at the Sparrows Point plant. He wasn't going to waste time lying about that. He sold enough to make a living, most of it down by the Poe Homes low-rises, but it wasn't like he was working out all the time.

Yeah, he had a gun. A .38 revolver, but it wasn't even loaded. He kept it at his other girlfriend's house on Amity Street. She held it for him, and that's where it was now.

Yeah, he had heard about Vincent Booker's father, too. Didn't know Purnell Booker, but he had heard on the street that the same gun had been used in both murders. True, the boy Vincent had worked for him for a while, selling dope on consignment. But the boy often fucked up the money, and he had a bad habit of snorting up profit, so Frazier had found it necessary to let him go.

Yeah, Vincent had access to Lena's place. In fact, Frazier would often send him there for dope, or bags, or cut. Lena would let him in because she knew he worked for Frazier.

Garvey moves to the meat of the interview: "Frazier, tell me what you can about that night."

Here, too, Frazier is more than helpful, and why shouldn't he be? After all, he last saw Lena alive on Saturday, the evening before the night of the murder, when he stayed with her on Gilmor Street. On Sunday, he spent the entire evening ten blocks away in the projects on Amity Street, where his new girlfriend threw a dinner party for several friends. Lobster, crabs, corn on the cob. He was there all night, from seven or eight o'clock on. Slept in the back bedroom, didn't leave until morning. He went by Lena's on the way to work that day and saw that the front door of the rowhouse was open, but he was late, and when Lena didn't answer the buzzer, he didn't go in. That afternoon, he tried calling Lena's house a couple of times but got no answer, and by early evening, the police were already over there about the murder.

Who, Garvey asks, can confirm your whereabouts on Sunday night?

Nee-Cee—Denise, that is, his new girl. She was on Amity Street with him all night. And of course, the people at the dinner party saw him there. Pam, Annette, a couple others.

Here, Frazier puts in another good word for young Vincent Booker, who, he says, showed up on Amity Street at the height of the party, knocking on the door just after ten o'clock and asking to speak with Frazier. The two men talked on the stoop for a few minutes, Frazier says, long enough for him to see that the boy was all nervous and wild-eyed. Frazier asked what was the matter, but Vincent ignored the question, asking instead for some cocaine. Frazier asked him if he had any money; the boy said no.

Frazier then told him that there would be no more drugs, not when he kept fucking up the money. At which point, according to Frazier, young Vincent got mad and stormed off into the night.

As the interview winds to a close, Frazier offers one last observation about Booker: "I don't know how things were between him and his father, but since they found the old man dead, Vincent hasn't been real upset about it."

Was Vincent sleeping with Lena?

Frazier looks surprised at the question. No, he answers, not that he knew about.

Did Vincent know where Lena kept the dope?

"Yeah," says Frazier, "he knew."

"Would you be willing to take a lie detector test, a polygraph?"

"I guess. If you want."

Garvey doesn't know what to think. Unless Vincent is fooling around with Lena Lucas, there is nothing to explain her nudity or the nested clothes at the bottom of the bed. On the other hand, there isn't any obvious connection between Frazier and old man Booker, though it's certain that both murders were committed by the same hand, wielding the same gun.

The detective asks a few more questions, but there isn't much you can do when a man answers everything put to him. As a measure of good faith, Garvey asks Frazier to bring in his .38 handgun.

"Carry it down here?" Frazier asks.

"Yeah. Just bring it in."

"I'll get a charge."

"We won't charge you with that. You got my word on it. Just make sure the gun's unloaded and bring it down here so we can get a look at it."

Reluctantly, Frazier agrees.

At the end of the interview, Garvey gathers up his notepaper and follows Frazier out into the hall. "All right, Frazier, thanks for coming down."

The man nods, then holds the yellow visitor pass issued to him by building security. "What . . ."

"You just give that to the man at the booth on your way out of the garage."

Garvey begins walking his witness toward the elevator, then stops near the water cooler. Almost as an afterthought, he leaves Frazier with something that is part warning and part threat.

"I'll tell you, Frazier, if anything you're saying isn't right, now's the time for you to deal with that," Garvey says, looking impassively at the man. "Because if this is bullshit, it's going to come back on you in a bad way."

Frazier takes this in, then shakes his head. "Told you what I know."

"All right, then," says Garvey. "See you 'round."

The man catches the detective's eyes briefly, then turns down the corridor. His first few steps are short, uncertain movements, but those that follow gather speed and rhythm until he's moving hip to shoulder, shoulder to hip, sailing forward in a full roll. By the time he clears the headquarters garage, Robert Frazier is once again ready for the street.

Thursday, March 3

D'Addario turns page after page on a cluttered clipboard, his voice locked in the monotone of another morning's roll call:

". . . is wanted in connection with a homicide in Fairfax, Virginia. Anyone with information about the suspects or the vehicle should call the Fairfax department. Number is on the teletype.

"What's next here?" says the lieutenant, scanning a fresh printout. "Oh yeah, we got another teletype from Florida . . . No . . . um, check that. It's three weeks old.

"Okay, one last item here . . . As a result of the ISD inspection, I'm informed that you need to write down the number of the gas cards on your run sheets, even if the cards aren't used."

"What for?" asks Kincaid.

"They need the number of the gas card."

"Why?"

"It's policy."

"Jesus, come on twenty-year pension," cracks Kincaid, disgusted.

D'Addario breaks up the laughter. "Okay, the colonel would like to say a couple words to you all."

Well, thinks every cop in the room, the shit must have really caught the fan. As CID commander, Dick Lanham rarely has call to address any particular unit on any particular case; God made captains and lieutenants and sergeants for that exact purpose. But a homicide clearance rate that is reaching new depths with every passing day is apparently enough to make even full colonels wince.

"I just wanted to say a few words to you all," Lanham begins, looking around the room, "to let you know that I've got absolute confidence in this unit . . . I know that this has been a rough time for you people. In fact, the whole year has been rough, but that's nothing new for this unit, and I don't have any doubt that it will bounce back."

As the detectives rustle uncomfortably and stare at their shoes, Lanham presses on with his pep talk, carefully straddling the fence between high praise and open acknowledgment of an ugly truth understood by everyone in the room: The Baltimore Police Department's homicide unit is getting thumped.

Never mind the Latonya Wallace probe or, for that matter, the Monroe Street investigation, both of which are still as open as the days are long. At least in those cases, the department could say that it reacted properly, pouring men and overtime into the search for suspects, and Lanham, looking for silver linings, can't help but bring that up.

"Anyone who knows anything about those investigations knows how hard they've been worked," he tells the gathering.

And never mind the newspaper articles this morning, in which the NAACP, in a letter to the mayor's office, has roundly criticized the Baltimore department for failing to curb racial abuses and—a charge unsupported by the evidence—for being slow to solve crimes involving black victims.

"I don't want to tell you what I think about those allegations," the colonel assures his detectives.

"But let's face it," he says, turning the corner, "the clearance rate is very low, and unless we get you all some help we're going to have a hard time bringing it back up to where we want it. Particularly if we have another night like the last one . . . Most of all, we got to crack some of these goddamn killings of women in the Northwest."

The room stirs uncomfortably.

"After talking with the captain, we've decided to bring in some extra men from around the sixth floor to work with the primary detectives on those cases . . . But I want you to understand that this is to help you in a rough time. Everyone has absolute confidence in the detectives assigned to those cases.

"At least," says the colonel, trying to close on a positive note, "at least it's not as bad as what's going on in Washington." Lanham then nods to D'Addario, who opens the floor to the robbery and sex offense supervisors.

"Is that it?" says D'Addario. "Lieutenant, you have anything to add? Joe? . . . All told."

Roll call ends and the homicide unit's dayshift breaks down into smaller clusters of detectives, some arguing and bartering for one of the Cavaliers, some heading for city court, some cracking jokes by the coffee machine. A day like any other, but every man on D'Addario's shift now understands that things have scraped bottom.

The clearance rate—murders closed by arrest—is now 36 percent and falling, a statistic that doesn't begin to explain the threat to Gary D'Addario's tenure. The board that gave His Eminence reason for concern six weeks ago has continued to fill with open murders, and it is on D'Addario's side of the wall that the names of the victims are writ in red. Of the twenty-five homicides handled by Dee's three squads, only five are down; whereas Stanton's shift has cleared ten of sixteen.

Of course, there are reasons for any statistical variation, but in the last analysis, the only fact that matters to the command staff is that Stanton's detectives know who killed their victims; D'Addario's men do not. There is no point in explaining that three fifths of D'Addario's homicides happen to be drug-related, just as seven of those solved by Stanton's shift are domestics or other arguments. Nor does it do any good to note that two or three case files were sacrificed to free men for the Latonya Wallace detail, or to point out that Dave Brown has a warrant out for one of the Milligan murders, while Garvey has a decent shot at clearing both the Lucas and Booker files.

All of that is commentary, and a Talmudic, murder-by-murder analysis of the board doesn't mean a damn thing to anyone when it comes to the clearance rate. It is the unrepentant worship of statistics that forms the true orthodoxy of any modern police department. Captains become majors who become colonels who become deputies when the numbers stay sweet; the command staff backs up on itself like a bad stretch of sewer pipe when they don't. Against that truth, which everyone above the rank of sergeant holds to be self-evident, D'Addario is in deep water—not only because his rate compares poorly to Stanton's, but because it compares poorly to expectations.

The clearance rate for murders in Baltimore has been slipping for seven years, from 84 percent in 1981 to 73.5 percent registered in 1987. Fortunately for the careers of several commanders, at no point in the decade did the homicide unit ever post a solve rate lower than the national average for murder clearances, which has also fallen—from a high of 76 percent in 1984 to a low of 70 in 1987.

The Baltimore unit has maintained its rate both through good, solid police work and through a gentle manipulation of the clearance rate itself. Whoever declared that there are lies, damn lies and statistics could just as easily have granted law enforcement data a category unto itself. Anyone who ever spent more than a week in a police department's planning and research section can tell you that a burglary clearance doesn't mean that anyone was actually arrested, and that a posted increase in the crime rate can have less to do with criminal proclivity than with the department's desire for a budget increase. The homicide clearance rate is equally vulnerable to subtle forms of manipulation—all of which are permitted under the FBI's guidelines for uniform crime reporting.

Consider the fact that a case is regarded to be cleared whether it arrives at the grand jury or not. As long as someone is locked up—whether for a week or a month or a lifetime—that murder is down. If the charges are dropped at the arraignment for lack of evidence, if the grand jury refuses to indict, if the prosecutor decides to dismiss the case or place it on the inactive, or stet, docket, that murder is nonetheless carried on the books as a solved crime. Detectives have a tag line for such paper clearances: Stet 'em and forget 'em.

Consider, too, that the federal guidelines allow a department to carry a previous year's clearance as a solved crime. This, of course, is as it should be: The mark of any good homicide unit is its ability to work back on open cases that are two, three or five years old; the clearance rate should reflect that persistence. On the other hand, the guidelines don't require departments to include the crime itself in the current year's statistics; clearly, the crime itself actually occurred in a prior year. Theoretically therefore, an American homicide unit can solve 90 of 100 fresh murders, then clear twenty cases from previous years and post a clearance rate of 110 percent.

Such card-up-the-sleeve tactics make every year's end an adventure in statistical brinksmanship. If the clearance rate is high enough, a shift commander or squad sergeant who knows his business can save an arrest on a December case until January to get a jump on the new year. Alternatively, if the clearance rate is a bit low, a commander might allow a two-or three-week grace period in which January clearances of December cases are credited to the prior year. The paper clearances and calendar tricks can give a homicide unit an extra 5 to 10 points on the sheet, but when the true solve rate takes a dive, no amount of statistical massage can help.

This was D'Addario's predicament and, over the last twenty-four hours, bad had become worse. His detectives clocked five fresh murders—only one of which was a dunker. That case, Kincaid's, featured a fifty-two-year-old man stretched out on the floor of a Fulton Avenue apartment. His skull had been crushed in an argument with a younger man, a boarder who used a steam iron to demonstrate the law of physics that allows no two objects to occupy the same space at the same instant. But things were not so tidy on the earlier midnight shift, when McAllister and Bowman caught a bludgeoning in the Northeast, only hours before Bowman learned that his shooting victim from three nights earlier had rolled a seven at University Hospital. There was no hint of a suspect in either case, and Fahlteich faced much the same problem later that same evening when he caught a fatal shooting off Wabash Avenue.

But all this was just a prelude to the one that really mattered: They'd found the body of another taxi driver in a wooded park on the city's northwest edge. As the fifteenth murder of a cab driver in eight years, the beating death of a Checker Cab employee got the full red-ball treatment, not only because it looks bad for a city to permit an open season on its taxi drivers, but because the hack was a woman. Found nude from the waist down. Murdered. In Northwest Baltimore.

That made six dead women in that district since December, all of them unsolved. The Northwest murders were decidedly unrelated: two were rape-murders with markedly different characteristics, two were drug killings, one an apparent argument, and this latest a cab robbery and possible rape. But the string of open cases was beginning to attract newspaper headlines and therefore dead women in the Northwestern District had suddenly acquired real prestige with the department brass.

As if to acknowledge his sudden vulnerability, D'Addario himself went to the scene of the cabbie murder. So, too, did the captain. Not to mention the district commander from the Northwest and the police department's chief spokesman. Donald Worden was off, but the rest of McLarney's squad took the call, with Rick James as the primary and Eddie Brown as secondary investigator. Never mind that he would be without the Big Man on this call, James was a man who counted his overtime, and by that reckoning alone he was due for a fresh murder. For three weeks he had wallowed at his desk near the front of the office, cursing every phone extension, silently willing the communications unit to send him a major case, a red ball with many hours involved.

"Incoming . . . I got it," he shouted time and again, grabbing every call on the first bleat. And then, in a mood blackened by poverty: "Edgerton, pick up line one. Sounds like your wife."

The ancient Greeks were fond of saying that the gods punish a man most by answering his prayers, and on Powder Mill Road, James was saddled with a stone whodunit. Face down at the edge of a wooded trail was a black woman in her thirties, wearing only a brown jacket with "Checker Cab" and "Karen" on either side of the chest. There was no wallet, purse, or identification, although her shoes, pants and panties lay near the body. Three hours after she was discovered, a Baltimore County unit found Checker Cab 4 in a garden apartment parking lot in Owings Mills, six to eight miles west of the city line. Abandoned with its hazard lights flashing, the cab caught the attention of neighbors; when contacted, cab company officials confirmed that neither cab 4, nor its driver, Karen Renee Smith, had been seen or heard from since nine o'clock that morning. The positive ID followed soon after.

Nothing about the murder of Karen Smith resembled any of the previous Northwest killings, but to argue such subtleties in the face of a departmental mood swing is futility defined. Now, a day later, the colonel is calling in the troops, ordering special details for each of the open murders of Northwest women while trying to avoid suggesting a lack of confidence in the homicide unit. Within twenty-four hours, a dozen fresh uniforms and detectives from other CID sections will be assigned to homicide—two for each of the six primary investigators in the Northwest murders. The annex office interrogation room will be converted into a cramped command post of sorts, with maps and charts, photographs of the victims, in and out boxes for the paperwork generated by the detail. Reward sheets for information on each of the murders will be printed for distribution in the neighborhoods near each crime scene.

The primary detectives are to use the extra manpower to generate new leads and run down any loose ends in the case files. They are to make the Northwest murders their first priority and, with a nod to a recent newspaper article that began the campaign by hinting at the possibility of a serial killer, they are to be especially vigilant for anything that might link these murders.

One of the six cases—the murder of Brenda Thompson, stabbed to death in the back of a Dodge in early January—runs into a conflicting priority: Latonya Wallace. Harry Edgerton is the primary detective in the Thompson murder, the secondary in the slaying of the little girl. As a result, the Thompson case is farmed out to Bertina Silver.

Edgerton and his sergeant, Roger Nolan, argue briefly with both D'Addario and the captain against the change, maintaining that it serves no purpose to change the primary detective in the middle of an investigation for the sake of creating some immediate activity. Edgerton knows the case file and the players, and most important, he has spent hours creating a working relationship with his best suspect, a young street dealer who sold for Brenda Thompson and owed her money. The kid has already been willing to subject himself to a couple of long interrogations. Edgerton argues that the Thompson murder is already two months old, and anything the special detail may do now can just as easily be done two or three or four weeks down the road, after the Latonya Wallace case has resolved itself.

Edgerton has on his side the prevailing wisdom and tradition of the homicide unit, both of which argue that no one can know a murder as well as the detective who handles the scene and its aftermath. The bosses, however, are adamant. A police department is a reactive beast, and with the newspapers and television both crowing about the possibility of multiple murders in the Northwest, tradition and wisdom are both being sold off at basement prices. The Thompson case goes to Bert Silver.

In happier times, Edgerton might have appealed personally to D'Addario, but now that the lieutenant has problems of his own, that appeal would be pointless. Latonya Wallace, the subterranean clearance rate, the Northwest murders—any and all are reason enough for D'Addario to feel vulnerable. Already there has been one meeting with the colonel and Deputy Mullen on the Latonya Wallace detail, an hour-long summary in which Jay Landsman outlined the efforts undertaken by the detectives and then fielded questions until the bosses seemed mollified. The meeting was a seamless piece of departmental politics, but D'Addario has to know that unless the solve rate rises, Landsman's performance is no more than a temporary reprieve.

If D'Addario had stayed tight with the captain, the threat wouldn't be so severe. Lately, however, a conflict that had been percolating for months has suddenly come to full boil. Simply put, the captain doesn't want D'Addario as one of his shift lieutenants; to D'Addario, the decision to bypass him on the Monroe Street probe said as much. And now, with his solve rate so low, the captain has leverage with which he can press the point—unless D'Addario can, like a cat with a canary locked in its jaw, go to the colonel with a fresh victory in one of the major cases, or at least a hint that the solve rate is turning around. It matters not at all that D'Addario has done the job for eight years; the consciousness of the command staff rarely strays beyond the latest red ball and as a result, the departmental hierarchy often expresses itself in that timeless query of practical politics: What have you done for me lately?

If the rate is good, if the red balls fall, it doesn't matter how D'Addario runs his shift. You say your detectives and sergeants are told to follow their own judgment on cases? Obviously, a fine example of a leader emphasizing confidence and responsibility. You say you leave it to the sergeants to train and discipline their men? Obviously, a man who knows the value of delegated responsibility. You say your overtime is running 90 percent over budget? That's fine, you've got to break some eggs for that omelette. Court time, too? Well, that just proves that more of these murders are going to trial. But let the rate slip and the lieutenant's image is suddenly transformed into that of a man incapable of directing and disciplining his men, a commander who leaves too much in the hands of his subordinates, a manager who can't control his budget.

On the midnight shift just before the colonel's brief oratory, five or six detectives were adrift in the admin office, floating on a sea of paperwork from the fresh spate of open murders. Eddie Brown, James, Fahlteich, Kincaid, Nolan—a fair cross section, a gathering of veterans who had all seen both good times and bad in the homicide unit. Inevitably, the talk turned to whether this year would really turn out any worse. Some argued that it always evened out, that for every stretch of stone whodunits there was a supply of dunkers waiting to take up the slack. Others pointed out that the rate would be higher if the shift had bothered to save a few

December clearances to pump up the current year's stats. But for all of their talk, none of the detectives could remember a rate as low as 36 percent.

"And I'll tell you something," said Fahlteich, "I have a feeling it's only going to get worse."

"Oh, it's going to get a helluva lot worse," Nolan agreed. "We've been coasting around here for a long time and now it's catching up to us."

Suddenly no one in the room was typing or collating anymore as voices competed with one another in a recitation of longstanding grievances. They complained about the equipment, about cars without radios and about a major urban department that still doesn't provide a polygraph examiner suitable for criminal investigations, requiring detectives to use the state police facilities. They complained about the cutbacks in overtime, about the department's reluctance to pay for pretrial preparation so that good cases wouldn't come unglued in the months between arrest and trial. They complained about the lack of money to pay informants and, consequently, the lack of informants. They complained about the inability of the trace and ballistics labs to keep up with the violence, about how the state's attorney's office no longer charged anyone with perjury when they lied to a grand jury, about how too many prosecutors allowed witnesses to back up on their grand jury testimony. They complained about the growing number of drug-related murders, about how the days of the domestic dunker and 90-plus clearance rates were long gone. They complained that the phone didn't ring the way it used to after a murder, that fewer people were willing to drop a dime and risk becoming a witness to an act of violence.

As a bitch-and-moan session, it was entirely satisfying. After a good forty minutes, the group was still thumping on dead horseflesh: "Look at Washington," said Brown. "That ain't but thirty miles away from us."

For a police detective, a detail with the District of Columbia's homicide unit had suddenly become synonymous with being assigned to hell itself. Washington was well on the way to becoming the U.S. murder capital in 1988; only two years earlier, the capital and Baltimore had posted similar rates and fought for whatever distinction comes with being the nation's tenth deadliest city. Now, in the wake of a cocaine epidemic and a series of Jamaican drug wars in the capital's Northeast and Southeast quadrants, the District's police department was contending with an incidence of homicide double that of Baltimore. As a result, Washington's homicide squad—once one of the best-trained investigative units in the nation—was now posting a clearance rate in the low 40s. Awash in a deluge of violence, there was no time for follow-up investigation, no time for pretrial preparation, no time for anything but picking up bodies. From what the Baltimore detectives gathered in passing encounters, morale in the D.C. unit was nonexistent.

"The same thing's going to happen here and nobody's doing a damn thing about it," said Brown. "Wait until we start seeing some of that crack up here. We already got the Jamaican problem up in the Northwest, but does anyone give a damn about that? Hell, no. This town's gonna break wide open and this department isn't even gonna know what hit it."

Fahlteich pointed out that in some ways the homicide unit was its own worst enemy: "Every year we give them a clearance rate above the average, so every year they figure we can make do with what we have."

"That's it exactly," said Nolan.

"So," Fahlteich continued, "when we come back and ask for more detectives, or better cars or radios or training or whatever, the bosses can look at the rate and say, 'Shit on that, they don't need anything more than they got last year.' "

"We've done with so little for so long that now it's coming back to haunt us," Nolan said. "I'll tell you, if we get two more nights like this last one, we'll never climb out of the hole."

"We might not climb out anyway," said Fahlteich. "We'll be lucky to get above sixty percent from where we are now."

"Hey, if we don't," said Ed Brown, "it won't just stop with the lieutenant. They'll go and have themselves a housecleaning, and a lot of people up here are gonna be out the damn door."

"No shit," agreed Fahlteich.

Then Nolan brought the room to silence. "I think this just might be the year," he said with the barest of smiles, "when the wheels fall off the cart."

You are a citizen of a free nation, having lived your adult life in a land of guaranteed civil liberties, and you commit a crime of violence, whereupon you are jacked up, hauled down to a police station and deposited in a claustrophobic anteroom with three chairs, a table and no windows. There you sit for a half hour or so until a police detective—a man you have never met before, a man who can in no way be mistaken for a friend—enters the room with a thin stack of lined notepaper and a ballpoint pen.

The detective offers a cigarette, not your brand, and begins an uninterrupted monologue that wanders back and forth for a half hour more, eventually coming to rest in a familiar place: *"You have the absolute right to remain silent."*

Of course you do. You're a criminal. Criminals always have the right to remain silent. At least once in your miserable life, you spent an hour in front of a television set, listening to this book-'em-Danno routine. You think Joe Friday was lying to you? You think Kojak was making this horseshit up? No way, bunk, we're talking sacred freedoms here, notably your Fifth Fucking Amendment protection against self-incrimination, and hey, it was good enough for Ollie North, so who are you to go incriminating yourself at the first opportunity? Get it straight: A police detective, a man who gets paid government money to put you in prison, is explaining your absolute right to shut up before you say something stupid.

"Anything you say or write may be used against you in a court of law."

Yo, bunky, wake the fuck up. You're now being told that talking to a police detective in an interrogation room can only hurt you. If it could help you, they would probably be pretty quick to say that, wouldn't they? They'd stand up and say you have the right not to worry because what you say or write in this godforsaken cubicle is gonna be used to your benefit in a court of law. No, your best bet is to shut up. Shut up now.

"You have the right to talk with a lawyer at any time—before any questioning, before answering any questions, or during any questions."

Talk about helpful. Now the man who wants to arrest you for violating the peace and dignity of the state is saying you can talk to a trained professional, an attorney who has read the relevant portions of the Maryland Annotated Code or can at least get his hands on some Cliff's Notes. And let's face it, pal, you just carved up a drunk in a Dundalk Avenue bar, but that don't make you a neurosurgeon. Take whatever help you can get.

"If you want a lawyer and cannot afford to hire one, you will not be asked any questions, and the court will be requested to appoint a lawyer for you."

Translation: You're a derelict. No charge for derelicts.

At this point, if all lobes are working, you ought to have seen enough of this Double Jeopardy category to know that it ain't where you want to be. How about a little something from Criminal Lawyers and Their Clients for $50, Alex?

Whoa, bunk, not so fast.

"Before we get started, lemme just get through the paperwork," says the detective, who now produces an Explanation of Rights sheet, BPD Form 69, and passes it across the table.

"EXPLANATION OF RIGHTS," declares the top line in bold block letters. The detective asks you to fill in your name, address, age, and education, then the date and time. That much accomplished, he asks you to read the next section. It begins, "YOU ARE HEREBY ADVISED THAT:"

Read number one, the detective says. Do you understand number one?

"You have the absolute right to remain silent."

Yeah, you understand. We did this already.

"Then write your initials next to number one. Now read number two."

And so forth, until you have initialed each component of the Miranda warning. That done, the detective tells you to write your signature on the next line, the one just below the sentence that says, "I HAVE READ THE ABOVE EXPLANATION OF MY RIGHTS AND FULLY UNDERSTAND IT."

You sign your name and the monologue resumes. The detective assures you that he has informed you of these rights because he wants you to be protected, because there is nothing that concerns him more than giving you every possible assistance in this very confusing and stressful moment in your life. If you don't want to talk, he tells you, that's fine. And if you want a lawyer, that's fine, too, because first of all, he's no relation to the guy you cut up, and second, he's gonna get six hours overtime no matter what you do. But he wants you to know—and he's been doing this a lot longer than you, so take his word for it—that your rights to remain silent and obtain qualified counsel aren't all they're cracked up to be.

Look at it this way, he says, leaning back in his chair. Once you up and call for that lawyer, son, we can't do a damn thing for you. No sir, your friends in the city homicide unit are going to have to leave you locked in this room all alone and the next authority figure to scan your case will be a tie-wearing, three-piece bloodsucker—a no-nonsense prosecutor from the Violent Crimes Unit with the official title of assistant state's attorney for the city of Baltimore. And God help you then, son, because a ruthless fucker like that will have an O'Donnell Heights motorhead like yourself halfway to the gas chamber before you get three words out. Now's the time to speak up, right now when I got my pen and paper here on the table, because once I walk out of this room any chance you have of telling your side of the story is gone and I gotta write it up the way it looks. And the way it looks right now is first-fucking-degree murder. Felony murder, mister, which when shoved up a man's asshole is a helluva lot more painful than second-degree or maybe even manslaughter. What you say right here and now could make the difference, bunk. Did I mention that Maryland has a gas chamber? Big, ugly sumbitch at the penitentiary on

Eager Street, not twenty blocks from here. You don't wanna get too close to that bad boy, lemme tell you.

A small, wavering sound of protest passes your lips and the detective leans back in his chair, shaking his head sadly.

What the hell is wrong with you, son? You think I'm fucking with you? Hey, I don't even need to bother with your weak shit. I got three witnesses in three other rooms who say you're my man. I got a knife from the scene that's going downstairs to the lab for latent prints. I got blood spatter on them Air Jordans we took off you ten minutes ago. Why the fuck do you think we took 'em? Do I look like I wear high-top tennis? Fuck no. You got spatter all over 'em, and I think we both know whose blood type it's gonna be. Hey, bunk, I'm only in here to make sure that there ain't nothing you can say for yourself before I write it all up.

You hesitate.

Oh, says the detective. You want to think about it. Hey, you think about it all you want, pal. My captain's right outside in the hallway, and he already told me to charge your ass in the first fuckin' degree. For once in your beshitted little life someone is giving you a chance and you're too fucking dumb to take it. What the fuck, you go ahead and think about it and I'll tell my captain to cool his heels for ten minutes. I can do that much for you. How 'bout some coffee? Another cigarette?

The detective leaves you alone in that cramped, windowless room. Just you and the blank notepaper and the Form 69 and . . . first-degree murder. First-degree murder with witnesses and fingerprints and blood on your Air Jordans. Christ, you didn't even notice the blood on your own fucking shoes. Felony murder, mister. First-fucking-degree. How many years, you begin to wonder, how many years do I get for involuntary manslaughter?

Whereupon the man who wants to put you in prison, the man who is not your friend, comes back in the room, asking if the coffee's okay.

Yeah, you say, the coffee's fine, but what happens if I want a lawyer?

The detective shrugs. Then we get you a lawyer, he says. And I walk out of the room and type up the charging documents for first-degree murder and you can't say a fucking thing about it. Look, bunk, I'm giving you a chance. He came at you, right? You were scared. It was self-defense.

Your mouth opens to speak.

He came at you, didn't he?

"Yeah," you venture cautiously, "he came at me."

Whoa, says the detective, holding up his hands. Wait a minute. If we're gonna do this, I gotta find your rights form. Where's the fucking form? Damn things are like cops, never around when you need 'em. Here it is, he says, pushing the explanation-of-rights sheet across the table and pointing to the bottom. Read that, he says.

"I am willing to answer questions and I do not want any attorney at this time. My decision to answer questions without having an attorney present is free and voluntary on my part."

As you read, he leaves the room and returns a moment later with a second detective as a witness. You sign the bottom of the form, as do both detectives.

The first detective looks up from the form, his eyes soaked with innocence. "He came at you, huh?"

"Yeah, he came at me."

Get used to small rooms, bunk, because you are about to be drop-kicked into the lost land of pretrial detention. Because it's one thing to be a murdering little asshole from Southeast Baltimore, and it's another to be stupid about it, and with five little words you have just elevated yourself to the ranks of the truly witless.

End of the road, pal. It's over. It's history. And if that police detective wasn't so busy committing your weak bullshit to paper, he'd probably look you in the eye and tell you so. He'd give you another cigarette and say, son, you are ignorance personified and you just put yourself in for the fatal stabbing of a human being. He might even tell you that the other witnesses in the other rooms are too drunk to identify their own reflections, much less the kid who had the knife, or that it's always a long shot for the lab to pull a latent off a knife hilt, or that your $95 sneakers are as clean as the day you bought them. If he was feeling particularly expansive, he might tell you that everyone who leaves the homicide unit in handcuffs does so charged with first-degree murder, that it's for the lawyers to decide what kind of deal will be cut. He might go on to say that even after all these years working homicides, there is still a small part of him that finds it completely mystifying that anyone ever utters a single word in a police interrogation. To illustrate the point, he could hold up your Form 69, on which you waived away every last one of your rights, and say, "Lookit here, pistonhead, I told you twice that you were deep in the shit and that whatever you said could put you in deeper." And if his message was still somehow beyond your understanding, he could drag your carcass back down the sixth-floor hallway, back toward the sign that says Homicide Unit in white block letters, the sign you saw when you walked off the elevator.

Now think hard: Who lives in a homicide unit? Yeah, right. And what do homicide detectives do for a living? Yeah, you got it, bunk. And what did you do tonight? You murdered someone.

So when you opened that mouth of yours, what the fuck were you thinking?

Homicide detectives in Baltimore like to imagine a small, open window at the top of the long wall in the large interrogation room. More to the point, they like to imagine their suspects imagining a small, open window at the top of the long wall. The open window is the escape hatch, the Out. It is the perfect representation of what every suspect believes when he opens his mouth during an interrogation. Every last one envisions himself parrying questions with the right combination of alibi and excuse; every last one sees himself coming up with the right words, then crawling out the window to go home and sleep in his own bed. More often than not, a guilty man is looking for the Out from his first moments in the interrogation room; in that sense, the window is as much the suspect's fantasy as the detective's mirage.

The effect of the illusion is profound, distorting as it does the natural hostility between hunter and hunted, transforming it until it resembles a relationship more symbiotic than adversarial. That is the lie, and when the roles are perfectly performed, deceit surpasses itself, becoming manipulation on a grand scale and ultimately an act of betrayal. Because what occurs in an interrogation room is indeed little more than a carefully staged drama, a choreographed performance that allows a detective and his suspect to find common ground where none exists. There, in a carefully controlled purgatory, the guilty proclaim their malefactions, though rarely in any form that allows for contrition or resembles an unequivocal admission.

In truth, catharsis in the interrogation room occurs for only a few rare suspects, usually those in domestic murders or child abuse cases wherein the leaden mass of genuine remorse can crush anyone who is not hardened to his crime. But the greater share of men and women brought downtown take no interest in absolution. Ralph Waldo Emerson rightly noted that for those responsible, the act of murder "is no such ruinous thought as poets and romancers will have it; it does not unsettle him, or frighten him from his ordinary notice of trifles." And while West Baltimore is a universe or two from Emerson's nineteenth-century Massachusetts hamlet, the observation is still useful. Murder often doesn't unsettle a man. In Baltimore, it usually doesn't even ruin his day.

As a result, the majority of those who acknowledge their complicity in a killing must be baited by detectives with something more tempting than penitence. They must be made to believe that their crime is not really murder, that their excuse is both accepted and unique, that they will, with the help of the detective, be judged less evil than they truly are.

Some are brought to that unreasoned conclusion by the suggestion that they acted in self-defense or were provoked to violence. Others fall prey to the notion that they are less culpable than their colleagues—I only drove the car or backed up the robbery, I wasn't the triggerman; or yeah, I raped her, but I stayed out of it when them other guys started strangling her—unaware that Maryland law allows every member of the conspiracy to be charged as a principal. Still others succumb to the belief that they will get a better shake by cooperating with detectives and acknowledging a limited amount of guilt. And many of those who cannot be lured over the precipice of self-incrimination can still be manipulated into providing alibis, denials and explanations—statements that can be checked and rechecked until a suspect's lies are the greatest evidentiary threat to his freedom.

For that reason, the professionals say nothing. No alibis. No explanations. No expressions of polite dismay or blanket denials. In the late 1970s, when men by the names of Dennis Wise and Vernon Collins were matching each other body for body as Baltimore's premier contract killers and no witness could be found to testify against either, things got to the point where both the detectives and their suspects knew the drill:

Enter room.

Miranda.

Anything to say this time, Dennis?

No, sir. Just want to call my lawyer.

Fine, Dennis.

Exit room.

For anyone with experience in the criminal justice machine, the point is driven home by every lawyer worth his fee. Repetition and familiarity with the process soon place the professionals beyond the reach of a police interrogation. Yet more than two decades after the landmark Escobedo and Miranda decisions, the rest of the world remains strangely willing to place itself at risk. As a result, the same law enforcement community that once regarded the 1966 Miranda decision as a death blow to criminal investigation has now come to see the explanation of rights as a routine part of the process—simply a piece of station house furniture, if not a civilizing influence on police work itself.

In an era when beatings and physical intimidation were common tools of an interrogation, the Escobedo and Miranda decisions were sent down by the nation's highest court to ensure that criminal confessions and statements were purely voluntary. The resulting Miranda warning was "a protective device to dispel the compelling atmosphere of the interrogation," as Chief Justice Earl Warren wrote in the majority opinion. Investigators would be required to assure citizens of their rights to silence and counsel, not only at the moment of arrest, but at the moment that they could reasonably be considered suspects under interrogation.

In answer to Miranda, the nation's police officials responded with a veritable jeremiad, wailing in unison that the required warnings would virtually assure that confessions would be impossible to obtain and conviction rates would plummet. Yet the prediction was soon proved false for the simple reason that those law enforcement leaders—and, for that matter, the Supreme Court itself—underestimated a police detective's ingenuity.

Miranda is, on paper, a noble gesture which declares that constitutional rights extend not only to the public forum of the courts, but to the private confines of the police station as well. Miranda and its accompanying decisions established a uniform concept of a criminal defendant's rights and effectively ended the use of violence and the most blatant kind of physical intimidation in interrogations. That, of course, was a blessing. But if the further intent of the Miranda decision was, in fact, an attempt to "dispel the compelling atmosphere" of an interrogation, then it failed miserably.

And thank God. Because by any standards of human discourse, a criminal confession can never truly be called voluntary. With rare exception, a confession is compelled, provoked and manipulated from a suspect by a detective who has been trained in a genuinely deceitful art. That is the essence of interrogation, and those who believe that a straightforward conversation between a cop and a criminal—devoid of any treachery—is going to solve a crime are somewhere beyond naive. If the interrogation process is, from a moral standpoint, contemptible, it is nonetheless essential. Deprived of the ability to question and confront suspects and witnesses, a detective is left with physical evidence and in many cases, precious little of that. Without a chance for a detective to manipulate a suspect's mind, a lot of bad people would simply go free.

Yet every defense attorney knows that there can be no good reason for a guilty man to say anything whatsoever to a police officer, and any suspect who calls an attorney will be told as much, bringing the interrogation to an end. A court opinion that therefore requires a detective—the same detective working hard to dupe a suspect—to stop abruptly and guarantee the man his right to end the process can only be called an act of institutional schizophrenia. The Miranda warning is a little like a referee introducing a barroom brawl: The stern warnings to hit above the waist and take no cheap shots have nothing to do with the mayhem that follows.

Yet how could it be otherwise? It would be easy enough for our judiciary to ensure that no criminal suspect relinquished his rights inside a police station: The court could simply require the presence of a lawyer at all times. But such a blanket guarantee of individual rights would effectively end the use of interrogation as an investigative weapon, leaving many more crimes unsolved and many more guilty men and women unpunished. Instead, the ideals have been carefully compromised at little cost other than to the integrity of the police investigator.

After all, it's the lawyers, the Great Compromisers of our age, who have struck this bargain, who still manage to keep cuffs clean in the public courts, where rights and process are worshiped faithfully. It is left for the detective to fire this warning shot across a suspect's bow, granting rights to a man who will then be tricked into relinquishing them. In that sense, Miranda is a symbol and little more, a salve for a collective conscience that cannot reconcile libertarian ideals with what must necessarily occur in a police interrogation room. Our judges, our courts, our society as a whole, demand in the same breath that rights be maintained even as crimes are punished. And all of us are bent and determined to preserve the illusion that both can be achieved in the same small room. It's mournful to think that this hypocrisy is the necessary creation of our best legal minds, who seem to view the interrogation process as the rest of us look upon breakfast sausage: We want it on a plate with eggs and toast; we don't want to know too much about how it comes to be.

Trapped in that contradiction, a detective does his job in the only possible way. He follows the requirements of the law to the letter—or close enough so as not to jeopardize his case. Just as carefully, he ignores that law's spirit and intent. He becomes a salesman, a huckster as thieving and silver-tongued as any man who ever moved used cars or aluminum siding—more so, in fact, when you consider that he's selling long prison terms to customers who have no genuine need for the product.

The fraud that claims it is somehow in a suspect's interest to talk with police will forever be the catalyst in any criminal interrogation. It is a fiction propped up against the greater weight of logic itself, sustained for hours on end through nothing more or less than a detective's ability to control the interrogation room.

A good interrogator controls the physical environment, from the moment a suspect or reluctant witness is dumped in the small cubicle, left alone to stew in soundproof isolation. The law says that a man can't be held against his will unless he's to be charged with a crime, yet the men and women tossed into the interrogation room rarely ponder their legal status. They light cigarettes and wait, staring abstractedly at four yellow cinderblock walls, a dirty tin ashtray on a plain table, a small mirrored window and a series of stained acoustic tiles on the ceiling. Those few with heart enough to ask whether they are under arrest are often answered with a question:

"Why? Do you want to be?"

"No."

"Then sit the fuck down."

Control is the reason a suspect is seated farthest from the interrogation room door, and the reason the room's light switch can only be operated with a key that remains in possession of the detectives. Every time a suspect has to ask for or be offered a cigarette, water, coffee or a trip to the bathroom, he's being reminded that he's lost control.

When the detective arrives with pen and notepaper and begins the initial monologue to which a potential suspect or witness is invariably subjected, he has two goals in mind: first, to emphasize his complete control of the process; second, to stop the suspect from opening his mouth. Because if a suspect or witness manages to blurt out his desire for a lawyer—if he asks for counsel definitively and declines to answer questions until he gets one—it's over.

To prevent that, a detective allows no interruption of his soliloquy. Typically, the speech begins with the detective identifying himself and confiding that this is some serious shit that the two of you have to sort out. In your favor, however, is the fact that he, the detective, is a fair and reasonable man. A great guy, in fact—just ask anyone he works with.

If, at this moment, you try to speak, the detective will cut you off, saying your chance will come in a little while. Right now, he will invariably say, you need to know where I'm coming from. Then he'll inform you that he happens to be very good at what he does, that he's had very few open cases in his long, storied career, and a whole busload of people who lied to him in this very room are now on Death Row.

Control. To keep it, you say whatever you have to. Then you say it over and over until it's safe to stop, because if your suspect thinks for one moment that he can influence events, he may just demand an attorney.

As a result, the Miranda warning becomes a psychological hurdle, a pregnant moment that must be slipped carefully into the back-and-forth of the interrogation. For witnesses, the warning is not required and a detective can question those knowledgeable about a crime for hours without ever advising them of their rights. But should a witness suddenly say something that indicates involvement in a criminal act, he becomes—by the Supreme Court's definition—a suspect, at which point he must be advised of his rights. In practice, the line between a potential suspect and a suspect can be thin, and a common sight in any American homicide unit is a handful of detectives standing outside an interrogation room, debating whether or not a Miranda warning is yet necessary.

The Baltimore department, like many others, uses a written form to confirm a suspect's acknowledgment of Miranda. In a city where nine out of ten suspects would otherwise claim they were never informed of their rights, the forms have proven essential. Moreover, the detectives have found that rather than drawing attention to the Miranda, the written form diffuses the impact of the warning. Even as it alerts a suspect to the dangers of an interrogation, the form co-opts the suspect, making him part of the process. It is the suspect who wields the pen, initialing each component of the warning and then signing the form; it is the suspect who is being asked to help with the paperwork. With witnesses, the detectives achieve the same effect with an information sheet that asks three dozen questions in rapid-fire succession. Not only does the form include information of value to the investigators—name, nickname, height, weight, complexion, employer, description of clothing at time of interview, relatives living in Baltimore, names of parents, spouse, boyfriend or girlfriend—but it acclimates the witness to the idea of answering questions before the direct interview begins.

Even if a suspect does indeed ask for a lawyer, he must—at least according to the most aggressive interpretation of Miranda—ask definitively: "I want to talk to a lawyer and I don't want to answer questions until I do."

Anything less leaves room for a good detective to maneuver. The distinctions are subtle and semantic:

"Maybe I should get a lawyer."

"Maybe you should. But why would you need a lawyer if you don't have anything to do with this?"

Or: "I think I should talk to a lawyer."

"You better be sure. Because if you want a lawyer then I'm not going to be able to do anything for you."

Likewise, if a suspect calls a lawyer and continues to answer questions until the lawyer arrives, his rights have not been violated. If the lawyer arrives, the suspect must be told that an attorney is in the building, but if he still wishes to continue the interrogation, nothing requires that the police allow the attorney to speak with his client. In short, the suspect can demand an attorney; a lawyer can't demand a suspect.

Once the minefield that is Miranda has been successfully negotiated, the detective must let the suspect know that his guilt is certain and easily established by the existing evidence. He must then offer the Out.

This, too, is role playing, and it requires a seasoned actor. If a witness or suspect is belligerent, you wear him down with greater belligerence. If the man shows fear, you offer calm and comfort. When he looks weak, you appear strong. When he wants a friend, you crack a joke and offer to buy him a soda. If he's confident, you are more so, assuring him that you are certain of his guilt and are curious only about a few select details of the crime. And if he's arrogant, if he wants nothing to do with the process, you intimidate him, threaten him, make him believe that making you happy may be the only thing between his ass and the Baltimore City Jail.

Kill your woman and a good detective will come close to real tears as he touches your shoulder and tells you how he knows that you must have loved her, that it wouldn't be so hard for you to talk about if you didn't. Beat your child to death and a police detective will wrap his arm around you in the interrogation room, telling you about how he beats his own children all the time, how it wasn't your fault if the kid up and died on you. Shoot a friend over a poker hand and that same detective will lie about your dead buddy's condition, telling you that the victim is in stable condition at Hopkins and probably won't press charges, which wouldn't amount to more than assault with intent even if he does. Murder a man with an accomplice and the detective will walk your co-conspirator past the open door of your interrogation room, then say your bunky's going home tonight because he gave a statement making you the triggerman. And if that same detective thinks you can be bluffed, he might tell you that they've got your prints on the weapon, or that there are two eyewitnesses who have picked your photo from an array, or that the victim made a dying declaration in which he named you as his assailant.

All of which is street legal. Reasonable deception, the courts call it. After all, what could be more reasonable than deceiving someone who has taken a human life and is now lying about it?

The deception sometimes goes too far, or at least it sometimes seems that way to those unfamiliar with the process. Not long ago, several veteran homicide detectives in Detroit were publicly upbraided and disciplined by their superiors for using the office Xerox machine as a polygraph device. It seems that the detectives, when confronted with a statement of dubious veracity, would sometimes adjourn to the Xerox room and load three sheets of paper into the feeder.

"Truth," said the first.

"Truth," said the second.

"Lie," said the third.

Then the suspect would be led into the room and told to put his hand against the side of the machine. The detectives would ask the man's name, listen to the answer, then hit the copy button.

Truth.

And where do you live?

Truth again.

And did you or did you not kill Tater, shooting him down like a dog in the 1200 block of North Durham Street?

Lie. Well, well: You lying motherfucker.

In Baltimore, the homicide detectives read newspaper accounts of the Detroit controversy and wondered why anyone had a problem. Polygraph by copier was an old trick; it had been attempted on more than one occasion in the sixth-floor Xerox room. Gene Constantine, a veteran of Stanton's shift, once gave a mindless wonder the coordination test for drunk drivers ("Follow my finger with your eyes, but don't move your head . . . Now stand on one foot"), then loudly declared that the man's performance indicated obvious deception.

"You flunked," Constantine told him. "You're lying."

Convinced, the suspect confessed.

Variations on the theme are limited only by a detective's imagination and his ability to sustain the fraud. But every bluff carries a corresponding risk, and a detective who tells a suspect his fingerprints are all over a crime scene loses all hope if the man knows he was wearing gloves. An interrogation room fraud is only as good as the material from which it was constructed—or, for that matter, as good as the suspect is witless—and a detective who underestimates his prey or overestimates his knowledge of the crime will lose precious credibility. Once a detective claims knowledge of a fact that the suspect knows to be untrue, the veil has been lifted, and the investigator is instead revealed as the liar.

Only when everything else in the repertoire falls does a detective resort to rage. It might be a spasm limited to a well-chosen sentence or two, or an extended tantrum punctuated by the slamming of a metal door or the drop kick of a chair, perhaps even a rant delivered as part of a good-cop, bad-cop melodrama, although that particular routine has worn thin with the years. Ideally, the shouting should be loud enough to suggest the threat of violence but restrained enough to avoid any action that could jeopardize the statement: Tell the court why you felt threatened. Did the detective hit you? Did he attempt to hit you? Did he threaten to hit you? No, but he slammed his hand down on the table, real loud.

Oh my. Motion to suppress denied.

What a good detective will not do in this more enlightened age is beat his suspect, at least not for the purpose of obtaining a statement. A suspect who swings on a homicide detective, who raves and kicks furniture, who tries to fight off a pair of handcuffs, will receive as comprehensive an ass-kicking as he would out on the street, but as a function of interrogation, physical assault is not part of the arsenal. In Baltimore, that has been true for at least fifteen years.

Simply put, the violence isn't worth the risk—not only the risk that the statement obtained will later be ruled inadmissible, but the risk to a detective's career and pension. It would be another thing entirely in those instances in which an officer or an officer's family member is the victim. In those cases, a good detective will anticipate the accusation by photographing a suspect after interrogation, to show an absence of injuries and to prove that any beating received prior to the suspect's arrival at the city jail had nothing to do with what occurred in the homicide unit.

But those are rare cases and, for the vast majority of murders, there is little for a detective to take personally. He doesn't know the dead man, he just met the suspect and he doesn't live anywhere near the street where the violence occurred. From that perspective, what civil servant in his right mind is going to risk his entire career to prove that on the night of March 7, 1988, in some godforsaken tract of West Baltimore, a drug dealer, Stinky, shot a dope fiend, Pee Wee, over a $35 debt?

Still, circuit court juries often prefer to think in conspiratorial terms about back rooms and hot lights and rabbit punches to a suspect's kidneys. A Baltimore detective once lost a case because the defendant testified that his confession was obtained only after he had been mauled by two detectives who beat him with a phone book. The detective was sequestered and did not hear that testimony, but when he took the stand, the defense attorney asked what items were in the room during the interrogation.

"The table. Chairs. Some papers. An ashtray."

"Was there a phone book in the room?"

The detective thought about it and remembered that yes, they had used a phone book to look up an address. "Yeah," he acknowledged. "A yellow pages phone book."

Only when the defense attorney looked approvingly at the jury did the cop realize that something was wrong. After the not guilty verdict, the detective swore he would never again begin an interview until he had cleared the room of every unnecessary item.

The passage of time can also damage the credibility of a confession. In the privacy of the interrogation room, it requires hours of prolonged effort to break a man to a point where he's willing to admit a criminal act, yet at some point those hours begin to cast doubt on the statement itself. Even under the best conditions, four to six hours of interrogation are required to break a suspect down, and eight or ten or twelve hours can be justified as long as the man is fed and allowed the use of a bathroom. But after a suspect has spent more than twelve hours in an isolated chamber without benefit of counsel, even a sympathetic judge will have qualms about calling a confession or statement truly voluntary.

And how does a detective know he has the right man? Nervousness, fear, confusion, hostility, a story that changes or contradicts itself—all are signs that the man in an interrogation room is lying, particularly in the eyes of someone as naturally suspicious as a detective. Unfortunately, these are also signs of a human being in a state of high stress, which is pretty much where people find themselves after being accused of a capital crime. Terry McLarney once mused that the best way to unsettle a suspect would be to post in all three interrogation rooms a written list of those behavior patterns that indicate deception:

Uncooperative.

Too cooperative.

Talks too much.

Talks too little.

Gets his story perfectly straight.

Fucks his story up.

Blinks too much, avoids eye contact.

Doesn't blink. Stares.

And yet if the signs along the way are ambiguous, there can be no mistaking that critical moment, that light that shines from the other end of the tunnel when a guilty man is about to give it up. Later, after he's initialed each page and is alone again in the cubicle, there will be only exhaustion and, in some cases, depression. If he gets to brooding, there might even be a suicide attempt.

But that is epilogue. The emotive crest of a guilty man's performance comes in those cold moments before he opens his mouth and reaches for the Out. Just before a man gives up life and liberty in an interrogation room, his body acknowledges the defeat: His eyes are glazed, his jaw is slack, his body lists against the nearest wall or table edge. Some put their heads against the tabletop to steady themselves. Some become physically sick, holding their stomachs as if the problem were digestive; a few actually vomit.

At that critical moment, the detectives tell their suspects that they really are sick—sick of lying, sick of hiding. They tell them it's time to turn over a new leaf, that they'll only begin to feel better when they start to tell the truth. Amazingly enough, many of them actually believe it. As they reach for the ledge of that high window, they believe every last word of it.

"He came at you, right?"

"Yeah, he came at me."

The Out leads in.

Thursday, March 10

"Sixty-four thirty-one."

Garvey listens to ten seconds of silence, then keys the mike a second time: "Sixty-four thirty-one."

More dead air. The detective cranks the volume control on the Cavalier's radio, then leans over to check the frequency indicator on the front of the set. Channel 7, just as it should be.

"Sixty-four thirty-one," he says again, releasing the key on the hand mike before adding the less procedural "oooh, yoo-hoo. . . . Anybody home in the Western? Helloooo . . ."

Kincaid laughs from the passenger seat.

"Sixty-four thirty-one," repeats the dispatcher, acknowledging the detective in a mumble that suggests only mild irritation. It's a known fact that those assigned to a police communications unit are carefully screened to ensure that they will sound as if they've been watching televised bowling tournaments for a month. Perhaps it's the job, perhaps it's the metallic squawk of the broadcast itself, but the speaking voice of the average police dispatcher falls somewhere between tedium and slow death. In Baltimore, at least, the world will not end with a bang but with the weary, distracted droning of a forty-seven-year-old civil servant who will ask a patrol unit for the 10-20 on that mushroom cloud, then assign the incident a seven-digit complaint number.

Garvey keys the mike again. "Yeah, we're in your district and we're gonna need uniforms for a paper," he says, "and also a DEU at Calhoun and, ah, Lexington."

"Ten-four. When do you need them?"

Unbelievable. Garvey suppresses an impulse to ask if the weekend after Labor Day is convenient for everyone involved.

"We need them as soon as possible."

"Ten-four. What's your ten-twenty again?"

"Calhoun and Lexington."

"Ten-four."

Garvey returns the radio mike to its metal retainer and settles back into the driver's seat. He slips a pair of wide-framed glasses down the bridge of his nose, then begins rubbing his dark brown eyes with one thumb and forefinger. The glasses are an incongruous accessory. Without them, Garvey looks like a Baltimore cop; wearing them, he looks for all the world like the proper businessman his father wanted him to be.

Garvey's appearance is, on the whole, decidedly corporate: dark blue suit, blue dress shirt, a necktie of red and blue Republican stripes, well-shined Bostonians—a businessman's ensemble made whole by the addition of a dark brown briefcase that travels between home and office, crammed with files and reports. Tasteful, nondescript, the clothes cover a tall but well-proportioned frame that is at first glance equal to the wardrobe in its ordinariness. Like his body, the detective's face is long and thin, with a well-trimmed mustache and high forehead that ascends to a carefully combed crop of thinning black hair.

Except for the small lump that a .38 revolver produces on the back of one hip, Garvey fairly reeks of sales manager or, on a day when his blue pinstripe suit has been deployed, vice president for marketing. At first encounter, an untutored visitor to the homicide office might reasonably mistake Garvey for something from the police department's planning and research department, a middle-management type who at any moment will begin pulling flow charts and quarterly projections from his briefcase, explaining that domestics and robbery shootings are down, but drug-related futures will continue to ascend through the last quarter. This image would shatter, of course, at the very moment Mr. Clean opens his mouth and emits the usual station house effluence. For Garvey, as for nearly all of the detectives in the unit, obscenities roll off the tongue in that practiced, fucking-this-motherfucker cadence that becomes, against a backdrop of violence and despair, a kind of strange poetry.

"Where are these motherfucking uniforms?" Garvey says, replacing his glasses and looking in both directions on Calhoun. "I don't want to spend all fucking day hitting this house."

"Sounded like you fuckin' had to wake that goddamn dispatcher up," Kincaid says from the passenger seat. "Now he's trying to wake up some other poor motherfucker."

"Well," says Garvey, "a good police officer is never cold, tired, hungry or wet."

The Patrolman's Creed. Kincaid laughs, then jerks open the passenger door and pushes himself up and out to stretch his legs on the sidewalk. Two more minutes pass before one radio car, then another, then a third, pull behind the Cavalier. Three uniforms gather on the corner, conferring briefly with the detectives.

"Anybody here know where your DEU is today?" asks Garvey. It would help to have the district drug enforcement unit around in the event the raid produces dope for the simple, selfish reason that submitting narcotics to evidence control, even in small quantities, is a pain-in-the-ass process.

"Dispatch said they won't be available," says one officer, the first to arrive at the intersection. "Not for an hour or so."

"Fuck it then," says Garvey. "But that means somebody here is going to have to submit whatever drugs we find in there."

"So let's not find any," says the first officer's side partner.

"Well, I wanna take it if it's there, just to have something on the guy," says Garvey. "Normally, I wouldn't care—"

"I'll take the dope," says the second patrolman. "I gotta run by headquarters anyway."

"You're a gentleman and a scholar," says a third uniform, smiling. "I don't care what them other guys say about you."

"Which house is it?" asks the first officer.

"Fifth house in. North side of the street."

"Three-seven?"

"Yeah, one family in there. Mother, daughter and a young boy named Vincent. He's the only one we might have to worry about."

"Is he getting locked up?"

"No, but if he's there, he's going downtown. We're here for search and seizure."

"Gotcha."

"Which one of you is taking the back of the house?" Garvey asks.

"I got the back."

"Okay, then you two go in the front with us."

"Uh-huh."

"Let's do it."

And then the district men are back in their cars, wheeling around the corner and onto Fayette. The first car rolls around the block and into the back alley that leads to the rear of the rowhouse; the other two screech to a halt in front of the stoop, with the Cavalier in between. Garvey and Kincaid race the younger patrolmen up to the marble stoop.

If this were an arrest warrant, if Vincent Booker were now charged with the murders of his father and Lena Lucas, the detectives would be wearing their vests, their guns drawn, and the front door to Vincent's home would be answered on the first knock or it would come down hard under a steel maul or patrolman's boot. So, too, would the raid be an act of controlled violence if the warrant had been written by a narcotics detective. But at this moment there is no reason to think Vincent Booker will play the role of desperado. Nor is the evidence sought in this warrant likely to be swallowed or flushed down a toilet.

Loud knocking brings a young girl to the door.

"Police. Open up."

"Who's there?"

"Police officers. Open this door now."

"What you want here?" asks the girl angrily, opening the door halfway. The first uniform pushes the door full open and a crowd rushes past the girl.

"Where's Vincent?"

"Upstairs."

The uniforms race up the center steps to meet a lanky, wide-eyed young man at the second-floor landing. Vincent Booker says nothing and takes the handcuffs without protest, as if he long ago readied himself for this moment.

"What you want to arrest him for?" shouts the girl. "You supposed to be arresting the man done killed his father."

"Calm down," says Garvey.

"Why you lockin' him up?"

"Just take it easy. Where's your mother?"

Kincaid gestures toward the middle room on the first floor. The matriarch of the Booker clan is a fragile, diminutive woman sitting in one corner of a worn, flower-print sofa. She is watching beautiful people coupling and uncoupling on a black-and-white television. Against the background noise of a soap opera, Garvey introduces himself, shows the warrant and explains that Vincent is going downtown.

"I don't know nothing about all that," she says, waving the paper away.

"This just says that we can search the house."

"Why you want to search my house?"

"It's here in the warrant."

The woman shrugs. "I don't see why you got to search my house for anything."

Garvey gives up, leaving a target copy on an endtable. Upstairs, in Vincent Booker's room, drawers are jerked open and mattresses upended. By now, Dave Brown, the primary on the Booker murder, has arrived, and the three detectives move slowly, methodically, through the room. Brown guts the boy's dresser as Garvey begins pushing each ceiling tile upward, probing for any objects hidden above. Kincaid takes apart the closet, pausing only to leaf through a skin magazine hidden on the top shelf.

"This thing didn't get much use," says Kincaid, laughing. "Ain't but a couple pages stuck together."

They strike gold after a little less than fifteen minutes, lifting the box spring of the double bed and shoving it against the long wall to reveal a locked metal tackle box. Garvey and Brown begin scanning every key ring discovered in the search, looking for anything that might match the small padlock.

"This one here."

"No, that's too big."

"How 'bout the brown one next to it?"

"Shit on this," says Brown. "I'm about to open this bitch up with a thirty-eight bullet."

Kincaid and Garvey laugh.

"Did he have any keys on him?"

"Those are them right here."

"How 'bout this one?"

"No, try the silver one."

The padlock slips open, and the tackle box comes apart to reveal several banded packages of glassine bags, a portable scale, some cash, a small amount of marijuana, a healthy collection of jackknives, and a plastic soap dish. Pried open carefully, the knives show not a sign of red-brown residue, but the soap dish opens to reveal a dozen or more .38-caliber rounds, most of them ass-backward wadcutters.

When the detectives are nearly ready to leave, Garvey takes the knives and the soap dish down to Mother Booker, who remains bathed in the blue-gray glow from the television.

"I just want you to see what we're taking with us. So there's no problem later."

"What is that you got?"

"These knives," says Garvey, "and these here in the dish are bullets."

The woman briefly contemplates the contents of the plastic dish, glancing for a second or two at stubby lead lumps of the same sort used not a dozen blocks from here to murder her estranged husband, the father of her children. The same type of bullets that killed a mother of two in a rowhouse just around the corner.

"You takin' those with you?"

"Yes, ma'am."

"Why?"

"Evidence."

"Well," asks the woman, returning her attention to the television, "he gonna get them back, ain't he?"

The warrant for the Booker home has brought Garvey to within a step of turning two murders from red to black on D'Addario's side of the board, but ironically, Vincent Booker—if he plays his cards right—is no longer the target of the last seventeen days of pursuit. Instead, he is the weakest link in Robert Frazier's jerry-rigged story.

Straight legwork took them half the distance: Garvey and Kincaid have run down every element of Frazier's statement and found, among other things, that the alibi of the dinner party wasn't worth much. Frazier's second girlfriend, Denise, the party's hostess, was decidedly unwilling to go the distance for her man; she readily recalled that on the night of the murder, Frazier had left the party before eleven o'clock after an argument. She also said that Vincent Booker had come by the projects not once, but twice; the second time Frazier left with the boy and didn't return until morning. Denise remembered this because she had slept alone that night, upset about the party. She had planned all week, buying lobster and Chesapeake blue crabs and corn on the cob. Frazier had ruined her evening.

Denise even volunteered that Frazier kept his .38 revolver at her Amity Street rowhouse and further appalled the detectives by mentioning that she hid the loaded weapon in her children's toy box in the back bedroom. The gun wasn't there now, she assured them; Frazier had come by and taken it a week ago, telling her that he was afraid she would be weak and give it to the police.

The detectives also learned that Frazier hadn't shown up for work at the Sparrows Point plant on the morning after the murder, although he had claimed that he didn't bother entering Lena's open apartment door because he was already late for work that morning. Nor had Frazier carried through on his promise to bring in his .38. Garvey wondered why Frazier would even mention that he owned such a gun or, for that matter, why he would offer the police any story at all. Pop quiz: You've just killed two people and there is no physical evidence or witness that can link you directly to either crime. Do you: (A) Shut your mouth or (B) Visit the homicide unit and lie your ass off?

"The only answer," mused Garvey as he typed the warrant for Vincent Booker's house, "is that crime makes you stupid."

Frazier's story was further shattered by the arrival of one additional piece of evidence, a break that owed as much to luck as to legwork.

On the Sunday night of the murder, a sixteen-year-old high school student in the rowhouse next door to Lena Lucas had been staring out of her third-floor window, watching the traffic on Gilmor Street slow to a trickle in the late evening. At about 11:15—she was sure because she had been watching the local news for several minutes—the girl saw Lena and a tall, dark-skinned man wearing a brimmed cap walking from a red sports car parked on the other side of Gilmor Street. The couple walked toward her, toward Lena's rowhouse, though the young girl couldn't see much more than that because of the angle from her window. But she heard Lena's front door close, and an hour later, through the common wall, she heard what sounded like a brief argument between a man and a woman. The noise sounded as if it was coming from below, perhaps from one of the apartments on the second floor of the adjacent house.

For a time, the girl told no one about what she had seen. And when she did finally speak, it was not to the police but to an employee at her school's cafeteria who she happened to know was Lena's sister. Upon hearing the story, the woman urged the young girl to call the police. But the witness was reluctant and so, the following day, the woman herself called the homicide unit. The young girl was named Romaine Jackson, and for all her fear, she needed only a little prodding to do the right thing. When the detectives showed her the array of six photographs, she hesitated for only a moment or two before picking out Robert Frazier. Then, after the young girl read and signed her statement, Rich Garvey drove her back to West Baltimore, letting her out of the Cavalier a block or two from Gilmor Street so that no one would see her with a detective. The following day, Garvey and Kincaid cruised the streets near Frazier's Fayette Street home and found a red car similar to the one described by Romaine. It was registered to Frazier's mother.

Even with the arrival of a living witness, however, Vincent Booker remained an open door, an escape hatch for Robert Frazier. As much as he was now convinced of Frazier's guilt, Garvey had to admit that any good defense lawyer could take Vincent's connections to the case and run wild in front of a city jury. Vincent was somehow involved—the .38 wadcutters in the soap dish made that clear—but as the killer, he simply didn't add up.

For one thing, there were the nested clothes and the blade marks on the headboard above the bed in Lena's room; the woman would not have undressed casually and stretched out on the bed for anyone but a lover. That played not to Vincent, but to Frazier. On the other hand, the same gun used to shoot Lena also killed Purnell Booker. What possible connection was there between Frazier and the father of a boy who sold Frazier's cocaine? Why would anyone want to kill old man Booker? The man who killed Lena took cocaine from that bag of rice hidden in the bureau, but for what did he ransack Purnell Booker's apartment?

Vincent is the key, and Garvey, looking at the boy beneath the barren white light of the large interrogation room, doesn't see someone capable of the act. No way did this kid do what was done to his father. Murder, maybe. But not the dozen or more superficial blade wounds to the old man's face. Even if Vincent could manage something like that with Lena, Garvey is certain that the kid doesn't have ice enough in his veins to conduct a prolonged torture of his father. Few people do.

Vincent has been stewing in the cubicle for more than an hour when Garvey and Kincaid finally walk into the room and begin the monologue. Wadcutters in the soap dish, drug paraphernalia, jackknives, and your man Frazier's putting you in for both these murders. Deep shit, Vincent, deep shit. Five minutes of this talk produce the desired level of fear, ten minutes produce a completed rights form, signed and witnessed.

The detectives carry the form out of the room and confer briefly in the hall.

"Hey, Rich."

"Hmm?"

"That boy don't stand a chance," says Kincaid in a stage whisper. "You're wearing your power suit."

"That's right. I am."

Kincaid laughs.

"The dark blue pinstripe," says Garvey, lifting one lapel. "He won't know what the fuck hit him."

Kincaid shakes his head and gives Garvey's attire a last look. A Kentucky native, Donald Kincaid addresses the world in a loud, backwoods drawl and sports a tattoo of his initials above his left wrist. Garvey plays golf at Hilton Head and speaks of power suits; Kincaid trains hunting dogs and dreams of deer season in West Virginia. Same squad, different world.

"You want to have a go at him alone?" asks Kincaid as the two move back toward the interrogation room.

"Nah," says Garvey, "we'll gang-bang him."

Vincent Booker waits for the second round with his back against the near wall, his hands cupped in the folds of his sweatshirt. Kincaid takes the far seat, facing the kid. Garvey sits between the two, closer to Vincent's end of the table.

"Son, lemme tell you something," says Garvey in a tone that suggests the interrogation is already over. "You have one shot here. You can tell us what you know about these murders and we'll see what we can do. I know you're involved in some way, but I don't know how much, and the thing for you to think about is whether you want to become a witness or a defendant."

Vincent says nothing.

"Are you listening to me, Vincent? You better start thinking about every fucking thing I'm saying here because a lot of shit is going to be coming down."

Silence.

"Are you worried about Frazier? Listen to me, son, you better start worrying about yourself. Frazier's been in here already. He's trying to fuck you. He's telling us about you."

That gets it. Vincent looks up. "What's Frazier sayin'?"

"What do you think?" says Kincaid. "He's trying to put you in for these murders."

"I didn't . . ."

"Vincent, I don't believe this motherfucker Frazier," says Garvey. "Even if you're involved in one or the other, I don't believe you killed your father."

Garvey pushes his chair closer to Vincent's corner of the room and drops his voice to little more than a whisper. "Look, son, I'm just trying to give you a chance on this. But you've got to tell us the truth now and we'll see what we can do with that. You can be at the defense table, or you can be on the prosecution side. That's what we can do. We do a few favors now and then and we're doing you one right now. Are you smart enough to see that?"

Probably not, thinks Garvey. And so the two detectives begin to lay it out to young Vincent Booker. They remind him that his father and Lena were both shot with the same kind of ammunition, that both murder scenes are identical. They explain that right now, he's the only suspect who was known to both victims. After all, they ask him, what was your father to Robert Frazier?

At this, the boy looks up, puzzled, and Garvey stops talking long enough to reduce this abstraction to paper. On the back of a lined statement sheet, he draws one circle on the left-hand side of the page, then writes "Lena" inside the circle. On the right-hand side he draws a second circle with "Purnell Booker" written inside. Garvey then draws a third circle that intersects the circles of the two victims. Inside that third circle he writes "Vincent." It's a crude little creation, something any algebra teacher would know as a Venn Diagram, but it gets Garvey's point across.

"This is our case. Look at it," he says, pushing the sheet in front of the boy. "Lena and your father are killed by the same gun, and right now the only person who has any connection to both of the victims is Vincent Booker. You're right in the fuckin' middle of this thing. You think about that."

Vincent says nothing and the two detectives leave the room long enough to allow the geometry to sink in. Garvey lights a cigarette and watches through the one-way window in the door as Vincent holds the crudely drawn diagram to his face and traces the three circles with his finger. Garvey shakes his head, watching Vincent turn the diagram upside down, then right side up, then upside down again.

"Look at this fuckin' Einstein in here, will you?" he says to Kincaid. "He's about the dumbest motherfucker I ever seen."

"You ready?" says Kincaid.

"Yeah. Let's do it."

Vincent doesn't look up from the diagram when the door opens, but his body gives an involuntary shake when Garvey enters and immediately begins another rant, his voice louder this time. Vincent can no longer manage eye contact; he grows smaller, more vulnerable with each accusation, a bleeder in the corner of the shark tank. Garvey sees his opening.

"You've got a knot in your fuckin' stomach, don't you?" Garvey asks abruptly. "You're feeling like you're going to be sick. I've seen a hundred or so just like that in here."

"I seen 'em throw up," says Kincaid. "You ain't gonna throw up in here, are you?"

"No," says Vincent, shaking his head. He is sweating now, one hand clutching the end of the table, the other wrapped tight in the hem of his sweatshirt. Part of the sickness is the fear of being pegged for two murders; part is the fear of Robert Frazier. But the greater share of what's holding Vincent Booker on the precipice is a fear of his own family. Right here and now, Garvey can look at Vincent Booker and know, with even greater certainty than before, that there is no way this boy killed his father. He doesn't have that in him. Yet the bullets connect him to the crime, and his rapid reduction to a speechless wreck in less than an hour of interrogation testifies to guilty knowledge. Vincent Booker is no killer, but he played a role in the death of his father, or at the very least, he knew the murderer and said nothing. Either way, there is something that cannot be faced.

Sensing that the boy needs one more good shove, Garvey walks out of the interrogation room and grabs the plastic soap dish from Vincent's bedroom.

"Gimme one of these," he says, taking a .38 cartridge from the dish. "This motherfucker needs some show-and-tell."

Garvey walks back into the cubicle and deposits the .38 round in Kincaid's left hand. The older detective needs no further prompting; he stands the round on its end in the center of the table.

"See this here bullet?" Kincaid asks.

Vincent looks at the cartridge.

"This isn't your ordinary thirty-eight ammunition, is it? Now we can get them to type this for us at the FBI lab, and it usually takes 'em two or three months, but on a rush job they can have it back in two days. And they're gonna be able to tell us which box of fifty this bullet came from," says Kincaid, pushing the round slowly toward the boy. "So, you tell me, is it going to be just coincidence if the FBI says this bullet comes from the same box as the one that killed your daddy and Lena both? You tell me."

Vincent looks away, his hands clasped tightly in his lap. A perfect deceit: even if the FBI could narrow the .38 ammunition to the same manufacturer's lot number of a couple hundred thousand boxes or more, the process would probably take half a year.

"We're just trying to lay it out for you, son," says Garvey. "What do you think a judge is going to do with evidence like that?"

The boy is silent.

"Death penalty case, Vincent."

"And I'm gonna be the one to testify," adds Kincaid in his Kentucky drawl, " 'cause that's my thing."

"Death penalty?" asks Vincent, startled.

"No contest," says Kincaid.

"Honest, son, if you're lying to us . . ."

"Even if we let you leave here today," says Kincaid, "you'll never know the next time there's a knock on your door whether it's us coming back to lock you up."

"And we will come back," says Garvey, pulling his chair closer to Vincent. Wordlessly, he brings himself face-to-face with the boy, leaning forward until their eyes are less than a foot apart. Then, softly, he begins describing the murder of Purnell Booker. An argument, a brief struggle, perhaps, then the wounds. Garvey moves closer still to Vincent Booker and tells of the twenty or so blade wounds to the face; as he does so, he taps the boy's cheek lightly with his finger.

Vincent Booker sickens visibly.

"Get this off your chest, son," says Garvey. "What do you know about these murders?"

"I gave the bullets to Frazier."

"You gave him bullets?"

"He asked me for bullets . . . I gave him six."

The boy comes close to crying but quickly steadies himself, resting both elbows on the table and hiding his face behind his hands. "Why did Frazier ask for bullets?"

Vincent shrugs.

"Dammit, Vincent."

"I didn't . . ."

"You're holdin' back."

"I . . ."

"Get it off your chest, son. We're trying to help you to start over here. This'll be the only chance you're going to have to start over."

Vincent Booker breaks.

"My daddy . . ." he says.

"Why would Frazier kill your father?"

First he tells them about the drugs, the packaged cocaine that was in his room at his mother's house, ready for street sale. Then he tells about his father finding the dope and taking it away. He tells them about the argument, about how his father wouldn't listen and drove off to his apartment on Lafayette Avenue with the cocaine in the car. Vincent's cocaine. Frazier's cocaine.

He tells them about how he went to Denise's house on Amity Street to tell Frazier, to admit that he'd fucked up, to reveal that his father had stolen their dope. Frazier listened angrily, then asked for bullets, and Vincent, afraid to refuse, gave him six wadcutters that he had taken from the tobacco can on top of the bureau in his father's apartment. Frazier went alone to Lafayette Avenue, Vincent tells them.

He expected his father would be threatened, he tells them, just as he expected that Frazier would get back the drugs. He did not expect a murder, he says, and he does not know what happened at his father's apartment.

Shit on that, Garvey thinks as he listens to the story. We know damned well what happened. I know it, you know it, Kincaid here knows it. Robert Frazier showed up at your daddy's house wired tight on cocaine from Denise's party, armed with a loaded .38 and a short blade and desirous of some missing drugs. Your daddy must have told Frazier to go to hell.

That scenario explained the ransacking of Purnell Booker's apartment as well as the repeated superficial stab wounds to the old man's face. The torture was inflicted to make Purnell Booker talk; the ransacking suggested he didn't.

But why kill Lena that same night? And in the same way? Vincent claims no knowledge of that murder, and from everything he's learned, Garvey has no idea either. Maybe Frazier was led to believe that Lena was somehow involved in the missing drugs. Maybe she was dipping into some of the dope Frazier kept on Gilmor Street. Maybe she answered the door saying something Frazier didn't particularly like. Maybe the cocaine rush got good to Frazier and he just kept on killing. Maybe A and B, or B and C, or all of the above. Does it matter? Not to me, thinks Garvey. Not anymore.

"You were there, weren't you, Vincent? You went with Frazier to your father's."

Vincent shakes his head and looks away.

"I'm not saying you were involved in the murder, but you went there, didn't you?"

"No," the boy says, "I just gave him those bullets."

Bullshit, thinks Garvey. You were there when Robert Frazier killed your father. Why else would this be so hard? It's one thing to live in fear of a man like Frazier, another to be afraid of telling the truth to your own family. Garvey pushes the boy for a half hour or more, but it's no use; Vincent Booker has come as close to the cliff as he dares. It is, Garvey reasons, close enough.

"If you're holding out on us, Vincent . . ."

"No, I ain't."

" 'Cause you will go before a grand jury, and if you lie to them, it'll be the worst mistake you ever make."

"No, sir."

"All right. Now I'm gonna write this up and have you sign it as a statement," says Garvey. "We're gonna start at the beginning and go slow so I can write this down."

"Yes sir."

"What is your name?"

"Vincent Booker."

"Your date of birth . . ."

The official version, short and sweet. Garvey exhales softly and puts pen to paper.

Friday, March 11

With his right hand, Garvey pulls the .38 from his waist holster and drops it down against his trouser leg, shielding it from view.

"Frazier, open up."

The uniform closest to the detective motions toward the front door of the Amity Street rowhouse.

"Kick it?" he asks.

Garvey shakes his head. No need. "Frazier, open the door."

"Who is it?"

"Detective Garvey. I got to ask you a couple questions."

"Now?" says a voice behind the door. "I got to—"

"Yeah, now. Open the damn door."

The door opens halfway and Garvey slips through, the gun still tight against his thigh.

"What's up," says Frazier, stepping back.

Suddenly, Garvey brings the snubnose up to the left side of the man's face. Frazier looks at the black hole of the barrel, then back at Garvey strangely, squinting through a cocaine haze.

"Get the fuck up against that wall."

"Wha . . ."

"MOVE, MOTHERFUCKER. AGAINST THAT FUCKING WALL BEFORE I BLOW YOUR FUCKIN' HEAD OFF."

Kincaid and two uniforms follow Garvey through the opening as Frazier is shoved roughly against a living room wall. Kincaid and the younger uniform check the back rooms as the older patrolman, a veteran of the Western, cocks his own weapon against Frazier's right ear.

"Move," says the uniform, "and your brains are on the floor."

Christ, thinks Garvey, staring at the cocked weapon, if that bad boy goes off we'll all be writing reports for the rest of our careers. But the threat works: Frazier stops bucking and leans into the plasterboard. The uniform uncocks and reholsters his .38 and Garvey once again begins to breathe air.

"What's this about?" says Frazier, working hard to approximate a picture of innocent confusion.

"What do you think it's about?"

Frazier says nothing.

"What do you think, Frazier?"

"I don't know."

"Murder. You're charged with murder."

"Who'd I murder?"

Garvey smiles. "You killed Lena. And the old man, Booker."

Frazier shakes his head violently as Howe opens one ring of his handcuffs and pulls Frazier's right arm off the wall. Suddenly, at the first touch of the metal bracelet, Frazier begins to buck again, pushing away from the wall and pulling his arm away from Howe. With surprising speed, Garvey moves a step and a half across the living room and lands a punch hard against Frazier's face.

The suspect looks up, stunned.

"What was that for?" he asks Garvey.

For a second or two, Garvey lets himself think about the question. The official answer, the one required for the reports, is that this detective was required to subdue a homicide suspect who attempted to resist arrest. The righteous answer, the one that is soon lost to any detective with time on the street, is that the suspect was struck because he is a cold-blooded piece of shit, a murderous bastard who in a single evening took the lives of an old man and a mother of two. But Garvey's own answer falls somewhere in between.

"That," he tells Frazier, "is for lying to me, motherfucker." Lying. To a detective. In the first degree.

Frazier says nothing more, offering no resistance as Howe and Kincaid guide him to the sofa, where he sits with his hands cuffed behind him. On the off chance that Frazier's .38 might be lying around, the detectives do a quick, plain-view search of the apartment. The murder weapon remains unaccounted for, but on the kitchen table is a night's work for Robert Frazier: a small amount of rock cocaine, quinine cut, a couple dozen glassine bags, three syringes.

The detectives look at the uniforms and the uniforms look at each other.

"You guys want to take it?" asks the younger uniform.

"Nah," says Garvey. "We're charging him with two murders. Besides, we don't have a warrant for this place."

"Hey," says the patrolman, "fine by me."

They leave it on the kitchen table, a West Baltimore still life waiting for the successor to Frazier's squalid, street-corner business. Garvey walks back into the living room and asks the younger uniform to radio for a wagon. Frazier finds his voice again.

"Officer Garvey, I didn't lie to you."

Garvey smiles.

"You ain't never told the truth," says Kincaid. "You ain't got the truth in you."

"I ain't lyin'."

"Sheeeet," says Kincaid, pushing the word to two and a half syllables. "You ain't got the truth in you, son."

"Hey, Frazier," says Garvey, smiling, "remember how you promised to bring me that thirty-eight? What ever happened to that gun anyway?"

"That's right," says Kincaid, picking up on it. "If you're so fuckin' honest, how come you never brought that gun in for us?"

Frazier says nothing.

"You ain't got the truth in you, son," says Kincaid again. "No sir. It ain't in you."

Frazier simply shakes his head, seeming to gather his thoughts for a moment or two. Then he looks up at Garvey, genuinely curious. "Officer Garvey," he asks, "am I the only one charged?"

The only one. If ever Garvey wondered whether Vincent Booker had anything to do with these murders, that utterance alone was enough to answer the question.

"Yeah, Frazier. You're it."

Vincent was involved, no doubt about it. But Vincent wasn't the triggerman—not for Lena, not for his father. And in the end, it was a hell of a lot better to keep Vincent Booker as a witness than give him a charge and let Frazier use him in front of a jury. Garvey saw no point in providing Frazier's attorney with an alternative suspect, a living, breathing piece of reasonable doubt. No, thought Garvey, for once they had told the truth in the interrogation room: You can either be a witness or a suspect, Vincent. One or the other.

Vincent Booker gave it up—or at least gave as much of it as he dared—and went home as a result. Robert Frazier lied his ass off and now he's going to the Western District lockup. In Garvey's mind, there is a certain symmetry to all this.

At the booking desk of the Western, the contents of Frazier's pockets are arrayed on the counter, then catalogued by the desk sergeant. From a front pocket comes a thick roll of drug money.

"Christ," says the sergeant, "there's more than fifteen hundred dollars here."

"Big fuckin' deal," says Garvey. "I make that in a week."

Kincaid shoots Garvey a look. The governor, the mayor and half of the British royal family would have to be bludgeoned to death in the men's room of the Fayette Street bus station before a Baltimore detective would see that kind of money. The desk sergeant understands.

"Yeah," he tells Garvey, loud enough for Frazier to hear. "And you didn't have to sell no dope for your paycheck, did you?"

Garvey nods.

"Officer Garvey . . ."

"Hey, Donald," says Garvey to Kincaid. "How 'bout I buy you a beer."

"Officer Garvey . . ."

"I might just have one tonight," says Kincaid. "I might just take you up on that."

"Officer Garvey, I ain't lied to you."

Garvey wheels around, but the turnkey is leading Frazier toward the rear cage door of the Western lockup.

"Officer Garvey, I ain't lied."

Garvey looks impassively at his suspect. "Bye, Frazier. See you 'round."

For a few moments, Robert Frazier is framed by the cage door, waiting at the edge of the lockup as the turnkey prepares a fingerprint card.

Garvey finishes playing with the paperwork on the booking desk and walks toward the back door of the station house. He glides past the lockup without looking inside, and so doesn't see the final, unmistakable expression on Robert Frazier's face.

Pure, murderous hate.

FIVE

Saturday, April 2

A detective's prayer: Blessed be the truly unwise, for they bring hope to those obligated to pursue them. Blessed be those of dim understanding, for by their very ignorance they bring light to those who labor in darkness. Blessed be Dennis Wahls, for though he believes otherwise, he is cooperating fully in the campaign to put him in prison for the month-old murder of Karen Renee Smith, the cab driver beaten to death in Northwest Baltimore.

"This house right here?" says Eddie Brown.

"Next one."

Brown nods and Wahls tries to open the back door of the Cavalier. The detective, sitting next to him in the rear seat, reaches over and pulls the door shut. Harris, one of the officers assigned to the Northwest detail, walks from his own car to Brown's window.

"We'll stay here," says Brown. "You and Sergeant Nolan go up and get him to come out."

Harris nods, then walks with Roger Nolan to the front of the red brick building. The Madison Avenue address is a downtown group home for those charged with delinquency, which in Baltimore means anything up to and including armed robbery and manslaughter. Inside that home is Dennis Wahls's younger brother, on whose person is a wristwatch that belonged to Karen Smith.

"How do you know he still has the watch?" asks Brown as he watches Nolan and the detail officer make their way up the front steps.

"I saw him yesterday and he had it then," says Wahls.

Thank God, thinks Brown. Thank God they're so stupid. If they were smart, if they regarded murder as a secret and heinous act, if they told no one, if they got rid of the clothing and the weapon and the possessions taken from the victim, if they refused to listen to bullshit in the interrogation rooms, what the hell would a detective do?

"This is giving me a headache," says Wahls.

Brown nods.

"I'm going to need a lift home after we get finished with this."

A lift home. This kid actually thinks he's going to go home and sleep it off, as if it were some kind of hangover. O. B. McCarter, another detail officer from the Southwest, bites his tongue in the driver's seat, trying hard not to laugh.

"You think you all could get me a lift home?"

"We'll see what happens," says Brown.

What happens is this: The younger brother of Dennis Wahls, a fourteen-year-old urchin with twice the sense of his sibling, comes out of the group home and is escorted to the side of the Chevrolet. He looks into the car, looks at his brother, looks at Eddie Brown and manages to assess the situation for what it really is. He nods.

"Hey," says Dennis Wahls.

"Hey," says his brother.

"I told them about the watch—"

"What watch?"

"Hey," Brown interrupts. "Your ass is going to be in this if you don't listen to your brother."

"Man, c'mon," says Dennis Wahls. "You got to give it up. They gonna let me go if you give it to him. If you don't, they gonna put a murder charge on me."

"Hmm," says the kid, obviously wondering how this can be. If they don't get the evidence, they charge you, but if they get the evidence, you go free. Yeah. Right.

"Go on," says Roger Nolan, standing beside the car.

The boy looks at his brother. Dennis Wahls nods and the young boy races back into the red brick building, returning three minutes later with a woman's timepiece on a black leather band. The boy tries to hand the watch to his brother, but Brown interjects his own hand. The boy takes a step away from the car.

"See you soon, yo," says Dennis Wahls.

The boy nods again.

They proceed to Reservoir Hill, where the two cars pull to the curb outside the Section 8 housing on Lennox Avenue. Again Brown and Wahls wait in the Cavalier; this time, Nolan pays a visit to Wahls's young girlfriend, who received a gift of Karen Smith's gold necklace.

In the driver's seat, McCarter plays with the radio. Eddie Brown, still in the back seat with his prisoner, watches Nolan bullshitting with the girlfriend's mother in the project parking lot. When Nolan gets wound up, he can talk your ear off.

"C'mon, Roger," mutters Brown. "What the fuck are you doing there anyway?"

A minute or two more and the girl returns from her apartment with the jewelry, walking across the lot to Nolan waving nervously at Wahls, who is peering out the rear passenger window.

"Man, I wish she hadn't seen me like this."

The detective grunts.

"Her momma's gonna be upset with me now."

McCarter pushes the radio buttons until rock 'n' roll spills out in a crackling AM static: the Bobby Fuller Four from about a dozen years back. The detail officer listens to the song for a moment; suddenly, he's dying in the front seat, trying hard not to laugh aloud.

"Oh man," says McCarter.

"Breakin' rocks in the hot sun . . ."

McCarter starts snapping two fingers, mugging for Brown and Harris, who is standing at the driver's window.

". . . I fought the law and the law won."

Brown steals a look at Wahls, but the kid is oblivious.

"Robbin' people with a six-gun . . ."

McCarter keeps time on the steering wheel.

". . . I fought the law and the law won."

"Can you believe it?" says McCarter.

"Believe what?" asks Wahls.

McCarter shakes his head. On the night when he has greatest need of a functioning mind, Dennis Wahls is suddenly struck deaf, dumb and blind. The radio could be playing back his own confession and he wouldn't notice.

Which is not to say that Wahls, at the age of nineteen, has a deep reservoir of intelligence from which to draw. First of all, he let some other brain-dead talk him into killing a woman cabbie for a few dollars and some jewelry, and then he settled for the jewelry, letting his partner keep the cash. Next, he gave away the jewelry and began bragging about being right there when the woman was pulled into the woods and beaten to death. He didn't kill her, no sir. He watched.

The first few people within earshot didn't believe it; either that or they didn't much care. But eventually some young thing that Dennis Wahls tried hard to impress went to school and told a friend, who told someone else, who finally decided that maybe some sort of authority figure ought to hear about it. And when line 2100 lit up in the homicide unit, Rick James was there to take the call.

"I did one thing right in this whole investigation," James, the primary for the Smith murder, will later declare. "I picked up the phone."

In truth, he did a lot more than that. With the detail officers to help him, James ran down every lead that came in, checking and rechecking the stories provided by Karen Smith's coworkers, boyfriends and relatives. He spent days going over the cab company's service logs, looking for fares or locations that seemed out of the ordinary. He sat at his desk for hours, listening to tapes of the cab dispatcher's calls, trying to pick up a location where Karen Smith may have gone before she disappeared into the woods of Northwest Baltimore. He checked every recent robbery or assault report involving a taxi driver anywhere in the city or county, as well as the robbery reports from anywhere close to the Northwest. When he found out that one of the victim's boyfriends had a cocaine habit, he went at him hard in a series of interviews. The alibi was checked. The boyfriend's acquaintances were all interviewed. Then they brought the man downtown and went at him again: Things weren't so good between you two, right? She made a lot of money, didn't she? You spend a lot of money, don't you?

Even Donald Worden, as harsh a judge of the younger detectives as any, was impressed with his partner's effort.

"James is learning," Worden said, watching the case from a distance, "what it means to be a detective."

Rick James did everything conceivable to solve the case, yet when the phone finally rang, the two binders of office reports from the cabbie killing contained not a single mention of Dennis Frank Wahls. Nor was Clinton Butler, the twenty-two-year-old wonder who conceived the slaying and struck the fatal blow, a name in the file. There was nothing new to that kind of twist, no lesson to be learned by the detective. It was merely a textbook example of Rule Five in the homicide lexicon, which states:

It's good to be good; it's better to be lucky.

James was actually on his way to the airport, waiting for a morning flight and a week's vacation, when detectives finally located Wahls and brought him downtown. Wahls gave up the murder in little more than an hour of interrogation, during which Eddie Brown and two detail officers offered him the most obvious out. You didn't hit her; Clinton did, they assured him, and Wahls went for the whole apple. No sir, he didn't even want to do the robbery. That was Clinton's idea, and Clinton called him names when he didn't initially agree. He didn't even get any of the money; Clinton took that, arguing that he was the one who had done all the work, leaving Wahls only the jewelry. After she fainted from fear, it was Clinton who dragged the cabbie out of her taxi and down the wooded path, Clinton who found the tree branch, Clinton who challenged him to do it, then teased him when he did not. So it was Clinton Butler who finally smashed the wooden limb against the woman's head.

In the end, the only thing that Wahls would admit was that it was he, not Clinton, who pulled off the woman's pants and attempted oral sex with their unconscious victim. Clinton was homosexual, Wahls assured the detectives. He didn't want none of that.

When Wahls had signed and initialed the statement, the detectives asked about the jewelry. We believe what you're telling us, Brown said, but we need a show of good faith. Something that proves you're telling us the truth. And Wahls nodded his understanding, suddenly confident that the return of the dead woman's watch and necklace would buy his freedom.

Solved by chance rather than perseverance, the Karen Smith case was as much a message for Tom Pellegrini as anything else. Just as he was replaying the Latonya Wallace murder in his mind like a tape loop, James had lost himself in the details of the cabbie slaying. And to what end? Sweat and logic can solve a case in those precious days that follow a murder, but after that, who the hell knows? Sometimes a late phone call can break a case. Sometimes a fresh connection to another crime—a ballistics match or print hit—can change the outcome. More often, however, a case that stays open a month will stay open forever. Of the six female slayings that provoked the department brass to create the Northwest detail, the Karen Smith case would be only one of two to end in arrest and the only case to reach trial. By the end of March, the detail officers in the other five cases had returned to their districts; the case files were back in the cabinets—a little thicker than before, perhaps, but no better for all the effort.

But Pellegrini has no time for any lesson offered by the Northwest cases. He spends the night of Dennis Wahls's confession handling shooting calls and rereading portions of the Latonya Wallace office reports. In fact, he is out on a call when they bring Wahls back into the homicide unit and begin typing the warrant for Clinton Butler. And he is long gone in the early hours of the morning when Eddie Brown, flush with the victory, sends the recovered jewelry down to the ECU and offers up for bid the opportunity to tell Dennis Wahls that he, too, will be charged with first-degree murder.

"Hey," says Brown, standing at the interrogation room door, "someone's got to go in there and tell this fool he ain't leaving. He's still asking about a ride home."

"Let me do it," says McCarter, smiling.

"Go 'head."

McCarter walks into the large interrogation room and closes the door. From the wire mesh window, the scene becomes a perfect pantomime: McCarter's mouth moving, his hands on his hips. Wahls, shaking his head, crying, pleading. McCarter waving one arm in the air, reaching for the door handle, smiling, turning back into the hallway.

"Ignorant motherfucker," he says, closing the door behind him.

TUESDAY, APRIL 5

Two months after the murder of Latonya Wallace, only Tom Pellegrini remains.

Harry Edgerton, the secondary investigator, left to help Bertina Silver pursue another interrogation of his best suspect in the January murder of Brenda Thompson, the woman found stabbed in the car on Garrison Boulevard. Eddie Brown was swallowed up by the sudden break in the Karen Smith case and has now moved on to fresh murders. And Jay Landsman, as much an investigator on the Latonya Wallace murder as any of them, he's gone too. No one expected otherwise: Landsman has a squad to run, and come the next three weeks of nightwork, all of his detectives are working a fresh spate of murders.

The detail men are also gone, back to the tactical section or to the district commanders who loaned them to homicide for the murder of a little girl. First the tac units were sent down, then the youth section detectives, then the Central men, and then, finally, the two plainclothesmen on loan from Southern District operations. Slowly, inexorably, the Latonya Wallace investigation has become the exclusive preserve of one detective.

Beached by the ebbing tide, Pellegrini sits at his desk in the annex office, surrounded by three cardboard crates of office reports and photographs, lab examinations and witness statements. Against the wall behind his desk is the bulletin board that the men on the detail created but never found the time to hang on a wall. Pinned to its center is the best and most recent photograph of the child. On the left is Edgerton's rooftop diagram of Newington Avenue. On the right, a map of the Reservoir Hill area and a series of aerial photographs taken from the police helicopter.

On this dayshift as on two dozen others, Pellegrini moves slowly through one of the bound case folders, reading reports that are weeks old, searching for any loose fragment of information that he failed to digest the first time around. Some of the reports are his own, others are signed by Edgerton or Eddie Brown, Landsman or the detail men. That's the trouble with the red-ball treatment, Pellegrini tells himself, scanning one typewritten page after another. By virtue of their importance, red balls have the potential to become David O. Selznick productions, four-star departmental clusterfucks beyond the control of any single investigator. From almost the moment the body was found, the Latonya Wallace case became the property of the entire police department, until door-to-door canvasses were being done by patrolmen and witness statements were being taken by detail officers with no more than a few days' experience in death investigation. Knowledge of the case file was soon scattered among two dozen people.

On one level, Pellegrini accepts the logic of unlimited manpower. In the weeks after the little girl's murder, the red-ball express made it possible to cover the longest piece of ground in the shortest stretch of time. By the end of February, the men on the detail had twice canvassed a three-block radius from the crime scene, had interviewed nearly two hundred people, had executed warrants for three addresses and had done walk-through consent searches in every rowhouse on the north side of Newington Avenue. But now, the paperwork from that massive campaign has congealed on Pellegrini's desk. The witness statements alone fill one file, while information about the Fish Man—still the best suspect—is relegated to a manila folder all its own.

Leaning forward in his chair, Pellegrini looks through the scene photos for what must be the three hundredth time. The same child stares out across the rainy pavement with that same lost look. Her arm is still extended in that same reaching motion, palm open, fingers slightly curled.

For Tom Pellegrini, the 3-by-5 color shots no longer produce anything that remotely resembles an emotion. In fact, he concedes to himself, they never really did. In some strange way that only a homicide detective can understand, Pellegrini psychologically stepped away from his victim at the very outset. It was not a conscious decision; it was more the absence of a decision. In some elemental, almost preordained way, the switch in his mind was thrown when he walked into that yard behind Newington Avenue.

The detachment came naturally enough, and Pellegrini still has no reason to question it. If he did, the easy answer would be that a detective can only function properly by accepting the most appalling tragedies on a clinical level. On that basis, the sight of a young child sprawled across the pavement—her torso gutted, her neck contorted—becomes, after an initial moment of shock, a matter of evidence. A good investigator, leaning over a fresh obscenity, doesn't waste time and effort battering himself with theological questions about the nature of evil and man's inhumanity to man. He wonders instead whether the jagged wound pattern is the result of a serrated blade, or whether the discoloration on the underside of the leg is indeed an indication of lividity.

On the surface, that professional ethos is part of what keeps any detective from the horror, but Pellegrini knows there is something more to it, something that has to do with the act of bearing witness. After all, he never knew the little girl. He never knew her family. Most important, perhaps, he never really felt their loss. On the day the body was found, Pellegrini left the crime scene to go directly to the ME's offices, where the autopsy of a little girl demanded the most clinical kind of mind-set. It was Edgerton who told the mother, who watched the family suddenly dissolve in anguish, who represented the homicide unit at the funeral. Since then, Pellegrini had spoken to members of the Wallace family on occasion, but only about details. At those moments, the survivors were both helpful and numb, their pain no longer apparent to a visiting detective. That Pellegrini had not borne witness to their grief somehow kept him from truly seeing the photographs in front of him.

And maybe, Pellegrini concedes, maybe there was distance because he was white and the little girl was black. It made the slaying no less a crime, Pellegrini knew, but it was in some way a crime of the city, of Reservoir Hill's ghetto, of a world to which he had no ties. Pellegrini could try to make himself believe that Latonya Wallace could have been his little girl, or Landsman's, or McLarney's, but the distinctions of race and class were always there, unspoken but acknowledged. Hell, for the past year and a half Pellegrini has listened to his sergeant say as much at dozens of ghetto crime scenes.

"Hey, it don't matter to me," Landsman would tell the locals when witnesses refused to come forward. "I don't live around here."

Well, it was true; Pellegrini didn't live in Reservoir Hill. Given that distance, he can tell himself that as an investigator, his interest is limited to that of the technician. From that view, the death of Latonya Wallace is nothing more or less than a crime, a singular event that with two beers and a warm dinner will seem a universe away from a brick ranch house, a wife and two children in the Anne Arundel suburbs south of the city.

Once, talking with Eddie Brown about the case, Pellegrini actually caught hold of his own detachment. He and Brown had been bouncing theories back and forth when the strangest word slipped out, falling like a brick on the conversation.

"She had to know this guy in the first place, we know that much. I think this broad . . ."

This broad. Pellegrini stopped almost immediately, then began searching for some other word.

". . . this girl let her killer take her off the street because she knew him from somewhere else."

Pellegrini's sergeant was no different, of course. When one of the detail officers was looking at scene photos and asking questions, Landsman suddenly slipped into his standard deadpan.

"Who found her?" the detail officer asked.

"Post officer from the Central."

"Did the guy rape her?"

"The officer?" asked Landsman, feigning confusion. "Um, I don't think so. Maybe. We didn't ask him 'cause we figured the guy who killed her did that."

In any other world, the comedy would be appalling. But this is the annex office of CID homicide in the city of Baltimore, where everyone—Pellegrini included—manages to laugh at the cruelest kind of humor.

In his heart, Pellegrini knows that solving the Latonya Wallace case will not be a response to the death of a young girl as much as a matter of personal vindication. His obsession is not with the victim but with the victimizer. A child—any child—had been murdered on a February dayshift and, as the man who took the call, Pellegrini accepted the murder as a professional challenge. If the Latonya Wallace case goes down, then a child-killer has been beaten. The alibis, the deceit, the hiding—all of it means nothing at the point of arrest. At the sweet instant that those metal bracelets click, Pellegrini will know he has truly arrived, that he is—like any other man in that unit—worth a detective's shield and 120 hours of paid overtime. But if the case stays open, if somewhere in this world the killer lives to know he has beaten the detective, then Pellegrini will never be quite the same. Watching him sink into the case files day after day, the other men in the unit know that.

For the first month of the investigation, he had come as close to working around the clock as possible: sixteen hours a day, seven days a week. Sometimes he left for work with the sudden awareness that for several days running, he had come home only to sleep and shower, that he hadn't really spoken to his wife or enjoyed the new baby. Christopher had been born in December, the second son in three years, but Pellegrini had done little to help with the child in the last two months. He felt guilty about that, but a little bit relieved as well. At least the infant kept his wife occupied; Brenda had every right to insist on something more than an absentee husband, but so far, between feedings and diapers and everything else, little had been said.

His wife knew he was working the Latonya Wallace case, and somehow, in a year's time, she had accustomed herself to a detective's hours. In fact, the whole household seemed to revolve around the little girl. Once, as Pellegrini was walking out the door on a Saturday morning, heading downtown for the third consecutive weekend, his older boy ran up to him.

"Play with me," Michael said.

"I have to go to work."

"You're working on Latonya Wallace," the three-year-old said.

By the middle of March, Pellegrini saw his health begin to suffer. He coughed in fits: a deep, rasping hack, worse than his usual smoker's wheeze, and it stayed with him through the day. At first he blamed the cigarettes; later, he complained about the aging ventilation system in the headquarters building. The other detectives were quick to join in: Never mind the cigarettes, they told him, the asbestos fibers set loose by cracking acoustic tile were enough to kill a man.

"Don't worry, Tom," Garvey told him after one morning roll call. "I hear that cancer you get from breathing asbestos is slow and lingering. You'll have plenty of time to work the case."

Pellegrini tried to laugh, but a thin wheeze gave way to the hacking. Two weeks later, he was still coughing. Worse, he was having trouble getting out of bed and more trouble staying awake at the office. No matter how much he slept, he managed to wake up exhausted. A short visit to the doctor yielded no obvious reasons, and the other detectives, armchair psychiatrists one and all, were quick to blame the Latonya Wallace file.

Veterans on the shift told him to forget the goddamn thing, to get back in the rotation and pick up a fresh murder. But the cutting in the Southeast only pissed him off—all that argument and aggravation just to prove that some Perkins Homes dope dealer cut up a customer over $20. Likewise that dunker from the Civic Center, the one where the maintenance employee responded to complaints about his tardiness by killing his boss.

"Yeah, I stabbed him," the guy says, covered with the victim's blood. "He hit me first."

Christ.

A little girl has been raped and killed and the detective charged with solving the crime is in some other part of the city putting handcuffs on the most mindless shitbirds. No, Pellegrini tells himself, the cure is not the next case, or the next case after that.

The cure is on his desk.

As the dayshift ends and the rest of D'Addario's detectives drift toward the elevators, Pellegrini stays put in the annex office, turning the stack of color photos in his hand and scanning the collection one more time.

What has he missed? What has been lost? What is still waiting for him up on Newington Avenue?

Holding one of the straight-on photographs of the body, Pellegrini stares at a thin metal rod resting on the sidewalk a few feet from the child's head. It isn't the first time he's looked at that metal rod and it won't be the last. To Pellegrini, that particular detail has come to symbolize everything that has gone wrong with the case.

Pellegrini noticed the metal rod almost immediately after the photographs came upstairs from the crime lab, two days after the body was discovered. There was no doubt about it: the metal rod in the picture was the same one that Garvey had recovered during the trainees' second-day search on Newington Avenue. When Garvey pulled the tubing out of that rear yard, it still carried a hair and a clot of coagulated blood—blood that had since been matched to the victim. Yet the day the body was found, the metal tubing had somehow been overlooked.

Pellegrini remembers that morning at the scene and the vague premonition that warned him to slow everything down. He remembers that moment when the ME's people came for the body and asked if everyone was ready. Yeah, they were ready. They had walked every inch of that yard and checked every detail twice. So what is that goddamn piece of metal doing in the photographs? And how the hell had they missed it in those early hours?

Not that Pellegrini has any idea what the metal tubing has to do with his murder. Maybe it was dumped there with the body. Maybe it was used by the killer, perhaps to simulate sexual intercourse. That would explain the blood and hair, as well as the vaginal tearing discovered at autopsy. Or maybe the damn thing was lying in the yard earlier, jetsam from a broken television stand or curling iron that somehow got mixed up in his crime scene. Perhaps the blood and hair were swept into the tube when the old man came out to clean his yard after the body was removed. There was no way of knowing, but the fact that a piece of evidence had not been noticed for twenty-four hours was unnerving. What else had they missed?

Pellegrini reads further into the case file, reviewing some of the reports from the canvass of the 700 block. Some of the interviews seemed to have been carefully performed, with detectives or detail men asking follow-up questions or encouraging witnesses to elaborate on answers. Others, however, seem perfunctory and halfhearted, as if the officer involved had already convinced himself that the interview was a wasted effort.

Pellegrini reads the reports and thinks of questions that could have been asked, should have been asked, in those first days, when memories are fresh. A neighbor says she doesn't know anything about the murder. Fine, but does she remember any noise in the alley that night? Voices? Cries? Automobile sounds? Car headlights? Nothing that night? What about in the past? Any problems with anyone in the neighborhood? You've got a couple of people living nearby that make you nervous, right? Why's that? Did your children ever have any problems with these people? Who don't you want them going near?

Pellegrini includes himself in this critical assessment. There are things he wished he had done in those early days. For example, the pickup truck that the Fish Man used the week of the murder to carry junk from his burned-out store—why hadn't they taken a better look at that vehicle? Too quickly they had bought into the argument that the little girl had been carried into the alley, presumably by someone traveling no more than a block. But what if the Fish Man had done the murder up on Whitelock Street? That was too far away to carry the body, but it was the same week that he had access to a neighbor's truck. And what might a careful search of the truck have yielded? Hairs? Fibers? The same tarlike substance that stained the little girl's pants?

Landsman had left the investigation believing that the Fish Man was not the killer, that they would have broken the store owner in the long interrogation if he were indeed their man. Pellegrini still isn't sure. For one thing, the Fish Man's story has too many inconsistencies and not enough alibi—a combination sure to keep a man on any detective's list. And then, five days ago, he had blown his polygraph.

They performed the lie detector test at the State Police barracks in Pikesville—their first opportunity to schedule it since the investigation had centered on the store owner. Incredibly, the Baltimore department did not have a qualified polygraph examiner of its own; although it handled close to half the homicide investigations in Maryland, the BPD had to rely on the State Police to accommodate its cases on an ad hoc basis. Once the test had been scheduled, they needed to find the Fish Man and convince him to take the examination voluntarily. In a manner as convenient as it was coercive, this was accomplished by locking the old man up on an outstanding marital support warrant—now several years old—that Pellegrini had discovered in the computer. The warrant had never been served and the legal issue was very likely moot; nonetheless, the Fish Man was soon in police custody. And once a man lands at City Jail, even a lie detector test begins to seem like a reasonable diversion.

At the State Police barracks, the Fish Man proceeded to blow the box, sending the polygraph needle soaring on every key question about the murder. The polygraph result was not, of course, admissible as evidence, nor did every homicide detective believe in lie detection as an exact science. Still, the result added to Pellegrini's suspicions.

So, too, did the arrival of an unexpected, if not entirely credible, witness. The man was a smokehound all right, as unbelievable a character as a detective might find. Arrested for assault in the Western District six days ago, he tried to make friends by assuring the booking officer that he knew who killed Latonya Wallace.

"And how do you know that?"

"He told me he did it."

When Pellegrini got to the Western District that day, he heard a story about two old acquaintances drinking at a west side bar, about one acquaintance saying that he had recently been picked up and questioned for the murder of a little girl, about the other acquaintance asking whether he had committed the crime.

"No," the first man said.

But later in the conversation the liquor got good to that man, who turned to his companion and said he would tell the truth. He did kill the child.

In the course of several interviews, the new witness related the same story to the detectives. He had known the man with whom he had been drinking for years. The man ran a store up on Whitelock Street, a fish store.

And so a second polygraph was scheduled for the day after tomorrow. Leaning back in his chair, Pellegrini reads the reports of the new witness's interrogation with a mind balanced between serene hope and committed pessimism. In two days, he is sure, the man will also blow his box, failing the polygraph just as miserably as the Fish Man did. He will do this because his story is so perfect, so valuable, that it can't possibly be true. A barroom confession, Pellegrini tells himself, is almost too easy for this case.

Pellegrini knows, too, that soon he will have a separate suspect file on the new witness as well. Not only because the willingness to implicate someone in a child killing is unusual behavior, but also because the new man himself knows the Reservoir Hill area and has a police record. For rape. With a knife. Nothing, Pellegrini tells himself again, is ever easy.

Closing the file with the office reports, Pellegrini reads through a draft report of his own, a four-page missive to the captain outlining the status of the case and arguing for a complete, prolonged review of the existing evidence. Without any primary crime scene or physical evidence, the report argued, there wasn't much point in looking at any particular suspect and then attempting to connect him to the murder.

"This tactic might be successful in certain circumstances," Pellegrini had written, "but not in a case where physical evidence is lacking."

Instead, the memo urged a careful review of the entire file:

> Since the collection of that data was accomplished by no less than twenty detail officers and detectives, it is reasonable to believe that a significant piece of information may exist, but has not yet been developed. It is the intent of your investigator to limit the number of investigators to the primary and secondary detectives.

In simple terms, Pellegrini wants more time to work the case and he wants to work it alone. His report to the captain is clear, yet bureaucratic; generally succinct, yet written in the departmental prose that makes anyone with a rank higher than lieutenant feel warm and fuzzy all over. Still, it could be better, and if he is going to get the time to review the case properly, the captain will have to be on board.

Pellegrini pulls the staple from the top page and spreads the draft on his desk, prepared to spend another hour or so at the typewriter. But Rick Requer has other ideas. On his way out of the annex office, he catches Pellegrini's attention and cups his hand to his mouth in a repetitive, arclike motion—the international hand signal for uninhibited alcohol consumption.

"C'mon, bunk, let's go have a couple."

"You leaving?" asks Pellegrini, looking up from the file.

"Yeah, I'm out of here. Barrick's squad is already in on four-to-twelve."

Pellegrini shakes his head, then waves at the sea of paper on his desk. "I got some stuff here I wanted to go through."

"You working over on that case?" asks Requer. "It'll wait 'til tomorrow, won't it?"

Pellegrini shrugs.

"C'mon, Tom, give it a night off."

"I don't know. Where you going to be?"

"At the Market. Eddie Brown and Dunnigan are already down there."

Pellegrini nods, mulling it over. "If I get a few things done," he says finally, "I might see you down there."

No way, thinks Requer, walking toward the elevators. No way are we going to see Tom Pellegrini at the Market Bar when he could just as easily spend four hours beating himself up over Latonya Wallace. So when Pellegrini sidles up to the bar a half hour later, Requer is momentarily startled. Suddenly, without warning, Pellegrini has let go of the Case Without Pity and come up for a little air. By any reckoning, a drinking session at the Market Bar is a fine time and place for some back slapping and confidence building; Requer, already half-smoked on good Scotch, is just the man for the job.

"My man Tom," Requer says. "What are you drinking, bunk?"

"A beer."

"Hey, Nick, gave this gentleman what he wants on me, man."

"What're you drinking there?" asks Pellegrini.

"Glenlivet. Good shit. You want one?"

"No. Beer's fine."

And so they settle down, one round after another, until other detectives arrive and the scene photos and witness statements and office reports seem a little less real, and Latonya Wallace becomes more cosmic joke than tragedy. Sisyphus and his rock. De Leon and his fountain. Pellegrini and his little dead girl.

"I'll tell you this," says Requer, holding court and bringing the liquor to his lips. "When Tom first got up there, I thought he wasn't any good at all. I mean that . . ."

"And now that you seen me work," says Pellegrini, half serious, "you know you were right."

"No, bunk," says Requer, shaking his head, "I knew you were all right when you put down that case in the projects. What was that boy's name?"

"Which case?"

"The one from high-rise. East side."

"George Green," says Pellegrini.

"Yeah, right, Green," agrees Requer, waving the empty shot glass in a brief semaphore at Nicky the bartender. "Everyone told him that the case was a loser. I even told him that. I told him to . . ." Requer pauses as Nicky pours, downs half the shot and tries to continue. "What was I sayin'?"

Pellegrini shrugs, smiling.

"Oh yeah, this case was no fuckin' good, no fuckin' good at all. Drug murder up in the high-rises, right. Black kid over on Aisquith Street, so nobody's gonna give a damn anyway. No witnesses, no nothing. I told him to forget the motherfucker and go on to something else. He doesn't listen to me or anyone else. Stubborn motherfucker didn't listen to Jay neither. He just goes out on his own and works the case for two days. Didn't listen to none of us and guess what happened?"

"I dunno," says Pellegrini sheepishly. "What happened?"

"You solved the motherfucker."

"I did?"

"Stop fuckin' with me," says Requer, turning back to an audience of CID detectives. "He went out and solved the motherfucker on his own. That's when I knew Tom was going to work out."

Pellegrini says nothing, embarrassed.

Requer gives a quick glance over his shoulder and realizes that even with half a drink on, the younger detective isn't buying any of it.

"No, seriously, Tom, seriously."

"Seriously?"

"Seriously. Listen to me."

Pellegrini sips his beer.

"Fuck it, I'm not sayin' this 'cause you're here, bunk. I'm sayin' it for the truth. When you came up, I thought you were gonna be bad, I mean no good at all. But you've done a helluva job. Really."

Pellegrini smiles and hails Nicky for one last one, pushing his empty across the bar and pointing to the shot glass in front of Requer. The other detectives turn to another conversation.

"I wouldn't say the same thing about Fred," says Requer quietly enough so that the comment goes no farther than Pellegrini. "I wouldn't."

Pellegrini nods, but he is suddenly uncomfortable. He and Fred Ceruti had transferred into Landsman's squad together, filling vacancies that occurred within weeks of each other. Like Requer, Ceruti is black, but unlike Requer—who had six years' seasoning in narcotics before the transfer to homicide—Ceruti is fresh from the Eastern District with only four years on the force. He has been pushed up to the sixth floor of headquarters by the captain, who saw him do good plainclothes work at the district level. But to Requer, those credentials aren't enough.

"I mean I like Fred. I really do," says Requer. "But he isn't ready for homicide. We've walked him through cases and shown him what needs to be done but it doesn't get through. He's not ready yet."

Pellegrini says nothing, aware that Requer is the veteran investigator in his squad and one of the most tenured black detectives in the homicide unit; he made his way up to CID at a time when black officers were still hearing racial jokes in the district roll call rooms. Pellegrini knows for a guy like that to sit here and punch the Italian kid's dance card while letting Ceruti pass is not an easy thing.

"I'll tell you this," Requer tells the other CID men at the bar. "If someone in my family got killed, if I got killed, I'd want Tom to work it." A detective's compliment.

"You really must be drunk," says Pellegrini.

"No, bunk."

"Well, Rick," says Pellegrini, "thank you for that vote of confidence. I might not solve your murder, but I'd definitely make some overtime on it."

Requer laughs, then calls for Nicky. The bartender pours one last shot, on the house, and the detective sends the Scotch sailing down his throat in one fluid, practiced motion.

The two men leave the bar, walking through the restaurant and out the double doors on the Water Street side. In three months, the Market Bar and Seafood Restaurant will become Dominique's, a French restaurant of considerable means. The clientele will be dressed better, the food more expensive, the menu a little less comprehensible to the average homicide detective. Nicky will be gone, the price of a drink will climb into the four-dollar range and the departmental crowd that frequents the bar will be told that their patronage no longer suits the restaurant's image. But for now, the Market Bar is as much BPD territory as Kavanaugh's or the FOP lodge.

Pellegrini and Requer turn on Frederick Street and saunter down the same stretch of pavement where Bob Bowman made his legendary midnight ride. No homicide detective can pass the spot without smiling at the thought of a drunken Bowman, borrowing a mounted man's horse long enough to parade back and forth in front of the Market Bar's plate glass windows, through which a half-dozen other detectives could be seen losing control. On a good day, Bo was five-foot-six. Perched on that stallion, he looked like a cross between Napoleon Bonaparte and Willie Shoemaker.

"You all right to drive?" asks Pellegrini.

"Yeah, bunk, I'm good."

"You sure?"

"Fuck yes."

"Okay then."

"Hey, Tom," says Requer before crossing to the Hamilton Street lot, "if the case is gonna go, then it's gonna go. Don't let it get you down."

Pellegrini smiles.

"I mean that," says Requer.

"Okay, Rick."

"Really."

Pellegrini smiles again, but with the look of a drowning man no longer willing to fight against the current.

"Really, bunk. You do what you can do and that's it. If the evidence ain't there, you know, it ain't there. You do what you can . . ."

Requer hits the younger detective's shoulder with an open hand, then fishes in a pants pocket for his car keys. "You know what I mean, bunk."

Pellegrini nods, smiles, then nods again. But he keeps his silence.

Friday, April 8

"Brown, you piece of shit."

"Sir?"

"I called you a piece of shit."

Dave Brown looks up from the current issue of *Rolling Stone* and sighs. Donald Worden is on a tear, and nothing good can come from that.

"Gimme a quarter," says Worden, palm open.

"Let me understand this," says Brown. "I'm here at my desk reading a magazine—"

"One of them art school magazines," Worden interjects.

Brown shakes his head wearily. Although his most recent creations have been limited to renderings of dead stickmen in his crime scene sketches, David John Brown is indeed the product of the Maryland Institute of Art. In Worden's mind, this fact alone makes suspect his credentials as a homicide detective.

"Reading a magazine of rock 'n' roll and popular culture," Brown continues, "interfering with no one, and you walk through the door and address me as fecal matter."

"Fecal matter. What the hell is that? I didn't go to college. I'm just a poor dumb white boy from Hampden."

Brown rolls his eyes.

"Gimme a quarter, bitch."

This has been going on ever since Dave Brown arrived in homicide. Time and time again, Worden demands 25-cent pieces from younger detectives, then simply pockets the money. No trip to the Macke machines downstairs, no donation to the coffee fund—the money is taken as tribute, plain and simple. Brown digs in his pocket, then tosses a quarter at the older detective.

"What a piece of shit," Worden repeats, catching the coin. "Why don't you start handling some calls, Brown?"

"I just handled a murder."

"Yeah?" says Worden, strutting over to Brown's desk. "Well, handle this."

The Big Man leans over Brown's chair, his crotch even with the younger detective's mouth. Brown screams in mock hysteria, bringing Terry McLarney into the room.

"Sergeant McLarney, sir," shouts Brown, with Worden now almost on top of him. "Detective Worden is forcing me to engage in sexual acts prohibited by law. As my immediate supervisor, I appeal to your . . ."

McLarney smiles, salutes, then turns on his heel. "Carry on, men," he says, walking back into the main office.

"Get off me, goddammit," yells Brown, tiring of the joke. "Leave me alone, you polar-bear-looking bitch."

"Oooooooo," says Worden, backing off. "Now I know what you really think of me."

Brown says nothing, trying hard to return to the magazine.

The Big Man won't let him. "Piece . . . of . . ."

Brown glares at the older detective, his right hand making a furtive move toward a shoulder holster burdened by the long barrel .38. "Careful," says Brown. "I brought the big gun today."

Worden shakes his head, then walks to the coat rack, looking for his cigars. "What the hell are you doing with that magazine, Brown?" he says, lighting up. "Why aren't you out there working on Rodney Tripps?"

Rodney Tripps. Dead drug dealer in the driver's seat of his luxury car. No witnesses. No suspects. No physical evidence. What the hell was there to work on?

"You know, I'm not the only person around here with an open one," says Brown, exasperated. "I see a couple names up there in red ink that belong to you."

Worden says nothing, and for just a second Brown wishes he could take back the last two sentences. The office banter always has an edge, but every now and then the line gets crossed. Brown knows that for the first time in three years the Big Man is truly slumping, carrying two consecutive open cases; more important, the mayhem that is the Monroe Street investigation is dragging on interminably.

As a consequence, Worden spends his days shepherding two dozen witnesses into the grand jury room on the second floor of the Mitchell Courthouse, then waiting outside while Tim Doory, the lead prosecutor in the case, does his best to recreate the mysterious slaying of John Randolph Scott. Worden, too, has been called before the same panel, with several of the grand jurors asking pointed questions about the actions of the officers involved in the pursuit of Scott—particularly after those jurors listened to the Central District radio tape. And Worden has no answers; the case begins and ends with a young man's body in a West Baltimore alley and a cast of Western and Central District officers, all claiming no knowledge of the event.

Not surprisingly, Worden's only civilian witness—the man identified in newsprint as a potential suspect—has gone before the grand jury and refused to testify, invoking his Fifth Amendment right against self-incrimination. Sergeant Wiley, the officer who found the body and who would be made to explain his prior radio transmission canceling the suspect's description, has not been called as a witness.

We call Wiley as a last resort, Doory explained to Worden at one point, because if he's culpable, he'll also take the Fifth. And at that point, the prosecutor argued, there are few options left: If we let him refuse to testify, he walks out of the grand jury room, leaving us with insufficient evidence for any kind of indictment. But if we offer him immunity to compel his testimony, then what? What if John Wiley, under a grant of immunity, tells us he shot that kid? Then, Doory explained, we've solved a crime we can't prosecute.

Returning from the courthouse every weekday afternoon, Worden's nights are spent in the rotation, handling shootings, suicides and, ultimately, fresh murders. And for the first time since his transfer to homicide, Worden has no answers for those either.

Given that his squad is built around Worden, even McLarney is a little unnerved by the trend. Every detective gets his share of unsolved cases, but for Worden, two consecutive open files simply don't happen.

During a recent midnight shift, McLarney pointed to the red names on the board and announced: "One of those is going down," adding, as much to hear himself say it as to convince anyone else, "Donald won't stand for two in a row like that."

The first case was a drug murder from Edmondson Avenue back in March, a street shooting in which the only potential witness was a fourteen-year-old runaway from a juvenile detention center. Whether the kid could be found and whether he would tell his story was uncertain. But the second murder, an argument up on Ellamont which escalated into the slaying of a thirty-year-old man—that one ordinarily should have been a dunker. Dwayne Dickerson had been shot once in the back of the head when he tried to intervene in a street dispute, and when everyone involved had been shipped downtown and interviewed, Worden was left with one depressing truth: No one seemed to know the shooter or, for that matter, what he was doing in Baltimore with a gun in his hand. By all accounts—and the witnesses were consistent—the shooter had nothing to do with the original argument.

McLarney may like to think that Worden isn't capable of letting two murders stay red, but unless the phone rings on the Dickerson murder, there isn't much left for an investigator to do but check other assault-by-shooting reports from the Southwest and hope something matches. Worden has told his sergeant just that, but McLarney heard instead the echo of Monroe Street. To his way of thinking, the department had used his best detective to go after other cops, and God knows that kind of thing has an effect on a man like Worden. For two months, McLarney has been trying to get his best detective away from the Scott murder, easing him back into the rotation. Get the man back on his horse with some fresh murders, McLarney figures. Get him back on the street and he'll be the same.

But Worden is not the same. And when Brown lets slip the comment about the red names on the wall, Worden suddenly lapses into cold silence. The banter, the bitching, the locker room humor, give way to brooding.

Brown senses this and changes tone, trying to bait the Big Man rather than fight him off. "Why are you always fucking with me?" he asks. "Why don't you ever go after Waltemeyer? Does Waltemeyer go out to Pikesville on Saturday dayshifts to get you bagels?"

Worden says nothing.

"Why the hell don't you ever fuck with Waltemeyer?"

Brown knows the answer, of course. Worden isn't going to fuck with Waltemeyer, who has more than two decades in the trenches. He's going to fuck with Dave Brown, who has a mere thirteen years on the force. And Donald Waltemeyer isn't going to drive up to Pikesville at seven A.M. to get bagels for the same reason. Brown gets the bagels because Brown is the new man and Worden is breaking him in. And when the likes of Donald Worden wants a dozen bagels and half a pound of veggie spread, the new man gets in a Cavalier and drives to Philadelphia if need be.

"This is the thanks I get," says Brown, still goading the older detective.

"What do you want me to do, kiss you?" says Worden, finally responding. "You didn't even get garlic for me."

Brown rolls his eyes. Garlic bagels. Always with the goddamn garlic bagels. They're supposed to be better for the Big Man's blood pressure, and when Brown brings back onion or poppy on weekend dayshifts, he never hears the end of it. Excluding the image of Waltemeyer locked in the large interrogation room with six drunken Greek stevedores, Brown's most fully formed fantasy delivers him to Worden's front lawn at five on a Saturday morning to lob sixty or seventy garlic bagels against the master bedroom windows.

"They didn't have garlic," says Brown. "I asked."

Worden looks at him with contempt. It is the same expression he carries in that crime scene photograph from Cherry Hill, the one that Brown liberated for his personal collection, the one that said, "Brown, you piece of shit, how can you possibly believe those beer cans have anything to do with your crime scene." One day, Worden just may retire and Dave Brown just may become the next centerpiece of McLarney's squad. But until then, the younger man's life is consigned to any hell of Worden's choosing.

For Worden, however, the hell is entirely the creation of his own mind. He has loved this job—loved it too much, perhaps—and now, finally, he seems to be running out of time. That it is hard for Worden to accept this is understandable; for twenty-five years, he came to work every day armed with the knowledge that wherever the department decided to put him, he would shine. It had always been so, beginning with all those years in the Northwest, an extended tour that made working that district second nature to him. Hell, he still can't work a homicide up there without making some connection to places and people he knew back when. From the beginning, he had never been much on writing the reports, but damned if there was anyone better at reading the street. Nothing happened on his post that escaped Worden's notice: his memory for faces, for addresses, for incidents that other cops had long forgotten, is simply amazing. Unlike every other detective in the unit, Worden never carries notepaper to his crime scenes for the simple reason that he remembers everything; a standard joke in the unit was that Worden needed a single matchbook to record the particulars of three homicides and a police shooting. On the witness stand, attorneys would often ask to see Worden's notes, then be incredulous when he claimed to have none.

"I just remember things," he told one defense attorney. "Ask your question."

On slow nights, Worden would take out a Cavalier and ride through a drug market, or downtown through the Meat Rack on Park Avenue, where hustlers sold themselves outside the gay pickup bars. Each tour provided another four or five faces for his memory bank, another four or five victims or victimizers who might one day matter to a case file. It wasn't a purely photographic memory but it was mighty close, and when Worden finally brought it downtown to the old escape and apprehension unit, it was clear to everyone that he would never go back to Northwest plainclothes. The man was born to be a detective.

It wasn't just his superb memory that kept him in CID, though that asset alone was formidable enough when someone was trying to track a prison escapee, or match up a string of city and county robberies, or remember which west side shootings involved a .380 automatic. But the elephant's memory was part and parcel of Worden's whole approach to police work, his clarity of thought and purpose, his insistence on dealing with people directly and demanding, in a quiet and formidable way, that they do the same.

Worden had fought his share of battles but his size had never marked him for violence, and his gun—which time and again he threatened to pawn—had been almost irrelevant to his career. His bluster, his taunting insults in the squadroom, were as much an act as anything else, and everyone—from Brown to McLarney—knew it.

His size could be intimidating, of course, and Worden used that fact on occasion. But ultimately he did the job using his mind, with a thought process as fluid as it was refined. At a crime scene, he absorbed not only the physical evidence, but everything and everyone on the periphery. Often, Rick James would be doing the boilerplate work at a scene only to look up and see Worden standing a block away, a mass of whiteness in a sea of black faces. And damned if he didn't always come back with some piece of information about the dead man. Any other detective would get eyefucked and maybe cursed, but Worden somehow managed to take the corner boys beyond that, to make it clear that he was there to put something right. If they had any respect for the victim, if they ever even thought about saying anything that a police detective might like to overhear, this was their chance.

Some of it was Worden's gruff, paternalistic manner. Those blue eyes, those jowls, that thinning white hair—Worden looked like the father whose respect no man could bear to lose. During interviews and interrogations he spoke softly, wearily, with a look that made lying seem like an inexplicable sin. That held true for black or white, man or woman, gay or straight; Worden carried a credibility that somehow transcended the excesses of his profession. On the street, people who had contempt for every other law officer often made a separate peace with Donald Worden.

Once, when he was already downtown, working robberies with Ron Grady, the mother of a boy they had arrested was threatening to file a brutality complaint with the internal affairs division. Grady, she was told, had beat the kid in the district lockup.

"Grady didn't hit your boy," Worden told the mother. "I did."

"Awright, Mr. Donald," the woman declared. "If you had to hit him, then I knowed he needed it."

But he rarely hit anyone. He rarely needed to. Unlike many of the cops he came on with—and a good many younger officers, too—he was no racist, though any kid born and raised in the white, working-class enclave of Hampden had ample opportunity to acquire the taste. Nor was the Baltimore department the most tolerant environment in which to come of age; there were cops twenty years younger who reacted to what they saw on the streets by crawling into a psychological cave, damning every nigger and liberal faggot to hell for screwing up the country. Yet somehow, with nothing more than a high school education and his Navy training, Worden grew with the job. His mother had something to do with that; she was not the kind of woman to bring prejudice into a house. His long partnership with Grady also had good effect; he could not, on the one hand, respect and care for a black detective, then go dropping words like nigger and toad as if they meant nothing.

That sensitivity was another strength. Worden was one of the few white detectives in homicide who could sit across the desk from a fifteen-year-old black kid and make it clear—with nothing more than a look and a word or two—that they were both beginning with a blank page. Respect brought respect, contempt the same. Anyone with eyes could see that the bargain being offered was a fair one.

It was Worden, for example, who won the gay community's trust when a series of homosexual murders began plaguing the Mount Vernon neighborhood downtown. The department as a whole was still shunned by many in the gay community for a history of harassment, both real and perceived. But Worden could walk into any Park Avenue club, show a bartender a series of BPI photos and get some truthful answers. His word was his bond and it wasn't his job to judge or threaten. He didn't need anyone to come out of any closets or file any official report of crimes. He just needed to know: Is the guy in the photo the same one out hustling in the bars, the same one who's been beating and robbing the men who pick him up? When the Mount Vernon murders went down, Worden made his point by taking his whole squad to a gay bar on Washington Boulevard, where he bought one round for the place and then, to the delight of the other detectives, drank free for the rest of the night.

Even in the homicide unit, where a measure of talent and intelligence was assumed, Worden was recognized as a precious commodity—a cop's cop, a true investigator. For his three years in homicide, he had worked the midnight shifts and double shifts beside younger men. He showed them what twenty-five years can teach and, at the same time, he learned the new tricks that homicide work could teach him. Until Monroe Street,

Worden seemed indestructible if not infallible. Until Monroe Street, it had seemed as if the man would go on handling calls forever.

John Scott, dead in an alley with a handful of Western men standing over his body, was, quite simply, the one that got away. Beyond the emotional cost of investigating other cops, of having them lie to you like any other shithead off the street, the Monroe Street probe had become for Worden what the Latonya Wallace murder was for Pellegrini. A man solves ten consecutive murders and begins to believe that he can stay out on the edge forever. Then comes the red ball, the one with a bad bounce, and the same man suddenly begins to wonder where it ends—all the case files, all the reports, all the wounds on all the dead men from all the scenes—so many crimes that the names and faces lose their meaning, until those deprived of liberty and those deprived of life blur into the same sad image.

That alone might be reason enough for Worden to quit, but there were others too. For one thing, he no longer had a family to support. His children were grown, and his wife was long accustomed to what had become a ten-year separation. They had reached an equilibrium: Worden had never filed for a divorce; his wife, he knew, would never file either. As far as his own finances were concerned, Worden was guaranteed a 60 percent pension as soon as he put in his retirement papers, so he was actually earning less than half of his paystub. On his days off, he made better money delivering furs to customers from summer storage, or he worked on the home he had bought down in Brooklyn Park. He was good with his hands and tools, and there was certainly money to be made in home improvements. No less a homicide fixture than Jay Landsman was making thousands of dollars from a company he operated in his spare time; the joke was that Landsman could solve your mother's murder in a week—or four days if you also wanted to run a new deck off the back patio.

On the other side of the ledger were two good reasons to stay. First there was Diane, the red-headed secretary from the Special Investigations Section down the hall, who by bravely endeavoring to domesticate Worden had won the awe and sympathy of the entire homicide unit. The truth was that Worden was hooked; the gold "D&D" signature ring on his left hand said as much. But even if they got married tomorrow—and Worden was still coming to terms with the idea of something permanent—Diane would not be eligible for full benefits unless he stayed with the department for another year. As a forty-nine-year-old cop with hypertension, Worden had to think about that sort of thing.

Less practically, there was also the small, clear voice in the back of Worden's head that told him he was meant for this job and no other, the voice that told him that he was still having a helluva time. In his heart of hearts, Worden wanted very much to keep hearing that voice.

A week ago, Waltemeyer had pulled a 1975 murder case out of the back files, a Highlandtown bar robbery in which the shooter had been charged in a warrant but never apprehended. Who would have believed that thirteen years could pass before the suspect finally surfaced in Salt Lake City, telling a friend about a crime he thought everyone had forgotten? Who would have believed that the case file would still contain a photograph of an identification lineup from 1975, a lineup in which five detectives stood shoulder-to-shoulder with one genuine suspect? And check out the face on that heavyset young man, the one with thick blond hair and deep blue eyes, the one staring at the camera, trying hard to look more felon than robbery detective? Donald Worden was thirty-six in that photograph—harder, thinner, gaudily dressed in the kind of checked pants and polyester sport coat that marked an up-and-coming Baltimore detective of an earlier epoch.

Waltemeyer, of course, paraded the photograph around the squadroom, as if he had unearthed the mummified remains of some ancient king. No, Worden told him, I don't want it for a goddamn souvenir.

The only thing that saved him that day was a ringing phone line and a west side cutting. Worden, like any old fire dog, was out at the sound of the bell. He grabbed the index card with the address and time-of-dispatch and was halfway to the elevators before any other detective could even think about taking the call.

Appropriate to the moment, his partner on the call was Kincaid, another twenty-year man, and together they worked the scene on Franklintown Road. It was a straight-up domestic stabbing, with the knife on the front lawn and a blood trail leading all the way back into the rowhouse. On the living room floor, immersed in a ten-foot-wide lake of purple-red blood, was the phone used by the husband to call for help.

"Christ, Donald," said Worden. "This bad boy must've caught a vein."

"Aw yeah," said Kincaid. "Must have."

Outside on the stoop, the first officer was writing down particulars for his report with an expected air of indifference. But when he got to the two detectives' sequence numbers—the departmental code that identifies officers in chronological order—he looked up in wonder.

"A-seven-o-three," Worden told him.

"A-nine-o-four," said Kincaid.

To make the A sequence, a man had to come on the force no later than 1967. The uniform, a D sequence himself, shook his head. "Isn't there anyone up there in homicide with less than twenty years on?"

Worden said nothing and Kincaid went right to work. "This guy's at University?" he asked.

"Yeah. The ER."

"How was he doing?"

"They were trying to get him stabilized when I got here."

The detectives walked back toward the Cavalier, but turned abruptly when another uniform, accompanied by a six-year-old boy, motioned them over to the spot where the knife had been found.

"This young man saw what happened," said the uniform, loud enough for the child to hear, "and he would like to tell us about it."

Worden knelt down. "You saw what happened?"

The boy nodded.

"GET AWAY FROM THAT BOY," screamed a woman from the other side of the street. "YOU CAN'T TALK TO HIM WITHOUT NO LAWYER."

"Are you his mother?" asked the uniform.

"No, but she don't want him talkin' to no police. I know that. Tavon, don't you say nothin'."

"So you're not the mother?" asked the uniform, now seething.

"No."

"Then get the hell out of here before I lock your ass up," muttered the patrolman, soft enough to be out of the boy's earshot. "You hear me?"

Worden turned back to the child. "What did you see?"

"I saw Bobby run out after Jean."

"You did?"

The boy nodded. "And when he got up close she cut him."

"Did he run into the knife? Did he run into it by accident or did Jean try to cut him?"

The boy shook his head. "She went like this," he said, holding his hand steady.

"She did? Well, what's your name?"

"Tavon."

"Tavon, you've helped us a lot. Thank you."

Worden and Kincaid liberated their Cavalier from a growing mass of patrol cars and drove east to the emergency room at University, both of them certain in the knowledge that Rule Six in the homicide lexicon now applied. To wit:

When a suspect is immediately identified in an assault case, the victim is sure to live. When no suspect has been identified, the victim will surely die. Indeed, the rule was confirmed in this instance by the subsequent discovery of Cornell Robert Jones, age thirty-seven, lying on his back in a rear examination room, conscious and alert, as a blonde surgical resident—an especially attractive blonde surgical resident—applied pressure to the wound on his inner left thigh.

"Mr. Jones?" asked Worden.

Wincing with pain, the victim nodded briefly from beneath an oxygen mask.

"Mr. Jones, I'm Detective Worden from the police department. Can you hear me?"

"I hear you," said the victim, his voice almost muzzled by the mask.

"We've been down to your house and the people there say your girlfriend, or is it your wife . . ."

"My wife."

"They say your wife cut you. Is that what happened?"

"Goddamn right she cut me," he said, wincing again.

"You didn't just run into the knife or anything like that?"

"Hell no. She stabbed me."

"So if we tell the officer to get a warrant on your wife, you're not going to change your mind about this tomorrow?"

"No I ain't."

"All right, then," said Worden. "Do you have any idea where your wife might be now?"

"I don't know. Maybe a girlfriend's house or something."

Worden nodded, then looked at Kincaid, who had spent the last five minutes undertaking as comprehensive a review of the surgical resident as could be accomplished under the circumstances.

"I'll say this, Mr. Jones," drawled Kincaid. "You're in good hands now. Real good hands."

The resident looked up, irritated and a little embarrassed. And then Worden was smiling wickedly at his own thoughts. He leaned low to the victim's ear. "You know, Mr. Jones, you're a lucky man," he said in a stage whisper.

"What?"

"You're a lucky man."

Wincing with pain, the victim looked sideways at the detective. "How the hell you figure that?"

Worden smiled. "Well, from the look of things, your wife was going for your Johnson," said the detective. "And from what I can see, she only missed by a couple inches."

Suddenly, from beneath the oxygen mask, Cornell Jones was laughing uproariously. The resident, too, was losing it, her face contorted as she struggled against herself.

"Yeah," said Kincaid. "A big guy like yourself, you was pretty damn close to singin' soprano, you know that?"

Cornell Jones rocked up and down on the gurney, laughing and wincing at the same time.

Worden held up his hand, signing off with a short wave. "You have a good one."

"You too, man," said Cornell Jones, still laughing.

The shit you see out here, thought Worden, driving back to the office. And my God, he had to admit, there are still moments when I love this job.

SUNDAY, MAY 1

"Something's gone wrong," says Terry McLarney.

Eddie Brown answers without looking up, his mind fully absorbed by mathematical endeavors. Statistical charts and spread sheets arrayed in front of him, Brown will figure a way to predict tomorrow night's four-digit lotto number or he will die trying.

"What's wrong?"

"Look around," says McLarney. "The phone is ringing with information on every kind of case and we're getting double-dunkers left and right. Hey, even the lab is coming up with print hits."

"So," says Brown, "what's wrong with that?"

"It's not like us," says McLarney. "I get the feeling that we're going to be punished. I have this feeling that there's a rowhouse somewhere with about a dozen skeletons in the basement, just waiting for us."

Brown shakes his head. "You think too much," he tells McLarney.

A criticism rarely leveled at a Baltimore cop, and McLarney laughs at the absurdity of the notion. He's a sergeant and an Irishman; by that reckoning alone, it's his responsibility to rip the silver linings out of every last little cloud. The board is going from red to black. Murders are being solved. Evil is being punished. Good Lord, thinks McLarney, how much is this going to cost?

The streak began a month ago up on Kirk Avenue, in the gutted remains of a torched rowhouse, where Donald Steinhice watched firefighters pull at the cracked and blackened debris until all three bodies were distinguishable. The oldest was three, the youngest, five months; their remains were discovered in an upstairs bedroom, where they stayed after every adult fled from the burning house. For Steinhice, a veteran of Stanton's shift, the accelerant pour-patterns on the first floor—identifiable as darker splotches on the floors and walls—told the story: Mother dumps boyfriend, boyfriend returns with kerosene, children pay the price. In recent years, the scenario had become strangely common to the inner city. Four months back, in fact, Mark Tomlin caught a rowhouse arson that claimed two children; then, little more than a week ago and less than a month after the Kirk Avenue tragedy, another boyfriend torched another mother's home, murdering a twenty-one-month-old toddler and his seven-month-old sister.

"The adults always make it out," explained Scott Keller, the primary on the most recent case and a veteran of the CID arson unit. "The kids always get left behind."

More than most homicides, the Kirk Avenue arson had an emotional cost; Steinhice, a detective with perhaps a thousand crime scenes behind him, suffered nightmares about a murder for the first time—graphic images of helplessness in which the dead children were at the top of a rowhouse stairway, crying, terrified. Nonetheless, when the boyfriend came downtown in handcuffs, it was Steinhice who mustered empathy enough to prompt a full confession. And it was Steinhice who intervened when the boyfriend tore apart an aluminum soda can after his confession and tried to use the rough edges against his wrists.

Kirk Avenue was hard for Steinhice to swallow, but it was nonetheless medicine for what ailed both shifts of the homicide unit. Three dead, one arrest, three clearances—a stat like that can start a trend all by itself.

Sure enough, the following week brought Tom Pellegrini his dunker at the Civic Center, the labor dispute that became a one-sided knife fight. Rick Requer followed that case with two more clearances: a double murder-suicide from the Southeastern in which an emotionally distraught auto mechanic shot his wife and nephew in the kitchen, then wrapped things up tidily by reloading the .44 Magnum and shoving the barrel in his mouth. In human terms, the scene at 3002 McElderry Street was a massacre; in the statistical terms of urban homicide work, it was the stuff from which a detective fashions dreams.

One week more and the trend was clear: Dave Brown and Worden caught a poker game dispute in the Eastern in which a sixty-one-year-old player, arguing over the proper ante, suddenly grabbed a shotgun and blew up a friend. Garvey and Kincaid followed suit, taking a shooting call on Fairview and getting a father murdered by his son, killed in an argument over the boy's unwillingness to share drug profits. Barlow and Gilbert again hit the jackpot for Stanton's shift in the Southwest, where yet another angry young boyfriend fatally wounded both the woman he loved and the infant daughter in her arms, then trained the same weapon on himself.

Five nights later, Donald Waltemeyer and Dave Brown clocked in with yet another death-by-argument, a bar shooting from Highlandtown in which the subsequent performance of the two suspects in the homicide office resembled nothing so much as outtake from a B-grade Mafia film. They were Philly boys, short, dark Italians named DelGiornio and Forline, and they had killed a Baltimore man in a dispute that centered on the relative accomplishments of their respective fathers. The victim's father ran an industrial firm; DelGiornio's father, however, had done well in the Philadelphia Mafia until events beyond his control forced him to become a federal witness against the heads of the Philly crime family. This, of course, necessitated the relocation of family members from South Philly, which, in turn, explained the appearance of the younger DelGiornio and his friend in Southeast Baltimore. The Baltimore detectives were biting their lips when DelGiornio made his phone call to Dad.

"Yo, Dad," mumbled DelGiornio, crying into the receiver in what appeared to the detectives to be a rank Stallone impersonation. "I fucked up. I really fucked up . . . Killed him, yeah. It was a fight . . . No, Tony . . . Tony shot him . . . Dad, I'm really in some trouble here."

By morning, a herd of well-cropped FBI agents had arrived at the Formstone rowhouse that the government had rented for the DelGiornio kid only forty-eight hours earlier. The kid's belongings were crated up, his bail was set at a ridiculously low amount and by the following evening he was living in some other city at the government's expense. For his role in the death of a twenty-four-year-old man, Robert DelGiornio will eventually receive probation; Tony Forline, the shooter in the incident, will get five years. Both plea agreements will be set only weeks before the elder DelGiornio testifies as the key government witness in the federal conspiracy trial in Philadelphia.

"Well, we taught him a lesson," declared McLarney, after the Italian kids were given light bails by a court commissioner and herded out of Maryland. "They're probably up in Philly now, warning all their little Mob friends not to do a murder in Baltimore. We might not lock them up for it, but hey, we'll take away their guns and refuse to give them back."

Regardless of the outcome, the DelGiornio case was another clearance in what had suddenly become a month of clearances. For Gary D'Addario, it was a good sign, but one that could only be called belated. In a world ruled by statistics, he had been exposed for far too long and, as a result, his conflict with the captain had made its way down the sixth-floor hall to Dick Lanham, the CID commander. D'Addario wasn't surprised to find out that in conversations with Lanham, his captain had attributed the low clearance rate and other problems to D'Addario's management style. Things were getting ugly, so ugly in fact that one late April morning, the captain approached Worden, arguably D'Addario's best detective.

"I'm afraid the colonel is talking about making changes," said the captain. "How do you think the men would feel about working for another lieutenant?"

"I think you'd have a mutiny on your hands," answered Worden, hoping to shoot down the trial balloon. "Why are you asking?"

"Well, I want to know how the men feel," explained the captain. "Something may be in the works."

In the works. Within an hour, D'Addario had heard about that exchange from Worden and three other detectives. He went directly to the colonel, with whom he believed he had credibility. Eight successful years as a homicide supervisor, he reasoned, had to count for a little something.

To D'Addario, the colonel confirmed that the pressure to move him was coming from the captain. Moreover, the colonel seemed noncommittal and expressed concern about the low clearance rate. D'Addario could hear the unasked question: "If you aren't the problem, then what is?"

The lieutenant returned to his office and typed a long memo that sought to explain the statistical difference between Stanton's rate and his own. He noted that more than half of the murders taken by his shift were drug-related, noting further that some of those cases had been sacrificed to staff the Latonya Wallace probe. Moreover, he argued, one critical reason for the low rate was that neither lieutenant managed to save any December clearances for the new year—something that always gives the unit a January cushion. The rate will rise, D'Addario predicted, it's rising now. Give it some time.

To D'Addario, the memo seemed to convince the colonel; others on his shift weren't sure. The choice of a shift lieutenant as a likely scapegoat might not be so much the work of the captain as the result of criticism from above, perhaps the colonel and maybe even the deputy. If that was the case, then D'Addario was being pressured by more than the clearance rate. It was Monroe Street, too. And the Northwest murders and Latonya Wallace. Especially Latonya Wallace. By itself, D'Addario knew, the absence of charging documents in the little girl's murder could be enough to send the brass on a head-hunting sortie.

Shorn of political allies, D'Addario had two options: He could accept a transfer to another unit and learn to live with the taste that such a transfer would leave. Or he could tough it out, hoping the clearance rate would continue to climb and a red ball or two would get solved in the process. If he stayed on, his superiors could try to force a transfer, but that, he knew, was a messy process. They would have to show cause, and that would result in a nasty little paper war. He would lose, of course, but it would not be pretty—and the colonel and captain both had to know that.

D'Addario also understood that there would be another cost if he remained in homicide. Because as long as that rate stayed low, he would no longer be able to protect his men from the whims of the command staff, at least not to the extent he had protected them in the past. Appearances would count: Every detective would have to toe closer to the line, and D'Addario would have to make it appear that he was the one compelling them to do so. The overtime would no longer flow as freely; the detectives handling fewer calls would have to pick up their pace. Most important, the detectives would have to cover themselves, writing follow-ups and updates to every case file so that no supervisor could come behind them, arguing that leads had not been pursued. This, D'Addario knew, was pure departmental horseshit. The make-work required for a half-dozen cover-your-ass office reports would waste valuable time. Still, that was the game, and now the game would have to be played.

The most complicated part of that game would be the crack-down on the unit's overtime pay, a ritual that often marked the end of a budget year in the Baltimore department. The homicide unit consistently came in almost $150,000 over budget on straight overtime and courtside pay for its detectives. Just as consistently, the department tried to crack the whip in April and May, exerting a minimal effect on the unit that disappeared entirely in June, when the new budget year began and the money once again flowed freely. For two or three months each spring, captains told lieutenants who told sergeants to authorize as little OT as possible so that the numbers would look a little better to the brass upstairs. This was possible in a district where, on any given night, one or two fewer radio cars might be handling calls during an overtime crunch. In the homicide unit, however, the practice created surreal working conditions.

The overtime cap was premised on a single rule: Any detective who reached 50 percent of his base pay in accumulated OT and court time was taken out of the rotation. The logic made perfect sense to fiscal services: If Worden hits his limit and is put on permanent daywork, he can't handle calls. And if he can't handle calls, he can't earn overtime. But in the opinion of the detectives and their sergeants, the rule had no logic. After all, if Worden is out of the rotation, then the other four detectives in his squad are catching more calls on the nightshift. And if, God forbid, Waltemeyer is also near his OT limit, then this squad is down to three men. In CID homicide, a squad that goes into a midnight shift with no more than three detectives is asking to be punished.

More important, the overtime cap was a frontal assault on quality. The best detectives were inevitably those who worked their cases longest, and their cases were inevitably those that were strong enough to go to court. Granted, an experienced detective could milk any case for extra hours, but it usually cost a great deal more money to solve a murder than to keep it open, and even more money to actually win that case in court. A cleared homicide is a money tree, a truth recognized by Rule Seven in the pantheon of homicide wisdom.

In reference to the color of money, and the colors by which open and solved murders are chronicled on the board, the rule states: First, they're red. Then they're green. Then they're black. But now, because of D'Addario's vulnerability, there would be less green in the equation. This spring, the 50 percent overtime rule threatened to do some real damage.

Gary Dunnigan hit the 50 percent mark first and suddenly found himself on a permanent dayshift, working follow-ups to old cases and nothing else. Then Worden hit the wall, then Waltemeyer, then Rick James began edging up over 48 percent. Suddenly, McLarney was looking at three weeks of nightwork with two detectives to call on.

"There's no limit to how many they can kill," said Worden cynically. "There's only a limit to how long we can work them."

D'Addario played the game as it had to be played, sending warning letters—copied to the colonel and captain—to the detectives approaching the 50 percent cap, then benching those who exceeded the limit. Remarkably, his sergeants and detectives were willing to cooperate in this nonsense. Any one of them could have thwarted the restrictions by calling in more detectives to help with a bad midnight shift and then claiming that events overran policy. Murder, after all, is one of the least predictable things in this world.

Instead, the sergeants sidelined detectives and juggled the schedules because they understood the risk to D'Addario and, beyond that, to themselves. There were a lot of lieutenants in the department and in the estimate of McLarney and Jay Landsman, at least, a good 80 percent of them had the ability, the will and the ambition to do a superior job of screwing up the CID homicide unit if ever given any chance.

But if McLarney and Landsman played the game out of genuine loyalty to D'Addario, Roger Nolan's reasons were altogether different.

Nolan took seriously his role as a sergeant and he clearly enjoyed working in what was essentially a paramilitary organization. More than most of the men in homicide, he took satisfaction in the protocols of police work—the deference to rank, the institutional loyalty, the chain of command. This peculiarity did not necessarily make him a company man; Nolan protected his detectives as well or better than any other supervisor in homicide, and a detective who worked for him could be assured that only his sergeant would mess with him.

Even so, Nolan was an enigma to his own men. A product of the West Baltimore ghetto with twenty-five years on the force, he was said to be the only practicing black Republican in the city of Baltimore. He repeatedly denied this, to little avail. Heavyset and bald, with wide, expressive features, Nolan looked very much like an aging boxer or perhaps the aging ex-Marine that he truly was. Growing up had not come easy to him; his parents had been tormented by alcoholism, other relatives had become players in the West Baltimore drug trade. To a great extent, it was the Marines that saved Nolan, plucking him off North Carrollton Street and providing him with a surrogate family, a bed of his own and three balanced meals a day. He served in both the Pacific and Mediterranean, but then put in his papers before Vietnam heated up. Semper Fi shaped him: Nolan spent his spare time leading a Boy Scout troop, reading military history and watching reruns of Hopalong Cassidy movies. This was not, to any detective's thinking, a behavior pattern consistent with that of the average West Baltimore native.

Still, Nolan's perspective was unique to the homicide unit. Unlike Landsman and McLarney, Nolan had never been a homicide detective; in fact, he had spent much of his career in patrol, working as a sector supervisor in the Northwestern and Eastern districts—a lengthy exile from headquarters that began when, as a promising young plainclothesman, he crossed the powers-that-be in a celebrated corruption case in the early 1970s.

Those were the years when the Baltimore department was truly rough-and-tumble. In 1973, almost half of the entire Western District and its commander were either indicted or fired for taking protection for the local gambling action. The CID vice unit met with a similar fate, and in the tactical section, rumors were swirling about the ranking black officer on the force, Major James Watkins, who was otherwise a rising candidate for the commissioner's post. Watkins had grown up with several of Pennsylvania Avenue's more notable narcotics dealers and, before the end of the decade, he would stand trial as a full colonel, charged with accepting protection from the drug trade.

Nolan was working plainclothes under Watkins's command, and he knew that things weren't right in the tac unit. On one occasion, when one of his raids netted more than five hundred glassine bags of heroin, other plainclothesmen offered to take the contraband to evidence control. Nolan balked. He counted the bags himself, photographed them, then got his own voucher for the submission. Sure enough, the heroin—$15,000 worth—disappeared from the ECU a short time later and two tac officers were ultimately indicted. But for all of that, Nolan didn't believe that Watkins knew about the corruption or was in any way involved. Against all advice and the wishes of the police commissioner, he testified as a character witness for Watkins at the subsequent trial.

The colonel was convicted, then granted a retrial on appeal, then acquitted. The verdict on Nolan's career was equally divided: before his testimony, he had been a sergeant assigned directly to the state's attorney's investigative unit; afterward, he was running a patrol sector in the Northwest with no hope of seeing the headquarters building for as long as the current department administration held office. The exile, the political machinations, the unwarranted taint of other men's corruption—all of that shaped Nolan, so much so that the men in his squad would groan in unison whenever their sergeant began another retelling of the missing heroin story.

That Nolan had made his way back to CID after so many years in the trenches was something of a personal testament to human perseverance. And although he had no experience with death investigation, it made sense that his ultimate destination would be homicide, where organized corruption was never much of an issue. Over the last fifteen years, the Baltimore department had stayed generally clean—remarkably so when compared to its counterparts in New York, Philadelphia and Miami. But even if a cop had it in mind to make real money, the place to do that was CID narcotics or gambling enforcement or any other unit in which a detective might kick in a door and find $100,000 under a mattress. In homicide, the only recognized scam was overtime pay; no one ever figured out how to make dead bodies pay serious money.

More than anything else, Nolan was a survivor, proud of his rank and his position in the homicide unit. Consequently, he took the supervisory aspects of his job seriously and was frustrated when Landsman, McLarney or D'Addario seemed less interested in the rituals of command. Supervisors' meetings on the shift inevitably began with Nolan proposing new ideas for the operation of the shift—some good, some bad, but all of them involving a more formal process of supervision. The meetings would never last long: Landsman would respond to Nolan's ideas by recommending either serious psychological help or a better grade of marijuana. Then McLarney would make a joke about something completely unrelated to the topic at hand and, to Nolan's dismay, D'Addario would adjourn the session. Basically, Landsman and McLarney would rather be working the cases; Nolan preferred the role of full-time supervisor.

As a result, D'Addario's sudden tactical shift toward closer supervision was, from Nolan's vantage point, both correct and belated. The lieutenant, he reasoned, should take control of his sergeants, and the sergeants, in turn, should get a rein on the men. In Nolan's mind, D'Addario had not only abdicated much of his own authority, but that of his sergeants as well.

And yet Nolan's detectives—Garvey, Edgerton, Kincaid, McAllister, Bowman—were operating with as much or more freedom than the men in the other squads. Documentation, administrative issues, personnel problems—Nolan held sway over such matters. But the essential purpose of CID homicide was to solve murders, and for that, chain of command mattered no more to Nolan and his men than anyone else. Nolan's detectives worked their cases in their own speed and fashion, and Nolan would never demand otherwise. Edgerton's personality required that kind of approach, but even the methodical Garvey would respond to a hovering, micromanaging sergeant by delivering twelve clearances a year. With no sergeant at all, he'd manage an even dozen.

"I wouldn't want to work for any other sergeant up there," conceded

Garvey, explaining the squad dynamics to another detective. "It's just that every now and then, you've got to slap the shit out of Roger and bring him back down to earth."

For the detectives themselves, the OT cutbacks and scheduling changes were tolerable only because they, too, understood D'Addario's predicament. And when D'Addario began trailing behind the detectives, checking the case files and asking for additional paperwork, no one took any real offense. Working a midnight shift one man short, Rick Requer summed up the sentiment sweetly:

"If it wasn't for Dee," he told two other detectives, "we wouldn't be putting up with any of this fuckin' bullshit."

Yet they continued to put up with it all through April and into May as D'Addario tried to come to terms with the required pain-in-the-ass persona. The extra paperwork and scheduling changes were cosmetic and could be suffered for as long as it took the lieutenant to weather the storm. As for the overtime, that would flow again in mid-June, when the new budget year began. They cursed, they grumbled, but they played out D'Addario's string. Most important, they continued to do the one thing absolutely essential to their lieutenant's future: They solved murders.

Ceruti contributed with a lockup on a fatal beating from the Southwestern, and Waltemeyer put down a shooting in a house on North Wolfe Street, near the Hopkins hospital complex. On Stanton's shift, Tomlin caught a cutting that ended with the arrest of a new police cadet, a man scheduled to attend the academy the following month.

"Do you think I should call the personnel office about this?" the man asked after confessing.

"Might be a good idea," Tomlin told him. "Although I'm sure they'll hear about it somehow."

Garvey and Kincaid caught one up on Harlem Avenue, where they were blessed with witnesses and a suspect still lingering at the scene. Arriving at University Hospital to check on their victim, the two detectives watched surgeons crack the kid's chest in a desperate effort at open-heart massage. The line on the EKG was irregular, and blood was pouring out of the chest cavity onto the white tile floor. Ten-seven within an hour or two, the ER resident predicted, morning at the latest. No shit, thought the detectives, who weren't exactly strangers to the medical aspects of violent death. A surgeon who cracks the chest is on the last roll of the dice; any detective knows that 97 percent of all such efforts fail. Rule Six had been upended and Garvey arrived back at the office unable to contain his wonder.

"Hey, Donald," shouted Garvey, bounding across the office and then waltzing Kincaid around a metal desk. "He's gonna die! He's gonna die and we know who did it!"

"You," said Nolan, shaking his head and laughing, "are one cold motherfucker." Then the sergeant turned crisply on his heel and danced a jig into his own office.

A week later, Waltemeyer and an assistant state's attorney caught a flight for Salt Lake City, where an upstanding, pillar-of-the-community type had confessed to his closest friend about being wanted for a murder committed in Baltimore thirteen years earlier. Daniel Eugene Binick, age forty-one, had been in Utah for a dozen years, married for most of that time and working as a drug and alcohol counselor under an assumed name. And though his photograph still adorned the "Wanted for Homicide" poster in the homicide unit's main office, it was a picture of a much younger, reckless man. The Daniel Binick of 1975 had long, stringy hair, a thick mustache and a respectable police record; the late eighties version wore his hair close-cropped and ran the local AA chapter. Even after a week's investigation, Waltemeyer found only one living witness to the bar robbery and shooting. But one was enough, and a clearance by any name still smelled as sweet.

By early May, the clearance rate is a fatter, happier 60 percent. Likewise, the flow of overtime and court pay will be at least temporarily staunched to a point that the brass can't help notice. If not entirely secure, D'Addario's position has stabilized, or so it seems to his men.

During one brief encounter in the homicide office, Landsman acknowledges the lighter mood on the shift by risking a joke at the lieutenant's expense—something that even Landsman would not have attempted a month earlier.

Late one afternoon, D'Addario, Landsman and McLarney are huddled in front of the television, the lieutenant and McLarney checking the roll book, Landsman absorbing gynecological mysteries from a skin magazine. Wandering across the sixth floor, Colonel Lanham happens to step into his homicide unit and all three supervisors snap to attention.

Landsman waits a good three seconds before handing the magazine, centerfold splayed open, to Gary D'Addario.

"Here's your magazine, lieutenant," he says. "I appreciate you letting me look at it."

D'Addario, unthinking, holds out his hand.

"Fucking Jay," says McLarney, shaking his head.

Even the colonel has to laugh.

MONDAY, MAY 9

Harry Edgerton needs a murder.

He needs a murder today.

Edgerton needs a human body, any human body, still and stiff and void of all life force. He needs that body to fall within the established limits of Baltimore city. He needs that body shot, stabbed, bludgeoned, battered or otherwise rendered inoperative through any act of human intervention. He needs a 24-hour homicide report with his name typed at the bottom, a red-brown case binder that declares Harry Edgerton to be the primary investigator. You say Bowman is handling a shooting call up in the Northeast? Tell him to hang on to that crime scene, because Harry Edgerton, his friend and personal savior, is already in a Cavalier and racing up Harford Road. You say the county police are working a murder in Woodlawn? Well, drag that poor bastard back over the city line and let Edgerton work on him. You got a questionable death in an apartment with no overt trauma or forced entry? No problem. Give the Edge a chance to write on that bad boy and it can be a murder before the next morning's autopsy.

"If I don't get one soon," says Edgerton, jumping red lights on Frederick Road in the early morning darkness, "I'm going to have to kill someone."

For two full weeks, Edgerton's name has been affixed to the board's wooden frame with a thumbtack, scrawled with a certain infamy on sheets of yellow legal paper that list the squad and detective expected to handle the next homicide call. The daily postings are another indication of D'Addario's change in demeanor; detectives who have handled fewer murders are now being identified and designated as candidates for the next call. Most especially that means Edgerton. Having handled only two homicides this year, the veteran's pace is not only a controversy within his squad but a loaded issue for D'Addario as well. For the last two weeks, every one of his postings began and ended with Edgerton's name. It has become something of a daily joke in the coffee room:

"Who's up today?"

"Harry's up."

"Christ. Harry's gonna be up 'til October."

For days now, Edgerton has bounced from shootings to stabbings to questionable deaths to overdoses, waiting earnestly for something—anything—to come back as a murder.

And it hasn't worked. On days when he has handled three or four calls, running from one end of the city to the other looking at bodies, other detectives have picked up the phone and been blessed with double-dunker massacres. Edgerton handles a shooting call and the victim is guaranteed to survive. He works an apparent bludgeoning and the ME is guaranteed to rule the cause of death an overdose, followed by injuries sustained when the victim collapsed on the cement floor. Edgerton goes to the scene of an unattended death and it's A-1-guaranteed to be an eighty-eight-year-old retiree with a chronic heart condition. None of which means a thing to D'Addario. Edgerton is up until he gets a murder, the lieutenant repeats. If it takes the rest of his career, fine.

This makes for one very irritable homicide detective. It's one thing, after all, to be considered the resident flake on the shift and the problem child in the squad. And to have Kincaid and Bowman and God knows who else bitching about sharing the workload—normally Edgerton can handle that, too. But, he thinks, normal can be tossed out a window when I'm being made to handle three calls a day every goddamn day for what is beginning to seem like the rest of my life.

Edgerton's urgent need for a murder was evident a week ago, when he began cursing at an overdose victim in the Murphy Homes, demanding from the cadaver a little more cooperation and consideration than had thus far been shown to him.

"You degenerate motherfucker," Edgerton said, berating the dead man as two housing authority cops stared on in amazement. "Where the fuck did you fire up? I don't have all fucking day to look at your fucking arms. Where the fuck is that fresh track?"

It wasn't just the aggravation of a missing needle mark, but the frustration that had been building with each successive call. And at that moment, standing over yet another body in a Murphy Homes stairwell, Edgerton was deeply disturbed that the dead man had done nothing more than kill himself with heroin. What the hell, he pleaded silently, was a murder too much to ask anymore? This was Baltimore, for Chrissakes. This was a dead man in a stairwell at the George B. Murphy Homes housing project. What better place to be shot down with a high-caliber weapon like a dog? What the fuck is this asshole doing with a syringe by his left hand, staring up from the cement floor with that ridiculous half-grin on his face?

"What are you, left-handed?" said Edgerton, rechecking the right arm. "Where the fuck did you shoot your shit?"

The dead man answered with his grin.

"Why," Edgerton asked the corpse, "are you doing this to me?"

A week later and Edgerton is still the point man for D'Addario's shift, racing across Southwest Baltimore to yet another shooting call that will, if bad luck holds, be nothing more than a grazing. There will be no crime scene, no suspect, no dead man sprawled at the intersection of Hollins and Payson. Edgerton conjures up not a corpse, but an eighteen-year-old sitting on a gurney in the ER at Bon Secours, fully alert, talking, with nothing more than an Ace bandage wrapped around one arm.

"The El Supremo's gonna have to give me a break already," he says, weaving between two lanes in the emptiness of Frederick Avenue. "I just can't buy a murder."

He does a Texas stop at the Monroe Street signal, then wheels right onto Payson. Blue strobes from the radio cars greet him, but Edgerton immediately notices the absence of fire department cherry tops. No body on the ground, either. If there was an ambo, Edgerton tells himself, it's long gone.

The detective marks his time of arrival and slams the driver's door. A Southwest uniform, a young white kid, sidles up with an earnest look on his face.

"He's alive, right?" Edgerton says.

"Who? The victim?"

No, thinks Edgerton, Elvis fucking Presley. Of course the victim. The detective nods.

"I don't think so," says the uniform. "Not for long anyway. He looked pretty bad in the ambo."

The detective shakes his head. The kid doesn't understand what he's dealing with. I don't do murders, Edgerton wants to tell him. I just handle calls.

"We got you a witness, though."

A witness. Now it's definitely not a murder.

"Where's this witness?"

"Over there by my car."

Edgerton looks across the intersection at a short, wire-thin doper who stares back and nods with what appears to be mild interest. This strikes Edgerton immediately, because eyewitnesses forced to remain at the scene of a murder are generally uncooperative and sullen.

"I'll be over there in a minute. Where's the victim?"

"Bon Secours. I think."

"This is the scene right here?"

"This here, and over that way you've got some more shell casings. Twenty-twos, I think."

Edgerton moves slowly into the street, carefully gauging his own steps. Ten shell casings—.22 rifle by the look of them—are scattered across the asphalt, each circled by a yellow chalk mark. The pattern of the spent shells seems to travel west across the center of the intersection, with most of the casings lying near the southwest corner. And at that corner, two more chalk marks note the location of the body when the paramedics arrived. Head east. Feet west at the curb's edge.

The detective walks the scene for another ten minutes, looking for anything out of the ordinary. No blood trail. No fresh scuff marks. No tire patches. Truly an unremarkable crime scene. In the gutter near the northeast corner, he finds a broken gelatin cap with traces of white powder. No surprise here—the intersection of Hollins and Payson is a drug market after dark. Moreover, the capsule is yellowed and dirty enough to make Edgerton believe it's been in the street for several days and has nothing to do with his shooting.

"Do you have this post?" he asks the uniform.

"Not usually. But I'm in the sector, so I know this corner pretty well. What do you need to know?"

What do I need to know. Edgerton is beginning to like this kid, who not only knows enough to grab hold of anything at the scene that resembles a witness but is also talking like he knows the area he's working. In the Baltimore department, this is a situation worthy of nostalgia. Ten or fifteen years ago, a homicide detective could ask a uniform a question and expect an answer. Those were the days when a good man owned his post and one dog couldn't fuck another at Hollins and Payson without word getting back to the Southwest station house. In that era, a patrolman who worked a post and caught a murder could expect to be asked who hung on that corner and where they could be located. And if he didn't know, he found out in a hurry. Nowadays, Edgerton tells himself, we're lucky if the post man can get the street names right. This kid here is a real police. A throwback.

"Who lives in that corner house there?"

"Bunch of drug dealers. It's a fucking shooting gallery is what it is. Our DEU hit it last week and locked up about a dozen of those fuckers."

Fuck that. No likely witnesses there.

"What about that corner?"

"Corner house has junkies. Junkies and an old wino. No, the wino lives one house down."

Priceless, Edgerton thinks. The kid is priceless.

"What about over there?"

The uniform shrugs. "I'm not sure on that one. That might be a real person living there."

"Did you canvass?"

"Yeah, we did half the block. No answer at that house, and the assholes over there say they didn't see shit. We can lock 'em up if you want."

Edgerton shakes his head, writing a few lines in his notepad. The uniform leans over to get a look, just a little bit curious.

"You know this guy you grabbed?" Edgerton asks.

"Not by name, but I've seen him around. He sells off this corner and he's been locked up, I know that. He's a piece of shit, if that's what you're asking."

Edgerton smiles briefly, then crosses the intersection. The wire-thin dealer is leaning against the radio car, a black beret pulled down straight across his forehead. High-top Air Jordans, Jordache jeans, Nike sweatshirt—a walking pile of ghetto status. He actually smiles when Edgerton walks up to the car.

"I guess I hung too long," the dealer says.

Edgerton smiles. A homeboy who knows the drill.

"I guess you did. What's your name?"

The dealer gives it up in a mumble.

"Any ID?"

The dealer shrugs, then pulls out a state proof-of-age card. The name checks.

"This your right address?"

The dealer nods.

"What was the shooting about?"

"I can probably say what it's about. And I can say what it looked like from down the street, but I didn't see who it was did it."

"What do you mean you didn't see them?"

"I mean I was too far. I was down in the middle of the block when they came up shooting. I didn't—"

Edgerton cuts him off as another radio car, cruising south on Payson, pulls to the curb. O. B. McCarter, having returned to Southwest patrol after being detailed to homicide for the Karen Smith case, leans out the driver's window and laughs.

"Harry Edgerton," he says, unable to contain himself, "is this your call, man?"

"Yeah, 'fraid so. You been to the hospital?"

"Yeah, I been there."

Fucking McCarter, thinks Edgerton. He's been gone from homicide three weeks and I haven't missed him even a little bit.

"So? Is he dead?"

"You got a suspect?"

"No."

McCarter laughs. "He's dead. You got yourself a murder, Harry."

Edgerton turns back to the dealer, who is shaking his head at the news. The detective wonders whether his witness is putting on appearances or is genuinely upset about the murder.

"Did you know the guy?"

"Pete? Yeah, I knew him."

"I got his name as Greg Taylor," says Edgerton, checking his notes.

"Naw man, 'round here, he was Pete. I just talked to him a couple hours ago. This is some shit."

"What was he about?"

"He was selling burn bags, you know. He was selling people shit. I told him that shit would get his ass killed . . ."

"You told him, huh?"

"Yeah. You know."

"You kind of liked the guy, didn't you?"

The dealer smiles. "Yeah, Pete was okay."

Almost despite himself, Edgerton is amused. His victim was working out on Payson Street, selling baking soda to junkies at $10 a cap—an act of unrestrained capitalism guaranteed to bring a man more enemies than can ever be put to good use. Christ, Edgerton tells himself, my luck is turning. Every doper along Frederick Avenue must have hated this sonofabitch and I find the one guy who's a little sorry to see him dead.

"Was he out here tonight selling burn bags?" Edgerton asks.

"Yeah. Off an' on, you know."

"Who'd he sell to?"

"Boy named Moochie bought some. And a girl with Moochie, she lives over on Pulaski. And then these other two came by in a car. I didn't know them. Quite a few people paid money for that shit."

"What happened with the shooting?"

"I was down the block. Didn't really see from where I was at, you know."

Edgerton shakes his head, then gestures to the back seat of the radio car. The dealer climbs in and Edgerton follows, slamming the right rear door behind him. The detective cracks the window, lights one cigarette and offers another to the dealer. The kid takes the offering with a soft grunt.

"You been doing all right with me so far," says Edgerton. "Don't start fucking up now."

"What do you mean?"

"I mean you've been straight with me up to this point, so I haven't dragged your ass downtown like I normally would. But if you're gonna hold back . . ."

"No, man, no," says the dealer. "It's not like that. I told you I saw the shooting, but I was down the street coming up from where my girl lives. I saw them chasing Pete and I heard the shots, but I can't tell you who they were."

"How many were there?"

"I saw two. But only one was shooting."

"Was it a handgun?"

"No," says the dealer, stretching his arms to the length of a long gun. "It was one of these."

"A rifle?"

"Yeah."

"Where'd he come from?"

"I don't know. He was right there when I first seen him."

"Where'd he go afterward?"

"After?"

"After Pete got shot. Where'd the boy with the rifle run?"

"Back down Payson."

"South? That way? What'd he look like? What was he wearing?"

"Dark coat and hat, I think."

"What kind of hat?"

"You know, like with a brim."

"Baseball cap?"

The dealer nods.

"How was he built?"

"Average. Six feet, you know."

Edgerton throws the last third of his cigarette out the window and reads through the last two pages in his notepad. The dealer breathes deep, then sighs.

"Ain't this some shit."

Edgerton grunts. "What?"

"I just talked to him a couple hours back. I told him that this shit was gonna get his ass killed. He just laughed, you know? He laughed and said he was gonna make a little money and then go buy his own shit."

"Well," says Edgerton, "you were right."

At the sound of voices on the adjacent sidewalk, the dealer slumps down inside the car, suddenly aware that he has been talking on the street with a police detective for a quarter of an hour. Two young boys glide past the car and turn the corner onto Hollins Street, eyefucking the uniforms but never bothering to look into the back seat. Except for the uniforms, the intersection is once again empty.

"Let's hurry this up," the dealer says, suddenly uncomfortable. "A lot of people know me around here and this don't look right."

"Tell me this," says Edgerton, still scanning his notes. "There had to be some people out on that corner, right?"

The dealer nods almost gratefully, content to know the price of his own noninvolvement.

"There were five or six people around," he tells the detective. "A couple girls that live over that way on Hollins with some other boy I don't know. I don't know their names but I see them around. And there was another guy who I do know. He was right there when it happened."

Edgerton flips to a fresh page of his notepad and clicks the top of his city-issue pen. With nothing else said, both men understand that the price of anonymity will be another witness's identity. The dealer asks for another cigarette, then a light, then expels both the smoke and the name.

"John Nathan," Edgerton repeats, writing it down. "Where's he live?"

"I think Catherine Street, right off Frederick."

"He deals?"

"Yeah. You all have locked him up."

The detective nods, then closes the notepad. There is only so much cooperation that a detective can expect at the scene of a drug murder, and this kid has just exceeded Edgerton's monthly quota. Instinctively, the dealer reaches over to close the bargain with a handshake. A strange gesture. Edgerton responds, then offers a last warning before opening the car door.

"If this doesn't check out," he says, sliding off the seat with the kid following him out of the car, "I know where to find you, right?"

The dealer nods agreement, then pulls the beret down on his forehead and disappears into the darkness. Edgerton takes another ten minutes to sketch his crime scene and asks the Southwest uniforms a few questions about the name he has just been given. If you see him on the street, he tells the patrolmen, pick his ass up and call homicide.

At half past three in the morning, Edgerton finally manages to get free for the four-block drive to Bon Secours and a visit with his dead man. He's a big one, too—six-foot-one or so with a linebacker's upper body and a tailback's legs. A thirty-year-old addict who lived not a block from where he was shot, Gregory Taylor looks up at the ceiling of the ER through one glazed eye, the other having swollen shut from the fall on Payson Street. Catheters and tubes hang limply from every appendage, lifeless as the body to which they were attached. Edgerton notes the needle tracks on both arms as well as gunshot wounds to the right chest, left hip and upper right arm. All of the wounds appear to be entrances, though with a .22 slug, Edgerton knows, it's hard to tell.

"He looks pretty mean, doesn't he?" says the detective to a nearby uniform. "Big and mean. I guess that explains why there were two of them. I wouldn't want to go out looking for this guy alone, even with a rifle. I'd definitely bring a friend."

The physical evidence suggests two other things to the detective. One: The killing was an act of impulse rather than premeditation. Edgerton knows that from the weapons involved; no shooter with any semblance of professionalism would carry something as cumbersome as a .22 rifle to a planned drug killing. Two: The shooter was mightily pissed off at Gregory Taylor, ten shots fired being an obvious indication of displeasure.

Leaning over the dead man's torso, Edgerton draws a human form on a fresh page of his notepad and begins marking wound sites. As he does, a heavyset trauma nurse, her face locked in that unmistakable get-out-of-my-emergency-room expression, walks across the ER, closing the plastic curtain behind her.

"Are you the detective for this one?"

"Yes."

"Do you need his clothes?"

"Yeah, we do, thanks. There should be a uniformed officer here to bag those. I'll see—"

"There's one out in the waiting room with the mother," says the nurse, obviously torn between the joys of irritation and the satisfactions of efficiency. "We're going to need this bed soon."

"The mother is here?"

The nurse nods.

"Okay, then. I need to see her," says Edgerton, opening the curtain. "One other thing. He didn't say anything in the ambulance or once he got here?"

"A-D-A-S-T-W," says the nurse.

"What?"

"A-D-A-S-T-W," she says with a certain pride. "Arrived dead and stayed that way."

Beautiful. Is it any wonder that the easiest extramarital affair for a cop is with an emergency room nurse? What other relationship could be so psychologically symbiotic, so happily diseased in its perspective? Hell, if they ever get bored with the sex, they can always go to a motel room and give each other attitude. A-D-A-S-T-W.

Edgerton swallows his smile before pushing through the double doors to find the fifty-eight-year-old mother in the waiting room.

Pearl Taylor takes the detective's hand but says nothing. Edgerton is usually good with the grieving mothers. An attractive, well-dressed man with carefully coifed salt-and-pepper hair and a rich, sonorous voice, he is a walking, talking reminder of the son they never managed to raise. Faced with black male defendants and juries of black women, city prosecutors love to get Edgerton on the witness stand for that very reason.

"I'm very sorry about your son."

The mother shakes her head quickly, then releases the detective's hand.

"We think this happened," says Edgerton, choosing his words with care, "because of an argument that might have had to do with—"

"Drugs," she says, finishing the sentence. "I know it."

"Is there anyone your son might have had a disagreement . . ."

"I don't know anything about his business," she says. "I can't help you with that."

Edgerton contemplates another question, but the woman's plaintive expression changes his mind. It's as if she's waited for this moment for years, waited so long that its arrival can be greeted with familiarity as much as grief.

"I'll do my best," Edgerton tells her, "to find the person responsible."

She looks at him strangely, then shrugs a shoulder before turning away.

TUESDAY, MAY 10

"Homicide," says Edgerton. "How's it going?"

"It's going," says the desk sergeant, unimpressed. "Nah, fuck that. It's more than going. It's gone. It's fuckin' history."

"That bad, huh?"

"What can I do you for?"

"Got a writ for a prisoner," says Edgerton, pulling out a custody form signed by a state's attorney and tossing it on the Southwestern booking desk. Peering at the writ over the top of his reading glasses, the desk sergeant grunts, coughs, then grinds a cigarette into an overburdened ashtray. He takes the paper slip and steps back, checking the name against the cellblock prisoner log.

"Gone to city jail," the sergeant says.

"You all just called and told me he was here," says Edgerton. "When was your wagon run?"

The sergeant rechecks the name, then walks over to the cellblock door. Calling for the turnkey, he passes the paper through the bars, nods an acknowledgment to the man on the other side, then walks back toward the detective. Edgerton watches each labored movement, caught between amusement and exasperation. The Midnight Dance of the Universal Desk Sergeant, a performance that is somehow the same whether the precinct house is in Boston or Biloxi. Was there ever a desk sergeant who didn't peer out over reading glasses? Was there ever a desk man who wanted to be bothered with police work at three in the morning? Was any station house desk ever manned by anything but aging civil servants, six months from their pensions, whose every movement seemed slower than death itself?

"Yeah, John Nathan. We got him," the sergeant says finally. "He gave us a slightly different name."

"Okay then."

"You want him carryout, right?"

"Yeah, he's going downtown."

Five minutes more and the cage door opens for a dark-skinned, pear-shaped kid, who steps slowly into the light of the booking area. Edgerton looks at the bloated little wonder that is his eyewitness and knows immediately that the Hollins Street murder is going down. He knows this from the kid's demeanor. Because not only was this brain-dead corner boy clever enough to get locked up on a drug charge two hours after the shooting, he's now standing here looking more sheepish than sullen. Three A.M. and the boy can't even manage a decent eyefuck; when Edgerton pulls out his cuffs, the kid actually pushes his arms forward, palms up.

"Don't keep him out too late," says the desk sergeant. "It's a school night."

An old station house line, and Edgerton doesn't laugh. The fat kid says nothing for a moment, then manages a sentence that is more of a statement than a question:

"You want to talk to me about Pete, too, man."

"I'm the one who's gonna talk to you for real," says Edgerton, walking his prisoner out the booking area door and into the back seat of the Cavalier. Heading west on Lombard Street, Edgerton makes a point of gesturing toward the medical examiner's building at the intersection of Penn Street.

"You want to wave to your friend?"

"Who's my friend?"

"Pete. The boy from Payson and Hollins."

"He ain't my friend."

"No, huh?" says Edgerton. "So I guess you don't want to wave to him?"

"Where he now?"

"Right there. The white building."

"What's he doing there?"

"Not a helluva lot," says Edgerton. "That's the morgue, yo."

The detective checks the rearview mirror and satisfies himself that there isn't a trace of surprise in the fat kid's face. He's been locked up at the Southwest since early yesterday morning, but he knows about the murder.

"I don't know no more about that shit," the kid offers after a five-second delay. "Don't know why you got to take me from the Southwest District to talk to me."

Edgerton slows the Cavalier to the curb lane, then wheels around in his seat and glares hard at the kid's dark, bloated face. The kid looks back evenly, but Edgerton can already sense some small kernel of fear.

"You don't need to know," says Edgerton coldly, turning back and speeding up again. "We're going to start over like you never met another cop in your whole life. Just forget you ever dealt with a cop any other time in your life because they ain't never talked to you like I'm gonna talk to you."

"You gonna talk to me."

"You got it."

"I don't know shit."

"You were there," says Edgerton.

"I wasn't nowhere."

Edgerton slows the car and turns around again. The kid actually flinches a bit.

"You were there," says Edgerton slowly.

This time the fat kid says nothing, and Edgerton drives the remaining six blocks in cold silence. Two hours, the detective tells himself. One hour and forty minutes for fat boy here to tell me everything that happened on Payson Street; twenty minutes to write it up and initial each page.

Predictions don't mean much in the interrogation room; Edgerton proved as much to himself three weeks ago when he went at his best suspect in the Brenda Thompson killing in a third and final interview. That day, Edgerton went into the box predicting a confession and emerged six hours later with nothing but lies. Still, he can't help but be optimistic this time around. For one thing, the kid in the back seat isn't the target but merely a witness. For another, he has managed to collect a drug charge that can be used for leverage. Lastly, John Nathan has no heart; he proved as much a minute ago.

Back at the homicide office, Edgerton shepherds the kid into the large interrogation room, then goes into his monologue. Twenty minutes later, the boy is nodding in semiagreement. In all, it requires a little more than ninety minutes before Edgerton has a viable account of the shooting on Payson Street, an account that conforms to everything he learned at the scene.

By Nathan's account, Gregory Taylor was indeed burning customers with fake dime bags, then firing the profits into his own arms. Even judged against the fleeting standards of the urban drug trade, this was not exactly a long-term career move. Taylor eventually burned a couple boys from down by the Gilmor Homes, then made the mistake of staying out on the corner too long. The boys came back in an old pickup, jumped on Taylor with rifles and demanded their money back. Sizing up the situation correctly, the victim coughed up two $10 bills, but one customer was still unsatisfied. He opened up with the rifle, chasing Taylor across the intersection, firing one round after another as the victim collapsed on the asphalt. The two gunmen then ran back to the pickup and drove south on Payson toward Frederick.

During the brief interrogation, Nathan gives up real names, street names, physical descriptions and approximate addresses—every last little detail. When Edgerton walks back into the main office, he has everything he needs for a pair of search and seizure warrants.

And yet none of that seems to matter the following morning when the administrative lieutenant—the supervisor who serves as a direct aide to the captain—reads the 24-hour report and learns that Edgerton questioned a witness at the scene without bringing the man downtown. Inappropriate, the lieutenant complains. Irregular. Against standard procedure. Such behavior shows bad judgment, perhaps even laziness.

"What the fuck does he know about investigation?" says Edgerton angrily when Roger Nolan tells him of the complaints on the following midnight shift. "He sits in that office and does arithmetic. When did he ever get out on the street and work a case?"

"Easy, Harry. Easy."

"I got everything I needed from that guy at the scene," storms Edgerton. "What the fuck does it matter whether I talk to him there or here?"

"I know . . ."

"I'm sick of these fucking politicians."

Nolan sighs. As Edgerton's sergeant, he's caught between the captain and D'Addario, for whom Edgerton has become ammunition in a shooting war. If Edgerton handles calls and solves murders, he vindicates his shift lieutenant; if he doesn't, he serves the captain and the admin lieutenant as prima facie evidence of lax supervision on D'Addario's shift.

But now the situation is even worse. Not only does Nolan have to contend with the external politics, but he's also got serious problems in his squad. Edgerton has become a lightning rod; Kincaid, in particular, can't abide the younger detective.

A veteran investigator of the old school, Kincaid puts stock in the way a man serves his unit. By that reckoning, a good detective shows up early for work to relieve the previous shift; he answers the phone, handling as many calls as come his way; he covers for his partner and his squad members, helping them with witnesses or even scenes without having to be asked. It is a gratifying portrait of the investigator as a cooperative entity, a team player, and Kincaid has spent twenty-two years fashioning himself in that image. For seven of those years, he worked murders with Eddie Brown, an interracial team made especially amusing by Kincaid's hillbilly drawl. And for the last two years, he has partnered with anyone and everyone on D'Addario's shift willing to share a call with him.

All of which makes Edgerton simply incomprehensible to Kincaid. It isn't so much a personal dislike, the older detective tells others in the office. After all, not two weeks ago he spent time with Edgerton at McAllister's squad party, a summer barbecue to which Edgerton brought his wife and young son. Harry was good company that afternoon, even a little bit charming, Kincaid had to concede. Granting the differences in youth, in race, in his New York urbanity, Edgerton might not be Kincaid's first choice for a drinking buddy, but in the end, the feud had less to do with personalities than with Edgerton's lack of any communal instinct, his indifference to the station house camaraderie that had always been so valuable to Kincaid.

To Edgerton, the consummate loner, homicide investigation is an isolated, individual pursuit. It is, in his mind, a singular contest between one detective and his killer, a contest in which the other detectives, the sergeants, the lieutenants and every other organism in the police department have no appropriate role beyond getting out of the primary detective's path. This was, in essence, Edgerton's strength and at the same time his weakness. Share and share alike would never be his credo, and consequently Edgerton would always be a source of discontent to his squad. But when he did catch a murder, he wouldn't shirk. Unlike many detectives who learn to work a murder only until the phone rings with the next dispatcher's call, Edgerton would bury himself in a case file until a sergeant came along to drag him kicking and screaming to the next assignment.

"It's hell getting Harry to take a case," explained Terry McLarney on one occasion. "You've got to grab him by the shoulders and yell, 'Harry. This one's yours.' But once you do that, he'll work it to death."

No, Edgerton will not handle his share of suicides, overdose deaths, or cellblock hangings. He will not take orders for anyone else when traveling to Crazy John's for a cheesesteak, and if asked to bring something back, he will surely forget. No, he will not be a workhorse like Garvey or Worden, a central force around whom the rest of a squad establishes its orbit. And it is true that when some rookie cop fires six-on-the-whistle at the scene of some gas station robbery, Edgerton will probably not volunteer to help sort through witness statements and collate reports. But, if left alone, he will give a squad eight or nine good clearances a year.

Having supervised Edgerton when the two were in the Eastern District, Nolan has for a long time understood the necessary tradeoff. Edgerton was one of the most talented, intelligent patrolmen in Nolan's sector—even if the rest of the uniforms didn't know what to make of him. He could be inconsiderate, at times even a little irresponsible, but nothing happened on that Greenmount Avenue post that he didn't know about. The same was true up in homicide; Edgerton may drift off into the ether for a day or two, but Nolan could be assured that in the end, Harry's cases would get worked. Hard.

"Don't worry about it," Nolan told Edgerton after one of Kincaid's angry tirades. "You just keep doing what you're doing."

For Nolan, the trick was to keep his squad together by keeping the friction points apart. Everyone to his proper orbit: Kincaid with Bowman and Garvey, Edgerton, alone or with Nolan himself when he occasionally needed a secondary. Suddenly, however, that had become impossible.

Twice in the last week, Nolan had overheard Kincaid and Bowman ranting about Edgerton in the main office. That fact alone was unremarkable; everyone threw shit on everyone else in the squadroom. But it was notable that the administrative lieutenant—a pipeline to the captain—was present on each occasion.

A boss was a boss. For one detective to talk trash about another in front of a lieutenant was going too far. And while Nolan, alone among the sergeants, had no great love for D'Addario, he had no intention of seeing Edgerton used as ammunition in any prolonged power struggle.

At least one detective in the squad, Rich Garvey, was equally uncomfortable with that notion. As the man who handled the most calls in Nolan's squad, Garvey was less than impressed by Edgerton's work ethic. But he also didn't want to see a fellow detective, a competent detective, burned over things that should never go further than the squad. Three days ago, at a quiet lunch in a Fells Point diner, he had said as much to Kincaid.

"Nolan lets him get away with too much," Kincaid said bitterly. "Last midnight shift, that motherfucker was late every day but one."

Garvey shook his head. "I know it. I know you're pissed off, Donald," he told the older detective. "But you have to remember that Nolan would do the same for you. He'd cover for you, too."

Kincaid nodded, understanding. "I know what you're saying," he said finally. "But I'll tell you, if I was his sergeant, I'd bust his ass so quick he wouldn't know what hit him."

"I know you would, Donald."

The lunch discussion helped establish a temporary truce; there would be no additional scenes in front of the admin lieutenant or any other boss. But Garvey and Nolan both knew that with Edgerton and Kincaid as the players, the problem wasn't really solved. Sure enough, things are ugly again today, with the admin lieutenant asking questions about Edgerton's performance on the Payson Street murder. By Nolan's reckoning, the lieutenant wouldn't even know to ask about Edgerton's questioning of that witness at the scene. Not unless some other detective mentioned it.

Edgerton is still fuming about the lieutenant's comment: "I'd like to hear what it is that he knows about investigating a murder. He wasn't even there and he's going to come out of that office and tell me how to do my job."

"Harry . . ."

"I got more out of that guy out on the street than he'd get if he brought him in here and talked to him for two days."

"I know, Harry, just . . ."

Nolan spends another five minutes trying to placate his detective, but to little effect. When Edgerton goes ballistic, nothing can bring him back down for a few hours, at the minimum. Reaching a pause in his rant, Edgerton wanders off to a typewriter, where he begins pecking brutally at his search warrants.

It doesn't matter that the PC in both warrants will be strong enough to obtain a judge's signature. It doesn't matter that the house on Laurens Street will yield .22 cartridges of a similar make and composition to those found at the scene. It doesn't matter that when Edgerton and Nolan confront the young man living at that address and take out a pair of handcuffs, the suspect will nod knowingly and say, "I was wondering when you'd come."

It doesn't even matter when the same young man breaks down after three hours' interrogation, implicating himself as the shooter in a full, seven-page statement. Somehow, none of that matters.

Because less than a week after Edgerton's arrests in the Payson Street murder, the same argument is still raging on. This time it's Bob Bowman, who shares Kincaid's opinions when it comes to Edgerton, sitting in the coffee room, telling five or six other detectives that Harry's case isn't going to court.

"He has one murder that's gone down this whole year," he says. "And I heard from Don Giblin that the case is so weak they're not even going to take it into a grand jury."

"You're kidding me."

"That's what I heard from Giblin."

Only it isn't true. The grand jury does indeed indict two men for shooting down Gregory Taylor on Payson Street, even after he tried to compensate them for the burn bags. And a prosecutor from the trial division is assigned to bring the case into court. And come fall, a circuit court judge will accept a twenty-year sentence and second-degree plea from the shooter, along with five years and fifteen suspended from the codefendant.

Even so, all of that is irrelevant to the politics. Because in the homicide unit, in his own squad especially, Harry Edgerton has become the accepted target. For the captain, he is ammunition; for D'Addario, a potential liability; for his fellow detectives, an aloof, enigmatic pain in the ass.

On the same morning that the Taylor case goes into the black, Edgerton arrives for roll call to find that his lieutenant has posted a new sheet of yellow legal paper next to the board.

"Hey, Harry," says Worden, pointing to the slip of paper. "Guess what?"

"Aw no," moans Edgerton. "Say it ain't so."

"It's so, Harry. You're still up."

SIX

THURSDAY, MAY 26

By measured steps, Patti Cassidy walks her husband into the crowded courtroom, where all is suddenly silence. The jury, the judge, the lawyers—the entire assembly sits transfixed as Police Agent Gene Cassidy stretches his right hand, touches a wooden beam, then guides himself into the witness stand. Patti touches his shoulder, whispers, then retreats to a seat behind the prosecution table.

The clerk rises. "Do you swear to tell the truth and nothing but the truth?"

"I do," says Cassidy, his voice clear.

In a place where partial victories and gray equivocations always seem to dominate, Gene Cassidy's appearance on the witness stand is a startling moment. Cassidy did not see Terry McLarney and Corey Belt and the other Western men in the hallway, gripping his shoulders with a few attaboys and go-get-'ems before the courtroom doors opened. He cannot see his wife, primly dressed and eight months' pregnant, in the gallery's front row. He cannot see one of the jurors, the young white girl, crying softly in the back tier. He cannot see the cold rage on the judge's face, and he cannot see Butchie Frazier, the man who blinded him with two .38 rounds, staring with strange fascination from the defense table a few feet away.

The courtroom is crowded, the gallery packed with Western officers in uniform, a show of solidarity that does not extend to the departmental brass. The Western District commander is not in attendance, nor is the chief of patrol or any of the deputy commissioners—a fact noted with some bitterness by the rank and file. Take a bullet for the company and you're on your own; the bosses may show up at the hospital and they'll definitely be on hand for the funeral, but the departmental memory is short. Cassidy's appearance in court will be witnessed by no one above the rank of sergeant. The space remaining in the gallery is occupied by the Cassidy family, a handful of reporters, curious courthouse regulars and a few friends and relatives of Butchie Frazier's.

At one point during the jury selection, his younger brother, Derrick, appeared in the corridor just outside the courtroom, where prosecution witnesses are seated before their testimony. He eyefucked one, talked trash to another and then was suddenly confronted by McLarney and two Western men, who offered him an opportunity to leave as a free man. Given the alternative of becoming a projectile launched into the rear of a police wagon, Derrick Frazier issued a few more obscenities and then turned on his heel toward the St. Paul Street exit.

"Okay," said McLarney to a Western officer. "I guess we put him on the list, too."

The uniform shook his head. "That motherfucker . . ."

"Fuck him," said McLarney, unsmiling. "One of these days, we'll be chalking him off."

For McLarney, the Cassidy trial was unrelieved agony, an ordeal of empty hours spent in courtroom hallways and prosecutors' offices. Because he was at the Clarence M. Mitchell Jr. Courthouse as a witness, McLarney was sequestered, and whatever happened behind the thick double doors of that second-floor courtroom was lost to him. As the most important criminal trial of his life lurched toward a verdict, McLarney could only watch a parade of witnesses from a bench in the hall, then buttonhole the prosecutors, Howard Gersh and Gary Schenker, during breaks:

"How's it going in there?"

"Are we winning?"

"How'd Gene do?"

"Is Butchie gonna testify?"

Yesterday, McLarney spent the hours pacing the length of the second-floor hall and trying to calculate the odds. A 40 percent chance for first-degree, maybe 50 percent if Yolanda sticks to the grand jury testimony she gave against Butchie in February after passing the polygraph. Another 40 percent for second-degree attempted murder or attempted manslaughter. Maybe 20 percent for a hung jury or acquittal. At least, McLarney reasoned, they managed to land a decent judge. If you were a lawyer, Elsbeth Bothe could drive you crazy with her penchant for questioning witnesses from the bench, and, true, she had a few convictions reversed on appeal for commentary from the bench. But more important, from McLarney's point of view, Bothe never got soft at the point of sentencing. If Butchie Frazier lost on points, Bothe would surely bang him.

Like any other appointee to the Baltimore circuit court, Bothe could judge men with the confidence that comes from incumbency and an elective term of fifteen years. Her voice was a quiet rasp, a perfect vehicle to express an undying irritation with prosecutors, attorneys, defendants and the criminal justice system in general.

From the bench, she was master of all she saw, and what she saw was a courtroom carved from the northwestern corner of the ornate courthouse, a paneled courtroom with high ceilings and portraits of long-dead judges glaring down from the walls. At first glance, it was not the sort of place where questions of life and death ought to be decided; whatever dignity was conveyed by the dark woods of the judge's bench and trial tables was utterly corrupted by the jumble of insulated pipe and metal ventilation work suspended from the ceiling. From certain angles, the judge appeared to preside in a courtroom created from a government office building's basement.

Elsbeth Bothe came to the Baltimore bench from the defense bar, where she had been one of the most talented attorneys in what was then a fledgling public defenders office. Many a man walked free of the Baltimore City Jail because Bothe had been his advocate, yet she could recall only one client among the hundreds she had defended whom she actually knew with any certainty to be innocent. It was, on reflection, the most appropriate history for a judge whose courtroom had become a cluttered stage for a large share of Baltimore's homicide prosecutions. Black, or brown, or on select occasions an occasional white stray, they were brought to the Calvert Street courthouse in dull, dirty jail vans, then led in handcuffs and legchains from lockup to courtroom and back again to lockup. Poor, huddled masses yearning to be free, they were the daily feed for the trough, and whether by plea or verdict, they existed only to be consumed. Day after day, the lawyers were fed, the prisons were filled, the machine rattled forward. By choice and circumstance, Bothe was one of three city judges who, among them, handled more than 60 percent of the hundred and fifty or so murder prosecutions that made their way to circuit court each year. It was a grim, pathetic parade, a chain of human misery for which Bothe was psychologically as well as temperamentally suited.

Her chambers said as much: Amid the Maryland code books and legal texts rested a collection of human skulls—mostly manufactured caricatures, one the real McCoy—to rival any anthropologist's closet. On the walls were original front pages from old turn-of-the-century *Police Gazettes*, each one recounting the details of some shocking spasm of violence. To homicide detectives, such a peculiarity was especially comforting, assuring them that Elsbeth Bothe—like any self-respecting cop—was capable of enjoying the best parts of a good murder.

Not that Bothe was some kind of hanging judge. Like everyone else compelled to deal with murder on wholesale basis, she was not above taking a light plea if it helped clear a crowded court docket of a cheap murder or two. This is the reality in Baltimore and every other American jurisdiction, where plea bargaining is the only way to keep the criminal justice system from strangling on its own caseload. The trick—for prosecutors as well as judges—is knowing which cases cannot be pled down.

By any reasoning, the case against Butchie Frazier could not be pled—not for anything that Butchie's attorney could in good conscience accept. Prosecuting the case in tandem, Gersh and Schenker had offered fifty years, knowing that the maximum for first-degree attempted murder and a handgun charge would be life and twenty, which shakes out to about eighty years in all. Given the state's parole guidelines, the ultimate difference to Butchie was maybe five years or so, but with any career criminal that kind of margin isn't worth talking about. Guys like Butchie Frazier hear prosecutors talking double digits and their eyes glaze over.

As a result, the case went to a jury of twelve: eleven women, one man; nine black, three white. It was a fairly typical city panel, which, if it did nothing else of note, had managed to at least stay awake throughout the state's case—no small accomplishment in a courthouse where judges are occasionally obliged to have a sheriff's deputy nudge juror number three back into lucidity.

The jurors were downright fascinated by Yolanda Marks, who was a picture of both anger and fear on the witness stand. Yolanda had tried time and again to back away from her grand jury testimony in her pretrial interviews with prosecutors. Her courtroom answers to Schenker's questions were all cold and monosyllabic and much of her testimony was laced with tears. Still, she gave up Appleton Street as Butchie glared at her from a few feet away.

Yolanda was followed by others, by McLarney testifying about the crime scene and Gary Tuggle, one of the two detail officers, testifying to the search for a suspect. Young, black, attractive, Tuggle was a necessity for this jury—a racial counterweight to Butchie Frazier, a subtle suggestion to black jurors that the system itself wasn't altogether white. Then came the couple who had been walking south on Appleton Street from the corner bar, both of whom recounted the same shooting scenario as Yolanda, though both testified that they were too far away to identify the gunman. Still, they confirmed Yolanda's account.

Finally, there was the kid from the City Jail, another murder defendant who had quarreled with Butchie when both were in pretrial detention. Butchie had told him about the shooting, offering details that only the shooter could know.

"What else did the defendant tell you?" asked Schenker.

"He said the police was roughing him up, so he pulled out his gun and shot him in the head. He said he wished he would have killed the bitch."

The ultimate ghetto insult, it hung there in the courtroom for a moment and then fell on dead silence. A young man, blind for life, so casually denigrated by the man who had held the gun. Cassidy. A bitch.

Gary Schenker paused for effect as two jurors shook their heads and Bothe lifted a hand to her mouth. Asked whether he was offered a reduced sentence in exchange for his testimony, the kid shook his head. This, he told the jury, was personal.

"I showed him a picture of my girl," the kid explained. "He said when he got out he was going to have her."

That was their case. Everything that could be done had been done before Gene Cassidy made his way to the stand. Cassidy was the emotional kicker, the unspoken appeal to a jury of Butchie Frazier's peers, a jury that now sits staring at the young man on the witness stand, a young man who cannot stare back. Gene Cassidy is the psychological culmination of the state's case, the last tug on the jury's heartstring before the defense takes over.

Already the jury has heard the University of Maryland surgeon describe the path of each bullet in clinical detail and assess the slim chance of anyone's surviving such wounds. Yet here is Cassidy, back from the grave in his dark blue suit to face the man who failed to kill him.

"Agent Cassidy," says Bothe, solicitous, "there's a microphone in front of you . . . if you could speak into it."

Cassidy reaches forward and touches the metal.

Schenker then asks the preliminary questions. "Agent Cassidy, how long have you been a Baltimore city police officer . . ."

As Schenker continues, the eyes of several jurors bounce from Cassidy to Frazier, then back to Cassidy. The two men are close to each other, separated by no more than six feet, and Frazier is staring with genuine curiosity at the side of Cassidy's head. Jet black hair covers the temple wound, and the facial injuries have healed perfectly. Only the eyes reveal the damage: one blue and vacant, the other translucent and distorted.

"And you are totally blind, correct?" asks Schenker.

"Yes, I am," says Cassidy. "I've also lost my senses of smell and taste."

It is the most precious kind of testimony. In every murder trial, the victim exists for the jury as an abstract entity, as a part of the process represented by nothing more than an autopsy report and some 3-by-5 crime scene photographs. The defendant, however, remains flesh and blood for the duration of the trial. In the hands of a competent defense attorney, his humanity is better displayed than the inhumanity of the crime, his ordinariness is more apparent than the extraordinary acts of which he is accused. A good defense attorney sits close to his client, touches him on the shoulder to get his attention, puts an arm around him to show the jurors that he likes this man, that he believes in him. Some lawyers go so far as to give defendants mints or hard candies, telling clients to pull them out at a quiet moment and offer one to the lawyer, perhaps even to the prosecutor, seated a few feet away. See, ladies and gentlemen, he's human. He likes mints. He can share.

But Gene Cassidy denies Butchie Frazier the advantage. In this courtroom he, too, is flesh and blood.

Schenker continues: "On that particular evening, what if anything do you recall . . ."

Cassidy grimaces slightly before answering. "I have no recollection of the incident . . . the shooting," he says slowly. "The last thing I remember is being at my father-in-law's house in Pennsylvania earlier that afternoon."

"Can you recall going to work that day?"

"I know that I must have," says Cassidy. "But I can't remember anything after my father-in-law's house. They tell me that's pretty common with these kinds of injuries—"

"Officer Cassidy," asks Bothe, interrupting. "I take it that's your wife who escorted you to the stand."

"Yes, your honor."

"And by the look of things," the judge says, unwilling to let the moment pass, "I would say that she's expecting . . ."

"Yes. Due on the Fourth of July."

The Fourth of July. The defense attorney shakes his head.

"Is this your first child?" asks the judge, glancing toward the jury box.

"Yes it is."

"Thank you, Officer Cassidy. I was curious."

The beleaguered defense counsel has nowhere to go. What do you do with the testimony of a blinded police officer whose pregnant wife waits on a nearby bench? What do you ask on cross examination? Where do you make your points? Where, in such a scene, do you find a place for your client to breathe?

"No questions, your honor."

"The witness is excused. Thank you, Agent Cassidy."

Out in the corridor, McLarney watches the double doors open at the recess. The jurors are already upstairs in the jury room, Bothe is already back in chambers. Patti walks out with Gene on her arm, followed by Schenker.

"Hey, Gene, how'd it go?" asks McLarney.

"Okay," says Cassidy. "I think I was good. What'd you think, Patti?"

"You were great, Gene."

"What did Butchie do? Did he look at me?"

"Yeah, Gene," says a friend from the Western. "He was staring right at you."

"Staring? Was he eyefucking me?"

"No," says the officer. "He just looked real strange, you know."

Cassidy nods.

"You hurt him, Gene," says a Western man. "You got him good."

McLarney claps Cassidy on the back, then walks down the hall with Patti and Gene's mother and brother, both down from New Jersey for the trial. As the family heads upstairs to the law library to wait out the defense case, McLarney puts a hand on Cassidy's arm and asks a string of questions about the testimony.

"I wish I could have been in there, Gene," McLarney tells him on the stairs.

"Yeah," says Cassidy. "I think I did okay, though. What did you think, Patti?"

Patti Cassidy reassures her husband again, but McLarney is too nervous to be satisfied by one opinion. Minutes later, he's again pacing the courthouse corridor, buttonholing every lawyer, spectator and sheriff's deputy who walks out of Bothe's court.

"How'd Gene do? What was the jury's reaction?"

McLarney frowns at every assurance. The cost of following the most important jury trial of your life from a corridor is that you're never willing to believe what you hear. Cassidy endured months of speech therapy, McLarney reminds the others. Did he hear the questions? How was his speech?

"He did great, Terry," says Schenker.

"What'd Butchie do?" asks McLarney.

"He just kept staring at him," says a Western man. "He kept staring at the side of Gene's face."

The side of Gene's face. The wound track. Butchie Frazier staring at his handiwork, wondering what the hell went wrong. That son of a bitch, thinks McLarney, frowning at the image.

The defense takes the rest of the afternoon, calling a couple of witnesses who insist that Butchie Frazier is the wrong man, that he wasn't out there at Mosher and Appleton on that fall night. But Frazier himself does not take the stand; his criminal history makes such an act problematic.

"What happened to Officer Cassidy is a tragedy," declares the defense attorney in his closing argument. "But it is a tragedy we can do nothing about. It would be adding to that tragedy to convict Clifton Frazier based on the evidence the state presented."

For their own closing, Schenker and Gersh counter in tandem, with Schenker taking the high road and Gersh going low. The high road asks for an impartial examination of the evidence; the low road calls to a communal instinct that may or may not exist.

"Don't convict Clifton Frazier because the victim in this case is a police officer," Schenker tells the jurors. "Do so because the evidence demands it . . . Because Clifton Frazier did not want to go to jail, he shot Officer Cassidy."

Yet ten minutes later, Gersh stands before the same jury, reminding them that "when a police officer is shot, a little bit of each of us is killed."

The "thin blue line" speech, thinks McLarney, listening to the closing arguments from the back bench. Every time a cop is shot, the prosecutors wheel out the protect-and-serve imagery. Does the jury believe it? Does anyone believe it anymore? McLarney looks at the twelve faces. They're listening, at least—all except number nine. She's looking right through Gersh, McLarney thinks. She's going to be trouble.

"We can send a message to the Butchie Fraziers of the world that they cannot go out on the street and shoot police officers . . ."

And then it's over. Walking single file, the jurors move past the prosecutors, past the defense attorney, past Butchie Frazier, to climb the stairwell to the deliberation room.

Standing with Gersh and Schenker near the courtroom doors, McLarney suddenly encounters Frazier as the defendant, in handcuffs and leg irons, is under escort to the basement lockup. Frazier actually sneers as the two face each other at the edge of the hallway.

"Yeah. Right," McLarney mutters, fighting hard for control. "Who the . . ."

Gersh pulls McLarney away. "I think we've got it," the prosecutor tells him. "It'll take a few hours, but I think we've got it. How'd you like our closing?"

McLarney ignores him, staring instead at the procession of Butchie Frazier and his two guards out the courtroom doors and down the second-floor stairs.

"C'mon," says Gersh, with a light touch on McLarney's shoulder. "Let's go find Gene."

Cassidy is already settled in for the wait, seated with his wife, his mother and his older brother in the back of the nearby jury assembly room. Western uniforms, fresh from their eight-to-four shift, hover around the family, issuing congratulations on the victory sure to come. Out in the hallway, Gersh and Schenker accept congratulations from spectators. As the evening sky fades outside the courtroom windows, two of the Western men organize a pizza run.

"Gene, what do you want on yours?"

"I don't care, as long as it's anchovy."

"What's the name of the place again?"

"Marco's. On Exeter Street."

"We better order now," says one officer, smiling. "We'll not be hanging around here long."

For an hour or so, they are the picture of confidence. For an hour, they are laughing and joking and telling stories from the streets of the Western, stories that always manage to end with someone in handcuffs. Waiting for a verdict they are sure will come quickly, they busy themselves by recounting the best parts of the closing arguments and the details of Gene's testimony.

But suddenly their optimism is shattered by the news that shouting can be heard near the door to Bothe's courtroom, shouting that comes from the jury room upstairs. At times, the loudest voices carry out into the courthouse hallway, just outside the room where Gene Cassidy and his family sit amid empty pizza boxes and Styrofoam cups. The mood of the Western men darkens.

Two hours go by, then three. The shouting in the jury room continues, and the wait becomes agonizing.

"I don't know what to say, Gene," says Gersh, losing faith. "I gave it my best and I'm afraid it wasn't enough."

Four hours brings only a note from the jury forewoman, indicating that the panel is hopelessly deadlocked. Bothe reads the note to the attorneys, then brings the jury downstairs and gives a standard instruction, urging the jurors to return and attempt to reach a verdict.

More shouting.

"This is a crime, Gene," says Corey Belt. "I can't believe it."

Raw doubt is sticking in their throats as the angry voice of one juror carries above the others and is heard at the bottom of the jury room stairs. They always lie, shouts the juror. You got to convince me.

They always lie. Who does? The police? The witnesses? The defendants? Butchie didn't even testify, so it can't be him. So who in hell is she talking about? McLarney hears about the remark from a clerk and immediately thinks of juror number nine, the woman who seemed to be looking through Gersh during the closings. It's her voice, he tells himself. Goddammit, she's the one.

McLarney swallows hard and retreats to the second-floor corridor, where he paces back and forth in a smoldering rage. There wasn't enough, he tells himself. I'm losing this jury because I didn't give them enough. An eyewitness. Corroboration. A jail-house confession. Somehow, it wasn't enough. As late evening arrives, McLarney finds it harder and harder to go back into the room where Gene is waiting. As he walks back and forth in the marble hallway, several men from the Western come outside to assure him that it doesn't matter either way.

"Guilty, he goes to prison," declares one uniform, a man who once served under McLarney in Sector 2. "Not guilty, he goes back out on the street."

"If he comes back to the Western, he's dead," says another, agreeing. "That piece of shit will wish he'd been found guilty."

Reckless words, but McLarney nods in agreement. In truth, there would be no need for a plan, no elaborate conspiracy. It would simply happen. Butchie Frazier was a stone criminal, and a criminal is nothing if not predictable. Back on the streets of the Western, he would surely do his dark little deeds, and just as surely, every last uniform would be there waiting. No trial, no lawyers, no jury. If Butchie Frazier is set free today, McLarney tells himself, he'll be dead within a year.

Back in the courtroom, Gersh and Schenker contemplate the alternatives. Fearing the worst, they could go to Frazier's attorney and offer a plea before the jury returns. But what kind of plea? Frazier already balked at fifty. Thirty? Thirty means parole in as little as ten. Cassidy said from the outset he couldn't live with ten. But can he live with an acquittal? In the end, the entire discussion is academic; sensing perhaps the same thing as the prosecutors, Butchie Frazier turns down any notion of a negotiated plea.

But the six-hour mark brings another, different note from the forewoman, this one inquiring about the difference between first- and second-degree attempted murder. Guilty. They're talking guilty in there.

Hearing the latest, the cops in the jury assembly room are suddenly breathing again; a few sidle up to Cassidy and offer congratulations. He shrugs them off. Second-degree, he says, shaking his head. How can they be thinking about second-degree?

"Never mind that, Gene," says Gersh, a veteran prosecutor who has been through this wait a hundred times. "They've turned the corner. They're coming around."

Cassidy smiles at the thought. As if to lighten his mood, he asks permission to tell his joke.

"Which joke is this?" asks Belt.

"You know," says Cassidy. "My joke."

"Your joke? The one you told before?"

"Yeah," says Cassidy. "That one."

Belt shakes his head, smiling. "What do you want to do, Gene? Clear the room?"

"What the hell," says Biemiller, another Western man. "Tell the joke, Gene."

Cassidy launches into an unlikely tale of three pieces of string standing outside a barroom, all of whom are thirsty and in want of a beer. A sign on the door says no string will be served.

"The first piece of string goes into the bar and orders a beer," explains Cassidy, "and the bartender says, 'Hey, are you a piece of string?' "

The string answers in the affirmative and is escorted from the premises. Some of the cops offer loud, audible yawns. Ignoring them, Cassidy recounts the plight of the second piece of string, which happens to be markedly similar to the first.

"So then the third piece of string rolls around on the ground and ties himself up and gets all messed up before going into the bar, right?"

McLarney wanders in from the hallway, just in time for a punch line he can't possibly understand.

"And the bartender asks him, 'Are you a piece of string?' And the string says, ' 'Fraid not.' "

Groans all around.

"Christ, that's a terrible joke, Gene," says one of the Western men. "Even for a blind guy, that's a terrible joke."

Cassidy laughs. Inside the jury assembly room the tension is gone, the pall of defeat lifted suddenly by the jury forewoman's casual question. McLarney, too, is relieved, though the idea of a second-degree verdict still doesn't sit well. As Cassidy launches into another joke, McLarney wanders back into the corridor and slumps onto a hallway bench, his head resting against the cold marble wall. Belt follows him out.

"Butchie's going to prison," says McLarney, as much to hear himself say it as for any other reason.

"We need first-degree, bunk," says Belt, leaning over the bench. "Second-degree don't cut it."

McLarney nods in agreement.

Upon the arrival of the forewoman's note, Gersh and Schenker immediately withdrew any and all plea offers. Judge Bothe tells the prosecutors in her chambers that she's ready to take a second-degree finding right now if the jurors are unanimous.

"No," says Gersh with a trace of anger. "Let them do their job."

The deliberations stretch to more than eight hours, and it is closing on 10:00 P.M. when the courtroom reconvenes and Butchie Frazier is returned from the basement lockup. Cassidy sits in the front bench with his wife, directly behind the prosecutors. McLarney and Belt find seats in the second bench, closer to the door. The jurors come downstairs silently. They do not look at the defendant—a good sign. They do not look at Cassidy—a bad sign. McLarney watches them settle into the jury box, his hands gripping the crease of his pants at both knees.

"Madam forelady," asks the clerk. "Have you reached a unanimous verdict on the charge of attempted murder in the first degree?"

"Yes we have."

"How say you to that charge?"

"We find the defendant guilty."

Gene Cassidy nods slowly, gripping his wife's hand, as each juror is polled and the Western uniforms give up a soft cheer from the gallery.

Several jurors begin to cry. From the trial table, Gersh turns around to scan the crowd, then gives McLarney a thumbs-up sign; McLarney smiles, shakes Belt's hand and then pumps a fist in the air and leans forward, exhausted by the moment. Butchie Frazier shakes his head, then begins a careful examination of his fingernails.

As Bothe sets a sentencing date and then concludes the proceedings, McLarney is out of his seat and moving toward the hallway, hoping to grab a juror or two and find out what the hell happened up in that room. Near the top of the stairs, a black juror, a younger woman still trying to control her tears, looks at the badge and shrugs off his question.

"I don't want to talk about it," she says.

McLarney moves on and catches one of the three white jurors; he recognizes her as the girl who was crying during Cassidy's testimony.

"Miss . . . miss."

The girl looks back.

"Miss," says McLarney, catching up. "I was one of the investigators in the case and I was wondering what happened with the jury."

The girl nods.

"Could I talk to you for a few minutes?"

Reluctantly, the girl agrees.

"I was the lead investigator," McLarney tells her, a little embarrassed at the intensity he can in no way conceal. "What was it that hung you all up for so long?"

The girl shakes her head. "A lot of them didn't care. I mean not at all. It was crazy."

"They didn't care?"

"Not at all."

"What didn't they care about?"

"The entire thing. They didn't care about any of it."

McLarney is stunned. Bombarding the young girl with questions, he begins piecing together eight hours of rancorous debate in which race and indifference played dominant roles.

The girl explains that two of the three white jurors argued from the beginning for a first-degree verdict, just as two of the younger black jurors had insisted on acquittal, contending that the police had put every witness up to testifying in an effort to convict someone—anyone—of shooting a white officer. That, they explained, was why all the police were sitting in court. Frazier's girlfriend had cried because she had been forced to lie. The other two witnesses were probably drunk, coming from the bar. The kid from the city jail testified because he had cut a deal for himself.

The girl remembers that a younger black juror declared at one point that she didn't like police, which prompted another juror to ask what that had to do with anything. I just don't like them, the first juror replied, adding that anyone who lived in her neighborhood wouldn't like them either.

The other eight jurors offered little opinion except to say that they would vote for whatever was agreed upon, the young girl tells McLarney. It was Friday, they pointed out, and the beginning of the Memorial Day weekend. They wanted to go home.

McLarney listens in amazement. "What brought you all around to first-degree?" he asks.

"I wasn't going to budge and that other woman, the one in the back row, she wasn't going to change her mind either. She was for first-degree from the very beginning, too. After a while, everyone wanted to go home, I guess."

McLarney shakes his head, incredulous. He has been a cop long enough to know that there is no understanding juries, but this is somehow more than he can take. The man who tried to kill Gene Cassidy has been given the right verdict for the wrong reasons.

The girl seems to read his mind. "I swear," she says, "if that's the way the system works, you can have it."

Two hours later at the Market Bar, the beer gets good to McLarney and he asks the girl to tell him the whole sordid story again. The girl obliges. A nineteen-year-old waitress at a downtown sports bar, she came to the Market with the cops and prosecutors and the Cassidy family at McLarney's insistence. She was a hero, he told her, and she deserved a beer. He listens to her alone for a few minutes, then begins calling over others from the Western to add to the audience.

"Vince, c'mere."

Moulter walks over from the bar.

"This is Vince Moulter," he says to the young juror. "He worked with Gene. Tell him the part about how the one juror said she thought Butchie was cute."

Two tables away, Gene Cassidy sips quietly at a soda, laughing at the occasional joke. He and Patti will be there for an hour or two, long enough for McLarney to bring the young juror by for an introduction an hour or so later.

"Thank you," says Cassidy to the girl. "You know you did the right thing."

"I know it," she says, a little unnerved. "Good luck to you, with the baby and all."

McLarney listens to the exchange and smiles from the bar, already a little bit drunk. The gathering plays out until it is soon a little after one in the morning and Nicky comes out from behind the bar to begin cleaning tables. Cassidy is gone, followed by Belt and Tuggle and Gersh. McLarney, Moulter, Biemiller and a few others remain as the young juror finally gathers up her things.

"We're going down to Clinton Street after we close this place," McLarney tells her. "You're welcome to come."

"What's Clinton Street?"

"Hallowed ground," jokes another cop.

Even before the girl can answer, McLarney feels the awkwardness of his own suggestion. The end of Clinton Street is the best hole in the Southeastern District, but it's nothing more than a rotting wharf. This girl here is normal. A civilian.

"Clinton Street is this pier a few minutes from here," McLarney explains, embarrassed. "Vince is going to go get some beer and we're going to meet him there. It's no big deal."

"I've got to get home," she says, uncomfortably. "Really."

"Okay, then," says McLarney, relieved in a way. "Vince can drive you to your car."

"Thanks for the beer," she says. "I've got to say, I wouldn't want to go through it again, but it's been an interesting experience. Thanks."

"No," says McLarney. "Thank you."

Vince Moulter leaves with the girl. McLarney finishes his beer and drops a tip on the bar for Nicky. He checks himself for car keys, wallet, badge, gun—the usual barroom inventory that tells McLarney he's good to go.

"You thought she'd want to go to Clinton Street?" asks Biemiller, looking at him with raised eyebrows.

"You don't get it," McLarney tells him, irritated. "She's a hero."

Biemiller smiles.

"Who's coming?" asks McLarney.

"You, me, Vince, maybe a couple of the others. I told Vince to get a couple cases."

They leave in separate cars, driving east and south through the rowhouse neighborhoods of Fells Point and Canton. They pick up Clinton Street at the harbor's edge, then drive south for a quarter mile, where the road dead-ends in the shadow of the Lehigh Cement towers. To the right, as they spill from their cars, is a corrugated iron warehouse. To the left, a battered shipping terminal. The night is warm and the harbor water gives off a slight, garbage scow stench.

Ten minutes behind the others, Moulter shows up with two cases of Coors Light. McLarney and the other Western hands pick up where they left off, their voices growing louder, less restrained, in the warm spring night. Moulter finds an FM station and cranks the car stereo. An hour passes with nothing more than shop talk and station house humor; McLarney does his bit, tossing a few amusing homicide tales into the kitty.

Soon there are two dozen silver empties bobbing in the harbor waters or lying dead against the metal side of the warehouse.

"A toast," says Biemiller.

"To the Western."

"No. To Gene."

"To Gene."

They drink and Moulter cranks the radio higher. It is several minutes before they notice a lone figure, a foreman perhaps, near the warehouse gate.

Biemiller sees him first.

"Sarge. Over there."

McLarney pushes his glasses back up the bridge of his nose. The foreman is just standing there, staring at them.

"Don't worry about it," McLarney tells them. "I'll handle this."

McLarney grabs a fresh can—a peace offering of sorts—and walks toward the warehouse gate. Leaning over the railing of a metal landing, the foreman stares down with undisguised contempt. McLarney smiles back apologetically. "How's it going?" he says.

The man spits. "Ain't you assholes got nothing better to do than come down here all drunk and raising hell? Who the hell you think you are?"

McLarney looks down at his shoes, then back up at the foreman's face. His voice is only a little bit better than a whisper. "I don't suppose," he says, "that you'd want to come down here and say that."

The foreman doesn't move.

"I didn't think so."

"Fuck you," the man replies, turning back through the gate. "I'm calling the cops."

McLarney saunters back to the end of the pier, where the other revelers look at him quizzically.

"What'd he say?" asks Moulter.

McLarney shrugs. "We reached an understanding. He's calling the police and we're getting the hell out of here."

"Where to?"

"Somewhere close."

"Calverton?"

"Calverton."

The beers are quickly divided and they pile into three cars. At the sound of the engines, the foreman runs back to the gate, checking license tags. They race up Clinton Street with their headlights out, fugitives in their own city.

"Terry, maybe we ought to go home," says a younger officer in McLarney's car. "We keep going like this and we'll get an IID number. Hell, we might even get locked up at this rate."

McLarney offers a look of contempt. "No one's gonna get locked up," he says, wheeling his Honda Civic west along the Boston Street waterfront. "Have you forgotten that you're in Baltimore? Nobody ever gets locked up in this fucking city. Why should we get treated different than any other criminal?"

McLarney laughs at his own logic, then guns the Civic through the streets just south of Little Italy, then west across the early morning vacancy of the city's downtown. Street cleaners and newspaper delivery trucks own the streets now, and the traffic signals have gone from green and red to flashing yellow. Across from the Omni on Fayette, a lone derelict is dissecting the contents of a trashcan.

"It's four A.M., Terry."

"Yes," says McLarney, checking his watch. "It is."

"Where the hell are we going?"

"Where every wanted criminal goes to hide."

"The Western?"

"The Western District," says McLarney, triumphant. "They'll never find us there."

And soon enough, it is 5:00 A.M. and eight or nine more 16-ounce cans are lying spent in a Calverton Road gutter. The party is down to a foursome now, the others having fled before the threat of sunrise. Of the group, only Bob Biemiller is still a Western man. McLarney has been downtown in homicide ever since he took that bullet on Arunah Avenue; Moulter has transferred to Southeastern patrol. But they are together again on Calverton Road because it is the morning after the night after a city jury brought the Cassidy case to an end. And even after being chased off the Clinton Street pier, they still cannot go home.

McLarney rolls another empty into the pile, where it clatters against its brethren. Biemiller grabs a replacement from the back seat and hands it to McLarney, who shifts his weight against the car's front fender.

"So, So, Vince, what do you think?" McLarney says, pulling the metal tab. White foam races around the rim of the can and down its sides. The sergeant mumbles an obscenity and shakes the wetness from his hand.

Moulter smiles vaguely. "What do I think?"

"About Gene."

About Gene. All this drinking, all this bullshitting, all this riding around Baltimore like a pack of motorized Gypsies but McLarney still isn't satisfied. Somehow the damn thing is still there to be reckoned with. At this moment, Appleton Street is the only station house story worth telling, and at this moment it demands some kind of moral.

Moulter shrugs, staring at the undergrowth and trash that mark the dead end of Calverton Road and the edge of the Amtrak railbed. The place has long been the favored hole in Sector 2 of the Western—a deserted spot to drink coffee and write reports, or share a six-pack, or maybe get a little sleep if you were scheduled for court in the morning.

McLarney turns to Biemiller. "What do you think?"

"What do I think?" asks Biemiller.

"Yeah. We won it for him, didn't we?"

"No," says Biemiller. "We didn't win."

Moulter nods his head in agreement.

"I don't mean it like that," McLarney says, backing up. "I mean we got the verdict. Gene's got to be pleased with that."

Biemiller says nothing; Moulter heaves an empty can into the underbrush. From the railbed comes a sudden flourish of noise and light as a metroliner races east along the center track. The train disappears in a long wail that sounds very much like a human voice.

"It's fucked up, isn't it?" says McLarney after a time.

"Yeah, it is."

"I mean here's a guy that's like a war hero," says McLarney. "This is a war and he's a hero. You know what I mean?"

"No."

"Vince, you see what I'm saying?"

"What do you mean, Terry?"

"Lemme tell you something," says McLarney, his voice catching up to his anger, "and this is something that I told Gene. I told him he has to see that he didn't get shot for Appleton Street. Fuck Appleton Street. Fuck that. Fuck Baltimore. He didn't get shot for Baltimore."

"What did he get shot for?"

"It's like this," says McLarney, "and I told this to Gene. I told him that there's this war going on in America. It's a fucking war, right? And Gene was a soldier who got shot. He was defending his country and he got shot. Like any other fucking war."

Biemiller throws an empty can toward the undergrowth. Moulter rubs his eyes.

"What I'm saying is that you have to forget it's Baltimore," says McLarney, very angry now. "This city is fucked up and it will always be fucked up, but that isn't normal. Fuck Baltimore. Gene was a police in America who got shot and there are places where he would get treated like a war hero. Do you see that?"

"No," says Biemiller. "Not really."

McLarney slowly deflates, unable to sustain the rage without help. "Well, Gene does," he says quietly, staring across the railbed. "That's the important thing. Gene does and I do, too."

McLarney wanders back toward the other side of the car as sunrise streaks the eastern sky red. An early work crew opens the gates to the city yard on Calverton Road; ten minutes later, a public works truck rumbles down to the pumps. At the sound of the truck, Biemiller looks across the asphalt, squinting through an alcohol haze.

"Who the fuck is that?"

A lone figure in blue is standing a few feet from the city yard entrance, glaring at them.

"Security guard," says McLarney.

"Christ. Not again."

"What the fuck does he want?"

"He saw the beer."

"So what? Why should he give a fuck?"

The man in blue pulls a notepad and pencil, then begins writing. The cops respond with obscenity.

"Christ, he's taking tag numbers."

"Well," says Biemiller. "Party's over. See you boys around."

"No point waiting around for the IID number," says another. "Let's get gone."

They toss the last few cans in the underbrush, then climb into their cars. Two cars and a pickup peel off and run a gauntlet past the security guard and out onto Edmondson Avenue. Back behind the wheel of his Honda, McLarney gauges the effects of the beer, then calculates the number of state troopers between his current location and his home in Howard County. The resulting odds seem improbable, so he drives east through the scattered Saturday morning traffic, turning south on Martin Luther King Boulevard and arriving minutes later at the South Baltimore rowhouse that is the home of a friend who had been among them on Calverton Road. McLarney stands on the stoop in the new day's light, the morning paper rolled in his right hand. The friend arrives a few minutes later.

"Got a beer?" asks McLarney.

"Jesus, Terry."

McLarney laughs, handing the younger man the paper. The two make their way through the door and McLarney wanders into the first-floor living room.

"What a dump," says McLarney. "You need to get a maid or something."

The younger man comes back from the refrigerator with the paper and two bottles of Rolling Rock. McLarney sits on the sofa and pulls apart the newspaper, looking for a story about the Cassidy verdict. He scatters sections across the table before finding the article on the front of the local section, below the fold. The story is brief, maybe a dozen paragraphs.

"Kind of short," he says, reading slowly.

He finishes the story, then rubs his eyes and takes a long drag on his beer. Suddenly, finally, he is exhausted. Very drunk and very exhausted.

"It's so fucked up," he says. "You know what I'm saying? Does everybody else see how fucked up it is? Does anyone see that? Do normal people see something like this and get pissed off?"

Normal people. Citizens. Human beings. Even among the believers, there is a pathology to being a cop.

"Fuck, I'm tired. I got to get home."

"You can't drive."

"I'm okay."

"Terry, you're fucking blind."

McLarney looks up, startled at the word. Again he picks up the local section. Again he scans the story, looking for the things that never manage to find their way into newspaper accounts.

"I thought they'd do more," he says finally. McLarney tries to fold the paper, crushing it awkwardly in his left hand.

"Gene did good though, didn't he?" he says after a pause. "He was good on the stand."

"He was."

"He got respect."

"He did."

"Good," says McLarney, his leaden eyes closing. "That's good."

The sergeant leans his head back against the wall behind the sofa. His eyes close at last.

"Gotta go," he says in a slur. "Wake me in ten . . ."

He sleeps like a still life, sitting up, his right ankle to his left knee. The crushed newspaper is in his lap, the half-empty beer can is surrounded by the meat of his right hand. The sport coat stays on. The tie is twisted but intact. The wire-frame eyeglasses, bent and battered from a half dozen near-misses, have slipped down his nose. The badge remains in the upper right coat pocket. The gun, a silver .38 snubnose, stays holstered to his belt.

WEDNESDAY, JUNE 8

Print hit.

When the human mind has exhausted itself, technology flexes a muscle and creates a clue of its own. Diodes and transistors and silicon chips produce a connection as the swirl pattern on a right index finger is matched to a name and address. Each ridge, each curve, each imperfection is noted, catalogued and compared until the verdict of the Printrak computer is certain:

Kevin Robert Lawrence

D.O.B. 9/25/66

3409 Park Heights Avenue

Like any of its species, the Printrak is an unthinking beast. It knows nothing of the case file, nothing of the victim, and virtually nothing of any suspect it happens to identify. And it cannot ask the questions that necessarily follow from its discoveries. That is left to a detective, who stretches his cramped legs across a metal desk and stares at a printout sent upstairs from the lab's ident section. Why, he wonders, does Kevin Robert Lawrence's fingerprint appear on the inside cover of a library book on Afro-American heroes, *Pioneers and Patriots*? And how can it be, he inquires further, that this same book is somehow one of those found in the satchel of a murdered child in Reservoir Hill?

Good and simple questions, to which a detective can have no immediate response. The name of Kevin Robert Lawrence appears nowhere in the Latonya Wallace case file, nor does it stir the memory of any detective or detail officer involved in the case. And but for the fact that Mr. Lawrence was arrested yesterday for attempting to shoplift some veal cutlets from a Bolton Hill grocery store, his name would not correlate with any criminal history within easy reach of the Baltimore Police Identification computer.

This, the detectives must concede, is not a promising fact. Generally speaking, the ideal rape-murder suspect usually manages to post on his BPI sheet something more substantive than a single shoplifting charge. Yet this Lawrence kid managed to get his hands on a dead little girl's library book without ever acquiring a police record. In fact, if it wasn't for his little shopping spree, the name of Kevin Robert Lawrence would probably never be uttered by any homicide detective. But Mr. Lawrence wanted veal for dinner and he apparently wanted it on the cheap, and by that limited ambition alone, he is now the leading suspect in the murder of Latonya Wallace.

Caught by a store security guard and held for a Central District wagon, the twenty-one-year-old Lawrence was taken to the lockup late yesterday, where a turnkey applied the appropriate amount of ink and produced a fingerprint card with a freshly minted BPI number. Overnight, the card traveled the usual route to the fourth-floor records section at headquarters, where it got the requisite run through the Printrak, which can compare a latent print with the hundreds of thousands of print cards on file with the Baltimore department.

In a perfect world, this wondrous process would produce evidence on a regular and routine basis. But in Baltimore, a city that can in no way be called perfect, the Printrak—like any other technological marvel in the department's crime laboratory—functions in accordance with Rule Eight in the homicide lexicon:

In any case where there is no apparent suspect, the crime lab will produce no valuable evidence. In those cases where a suspect has already confessed and been identified by at least two eyewitnesses, the lab will give you print hits, fiber evidence, blood typings and a ballistic match. And yet in the case of Latonya Wallace, a murder that genuinely matters, this rule seems not to apply. For once, the lab work has suddenly propelled a stalled investigation forward.

Not surprisingly, the sudden print hit found the Latonya Wallace case flat on its back because Tom Pellegrini was in precisely the same condition. His coughing had continued without respite, and the exhaustion seemed to leave him with less and less each day. One morning, trying to get out of bed, he felt as if his legs were barely moving. It was like one of those dreams in which you're trying to run from something but you just can't get started. Again, he went to a physician, who diagnosed the respiratory problem as an allergic reaction. But allergic to what? Pellegrini had never had an allergy before in his life. The doctor suggested that stress can sometimes trigger an allergy that might ordinarily be contained by the body's defenses. Then: Have you been under any particular kind of stress lately?

"Who? Me?"

Every day for three months, Pellegrini had come dragass into the office to stare at the same photographs and read the same office reports. And every day the thing looked exactly the same. Every other day he was out wandering the streets of Reservoir Hill, checking the basement of a vacant rowhouse or the back of an abandoned car or truck, searching for his lost crime scene. He worked back on every significant suspect, interviewing friends, relatives and acquaintances of the Fish Man; and Ronald Carter, who tried to implicate the Fish Man; and Andrew, who parked his car in the back alley and admitted to having been out there on the night the body was dumped. He worked the fresh leads, too, checking out this sex offender locked up for a child rape in Baltimore County, or that pedophile caught playing with himself outside an elementary school. He went to the polygraph examinations at the State Police barracks in Pikesville, where each successive test of a potential suspect seemed to leave him with only a little more ambiguity. And when everything else failed, he went downstairs to the trace lab and argued with Van Gelder, the chief analyst. What about those black smudges on the dead girl's pants? Roofing tar? Road tar? Can't we narrow the field a little bit?

Meanwhile, Pellegrini tried to keep up with the rotation, working those calls that came his way and struggling to stay interested in the cheap shootings and domestic cuttings. Once, while interviewing a witness to one particularly unimportant bit of violence, he found that he had to force himself to ask even the requisite questions. It was scary. At that moment, he had been in homicide for less than two years and yet, for all practical purposes, he'd become a genuine case of burnout. The well is dry, Pellegrini had to concede. There is no more.

In early June, he took himself out on sick leave for more than two weeks, trying to recover whatever it was that had brought him to homicide in the first place. He slept and ate and played with the baby. Then he slept some more. He did not go downtown, he did not call the office and he tried, for the most part, not to think about dead little girls.

And when the print hit lands on Gary D'Addario's desk, Tom Pellegrini is still on leave and the lieutenant decides—for reasons more humanitarian than tactical—not to call him back in. To the other detectives, it seems at first sad, and a little ironic, that the primary investigator is not there as they swarm into Kevin Lawrence's life, learning everything they can about this nonentity who has somehow fallen upon them like manna from heaven. More than any man in the unit that year, Pellegrini has earned a shred of hope, and his absence is very much noticed when Donald Kincaid and Howard Corbin begin tracing the new suspect's movements, trying to link him to friends or relatives in the Reservoir Hill area. Others on the shift tell themselves and one another that Pellegrini should be here as they're running the NCIC check on the new man, or when they search the city computer for a criminal history that can't be found, though they feel sure that it exists under some other name or alias. Pellegrini should be here, too, when they talk to Lawrence's family and friends. In the hours after the print hit, they tell themselves that Pellegrini deserves to be on hand for that righteous moment when this bastard case finally falls.

Instead, the case file is transferred to Kincaid and Corbin: Kincaid, because he arrived early for the dayshift and D'Addario grabbed him first with a fresh copy of the Printrak report; Corbin, one of the true ancients on the detectives' floor, because the Latonya Wallace murder has become an obsession for him as well.

An aging, snaggle-toothed wonder, Corbin is the product of twenty years in the homicide unit and another fifteen in the department. The man is edging away from sixty-five years, well beyond the point at which most cops see retirement as the reasoned alternative, yet he refuses to miss so much as a day of work. A veteran of perhaps three thousand crime scenes, Corbin is a walking piece of history. Older detectives remember a time when Corbin and Fury Cousins, two of the earliest black recruits to the homicide unit, knew everyone and anyone in Baltimore's inner city and could put that knowledge to use on any kind of case. It was a smaller, tighter city back then, and Corbin owned most of it. If your shooter went by the street name of Mac, Corbin could ask you whether you meant the east side Mac or the west side Mac, or whether you were talking about Big Mac Richardson or maybe Racetrack Mac, from up on the Avenue. And your answer wouldn't matter, because Corbin had two or three addresses for every one of them. In his time, he was that good.

But twenty years has transformed the city and Howard Corbin both, pushing Corbin to the career criminals unit at the other end of the sixth floor: For the last several years, in fact, Corbin has been fighting a rear-guard action against change itself, trying to prove to the chain of command that age and a diabetic condition have done nothing to slow him down. It is a noble fight, but in some ways painful to watch. And in the mind of any younger detective, Corbin has become a living, breathing reminder of the price you can be made to pay for giving too much of your life to a police department. He still shows up early every morning, still fills out his run sheets, still works a case or two, but the truth is that career criminals is a paper unit with half an office and a handful of men. Corbin knows it, too, and he doesn't work a day there without wearing his heart on his sleeve. For him, the homicide unit will always be the promised land, and the Latonya Wallace case is his chance for an exodus.

A month into the case, Corbin asked Colonel Lanham if he could look at the case file, and the colonel couldn't come up with any reason to deny the request, though he and everyone else could plainly see the motive behind it. But so what? Lanham reasoned that it couldn't hurt to have an experienced detective review the file. You never knew what a fresh mind might notice. And if, by some chance. Corbin actually managed to solve the case, then maybe he had every right to come back to the other end of the hall.

To Pellegrini's dismay, when the request was approved, Corbin immediately moved into the annex office and appropriated the Latonya Wallace case file. A blizzard of follow-up reports came on the heels of Corbin's arrival as he documented his daily effort in lengthy, typewritten reports about whatever investigative leads he happened to be pursuing. For Pellegrini, the case file soon became unmanageable through sheer bulk, much of it unnecessary, to his mind. More important to Pellegrini, Corbin's involvement was exactly the opposite of the approach he had argued in his memo to the captain. He had urged a careful, thorough review of the existing evidence, a review to be conducted by the primary and secondary detectives who were most familiar with the case. Instead, the file seemed once again to have become community territory.

And now Corbin will serve as Pellegrini's proxy in the pursuit of Kevin Lawrence, or at least for as long as it takes to confirm that the suspect is viable. "If this guy looks good," Landsman assures the others in his squad, "we're definitely going to give Tom a call at home."

But the next day, no one thinks about calling Pellegrini when the detectives check with the principal at Eutaw-Marshburn Elementary and are told that Kevin Robert Lawrence was enrolled there from 1971 to 1978. Nor do they think of calling when the more comprehensive computer search produces nothing remotely resembling a criminal record. Nor do they think of bothering him when the Wallace family says that they know nothing of this Kevin Lawrence and cannot remember his having anything to do with the victim.

Eight days after a police computer took his name in vain, Kevin Lawrence is brought down to the homicide unit, where he tells detectives that he knows nothing about any girl named Latonya Wallace. He does, however, remember a book about black American heroes with the title of *Pioneers and Patriots*. Shown the text itself, he can even recall the school report he prepared long ago using that same book, which he had borrowed from the Eutaw-Marshburn school library. The paper was on great black Americans and, as the young man recalled, it earned him an A. But that, he says, was more than ten years ago. Why are they even asking about it?

The investigation that exonerates Kevin Lawrence is still wrapping up when Pellegrini returns to duty. But by luck or mercy or both, the primary investigator is allowed to watch from the periphery as other detectives slam into a wall. He is, in a very real sense, spared the anguish of seeing a precious piece of physical evidence reduced to fantastic coincidence—a fingerprint that sat undisturbed on a book for more than a decade, waiting for a million-dollar computer to give it life enough to taunt a few homicide detectives for a week and a half.

Instead of riding the print hit into another psychological trough, Pellegrini manages to come back to work a little stronger. The cough is still there, but the exhaustion, less so. Within a day or two of his return, the manila folder that contains the information gleaned on the Fish Man is back on his desk in the annex office. And at the same time that the detectives are busy returning a blissfully unaware Kevin Lawrence to freedom and anonymity, Pellegrini is back up on Whitelock Street, interviewing other merchants about the habits of the man who still remains his most promising suspect.

On the same day, in fact, that Lawrence is boring other detectives with his grade school adventures, Pellegrini grabs a set of Cavalier keys and a handful of plastic evidence bags and makes his way inside the burned-out Whitelock Street store where the Fish Man had made a living until perhaps a week before the murder. The detective had been through the derelict property several times before, looking for anything to indicate that the little girl—alive or dead—had ever been inside the place, but to his frustration, the building had always seemed nothing more than a blackened shell. Neighboring merchants had in fact told him that the Fish Man had cleaned most everything out in the day or two before the discovery of the little girl's body.

Still, Pellegrini takes another look around before getting down to the business at hand. Satisfied that nothing in the wreckage has gone unnoticed, he sets about prying up blackened soot and debris from several locations. In places, the stuff is thick and oily and mixed, perhaps, with the tar from portions of the collapsed roof.

The thought had occurred to Pellegrini while he was out on leave and it was, he had to concede, something of a long shot, considering how little the trace lab had so far been able to learn about the black smudges on the dead girl's pants. But what the hell, he tells himself, if they have something specific with which to compare those smudges, Van Gelder's people may be able to make something happen.

Every now and then a long shot does come in, the detective muses, a little hopeful. But even if the samples from the store never amount to anything, they are important to Pellegrini for another reason: It is his idea. It is his own thinking that the stuff on the little girl's pants may match the soot from the Fish Man's store. Not Landsman's. Not Edgerton's. Not Corbin's.

In all probability, Pellegrini tells himself, this will be another dead end in the maze, another single-page report in the folder. But even so, it would be his dead end, his report.

Pellegrini is the primary and he is thinking like the primary. He drives back from Reservoir Hill with the soot samples beside him on the passenger seat, feeling, for the first time in weeks, like a detective.

Wednesday, June 22

Clayvon Jones lies face down in the courtyard of the housing project, his torso covering the loaded 9mm Colt he never had a chance to use. The gun is cocked, with a live round in the chamber. Someone was looking for

Clayvon and Clayvon was looking for someone, and Clayvon got rained on first.

Dave Brown rolls the body and Clayvon stares up at him, white foam at the edges of his mouth.

"Damn," says Dave Brown. "That's a nice gun."

"Hey, that is pretty," says Eddie Brown. "What is that? A forty-five?"

"No, I think it's one of those Colt replicas. They're making nine-millimeters with that classic forty-five mold."

"That's a nine-millimeter?"

"Either that or a three-eighty. I saw an ad for one of these bad boys in the FBI magazine."

"Uh-huh," says Eddie Brown, giving the gun a last look. "She does look nice."

It is daylight now, a little before six on a day that promises to be hot. In addition to having been the proud owner of a 9mm Colt replica, the dead man is a twenty-two-year-old east-sider with a thin, athletic frame. The corpse has already got a decent rigor to it, with the lone gunshot wound visible at the top of the head.

"Like he was duckin' down and didn't get low enough," says Eddie Brown, a little bored.

A crowd has already gathered at both ends of the courtyard, and though a canvass of the neighboring rowhouses will produce not a single witness, half the neighborhood seems to be out bright and early for a glimpse of the body. Within hours there will be four anonymous calls—"I want to remain monogamous," one caller will insist—as well as a report from one of Harry Edgerton's paid informants on the east side. Together they will provide a full chronicle of the death of Clayvon Jones. Classify it as scenario number 34 in the catalogue of life-and-death ghetto drama: an argument between two dopers over a girl; a fistfight in the street; threats back and forth; young kid paid in cocaine to go shoot Clayvon in the head.

To Dave Brown's amusement, three of the callers will insist that the shooter placed a white flower on Clayvon's mouth after the murder. The flower, Brown will realize, was nothing more than the foam at the corners of the dead man's mouth, which was undoubtedly visible to the crowd that greeted the detectives on their arrival at the scene.

At this moment, however, all of that is still to come. At this moment, Clayvon Jones is simply a dead yo with a quality weapon he never got to use. No witnesses, no motive, no suspects—the standard whodunit mantra.

"Hey, guy."

Dave Brown turns around to see a familiar face on one of the Eastern uniforms. Martini, isn't that it? Yeah, the kid who took a bullet for the company in a drug raid at the Perkins Homes last year. Good man, Martini.

"Hey, how you doing, bunk?"

"Okay," says Martini, pointing to another uniform. "My buddy here needs a sequence number for his report."

"You're Detective Brown, right?" asks the other uniform.

"We both be Detective Brown," says Dave Brown, wrapping his arm around Eddie Brown's shoulder. "This here's my daddy."

Eddie Brown smiles, his gold tooth shining in the morning sun. Smiling back, the uniform takes in the salt-and-pepper family portrait.

"He looks like me, don't he?" says Eddie Brown.

"A little bit," says the uniform, laughing now. "What's your sequence?"

"B as in boy, nine-six-nine."

The patrolman nods and steps away as the ME's van pulls to the edge of the courtyard.

"We done here?" asks Dave Brown.

Eddie Brown nods.

"Okay," says Dave Brown, walking back toward the Cavalier. "But we can't forget the most important thing about this case."

"What's that?" says Eddie Brown, following.

"The most important thing about this case is that when we left the office, the Big Man told us to bring him back an egg sandwich."

"Oh yeah."

Back in the homicide unit's coffee room. Donald Worden waits for his sandwich in a cloud of Backwoods cigar smoke, nursing a rage that has been his for a week and a half. He does this silently, stoically, but with such energy and determination that no other man dares approach him with so much as a platitude during the morning shift change.

And what, in truth, can anyone really say? What do you tell a man who has tailored a career to his own sense of honor, his own code, when that honor is being bartered back and forth by politicians? What do you say to a man for whom institutional loyalty is a way of life when the police department in which he has spent twenty-five years is now offering fresh lessons in betrayal?

Three weeks ago, the brass had gone first to Rich Garvey. They went to him with a 24-hour report and some notes and a manila folder without a name or case number. State senator, they explain. Threats. Mysterious assailants. A possible abduction.

Garvey listened patiently. Then he looked at the initial report from two detectives on Stanton's shift. It was not pretty.

"Just one question," asked Garvey. "Can I polygraph the senator?"

No, the supervisors told themselves, perhaps Rich Garvey isn't the best man for this case. They excused themselves quickly, taking the report and the manila folder to Worden.

The Big Man let them talk, then arrayed the facts in his mind: State senator Larry Young. A Democrat from West Baltimore's 39th legislative district. A product of the Mitchell family's west side political machine and the chairman of the General Assembly's influential House Environmental Matters Committee. A leader of the Black Legislative Caucus with ties to City Hall as well as some of the police department's ranking blacks. A forty-two-year-old bachelor living alone on McCulloh Street.

That much made sense, the rest was bizarre. Senator Young had called a friend, a highly respected black physician, and told of being abducted by three men. He had been leaving McCulloh Street alone and they had a van, he explained. He was forced inside, blindfolded, threatened. Stay away from Michael and his fiancée, they told him, referring to a longtime political aide who was planning to marry. Then these unnamed assailants dumped him out of the rear doors, up near Druid Hill Park. He had hitched a ride back home.

Outrageous, the friend had told him. You have to call the police. No need, Larry Young assured him. Why involve the police department? I can deal with this on my own but I just wanted to tell you about it, he explained to the friend, who nonetheless remained insistent, arranging for a conference call with Eddie Woods, the deputy commissioner for services and a political ally of the senator. Deputy Woods listened to the tale, then rightly insisted that an abduction of a state senator had to be investigated. Homicide was called.

"Will you take it?" they asked again.

Worden calculated the unspoken facts: powerful legislator, powerful friends. A reluctance to report a crime. A ridiculous story. Nervous bosses. The selection of an aging white homicide detective, a cop with a clean performance sheet and enough time on to take a pension should the thing get nasty.

Okay, Worden told them. I'll eat it.

After all, someone had to take the file, and Worden reasoned that a younger man would have more to lose. The detectives on Stanton's shift who originally took the call wanted nothing whatsoever to do with it. Nor was Garvey looking to lean into any punches. But what could they do to Worden? It made sense, and yet when Worden talked like that it sounded as though he was trying to convince himself more than anyone else.

Closer to the point, Worden was truly the product of the department's old school: Give him an assignment and he works it. And if some believed that loyalty to command had burned Worden in the Monroe Street investigation, everyone understood that he would never duck a request from a superior even if it meant getting burned again.

With Rick James in tow, Worden went first to the home of the political aide in Northeast Baltimore, where he spoke with the aide's parents, a gracious, elderly couple fairly mystified at their playing host to a homicide detective. They told Worden that they knew nothing about any abduction. In fact, earlier on the evening of the alleged incident, the senator had come by the house to visit their son, who had not been home at the time. Mr. Young waited, chatting amiably with the couple, until their son returned. Then the two younger men walked out the back door and into the yard to discuss a private matter. A short time later, their son came back into the house without the senator, who had left. Then their son said he had hurt his arm and needed a lift to the emergency room.

Worden nodded, listening carefully. With each additional fact, the senator's story was becoming both a little more ridiculous and a little more understandable. The ensuing interview with the aide confirmed the scenario that had already taken shape in Worden's mind. Yes, the aide admitted, the senator had become angry during that discussion in the yard. At one point, he picked up a tree branch and struck the aide across the arm. Then he had fled.

"I guess the argument between you and the senator was over a personal matter," said Worden, speaking with great care, "one that you would rather keep private."

"That's right."

"And I take it you don't want to press charges on the assault."

"No. I don't want that."

The two men exchanged glances and a handshake. Worden and James drove back to the office, discussing the alternatives left to them. First option: They could spend days or even weeks investigating an abduction that had never occurred. Second option: They could confront the senator, perhaps with the implied threat of a grand jury investigation or maybe even a charge of false report, yet that would be dangerous because things would get ugly in a hurry. There was a third option, however, and Worden pushed it back and forth in his brain, weighing the risks and benefits. And when the two men and Lieutenant D'Addario were called into the captain's office for a review of the case, Worden offered the third choice as the most sensible alternative.

If they treated the abduction report as genuine, Worden told the captain, trained homicide detectives would be wasting their days looking for some mystery men in a mystery van that would never be found. If they tried to go to a grand jury, that would be an even bigger waste of government time. A false report charge was penny ante stuff, and who in the homicide unit really wanted to waste his days trying to stick some politician with a misdemeanor, particularly when it wasn't even clear that the politician had made any official complaint? After all, it was the senator's doctor friend who made the original call to Deputy Woods; technically, that was reason enough to suggest that there wasn't any real intent of filing a false report. The third choice was the best, Worden argued, though he had no intention of pursuing that course on his own.

The captain asked how Worden would proceed and what would be said. Worden gave him as clear a picture as possible. The captain then ran Worden's proposal through once more for clarity and the four men in the room agreed that it made sense. Go ahead, the captain said. Do it.

Worden arrived at Senator Young's office that same afternoon. He left James back at the office; the younger detective was six years shy of a pension and therefore at greater risk. Instead, Roger Nolan volunteered to go, telling Worden that he might need a witness to whatever occurred. And not only did Nolan have time enough to weather any storm, but, like the senator, he was black. Should anything said in this meeting ever become public, Nolan's presence might diffuse any issue of race.

At his office downtown, Larry Young welcomed both men and said again that he saw no reason for the police to waste their time investigating the incident. It was a personal matter, the senator explained, and he had every intention of investigating it privately.

Worden seemed to nod in agreement, then offered the senator a review of the investigation thus far. Detectives had failed to locate anyone on McCulloh Street who had seen the abduction, nor had they discovered any physical evidence at the Druid Hill Park site where the senator claimed he had been pushed from the van. The pants that the senator claimed to have worn that night didn't have so much as a grass stain on them. Likewise, Worden explained, the interview with the senator's aide and the aide's parents had raised additional questions. The detective recounted the details of that interview, then gave the senator his out.

"It's my impression that this is something private between the two of you," said Worden, "something that you would like to deal with privately."

"That's correct," Young told him.

"Well, if a crime has been committed, then we will investigate it fully," Worden said. "But if no crime was committed, then that puts an end to it."

The senator took the offer for what it was, but asked a few questions to be sure. If he told them that no crime had occurred, that would end the investigation, correct? And if he told them here and now that there was no crime, that admission would not be used against him, correct?

"Not by me," Worden told him.

"Then," the senator replied, "there was no abduction. I would prefer that the matter be dealt with privately."

Worden told the senator that he could regard the police department's investigation as a closed file. The original abduction report had been written up as a police-information-only report, as was the case with all threat cases involving public officials. And because there is no incident report, there should be nothing in the newspapers.

"Our part in this is over," Worden said.

Worden and Nolan shook hands with the senator, concluding the bargain. There would be no grand jury probe, no red-ball moneymaker for which a squad of homicide detectives could clock overtime, no awkward questions about the senator's private life, no public revelations about a politician's bungled attempt to fabricate a counterweight to his own assault and battery. Instead, the homicide unit would go back to the more parochial task of working murders. Worden returned to headquarters and typed the requisite report of the meeting for the captain, believing he had done the right thing.

But on June 14, a week and a half after his journey to the senator's office, Worden's quiet solution to the whole sordid affair was shattered by a news leak of the incident to a television reporter for the local CBS affiliate. From the amount of information about the case in the reporter's broadcast, Worden and James both suspected that the leak had come from within the department. That scenario made sense; not everyone in the chain of command could be considered the senator's political ally and the bizarre abduction report made for a pretty embarrassing picture.

Of course, once the confidential information was revealed, police officials and prosecutors alike were suddenly tripping over one another in an attempt to avoid the appearance of covert deals and cover-ups. Confronted by the reporter, the mayor himself got into the act, ordering the department to make public its incident report for the original abduction complaint. With the press suddenly baying outside City Hall, the original priorities were all immediately inverted. A week earlier, the brass had been content to have Worden end the probe of a nonexistent crime with some discretion, allowing the homicide detectives to return to their primary responsibilities; now, these same bosses were being asked in public why an influential West Baltimore senator who had admitted to making a false report had not himself been charged. Was some sort of deal cut? Was the incident kept secret to protect the senator? What kind of influence was used on behalf of the senator?

A steady deluge of newspaper headlines and TV broadcasts prompted city officials to begin a full review by the state's attorney's office, followed by a grand jury investigation. For the next week, there were meetings between prosecutors and police officials, followed by more meetings between prosecutors and an influential trial attorney retained by the senator. One particular afternoon, when Worden and James were leaving a meeting between prosecutors and the senator's attorney at a private law office, they walked out of the building only to be confronted by the same television reporter who had been leaked the story.

"I wonder who even told her there was a meeting," said James, amazed. "She fucking knows what's going to happen even before we do . . ."

Everything that Worden had tried to avoid instead came to pass. He had wanted to work murders; now murders were not the priority. He had wanted to avoid spending time and effort wandering around in a public man's private life for no valuable reason; now he and three or four other detectives would waste even more time prying up large pieces of the man's privacy. Worden, James, Nolan—they were all pawns in a ridiculous game of brinksmanship as the bureaucrats tossed Larry Young's political future around like a hot potato. And to what end? On the day that he had convinced the senator to recant his story, Worden had two open murders and was still actively involved in the grand jury probe of the Monroe Street shooting. Now, none of that meant a damn thing. Now, the bosses wanted nothing more than a complete investigation of state Senator Larry Young and his recantation of an alleged abduction. The department would be sending some of its best investigators out on the street to prove a negative, to show that a state legislator had not been abducted by three men in a mystery van. Then the senator would be charged with filing a false report—a paltry misdemeanor—in preparation for a court trial that the prosecutor's office and police department had no real interest in winning. By tacit agreement, the trial would be nothing more than a public display, a show to appease public opinion. And Worden's word—given honestly in the solitude of a beleaguered man's office—now meant nothing. To the department, it was an utterly expendable commodity.

In a brief conversation that occurred a few days after the Larry Young imbroglio broke in the press, the captain mentioned Worden's plight to Gary D'Addario and Jay Landsman. "You know," he remarked, "I'd hate to see a good detective like Worden get jammed up over this Larry Young thing . . ."

Hate to see it? You'd hate to see it? What the hell does that mean? D'Addario wondered. The captain had signed off on the back door approach to Larry Young; they all had. How could this thing fall on Worden? D'Addario wondered whether the captain was trying to send a message or merely talking off the top of his head. With Landsman listening, D'Addario spoke up cautiously, trying to give the captain the benefit of the doubt.

"Why would Worden get jammed, captain?" he asked pointedly. "He was only following orders."

It would be unfair, the captain agreed. He didn't want to see it happen. At that moment, D'Addario was unsure what to believe and he held his tongue behind his teeth. If the captain's comment was a grant of immunity—a suggestion that they could both skate any controversy by sacrificing Worden—then D'Addario hoped that his own response was enough to sink the plan. If the captain was just spouting off and not thinking about the implications, better to just let it pass.

Landsman and D'Addario both left the captain's office confused. Perhaps the idea of Worden as a scapegoat was coming from the captain, perhaps from someone higher up. Perhaps they were misreading the comment. There was no way for D'Addario to know, but he and Landsman agreed that if the idea of burning Worden ever took solid form, they would have to go to war with the captain and burn every last bridge. Even to someone as jaded by command staff ethics as D'Addario, the idea of Worden as a sacrificial lamb was unbelievable. Worden was one of the best men in the unit, yet in a crisis, he was being considered as fodder.

The defense of Donald Worden in the captain's office was a subdued affair, but D'Addario's quiet refusal to burn a detective was soon known to the entire shift. It was, the detectives agreed, one of LTD's finer moments and proof positive that he was a man that other men could follow.

It had been one thing, after all, for D'Addario to cater a bit to the chain of command when the clearance rate was low; that cost nothing and allowed his detectives to do their work with only a minimum of interference from the bosses. Besides, the same clearance rate that had made D'Addario seem vulnerable earlier in the year was now his ally. Even with the summer homicide deluge on them, the rate was now hovering at 70 percent, and the lieutenant's leadership, which had earlier been open to question, was once again of some value to the bosses. For D'Addario, the worm had turned.

But even if the rate had been low, D'Addario would have felt obligated to speak up in the captain's office. Worden in a jackpot? Donald Worden? The Big Man? What the hell could the bosses be thinking? However seriously the idea had been considered, if it had really been considered at all, there was no further mention of it after D'Addario's conversation with the captain. And yet the lieutenant knew that his defense of Worden could only go so far; in the end, Worden might not be abused for his part in the Larry Young fiasco, but the detective was most certainly correct in believing that he had already been badly used.

Worden had given another man—a politician, of course, but a man nonetheless—his promise. And now, for the sake of its own public image, the police department and the mayor's office were proving just how much such a promise was worth.

Still, even a badly used detective has to eat, and on this summer morning, Worden mixes his anger with a little patience as he waits for Eddie and Dave Brown to return from their murder scene. When Dave Brown finally returns to the office, he glides gently into the coffee room, conscious of Worden's week-long anger. Wordless, he lays the egg sandwich directly in front of the Big Man, then swings back toward his own desk.

"What do I owe you?" asks Worden.

"I covered it."

"No. What do I owe you?"

"That's okay, bunk. I'll get you next time."

Worden shrugs, then sits back to pick at his breakfast. McLarney was off last night, and as senior man, Worden had worked the midnight shift as the acting supervisor. It had been miserable and now Worden can look forward to another full shift of shepherding witnesses to and from the grand jury that is hearing the Larry Young case. The whole fiasco would probably consume the rest of the week.

"What did you have out there?" Worden asks Dave Brown.

"Stone fucking whodunit."

"Hmmm."

"Dead yo in a low-rise courtyard. When we rolled him, he still had his own gun in his pants. That bad boy was cocked, too, with one in the chamber."

"Someone was quicker on the draw, huh?" offers Rick James from the other end of the room. "Where's he shot?"

"Top of the head. Like the shooter was above him or maybe caught him when he was ducking down."

"Ouch."

"He's got an exit wound in the neck and we got the bullet, but it's all fucked up, pancaked like. No good for comparison."

James nods.

"I need a car for the morgue," says Brown.

"Take this one," says James, tossing the keys. "We can walk over to the courthouse."

"I don't know about that, Rick," says Worden with bitter sarcasm. "I don't know if we can give him a car to do real police work. If he was investigating a senator or something like that, it would be one thing. But I don't think he gets a car for a murder . . ."

James shakes his head. "Hey, they can do whatever they want," he tells Worden. "I'm just happy to be making money again."

"Oh hell yeah," says Dave Brown. "More money than I'm gonna make on this murder, I'll bet."

"That's right," says Worden. "For purposes of the Larry Young investigation, the overtime cap has been lifted. From now on, I won't be working murders anymore. There's just no money in it . . ."

Worden lights another Backwoods and leans back against the green bulkhead, thinking that the joke is both funny and unfunny.

Three weeks ago, the officer who discovered the body of John Randolph Scott in the alley off Monroe Street went before the same grand jury and refused to answer any questions about the unexplained death of a man whom he had been pursuing. Sergeant John Wiley read a brief statement to the grand jury, complaining about having been treated like a suspect in the murder, then invoked his Fifth Amendment right against self-incrimination. Wiley was not offered immunity by the prosecutors and he subsequently walked out of the grand jury, effectively sending the Monroe Street investigation into a long, final stall. In the absence of any other definitive evidence, Tim Doory, the lead prosecutor, did not ask the grand jury for any indictment. In fact, Doory had to do some fast talking to keep the grand jurors from issuing any indictments; after hearing Worden and James testify about the contradictory statements made by officers involved in the pursuit of John Scott, several members of the panel were more than ready to hand up a charge until Doory convinced them that the case could not be successfully prosecuted. Indict it now and we'll lose it on the merits, he told them. And then, even if we get fresh evidence a year from now, we've played our hand. Double jeopardy says a man can't be tried twice for the same crime.

Doory's speech effectively closed the Monroe Street investigation, leaving both Worden and James with a bad taste. Doory was a good lawyer, a careful prosecutor, but both detectives were tempted to second-guess the decision not to indict: "If the suspect was Joe the Rag Man," James declared at one point, "he'd have been charged."

Instead, the Monroe Street investigation was consigned to a separate file drawer in the admin lieutenant's office—a burial apart from the other open cases, an interment that befitted the only unsolved police-involved shooting in the department's history.

After months of work, that outcome was hard enough for Worden to swallow. And on the board, meanwhile, the names of two March murder victims were still written in red next to Worden's initial. Sylvester Merriman waited for the Big Man to find that missing witness, the teenage runaway from the group home; Dwayne Dickerson waited for Worden to shake something loose from the neighborhood around Ellamont Avenue. And for the rest of this week as well, McLarney's squad would be working a midnight shift, virtually assuring Worden that he would catch a fresh one before Saturday. The last six months had left him with a full, heaping plate of bone and gristle. Yet the city of Baltimore was paying him unlimited OT to chew on a wounded politician's leg.

"I'll tell you this," the Big Man tells Rick James in between bites of the sandwich. "This is the last time I let myself be used. I'm not here to do their dirty work."

James says nothing.

"I don't give a damn about Larry Young, but you give a man your word . . ."

Worden's word. It was a rock in the Northwest District, and it was good as gold when he was back in the old escape and apprehension unit. Hell, if you found yourself in a room with a CID robbery detective by the name of Worden, you took anything said to you there as fact. But this was the homicide unit—land of the forgotten promise—and Worden is again being made to understand that at any given moment, the bosses own the rulebook.

"No matter what happens," he tells James, blowing cigar smoke toward the window. "They can't take your EOD away from you."

James nods; the comment is anything but a non sequitur. Worden's Entrance On Duty date is 1962. He's got the mandatory twenty-five plus one for good measure; Worden can go out on a full pension in the time it takes to type up the forms.

"I can always make money building decks and putting up drywall . . ."

The last natural police detective in America slinging spackle. It's a depressing image, and James says nothing.

". . . or delivering furs. There's a lot of money in furs."

Worden finishes breakfast with another cup of black coffee, followed by another cigar. Then he cleans the desk and waits for the 9:00 A.M. shift at the courthouse in cold, empty silence.

Wednesday, June 29

Fred Ceruti knows it's a bad one when he turns the corner on Whittier and sees the ambulance. Time of call was 0343 and that was a half an hour ago, he calculates, so what the hell is the guy still doing in the ambo?

The detective edges the Cavalier up behind the red glow of the medic unit's emergency lights, then stares for a moment at the frenzied paramedics in the rear of the ambulance. Standing on the ambo's rear running board, a Western uniform looks back at Ceruti and gives a quick thumb's down.

"He don't look so hot," says the uniform as Ceruti gets out of his car and steps toward the red strobes. "They've been here twenty minutes and he still ain't stable."

"Where's he hit?"

"Head shot. One in the arm too."

The victim is writhing on his litter, moaning, with his legs buckling back and forth in slow repetition—outward at the knees, inward at the toes—an involuntary movement that tells a homicide detective to post the vacancy sign. When a head-shot victim starts dancing on his ambo litter—"doing the Funky Chicken," Jay Landsman calls it—you can write it down as a murder.

Ceruti watches the paramedics struggle as they begin working a pair of pressure pants around the victim's legs. Fully inflated with air, the device greatly constricts blood flow to the lower extremities, thereby maintaining blood pressure in the head and torso. In Ceruti's mind, the pressure pants are as much of a threat as anything else; the damn things can keep a man alive until he arrives at an emergency room, but the trauma team eventually has to deflate those bad boys, and at that point, blood pressure takes a nose dive and all hell breaks loose.

"Where's he going?" Ceruti asks.

"Shock-Trauma, if we can stabilize him," says the ambo driver. "But I mean, shit, we haven't been able to get him leveled out."

Ceruti looks up and down Whittier Avenue and reads the scene like a short grocery list. Dark side street. Ambush. No witnesses. No physical evidence. Probable drug murder. Don't die on me, you bastard. Don't you dare go and die on me.

"Are you the first officer?"

"Yeah. Seven-A-thirty-four unit."

Ceruti begins collecting the particulars in his notebook, then follows the uniform to an alleyway between the rowhouses at 2300 and 2302.

"We got the call as shots fired and found him lying right there, head to the wall. He still had this in his waistband when we rolled him."

The patrolman holds up a .38 five-shot.

No good, thinks Ceruti, no good at all. His last case was also a drug murder from the Western. Boy by the name of Stokes shot down in an alley off Carrollton, skinny kid who turned out to be HIV-positive when they got him down to the ME's office. That case, too, is still open.

Ceruti fills a couple of pages in his notepad, then walks a block and a half east to a corner pay phone to call for reinforcements. Landsman answers the phone on the first ring.

"Hey, Jay," says the detective, "this guy didn't look good in the ambo."

"Oh yeah?"

"Yeah. He's shot in the head and it's gonna be a murder. You better wake Dunnigan up . . ."

No, Landsman tells him. Not this time.

"Whoa, Jay. I had the last one . . ."

"It's your call, Fred. Do what you got to do. Are you sending anyone down here?"

"There's no one to send. There aren't any witnesses or anything close."

"Okay, Fred. Gimme a call when you finish up at the scene."

Ceruti slams the receiver into its cradle, cursing his sergeant bitterly. The brief conversation has left him with no doubt that Landsman is trying to fuck him, sending him out on calls alone and holding back when he calls for help. It was the same thing on the Stokes homicide last month and on the beating in the Southwest back in April. Those are the last two homicides handled by Landsman's squad and Ceruti was the primary on both; this guy here on Whittier makes three in a row. Landsman reads the board, Ceruti tells himself. He knows what's up. So why the hell doesn't he get on Dunnigan and send his ass out here to pick up this murder?

Ceruti knows the answer. At least he thinks he does. He isn't the golden boy of Landsman's squad, not by a long shot. He and Pellegrini arrived at the same time, but it was Pellegrini who caught the interest of the sergeant, Pellegrini with whom Landsman preferred to handle calls. Tom is not only a prospect but a sidekick for his sergeant, a straight man for the situation comedy in which Landsman lives. Two or three good cases and Tom is suddenly a prodigy, a candidate for rookie of the year. Ceruti is simply the other one, the dime-a-dozen new kid from the districts. And now he is alone.

Ceruti makes his way back from the pay phone just as the ambo is pulling away. He tries to forget the conversation with Landsman and do what he needs to do, working what little there is of this murder-to-be. One of the uniforms manages to find a spent bullet on a nearby stoop, a .38 or .32 from the look of it, but too badly mutilated to be of any use in a ballistics comparison. A lab tech arrives a few minutes later to bag the bullet and take scene photos. Ceruti wanders back to the pay phone to tell Landsman that he's on his way in.

That's his intention, anyway, until he spots a heavyset woman on an Orem Avenue porch, watching him strangely as he walks toward the phone. He changes direction and saunters up to the house as casually as possible, given that it's four in the morning.

Incredibly, she saw them. More incredible still, she is willing to tell Ceruti what she saw. There were three of them running after the sound of shots, sprinting down the street toward one of the houses at the other end of Orem. No, she didn't recognize them, but she saw them. Ceruti asks several more questions and the woman becomes nervous—understandably, since she still has to live in this neighborhood. If he takes her off the porch now, Ceruti tells the whole street that she's a witness. Instead, he leaves with a name and phone number.

Back at the homicide office, Landsman is watching the overnight news channel when Ceruti returns and throws the notepad down on a desk.

"Hey, Fred," says Landsman coolly. "How'd it go out there?"

Ceruti glares at him, then shrugs.

Landsman turns back to the television. "Maybe you'll get a call on it."

"Yeah. Maybe."

From Ceruti's point of view, his sergeant is being senselessly cruel. But for Landsman, the equation is simple. A new man comes up and you show him the ropes, carrying him along on a few cases until he knows the game. If you can, you may even throw him a few dunkers to feed his confidence. But up in homicide, that's about it for the orientation program. After that, it's sink or swim.

It is true that Landsman thinks the world of Pellegrini; it is also true that he would rather work a murder with Pellegrini than with anyone else in the squad. But Ceruti has had a year of handling calls with Dunnigan or Requer watching over him; he isn't exactly being thrown naked to the wolves here. In that sense, he is right to find meaning in the fact that he has worked the squad's last three murders and worked them alone. They were homicides and he's a homicide detective and, in Landsman's mind, now is the time to see if Ceruti can find the meaning in that.

Fred Ceruti is a good cop, brought to homicide by the captain after four years' experience in the Eastern District. He did some respectable plainclothes work in the ops unit there, and in a department where affirmative action is a standing policy, a good black plainclothesman is going to get noticed. But still, CID homicide after only four years of experience is a hard road for anyone to walk, and the other sixth-floor units were littered with detectives who had been bounced from the Crimes Against Persons section. At crime scenes and during interrogations, things that could never slip past a more experienced investigator could still elude Ceruti. Such limitations weren't immediately noticeable when he was working cases as a secondary investigator with Dunnigan or Requer. Nor did they become immediately apparent when Landsman began sending him out alone on calls four months ago.

Many of Ceruti's first solo flights were successes, but those cases were largely stone dunkers—the February stabbing death of a Block prostitute came complete with three witnesses, and the suspect in the April bludgeoning from the Southwest was identified by patrol officers well before any detective's arrival.

But a double murder from January, a pair of drug killings at an east side stash house, had been cleared only after some acrimony between Ceruti and his sergeant. In that case, Ceruti had been reluctant to charge a suspect with a case that consisted of one reluctant witness. Landsman, however, needed to get those two murders off the board, and when Dunnigan was later able to pressure the witness into a full statement, the case was sent to the grand jury over Ceruti's objections. Substantively, Ceruti had been right—the weak case was ultimately dismissed before trial by prosecutors—but in practical, political terms, the late clearance made the new detective appear unaggressive. Likewise, the Stokes case, the back alley drug slaying from the Western, did not go well either. There, too, Ceruti had to his credit found a woman who had seen the fleeing gunmen, but he elected not to bring her downtown at the time. Considering the risk to a known witness, this was not the worst decision; Edgerton, for example, left his witness at the scene of that Payson Street shooting last month. The difference was that Edgerton put his case in the black, and in the real world, a detective can do anything he wants as long as the cases go down.

The fact that a new detective such as Ceruti was now looking at two consecutive open murders did not in itself constitute a threat. After all, neither Joseph Stokes nor Raymond Hawkins, the dying man on Whittier Street, was going to be mistaken for a taxpayer, and in practice, a homicide detective could go a fairly long time without typing a prosecution report so long as none of the cases was a red ball. In the end, therefore, Ceruti's sin would not be that two drug murders stayed open. The sin was more basic. Ceruti would be brought down by willful neglect of the police department's First Commandment: Cover Thine Ass.

A little more than a month from now, Ceruti will be down on the captain's carpet for the Stokes murder, in particular. Taxpayer or no, the thirty-two-year-old victim in that case turns out to be the brother of a civilian communications clerk for the department. By virtue of that position, she knows enough about the police department to find the homicide unit and make repeated inquiries about the status of the investigation. In truth, the status of the investigation is that it has no status. There are no fresh leads and the woman who witnessed the flight of the shooters can identify no one. Ceruti puts the clerk off for a time, but eventually the woman directs a complaint to his superiors. And when those superiors pull the case file, they find nothing. No office report, no follow-ups, no paper trail documenting either progress or lack of it. And when the captain learns that Ceruti left breathing witnesses at his last two murder scenes, things go from bad to worse.

"That's the first thing you're supposed to learn up here," Eddie Brown later tells Ceruti. "No matter what, you always cover yourself in the case file. You write up everything so that no one can come back and second-guess what you did."

In the end, it is not Landsman who brings the empty case file into the captain's office; he is on vacation at the time and Roger Nolan is the supervisor assigned to handle the woman's complaint. For that reason, Landsman will later insist to anyone who will listen that he played no part in Ceruti's misfortune. That is true in only the strictest sense, of course. In fact, Landsman sent him out alone on those murders with an air of practiced noncommitment, waiting to see if his detective would stand or fall. Ceruti may have been wrong to think that his sergeant was out to screw him, but he was right to believe that, in the end, Landsman did little to save him from being screwed.

It is altogether sad and painful, particularly because Ceruti is a decent guy, an intelligent, good-humored addition to the homicide unit's camaraderie. But by summer's end, the complaints about the Stokes case will reach a natural resolution. The captain and D'Addario will keep Ceruti on the sixth floor, of course; they owe him that much, though such considerations are of small consolation to Ceruti. By September, he will be a vice detective, honing himself on whores and pimps and numbers runners in an office three doors down the hall from homicide. And the proximity alone will make for hard moments.

A week after the transfer, Ceruti is standing with another vice detective in the sixth-floor lobby when an elevator suddenly disgorges Landsman, who looks blankly at the detective.

"Hey, Fred, how's it going?"

Ceruti stares angrily and Landsman moves past him, seemingly oblivious.

"You tell me," asks Ceruti, turning to his companion. "How cold was that?"

THURSDAY, JUNE 30

"I hear what you're saying," Terry McLarney tells him. "I just don't believe you really mean it."

Worden shrugs.

"You don't want to leave like this, Donald. You'd fucking hate it. You know you would."

"Watch me."

"No, you're just pissed off. Give it time."

"I've given it a lot of time. I've given it twenty-six years."

"That's what I mean."

Worden looks at him.

"What else are you gonna do with yourself? You'd be bored shitless."

Worden says nothing for a moment, then pulls out the keys to his pickup. "It's getting late, Terry. Time to be heading down the road."

"Wait a minute," says McLarney, turning toward a brick wall at the edge of the lot. "I gotta take a leak. Don't leave yet."

Don't leave yet. Don't give up on a long, dangling conversation between two white men in rumpled suits, two refugees who have been standing in an empty parking lot off the 200 block of West Madison Street for more than an hour. It is three in the morning, and the two-story Formstone structure on the opposite side of the street, an establishment that trades as Kavanaugh's Irish Tavern, sits dark and empty, having expectorated four or five homicide detectives more than an hour ago. The two white men are the only remaining patrons, and they have but one can of warm beer remaining. Why in the world would anyone even think of leaving?

"Listen to me, Donald," says McLarney, returning. "This is your job. This is what you do."

Worden shakes his head. "This is what I do now," he says. "I can always change jobs."

"You can't change."

Worden glares at his sergeant.

"I mean you don't want to change. Why would you want to change? How many other people can do what you do?"

McLarney pauses, hoping that some of this—any of it—will touch a nerve. God knows he means every word of it. Worden was struggling, true, but even the man's most mediocre year is worth any aggravation. For a squad sergeant, having Worden working for you was like having sex: When it was good it was great, and even when it wasn't so hot, it was still pretty damn good.

In the last week alone, Worden proved as much by clearing two murders on nothing less than instinct and talent. He made it all look effortless and elegant, even as the stink of the Larry Young debacle was still hanging in the air.

Six days ago, Worden and Rick James caught a stabbing up on Jasper Street, a twenty-three-year-old black kid half-naked under bloody sheets in a second-floor bedroom. The two detectives took one look at their victim and knew immediately that they were dealing with a dispute between homosexual lovers. The depth and number of the stab wounds told them that much; no motive other than sex produces that kind of overkill, and no woman can make those kinds of holes in a man.

The body was already coming out of rigor. It was a humid night, and the temperature in that rowhouse had to be 110 on the upper floors: still, the two men refused to rush their scene. Several times, when the heat became too much for him, Worden stepped out onto the street and sat for a moment on the corner bench, sipping quietly on a convenience store soda. They stayed with that scene for hours, with James working the second floor and the area immediately surrounding the body. Worden wandered through the rest of the house, looking for anything out of place. In the third-floor bedroom, the killer had apparently yanked a VCR off its table and pushed the appliance halfway into a plastic garbage bag before giving up on the theft and fleeing. Was it really a robbery? Or was someone trying to make it look like a robbery?

Eventually, Worden got down to the kitchen, where he found the sink half-filled with dirty water. Reaching down gingerly, he pulled the drain and the sink emptied slowly, revealing a cutting knife with its blade broken. Lying next to the murder weapon was a hand towel still pink from the blood; the killer had washed up before leaving. Worden looked down the kitchen counter at a dozen or so unwashed dishes, glasses and utensils—jetsam, it seemed, from the previous night's dinner. One glass, however, stood on the far edge of the counter, alone and distinct. Worden called the lab tech over and told him to check that glass in particular for prints. Hot as it was, Worden figured the killer might have wanted a drink of water before leaving.

The Jasper Street scene took five hours, after which James headed for the morgue and Worden locked himself in an interrogation room with the roommate of the victim, who also owned the house. The roommate had discovered the body after returning from his night job and told Worden that when he left to go to work, the victim was entertaining a friend he had met at a bar. He had never seen the guy before and didn't know his name.

Worden rode the roommate hard, seizing on the fact that he was out working while his bunky was lazing around the house with some new man.

"You didn't like that, did you?"

"I didn't care."

"You didn't care?"

"No."

"I know that would make me angry."

"I wasn't angry."

The man held firm to his story and Worden was left with nothing, or so it seemed until later that afternoon, when the Printrak got a solid hit off the drinking glass. The latent print matched that of a twenty-three-year-old west-sider with a long sheet of priors. With considerable reluctance, the owner of the house returned once again to the homicide unit and made the ID of the suspect from a photo array. For that clearance, Worden's eye—his ability to see that separate drinking glass as precious evidence—got the credit.

Four nights later, his remarkable memory sent another murder into the black when a tactical section officer locked up two east side men on auto theft charges and found that one of them, Anthony Cunningham, was wanted on a murder warrant written by Worden a month earlier. The warrant had been typed and signed shortly after detectives from the robbery unit locked up a crew of east-siders for a series of holdups centered around the Douglass Homes. Lew Davis, a long-time colleague of Worden's in robbery, had wandered across the hall with the news.

"We've got one of them in there now going for a whole bunch of holdups," Davis asked Worden. "You all have anything up there that might match up to these guys?"

Standing in front of the board, Worden needed exactly fifteen seconds before his elephantine memory settled on one name among fifty: Charles Lehman, the fifty-one-year-old killed on Fayette Street as he walked to his car with a Kentucky Fried Chicken dinner. Kincaid's whodunit from February.

"I got one right in that area," said Worden. "You're talking to this guy now?"

"Yeah, he's in the big interrogation room. Christ, Donald, he's already gone for about a dozen robberies."

After a brief parley with the kid in the large box, Worden knew that the kid could indeed put the Lehman murder down. The duty prosecutor that night, Don Giblin, was called down and the negotiations began. The prosecutor's bottom-line offer: for identifying and testifying against the shooter on the Lehman murder, eleven years on one of the robberies and no immunity if you're linked to any other murders or shootings.

Worden watched the kid mull over the deal, then attempt a counter-offer: "Five years."

"You're no good to me with five years," the prosecutor told the kid. "A jury won't believe you unless you get at least ten."

"Too much," said the kid.

"Oh, you don't think you should get any time," said Worden, disgusted. "What about all them people you robbed? What about that old lady you all shot on Monument Street?"

"We're not talkin' about them," the kid snapped. "This is me we're talkin' about."

Worden shook his head and walked from the room, leaving Giblin to cement the deal. It was ugly, all right, but the warrant for twenty-five-year-old Anthony Cunningham went to a court commissioner that same night. Now, with Cunningham locked up, that case, too, was down.

Four nights, two murders. McLarney has to wonder how many other detectives would have noticed that one drinking glass was a little too far from the others? And how many detectives would have made the connection between the Lehman case and the other east side robberies? Hell, McLarney tells himself, most detectives can't remember the cases worked by their own squad, much less those handled by some other squad five months back.

"You can't leave," McLarney tells Worden, renewing his appeal.

Worden shakes his head.

"You can't," says McLarney, laughing. "I won't let you."

"You're just talking like this 'cause you're losing a detective. That's what you're worried about, right? You just don't want to have to spend the time to break in a new guy."

McLarney laughs again and leans back against the front of his car. He reaches into the paper bag for the last can. "If you leave, there'll be no one around to fuck with Dave Brown and he'll go all derelict."

Worden gives back a half-smile.

"If you quit, Donald, he'll start thinking he knows what he's doing. It'll be dangerous. I'll be writing long reports for the captain every other week."

"Waltemeyer will keep on him."

McLarney shakes his head. "I can't believe we're even talking about this . . ."

Worden shrugs. "You're the one talking."

"Donald, you . . ." says McLarney, pausing to stare down the cross street toward Monument. Worden fidgets, rolling the keys to his truck back and forth on their ring.

"You see him?" asks McLarney suddenly.

"The boy in the gray?"

"Yeah, the sweatshirt."

"Yeah I seen him. He's only walked by here four times now."

"He's marking us."

"Yeah, he is."

McLarney stares back up the cross street. The kid is wiry and dark-skinned, sixteen or seventeen, wearing spandex bike shorts and a hooded sweatshirt. It's still eighty degrees or better and the kid has both hands in his pockets and the hoody zipped tight.

"He thinks we're victims," says McLarney, laughing under his breath.

"Two old white guys hanging in an empty lot at this hour," snorts Worden. "I'm not surprised."

"We're not old," says McLarney, objecting. "I'm not old anyway."

Worden smiles, tosses the key ring and catches it with the other hand. He told himself that he would be going straight home after the four-to-twelve shift; instead, he spent two hours on a Kavanaugh's barstool, hurting himself with Jack Black. But the last hour's temperance—Worden had no taste for the Miller Lite that McLarney bought carryout—was bringing him back down to earth.

"I got to get up early," he says.

McLarney shakes his head. "I don't want to hear this, Donald. You've had a bad year, all right, so what? So you get back in the saddle on another case and things change. You know how it is."

"I don't like being used."

"You weren't used."

"Yes," says Worden. "I was."

"You're still angry about Monroe Street, right? We disagreed about that and that's okay, but that's—"

"No. This isn't about Monroe Street."

"Then what?"

Worden grimaces.

"This Larry Young thing?"

"That's part of it," says Worden. "That's definitely part of it."

"Well, that was fucked, I have to admit."

"They used me," Worden repeats. "They used me to do their dirty work. I don't need that."

"They used you," McLarney agrees reluctantly.

Worden turns his head slightly, catching the kid in the gray hoody out of one eye. Like a shark circling the raft, the kid is once again edging down the opposite side of the cross street, hands still deep in his pockets, watching the two men without seeming to watch them.

"Enough is enough," says McLarney. He drains the can in one fluid motion, then reaches into his jacket pocket while starting across the lot. The kid has changed directions again, moving toward the detectives from the other side of the street.

"Don't go and shoot him, Terry," says Worden, mildly amused. "I don't wanna spend the first day of my vacation writing."

At McLarney's approach, the kid slows, suddenly confused. The sergeant pulls the silver shield out and waves it once in a way that suggests nothing more than irritation. "We're cops," he yells at the kid. "Go rob someone else."

One flash of silver and the kid is off on a new vector, bounding back to the other side of the street. He throws his hands in the air, palms open, as if to surrender.

"I ain't about robbin' nobody," the kid yells over his shoulder. "You got it wrong."

McLarney waits long enough for the kid to disappear onto Madison, then walks back to the conversation.

"We're cops and you're not," says Worden, amused. "That was good, Terry."

"I guess we pretty much fucked up his night," says McLarney. "He wasted half an hour on us."

Worden yawns. "Awright, sergeant. I think it's about time to be heading down the road here . . ."

"Guess so," says McLarney. "I'm outta beer."

Worden gives his sergeant a light chuck on the arm and begins sorting through the key ring.

"Where'd you park?"

"Up on Madison."

"I'll walk you."

"What're you? My date?"

McLarney laughs. "You could do worse."

"Not really."

"Listen, Donald," says McLarney abruptly. "Just give it some time. You're pissed off now and I don't blame you, but things will change. You know this is what you want to do, right? You don't want to do anything else."

Worden listens.

"You know you're the best man I've got."

Worden shoots him a look.

"Really, you are. And I'd hate like hell to lose you, but that's not why I'm saying this. Really."

Worden shoots him another look.

"Okay, okay, maybe that is why I'm saying it. Maybe I'm full of shit here and I just don't want to be alone in the office with a mental case like Waltemeyer. But you know what I'm saying. You really should give it some time . . ."

"I'm tired," says Worden. "I've had enough."

"You've had a terrible year. Monroe Street and the cases you got . . . You definitely haven't caught the breaks, but that will change. It'll definitely change. And this Larry Young thing, I mean, who the fuck cares?"

Worden listens.

"You're a cop, Donald. Fuck the bosses, don't even think about the bosses. They're always going to be fucked up and that's all there is to it. So what? So fuck them. But where else are you going to go and be a cop?"

"Careful driving home," says Worden.

"Donald, listen to me."

"I heard you, Terry."

"Just promise me this. Promise me you won't do anything without coming to me first."

"I'll tell you first," says Worden.

"Okay," says McLarney. "Then we can have this discussion a second time. I get another chance to practice my speech."

Worden smiles.

"You're off tomorrow, right?" asks McLarney.

"For ten days. My vacation."

"Oh yeah. Have a good one. You planning on going anywhere?"

Worden shakes his head.

"Staying around the house, huh?"

"I'm doing some work on the basement."

McLarney nods, suddenly speechless. Power tools, drywall and all other facets of home improvement have always been a mystery to him.

"Careful driving home, Terry."

"I'm fine," says McLarney.

"Okay then."

Worden climbs in the cab, pumps the ignition and edges the truck into the empty lanes of Madison Street. McLarney walks back to his own car, hoping against hope, wondering whether anything said tonight will make even the least bit of difference.

SEVEN

Summertime and the living is easy, says Gershwin. But he never had to work murders in Baltimore, where summer steams and swelters and splits open wide like a mile of the devil's sidewalk. From Milton to Poplar Grove, visible heat wriggles up from the asphalt in waves, and by noon, the brick and Formstone is hot to the touch. No lawn chairs, no sprinklers, no piña coladas in a ten-speed Waring; summer in the city is sweat and stink and $29 box fans slapping bad air from the second-floor windows of every other rowhouse. Baltimore is a swamp of a city, too, built on a Chesapeake Bay backwater by God-fearing Catholic refugees who should have thought twice after the first Patapsco River mosquito began chewing on the first pale patch of European skin. Summer in Baltimore is its own unyielding argument, its own critical mass.

The season is an endless street parade, with half the city out fanning itself on marble and stone stoops, waiting for a harbor breeze that never seems to make it across town. Summer is a four-to-twelve shift of nightsticks and Western District wagon runs, with three hundred hard cases on the Edmondson Avenue sidewalk between Payson and Pulaski, eye-fucking each other and every passing radio car. Summer is a ninety-minute backup in the Hopkins emergency room, an animal chorus of curses and pleas from the denizens of every district lockup, a nightly promise of yet another pool of blood on the dirty linoleum in yet another Federal Street carryout. Summer is a barroom cutting up on Druid Hill, a ten-minute gun battle in the Terrace, a daylong domestic dispute that ends with the husband and wife both fighting the cops. Summer is the season of motiveless murder, of broken-blade steak knives and bent tire irons; it's the time for truly dangerous living, the season of massive and immediate retaliation, the 96-degree natural habitat of the Argument That Will Be Won. A drunk switches off the Orioles game in a Pigtown bar; a west side kid dances with an east-sider's girl at the rec center off

Aisquith Street; a fourteen-year-old bumps an older kid getting on the number 2 bus—every one of them becomes a life in the balance.

In a detective's mind, the beginning of the summer can be marked with precision by the year's first warm weather disrespect murder. Respect being the rarest of commodities in the inner city, its defense by homicidal assault on an 85-degree-or-better day can suddenly seem required. This year, summer begins on a warm Sunday night in May, when a sixteen-year-old Walbrook High School student dies of a gunshot wound to the stomach, sustained during a fight that began when his friend was punched and forced to relinquish a 15-cent cherry Popsicle.

"This had nothing to do with drugs," says Dave Hollingsworth, one of Stanton's detectives, in a statement meant to reassure reporters and, through them, the sweltering masses. "This was over an ice cream."

Summertime.

True, the statistics show only a mild increase in the homicide rate during the hot months, at least if you consider a 10 or 20 percent jump worthy of the term mild. But in the mind of any homicide detective, the statistics can't say a goddamn thing until they get out in an Eastern District radio car for a Fourth of July weekend. Out in the streets, summer is something to be reckoned with no matter how much meat the shock-trauma units manage to salvage. To hell with the ones who die, a veteran detective will tell you, it's the assault-by-shootings and cuttings and beatings that can keep a squad running all summer long. Beyond that there are the suicides and overdoses and unattended deaths—routine garbage detail duty that suddenly becomes unbearable when the cadavers are going ripe in 90-degree weather. Don't even bother showing a homicide detective the charts and graphs because he'll shake them off. Summer is a war.

Just ask Eddie Brown on a hot July afternoon in Pimlico as the neighborhood girls dance with each other on rowhouse porches while lab techs and detectives clean up a crime scene. A young man is dead, shot while sitting in the passenger seat of a stolen car as he rode down Pimlico toward Greenspring in search of another homeboy who managed to find him first. A daylight murder on a main drag, but the driver of the car has fled and no one else saw a thing. Brown pulls a loaded .32 from the wrecked car as the girls move to a beat that has been brought to distortion by unlimited volume.

First a high wail: "*It takes two to make a thing go right . . .*"

Then the bass lick and another soprano shout: "*. . . it takes two to make it outta sight.*"

Number 1 with a bullet. The song is this summer's hands-down winner for Sound of the Ghetto, with that deep-bottom bass line and those high-pitched screams on the quarter beat. Thick drum track, def rhythm and some sweet-voiced yoette wailing out the same two-line lyric. East side, west side, and all around the town, the corner boys of Baltimore are fighting and dying to the same soundtrack.

You think summer's just another season? Then ask Rich Garvey about the Fourth of July shooting on Madeira Street in the Eastern, where a thirty-five-year-old woman ends a running dispute with her neighbor by firing one shot from a .32 at close range, then walks back to her rowhouse as the other woman lies dying.

"It takes two to make a thing go right . . ."

Ask Kevin Davis about Ernestine Parker, a middle-aged Pimlico resident who decides that it's not the heat but the humidity, then puts a shotgun to the back of her husband's head on a July night. And when Davis gets back to the office and punches Ernestine into the computer, he learns it's her second bite of the apple; she had killed another man twenty years ago.

"It takes two to make it outta sight . . ."

Ask Rick James after a summer morning in the Hollander Ridge housing project, where a resident lies dead on a bloodsoaked mattress, having calmly gone upstairs and put himself to bed after being cut by a ladyfriend the night before. Or ask Constantine at his scene down on Jack Street, half a block from the Brooklyn Homes projects, where the wreck of a ninety-year-old woman waits for him in a bedroom with blood spatter on every wall. Beaten, raped and sodomized, the old woman was then forced to breathe into a pillow, finally ending the ordeal.

"It takes two . . ."

Ask Rick Requer or Gary Dunnigan about that domestic from the Northeast, the one where the dead man has a hole in his throat so deep you can see the whole thorax, and his girlfriend claims that he routinely asked her to come at him with kitchen knives, the better to show off his martial arts skill. Or ask Worden and James about the loser who tries to break into an East Baltimore rowhouse only to have his own pistol used against him by the surprised but otherwise athletic male occupant. A single shot is fired during the struggle and the dying man sits down suddenly on the living room sofa.

"Get out of here before I blow your head off," the homeowner shouts, clutching the gun.

"You already did," says his assailant, losing consciousness.

". . . to make a thing go right . . ."

Summer needs no motive; it's a reason unto itself. Just ask Eddie Brown about the fifteen-year-old who shoots his friend with a defective .22 on Preakness Saturday night in Cherry Hill, then smugly refuses any statement to police, assured in his mind and in fact that he will only be charged as a juvenile. Then ask Donald Kincaid about Joseph Adams, who bled to death on the way to University Hospital after picking a fight with a fourteen-year-old and getting pushed through a convenience store window, the broken sheet glass falling on his neck like a guillotine.

"It takes two . . ."

Bodies everywhere as June bleeds into July, and even among men for whom a studied indifference to human weakness and misery is a necessary survival skill, summer produces its own special strain of the disease. This is CID homicide, mister, and neither heat nor rain nor gloom of night will stay these men from their rendezvous with callousness. Cruel jokes? The cruelest. Sick humor? The sickest. And, you ask, how can they possibly do it? Volume. That's right, volume. They won't be outsold, they won't be undersold; they will solve no crime before its time.

Picture Garvey and Worden sharing a smoke outside a second-floor apartment on Lanvale, where an aging alcoholic lies dead on the floor, his bottle empty, his neck cleanly broken. Chances are he was alive when he fell to the floor drunk, but was then killed accidentally by his equally intoxicated wife, who forced the door against his neck as she tried to enter the room.

"You want to make it a murder?" deadpans Worden, inspecting and then lighting his cigar.

"We could use the stat," jokes Garvey, equally dry.

"Then make it a murder. What do I know? I'm just an ignorant white boy from Hampden."

"It's a dunker . . ."

"I don't think she's strong enough to kill him."

"What the hell," says Garvey, as if sizing up a trout. "We'll throw this one back."

Or Jay Landsman doing another stand-up routine in lower Wyman Park, where the elderly occupant of a senior citizens' high-rise has done a header from a twentieth-floor balcony. From the look of things, the old woman stayed pretty much intact until she glanced off a second-floor landing, her head and torso staying upstairs, legs and rump falling to street level.

"She went her separate ways," Landsman tells the uniform at the scene. "So you'd better write separate incident reports."

"Sir?"

"Never mind."

"One guy on the sixth floor said he actually looked out his window and saw her falling," the patrolman says, reading from his notes.

"Oh yeah?" says Landsman. "Did she say anything?"

"Uh, no. I mean maybe. I mean I didn't ask."

"Right," says Landsman, "but have you found the pogo stick yet?"

"Pogo stick?" asks the flustered uniform.

"Pogo stick," says Landsman firmly. "I think it's pretty obvious this woman took a bad bounce."

Blame it on the heat, because what else can explain that rollercoaster midnight shift in August, when Harry Edgerton takes an unattended death call from a young Southwest uniform, listens for a minute or two, then tells the kid he doesn't have time to visit the scene.

"Listen, we're kinda busy right now," he says, cradling the phone on his shoulder. "Why don't you throw the body in the back of your car and bring him on downtown so we can take a look at him?"

"Right," says the kid, hanging up.

"Oh shit," says Edgerton, fumbling through a directory for the Southwest dispatch phone number. "He actually believed me."

A hellacious night it was, too, with a murder, two cuttings and a police-involved shooting. But two nights later, McLarney's detectives are again tempting fate. Waiting for the first call of the night, Worden, James, and Dave Brown gather around the coffee room desk, concentrating their psychic powers on the phone extensions, trying to will into existence something more than a ghetto homicide, something that will bring unlimited overtime.

"I feel it."

"Shut up. Concentrate."

"I feel it."

"Yeah, it's coming."

"A big one."

"A double," says Dave Brown.

"No, a triple," adds James.

"Stone whodunit."

"At a major tourist attraction . . ."

"Fort McHenry!"

"Memorial Stadium!"

"No," says Brown, reaching for the motherlode, "the Harborplace Pavilion."

"During lunch hour," adds Worden.

"Ooooooh," says Rick James. "A moneymaker."

Bad craziness.

Or picture Landsman and Pellegrini a week or so later in the Pennington Hotel in Curtis Bay, where refinery storage tanks tower above a battered working-class neighborhood at the harbor's southern approach.

"Third floor," says the desk man. "On the right."

The dead man is rigored and jaundiced, obviously diseased, with half a bottle of Mad Dog on the floor by his feet, an empty box of Hostess doughnuts on the facing table. In the last analysis, death at the Pennington Hotel is a sad redundancy.

A Southern District uniform, a young officer fresh to the street, nonetheless guards the scene with an earnest sincerity.

"I need you to tell the truth about something," says Landsman.

"Sir?"

"You ate those doughnuts, didn't you?"

"What?"

"The doughnuts. You finished 'em off, right?"

"No sir."

"You sure?" asks Landsman, deadpan. "You just had one, right?"

"No sir. They were gone when I got here."

"Okay then, good job," says Landsman, turning to leave. "Whaddaya know, Tom, a cop who doesn't like doughnuts."

More than any other season, summer holds its own special horrors. Consider, for example, Dunnigan and Requer on a 100-degree dayshift and an old man in the clutter of a basement apartment on Eutaw Street. A decomp case with attitude, cooking in there for a week or more until someone caught the scent and noticed a few thousand flies on the inside of a window.

"If you got 'em, smoke 'em," says the ME's attendant, lighting up a cigar. "It's bad now, but it's gonna be worse when we get to flippin' him."

"He'll burst on you," says Dunnigan.

"Not me," says the attendant. "I'm an artist."

Requer laughs, then laughs again when the attendants try to roll the bloated wreck gently only to have it explode like a bad melon, the skin sliding away from the chest cavity.

"Jesus fucking Christ," says the attendant, dropping the dead man's legs and turning to gag. "Jesus fuck-my-fucking-job Christ."

"That ain't pretty, bunk," growls Requer, puffing harder on the cigar and looking at a rolling mass of maggots. "His face is moving—pork fried rice. You know what I'm saying?"

"One of the worst I ever had," says the attendant, catching his breath. "By the number of flies, I'd say five or six days at least."

"A week," says Requer, closing his notebook.

Outside in the parking lot, a Central District officer, the first uniform in the apartment, has slipped away to eat lunch in the front of his radio car, a portable tape player on the dash blaring that same summer beat.

"It takes two to make a thing go right . . ."

"How the fuck can you eat after handling this call?" asks Dunnigan, genuinely amazed.

"Roast beef, rare," says the cop, displaying the second half of the sandwich with pride. "Hey, you only get one lunch a shift."

For summer, you need a scorecard to keep the lineup straight. Put Constantine and Keller in Pigtown, working a bar murder where the suspect turns out to be a kid who beat the robbery-murder of an elderly schoolteacher four years ago. Put Waltemeyer and Worden at a reggae dance club near the Metro tracks in the Northwest, its front walk covered by a dead Jamaican and a dozen spent 9mm casings, its interior cluttered by about seventy other Jakes who swear to Jah himself that they see not a blessed thing, mon. Put Dunnigan down in the Perkins Homes for a body in the closet; Pellegrini in the Central for a body in the gutter; Childs and Sydnor in the Eastern for a female skeleton beneath a rowhouse porch, a skeleton that is finally matched to a missing persons report three weeks later. She was the tiniest thing, barely eighteen and a hundred pounds dripping wet, and her bastard of a stepfather waited only long enough for his wife to go out of town for a week. He brought three friends home for Saturday night and after a six-pack, the four of them took turns on her, then strangled her by wrapping a towel around her neck and pulling in different directions.

"Why are you doing this?" she asked, pleading.

"Sorry," her stepfather told her. "We got to."

The shouts and screams and curses rise and fall with the temperature in the stagnant, fetid air. The crescendo comes in the last and hottest week of July, six straight days of boiler room heat that makes the citywide police frequency sound like an endless tape:

"Forty-five hundred Pimlico, odd side in the rear, for a woman screaming . . . Thirty-six hundred Howard Park, for an armed person . . . Twenty-four fifty-one Druid Hill, for an assault in progress . . . Signal thirteen. Calhoun and Mosher. Signal thirteen . . . Fourteen-fifteen Key Highway for a man beating a woman . . ."

And then, the dispatch call that everyone most fears, the dayshift broadcast that only comes when the heat has truly touched the wrong nerve in the wrong man in the wrong place.

"Signal thirteen. Seven fifty-four Forrest Street."

It begins with one inmate and one guard mixing it up in the security booth at the end of the No. 4 yard. They are joined by another inmate, then another, then a fourth—each one wielding an aluminum softball bat. Riot.

Detectives fly out of the homicide office in bunches—Landsman, Worden, Fahlteich, Kincaid, Dave Brown, James—heading for the Maryland Penitentiary at the eastern edge of the city's downtown, the gray stone fortress that has served as the state's maximum security prison since James Madison was president. The Pen is the end of the line for every lost cause in the state corrections system, the final repository for the men who somehow can't live within the limits of the prisons at Jessup and Hagerstown. Home to Death Row and the gas chamber, the Maryland Pen warehouses human beings who are facing an average sentence of life imprisonment, and its antiquated south wing has been called "the innermost circle of hell" by a state attorney general's report. By any reckoning, the population of the Maryland Pen has nothing whatsoever to lose; worst of all, they know it.

For fifteen minutes, the Pen correctional officers lose complete control of the recreation yards to more than three hundred inmates armed with homemade knives, clubs and every other available weapon. Two guards are beaten with bats in the No. 4 yard, another is bludgeoned with a metal cross bar from the weight room. A fourth is chased into the prison shop building only to find that the security area gate is locked shut. Unwilling to risk unlocking the metal gate, a female correctional officer watches, terrified, from the other side of the partition as six or seven inmates beat and stab the guard to within an inch of his life. Twenty other inmates drag another female officer out of a counseling clinic at the southern edge of the recreation yard, beating her badly, then rush into the clinic to batter a prison psychologist. Before being repulsed by a detachment of guards rushed through the Madison Street entrance, the inmates set fire to the clinic, torching as many psychological evaluations as they can find. Led by a deputy warden, the reinforcements arrive to retake the clinic and rescue the female officer and the psychologist, who has fallen to the floor of his office beneath a rain of blows from a metal pipe. The prisoners are pushed slowly back toward the yard—a retreat that only becomes a rout after two guards fire their shotguns from the clinic door. Two inmates fall wounded on the asphalt.

On the towers at the penitentiary's east and west walls, guards try to fire their shotguns over the heads of the rioters—which only adds to the carnage by striking several guards as well as rioters. Just outside a west wall tower, yet another correctional officer is felled by shotgun pellets fired by an east wall guard two hundred yards away. There are no attempts to escape, no effort to take hostages, no demands, no negotiations. It is violence for its own sake, the mirror image of the summer that exists in the city that surrounds the penitentiary walls. You can lock them up and you can lose the key, but the men inside the fortress on Forrest Street still march to the rhythm of the streets.

Fifteen minutes after the last prisoner has been hauled out of the yard and dragged to a tier for lockdown, Jay Landsman walks across the No. 3 and 4 yards, mentally noting the bloodstains that represent a half-dozen crime scenes. From the south wing tiers immediately above him, the focused rage of the prison comes down on him like rain. Walking alone in the open yard, Landsman is made for a city detective immediately, perhaps by prisoners who have been among his clientele.

"Yo, you white bitch, bring yo' tight ass up here and drop them trousers."

"Get out my yard, you fuckhead cop."

"Don't be down there after dark, yo, we'll fuck you good."

"Eat my shit, cop. Eat my shit."

The last comment catches Landsman's ear; for just a moment he pauses, staring up at the south wing tiers.

"C'mon up here, faggot. We'll fuck you like we fucked them bitch guards."

"Bring yo' white ass up here, faggot."

Landsman lights a cigarette and waves cheerfully at the stone facade, as if it were some kind of cruise ship pulling away from its moorings. In its moment, the perfect gesture—better than a hard look or the standard finger—and the catcalls fall away. Smiling maniacally, Landsman waves again and the message becomes clear: Yo, assholes. My white bitch ass is going home tonight to an air-conditioned rancher and a woman and a dozen steamed crabs and a six-pack of beer. You're going to a 98-degree prison cell for a steaming week of lockdown. Bon voyage, you simple motherfuckers.

Landsman finishes his tour of the yard and confers with the deputy warden. Nine correctional officers are hospitalized; three inmates have also been sent to emergency rooms. The prison authorities are responsible for security, but homicide will handle the prosecution of those inmates named as being part of the riot. That's the theory anyway. But it's hard for any guard to remember a single face when a crowd of men is beating on him with aluminum bats; after an hour, the tentative list of suspects stands at only thirteen inmates positively identified by authorities.

Landsman and Dick Fahlteich, the primary detective for the riot, have those suspects brought to the deputy warden's office. They come in one by one, shackled and cuffed and devoid of expression. A quick survey reveals that every last one is a product of Baltimore, and all but four are down on a city murder charge. In fact, every other name on the list manages to trigger a memory in some detective's mind. Clarence Mouzone? That crazy bastard beat three or four murders before Willis finally got him on one. Wyman Ushery? Didn't he kill that boy at the Crown station on Charles Street back in '81? Litzinger's case, I think. Fuck yeah, that was him.

The accused shuffle into the office and listen impassively as Landsman tells them they were seen assaulting this or that guard. Each inmate listens with practiced boredom, glancing back and forth among the faces of the detectives, searching for anything that seems familiar. You can almost hear them thinking aloud: That one I don't remember, but that one was there for my lineup, and that one in the corner took the stand on me in court.

"You want to say anything?" asks Landsman.

"I don't got shit to say to you."

"Okay," says Landsman, smiling. "See ya."

One of the last men to saunter down memory lane is a thick-framed nineteen-year-old monster, a kid with the kind of prize-fighter physique that can only come from a prison weight room. Ransom Watkins begins shaking his head halfway through Landsman's speech.

"I got nothin' to say."

"Okay then."

"But I want to know one thing from this man here," he says, looking hard across the room at Kincaid. "I bet you don't even remember me."

"Sure I do," says the detective. "I got a good memory."

Ransom Watkins was all of fifteen when Kincaid locked him up for the Dewitt Duckett murder in '83. Watkins was a smaller piece of a man then, but just as hard. He was one of three west side boys who shot a fourteen-year-old in a hallway at Harlem Park Junior High, then yanked a Georgetown athletic jacket off the dying kid's back. Other students recognized the trio as they ran from the school, and Kincaid discovered the missing jacket in a suspect's bedroom closet. The next morning, Watkins and the others were cracking jokes in the Western District lockup, charged as adults.

"You remember me, detective?" Watkins says now.

"I remember you."

"If you remember who I am, then how the hell do you sleep at night?"

"I sleep pretty good," says Kincaid. "How do you sleep?"

"How do you think I sleep? How do I sleep when you put me here for something I didn't do?"

Kincaid shakes his head, then picks a piece of lint from his pants cuff.

"You did it," he tells the kid.

"The hell I did," Watkins wails at him, his voice cracking. "You lied then and you lyin' now."

"No," says Kincaid quietly. "You killed him."

Watkins curses him again and Kincaid looks back placidly. Landsman calls to the outer room for the escorting guards even as Watkins begins to argue his case.

"We're done with this asshole," he says. "Send in the next guy."

It's another two hours before the detectives begin making their way back through the labyrinth of steel grates and metal detectors and checkpoints, back upstairs to the visiting area and the lockers in which their service revolvers have been stored.

Outside the main gate, the television reporters are doing standups for the early afternoon broadcasts, just as representatives of the guards' union show up to criticize prison administrators and demand yet another investigation of conditions at the Pen. Halfway down Eager Street, a young boy on a ten-speed stops at the wrought-iron gate to listen to the shouts coming from the inmates in the west wing tiers. He stays for a minute or two, soaking up the catcalls and obscenities, before punching the Play button on a tape machine wedged beneath his handlebars and pedaling toward Greenmount.

"It takes two to make a thing go right . . ."

Beat, scream, beat, scream. A mindless liturgy of another Baltimore summer, a theme song for a city that bleeds.

"It takes two to make it outta sight . . ."

Landsman and Fahlteich climb into the dry heat of a Cavalier's interior and roll slowly toward the expressway with the windows down, waiting on a breeze that just won't come. Fahlteich flips the AM radio dial to 1100 for the all-news station, where these and other stories are coming up on the hour. *Twelve seriously injured in today's disturbance at the Maryland Penitentiary. Night watchman found slain in North Howard Street store. And tomorrow's WBAL forecast calls for partly cloudy and hot, with highs in the mid-90s.*

Another day for bagging bent blades and chalking sidewalks. Another day for pulling semi-wadcutter projectiles from drywall, for photographing blood at the broken edge of the bottle. Another day's pay on the killing streets.

Friday, July 8

Another hot, humid night wears out its welcome in a South Baltimore rowhouse, where violence takes as its servant a lovers' quarrel. Edgerton walks the crime scene and sends a couple of witnesses downtown before jumping into the crowded rear of the ambulance.

"How you doin', Officer Edgerton?"

The detective looks down at the gurney to see the bloody face of Janie Vaughn smiling back at him. Janie from the Patch, as the locals call South Baltimore's Westport. A goodhearted kid, twenty-seven years old, who when Edgerton last knew her was running with a boy by the name of Anthony Felton. Felton's problem was his propensity for killing people, shooting them for money or drugs, mostly. The boy beat two of those murders, then went down for fifteen years on a third shooting. From the look of things in the ambo, Janie's new boyfriend wasn't exactly the epitome of self-control either.

"How you doin'?"

"Do I look real bad?"

"You've looked better," Edgerton tells her. "But if you're breathing now, you're gonna make it . . . They sayin' your boyfriend Ronnie cut loose."

"Yeah he did."

"He just went off or what?"

"I didn't know he'd go this far."

"You really can pick 'em, huh?"

Janie smiles, her white teeth shining for a moment amid the bloody wreckage. A tough kid, Edgerton thinks, not the kind of girl to go into shock. Stepping deeper in the ambo, Edgerton looks closely at her face and notices the stippling—dirt and metal residue from the gunshot—embedded in her cheek. A contact wound.

"Did you know he had the gun?"

"He told me he got rid of it. Sold it."

"What kind of gun did you think he sold?"

"A little cheap one."

"What color?"

"Silver."

"Okay, honey, they're getting ready to head for the hospital. I'll see you there."

The other victim, the twenty-eight-year-old boyfriend of Janie's older sister, is already dead on arrival at the University ER, a casualty for no other reason than that he tried to intervene when Ronnie Lawis began beating the hell out of Janie. Later, at the hospital, she tells Edgerton that it was over nothing, that it began because Ronnie saw her sitting in a car with another man.

"How's Durrell?" she asked Edgerton in the emergency room's code area, naming her sister's boyfriend. "He gonna make it?"

"I don't know. He's in another part of the hospital."

It's a lie, of course. At that moment, Durrell Rollins is dead on the gurney to Janie's immediate right, his mouth clamped around a yellow catheter, his chest pierced by a single shot. If Janie could move her head or see past the facial bandage, she'd know.

"I'm cold," she tells Edgerton.

He nods, stroking the girl's hand, then stops for a moment to wipe the blood from her left hand with a paper towel. Dark red dots speckle the lighter brown of his trousers.

"How'm I doin'?"

"Hey, if they're leaving you alone in here with me, you're okay," Edgerton tells her. "It's when about eight people are hovering over you that you're in trouble."

Janie smiles.

"What happened exactly?" Edgerton asks.

"It happened so fast . . . Him and Durrell was inside in the kitchen. Durrell had come in 'cause he was fightin' with me."

"Go back to the beginning. What started it?"

"Like I told you, he saw me in a car with this guy and got mad. He came in and went down, and when he come back he put the gun to my head and starts yellin' and all, so Durrell comes into the kitchen . . ."

"Did you see him shoot Durrell?"

"No, they went into the kitchen, and when I hear the shot I ran . . ."

"Did Durrell and him talk?"

"No. It happened too fast."

"No time for any words, huh?"

"Uh-uh."

"Then he came outside after you?"

"Uh-huh. Fired the first shot and I tried to duck, but I fell down in the street. He came up and was right over me."

"How long you been going together?"

"Almost a year."

"Where's he stay?"

"In the house."

"That wasn't all his clothes in there."

"No, he got more in the basement. He got another girl he stays with up on Pennsylvania Avenue, too. I seen her once."

"You know her?"

"I just seen her once."

"Where's he hang at? Where's he likely to go?"

"Downtown area. Park and Eutaw, 'round there."

"Any special place he'd go?"

"Sportsman's Lounge."

"At Park and Mulberry?"

"Yeah. He know Randy. The bartender."

"Okay, honey," says Edgerton, closing his notebook. "You rest easy now."

Janie squeezes his hand, then looks up at him.

"Durrell?" she asks. "He dead, right?"

He hesitates.

"It doesn't look good," he says.

Later this night, when Ronnie Lawis returns to the empty Westport rowhouse for his belongings, a neighbor is out on a porch to see him and call police. A responding Southern District uniform corners the man in the basement and, after applying the handcuffs, discovers a .32 Saturday Night Special behind the hot water heater. An NCIC fingerprint check the following day shows that Lawis is, in fact, a man named Fred Lee Tweedy who escaped from a Virginia prison a year ago, having been incarcerated on a previous murder conviction.

"If my name was Tweedy," says Edgerton, reading the report, "I'd have an alias, too."

Another summer call, another summer clearance. The season has brought out the new and improved Harry Edgerton, at least as far as the rest of his squad is concerned. He's answering phones. He's handling calls. He's writing 24-hour reports. After one police shooting, there was Edgerton in the middle of the coffee room, offering to debrief a witness or two. If not entirely convinced of Edgerton's character transplant, Donald Kincaid has at least been mollified. And while Edgerton isn't exactly winning awards for early relief on midnight shift and daywork, he has been getting to the office a little earlier and then, as usual, leaving later than the others.

Part of the change is Roger Nolan—the sergeant trapped in the middle of it all—who talked to Edgerton about avoiding acrimony and using some practical politics now and then. Part of it is Edgerton himself, who took some of Nolan's advice because he was getting damn tired of being the focal point for everyone else's backbiting. And part of it has been the other men in the squad—Kincaid and Bowman, in particular—who are also making some effort to uphold the existing truce.

Yet everyone in the room knows that it is a temporary and fragile peace, dependent on the goodwill of too many aggravated people. Edgerton is willing to placate his critics to a point, but beyond that, he is what he is and he does what he does. Likewise, Kincaid and Bowman are willing to hold their tongues so long as the lamb doesn't stray too far from the fold. Given these realities, the friendly banter can't last, though for now, Nolan's squad seems to be holding itself together.

In fact, Nolan's boys are on something of a roll, handling five or six more cases than either of the other squads on D'Addario's shift and solving a better percentage of those murders. Not only that, but Nolan's people have been saddled with nine of the seventeen police-involved shooting incidents this year. And more than the murders, it's the police shootings—with their incumbent issues of criminal and civil liability—that can bring the bosses down on the squad like a plague of locusts. This year's crop of shooting reports, however, has so far cleared the command staff without causing so much as a rustle. All in all, from Nolan's point of view, it's turning out to be a respectable year.

Rich Garvey and his eight clearances are, of course, a large share of Nolan's happiness, but Edgerton, too, is beginning a little streak of his own, one that began with that drug murder on Payson Street back in late May. After putting that case down, he found himself preoccupied with the Joe Edison trial in Judge Hammerman's court, a successful three-week legal campaign to get a nineteen year old sociopath life in prison for one of the four drug murders from 1986 and '87 in which he was charged. Edgerton returned to the rotation in time for nightwork and the shooting call in Westport, which would be followed by two more clearances before summer's end—one of them a whodunit street shooting from the Old York Road drug market. In the homicide unit, four clearances in a row is usually enough to mute anyone's critics, and for a brief time, the tension in Nolan's squad seems to ease.

During one four-to-twelve shift in midsummer, Edgerton is sitting at his desk in the main office, a phone receiver braced against a shoulder and a cigarette wedged into the corner of his mouth.

Worden walks by and Edgerton begins an exaggerated pantomime, causing the older detective to pull a Bic lighter from his pants and produce a flame; Edgerton leans across the desk to ignite the tobacco.

"Aw Christ," says Worden, holding the lighter steady. "I hope nobody sees me doing this."

Twenty minutes later and still a prisoner of the same phone conversation, Edgerton flags down Garvey for another light and Worden, watching from the coffee room, picks up on it again.

"Hey, Harry, you're getting awfully used to havin' white guys light your cigarette for you."

"What can I say?" says Edgerton, covering the mouthpiece of the phone with his hand.

"You tryin' to make a point, Harry?"

"What can I say?" repeats Edgerton, hanging up the phone. "I like how it looks."

"Hey," says Kincaid, cutting in. "As long as Harry keeps handling calls, we can light his cigarettes, right, Harry? You keep answering that phone and I'll start carrying a book of matches."

"Fair enough," says Edgerton, almost amused.

"We're bringing Harry along, ain't we?" says Kincaid. "We're breakin' him back into homicide. As long as we can keep him away from Ed Burns, he'll be all right."

"That's right," says Edgerton, smiling. "It was that nasty Ed Burns that messed me up, talking me into all these long investigations, telling me not to listen to you guys . . . It was all Burns. You should blame him."

"And where is he now?" adds Kincaid. "He's still over with the FBI and you're back here with us."

"He used you, Harry," says Eddie Brown.

"Yeah," says Harry, dragging on his cigarette. "I guess ol' Eduardo did a number on me."

"Used and abused and tossed away like a dirty condom," says Garvey, from the back of the room.

"You talkin' 'bout Special Agent Burns," says Ed Brown. "Hey, Harry, I hear Burns already has his own desk over at the FBI office. I hear he's all moved in."

"His own desk, his own car," adds Kincaid.

"Hey, Harry," says Ed Brown. "You ever hear from your partner? Does he call you up and tell you how things are going over there in Woodlawn?"

"Yeah, he sent me a postcard once," says Edgerton. "It said, 'Wish you were here' on the back."

"You stick with us, Harry," says Kincaid dryly. "We'll take good care of you."

"Yeah," says Edgerton. "I know you will."

Considering it's Edgerton, the banter is easy and almost affectionate. After all, this is the same homicide unit in which the diagnosis of Gene Constantine's diabetes was greeted by a coffee room chalkboard divided by two headings: "Those who give a shit if Constantine dies" and "Those who don't." Sergeant Childs, Lieutenant Stanton, Mother Teresa and Barbara Constantine topped the latter list. The shorter column featured Gene himself, followed by the city employees' credit union. By that standard of camaraderie, Edgerton isn't putting up with anything out of the ordinary on this slow four-to-twelve shift. In fact, the scene being played out in the main office is a rare performance of Harry Edgerton as Just One of the Guys, a homicide man among homicide men. Never mind that Edgerton still thinks the world of Ed Burns and the ongoing Boardley investigation. And never mind that Kincaid and Eddie Brown don't really believe that Edgerton wants to be working straight murders when his bunky is over at the FBI field office fleshing out a two-year conspiracy probe. Never mind all that bitching earlier in the year, because right now Edgerton is handling murders.

It's the new Harry who laughs when his colleagues assure him that they're going to make something out of him, the changed man who makes a point of announcing to the office that he's getting ready to answer a ringing phone.

"Go for it, Harry."

"Don't hurt yourself there, Harry."

"He got it on three rings. Someone call a fuckin' press conference."

Edgerton chuckles, the picture of tolerance. He cups one hand over the receiver, then turns in his chair, feigning confusion.

"What do I do?" he asks in mock earnest. "Just talk into this part?"

"Yeah, put the top to your ear and talk into the bottom."

"Homicide unit. Edgerton."

"Way to go, Harry, babe."

SATURDAY, JULY 9

Hotter than hell up here.

It's three in the morning and the coffee room is 90 degrees or better. Apparently, some bean counter in fiscal services decided that the midnight shift doesn't need any heat before February or air conditioning before August, and now Donald Kincaid is out in the main office, stalking back and forth in his shirttails, Jockey shorts and socks, threatening total nudity if the temperature doesn't fall before morning. And Kincaid without clothes on an overnight shift is a dangerous thing.

"Oh God," says Rich Garvey, his face a sickly blue from the television glow. "Donald's got his pants off. God help anyone who sleeps on his stomach tonight."

It's an old routine for Nolan's squad, this running joke about Kincaid looking for love on the overnight shift, forcing his attentions on the younger detectives. Last night, McAllister fell asleep on the green vinyl sofa only to wake in mortal terror an hour later: Kincaid was on top of him, cooing softly.

"Naw, not tonight," Kincaid says, pulling the tie from his collar and stretching himself across the sofa. "Too damn hot for that."

Every man in the room sends up the same prayer: Lord, let the telephone ring. Let that 2100 extension light up with death and mayhem before we all drown in our own sweat and stink. Every man in the room would take a drug murder right now. A double even, with two bleached skeletons in a basement somewhere and not a witness or suspect to be found. They don't care what the call is as long as they can get out on the street where, incredibly, it's ten degrees cooler.

Out in the main office, Roger Nolan has the video recorder wired up so that half the squad can watch some godawful movie in which everyone is chasing one another in automobiles. The first movie in Nolan's midnight shift triple feature is generally excellent, and the second is usually tolerable. But by three o'clock, Nolan always manages to come up with something guaranteed to induce sleep, and at that point, sleep begins to acquire a certain appeal.

The VCR is Nolan's concession to the hell of midnight shift, to the absurdity of six grown men spending a week of overnights together in a downtown office building. In Baltimore, a homicide detective works three weeks of eight-to-four, then two weeks of four-to-twelve, then one week of midnight. Which leads to a strange inversion: at any given moment, an entire shift of three squads is working daywork, two squads are working four-to-twelve, and the squad working midnight is on its own in those hours when nearly half of all homicides occur. On a jumping midnight tour, no one has time for movies or anything else. On a shift with two murders and a police shooting, for example, no one even presumes to think about sleep. But on the slow nights, on a night like this, the detectives learn what rigor mortis is all about.

"My back is killing me," says Garvey.

Of course it is. After all, he's trying to sleep sitting in a metal desk chair, his head horizontal to the top of the chair back. The sixth floor is hotter than the inside of a Weber grill on a Fourth of July weekend and Garvey still has his tie on. The man is not real.

Kincaid is now snoring on the green couch. Bowman is around the corner, out of sight, but when last seen he was also nodding, his chair propped against the wall, his short legs barely touching the floor. Edgerton is who the hell knows where, probably down on Baltimore Street blasting space critters on a video game.

"Hey, Rich," says Nolan, a foot and a half from the TV screen, "check this part out. This almost makes the movie."

Garvey lifts his head in time to see one tough guy blow another apart with something that appears to be a rocket launcher.

"That was great, Rog."

Nolan senses the ennui and slowly glides over to the television, using his legs to propel the wheeled chair. He scans the side of another videotape box. "How about a John Wayne movie?"

Garvey yawns, then shrugs. "Whatever," he says finally.

"I've got two on this tape where the Duke actually dies," says Nolan, still wide awake. "Trivia question: In how many movies did John Wayne's character actually die?"

Garvey looks at Nolan and sees, not his squad sergeant, but a large black man with a pitchfork and horns on his head. The innermost circle of hell, Garvey now knows, is a steaming municipal building with no beds, bile green walls and trivia questions from a superior at three in the morning.

"Thirteen," says Nolan, answering his own question. "Or is it fourteen? We figured it out last night . . . I think it's fourteen. The one everyone always forgets is *Wake of the Red Witch*."

Nolan knows. He knows everything. Ask him about the 1939 Academy Awards and he'll tell you about the catfight for Best Supporting Actress. Ask him about the Peloponnesian War and he'll explain the essentials of hoplite infantry tactics. Mention the western coast of Borneo and . . . well, Terry McLarney once made that mistake.

"You know," he blurted during one four-to-twelve shift. "I understand that the beaches in Borneo are made of black sand."

At the time, the statement might have seemed like a lonely non sequitur, but McLarney had recently read a five-hundred-page tome on the island of Borneo, his first conquest of a Howard County library book in perhaps three years. A fact is a fact, and McLarney had been trying to work this one into conversation for maybe a month.

"That's right," said Nolan. "They're black from the volcanic ash. Krakatoa did a number on all the islands around there . . ."

McLarney looked as though his dog had just died.

". . . but only on the western part of the island is it completely black. We practiced amphibious landings there when I was in the Corps."

"You were there?"

"In sixty-three or so."

"Well," said McLarney, stalking away, "that's the last time I ever bother reading a book."

For a career cop, Roger Nolan is positively scary and a force to be reckoned with in any game of trivia. Still trying to find comfort in that metal chair, Garvey succumbs to his sergeant's academic dissertation on the John Wayne mystique. He listens quietly because what else can he do. It's too hot to type that prosecution report. Too hot to read the *Evening Sun* sitting on Sydnor's desk. Too hot to go down to Baltimore Street and pay for a cheesesteak. Too goddamn hot.

Whoa. Incoming.

Garvey pushes the chair toward Edgerton's desk and grabs the receiver on the first bleat, fastest on the draw. His call. His moneymaker. His ticket out.

"Homicide."

"Northwest district, six-A-twelve unit."

"Yeah, whatcha got?"

"It's an old man in a house. No sign of wounds or anything like that."

"Forced entry?"

"Ah, no, nothing like that."

Garvey's disappointment seeps into his voice. "How'd you get in?"

"Front door was open. The neighbor came over to check on him and then found him in the bedroom."

"He live alone?"

"Yeah."

"And he's in bed?"

"Uh-huh."

"How old is he?"

"Seventy-one."

Garvey gives up his name and sequence number, knowing that if this officer has misread the scene and the case comes back from the ME as a murder, Garvey will have to eat it. Still, it sounds straight enough.

"Do I need anything else for the report?" the cop asks.

"No. You called for the medical examiner, right?"

"Yeah."

"That's everything then."

He drops the receiver back onto the phone and separates the sticky wetness that is his shirt from the back of the chair. Twenty minutes later, the phone rings again with a west side cutting—cheap stuff, too, with one kid in the University Hospital ER and the other in the Western lockup, staring out of his cell at Garvey and Kincaid through a cocaine haze.

"He just walked in here and said he stabbed his brother," says the Western turnkey.

Garvey snorts. "You don't think he's on drugs, do you, Donald?"

"Him?" says Kincaid, deadpan. "No way."

The cutting call keeps them on the street for no more than twenty minutes, and when they return to the office, Nolan is dismantling the VCR; all else is three-part snoring so regular that it takes on a hypnotic quality.

Edgerton has returned from videoland and the squad soon settles in for the worst kind of sleep, the kind where a detective wakes up more exhausted than before, covered by a layer of liquid homicide office that can only be scraped away by a twenty-minute shower. Still, they sleep. On a slow night, everyone sleeps.

At five, the telephone finally rings again, although now everyone is two hours past the desire to get a call—the general reasoning being that anyone inconsiderate enough to relinquish his life after the hour of three A.M. does not deserve to be avenged.

"Homicide," says Kincaid.

"G'morning. Irwin from the *Evening Sun*. What'd you have last night?"

Dick Irwin. The only man in Baltimore with a work schedule more miserable than that of a homicide detective. Five A.M. calls for seven A.M. deadlines, five nights a week.

"All quiet."

Back to sleep for a half hour or so. And then a moment of pure terror: some sort of thunderous machine, some kind of battering ram, is heaving against the hallway door. Metal hitting metal in the darkness to Garvey's immediate right. Shrill, high-pitched noises as a violent, nocturnal beast clatters toward a sleeping squad, bulling its way through the dark portal. Edgerton remembers the .38 in his top left drawer, a firearm fully stocked with 158-grain hollow-points. And thank God for that, because the beast is now entering the room, its steel lance projected, its leaden armor clanging against the bulkhead on the far side of the coffee room. Kill it, says the voice in Edgerton's head. Kill it now.

A sheet of light falls upon them.

"What the . . ."

"Aw, hell, I'm sorry," says the beast, surveying a room full of cowering, bleary-eyed men. "I didn't see you all in there where you was sleepin'."

Irene. The monster is a cleaning woman with an East Bawlmer accent and yellow-white hair. The steel lance is a mop handle; the clanging armor, the larger half of the floor buffer. They are alive. Blind, but alive.

"Turn out the light," Garvey manages to say.

"I will, hon. I'm sorry," she says. "You go back to sleep. I'll start out here 'n leave you alone. You get on back to sleep an' I'll tell when the lieutenant comes in . . ."

"Thank you, Irene."

She is the ancient janitress with a heart of gold and a vocabulary that could make a turnkey blush. She lives alone in an unheated rowhouse, earns a fifth of what they do and never arrives later than 5:30 A.M. to begin shining the sixth-floor linoleum. Last Christmas, she took what little money didn't go for food and bought a pressed-wood television table as her gift to the homicide unit. No amount of pain or aggravation could cause them to yell at this woman.

They will, however, flirt with her.

"Irene, honey," says Garvey, before she can shut the door. "Better watch out now. Kincaid had his pants off tonight and he was dreamin' about you . . ."

"You're a liar."

"Ask Bowman."

"It's true," says Bowman, picking it up from the rear of the office. "He had his pants off and he was calling your name . . ."

"You can kiss my ass, Bowman."

"You better not say that to Kincaid."

"He can kiss my ass too," says Irene.

As if on cue, Kincaid returns from the bathroom, albeit fully dressed, and requires only a little prodding from Bowman before he's once again wooing the hired help.

"C'mon, Irene. Gimme a little somethin'."

"Why should I, Donald?" she says, warming to the game. "You ain't even got anything I'd want."

"Oh yeah I do."

"What?" she says, looking down disdainfully. "That little tiny thing?"

The entire squad cracks up. Twice a midnight shift, Kincaid talks dirty to Irene. Twice a midnight shift, Irene manages to keep up with him.

Beyond the darkness of the main unit office, the coffee room and the outer offices are brightening with the lighter blue of morning. And like it or not, every man in the room is now wide awake, rattled from sleep by Kincaid's determined courtship.

But the phones stay quiet and Nolan cuts Bowman loose just after six; the rest of the squad sits quietly, trying not to move until the air conditioning kicks up again for the dayshift. The men lean back in their seats in some kind of communal trance. When the elevator bell rings at twenty after, it's the sweetest sound in the world.

"Relief's here," says Barlow, strutting into the room. "You all look like shit . . . Not you, Irene. You look as lovely as ever. I was talking to these ugly pieces of shit."

"Fuck you," says Garvey.

"Hey, mister, is that any way to talk to the man who's giving you early relief?"

"Eat me," says Garvey.

"Sergeant Nolan," says Barlow, feigning indignation, "did you hear that? I just stated a simple fact by saying that these guys look like pieces of shit, which they do, and I'm subjected to all kinds of abuse. Was it this fuckin' hot in here all night?"

"Hotter," says Garvey.

"Proud to know you, mister," says Barlow. "You know, you're one of my personal heroes. What'd you have last night? Anything?"

"Nothing at all," says Edgerton. "It was death up here."

No, thinks Nolan, listening from the corner of the room. Not death. The absence of death, maybe. Death means being out on the streets of Baltimore, making money.

"You all can take off," says Barlow. "Charlie'll be in here in a couple."

Nolan keeps Garvey and Edgerton waiting for the second dayshift man to arrive, letting Kincaid escape at half past.

"Thanks, Sarge," he says, shoving a run sheet into Nolan's mailbox.

Nolan nods, acknowledging his own mercies.

"See you Monday," says Kincaid.

"Yeah," says Nolan wistfully. "Daywork."

Friday, July 22

"Aw Christ, another Bible."

Gary Childs picks the open book up off a bureau and tosses it onto a chair with a dozen others. The bookmark holds the place even as pages flutter in the cool breeze of an air conditioner. Lamentations 2:21:

> *Young and old lie together*
> *In the dust of the streets;*
> *My young men and maidens*
> *Have fallen by the sword.*
> *You have slain them in the day of your anger;*
> *You have slaughtered them without pity.*

One thing about Miss Geraldine, she took her Good Book seriously, a fact confirmed not only by the Bible collection, but also by the framed 8-by-11 photographs of her in her Sunday finest, preaching the good news at storefront churches. If salvation is ours through faith rather than works, then perhaps Geraldine Parrish can find some contentment in the wagon ride downtown. But if works do count for anything in the next world, then Miss Geraldine will be arriving there with a few things charged to her account.

Childs and Scott Keller pull up the bed and begin riffling the stack of papers stuffed beneath it. Grocery notes, telephone numbers, social service forms and six or seven more life insurance policies.

"Damn," says Keller, genuinely impressed. "Here's a whole bunch more. How many does that make now?"

Childs shrugs. "Twenty? Twenty-five? Who the hell knows?"

The search warrant for 1902 Kennedy gives them the right to seek a variety of evidentiary items, but in this instance, no one is gutting a room in the hope of finding a gun or knife or bullets or bloody clothes. On this rare occasion, they are looking for the paper trail. And they are finding it.

"I got more of them in here," says Childs, dumping the contents of a paper grocery bag onto the upended mattress. "Four more."

"This," says Keller, "is one murderous bitch."

An Eastern District patrolman who has been downstairs for an hour, watching Geraldine Parrish and five others in the first-floor living room, knocks softly on the bedroom door.

"Sergeant Childs . . ."

"Yo."

"The woman down there, she's sayin' she feels faint . . . You know, she's sayin' that she's got some kind of heart condition."

Childs looks at Keller, then back at the uniform. "Heart condition, huh?" he says, contemptuous. "She's having a heart attack? I'll be down in a minute and you can really watch her fall out of her chair."

"Okay," says the patrolman. "I just thought I'd tell you."

Childs sorts through the jetsam from the grocery bag, then wanders downstairs to the front room. The occupants of the rowhouse are clustered together on a sofa and two chairs, staring up at him, waiting for answers. The sergeant stares back at the plump, sad-faced woman with the Loretta Lynn wig and red cotton dress, a genuinely comic vision under the circumstances.

"Geraldine?"

"Yes I am."

"I know who you are," says Childs. "Do you want to know why we're here?"

"I don't know why you're here," she says, patting her chest lightly. "I can't sit like this. I need my medicine . . ."

"You don't have any idea why we're here?"

Geraldine Parrish shakes her head and pats her chest again, leaning back in her chair.

"Geraldine, this is a search-and-seizure raid. You're now charged with three counts of first-degree murder and three attempted murders . . ."

The other occupants of the room stare as deep gurgling noises begin to rise in Geraldine Parrish's throat. She falls to the carpet, clutching her chest and gasping for air.

Childs looks down, moderately amused, then turns calmly to the Eastern uniform. "I guess you might want to call for that medic now," he says, "just to be on the safe side."

The sergeant returns upstairs, where he and Keller continue dumping every document, every insurance policy, every photo album, every slip of paper into a green garbage bag—the better to sort through it all in the relative luxury of the homicide office. Meanwhile, the paramedics arrive and depart within minutes, having judged Geraldine Parrish healthy in body if not in mind. And across town, at the Division Street rowhouse of Geraldine Parrish's mother, Donald Waltemeyer is executing a second warrant, digging out another thirty insurance policies and related documents.

It is the case to end all cases, the investigation that raises the act of murder to the level of theatrical farce. This case file has so many odd, unlikely characters and so many odd, unlikely crimes that it almost seems tailored for musical comedy.

But for Donald Waltemeyer, in particular, the Geraldine Parrish case is anything but comedic. It is, in effect, a last lesson in his own personal voyage from patrolman to detective. Behind Worden and Eddie Brown, the forty-one-year-old Waltemeyer is Terry McLarney's most experienced man, having come to homicide in '86 from the Southern District plainclothes unit, where he was a fixture of large if not legendary proportion. And though the last two years have taught Waltemeyer everything he needs to know about handling the usual run of homicide calls, this case is entirely different. Eventually, Keller and Childs and the other detectives assigned to the case will return to the rotation and it will be Waltemeyer's lot to serve as primary investigator in the prosecution of Geraldine Parrish—a probe that will consume half a year in the search for victims, suspects and explanations.

In a unit where speed is a precious commodity, it's the rare case that teaches a detective patience, providing him with those last few lessons that come only from the most prolonged and complex avenues of investigation. Such a case can transform a cop, allowing him to see his role as something more than that of an ambulance chaser whose task is to clean up one shooting after another in the shortest time possible. And after a month or two, or three, this sort of sprawling case file can also drive a cop to the brink of insanity—which for Waltemeyer isn't all that long a journey in the first place.

Just yesterday, in fact, he was gnawing on Dave Brown's leg about one case or another when Brown felt compelled to whip out Rule 1, Section 1, from the department's Code of Conduct and read verbatim, to wit:

" 'All members of the department shall be quiet, civil and orderly at all times and shall refrain from coarse, profane or insolent language.' And," added Brown, glaring at his partner, "I emphasize the word 'civil.' "

"Hey, Brown," said Waltemeyer, making an obscene gesture. "Emphasize this."

It isn't that Dave Brown doesn't respect his partner, because he does. And it isn't that they can't work together, because when they have to, they do. It's just that Waltemeyer is constantly trying to explain police work to Brown, an exercise in condescension that Brown will accept only when it comes from Donald Worden, no one else. But even on his best days, Waltemeyer is quite possibly the most volatile detective in homicide, with a hair-trigger temper that never ceases to amaze the rest of McLarney's squad.

Once, soon after Waltemeyer had come downtown, McLarney himself happened to be busy talking to one of several witnesses from a murder. He called Waltemeyer over and asked him to handle one of the interviews, but as he began explaining the details of the case, he quickly realized that it was simply easier for him to talk to the witness himself. Never mind, McLarney explained, I'll do it myself.

But later, at several points during the interview, McLarney looked up to see Waltemeyer's face staring at him from the hallway. Three minutes after the end of the interview, Waltemeyer was in the office, pointing a finger in McLarney's face and raving wildly.

"Goddammit, I know my job, and if you don't think I can handle it, to hell with you," he told McLarney, who could only watch with detached awe. "If you don't trust me, then send me back to the goddamn district."

As Waltemeyer stormed away, McLarney looked around the office at his other detectives, who were, of course, biting the sleeves of their sport coats to keep from laughing aloud.

That was Waltemeyer. He was the hardest worker in McLarney's squad, a consistently aggressive and intelligent investigator, and two days out of every five he was a confirmed mental case. A Southwest Baltimore boy and the product of a large German family, Donald Waltemeyer was a source of endless delight to McLarney, who would often distract himself on a slow shift by goading his new detective into a tirade against Dave Brown. If Brown could then be made to respond, the result was usually better than television.

Heavyset, with a ruddy face and a mop of thick, coal black hair, Waltemeyer suffered his most embarrassing moment in homicide one morning at roll call: a sergeant read an announcement that Waltemeyer had been named the hands-down winner in a look-alike contest for his portrayal of Shemp, the forgotten Stooge. In Waltemeyer's considered judgment, the author of that little item would survive only as long as he remained anonymous.

Neither temper nor appearance had prevented Waltemeyer from becoming a first-class street police in the Southern District, and he still liked to think of himself as the same down-in-the-trenches patrolman he had always been. Long after his transfer to homicide, he made a point of staying close to his old bunkies in the district, often disappearing at night with one of the Cavaliers to visit the Southern's holes or shift-change parties. It was as if there was something a little disreputable about his having gone downtown to CID, something for which a real cop ought to apologize. The vague embarrassment Waltemeyer so obviously felt at having become a detective was his most distinctive trait.

Once last summer, he made a point of taking Rick James out to lunch at Lexington Market, where the two bought tuna sandwiches from a carry-out vendor. So far, so good. But then, instead of taking the meal back to headquarters, the older detective drove to Union Square, parking the Cavalier in his old patrol post.

"Now," said Waltemeyer, pushing the driver's seat back and spreading a napkin over his trousers. "We're going to eat like real police."

In McLarney's opinion, Waltemeyer's unswerving adherence to the patrolman's ethic was his only real weakness. Homicide is a world unto itself, and the things that work out in the district don't always work downtown. Waltemeyer's written reports, for example, were no better than district quality when he first came to homicide—a typical problem for men who spent more time on the street than at the typewriter. But in homicide the reports genuinely mattered, and what fascinated McLarney was that after mentioning the value of coherent paperwork to Waltemeyer, the detective set out on a successful, systematic campaign to improve his writing ability. That was when McLarney first realized that Waltemeyer was going to be one hell of a detective.

Now, neither McLarney nor anyone else could teach Waltemeyer much that was new about working murders. Only the cases themselves could add to his education, and only a case such as Geraldine Parrish could qualify him for the advanced degree.

The case actually began back in March, though at the time, no one in the homicide unit recognized it for what it was. In the beginning, it appeared to be nothing more than a routine extortion case: a complaint from a twenty-eight-year-old heroin addict who claimed that her uncle wanted $5,000 to keep her from being murdered by a contract killer. Why anyone would want to kill a brain-dead like Dollie Brown was unclear; the girl was a fragile little wraith with no known enemies, tracks on every appendage and very little in the way of money. Nonetheless, someone had tried to kill her, not once, but twice.

The first attempt was almost a year ago, when she was shot in the head during an ambush in which her thirty-seven-year-old boyfriend had been slain. That, too, had originally been Waltemeyer's case, and though it was still an open file, Waltemeyer believed that the boyfriend had been the intended victim and that the shootings had been drug-related. Then, after being released from University Hospital's shock-trauma unit back in March, Dollie Brown had the misfortune to be standing on Division Street when an unknown assailant cut her throat and ran away. Again, the girl survived, but this time there could be no doubt of the intended victim.

In any other environment, two such assaults in a six-month period may have led an investigator to believe that a campaign to end Dollie Brown's life was indeed under way. But this is West Baltimore, a place where two such incidents—absent any other evidence—can be safely regarded as coincidence and nothing more. The more likely explanation, Waltemeyer reasoned, was that Dollie's uncle was simply trying to capitalize on her fears and cheat her out of the $5,000 check she had received after the shooting from the state's crime victims compensation board, a government agency that provides financial assistance to those seriously harmed by violent crime. Her uncle knew about that money and told his niece that in return for the cash, he would intervene by killing the man who had been trying to kill her.

Working with a special undercover unit of the Maryland State Police, Waltemeyer had Dollie and her sister, Thelma, wired up with Nagra recorders and sent under police surveillance into a meeting with her uncle. When the man again demanded the money to prevent the impending murder, the extortion attempt was captured on tape. A week or so later, Waltemeyer made an arrest and closed the file.

Only in July did the Dollie Brown case become truly bizarre, for only then did a murder defendant with the singularly appropriate name of Rodney Vice begin talking to prosecutors, trying to cut a deal for himself.

And when Rodney Vice opened his mouth, the plot didn't just thicken, it positively congealed.

Vice had been implicated as a go-between in the contract slaying of Henry Barnes, a middle-aged West Baltimore man who had been killed by a shotgun blast as he warmed up his car on a cool morning in October. The victim's wife had paid Vice a total of $5,400 for his services in procuring a gunman to kill her husband, thereby allowing her to collect on a series of life insurance policies. Vice had given a Polaroid photograph of Barnes and a shotgun to a tightly wound sociopath by the name of Edwin "Conrad" Gordon. Told that the intended victim usually warmed his car in front of his rowhouse every morning, Gordon was able to get close enough to use the shotgun at point-blank range. Henry Barnes left this world never knowing what hit him.

All would have gone according to plan had Bernadette Barnes been able to keep her silence. Instead, she admitted to a co-worker at the city social services building that she had arranged her husband's death, telling the woman, "I told you I was serious." Alarmed, the co-worker called the police department, and after several months of investigation by the detectives on Stanton's shift, Bernadette Barnes, Rodney Vice and Edwin Gordon were all in the Baltimore City Jail, tied together in a single prosecution report. Only then did Rodney Vice and his lawyer begin shopping some cooperation around, searching for a ten-years-or-less deal.

At a July 11 proffer session with lawyers and detectives at the Mitchell courthouse, Vice was asked how he had known that Edwin Gordon was a man capable of carrying out a contract murder. Nonplussed, Vice assured the detectives and prosecutors that Gordon had been in that line of work for some time. In fact, he had been killing people for an East Baltimore woman by the name of Geraldine for several years now.

How many people?

Three or four that Vice knew about. Not to mention that one girl—a niece of Geraldine's—who wouldn't die no matter how many times Gordon tried to kill her.

How many times did he try?

Three, said Vice. After the most recent occasion, when he had shot the girl in the head three times to little effect, Gordon was particularly disheartened, telling Vice, "It don't matter what I do, the bitch won't die."

Checking back with Dollie Brown that same day, Waltemeyer and Crutchfield confirmed that Geraldine Parrish was indeed her aunt and that the young woman had indeed been assaulted a third time. She had been walking with Aunt Geraldine back in May, when the older woman told her to wait on a Hollins Street stoop while she went to get something. Seconds later, a man ran up and shot her repeatedly in the head. Again, she was treated and released from University Hospital; incredibly, she mentioned nothing to the investigating officers about the previous attempts on her life. McAllister handled the Hollins Street shooting, and knowing little of Waltemeyer's extortion case two months earlier, he wrote nothing more than a brief 24-hour report.

As Vice spoke, a new tale was being added to the lore and legend of the BPD homicide unit, that of the Unsinkable Dollie Brown, the hapless, helpless niece of Miss Geraldine Parrish, alias the Black Widow.

Rodney Vice had a lot more to say about Miss Geraldine, too. After all, Vice told the gathering, it didn't exactly stop with Dollie Brown and the $12,000 in insurance policies that Aunt Geraldine had obtained in her niece's name. There were other policies, other murders. There was that man back in 1985, Geraldine's brother-in-law, who had been shot on Gold Street. Edwin Gordon had taken that contract as well. And then there was the old boarder who lived at Geraldine's house on Kennedy Street, the elderly woman whom Gordon had to shoot twice before he finally killed her off. It was Miss Geraldine herself who sent the old woman out to a Chinese carryout on North Avenue, then signaled Gordon, who walked calmly up to the target and fired one shot to the back at point-blank range, then issued a coup de grâce to the head after the victim fell to the sidewalk.

Veteran detectives left the courthouse with their heads spinning. Three murders, three attempted murders—and that was just what Vice happened to know about. On their return to the homicide office, open murder files dating back as many as three years were suddenly being yanked from the oblivion of the filing cabinets.

Incredibly, everything in those files conformed exactly to Rodney Vice's account. The November 1985 murder of Frank Lee Ross, the common-law husband of Geraldine's sister, had been handled by Gary Dunnigan, who at that time could find no motive for the slaying. Likewise, Marvin Sydnor had worked the fatal shooting of Helen Wright, sixty-five, who had been boarding with Geraldine on Kennedy Street; lacking any solid information about the murder, he had presumed that the old lady had been killed in a robbery attempt gone awry. Not that Sydnor hadn't found a few loose ends in a routine interview with Geraldine Parrish; he even tried to polygraph the landlady, but he gave up when she produced a cardiologist's note saying that her health could not stand the stress of a lie detector test. True to Vice's account, the old woman had been shot in the head several weeks before being murdered but had survived the first assault—a redundancy that had also been written off as inner-city coincidence.

The sheer amount of new information made clear the need for a special detail, and Waltemeyer—because he had handled the original March extortion complaint as well as the initial shooting of Dollie Brown—soon found himself reassigned to Gary Childs's squad on Stanton's shift. He was joined by Mike Crutchfield, the primary detective on the Bernadette Barnes case, and later by Corey Belt, the bulldog from the Western District who had done so well on the Cassidy investigation. At Stanton's request, Belt had been returned to homicide from the Western ops unit specifically for the investigation of Geraldine Parrish.

They began with detailed interviews of Dollie Brown and other relatives of Miss Geraldine's, and what they heard became more incredible with each telling. Everyone in the family seemed to know what Geraldine had been doing, yet everyone seemed to have regarded her campaign to trade human lives for insurance benefits as an inevitable, routine bit of family business. No one ever bothered to call the police—Dollie, for one, had said nothing about her aunt during the extortion probe—but worse than that, many family members had signed insurance policies for which Geraldine was the beneficiary. Nieces, nephews, sisters, brothers-in-law, tenants, friends and neighbors—the detectives began learning of hundreds of thousands of dollars in double-indemnity policies. Yet when people were being shot, no one who knew anything about it had bothered to voice so much as mild apprehension.

They feared her. At least they said they feared her—and not just because they knew of the sociopaths that Geraldine Parrish employed for her insurance killings. They feared her because they believed that she had a special power, that she knew voodoo and hexes and all kinds of Carolina backwoods garbage. She could bend a man to her will, make one marry her or make one kill for her. She told them that stuff and, after a time, when people began dying, they actually took to believing it.

But Aunt Geraldine's power wasn't at all obvious to anyone outside the family circle. She was a semiliterate lay preacher with a gray Cadillac and a white stone rowhouse with fake paneling and dropped tile ceilings. She was heavyset, and ugly, too—a thoroughly unattractive woman whose penchant for wigs and fire engine red lipstick suggested a $20

Pennsylvania Avenue prostitute. Geraldine was a hard fifty-five years old when the city homicide unit finally kicked in her front door and that of her mother's house on Division Street.

The search of both addresses takes hours, as Childs, Keller and Waltemeyer find policy binders and other papers strewn throughout the two rowhouses. Long before the search at Kennedy Avenue is complete, Geraldine departs in the back of an Eastern District wagon, arriving at the homicide office well before the investigators. She sits stoically in the large interrogation room as Childs and Waltemeyer arrive and spend another hour or so in the coffee room scanning the insurance policies, photo albums and documents seized in the two houses.

The two detectives immediately notice a proliferation of marriage licenses. As far as they can tell, the woman is married to five men simultaneously, two of whom were living with her on Kennedy Avenue and were taken downtown as witnesses following the raid. The two men sit together like bookends on the fishbowl sofa, each believing the other to be nothing more than a tenant at the East Baltimore home. Each is confident of his own place in the household. Each has signed a life insurance policy naming Geraldine Parrish or her mother as the beneficiary.

Johnnie Davis, the older of the two husbands, tells detectives that he met Miss Geraldine in New York and had, over his own objection, been intimidated into marriage and brought to Baltimore to live in the basement of the Kennedy Avenue rowhouse. Without fail, Miss Geraldine confiscated his disability checks at the beginning of every month, then returned a few dollars so that he could buy food. The other husband, a man by the name of Milton Baines, was in fact Miss Geraldine's nephew and had rightly objected on grounds of incest when his aunt insisted on marriage during a trip back home to Carolina.

"So why did you marry her?" Childs asks him.

"I had to," he explains. "She put a voodoo curse on me and I had to do what she said."

"How did she do that?"

Baines recalls that his aunt had cooked him a meal using her own menstrual discharge and watched as he ate. Afterward, she told him what she had done and explained that she now had power over him.

Childs and Waltemeyer exchange glances.

Baines rambles on, explaining that when he continued to express concern about marrying his mother's sister, Miss Geraldine took him to an old man in a neighboring town who spoke briefly with the bride-to-be, then assured Baines that he was not, in fact, related to Geraldine.

"Who was the old man?" Childs asked.

"I don't know."

"Then why did you believe him?"

"I don't know."

It was not to be believed—a murder case with cosmic insanity as the only common frame of reference. When the detectives tell Milton Baines that the old man living in the basement is also Geraldine's husband, he is stupefied. When they explain to him that both he and his rival were living in that house like hogs waiting for the slaughter, corralled by a madwoman who would eventually trade them in for a few thousand dollars of insurance benefits, the man's mouth drops in abject wonder.

"Look at him," says Childs from the other side of the office. "He was the next victim. You can almost see the H-file number stenciled on his forehead."

Waltemeyer guesses by the marriage licenses and other documents that husband number three is probably in Plainfield, New Jersey, though whether he is dead or alive isn't immediately clear. Husband number four is doing a five-year bit at Hagerstown on a gun charge. Husband number five is somebody by the name of the Reverend Rayfield Gilliard, whom Geraldine married this past January. The good reverend's whereabouts are uncertain until Childs goes to the blue looseleaf binder that lists unattended deaths for the year. Sure enough, the seventy-nine-year-old Gilliard's marriage to Miss Geraldine had lasted little more than a month; his sudden departure had been attributed by the medical examiner's office to natural causes, though no autopsy had been performed.

There are also the photo albums, in which Miss Geraldine had saved not only the Reverend Gilliard's death certificate but also that of her thirteen-year-old niece, Geraldine Cannon, who, according to an accompanying newspaper clipping, had been in her aunt Geraldine's care when she succumbed to an overdose of Freon in 1975—an overdose ruled accidental, though pathologists attributed it to a possible injection of Ban deodorant. On the following page of the album, the detectives find a $2,000 insurance policy in the child's name.

In the same album, they locate more recent pictures of Geraldine with an infant girl and soon learn that she had purchased that child from a niece. The baby would be found later that week at a relative's house and would be taken into custody by the Department of Social Services after the detectives match that infant to at least three life insurance policies totaling $60,000 in double-indemnity benefits.

The list of potential victims has no end. An insurance policy is found for a man who had been beaten and left to die in a wooded section of Northeast Baltimore; however, he survived the attack and was later located in a rehabilitative hospital. Another policy is found for Geraldine's younger sister, who died of unexplained causes several years back. And from one page of another album, Childs pulls out a death certificate, dated October 1986, for a man named Albert Robinson. The manner of death is listed as homicide.

Childs takes the document and walks to another blue binder that contains a chronological list of Baltimore homicides. He opens the binder to the '86 cases and scans the column of victims:

Robinson, Albert B/M/48

10/6/86, shot, NED, 4J-16884

Nearly two years later, the case is still open, with Rick James as the primary detective. Childs takes the death certificate back into the main office, where James is at his desk, absently poking at a chef's salad.

"This mean anything to you?" Childs says.

James scans the death certificate. "Where'd you get this?"

"Out of the Black Widow's photo album."

"Are you shittin' me?"

"Uh-uh."

"Hot damn," says James, jumping up to grip the sergeant's hand. "Gary Childs done solved my murder."

"Yeah, well, someone had to."

A smokehound from Plainfield, New Jersey, Albert Robinson had been found dead by the B&O railbed at the foot of Clifton Park, shot once in the head. The man's blood-alcohol level at the time of death was 4.0, four times the legal standard in drunk driving cases. Working on that murder, James never did figure out why an alcoholic from north Jersey was dead in East Baltimore. Perhaps, he had reasoned, the man was a hobo who had hitched a southbound freight only to be shot to death for some unknown reason as the train meandered through Baltimore.

"How does she connect with Albert?" asks James, suddenly fascinated.

"I don't know," says Childs, "but we know she used to live up in Plainfield . . ."

"No shit."

". . . and I got a feeling that somewhere in that pile of papers we're gonna find an insurance policy on your man."

"Oooooo, you makin' me feel all warm an' happy inside," says James, laughing. "Keep talkin' that nice talk."

Inside the large interrogation room, Geraldine Parrish adjusts her wig and applies another coat of makeup, using a small mirror. None of this has made her any less conscious of her appearance, such as it is. Nor has she lost her appetite; when detectives bring her a tuna sub from Crazy John's, she puts away the entire thing, chewing slowly, pinkies raised as she holds the ends of the sandwich to her mouth.

Twenty minutes later, she demands to use the ladies' room and Eddie Brown walks her as far as the door, shaking his head and smiling when his prisoner asks if he would be coming inside.

"You go on ahead," he tells her.

She is in there for a good five minutes, and when she steps back into the hallway, it's with a fresh coat of lipstick. "I need my medicines," she says.

"Well, which medicines do you need?" asks Brown. "You had about two dozen different ones in your purse."

"I need all of them."

Visions of an interrogation room overdose dance through Eddie Brown's head. "Well, you ain't getting all of them," he says, walking her back down the hallway. "I'll let you pick three pills."

"I got rights," she says bitterly. "Constitutional rights to my medicines."

Brown smiles, shaking his head.

"Who you laughing at? What you need to get is some religion . . . stand there laughing at people."

"You gonna give me religion, huh?"

Geraldine saunters back into the interrogation room, followed by Childs and Waltemeyer. In the end, four detectives will take a crack at this woman, laying the insurance policies on the long table and explaining over and over that it doesn't matter whether she actually pulled the trigger.

"If you caused someone to be shot, then you're guilty of murder, Geraldine," says Waltemeyer.

"Can I have my medicines?"

"Geraldine, listen to me. You're charged with three murders already, and before this is over you're probably going to be charged with some others. Now's the time to tell us what happened . . ."

Geraldine Parrish stares up at the ceiling, then begins babbling incoherently.

"Geraldine . . ."

"I don't know what you're talkin' 'bout, Mistah Poh-leeces," she says suddenly. "I didn't shoot no one."

Later, when the detectives have given up on the notion of a coherent statement, Geraldine sits alone in the interrogation room, waiting for the paperwork to catch up with her before she is transferred to the City Jail. She is leaning forward, her head resting on the table, when Jay Landsman walks by the one-way window and glances inside.

"Is that her?" says Landsman, who has just come on the four-to-twelve shift.

"Yeah," says Eddie Brown. "That's her."

Landsman's face creases into an evil grin as he slams an open palm hard against the metal door. Geraldine jumps in her seat.

"Whhhhooooaaaaaaaaaaa," wails Landsman in his best approximation of a ghost. "Whhhhoooooaa, mmuuurrder . . . MMMUUURRDER . . ."

"Aw Christ, Jay. Now you fuckin' did it."

Sure enough, Geraldine Parrish dives under the table on all fours and begins bleating like a crazed goat. Delighted with himself, Landsman keeps at it until Geraldine is prone on the floor, bellowing at the metal table legs.

"Whhhhhooooaaaaa," moans Landsman.

"Aaaaaaaaahhhhhh," screams Geraldine.

"Whhhhoooooaaaaaa."

Geraldine stays down on the floor, whimpering loudly, as Landsman strolls back into the main office like a conquering hero.

"So," he says, smiling wickedly, "I guess we're probably looking at an insanity defense."

Probably so, although everyone watching Geraldine Parrish's performance is now utterly convinced of her sanity. This writhing-on-the-floor nonsense is a calculated and naive version of the real thing, an altogether embarrassing performance, particularly when everything else about her suggests a woman vying for a special advantage, a manipulator measuring every angle. Her relatives have already told detectives how she would boast about being untouchable, about being able to kill with impunity because four doctors would testify to her insanity if need be. The musings of a sociopath? Perhaps. The mind of a child? Probably so. But a mind genuinely unhinged?

A week ago, before the search warrants were even typed, someone showed Waltemeyer an FBI psychological profile of the classic black widow serial killer. Prepared by the behavioral sciences unit at the Quantico Academy, the profile suggested that the woman would be thirty years or older, would not necessarily be attractive, yet at the same time would make great efforts to exaggerate her sexual prowess and manipulate her physical appearance. The woman would probably be a hypochondriac and would more likely than not enjoy portraying herself as a victim. She would expect special treatment, then pout if it was not forthcoming. She would greatly overestimate her ability to sway other people, men in particular. Measured against the profile, Geraldine Parrish seemed to be the product of Central Casting.

After the interrogation, Roger Nolan and Terry McLarney are both escorting Geraldine Parrish to the City Jail, following her down the sixth-floor hallway, with Nolan walking directly behind the woman.

"Just before the elevators, she stops suddenly and bends over," Nolan later tells the other detectives, "as if she's trying to make me run into her fat ass. I tell you, that's what she's really about . . . In her mind, she really believes that if I get a good feel of her ass, I'm gonna fall in love with her and shoot Terry McLarney with his own gun and ride off into the sunset in an unmarked Chevrolet."

Nolan's psychoanalysis may be sufficient to the occasion, but for Waltemeyer, the long journey into the mind and soul of Geraldine Parrish is just beginning. And while every other detective in the room is content to believe that they already know everything there is to know about this woman, it is now up to Waltemeyer to determine just how many people she killed, how she killed them and how many of those cases can be successfully prosecuted in court.

For Waltemeyer, it will be an investigation unlike any other, a career case that only a seasoned detective could contemplate. Bank statements, insurance records, grand jury proceedings, exhumations—these are things that no patrolman ever worries about. A street cop rarely takes the work beyond a single shift; one night's calls have nothing to do with those of the next. And even in homicide, a detective never has to worry the cases beyond the point of arrest. But in this investigation, the arrest is just the beginning of a long, labored effort.

Two weeks from now, Donald Waltemeyer, Corey Belt and Marc Cohen, an assistant state's attorney, will be in Plainfield, New Jersey, interviewing the friends and relatives of Albert Robinson, finding one of Geraldine's surviving husbands and delivering subpoenas for bank and insurance records. Much of the evidence involves an interstate paper trail, the kind of detail work that usually inspires a street cop to nothing more than tedium. But the three men will return to Baltimore with the explanation for the migration of Albert Robinson to East Baltimore and his subsequent murder.

Brought once again to the interrogation room from her jail cell, Miss Geraldine will once again confront a detective who lays the insurance policies in front of her and once again explains the truth about criminal culpability.

"You not makin' any sense," Geraldine will tell Waltemeyer. "I didn't shoot no one."

"Fine with me, Geraldine," the detective says. "It doesn't matter to me whether you tell the truth or not. We just brought you here to charge you with another murder. Albert Robinson."

"Who's he?"

"He's the man from New Jersey you had killed for ten thousand dollars of insurance money."

"I didn't murder no one."

"Okay, Geraldine. Fine."

Once again, Geraldine Parrish leaves the homicide unit in handcuffs and, once again, Waltemeyer goes back to working the case, expanding it further, searching this time for answers in the death of the Reverend Gilliard. It is a deliberate, often tedious process, this prolonged investigation of a woman who has already been arrested and charged with four murders. More than a string of fresh street shootings, it demands a professional investigator. A detective.

Months into the Parrish investigation, McLarney will walk by Waltemeyer's desk and overhear a lecture that the detective is delivering with calm sincerity. The beneficiary of Waltemeyer's newfound wisdom will be Corey Belt, the prodigy from the districts whose detail to homicide was extended for the Parrish investigation. At that moment, Belt wants very much to respond to a lying, recalcitrant witness in the Western District way.

"Back in the Western," Belt tells Waltemeyer, "we'd just throw the asshole against a wall and put some sense into him."

"No, listen to me. This isn't patrol. That kind of stuff doesn't work up here."

"That stuff always works."

"No, I'm telling you. Up here you got to be patient. You got to use your head."

And McLarney will stand there, listen a little longer, and then move on, delighted and amused at the notion of Donald Waltemeyer telling another man to shake off the lessons of the street. If there was nothing else to her credit, the Black Widow had at least taken a patrolman and turned him into a detective.

TUESDAY, AUGUST 2

It's a summer afternoon in the Woodland Avenue drug market, and suddenly, with a body on the ground, race becomes the dominant theme. The dead kid is decidedly black and the police, standing over their daylight scene, are decidedly white. The crowd grows restless.

"This could get out of hand in a hurry," says a young lieutenant, scanning the sea of angry faces on the other side of the police line. "I'd like to get that body outta here as soon as possible."

"Don't even worry about it," says Rich Garvey.

"I only got about six guys here," the lieutenant says. "I'd call for more, but I don't want to empty the other sector."

Garvey rolls his eyes. "Fuck them," he says softly. "They're not going to do shit."

They never do. And after a few hundred crime scenes, Garvey doesn't even hear the trash that gets thrown out from the crowd. The way a detective sees it, you just let the assholes run their mouths as long as they keep out of your way. And if one actually jumps into your scene, you throw his ass against a radio car and call for the wagon. No problem whatsoever.

"Why don't you cover that boy up and show some respect for the dead," shouts a fat girl on the other side of the Cavalier.

The crowd shouts its approval and the girl, encouraged, presses the point. "He just another dead nigger to you, right?"

Garvey turns to Bob McAllister, glowering, as a uniform pulls a white plastic sheet over the head and torso.

"Now, now," says McAllister, anticipating his partner's anger. "Let's have a little decorum here."

The body stays on the pavement, stranded there by the delayed arrival of a lab tech, who is rushing from another call on the other side of the city. A hot summer day in August and only four techs are working, one consequence of a municipal pay scale that doesn't exactly encourage careers in the fast-growing field of evidentiary processing. And though this fifty-minute delay is being regarded as yet another public display of the white racist police conspiracy that runs rampant on the streets of Baltimore, Garvey is somehow unrepentant. Fuck them all, he thinks. The kid is dead and he ain't getting any better and that's all there is to it. And if they think a trained homicide detective is going to dismantle a crime scene to satisfy a half a block's worth of agitated Pimlico squirrels, they don't know the game.

"How long you gonna leave a black man out in the street?" shouts an older resident. "You don't care who sees him like that, do you?"

The young lieutenant listens to all of this nervously, checking his watch, but Garvey says nothing. He takes his eyeglasses off, rubs both eyes and walks over to the body, slowly lifting the white sheet from the dead man's face. He stares down for half a minute or so, then drops the cloth and walks away. A proprietary act.

"Where the hell is the crime lab?" says the lieutenant, fingering his radio mike.

"Fuck these assholes," says Garvey, irritated that this is even being mistaken for an issue. "This is our scene."

And not much of a scene at that. A young drug dealer by the name of Cornelius Langley has been gunned down in a daylight shooting on the sidewalk in the 3100 block of Woodland, and no one in this crowd is rushing forward to provide any information. Nonetheless, it's the only crime scene around, and as such, it's real estate that now belongs to Garvey and McAllister. What the hell else does anyone need to be told?

The lab tech is another twenty minutes in arriving, but true to form, the crowd eventually loses interest in the confrontation well before that. By the time the tech gets busy taking photos and bagging spent .32 auto casings, the locals on Woodland Avenue are back to signifying, staring down the proceedings with nothing more than casual curiosity.

But just as the detectives are putting the finishing touches on the scene, the crowd on the far side of the street parts for the hysterical mother, who is already wailing inconsolably even before glimpsing her son's body. Her arrival ends the truce and gets the crowd going again.

"Why you got to make her watch?"

"Hey, that the mother, yo."

"They don't care. That's some cold poh-leece shit there, yo."

McAllister gets to the woman first, blocking her view of the street and imploring the relatives with her to go back home.

"There's nothing you can do here, really," he says over the mother's screams. "As soon as we can, we'll be down to the house."

"He was shot?" asks an uncle.

McAllister nods.

"Dead?"

McAllister nods again and the mother goes into a half-faint, leaning heavily against another woman, who helps her back into the family's double-parked Pontiac.

"Take her home," McAllister says again. "That's really the best thing right now."

At the other end of Woodland, closer to Park Heights, the spectators provide even more dramatics. A young kid points to a tall, gangly bystander and blurts out a vague accusation.

"He was there," the kid tells a friend, loud enough for a uniform to overhear. "He was right there and broke running when they shot the boy."

The uniform takes half a step toward the man, who turns and runs down the sidewalk. Two other uniforms join the chase and catch up to their quarry at the corner of Park Heights. A body search produces a small amount of heroin and a wagon is called.

Half a block away, Garvey is told of the arrest and shrugs. No, not the shooter, he reasons. Why would the shooter be hanging around an hour after the body hits the pavement? A witness, perhaps. Or maybe just a bystander after all.

"Yeah, okay, have the wagon take him on down to our office," says the detective. "Thanks."

Ordinarily, the routine lockup of a drug addict on Woodland Avenue—Pimlico's grand boulevard of drug addicts—would mean nothing to a detective's case. Ordinarily, Garvey would have every reason to stand over his latest body feeling a little like a lost ball in tall grass. But in the context of his summer, a sudden shout and a foot chase and a little bit of dope in a glassine bag are all it takes. It's everything required to make even the weakest sister get up and dance.

It began with the Lena Lucas case back in February and continued with a couple of misdemeanor homicides in April—one whodunit, two dunkers, but all of them cleared by arrest within a week or two. No deeper meanings there; every detective can expect a run of good luck now and then. But when the Winchester Street killing went down in late June, a pattern began to emerge.

Winchester Street was nothing more than a couple of blood smears and a mutilated bullet when Garvey and McAllister reached the scene, and undoubtedly there would have been little else if the first uniform there hadn't been Bobby Biemiller, McLarney's drinking buddy from the Western.

"I sent two down to your office," Biemiller told the arriving detectives.

"Witnesses?"

"I dunno. They were here when I showed up, so I fuckin' grabbed 'em."

Bob Biemiller, friend of the little man, hero to the unwashed masses, and the patrolman voted Most Desirable First Officer for a Ghetto Shooting by three out of five Baltimore homicide detectives. That cabbie slaying on School Street a few years back—Garvey's first case as a primary—also starred Biemiller as first officer. A happy memory for Garvey, too, because the case went down. Good man, Biemiller.

"So tell me," said McAllister, amused, "who are these unfortunate citizens that you've managed to deprive of their liberty?"

"One is your guy's girlfriend, I think."

"Oh yeah?"

"Yeah. She was hysterical."

"Well, that's a start," said Garvey, a man of faint praise. "So where's our boy?"

"University."

Down at the emergency room entrance, the ambo was still backed up to the door. Garvey looked inside and nodded to a black medic who was washing blood from the floor of Medic 15.

"How we doing?"

"I'm fine," said the medic.

"I know you're fine. How's he?"

The medic shook his head, smiling.

"You ain't makin' my night."

Dead on arrival, but the surgeons had cracked the chest anyway in an attempt to massage a spark or two into the guy's heart. Garvey stayed long enough to watch an intern yell for a charge nurse to move the dead man from the triage area.

"Right now," yelled the doctor. "We got a guy coming in eviscerated."

Saturday night in Bawlmer.

"Eviscerated," said Garvey, enjoying the sound of the word. "Is this a great city or what?"

University Hospital couldn't save the victim, so the rulebook called for a case in which no reliable witnesses or evidence would be recovered. And yet back at the homicide unit, the dead man's girlfriend readily gave up most of the murder and its origins in an $8 debt. No, she didn't see it, she claimed, but she begged the boy Tydee not to use his gun. The next morning, McAllister and Garvey both canvassed the 1500 block of Winchester Street and turned up a pair of eyewitnesses.

At that moment, Garvey did not immediately pause and go directly to the altar of the nearest Roman Catholic church. He should have, but he didn't. Instead, he merely typed out an arrest warrant and put himself back into the rotation, thinking that this happy little streak was merely a synthesis of investigative skill and random luck.

It took another week before Rich Garvey began to realize that the hand of God was truly upon him. It took a July tavern robbery in Fairfield, with an elderly bartender dead behind the bar of Paul's Case and every living occupant of the establishment too drunk to identify their own house keys, much less the four men who robbed the place. All except the kid in the parking lot, who happened to get the license tag of the gold Ford seen speeding off the bar's dirt lot.

Hail Mary, mother of God.

A quick records check on the tag came back with the name of Roosevelt Smith and an address in Northeast Baltimore; right as rain, the officers arrived at the suspect's home to find the automobile parked in front, its engine still hot. The very braindead Roosevelt Smith needed about two hours in the large interrogation room before making his first down payment on Out Number 3:

"Here's what I believe," offered Garvey, working without the benefit of his power suit. "This man was shot in the leg and bled out from his artery. I don't think anyone intended this man to die."

"I swear to God," wailed Roosevelt Smith. "I swear to God I didn't shoot anyone. Do I look like a killer?"

"I dunno," answered Garvey. "What does a killer look like?"

An hour more and Roosevelt Smith was admitting to having driven the getaway car for $50 of the robbery money. He also gave up the name of his nephew, who had been inside the bar during the holdup. He didn't know the names of the other two guys, he told Garvey, but his nephew did. As if he understood that it was up to him to keep the investigation neat and orderly, the nephew turned himself in that same morning and responded immediately to McAllister's classic interrogative technique, the Matriarchal Appeal to Guilt.

"My m-m-mother is really sick," the nephew told the detectives in a bad stutter. "I n-need to g-g-go home."

"Well, I'll bet your mother would be real proud to see you now, wouldn't she? Wouldn't she?"

Ten more minutes and the nephew was crying tears and banging on the interrogation room door for the detectives. He did his mother a good turn by giving up the names of the other two men in the stickup crew. Working around the clock, Garvey, McAllister and Bob Bowman wrote warrants for two East Baltimore addresses and hit the houses just before dawn. The house on Milton Avenue yielded one suspect and a .45-caliber rifle that witnesses said was used in the robbery; the second address produced the shooter, a sawed-off little sociopath named Westley Branch.

The murder weapon, a .38 revolver, was still missing and, unlike his codefendants, Branch refused to make any statement in the interrogation room, leaving the case against him a weak one. But three days later, the trace evidence lab made up the difference by matching Branch's fingerprints with those found on a Colt 45 malt liquor can near the Fairfield bar's cash register.

Print hits, license tag numbers, cooperating witnesses—Garvey had indeed been touched. Hands had been laid upon him as he bounced an unmarked car back and forth across the city, turning every criminal act into an arrest warrant. The fingerprint match on the Fairfield bar murder alone demanded some kind of Old Testament offering. At the very least, Garvey should have sacrificed a virgin or a police cadet or anything else that could be the Baltimore equivalent of an unblemished heifer. A few priestly blessings, a little lighter fluid, and the Big Shift Commander in the Sky might have been appeased.

Instead, Garvey simply went back to his desk and answered the phone—the impulsive act of a man ignorant of the demands of karma.

Now, standing over the shell of a Pimlico drug dealer, he has no right to invoke the gods. He has no right to believe that the thin man now wagonbound for homicide will know anything about this murder. He has no right to expect that this same man will be looking at a five-year parole backup for that small bag of dope in his possession. He certainly has no reason to think that this man will actually know one of the shooters by name, having served some time in the Jessup Cut with the gunman.

Yet an hour after clearing the Woodland Avenue crime scene, Garvey and McAllister are writing furiously in the large interrogation room, playing host to a truly cooperative informant named Reds.

"I'm on parole," the guy reminds Garvey. "Any kinda charge is going to back me up."

"Reds, I need to see how you're gonna do by us on this thing."

The thin man nods, accepting the unspoken agreement. With a felony, it takes a downtown prosecutor to cut the deal; with a misdemeanor like drug possession, any detective can maneuver on his own, killing the charge with a quick call to the state's attorney out at the district court. Even as Reds lays out the Woodland Avenue murder, a homicide detective is talking the Northwest District court commissioner into approving a pretrial release without bail.

"How many were there?" asks Garvey.

"Three, I'd say. But I only know two."

"Who were they?"

"The one's name is Stony. He's my rap buddy."

"What's his real name?"

"I dunno that," says Red.

Garvey stares at him, disbelieving. "He's your rap buddy and you don't know his real name?"

Reds smiles, caught in a stupid lie.

"McKesson," he says. "Walter McKesson."

"And the other guy?"

"I only know him by Glen. He's one of them boys from North and Pulaski. I think Stony be working for him now."

Little Glen Alexander, an up-and-comer in the shooting galleries along West North Avenue. McKesson is no slouch either; he beat a murder charge back in '81. Garvey knows all that and more after a half an hour on the BPI computer. Alexander and McKesson were up in Pimlico on business, putting out free testers for all the Park Heights fiends, trying to expand their market share at the expense of someone else's territory. A minion of one of the local Pimlico dealers, Cornelius Langley, took exception and there were some words on Woodland Avenue between Langley and Alexander that same morning. Like MacArthur, little Glen left the neighborhood declaring that he would return, and like MacArthur, he surely did.

When the gold Volvo pulled up on Woodland Avenue, Reds was walking through the alley from the Palmer Court apartments, where he had gone to score his dope. He came out on Woodland just as McKesson was taking aim at Cornelius Langley.

"Where was Glen?" asks Garvey.

"Behind McKesson."

"Did he have a gun?"

"I think so. But it was McKesson who I seen shoot the boy."

Langley stood his ground, a true stoic, refusing to run even when the men poured from the Volvo. The victim's younger brother, Michael, was with him when the shooting started, but ran screaming when Cornelius hit the pavement.

"Did Langley have a gun?"

"Not that I seen," says Reds, shaking his head. "He should've though. Them boys from North and Pulaski don't play."

Garvey runs through the scenario a second time slowly, picking up a few more details and committing the story to eight or nine sheets of interview paper. Even if they weren't going to get rid of his dope charge, Reds wouldn't make much of a court witness, not with his long arrest sheet and the HO-scale tracks running up and down each arm. Michael Langley, however, will be another story. McAllister goes downstairs and brings Reds a soda, and the man stretches his thin frame back from the table, his chair scraping across the tile floor.

"All this dopin' is running me down," he says. "You all took my shit and now I got to deal with that. Hard life, you know?"

Garvey smiles. In a half hour, the papers come downtown from the Northwest District Court and Reds signs the personal recog sheet and squeezes his gangly body into the cramped back seat of a Cavalier for the short trip up the Jones Falls Expressway. At Cold Spring and Pall Mall, he slumps down, head below the window's edge, so as not to be seen in an unmarked car.

"You want to get out at Pimlico Road or somewhere else?" Garvey asks, solicitous. "Is this safe for you?"

"I'm fine right here. Ain't nobody around. Just pull up on that side of the street."

"Take care, Reds."

"You too, man."

And then he is gone, sliding out of the car so quickly that he is a half block away and moving fast before the traffic light changes. He does not look back.

The next morning, after the autopsy, McAllister gives his patented do-right-by-the-victim speech to the dead man's mother, delivering it with so much apparent sincerity that as usual it makes Garvey want to throw up and has him wondering whether McAllister is going to finish by falling to one knee. No doubt about it, Mac is an artist with a grieving mother.

This time, the plea is for Michael Langley, who has not stopped running since the gunshots on Woodland Avenue. Rather than stand up as the eyewitness to his brother's murder, the boy raced two blocks to his room, packed a bag and headed south for the Langley ancestral lands in Carolina. Bring him back to us, McAllister will ask the mother. Bring him back and avenge your son's death.

And it works. A week later, Michael Langley returns to the city of Baltimore and its homicide unit, where he wastes no time identifying Glen Alexander and Walter McKesson from two photo arrays. Soon Garvey is back in the admin office, pecking out two more warrants on a secretary's IBM Selectric.

Eight cases, eight clearances. While summer bleeds the rest of the shift dry, Rich Garvey is once again communing with an electric typewriter, building the Perfect Year.

TUESDAY, AUGUST 9

Hell Night is three men on a midnight shift that never ends, with the office phones bleating and the witnesses lying and the bodies stacking up in the ME's freezer like commuter flights over La Guardia. It arrives without pity at a quarter before midnight, little more than a half hour after Roger Nolan's crew started walking through the door. Kincaid showed up first, then McAllister, and then Nolan himself. Edgerton is late, as usual. But before anyone can finish even one cup of coffee, the first call is on them. And this time it's a little more than the usual corpse. This time it's a police-involved shooting from the Central.

Nolan calls Gary D'Addario at home; protocol dictates that regardless of the hour, the shift lieutenant is to return to the office to supervise the investigation of any police-involved shooting. Then he calls Kim Cordwell, one of two secretaries assigned to the homicide unit. She, too, will have to come in on overtime so that the 24-hour report will be typed to perfection and copied for every boss by morning.

The sergeant and his two detectives then head for the shooting scene, leaving the phones to be answered downstairs in the communications center until Edgerton arrives to staff the office. No sense holding a man back, Nolan reasons. A police-involved shooting is by definition a red ball and, by definition, a red ball requires every warm body.

They take two Cavaliers, arriving at a vacant parking lot off Druid Hill Avenue, where half the Western District's plainclothes vice unit is standing around a parked Oldsmobile Cutlass. McAllister takes in the scene and experiences a moment of déjà vu.

"Maybe it's just me," he tells Nolan. "But this looks a little bit too familiar."

"I know what you mean," says the sergeant.

Following a brief conversation with the Western's vice sergeant, McAllister walks back to Nolan, quietly wrestling with the humor of it all.

"It's another ten seventy-eight," says McAllister, dryly creating a new

10 code for the occasion. "Your basic blowjob-in-progress interrupted by police gunfire."

"Damn," says Kincaid. "It's gettin' so a man can't even get blowed without gettin' himself shot."

"This is one tough town," agrees Nolan.

Three months ago, the same scene was played out on Stricker Street; McAllister was the primary detective for that one as well. The scenario in each case is the same: Suspect picks up a Pennsylvania Avenue prostitute; suspect parks at isolated spot, drops his pants and consigns his nether regions to $20 worth of fellatio. Suspect is approached by plainclothes vice officers from the Western District; suspect panics, doing something that seems to threaten the arresting officers; suspect is hit with a .38-caliber bullet and ends the evening in a downtown ER, reflecting on the relative joys of marital fidelity.

As law enforcement goes, it's downright ugly. And yet with the right amount of talent and finesse, both incidents will be ruled justifiable by the state's attorney's office. In a strictly legal sense, they can certainly be justified; before firing their weapons at the two men, both officers may well have believed they were in jeopardy. When ordered to surrender, the suspect on Stricker Street reached for something in the back of his truck and a plainclothes officer fired one shot into his face, fearing that he was trying to grab a weapon. The officer in tonight's incident fired one shot through the windshield after the suspect, attempting to drive away from the plainclothesmen, struck one of the officers with the car's bumper.

For homicide detectives, however, a justified police shooting means only that there was no criminal intent behind the officer's actions and that at the time he used deadly force the officer genuinely believed himself or others to be in serious danger. From a legal standpoint, this is a hole large enough for the proverbial truck, and in the case of these two vice squad shootings from the Western, the homicide unit will feel no qualms about using every inch of that chasm. The equivocation inherent in every police-involved shooting probe is understood by any cop with a year or two on the street: If Nolan or McAllister or Kincaid were asked at the scene whether they truly believed the shooting to be justified, they would answer in the affirmative. But if they were asked whether that shooting represented good police work, they would provide an altogether different answer or, more likely, no answer at all.

In the realm of American law enforcement, the deceit has been standardized. Inside every major police department, the initial investigation of any officer-involved shooting begins as an attempt to make the incident look as clean and professional as possible. And in every department, the bias at the heart of such an investigation is seen as the only reasonable response to a public that needs to believe that good cops always make good shootings and that bad shootings are only the consequence of bad cops. Time and again, the lie must be maintained.

"I take it the lady in question is already downtown?" says Nolan.

"Yes indeed," says McAllister.

"If it's the same girl as on Stricker Street, I'm going to bust a gut hearing about how every time she goes down on a guy, he gets shot."

McAllister smiles. "If we're all right here, I think I'm going to head for the hospital."

"You and Donald can both go," says the sergeant. "I'm going back to the office and get things started."

But before he can do so, a nearby uniform overhears the citywide dispatch call for a multiple shooting in the Eastern. The uniform turns up the volume and Nolan listens as the call is confirmed and an Eastern officer asks the dispatcher to notify homicide. Nolan borrows a hand-held radio and assures communications that he's responding from the shooting scene in the Central.

"We'll meet you back at the office," says McAllister. "Call if you need us."

Nolan nods, then heads across town as McAllister and Kincaid go to the emergency room at Maryland General. Twenty minutes later, the thirty-six-year-old suspect—"a working man," he is quick to assure them, "a happily married working man"—is sitting up in a back room, his upper right arm bandaged and encased in a canvas sling.

McAllister calls his name.

"Yes sir?"

"We're with the police department. This is Detective Kincaid and I'm Detective—"

"Listen," says the victim. "I'm really, really sorry, and like I wanted to tell the officer, I didn't know he was a police—"

"We understand . . ."

"I had my glasses off and I just saw him coming up to the car waving somethin' and I thought I was gettin' robbed, you know?"

"That's fine. We can talk later . . ."

"And I wanted to apologize to the officer but they wouldn't let me see him, but really, sir, I didn't know what—"

"That's fine," says McAllister. "We can talk about this later, but the important thing is that you and the officer are both all right."

"No, no," says the suspect, waving his sling in the air. "I'm fine."

"Okay, great. They'll be taking you down to our office and we'll talk there, okay?"

The suspect nods and both detectives walk toward the emergency room exit.

"Nice guy," says Kincaid.

"Very nice," says McAllister.

The guy is telling the truth, of course. Both detectives couldn't help but notice that the suspect's eyeglasses were still sitting on top of the Oldsmobile's dashboard. Parked in an isolated spot with his pants at his knees, the man probably felt particularly vulnerable at the sight of a young man in street clothes walking up to the car with something shiny in his hand. The victim on Stricker Street had the same fear of a robbery and, as a supermarket security guard, he impulsively reached for his nightstick in the back seat when the first officer jerked open the passenger door. Mistaking the stick for a long gun, the cop fired one round into the man's face, and only by the grace of the University ER did the poor guy survive. To the department's credit, the second shooting will be enough to prompt the deputy commissioner for operations to pull the district vice units off the street long enough to make changes in the prostitution detail procedures.

Over on the east side, Roger Nolan is dealing with the fallout from a triple shooting. The scene on North Montford is a wild one, too, with a young girl shot dead and two other family members wounded. The wanted man is the dead girl's estranged lover, who compensated for the end of the brief relationship by shooting everyone he could find in his girlfriend's rowhouse and then running away. Nolan is at the scene for two hours, prying witnesses from the neighborhood and sending them downtown, where Kincaid begins to sort through the early arrivals.

Returning to the homicide office, Nolan checks the small interrogation room, satisfying himself that tonight's streetwalker is not the same girl whose customer was shot on Stricker Street. He checks in with D'Addario, who has arrived, and with the twenty-six-year-old plainclothesman who pulled the trigger and is now a nervous wreck in D'Addario's office. Then he scans the bustling activity in the office and does not see the face he is looking for.

Sitting at Tomlin's desk, he dials Harry Edgerton's home number and listens patiently as the phone rings four or five times.

"Hullo."

"Harry?"

"Uh-huh."

"This is your sergeant," says Nolan, shaking his head. "What the hell are you doing asleep?"

"What do you mean?"

"You're supposed to be working tonight."

"No, I'm off. Tonight and Wednesday, I'm off."

Nolan grimaces. "Harry, I got the roll book right in front of me and your H-days are Wednesday-Thursday. You're on tonight with Mac and Kincaid."

"Wednesday and Thursday?'

"Yeah."

"No way. You're kidding me."

"Yeah, Harry, I'm calling you up at one A.M. just to fuck with you."

"You're not kidding me."

"No," says Nolan, almost amused.

"Shit."

"Shit is right."

"Anything going on there?"

"A police shooting and a murder. That's all."

Edgerton curses himself. "You want me to come in?"

"Fuck it, go back to sleep," says the sergeant. "We'll be all right and you'll work Thursday. I'll pencil it in."

"Thanks, Rog. I could swear I had Tuesday and Wednesday. I was sure of it."

"You're a piece of work, Harry."

"Yeah, sorry."

"Go back to sleep."

In a few hours, when events again overtake the squad, Nolan will regret his generosity. Now, however, he has every reason to believe that he can make do until morning with two detectives. McAllister and Kincaid have returned from the hospital with the wounded suspect, his arm in a sling, and an interview is already under way in the admin office. From the look of things, it is going pretty much as expected, too. After giving a half-hour statement to Kincaid and McAllister, the victim's most sincere desire is to apologize to the cop who shot him.

"If I could just see him for a moment, I'd like to shake his hand."

"That might not be a good idea right now," says Kincaid. "He's a little upset right now."

"I can understand that."

"He's very upset that he had to shoot you and all, you understand."

"I just want him to know that—"

"We told him," says McAllister. "He knows you didn't think he was a police officer."

Eventually, McAllister lets the suspect use the admin office phone to call his wife, who last saw her husband an hour and a half earlier, when he was leaving for a five-minute ride to an all-night video store. The detectives will listen sympathetically as the poor man tries to explain that he's been shot in the arm, arrested and charged with assault on a police officer and that it's all just a big misunderstanding.

"I'm going to have to wait to make bail," he tells her, "but I'll explain when I get home."

No mention is made of the perverted sex charge, and the detectives assure him that they have no reason to want to wreck his marriage.

"Just make sure she don't show up for court," Kincaid tells him. "If you can do that, you'll probably be all right."

Back in D'Addario's office, the young plainclothesman is writing his own report of the incident, electing on the advice of his district commander to give a voluntary statement to the detectives. By law, any attempt to compel an officer's statement makes that information inadmissible in court, and the detectives are under standing orders from prosecutors to do nothing more than request a statement from any officer involved in a shooting. Since the Monroe Street probe, however, the police union has been urging officers not to give any statements—a policy that in the long run is likely to breed trouble. After all, if a homicide detective can save another cop, he won't hesitate to do so; but any cop who refuses to explain his actions is just asking for a grand jury investigation. On this night, however, the major from the Western manages to convince his man to consent to an interview, thereby giving the detectives room to work.

The officer's report conforms to the suspect's own statement that the plainclothesman fell on the hood of the car, after it jerked forward three or four feet, then fired a single shot through the windshield. The interview with the prostitute provides further corroboration. Not that she saw all that much, she tells the detectives, her field of vision at the time being somewhat limited.

Slowly, methodically, the five-page report begins to come together beneath the hum of Kim Cordwell's word processor. Reading the draft,

D'Addario pencils a change or two and suggests the rewording of a few critical sections. When it comes to police-shooting reports, D'Addario is something of an artist; eight years in homicide have trained him to anticipate the likely questions from the command staff. Rarely, if ever, has a shooting report bounced down the ladder after the lieutenant put his mark on it. As awkward and excessive as the use of deadly force might have seemed out on that parking lot, it reads squeaky clean in the finished product.

Nolan watches the paperwork progress and again tells himself that they can do without Edgerton and that it's better, after all, to get a full night's work out of Harry on Thursday rather than call him downtown two hours into a shift.

But two hours later, just as the floodwaters have started to recede, the phone rings again, this time with a shooting call from North Arlington Avenue on the west side. Kincaid leaves the last of the paperwork from the police shooting behind, grabs the keys to a Cavalier and drives twenty or thirty blocks to watch the sun rise over a dead teenager, his long frame stretched across the white asphalt of a back alley. A stone whodunit.

When the dayshift detectives begin arriving a little after seven, they find an office in a state of siege. Nolan is at one typewriter, working on his 24-hour report as his witnesses wait in a back room for transport back to the Eastern. McAllister is down at the Xerox machine, copying and collating his police-shooting opus for everyone above the rank of major. Kincaid is in the fishbowl, haggling with three west-siders who are trying hard to avoid becoming witnesses to a disrespect shooting that happened right in front of their eyes.

McAllister manages to slip out a little after eight, but Kincaid and Nolan end their day in the afternoon rush at the ME's office, waiting for their respective bodies to be examined and disassembled. They wait together in the antiseptic sheen of the autopsy room corridor, and yet they are anything but together after this shift.

The issue, once again, is Edgerton. Earlier in the night, Kincaid overheard Nolan's telephone call to the missing detective; if he hadn't been knee deep in witnesses and incident reports, he would have boiled over on the spot. Several times during the night he had been ready to blast Nolan about it, but now, with the two of them alone in the Penn Street basement, he's too tired to argue. For the moment, he satisfies himself with the bitter thought that in his whole career, he never managed to forget when the hell he was supposed to be working.

But Kincaid will have his say; that much is certain. The air of compromise, the teasing banter, the rough acknowledgment of Edgerton's effort to handle more calls—all of that is out the window as far as Donald Kincaid is concerned. He's had it with that crap. He's had it with Edgerton and with Nolan and with his place in this goddamn squad. You're scheduled to be in at 2340 hours, you're in at 2340, no later. You're scheduled to work the Tuesday shift, you come to work on Tuesday. He didn't give the department twenty-two years to put up with this kind of bullshit.

Roger Nolan, for his part, simply doesn't want to hear it anymore. To his way of thinking, Edgerton is a good man who works his cases harder than most of the men in homicide, and besides, he's back to clearing murders. Okay, thinks Nolan, so every now and then Harry gets out there in the ozone. So he got his shifts wrong. So what should we do? Make him write a 95 explaining why he's a space cadet? Maybe dock him some vacation days? What the hell good is that? That shit didn't work in patrol and it sure wasn't the way to do business in homicide. Everyone knew the story about the time a supervisor had demanded that Jay Landsman write a 95 explaining why he was late for a shift. "I was late for duty," Landsman wrote, "because when I left the house to come to work there was a German submarine parked in my driveway." For better or worse, that was homicide, and Nolan simply wasn't going to jam it to one detective to make another feel better.

The middle ground is gone. On this, the morning after, Kincaid keeps the rein on his anger and says nothing. Nor does he give Edgerton more than a passing comment when both men show up for their shift on Friday.

"I don't even blame Harry," Kincaid tells the other squad members. "I fuckin' blame Roger for not making him straighten up."

But over the next few days, Kincaid's anger becomes white heat, and the others—McAllister, Garvey, even Bowman, who is more likely than not to side with Kincaid in this dispute—know enough to leave it alone and stay out of the way. In the end, the inevitable explosion comes on a four-to-twelve shift that marks Edgerton's next off-day. It's a shift comprised entirely of yelling and cursing, of accusation and counteraccusation, that finishes with Nolan and Kincaid shouting at each other in the main office, emptying all their guns in the kind of firefight that leaves few pieces to be picked up. Nolan makes it clear that he regards Kincaid as more trouble than anything else, telling the detective to mind his own business and then accusing him of failing to work his cases hard enough or long enough. And while it's true that Kincaid has a healthy share of open files over the last two years, it's also fair to say that Nolan is offering up the kind of criticism that no veteran detective is willing to hear. As far as Donald Kincaid is concerned, he's gone as soon as a vacancy opens up on either shift.

After showing its fault lines for more than a year, Roger Nolan's squad is finally breaking apart.

EIGHT

The sights, the sounds, the smells—there is nothing else in a detective's frame of reference to which that basement room on Penn Street can be matched. Even the crime scenes, no matter how stark and brutal, pale against the process by which the murdered are dissected and examined: that is truly the strangest vision.

There is a purpose to the carnage, a genuine investigative value to the gore of human autopsy. The legal necessity of the postmortem examination is understood by a detached and reasoning mind, yet the reality of the process is no less astonishing. To that part of the detective which calls itself professional, the medical examiner's office is a laboratory. And yet to that other part, which defines itself in hard, but human terms, the place is an abattoir.

The autopsy brings home the absolute finality of the event. At the crime scenes, the victims are most certainly dead, but at the point of autopsy, they become for the detectives something more—or less. It is one thing, after all, for a homicide detective to detach himself emotionally from the corpse that forms the center of his mystery. But it's another thing altogether to see that corpse emptied of itself, to see the shell reduced to bones and sinew and juices in the same way that an automobile is stripped of chrome and quarter panels before being hauled to the wrecker. Even a homicide detective—a jaded character indeed—has to witness his share of portmortems before death truly becomes a casual acquaintance.

For a homicide detective, the Office of the Chief Medical Examiner is both a legal necessity and an evidentiary asset. A pathologist's autopsy forms the baseline for any homicide prosecution simply because, in every murder case, it must first be proven that the victim died from human intervention and not from some other cause. But beyond that basic requirement, a good cutter's abilities can often mean the difference between an accident being mistakenly viewed as a homicide or, equally disastrous, a homicide being attributed to accidental or natural causes.

To the pathologist, every body tells a story.

Given a gunshot wound, a medical examiner can determine from the amount and pattern of soot, burned powder and other debris whether a particular bullet was fired at contact range, close range or a distance greater than two to two and a half feet. More than that, a good cutter can look at the abraded edges of the entrance wound and tell you the approximate trajectory of the bullet at the point of entrance. Given a shotgun wound, that same pathologist can read the pellet pattern and gauge the approximate distance between the barrel of the weapon and its target. From an exit wound, an ME can tell whether the victim was standing free or if the wound was shored because the victim was against a wall, or on a floor, or in a chair. And when presented with a series of wounds, a good pathologist can tell you not only which projectile proved lethal but, in many cases, which projectiles were fired first, or which wounds were sustained postmortem and which were antemortem.

Give that same doctor a knife wound and you'll learn whether or not the blade had one edge or two, was serrated or straight. And if the stab wound is deep enough, a medical examiner can look at the markings made by the knife hilt and tell you the length and width of the murder weapon. Then there are the blunt trauma injuries: Was your victim hit by a car or a lead pipe? Did that infant fall in the bathtub or was he bludgeoned by his babysitter? In either case, an assistant medical examiner has the key to the corporeal vault.

But if a forensic pathologist can confirm that a murder has been committed, if he can further provide some basic information about how the crime was done, he is rarely if ever able to lead a homicide detective from the how of it to the who of it. Too often the dead man comes to the detective as little more than a vessel emptied of life by persons unknown in the presence of witnesses unknown. Then the pathologist can provide all the detail in the world: wound trajectories, the sequence of wounds, the distance between shooter and victim—and none of it means a thing. Without witnesses, autopsy results become filler for the office reports. Without a suspect to be interviewed, the medical facts can't be used to contradict or confirm information gained in an interrogation room. And though a cutter may be an absolute pro at tracking wounds through a human body, though he may recover every piece of lead or copper jacketing left inside that body, it hardly matters when no gun has been recovered for a ballistics comparison.

At best, an autopsy provides information that can be used by an investigator to measure the veracity of his witnesses and suspects. An autopsy tells a detective a few things that definitely happened in the last moments of his victim's life. It also tells him a few things that could not have happened. On a few blessed occasions in a detective's career, those few somethings happen to matter.

A pathologist's death investigation is therefore never an independent process; it exists in concert with everything the detective has already learned at the crime scene and in interviews. An assistant medical examiner who believes that cause and manner of death can be determined in all cases solely by the examination of the body is just asking for pain. The best pathologists begin by reading the police reports and looking at Instamatic photos taken by the ME's attendants at the crime scene. Without that context, the postmortem examination is a meaningless exercise.

Context is also the reason that the homicide detective is generally required to be present in the autopsy room. Ideally, cutter and cop impart knowledge to each other, and both leave the autopsy room with a greater sum of information. Often, too, the relationship creates its own tension, with the doctors arguing science and the detectives arguing from the street. Example: A pathologist finds no semen or vaginal tearing and concludes that a victim found nude in Druid Hill Park was not raped. Yet a detective knows that many sex offenders never manage to ejaculate. Moreover, his victim was a part-time prostitute and mother of three. So what if there isn't any tearing? Alternatively, a detective looking at a body with a contact gunshot wound to the chest, a second contact wound to the head and multiple bruises and contusions to the torso may think that he's got to be dealing with a murder. But the two gunshot wounds are not inconsistent with a suicide attempt. Pathologists have documented cases in which a person taking his own life has fired a weapon repeatedly into his chest or head with inconclusive results—perhaps because he jerked his hand at the last second, perhaps because the initial shots were far from lethal. Likewise, the chest bruising—though it may seem to be the work of an assailant—could be from the efforts of family members who, on hearing the gunshots, rushed into the room and began performing cardiopulmonary resuscitation on the victim. No suicide note? The truth is that in 50 to 75 percent of all cases, suicide is never accompanied by a written note.

The relationship between the detective and the medical examiner is necessarily symbiotic, but the occasional tension between the two disciplines produces its own stereotypes. The detectives genuinely believe that every new pathologist comes out of medical school with a by-the-textbook mentality that bears only a casual resemblance to what occurs in the real world. A new doctor must therefore be broken in like a new shoulder holster. Likewise, the pathologists consider the vast majority of homicide detectives to be glorified beat cops, untrained and unscientific. The less experienced the detective, the more likely they are to be perceived as amateurs in the art of death investigation.

A year or two back, Donald Worden and Rich Garvey happened to be in the autopsy room on a shotgun murder just as John Smialek, Maryland's chief medical examiner, was leading a group of medical residents on the day's rounds. Smialek had only recently arrived in Baltimore, by way of Detroit and Albuquerque, and consequently Worden probably seemed to him no more or less knowledgeable than any other police investigator.

"Detective," he asked Worden in front of the group, "can you tell me if those are entrance wounds or exit wounds?"

Worden looked down at the dead man's chest. Small entrance-big exit is the rule of thumb for gunshot wounds, but with a 12-gauge, the entrances can also be pretty fearsome. At close range, it's never easy to say for sure.

"Entrance wounds."

"Those," said Smialek, turning to the residents with proof of a police detective's fallibility, "are exit wounds."

Garvey watched the Big Man go into a slow boil. It was, after all, Smialek's job to know any and all entrances from any and all exits, whereas it was Worden's to find out who put the holes there in the first place. Given the divergence in perspectives, several months and a dozen or so bodies are often required before a detective and a pathologist can work well together. After that initial encounter, for example, it took quite a while before Worden could see Smialek as a good cutter and investigator. Likewise, it took that long before the doctor began to regard Worden as something more than a poor dumb white boy from Hampden.

Because a medical examiner's report is required on any case in which murder is probable, the autopsy room has long been part of a Baltimore detective's daily routine. On any given day, the morning rounds may bring to Penn Street a state trooper handling a Western Maryland drowning or a Prince George's County detective with a drug murder from the D.C. suburbs. But the sheer volume of city violence has established the

Baltimore cops as fixtures at the ME's office, and as a result, the relationship between veteran detectives and the more experienced pathologists has grown close with time. Too close, to Smialek's way of thinking.

Smialek arrived in Baltimore with the belief that the natural ties to the homicide unit had allowed the medical examiner's office to sacrifice some of its status as an independent agency. Detectives, particularly those from the city, had too much influence over the manner-of-death rulings, too much say in whether something would be called a murder or a natural death.

Before Smialek's arrival, the autopsy room was indeed a less formal place. Coffee and cigarettes were bartered and shared in the cutting room and a few detectives had been known to show up on Saturday mornings with a six-pack or two, treating the cutters to some early relief from the weekend rush that always began with Friday night's violence. Those were the days when practical jokes and raw banter were an established part of morning rounds. Donald Steinhice, a detective on Stanton's shift who long ago had learned to throw his voice, was responsible for some notable feats, and many an ME or assistant began an autopsy by pausing for what seemed to be a dead man's complaint about cold hands.

Nonetheless, the casual ease of these years also had a down side. Worden, for one, could remember visiting the autopsy room and noticing the clutter and disorganization; sometimes, when the weekend rush used up all the metal gurneys, bodies were even laid out on the floor. Nor was it uncommon for evidence to get lost, and the integrity of trace evidence was often suspect, with the detectives unsure whether hairs and fibers found on the bodies were from the crime scene or from the ME's own freezer. Most important, to Worden's way of thinking, there had simply been a lot less respect for the dead.

In a campaign for investigative independence and better conditions, Smialek ended all that, although he did so in a way that damaged the camaraderie of Penn Street and made the place a hell of a lot less fun in the process. As if to emphasize the professionalism of the office, he insisted on being addressed as a doctor and would not tolerate even a passing reference to his office as a "morgue." To avoid acrimony, detectives learned to call the place—in Smialek's presence, at least—the Office of the Chief Medical Examiner. Subordinates who were used to less formal arrangements, many of them talented pathologists, soon ran afoul of the new chief, as did those detectives who couldn't sense the change in the weather.

Walking into the autopsy room on one occasion, Donald Waltemeyer made the mistake of wishing all the ghouls in the chopshop a fine good morning. Whereupon Smialek told other detectives that if Waltemeyer continued on that path, he would do so with a new and larger asshole. They were not ghouls, he declared, they were doctors; it was not a chopshop, it was the Office of the Chief Medical Examiner. And the sooner Waltemeyer learned these things, the happier a warrior he'd be. Ultimately, the detectives' verdict on the Smialek regime was divided: the ME's office certainly seemed to be better organized and more professional in some respects; on the other hand, it was a fine morning when you could share a cold one with Dr. Smyth while listening to Steinhice speak for the dead.

Of course, the application of criteria such as comfort and amusement to the autopsy room is—in and of itself—ample proof of a homicide man's peculiar and sustaining psychology. But for the detectives, the most appalling visions have always demanded the greatest detachment, and Penn Street, even on a good day, was one hell of a vision. In fact, quite a few detectives came close to being ill the first couple times around, and two or three aren't ashamed to say they still have a problem every now and then. Kincaid can handle anything unless it's a decomp, in which case he's the first one out the loading dock door. Bowman's okay until they pop the skull to remove the brain; the sight doesn't bother him so much as the clipped sound of the snapping bone. Rick James still gets a little unnerved when he sees a young child or an infant on the table.

But beyond those occasional hard moments, the daily routine at the ME's office is, for a detective, exactly that. Any investigator with more than a year in the unit has witnessed the postmortem examination so often that it has become utterly familiar. If they absolutely had to do it, half the men on the shift could probably pick up a scalpel and break a corpse down to parts, even if they didn't have any idea what, if anything, they were actually looking for.

The process begins with the external examination of the body, as important as the autopsy itself. Ideally, the cadavers are supposed to arrive at Penn Street in the same condition as they appeared on the scene. If the victim was dressed when found, he remains dressed, and the clothes themselves will be examined with great care. If there were indications of a struggle, the victim's hands will have been encased at the scene in paper bags (plastic bags produce condensation when the body is later removed from the freezer) to preserve any hairs, fibers, blood or skin beneath the fingernails or between the fingers. Likewise, if the crime scene was in a house or some other location where trace evidence could be recovered, the ME's attendants will wrap the body in a clean white sheet before removal, trapping any hairs, fibers or other trace material for later recovery.

At the beginning of the external examination, each body is removed from the walk-in freezer and weighed, then rolled on a metal gurney to the overhead camera that provides the photographs of record before the autopsy. Next, the body is rolled into the autopsy area, a long expanse of ceramic tile and metal that can accommodate as many as six examinations simultaneously. The Baltimore facility does not have, like many autopsy rooms, overhead microphones that allow the pathologists to record findings for later transcription. Instead, the doctors take notes periodically using clipboards and ball-points left on a nearby shelf.

If the victim was clothed, the pathologist will try to match the holes and tears in each item of clothing to the corresponding wounds: Not only does this help confirm that the victim was killed in the presumed manner—a good pathologist can spot a body that has been dressed after being shot or stabbed—but in the case of gunshot wounds, the clothes can then be checked visually or chemically tested for ballistic residue.

Once the victim's clothes have received a preliminary examination, each article is then removed carefully to preserve any trace evidence. As with a crime scene, precision is preferable to speed. Bullets and bullet fragments, for example, often manage to leave the body only to lodge in the victim's clothing, and often that evidence will be recovered as the body is slowly undressed.

In cases where sexual assault is suspected, the external examination includes a careful search for any internal trauma, as well as vaginal, oral or anal swabs for ejaculate, because semen recovered at the point of autopsy may be used later for comparison to link a suspect to the crime.

Other trace evidence can be extracted from the victim's hands. In a murder that follows a struggle or sexual assault, fingernail clippings may produce fragments of skin, hair or even the blood of the assailant. If the struggle involved a knife, defense wounds—a pattern of straight incisions, often relatively small—may be visible on the victim's hands. Likewise, if at any point the victim fired a weapon, particularly a large-caliber handgun, chemical tests for barium, antimony and lead deposits on the back of each hand might yield proof of that fact. The examination of a victim's hands may also mean the difference between a ruling of homicide or suicide; in about 10 percent of all self-inflicted gunshot wounds, the shooting hand will be speckled by blood and tissue particles—"blowback" from the wound track.

Just as a detective stares at a crime scene and tries to see those things that are out of place or missing entirely, a pathologist conducts an autopsy with a similar eye. Any mark, any lesion, any unexplained trauma to the body is carefully noted and examined. For that reason, hospital trauma teams are told to leave catheters, shunts and other tools of medical intervention intact so that the pathologist can differentiate between physical alterations that occurred in the effort to save the victim and those that occurred prior to the emergency room.

Once the external examination is complete, the actual autopsy begins: the pathologist makes a Y-shaped incision across the chest with a scalpel, then uses an electric saw to cut through the ribs and remove the breastplate. In the case of penetrating wounds, the doctor will follow the wound track at each level of the body's infrastructure, noting the trajectory of the bullet or the direction of the blade wound. The process continues until the full extent of the wound is known and, in the case of gunshot wounds, until either the entrance wounds are matched with exits or the spent projectile is recovered from the body.

The wounds are further evaluated in terms of their likely effect on the victim. A through-and-through wound to the head no doubt caused immediate collapse, but another wound, a chest shot that pierced a lung and the vena cava, might not have resulted in death for perhaps five to ten minutes, though it would have ultimately proven just as lethal. By this process, a pathologist can speculate about what actions may have been physiologically possible after a wound was inflicted. This is always a difficult guessing game, however, because shooting victims do not demonstrate the same reliable and consistent behavior depicted in television and film. Unfortunately for homicide detectives, a badly wounded person often refuses to limit the crime scene by simply falling down at the first wound and then waiting for the ambulance or morgue wagon.

The distortion of television and popular culture is nowhere more apparent than in the intimate relationship of bullets and bodies. Hollywood tells us that a Saturday Night Special can put a man on the pavement, yet ballistic experts know that no bullet short of an artillery shell is capable of knocking a human being off his feet. Regardless of a bullet's weight, shape and velocity and regardless of the size of the handgun from which it was fired, it is too small a projectile to topple a person by the impact of its own mass. If bullets truly had such power, the laws of physics would require that the shooter would also be knocked off his feet in similar fashion when he discharged the weapon. Even with the largest firearms, this doesn't occur.

In fact, a bullet stops a human being by doing one of two things: striking the brain, brain stem or spinal cord, causing immediate damage to the central nervous system; or damaging enough of the cardiovascular system to cause massive blood loss to the brain and eventual collapse. The first scenario has an immediate result, though the average shooter's ability to intentionally strike the brain or spinal cord of a target is largely limited to luck. The second scenario takes longer to play out because there is an awful lot of blood for a human body to lose. Even a gunshot wound that effectively destroys the victim's heart leaves enough blood to supply the brain with oxygen for ten to fifteen seconds. Although the popular belief that many people fall down upon being shot is generally accurate, experts have determined that this occurs not for physiological reasons, but as a learned response. People who have been shot believe they are supposed to fall immediately to the ground, so they do. Proof of the phenomenon is evident in its opposite: There are countless cases in which people—often people whose mental processes are impaired by drugs or alcohol—are shot repeatedly, sustaining lethal wounds; yet despite the severity of their injuries, they continue to flee or resist for long periods of time. An example is the 1986 shootout between FBI agents and two bank robbery suspects in Miami, a prolonged gun battle in which both suspects and two federal agents were killed and five other agents wounded. Pathologists later discovered that one of the gunmen sustained a lethal heart wound in the first minutes of the incident yet managed to remain ambulatory for close to fifteen minutes, firing at agents and attempting to escape by restarting two cars before finally collapsing. People with bullets in them, even a considerable number of bullets, do not always perform to expectations.

Neither, for that matter, do the bullets themselves. Once loosed upon the innards of a human being, these little lead bits also tend toward the unpredictable. For one thing, bullets often lose their shape. Hollow-point and wadcutter rounds tend to flatten out against tissue, and all ammunition can shatter against bone. Likewise, most projectiles do a lot less spinning and drilling after encountering resistance inside the body; instead, they yaw and tumble, battering tissue and organs along the way. As bullets enter a body, they also become less directional, glancing off bone and sinew and following the altered trajectories of their own changing shape. This is as true for the smallest slugs as for the larger ones. Out on the street, the big guns—the .38s, .44s and .45s—still get the greatest respect, but the lowly .22 pistol has acquired a reputation all its own. Any West Baltimore homeboy can tell you that when a .22 roundnose gets under a man's skin, it bounces around like a pinball. And every pathologist seems to have a story about a .22 slug that entered the lower left back, clipped both lungs, the aorta and the liver, then cracked an upper rib or two before finding its way out the upper right shoulder. It's true that a man who gets hit with a .45 bullet has to worry about a larger piece of lead cleaving through him, but with a good .22 round, he has to worry that the little bugger is in there for the grand tour.

Most big-city medical examiners employ a fluoroscope or X-ray to hunt down the tiny shards of metal alloy that travel to all sorts of unexpected destinations. In Baltimore, that technology is readily available and is occasionally used by a cutter in situations where multiple gunshot wounds or shattered bullets have complicated the recovery effort. For the most part, however, the veterans on Penn Street take pride in being able to locate most of the bullets and fragments without resorting to the scope, relying instead on a careful examination of the wound track and an understanding of a bullet's dynamics inside the body. For example, a bullet fired into the skull of a victim might not leave the head but instead ricochet off the inside of the skull at a point roughly opposite from the entrance wound; that much would be obvious from the absence of any exit wound. But an experienced pathologist begins his search knowing that projectiles bouncing off the interior skull rarely ricochet at acute angles. On the contrary, such a slug is more apt to strike the bone and then skate along the inside of the skull in a long arc, often coming to rest just inside the bone and a good distance from any point along the original trajectory. It's esoteric stuff and, in a perfect world, nothing that a human being should ever need to know. Such is the cumulative knowledge of the autopsy room.

The process continues with the removal of the breastplate and the examination of the internal organs. Linked together in the body's central cavity, the organ tree is lifted out as a single entity and placed on the steel sinks at the other end of the room. A careful vivisection of the heart, lungs, liver and other organs is then conducted, with the pathologist checking for any signs of disease or deformity while continuing to follow wound paths through the affected organs. With the organs removed, the remaining wound tracks can be followed into the posterior tissue of the body, and projectiles that have lodged in those muscles can also be removed. Bullets and bullet fragments, a critical category of physical evidence, are of course handled with great care, and they are removed by hand or with soft implements that cannot scratch the outer surface and thereby interfere with later ballistic comparisons of rifling marks.

In the final phase of the internal exam, the pathologist uses the electric saw to cut the circumference of the skull, the top of which is then popped upward with a lever-like tool. Pulling from behind the ears, the skin of the victim's scalp is then folded forward across the face so that any head wound can be tracked and the brain itself can be removed, weighed and examined for disease. For observers, the detectives included, this last stage of the autopsy is perhaps the hardest. The sound of the saw, the cranial pop from the lever, the image of the facial skin being covered by scalp—nothing makes the dead seem quite so anonymous as when the visage of every individual is folded in upon itself in a rubbery contortion, as if we've all been wandering this earth wearing dimestore Halloween masks, so easily and indifferently removed.

The examination concludes with a sampling of bodily fluids—blood from the heart, bile from the liver, urine from the bladder—to be used for toxicology tests that can identify poisons or measure alcohol and drug consumption. More often than not, a detective will request a second blood sample as well in order to identify blood at the crime scene or any bloodstained items that are seized in a later search warrant. Toxicology results take several weeks, as does neutron activation testing for gunshot residue, which is analyzed at the FBI lab in Washington. DNA testing, another aid to identification that was introduced in the late 1980s, can credibly match samples of the human genetic code using blood, skin or hair samples and has therefore become the new frontier for trace forensics. But the process is beyond the lab capabilities of both the medical examiner's office and the Baltimore department. When relevant to a case and requested by a detective, samples are instead sent to one of a handful of private labs used by Maryland authorities, but the backlog can be as bad as six months—a long time to wait for critical evidence.

A single autopsy can take less than an hour, depending on the complexity of the case and the extent of the wounds or injuries. When it is finished, an assistant returns the internal organs to the chest cavity, replaces the brain and skull top and closes the incisions. The body is then returned to the freezer to await a funeral home's hearse. The gathered evidence—

blood samples, swabs, nail clippings, bullets, bullet fragments—is then marked and bagged for the detective, who will take it to the evidence control unit or the ballistics lab, ensuring a clear chain of custody.

By its very efficiency, the process manages somehow to become less and less extraordinary. But what still has emotional force for even veteran detectives is the autopsy room as a panoramic vision, a sort of Grand Central Station of lifelessness in which human bodies are at varying stops along the disassembly line. On a busy Sunday morning, the hallway outside the cutting room might be filled with eight or nine metal tables and the freezer may hold a half dozen more. To stand amid the overnight accumulation of homicides and auto accidents, drownings and burnings, electrocutions and suicides, overdoses and seizures—that is always a little overwhelming. White and black, male and female, old and young, all come to Penn Street with no common denominator save that their deaths are officially unexplained occurrences within the geographic confines of the Old Line State. More than any other visual image, the weekend display in the tiled room reminds a homicide detective that he deals in a wholesale market.

Every visit to the autopsy room reaffirms a detective's need for a psychological buffer between life and death, between the horizontal forms on the gurneys and the vertical forms moving between the metal. The detectives' strategy is simple and it can be presented as an argument: We are alive; you are not.

It is a philosophy unto itself, a religion worthy of its own rites and rituals. Yea, though we walk through the valley of the shadow of death, we are breathing and laughing and sipping coffee from a Styrofoam cup, while you are stripped bare and emptied of vital pieces. We are wearing blue and brown and arguing with the attendant about last night's Orioles game, insisting that the Birds can't win without another RBI man in the lineup. Your clothes are torn and soaked with blood and you are refreshingly free of all opinion. We are contemplating a late breakfast on company time; you are having the contents of your stomach examined.

By that logic alone, we are entitled to a little arrogance, a little distance, even within the close confines of the autopsy room. We are entitled to walk among the dead with a false confidence, with a deceitful wit, with the self-sustaining assurance that it's still the greatest of chasms that separates us from them. We will not mock the shells of the dead, sprawled on their wheeled alloy cots; but neither will we humanize them, growing solemn and mortal at the very sight. We can laugh and joke and bear witness in this place only because we will live forever, and if we don't live forever, we will at least manage to avoid leaving this vale as an unattended death in the state of Maryland. In the safety of our imagination, we will only depart in wrinkled skin and a soft bed, with a signed death certificate from a licensed physician. We will not be bagged and weighed and photographed from above so that Kim or Linda or some other secretary in the Crimes Against Persons section can glance at the 8-by-10 glossy and remark that Landsman looked better with his clothes on. We will not be split and spliced and sampled only to have a civil servant note on a government-issue clipboard that our heart was moderately enlarged, our gastrointestinal system, unremarkable.

"Table for one," says an attendant, sliding a cadaver into an empty slot in the autopsy room. An old joke, but he, too, is alive and therefore entitled to an old joke or two.

Likewise for Rich Garvey, taking note of a rather well-endowed male cadaver: "Oh, my goodness, I'd hate to see that thing angry."

Or Roger Nolan, noticing a random racial configuration: "Hey Doc, how is that the white guys got their tables right away and the black guys are all waiting in the hall?"

"I think this is one time," muses an attendant, "when the black guys would rather see the white guys go first."

Only on rare occasions is the veil lifted, with the living compelled to acknowledge the dead honestly. It happened to McAllister five years back, when the body on the metal table was Marty Ward, a narcotics detective killed in a Frederick Street drug front when a hand-to-hand sale went bad. Ward was Gary Childs's partner back then and one of the most popular detectives on the sixth floor. McAllister was chosen to work that autopsy because someone in the unit had to do it, and the other homicide detectives had been closer to Ward. None of that made it easier, of course.

For the detectives, the rule of thumb is that if you think about it, if you allow the imagery to be about human beings rather than evidence, you will be led to some strange and depressing places. Insisting on this distance is an acquired skill, and for new detectives, an established rite of passage. New men are measured by their willingness to watch a body disassembled and then adjourn to the Penn Restaurant, on the other side of Pratt Street, for the three-egg special and a beer.

"The real test of a man," says Donald Worden, reading the menu one morning, "is whether or not he's willing to substitute that nasty pork roll for the bacon."

Even Terry McLarney, the closest thing to a philosopher in the homicide unit, has trouble finding anything more than black comedy in the autopsy room. When it is his turn to walk in that small space between the living and the dead, his empathy for the forms on the metal tables is largely limited to his ongoing and thoroughly unscientific survey of livers.

"I like to look for the more derelict-looking guys, the ones who look like they've had a hard life," explains McLarney, deadpan. "If they open 'em up and the liver is all hard and gray, I get depressed. But if it's pink and puffy, hey, I'm happy all day."

On one discomfiting occasion, McLarney was in the autopsy room when one case appeared on the rounds sheet with the explanation that although the victim had no medical history, he was known to drink beer every day. "I read that and figured, What the fuck," McLarney mused. "I might as well just find an empty table, lie down and unbutton my shirt."

Of course, McLarney knows better than to think it can all be laughed off. The line between life and death isn't so thick and straight that a man can stand on it every morning, cracking jokes with impunity as the doctors wield scalpel and knife. Once, in a rare moment, McLarney even tries to find words for something deeper.

"I don't know about anyone else," he says, serving up a platitude to the others in the homicide office one afternoon, "but whenever I'm down there for an autopsy, I can pretty much convince myself that there is a God and there is a heaven."

"The morgue makes you believe in God?" asks Nolan, incredulous.

"Yeah, well, if not heaven, then someplace where your mind or your soul goes after you die."

"Ain't no heaven," says Nolan to the rest of the group. "You look around that room down there and you know we're all just meat."

"No," says McLarney, shaking his head. "I believe we go somewhere."

"Why's that?" asks Nolan.

"Because when the bodies are all laid out like that, all the life is just gone and you know that there's nothing left. They're so empty. You can look at their faces and know they're completely empty . . ."

"So?"

"So, it's got to go somewhere, right? It doesn't just disappear. They've all got to have somewhere else to go."

"So their souls go to heaven?"

"Hey," says McLarney, laughing, "why not?"

And Nolan smiles and shakes his head, giving McLarney time to wander off with his seminal theologies intact. After all, only the living can argue for the dead, and McLarney is alive; they are not. By virtue of that one undeniable fact, he is entitled to win with the weakest argument.

Friday, August 19

Dave Brown pilots the Cavalier to within a block of the blue emergency lights, close enough to observe the general outline of the scene.

"I'll take this one," he says.

"You really are a piece of shit," says Worden from the passenger seat. "Why don't you just drive up and take a look at it first before deciding?"

"Hey, I'm deciding now."

"Maybe you want to see if there's a lockup first?"

"Hey," says Brown again, "I'm deciding now."

Worden shakes his head. Protocol demands that when two detectives are in a car and heading for a scene, one detective signs on as the primary before anything about the murder is known. By this unspoken agreement, those unseemly arguments in which one detective accuses another of grabbing dunkers and dumping whodunits are kept to a minimum. By waiting until the scene is within sight, Dave Brown is trampling around the edges of the rule, and Worden, true to form, is letting him know it.

"Whatever happens," Worden says, "I'm not helping you with this case."

"Did I ask for your fucking help?"

Worden shrugs.

"It's not like I got a look at the body."

"Good luck," says Worden.

Brown wants this murder for no other reason than the location of the crime scene, but as reasons go, it's pretty good. For one thing, the Cavalier is now parked in the 1900 block of Johnson Street in South Baltimore's bottom, and South Baltimore's bottom is deep in the bowels of Billyland. Stretching from Curtis Bay to Brooklyn and from South Baltimore on through Pigtown and Morrell Park, Billyland is a recognized geographic entity among Baltimore cops, a subculture that serves as the natural habitat for the descendants of West Virginians and Virginians who left the coal mines and the mountains to man Baltimore's factories during the Second World War. To the chagrin of the established white ethnic groups, the billies swarmed into the red brick and

Formstone rowhouses in the southern reaches of the city—an exodus that defined Baltimore as much as the northern movement of blacks from Virginia and the Carolinas during the same era. Billyland has its own language and logic, its own social framework. Billies don't reside in Baltimore, they live in Bawlmer; it is the Appalachian influence that gives the language in the white sections of the city much of its twang. And although the advent of fluoride has allowed even the truest of billies to retain more of their teeth with each passing generation, nothing prevents their allowing their bodies to be treated like virgin canvas by the East Baltimore Street tattoo artists. Similarly, a billy girl might feel compelled to call police when her boyfriend throws a National Premium bottle at her head, but she will just as surely leap with claws bared on a Southern District uniform's back the moment he arrives to take her man away.

For Baltimore's cops, hard-core billyness is generally regarded with as much disdain and humor as the hard-core ghetto culture. If nothing else, this attitude provides some proof that it is class consciousness, more than racism, that propels a cop toward a contempt for the huddled masses. And in the homicide unit in particular, the working coalition of black and white detectives tends to drive home the point. Just as Bert Silver is excepted from the general dislike of female officers, so are Eddie Brown and Harry Edgerton and Roger Nolan regarded as special cases by white detectives. If you are poor and black and your name is floating around somewhere in the BPI computer, then you are a yo and a toad and—depending on how unreconstructed the mind of the cop—maybe even a brain-dead nigger. If, however, you are Eddie Brown at the next desk over, or Greg Gaskins down at the state's attorney's office, or Cliff Gordy on the circuit court bench, or any other member of the taxpaying classes, then you are a black man.

A similar logic applies in Billyland.

You may come from the same mountain stock as the rest of Pigtown, but by a detective's reasoning, that alone doesn't make you a true billy. Maybe you're just another white boy; maybe you finished twelfth grade at Southern High and nailed down a decent job and moved out to Glen Burnie or Linthicum. Or maybe you're like Donald Worden, who grew up in Hampden, or like Donald Kincaid, speaking in a mountain drawl and sporting that tattoo on the back of one hand. On the other hand, if you've spent half your life drinking at the B&O Tavern on West Pratt

Street and the other half shuttling back and forth from the Southern District Court for theft, disorderly conduct, resisting arrest and possession of phencyclidine, then to a Baltimore detective you most certainly are a billy boy, a white-trash redneck, a city goat, a dead-brained cul-de-sac of heredity, spawned in the shallow end of a diminishing gene pool. And if you happen to get in the way of a Baltimore cop, he'll probably be happy to tell you as much.

Whatever their views on billy culture, the Baltimore detectives all agree that the best thing about working a murder on the white side of the tracks—aside from the sheer novelty—is that the billies talk. They talk at the scene, they talk in the interrogation rooms, they actually look up the number for the homicide office and then talk on the phone. And when asked whether he wants to remain anonymous, a good billy asks what the hell for. He gives up his real name, his correct address. He offers his work number, his girlfriend's name and phone number, his girlfriend's mother's phone number and every thought he's had in his head since the ninth grade. The code of the street—the ghetto rule that says a man never talks to a police under any conceivable circumstance—just doesn't mean as much in Billyland. Maybe it's because the cops have a little good ol' boy in them, maybe it's because the high-spirited Baltimore billy never managed to incorporate lying as an art form. Whichever, a detective working a white murder in the Southern or Southwestern District usually has more information than he knows what to do with.

Dave Brown knows all this, of course. As he takes in the swirl of bluetops surrounding his crime scene, he also knows that he needs a clearance to balance some nasty red on the board. He's been carrying a couple of open ones, most notably the Clayvon Jones killing, which can't be put down without a witness no matter how many anonymous callers offer up the suspect's name. Ordinarily, he might have shrugged young Clayvon off as a hard luck case, but the return of Corey Belt from the Western District for the Geraldine Parrish detail was, in Brown's mind, a reason for genuine angst. No doubt, Belt had obviously impressed McLarney in the Cassidy investigation, and now Belt was happily teamed with Donald Waltemeyer, Brown's usual partner, in a probe of the Parrish insurance killings that might take months.

Only last night, Brown had gone so far as to joke weakly about his status. Sitting at an admin office typewriter at the beginning of the overnight shift, he concocted a short, plaintive memorandum to McLarney, which he left in the sergeant's mailbox:

> With Officer Corey (I'm a superstar) Belt looming on the horizon, I thought I'd take just a moment to reintroduce myself to you.
>
> Until I came to your squad, I was just another long-haired, drug-infested, raving homosexual. Working under your knowledge, talent, skill, kindness and love I have become a detective of barely questionable means. Keeping this in mind, and to include the great feelings of my squad toward me (Worden: "He's a useless fuck" . . . James: "He never pays his fucking bar tab" . . . Ed Brown: "I doesn't even know the motherfucker") I was wondering what plans you had in mind for my CONTINUED service to you.
>
> I will remain ever vigilant, awaiting your response. Respectfully (everyone takes advantage of me),
>
> David John Brown, Detective.
> CID? Homicide? (Forever, Please God)

McLarney found the memo about an hour into the midnight shift and read it aloud in the coffee room, giggling at the more obsequious passages.

"Amusing," he declared in conclusion. "In a truly pathetic sort of way."

Fred Ceruti's troubles had not gone unnoticed, and Dave Brown, in his own, feverish brain at least, was feeling a little of the same heat. Driving out to Johnson Street, he had reasoned that an investigative sortie into Billyland might be just the cure.

"Well, Brown," says Worden, getting out of the passenger seat, "let's see what you've got."

She is face down in the hard mud and stone, a pale figure framed by a semicircle of radio cars. A short woman with straight reddish-brown hair, her red-and-white-striped tank top is pulled up to expose most of her back; her white corduroy cutoffs are torn at one side, revealing the buttocks. A pair of cream-colored panties, also torn from the left side, are down between her knees, and a single sandal rests a few feet from her right foot. Around her neck is a thin gold necklace and a pair of gold hoop earrings lie in the gravel on either side of her head. On closer inspection, one of the earrings is bloody, apparently because it was torn from the woman's left earlobe, which shows a laceration and some dried blood. Scattered near the body are a few coins; working carefully, Worden manages to liberate $27 in bills from a back pocket. Jewelry, money—if it was a robbery, it didn't get far.

Dave Brown looks at Worden, conscious of the fact that the Big Man is participating in this scene reluctantly.

"How old would you say, Donald?"

"Twenty-five. Maybe a little older. Can't really say until we roll her."

"I'd say twenty-five might be high."

"Maybe," says Worden, bending over the woman. "But I'll tell you what my first question is."

"Lemme guess. You want to know where that other sandal is."

"You got it."

The scene is a gravel lot that serves as a tractor-trailer turn-around and loading dock for an aging, red brick warehouse at the edge of the Chessie System railbed. Three trucks are parked at the eastern edge of the lot, but their drivers were sleeping in the rear of their cabs before the warehouse opened and they heard and saw nothing; whatever happened on the lot happened quickly or quietly enough that they stayed asleep. The body is on the western side of the lot, near the warehouse itself, perhaps ten or fifteen feet from the concrete wall of the loading dock. At the edge of the dock is a truck trailer that blocks any view of the body from Johnson Street.

She was found by two teenagers who live a few blocks away and were out running a dog at dawn. Both of them have already been sent downtown by uniforms, and McLarney will soon be busy taking statements. Both are billies tried and true, with Harley-Davidson tattoos and minor police records, but nothing about their story will arouse any suspicion.

While Worden deals with the lab tech, Dave Brown begins walking the length of the gravel lot, from the loading dock to the overgrown grass at the edge of the railbed. He jumps up on the concrete dock, then walks around both sides of the warehouse. No sandal. Brown walks a block and a half down Johnson Street, checking the gutter, then walks back to the southern boundary of the lot, where he jumps down to the railbed and searches a few hundred feet of the tracks. Nothing.

By the time he returns, the lab tech has recovered the money and jewelry, photographed the body in its original position and sketched the scene. The ME's attendants have also arrived and taken their Polaroids, followed by two television news cameras that are perched at the lot's entrance, shooting a few seconds of tape for the noon broadcasts.

"Can they see the body from up there?" asks Worden, turning to the sector sergeant.

"No. The trailer blocks the view."

Worden nods.

"We ready?" Brown asks.

"Let's do it," says the ME's lead attendant, putting on his gloves. "Slow and steady."

Gingerly, the two attendants roll the corpse, turning the dead woman slowly onto her back. The face reveals itself as a bloody, fleshy pulp. More surprising, black treadmarks cross the left upper torso and head in a consistent diagonal.

"Whoa," says Dave Brown. "Road kill."

"Well, what do you know," says Worden. "I guess it's a whole new ball game now."

The older detective walks back to the Cavalier for one of the handheld radios and opens the citywide channel.

"Sixty-four forty," says Worden.

"Sixty-four forty."

"I'm down at this homicide scene on Johnson Street and I need to get a supervisor in the traffic investigation section down here."

"Ten-four."

Half a minute later, a TIS sergeant is on the wire, explaining to the dispatcher that he is not needed on Johnson Street because the incident is a homicide, not an automobile accident. Worden listens to the conversation with growing irritation.

"Sixty-four forty," says Worden, interrupting.

"Sixty-four forty."

"I know it's a homicide. I want someone from TIS down here for their expertise."

"Ten-four," says the traffic man, cutting back in. "I'll be out there in a few minutes."

Unbelievable, thinks Worden, a perfect illustration of the not-my-job reflex. Traffic section handles any auto fatalities, including hit-and-runs, so they are reluctant to send a man down if it means they might get stuck with the case. McAllister and Bowman encountered something similar back in March when they called for traffic while working a body found mauled by the shoulder of Bayonne Avenue in the Northeast. The detectives were walking around that scene looking for chrome and paint chips; the traffic man was looking for shell casings.

"Did you catch that?" asks Worden, almost amused. "That guy wasn't going to come down here until he heard me say it was a homicide."

Dave Brown doesn't answer, preoccupied with the change in scenario. Death-by-auto requires an entirely different perspective, though neither detective believes that this was an accident. For one thing, the body is on a vacant gravel lot and was run over not ten feet from the concrete wall of the loading dock: It's hard to imagine a car whirling around in such a confined area for no reason. More important is the missing sandal. If the dead woman was a pedestrian, if she was merely the victim of a hit-and-run, then why wouldn't that other sandal be somewhere on the lot? No, the detectives reason, she wasn't a pedestrian; she arrived at the scene in the car that killed her, and chances are she had to get out of that car in a hurry, leaving behind one of her shoes.

On a closer inspection of the body, Worden also notices bruising in the approximate shape of fingers on both forearms. Was she grabbed? Was she attacked before the killer got back in the car and finished her? And the earrings: Were they pried out by the movement of the tire over her head, or were they pulled from her ears in an earlier struggle?

Freed from his fears about being saddled with the case, the TIS sergeant arrives a moment later and, after examining the treadmarks on the dead woman, begins waxing eloquent on radial tire design and the myriad distinctions between manufacturers. Before his brain turns to yogurt, Dave Brown interrupts the discourse.

"What do you think hit her?"

"Hard to say. But that tread would be most common on a sports car. A Two-eighty Z. A Camaro. Something along those lines."

"Nothing bigger?"

"Maybe a little bigger, but I'm saying it would have to be in that same class of sports cars. Those are like a high-performance tire, like you want for a car that's riding low to the ground."

"Thanks," says Worden.

"You got it."

Dave Brown squats down on his haunches to scan the treadmarks closely.

"No question it's a murder, Donald," he says. "No question in my mind."

Worden nods agreement.

But the drivers sleeping in the tractor cabs at the opposite end of the lot heard nothing; nor did the railroad workers at the yard office across the tracks remember any noise or headlights. Worden talks to the sector sergeant and learns that at about four A.M.—little more than two hours before the discovery of the body—there was a fire alarm at the warehouse. Trucks and engines from the Fort Avenue and Light Street stations drove right onto the gravel lot, confirmed the absence of any flame or smoke, and then drove off—presumably without noticing the body. Either she was killed after four o'clock or half the fire department all but drove over the corpse. On second thought, Worden muses, maybe they did that, too.

News of the fire alarm makes both detectives realize that half their crime scene has already been destroyed. If the weapon is an automobile, treadmarks are important, and on a mud and stone lot such marks should be easy enough to find—provided, of course, that a convoy of fire trucks didn't get a chance to roll across the scene, not to mention a half dozen radio cars, every last one of which made a point of pulling to within feet of the body. Dave Brown could spend a month matching tire prints to eliminate every vehicle that had been on the lot. Hoping for something easier, he checks the white cement of the loading dock and the scarred metal of a Dumpster, looking for fresh scrapes and dents.

"It's a tight spot," he says, hopeful. "Wouldn't it be great if the guy clipped a fender while rolling around in here?"

It would be manna from heaven, but even as he speaks, Brown knows that the only physical evidence he has is the body itself. And depending on what happens in the autopsy room in two hours, he may have precious little of that. Contrary to his initial expectations, Johnson Street was turning out to be a stone whodunit; Billyland was turning out to be no fun at all.

After the body has disappeared into the rear of the black van, the two detectives walk back up to the lot's Johnson Street entrance, where a crowd of onlookers has collected over the last two hours. A younger woman waves Dave Brown aside and asks for the name of the victim.

"We don't know yet. We don't have any ID."

"Was she in her forties?"

"Younger. Much younger, I think."

As the detective fights to remain patient, the woman slowly explains that her aunt left their home on South Light Street late last night and hasn't been seen since.

"We don't know who she is yet," Brown repeats, handing her his business card. "If you want to call me later in the day, I'll probably have something more."

The woman takes the card and opens her mouth with another question, but Brown is already in the driver's seat of the Cavalier. If the case was an ordinary shoot-'em-up, one of the detectives would be peeling off to work on the identification and interview relatives. But this case, more than most, hinges on the postmortem.

Brown guns the motor and races the Cavalier up South Charles Street; fifty miles an hour for no apparent reason. Worden looks at him.

"What?" asks Brown.

Worden shakes his head.

"What's the matter with you? I'm a police. I'm allowed to drive like that."

"Not with me in the car."

Brown rolls his eyes.

"Go by the Rite Aid up on Baltimore Street," says Worden. "I need cigars."

As if to make his point, Brown guns the motor again and catches every light across downtown. At Calvert and Baltimore, he double parks outside the drugstore and gets out of the driver's side before Worden can react. He waves off the older detective and returns a minute later with his own brand of cigarettes and a soft pack of Backwoods.

"I even got you one of them pink lighters you like so much. The bigger size."

A peace offering. Worden looks at the lighter, then back at Dave Brown. They are both large men, both squeezed beyond all dignity into the cramped interior of a two-door economy sedan. They are flesh under pressure in that car, a vision of cluttered humanity that somehow increases the comedic possibilities.

"They say it takes a big man to carry a pink lighter," says Brown. "A big man or a man familiar with alternative lifestyles."

"You know why I need the bigger size," says Worden, lighting a cigar.

"Because you can't get them fat stubby fingers around one of the little ones."

"That's right," says Worden.

The Cavalier bumps its way through the potholes and metal plates of Lombard Street in the late morning traffic. Worden blows smoke out the window and watches secretaries and businessmen coming out of office buildings for an early lunch.

"Thanks for the cigars," he says after a block or two.

"You're welcome."

"And the lighter."
"You're welcome."
"I'm still not helping you with this one."
"I know, Donald."
"And your driving still sucks."
"Yes, Donald."
"And you're still a piece of shit."
"Thank you, Donald."

"Dr. Goodin," says Worden, pointing to the metal gurney just outside the autopsy room door, "is this one yours?"

"That one there?" says Julia Goodin. "That's your case?"

"Well, actually Detective Brown here is the primary investigator. I'm here for moral support."

The doctor smiles. She is a small woman, tiny in fact, with close-cropped blonde hair and wire-rim glasses. And despite the additional authority of a white lab coat, she is a young woman with at least a passing resemblance to Sandy Duncan. To be blunt, Julie Goodin looks nothing like a cutter, and considering the prevailing stereotype, that's probably something of a compliment.

"And also," adds Worden, "because Brown promised to buy me breakfast across the street."

Dave Brown shoots Worden a look. Cigars. Lighters. Breakfast. You miserable old bastard, he thinks, why don't you just bring me your fucking mortgage payments?

Worden gives back a grin, then turns his attention to the pathologist, who now has her back to the two men. She is at the metal sink, cutting through the organ tree of this hour's client, a middle-age black man whose empty center yawns at them from the gurney just behind the doctor.

"I guess," says Worden, "that you're real glad to be working with me again, right?"

Julia Goodin smiles. "It's always interesting working on your cases, Detective Worden."

"Interesting, huh?"

"Always," she says, smiling again. "But I won't get to her for another half hour or so."

Worden nods and walks back out into the weighing room with Dave Brown.

"I'll bet she's real happy to see me."

"Why's that?"

"Tiffany Woodhous. The baby case."

"Oh yeah."

Doc Goodin has only been down at Penn Street for a few months, but already there is a history between her and Worden. It was a clusterfuck, of sorts, and it came three weeks back on a suspected child abuse call from Bon Secours, where the broken body of a dead two-year-old greeted Worden and Rick James in the rear examination room. Tiffany Woodhous had arrived at the hospital as a cardiac arrest case, but when the ER technicians forced a tube down into the child's stomach, the only liquid they brought up was old blood from an earlier injury. Doctors then noticed that rigor mortis was already developing in the face and extremities. Both detectives noted a large bruise on the right side of the forehead, as well as others on the shoulder, back and abdomen.

Assuming the worst, the detectives had both parents taken down to homicide, and when they learned that there were three other children at the family's Hollins Street home, they contacted the Department of Social Services. But after lengthy interviews, both mother and father remained insistent that they had no idea who could have caused those injuries. Then their thirteen-year-old daughter raised a new suspicion by mentioning an incident that had occurred when her ten-year-old cousin was caring for the baby. The daughter said that she was on the second floor of the house when she heard a smacking noise, and when she walked downstairs and asked about it, the younger boy explained that he had only clapped his hands. After that, she told Worden, she took Tiffany upstairs, but the little girl was quiet and listless. She put the infant back on the sofa and watched as she fell asleep.

Worden and James were both understandably eager to interview the boy, but he was suddenly nowhere to be found. He had been living with his aunt because he had already run away from his grandmother's house on Bennett Place, and now he had fled from Hollins Street as well. Consequently, when Julia Goodin got her first look at the tiny body at the next morning's autopsy, all she had to go on was the daughter's statement and the obvious trauma to the body, which included a severe blow to the head that had caused massive hemorrhaging. That added up to at least a preliminary ruling of homicide—a ruling that was promptly released to reporters.

Later that same morning, however, the ten-year-old was finally picked up by district officers in the alley behind his grandmother's house and taken to the homicide unit. In the presence of his mother and a juvenile division prosecutor, he gave a full statement. He told detectives that he had been alone with Tiffany shortly before 1:00 P.M. when she began to cry. He picked her up, played with her until she quieted down, then sat her on the arm of the reclining chair in the living room. But while the boy was watching television, the child fell backward off the chair, striking her head against a bicycle that was lying on the floor behind the chair. The little girl cried uncontrollably and the boy ran outside, looking for his cousin. He couldn't find her and began to panic. Just then, the thirteen-year-old returned and the two of them noticed that Tiffany's eyes were rolling back into her head. They put the child on a foam mat in the middle room of the rowhouse and listened to a gurgling noise coming from her throat. Then they noticed that Tiffany was not breathing.

They tried to resuscitate the child, a frantic and clumsy effort that explained the bruising to the chest, back and abdomen. The little girl began to breathe again and was put back on the sofa. Again she stopped breathing, and again the babysitters tried to revive her, this time by splashing her with cold water. Then they took the child to the middle room and laid her down beside her one-month-old brother. They did not call for an ambulance.

When the thirteen-year-old girl was interviewed again that same day, she recanted. She had lied in fear of her parents, and both teenagers had been reluctant to seek medical help for the same reason. Only when the parents returned home at eight that evening was an ambulance finally summoned. The children's behavior was witless and the result was tragic, but to Worden's mind, this was not by any stretch of the imagination a case of murder.

But the medical examiner's office, and Julia Goodin in particular, was not entirely convinced. As the chief pathologist, John Smialek noted that the head injuries were severe, more so, in fact, than a child would be likely to sustain in a fall from a chair. But Worden believed his young witness, who had described the little girl's fall as a backward flip from the armrest, straight down to the metal handlebars of the bicycle. And when the detectives convinced Tim Doory in the states attorney's office not to charge the crime, Smialek insisted on a meeting. The ME's office would not change the ruling, he told the prosecutor, and he was concerned that the case might seem to an outsider to be a cover-up by detectives who were reluctant to charge a ten-year-old defendant in a case that could never be won in court.

It was a standoff of sorts, and the problem for Goodin was simple: A forensic pathologist can't be wrong. Not once, not ever. Not even with a preliminary finding. Because it's a bedrock rule that any mistake by a professional expert in any criminal field—pathology, trace evidence, ballistics, DNA coding—once publicly acknowledged, becomes the domain of every defense attorney in town. Give a good lawyer a single case in which an expert's opinion is open to criticism, and he can ride that train straight down the track to reasonable doubt. And, more than most cases, the death of a two-year-old girl can always be expected to produce headlines.

"Death of girl ruled homicide; no charges due," declared the *Sun*. The paper quoted D'Addario as saying, "We have the basis for a case, but we can't say factually what actually took place in the house . . . We have to stick with the medical examiner's ruling."

Smialek provided some counterweight with the statement that the babysitters' explanation "is not consistent with the injuries . . . the child died as the result of an action on some other person's part." The ME did concede, however, that the death could have possibly resulted from accidental human intervention, but there was no way to tell. Trying hard for some middle ground, Smialek carefully explained that a medical ruling of homicide does not necessitate a criminal charge of murder. Meanwhile, the police department's spokeswoman summed things up cogently by telling reporters: "She was not murdered. That is all I have to say."

All in all, the Tiffany Woodhous investigation ended awkwardly for Worden, with a standing ruling of homicide for which no criminal charge would ever be filed. It also left the homicide unit and the ME's office struggling for common ground in the glare of publicity, and it was, in retrospect, about par for the kind of year Worden was having.

Now, three weeks later, the Big Man is back down on Penn Street with another body. And who but Julia Goodin is waiting for him in the autopsy room.

The two detectives watch their Jane Doe from Billyland go beneath the overhead camera in the outer room, with Worden asking the attendant for particular attention to the treadmarks on the left arm and upper torso. Fifteen minutes later, they follow their victim into the autopsy room, where the external examination begins in the first available space, which happens to be between a fire victim from Prince George's and an auto fatality from Frederick.

Doc Goodin is nothing if not cautious. And after the Tiffany Woodhous mess, she's now working with even more deliberation. She moves slowly around the corpse, noting the location of the treadmarks, of the bruises and contusions, of every visible injury. She notes each on the top sheet of her clip-pad, which is itself a silhouette of a prone female form. She carefully checks the hands for trace evidence, then scrapes the fingernails, though she can see nothing in the scrapings to indicate that the victim fought against any assailant. She pays particular attention to the victim's shins and thighs, looking for telltale bumper marks to indicate that she was struck while standing and then run over. Nothing there either.

Worden points out the finger-pattern bruising on each arm. "Like she was grabbed first?" he asks.

Goodin shakes her head. "Actually," she says, "those are contusions that could have been caused when the vehicle went over her."

Worden mentions the earrings, both found on either side of her head along with small clumps of hair. Could they have been pulled out by an angry assailant?

"More likely they were pulled out when her head was run over."

And the torn shorts? The torn panties? No, says Goodin, holding the two together to show that they both tore on the same side, at the point that would be weakest as the wheels rolled over her.

"The tires could have done that."

Worden sighs, steps away, and looks at Brown. Both detectives can now see where they're going with this thing; they may as well let the good doctor work and adjourn to the Penn Restaurant.

"Well," says Worden, "we'll be across the street and back in a half hour or so."

"You could make it an hour."

Worden nods.

The Penn Restaurant is mostly a lunchtime venue, a Greek family-owned establishment that draws most of its business from the hospital complex across the street. The decor is blue and white, heavy on the Formica, with the requisite number of wall murals depicting the Acropolis and the Aegean coastline. The gyros are exceptional, the breakfasts, acceptable, and the beer, cold. Brown orders the steak and egg combo; Worden, a beer.

"How do you want the steak cooked?" asks the waitress.

"He'd like it rare," says Worden, smiling.

Brown looks at him.

"Go on, David, get it bloody and show us how it doesn't bother you."

"Medium," says Brown.

Worden smiles and the waitress wanders back toward the kitchen. Brown looks up at the older detective. "What do you think?"

"I'll give you odds right now she won't make it a murder," Worden tells him.

"Not after what you put her through," says Brown dryly. "You went and ruined her for the rest of us."

"Yeah, well . . ."

They eat and drink in silence. Finishing his steak, Brown looks again at Worden.

"You know what I'm going to have to do?" he says. "I'm going to have to go out with her and show her the scene."

Worden nods.

"You think that'll help?"

Worden shrugs.

"I know it's a murder, Donald."

Brown finishes his coffee and snuffs out his second cigarette. Back in May, he was down to a couple of smokes a day on the Johns Hopkins clinic plan. Now, whenever he coughed, he sounded like a garbage disposal chewing on a spoon.

"You ready?"

"Yep."

They cross the street, heading down the ramp and up the loading dock entrance, past the bulkhead door that marks the entrance to the decomp room; there the nastiest cases are examined apart from the others to keep life on Penn Street as bearable as possible. Even from the loading dock, there is still the suggestion of unbelievable stench.

Inside the autopsy room, Julia Goodin is finishing her examination. As expected, she tells the detectives that nothing about the body points conclusively to a homicide. Particularly important, she says, is the absence of any visible contusions on the legs. In all probability, she explains, the woman was already lying down on that lot when she was run over. The toxicology will take weeks, but both Goodin and the detectives can guess that the results will come back positive for alcohol, if not for drugs as well. After all, she's a billy girl found dead on a Sunday morning; chances are she saw the inside of at least one or two bars the previous night. There's no semen, no direct evidence of sexual assault.

How do we know, Goodin argues, that she didn't just fall down drunk before someone ran her over? And what if one of those tractor-trailers didn't see her lying there and backed up to that loading dock?

Worden gives her the traffic man's opinion on the tires, suggesting that it's a sports car rather than any kind of truck.

"If a semi-truck rolled over her," says Worden, "it'd do a lot more damage than that, wouldn't it?"

"That's hard to say."

Dave Brown brings up the missing shoe. If she just fell down drunk, wouldn't that sandal be somewhere nearby? Intriguing thought, Goodin agrees, but she remains unconvinced, countering that if the victim was drunk, she could have lost the sandal two blocks away from where she eventually fell.

"Look, guys, if you bring me something conclusive, I'll rule it a homicide," she says. "Right now, I have no choice but to pend it."

Later that afternoon, Dave Brown returns to Penn Street and collects the good doctor for a tour of the crime scene, arguing once again that the isolated lot just isn't suited to the ordinary hit-and-run. Goodin listens carefully, scouts the scene and nods her understanding, but still refuses to call the death a murder.

"I need some solid evidence either way," she insists. "Bring me something definitive."

Brown accepts defeat graciously, and though he is still certain that the case is a murder, he understands on some level that it ought to be pended. Three weeks ago, after all, Goodin called a murder only to be overtaken by new evidence; now, the same bunch of cowboys are asking her to call another one without definitive proof. It's probably a murder, Brown reasons, but right now it probably should be pended.

Nonetheless, Goodin's ruling creates another kind of problem: A case in which the pathologist's finding is being pended is not, to the police department's way of thinking, a murder. And if it isn't a murder, it doesn't go up on the board. And if it isn't up on the board, it doesn't really exist. Unless the primary detective takes it on himself to pursue a pended case, it has every chance of falling through the cracks the moment that detective gets a call that *is* a murder. If this case goes down, it will go down because Dave Brown somehow managed to follow through, and Worden, for one, has doubts about Brown's ability to do so.

Arriving back at the homicide office, the two men find that McLarney has already dispensed with the preliminaries. The paperwork has been given a start and the two billies who found the body are asleep in the fishbowl, their statements completed. And the woman that Brown talked with at the scene has called back; she's heard a description of the victim on the neighborhood grapevine and it matches her aunt. Brown asks about the aunt's jewelry and the woman describes both the necklace and earrings. He explains that there's no need for the family to visit Penn Street for a positive identification; the facial injuries make that impossible. An hour or so later, fingerprint comparisons identify the dead woman as Carol Ann Wright, a young-looking forty-three-year-old who lived not two blocks from where she died. She was the mother of five children, and the last time her family saw her was a little before 11:00 P.M. on Saturday, when she walked over to Hanover Street to hitch a ride to the Southern District, where a friend of hers had been locked up.

By early afternoon, Brown has confirmed that his victim did indeed pay a brief visit to a prisoner at the Southern District holding cells before leaving for parts unknown. And by late afternoon the family is calling back with the rest of the story. True to Brown's most fervent hopes, the good country folk of South Baltimore are talking to one another and to the police, spewing out any and all relevant facts and rumors.

Tracking the tale backward, Brown learns that a short time after the television stations began identifying the victim, the dead woman's niece got a call from some friends over at Helen's Hollywood Bar, down on Broadway in Fell's Point. The bartendress and the manager both knew Carol, and both remember that she showed up close to 1:00 A.M. with some guy named Rick, who had long, dirty blond hair and drove a black sports car.

A short time later, the family calls again with more information: Before going to the bar that night, Carol went to a friend's house over in Pigtown a little after midnight, looking to buy a little marijuana. Brown and Worden roll back out of the headquarters' garage and drive first to South Stricker Street, where the friend confirms the visit but says she didn't get a good look at the guy who drove Carol because he stayed in the car. She thinks he was young and kind of greasy looking, with longish blond hair. His car, she says, was blue or green. Maybe like a bluish green. Definitely not black.

Later that night, at Helen's on Broadway, the two detectives get little more from the regular patrons and night employees. The guy had blond hair, kind of long and stringy, but with a little curl to it. And a mustache, too. Kind of thin.

"How tall?" Brown asks the bartendress. "My height?"

"No," she says. "Shorter."

"About *his* height?" he says, pointing to a customer.

"Maybe a little shorter than that."

"What about the car?"

The car. Nothing is more frustrating for Brown and Worden than to listen to these people try to describe the automobile that ran over Carol Ann Wright. The woman on Stricker Street says it was a blue or green compact. The manager of the bar says it was black and sporty, with a T-top and a round insignia on the front of the hood, like a 280Z. No, says the bartendress, it had those doors that open upward, like wings.

"Winged doors?" says Brown, incredulous. "Like a Lotus?"

"I don't know what you call it."

"Are you sure?"

"I think so."

It's hard to dismiss the employee because she actually went outside at closing time and listened to this guy talk about how he's a mechanic, a transmission expert, and does his own work on the car.

"He was real proud of it," she tells Brown.

But it's harder to believe her when she says that some greasy motor-head named Rick is running around South Baltimore in a custom $60,000 Lotus, giving billy girls a ride down to the Southern District. Yeah, right, thinks Brown, and Donald Worden is my personal love slave.

What's especially aggravating to the detectives is that if these witnesses can't get the car right—the car being a definite object with its make and model number displayed in chrome on its exterior—then they sure as hell can't be trusted to come anywhere close on the guy's description. Everyone mentions the shoulder-length blond hair, but some are saying stringy and others, curly. Only half of them have the thin mustache, and they're all over the map on the guy's height and weight. Eye color? Forget it. Distinctive features? Oh yeah, he was driving a Lotus.

Ordinarily, a bad description is par for the course. Any good detective or prosecutor knows that stranger-to-stranger identification is the weakest kind of evidence; in a crowded world, people just don't have the facility to commit a new face to memory. Many veteran detectives don't bother to include preliminary descriptions in their reports for that reason: A description of a six-foot-two, 220-pound suspect will hurt you in court when the guy turns out to be five-seven and 150. True to the stereotype, law enforcement studies have also shown that interracial identifications—blacks of whites, whites of blacks—tend to be the weakest because at first glance, both races have trouble distinguishing between members of the other. In Baltimore, at least, the reputation for the most ineffectual identifications goes to the Koreans, who run every other corner store in the inner city. "All rook arike" is the only credo they ever offer to a robbery detective.

But this case should have been different. For one thing, the identification is white-on-white. For another, the guy was in the bar for over an hour, hovering around Carol, making conversation with the other patrons and employees. Collectively, these people remember that the guy claimed to be a mechanic, a transmission expert actually, that he drank Budweiser, that he mentioned that a particular bar up in Parkville was for sale and that his uncle owned some bar in Highlandtown with a German-sounding name that no one can recall. They even remember that the guy got mad when Carol got up to dance to the jukebox with another girl. All of that has been committed to memory by the regulars at Helen's, and yet Brown is left with nothing better than a partial description.

Frustrated, Brown works the bartendress through her story a second time, then communes with Worden at the back of the tavern, near the pool table.

"These are our best witnesses?" says Brown. "We don't have dick."

Leaning against the pay phone on the back wall, Worden gives Brown a what-you-mean-we-Kemosabe look.

"The problem is that it was closing time and they were all shitfaced," Brown continues. "They're not going to remember this guy well enough for a composite."

Worden says nothing.

"You don't think there's any point in calling an artist, right?"

Worden looks at him skeptically. Even with good eyewitnesses, the composite sketches never manage to look like the suspect. Somehow, all the black guys resemble Eddie Brown and, depending on hair color, all the white guys are dead ringers for either Dunnigan or Landsman.

Brown persists. "There's not enough here for a composite, right?"

Worden holds out his hand. "Gimme a quarter."

Brown fishes up a twenty-five-cent piece, presuming that Worden wants to use the phone or maybe punch a song on the juke.

"Brown, you're a piece of shit," says Worden, pocketing the coin. "Finish your beer and let's go."

They are left with the worst kind of investigation, a needle-in-a-haystack search for blond-haired Rick and his black or maybe blue-green sports car. Reluctantly, Worden puts a description out on a teletype to the districts. He had hoped to keep that information from floating around too freely, because if word somehow gets back to the suspect that they have a partial description of the car, he'll paint it or ditch it or hide it in a garage somewhere for about four months. The car, both detectives understand, is essential evidence.

Ideally, the teletypes are read at every roll call citywide and maybe elsewhere in the state if a detective uses the MILES computer system. Hell, if an investigator thinks his man has gone on the wing interstate, he can go whole hog and put the thing on NCIC. But both the local and national teletype networks—like most everything else in the criminal justice system—are flooded to the point of absurdity. Usually, the only items a cop remembers from roll call will be red-ball items—cop killings, child murders—and the occasional punch line. At the beginning of a recent 8-to-4 shift, Jay Landsman made a point of reading a burglary teletype from Baltimore County in which the stolen property consisted of 522 gallons of ice cream.

"The suspects are believed to be a lot fatter than they were . . ."

In the Baltimore precincts, at least, a homicide lookout stands a good chance of being read at roll call, but whether anyone's actually listening or not is open to debate. In Brown and Worden's favor, however, is the fact that the girl was run over in the Southern District. In a detective's mind, the street police in certain districts are known for certain things: The Eastern cops protect a crime scene better than anyone, the Western operations unit has decent informants, and in the Southern and the Southeast, there are still some guys out on the street who will actually work a lookout.

Over the next several days, uniforms in those districts make traffic stops on anything close to the description. The paperwork comes downtown to Brown's desk, where names and license numbers are matched with motor vehicle registrations and BPI photos. There's a lot of data and Brown looks at each report carefully. Nothing seems to match: This guy's got a black 280Z with a T-top, but he's got thinning brown hair. This one's got a Mustang with some front end damage, but his long hair is jet black. This one's got long blond hair, but his Trans Am is a light copper color.

In addition to the district car stops, Brown and Worden spend the days and nights after the murder wedged into a Cavalier, following up on everything that the victim's family tells them. And with each passing day, the family comes up with a new suspect. First, there is the guy out in Middle River whose name is most definitely Rick and who had called for Carol about a week before she was killed. The family still has the guy's phone number.

When Brown and McLarney ride out to the Middle River address, a man with short, thinning blond hair answers the door. Hell, thinks Brown, hopeful, he could have cut it. But downtown in the large interrogation room, the detectives learn that he works at the Domino Sugar plant in Locust Point, not as an auto mechanic. Worse than that, his only car is an old yellow Toyota; Brown checks it that day on the company lot. The man readily acknowledges having given Carol Wright a ride down Fort Avenue on his motorcycle, but he's genuinely surprised to hear about the woman's death.

Another kid stopped by the district has blond hair and the right kind of car listed to his mother's address out on Washington Boulevard, but his alibi seems to hold. A third billy is a mechanic who goes by the name Rick and lives down in Anne Arundel: He even knew some of Carol's friends, according to the family. Brown sits on the house for two days, looking for that black sports car, only to pick the guy up and learn that the family had already called him first.

"They told me you might be coming by," he assures Brown. "What do you want to know?"

Billyland. Not only do they talk to the police, they babble to one another—so much so that there's no conceivable way for an investigator to work effectively. As soon as one family member learns about a potential suspect, another family member is asking a friend of a friend to ask the guy whether he has a black sports car and if so, whether he used it to run over Carol Wright. Twice, Brown goes back to South Baltimore to urge the family not to discuss the case with anyone. Twice, they assure him that they will shut up.

Two days later, Brown is alone in a Cavalier, watching a side street off Dundalk Avenue for yet another suspect. He is there for hours, drinking 7-Eleven coffee and feeding his smoker's cough and watching the billy boys come and go from their cars. Rarely does a homicide detective have time for this sort of endless surveillance, even if he has the patience. But so far no fresh murders have landed on Brown's desk, allowing him to sit for hours with the air conditioning running. With white powder from a Hostess doughnut in his mustache and Appalachian bluegrass on the AM radio, it soon occurs to him that he hasn't spent this long sitting on a house since his tour in narcotics. By the end of the day, in fact, he's damn proud of himself for being careful, patient and determined—just like any real detective.

Finally, only after two successive dayshifts in a Cavalier, when it's clear that there's no black car anywhere near the house, Brown picks the guy up for an interview. "Yeah," says his suspect. "They were sayin' that they gave you my name a few days back. I don't know why they did that, though."

Brown drove back to the homicide office, ready to chuck the case file into the nearest empty drawer. "Get me a murder in West Baltimore," he tells Worden. "I can't deal with these fucking white people anymore."

For his part, Worden has stayed with the case, but he has preserved a certain distance. Alongside the younger detective, he has cruised Highlandtown looking for a bar with anything resembling a German name. And he has also spent hours sitting with Brown on many of those same houses and parking lots, looking for that black mystery car. And yet there is a message to Worden's presence on this case, something that Brown understands instinctively.

"You want to go?" Brown asks him after three long hours of watching a garden apartment down in Marley Neck.

"It's your case," says Worden, masking the Socratic method with indifference. "What do you want to do?"

"We'll wait," says Brown.

Still, after a week they are no closer to a killer, and the Carol Ann Wright case remains an undetermined death, not even a murder. And both men know that without a fresh lead, their task is Herculean. Three days ago, a DMV printout arrived at the homicide unit with the names and addresses of the owners of 280Zs in central Maryland. Even if their best witnesses are right about that particular make of car, and even if their man happens to be the registered owner of record, the computer list is more than a hundred pages long.

On August 30, Worden inherits a true red ball, a fourteen-year-old kid shotgunned to death in the Northwest, killed without any apparent motive as he walked home from his job at a fast-food restaurant. Five days after that, Dave Brown and McLarney are working on the disappearance of a twenty-six-year-old west side woman who has not been seen for a week, though two dopers have been locked up for driving her car.

Fresh bodies. Fresh leads. From Brown's desk, you can listen close and hear a slow, grinding noise as the Carol Wright case slips out of gear.

THURSDAY, SEPTEMBER 15

The scene is a rowhouse basement, a dank, unfurnished place on East Preston Street, where an elderly white man is stretched across the floor in full rigor, covered by a few sheets of plastic tarp and a trio of die-cast, two-foot-tall Magi. Yessiree: the three wise men, those good souls who carry around myrrh and frankincense and visit blessed mangers on church lawns every Christmas. A nice, bizarre touch, thinks Rich Garvey. Someone blew a very big hole in this old man's head, stole his money, dragged the body downstairs and then threw a plastic wrap and three wise men over the corpse. A nativity scene, East Baltimore style.

The dead man is Henry Plumer, and it's immediately obvious to Garvey and Bob McAllister that the old man has encountered something very big—a .44 or .45 probably, and fired at point-blank range, too, judging from the powder burns. Plumer was in his late sixties and had for at least half his life been collecting for Littlepage's Furniture in the city, wandering around the ghetto all day long, calling in the monthly payments on furniture and appliances. It was mostly no-money-down credit stuff, which lures poor folk into paying $10 a week until their living room set ends up costing more than a college education, but old Mr. Plumer had been at it for so long that the people on his route all knew and liked him. He'd become something of a neighborhood institution in East Baltimore, riding around all day with that little collection book of his. Donald Kincaid actually knew the man, since his mother still lived in the 900 block of Collington, refusing to quit her east side home even as the neighborhood around her fell into ruin.

Garvey already knows all about Mr. Plumer, or at least he knows everything that was in a missing person's teletype sent out by county police yesterday, when the old man and his car disappeared into the wilds of Baltimore and his family began to panic. Garvey's already fairly certain that he knows who killed Mr. Plumer—knowledge that comes easily when the owner of the basement in question is a drug user with a long sheet.

From what he has gleaned thus far, an addict by the name of Jerry Jackson owns this two-story brick pile, was one of the last people to see a living Henry Plumer, and apparently left for his housecleaning job at Rosewood Hospital with Plumer's body still bleeding on his basement floor. As clues, these facts are decidedly unsubtle and suggest a certain lack of intellect on the part of the homeowner in question—a suggestion that is all but confirmed when the phone on the first floor suddenly begins ringing twenty minutes after the detectives' arrival. Garvey bounds up the stairs and picks up on the third ring.

"Hello?"

"Who's this?" asks the male caller.

"This is Detective Garvey from the homicide unit," he says. "Who's this?"

"This is Jerry," says the voice.

How considerate, thinks Garvey. A suspect who calls his own crime scene.

"Jerry," says Garvey, "how fast can you get over here?"

"About twenty minutes or so."

"I'll be waiting."

In his first statement on the matter at hand, Jerry Jackson doesn't even bother to ask what a homicide detective is doing at his house, doesn't think about denying anything or demonstrating shock and dismay. He hangs up the phone without ever expressing amazement or distress that a dead body is being examined in his basement. Nor does he express any immediate curiosity about why that body is there. Garvey hangs on until the phone line goes dead, delighted to be dealing with such an earnest, cooperative brain-dead.

"Hey Mac," says Garvey, hanging up the receiver and walking back to the top of the basement stairs. "That was Jerry calling."

"Oh really," says McAllister from the basement.

"Yeah. He's on his way over."

"That's nice," says McAllister, deadpan.

The detectives continue to work the crime scene. Two hours later, they stop waiting for Jerry Jackson, who, for all his seeming cooperation, has still not made an appearance. Late that night, with a county detective in tow, they drive out to Fullerton and break the news to the Plumer family, whereupon the elderly widow goes white and faints. By morning, she is dead of a heart attack, as much a homicide victim as her husband.

It's in the early morning hours that Jerry Jackson finally returns to the house on Preston Street, where he is greeted with some consternation by his own wife, a woman not at all pleased to be finding bodies in her basement. It was the wife who had located Henry Plumer and called police after hearing from friends in the neighborhood that the old bill collector was missing and had last been seen making his regular stop at the Jackson home. Rumors of the murder had been around the block a couple of times by then and a friend had urged Mrs. Jackson to check her basement carefully. The two got halfway down the stairs when they saw the shoes sticking out from under the tarp. The wife went no farther, but the friend managed to step forward and lift the plastic enough to convince herself that it was Mr. Plumer and that he'd definitely looked better. At that point, Jerry Jackson's wife saw where things were going; without waiting for her husband to return from work, she went to the phone and dialed 911.

And so, by the time Jerry Jackson returns home and confers with his wife, it's abundantly clear—even to him—that whatever the plan for this murder was, it definitely isn't working. He does not, however, disappear into the bowels of East Baltimore. Nor does he try to scrape together some cash for a bus ticket to Carolina. No, sir. For his last act as a free man, Jerry Jackson elects to call the homicide unit and ask for Rich Garvey. He'd like to talk about the body in his basement. Perhaps, he offers, he could be of some help to the investigation.

But when Jackson arrives in the large interrogation room, his pupils are the size of purely theoretical particles. Cocaine, thinks Garvey, but he decides his suspect may just be able to manage a few intelligible sentences. After negotiating the Miranda, the detectives' first question is the obvious one, of course.

"Ah, Jerry," asks Garvey, scratching the top of his head in feigned confusion, "why was Mr. Plumer's body in your house?"

Quietly, almost casually, Jackson tells the detectives that he made his monthly payment to Mr. Plumer yesterday afternoon; then the old man took the money and drove away.

"And I don't know nothing about no murder," he continues, his voice breaking, "until I called my mother's house from work and was told THAT THERE'S A MOTHERFUCKING BODY IN MY BASEMENT!"

The first half of the sentence is tense but quiet, but the last part is a wild rant, a shout that pierces the interrogation room doors and can be heard clear down at the other end of the sixth-floor hall.

Seated on either side of the suspect, the detectives look at each other for a moment, then down at the table. Garvey is biting his lip.

"Could, ah, you excuse us for just a moment," says McAllister, addressing the suspect as if he were Emily Post and the man had just used the wrong salad fork. "We just need to discuss something and we'll be right back with you in just a second, okay?"

Jackson nods, twitching.

The two detectives walk silently out of the room and close the metal door behind them. They manage to make it to the annex office before they both double over, convulsed by the force of suppressed laughter.

"THERE'S A BODY IN MY BASEMENT!" shouts Garvey, shaking his partner's shoulders.

"Not just a body," says McAllister, laughing. "A *motherfucking* body."

"THERE'S A MOTHERFUCKING BODY IN MY BASEMENT!" shouts Garvey again. "THERE'S A MADMAN ON THE LOOSE!"

McAllister shakes his head, still laughing. "Don't you just hate that?

You leave the house, you go to work, call your mom, and she tells you there's a body in your basement . . ."

Garvey grips a desk in the annex office with both hands, trying to regain his composure.

"It was all I could do not to laugh in his face," he tells McAllister. "God."

"You don't think he's high or anything like that," says McAllister dryly.

"Him? No way. He's a little high-strung. That's all it is."

"Seriously, should we even bother with a statement?"

The question is a legal one. Any statement taken now could be mitigated by the fact that Jerry Jackson is somewhat compromised, chemically speaking.

"What the hell?" says Garvey. "Let's go back in. We've got to charge him. We either talk to him now or not at all . . ."

McAllister nods, then leads the way toward the interrogation room. From outside the wire mesh window, the two detectives can see Jerry Jackson dancing a mad samba in his chair. Garvey begins laughing again.

"Wait a sec," he tells McAllister.

Garvey finds his poker face, then loses it, then finds it again. "This motherfucker is killing me."

McAllister grips the door handle, fighting hard for his own composure. "Ready?" he asks.

"Okay."

The two detectives return to the room and their seats. Jackson waits for another question but is instead treated to a long monologue by McAllister in which it is explained that he has no reason to be upset or angry at the existing circumstances. None at all. After all, they're just asking questions and he's just answering questions, right?

"We're not hurting you, are we?"

No, agrees the suspect.

"And we're not treating you badly, are we?"

No, agrees the suspect.

"You're being treated fairly, right?"

Yes, agrees the suspect.

"Okay then, Jerry. Why don't you tell us—calmly—why don't you calmly tell us why there was this body in your basement?"

Not that it matters what he says, because by daylight Garvey, McAllister and Roger Nolan have also obtained a complete statement from Jackson's wife. They've also interviewed the nephew who helped Jerry Jackson plan the robbery and then ditch Plumer's car. They've even interviewed the neighborhood dealer from whom Jackson bought $200 worth of cocaine, using the money he took off the old man's body. All in all, the Preston Street call is definitely not what comes to mind when a detective is asked to think of the perfect murder. Presumably, Jackson planned to show up for work so as not to arouse suspicion, then remove the body from his basement and dump it somewhere else in the early morning hours. That's assuming the man had any plan at all beyond robbing and killing a man in his living room for enough money to stay high all day.

Just before the morning shift change, Garvey is at his desk in the main office, battling the paperwork to a draw and listening to Nolan philosophize on just what it was that cracked this case. When we went back out and picked up the dealer who sold to Jackson, says Nolan, that's when we really cracked it wide open.

At which point Garvey and McAllister both drop their pens and look at their sergeant as if he's just stepped off the last Greyhound from Mars.

"Uh, Rog," says McAllister, "what cracked this case was the fact that the killer left the dead guy in his house."

"Well, yeah," says Nolan, laughing but a little disappointed. "That too."

So Rich Garvey's Perfect Year marches ever onward, a divine crusade seemingly impervious to the touch of reality, a campaign unfettered by the rules of homicide that somehow manage to afflict every other detective. Garvey is getting witnesses, he's getting fingerprint hits, he's getting the license tags off getaway cars. You do a murder in Baltimore when Rich Garvey's working and you may as well have a lawyer meet you at the district lockup an hour later.

Not long after Jerry Jackson returns to earth and a city jail tier, Garvey again picks up a telephone extension and writes down an East Baltimore address. This time it is the worst kind of call a murder police can get. Garvey is so certain of unanimity on this opinion that he actually puts down the phone and asks the other detectives in the office to name the call they least like to handle. McAllister and Kincaid need about a half second to say "arson."

For a homicide detective, an arson murder is a special type of torture because the police department is essentially stuck with whatever the fire department's investigator says is arson. To this day, Donald Kincaid is still carrying an open murder for a fatal fire that almost certainly began with nothing more sinister than an electrical short. At the scene, Kincaid could see the burn pattern running up the rowhouse wall where the wiring was, but some goof from FIB insisted on calling it arson. So what was he going to do then, arrest the goddamn fuse box? Not only that, but when a detective gets a genuine arson murder in front of a jury, he can never convince them that the fire wasn't an accident, not without a six-pack of witnesses, at least. Even if there's a pour pattern from gasoline or some other accelerant, a good lawyer can suggest that someone spilled the stuff by mistake and then accidentally dropped a cigarette. Juries like dead people who have bulletholes or steak knives attached to them; anything less is not convincing.

Knowing all this, Garvey and McAllister once again steer an unmarked car to a crime scene with fear and loathing in their hearts. It's a two-story dump on North Bond Street and, of course, there are no witnesses—just a bunch of burned furniture and one crispy critter in the middle room. Some smokehound, an old guy, maybe sixty.

The poor bastard is lying there like a piece of chicken that someone forgot to turn over, and the FIB investigator is showing Garvey a dark splotch on the other side of the room and calling it a textbook example of a pour pattern. Sure enough, when they clear all the soot away, the splotch really does look darker than the surrounding area. So Garvey has a dead guy and a pour pattern and some drunk woman who jumped out the rear window when the fire started and is now up at Union Memorial breathing from an oxygen tank. From the fire investigator, the detectives learn that the woman is supposedly the dead guy's girlfriend.

Having satisfied themselves that North Bond Street is indeed their worst nightmare come true, Garvey and McAllister drive to the hospital with the understanding that this blessed year of his has finally reached its terminus. They walk into the Union Memorial ER and greet two detectives from the arson squad who are standing out at the nurses station like a pair of bookends, telling them the injured woman's story is all bullshit. She's got the fire starting by accident in an ashtray or some nonsense like that.

The woman told the arson guys that much while she was being treated in the ER, but now she can't be interviewed further because she inhaled a lot of smoke and talking is a problem. Garvey may have his arsonist, but there's absolutely no way to prove the case. Given that conflict, the idea of getting an assistant medical examiner to pend the case for a little while—like maybe a decade—becomes more and more appealing in the minds of both detectives. At the following morning's autopsy, Garvey manages to accomplish this feat, whereupon he and McAllister return to the office with the sincere hope that if they just click their heels three times, the entire case will go away.

Given recent events, such thoughts in the mind of Rich Garvey can only suggest a certain lack of faith, a certain disregard for his own destiny. Because two weeks later, the woman at Union Memorial succumbs to smoke inhalation and related injuries; two days after that, Garvey pays a second visit to Penn Street and assures the good doctors that they can go ahead and rule the case a homicide. That done, he can immediately show the case as cleared due to the rather timely death of his solitary suspect. A good detective, after all, is never too proud to take a paper clearance.

The arson case makes it ten out of ten since February and the Lena Lucas murder. Drug murders, neighborhood disputes, street robberies, unprosecutable arson deaths—it matters not to Rich Garvey, the luckiest sonofabitch on D'Addario's shift of fifteen. Apparently the Perfect Year, like any force of nature, cannot be denied.

Saturday, October 1

Up and down the stoops he goes, a homicide detective banging on North Durham Street doors in search of a little cooperation, a little civic responsibility.

"Didn't see it," says the young girl at 1615.

"I heard a loud bang," says the man at 1617.

No answer at 1619.

"Lord," says the woman at 1621, "I don't know nothin' 'bout it."

Tom Pellegrini presses a few additional questions on these people, trying hard to get himself interested in this case, to find something that might make a detective care about the bloodstain in the center of the 1600 block.

"Were you home when it happened?" he asks another girl, at the door of 1616.

"I'm not sure."

Not sure. How can you not be sure? Theodore Johnson was hit by a shotgun blast fired at point-blank range, blown apart in the center of a narrow rowhouse street. The sound itself had to be audible all the way up to North Avenue.

"You don't know if you were home?"

"I might have been."

So much for the door-to-door canvass. Not that Pellegrini can blame the neighborhood for its reluctance to volunteer information. Word is out that the dead man crossed a local dealer on a drug debt and the dealer has just proven to everyone within earshot that he's a man to be reckoned with. The people behind these doors have got to live on Durham Street; Pellegrini is no more than an occasional tourist.

With nothing on the horizon even remotely resembling a witness, Pellegrini has a body on the way to Penn Street and a bloodstain on dirty asphalt. He's got a spent shotgun shell ejected by the shooter in the alley around the corner. He's got a street so dark that the emergency vehicle unit has been called to light up his scene for the photographs. An hour or so later, Pellegrini will have the sister of his victim sitting in Jay Landsman's office, feeding him a bit of rumor about some people that may or may not have had something to do with the shooting. He will have a headache, too.

Theodore Johnson joins Stevie Braxton and Barney Erely on the white rectangle in the coffee room. Braxton, the kid with a long sheet found stabbed up off Pennsylvania Avenue. Erely, the homeless man bludgeoned to death on Clay Street. Red names riding the board with Pellegrini's initial near them, casualties in the year-long campaign to close the Latonya Wallace murder. It's triage, plain and simple, but Pellegrini can live with that. After all, he's got an eleven-year-old raped and murdered, and neither Theodore Johnson nor a drug debt that has now been paid has any real weight when hung in the balance. Tonight's dead man will get one or two shakes from the homicide unit, one or two go-rounds in the interrogation rooms with a few reluctant witnesses. But then the primary investigator will set the file aside.

Months later, Pellegrini will feel some guilt about this, some concern about the number of cases sacrificed for the sake of one child. With much the same sort of self-recrimination that governs his thoughts on the Latonya Wallace murder, Pellegrini will wonder whether he should have pressed harder on that kid in the Western District lockup back in January, the one who claimed to know one of the shooters from Gold and Etting. He'll wonder about whether he should have gone harder at Braxton's girlfriend, who didn't seem all that upset about the murder. And he'll wonder, too, about the rumors that Theodore Johnson's sister is now feeding him—information that will never be fully checked.

True, he could dump this case on the secondary. Vernon Holley handled the scene with him and he would probably understand if Pellegrini ducked the call to stay focused on Latonya Wallace. Still, Holley is new to the squad, a veteran black detective transferred from the robbery unit to replace Fred Ceruti. He'd been out on one murder with Rick Requer a couple of weeks ago, but that wasn't enough to qualify as an orientation, even for an investigator as experienced as Holley. And the squad was a man short to begin with: Dick Fahlteich had voluntarily transferred to sex offense after six years in homicide. The body count had finally got to Fahlteich, a talented detective who nonetheless was handling fewer calls each year, working at a pace that others in Landsman's squad were quick to compare to Harry Edgerton's. The workload and the hours—coupled with a gnawing aggravation about his being passed over several times on the sergeant's lists—had at last pushed Fahlteich down to the other end of the sixth-floor hallway at about the same time that Ceruti traveled the same route. At least with Fahlteich it was a matter of choice.

No, Pellegrini reasons, with the squad down to three regulars and a fresh transfer, the Theodore Johnson case is his to eat. At the very least, he owes it to Holley to stay with the thing for a few days. A graphic display of job-related burnout isn't exactly the best lesson to be teaching a new man.

Bravely, Pellegrini fights his own impulses, doing a competent crime scene out on Durham Street, then canvassing the entire block for witnesses that he knows in his heart will never come forward. Holley peels off early, heading back to the homicide office to begin interviewing family members and a couple of kids at the scene who were sent downtown only because they were out there acting like squirrels when the first uniforms arrived.

The sudden role reversal—with Pellegrini now the tired veteran, breaking in the latest prodigy—is accepted without comment by everyone else in Landsman's squad. Nine months of Latonya Wallace has changed Pellegrini: His metamorphosis from fresh-scrubbed recruit to battered trench rat is complete. To say that he can look at Holley and see himself a couple years ago goes too far: Holley already had the experience of CID robbery behind him; Pellegrini had come to homicide with no investigative background whatsoever. Still, Holley is working this Durham Street case as if it mattered, as if it were the only murder in the history of the world. He is fresh. He is confident. He makes Pellegrini feel one hundred years old.

The two detectives chase the murder on Durham Street through into late morning, gathering the information from the sister, then trying to check her story against that provided by a former police officer who has family living in the block. His family will not come forward, but the ex-cop, though fired from the force twenty years ago in a corruption case, has enough residual instinct to call in with the name of a possible participant. Pellegrini and Holley find the kid that same morning, go at him in the large box for several hours and emerge with little to show for the effort. Then, slowly, after a few more laps around the case file, Holley accepts the unspoken verdict of his tutor. He drifts away, looking for better pickings with Gary Dunnigan and Requer.

He finds them, too, hooking up with Requer on a domestic from Bruce Street, a true tragedy in which a young girl has been bludgeoned to death by her cokehead of a boyfriend and her orphaned infant is left crying on a policewoman's shoulder, wailing at the world as the officer's hand-held radio squawks out citywide dispatch calls. Holley follows that with another domestic from Cherry Hill that he works to completion with Dunnigan. Both cases are dunkers and both bring a certain confidence. By December, Holley will be handling calls as a primary.

For Pellegrini, however, the milestones marked by his squad mean little. Ceruti's fall from grace, Fahlteich's departure, Holley's education—they are scenes from a play in which Pellegrini has no real part. Time stands still for one detective, leaving him alone on a stage of his own, trapped there by the same few props and the same few lines from the same sad scene.

Three weeks ago, Pellegrini and Landsman hit the Fish Man's Whitelock Street apartment a second time, working through a search warrant that was written more for Pellegrini's peace of mind than anything else. Months had passed and the chance of recovering any additional evidence from the apartment was minimal. Yet Pelligrini, now fixated on the store owner as his best suspect, was convinced that in their haste to hit the three-story shithouse on Newington back in February, they had blown off the earlier searches on Whitelock. In particular, Pellegrini vaguely remembered seeing a remnant of red carpeting in the Fish Man's living room during the February raid; months later, he thought of the hairs and fibers taken from the young girl's body at the morgue and recalled that one of those fibers was red cloth.

Red carpet, red fiber: Pellegrini suddenly had another reason to kick himself. For Pellegrini, the contents of file H88021 had become nothing less than an ever-changing landscape in which every tree, rock and bush seems to be moving. And it was no use explaining to him that this could happen to any detective on any case—this pit-of-the-stomach feeling that everything was being missed, that evidence was disappearing faster than an investigator could perceive it. Every detective in the unit had lived through the sensation of seeing something at a crime scene or during a search warrant and then looking twice to see that it was no longer there. Hell, maybe it never was there. Or maybe it's still there, but now you've lost the ability to see it.

It was the stuff from which the Nightmare was made, the Nightmare being that recurring dream that occasionally ruins the sleep of every good detective. In the throes of the Nightmare, you are moving through the familiar confines of a rowhouse—you've got a warrant, perhaps, or maybe it's just a plain-view search—and from the corner of your eye you glimpse something. What the hell is it? Something important, you know that. Something you need. A blood spatter. A shell casing. A child's star-shaped earring. You can't say for sure, but with every fiber of your being you understand that it's your case lying there. Yet you look away for a moment, and when you look back again, it's gone. It's an empty place in your subconscious, a lost opportunity that mocks you. The Nightmare scares the hell out of young detectives; some of them even live the dream at their first crime scenes, convinced that the entire case is evaporating into the ether. As for the veterans, the Nightmare just pisses them off. They've gone through it enough not to believe every voice that speaks from the back of the mind.

And yet on this case the Nightmare owns Pellegrini. It ordered him to write the second warrant for the Fish Man's apartment, it demanded that he collect enough probable cause to get back inside a door that had been opened to him once before. Not surprisingly, the September raid left the Fish Man as bored and indifferent as its predecessor. Nor did it produce a red cloth carpet fiber: Pellegrini found the remnant he remembered on the bedroom floor, but it proved to be plastic, an outdoor Astro-Turf carpet. Nor did a small blue pin earring found in a corner of the living room mean anything to the investigation. Contacted by detectives a few days later, Latonya Wallace's family members explained that they never recalled the young girl wearing a mixed set of earrings. If she had a star-shaped pin in one lobe, it was safe to assume that a star-shaped pin was missing from the other. To be sure, Pellegrini borrowed a Cavalier and drove the blue pin earring up to the little girl's mother; she seemed a little surprised that the case was still being worked after seven months, but confirmed that the blue earring did not belong to her daughter.

Around every corner of the maze, a fresh corridor began. A week after the second search of Whitelock Street, Pellegrini found himself tangled in a prolonged encounter with an auto thief arrested by Baltimore County police back in July. A disturbed young man with a history of mental illness, the thief had attempted suicide at the county detention center on three separate occasions, then blurted out to a county officer that he knew who had committed two murders in the city. One was a drug killing at a Northwest Baltimore bar. The other involved the death of a little girl in Reservoir Hill.

Howard Corbin went out to the county for the initial interview and came back with a story about a chance encounter in the alley behind the 800 block of Newington, where the auto thief said he had been snorting cocaine with his cousin. A little girl happened by the alley and the auto thief heard his cousin say something to the child. The girl—who carried a bookbag and wore her hair braided—said something back, and it seemed to the auto thief that they knew each other. But when his cousin jumped up and grabbed the girl, the auto thief became frightened and fled. Shown a picture of Latonya Wallace, the young man began crying.

Slowly, the scenario took on real life. The auto thief did indeed have a cousin at 820 Newington and the cousin did indeed have a substantial record, though nothing on it screamed sex offender. Still, Corbin was impressed that the young man had apparently remembered that the girl had her hair up in braids and was carrying a satchel. Those details had been released to the public early in the investigation, of course, but they helped establish some credibility for the thief's story.

Pellegrini and Corbin dutifully rechecked the vacant rowhouses in the 800 block of Newington and then towed a derelict Chevy Nova from the rear of an occupied house in that same block. The car had once belonged to the thief's cousin, and the thief claimed that his relative routinely kept a buck knife and a switchblade in the trunk of the car. That car and another vehicle belonging to the cousin's sister were both processed by lab techs at headquarters with negative results. Likewise, the auto thief was brought downtown for lengthy interviews.

Eventually, as facts began to get in his way, the thief's story changed. He suddenly remembered, for instance, that his cousin had at one point opened the trunk of his sister's car and shown him a zippered plastic bag. And then his cousin opened the zipper to reveal the face of the little girl. And then . . .

The auto thief was a mental case, no question about it. But his tale had been constructed with just enough detail to require a full investigation. The cousin would have to be confronted, and the story would have to be corroborated or knocked down. Eventually, the auto thief would have to be polygraphed.

Beyond that piece of business, Pellegrini also had another manila file on his desk with the name of a Park Avenue man on the heading—a raw mix of fact and rumor regarding a potential suspect known to have behaved strangely in recent months and on one occasion to have exposed himself to a schoolgirl. There were a few rape reports from the Central, too, along with notes from another five or six interviews with friends and former friends of the Fish Man.

All of that waits for Pellegrini as he pauses to work the shotgun murder of Theodore Johnson on Durham Street. And when that pause is over, he continues to wonder whether he should have kept working the drug killing rather than returning to obsess over Latonya Wallace. He tells himself that if he works the Durham Street murder hard, it might just go down. On the other hand, if he keeps on the dead little girl, there could be no telling when the case might break.

To every other detective on the shift, this is the worst kind of optimism. Latonya Wallace is history; Theodore Johnson is fresh. And in the minds of most of his colleagues, Pellegrini has gone over the hill on this one. Repeat warrants on a suspect's apartment, prolonged background investigations, protracted statements from suicidal shitbirds—all of it is understandable of a young detective, they concede. Hell, with a dead little girl it may even be required, in a way. But, they tell each other, let's not kid ourselves: Tom Pellegrini has lost it.

Then, a week after the murder of Theodore Johnson, this widely held opinion undergoes a sudden revision when a fresh lab report arrives on Pellegrini's desk and its contents become known to the shift.

The author of the report: Van Gelder in the trace section. The subject: black smudge marks on the dead girl's pants. The verdict: tar and soot with burned wood chips mixed in. Fire debris, plain and simple.

Taking its own sweet time, the trace lab has finally compared the black smudges on Latonya Wallace's pants to the samples that Pellegrini lifted from the Fish Man's burned-out store two months earlier. The report declares the two samples to be consistent, if not identical.

What can we say? Pellegrini asks, pressing the lab people. Is it similar or is it exactly the same? Can we say with any certainty that she was in that Whitelock Street store?

Van Gelder and the others in the trace section are equivocal. The samples can be sent to the Alcohol, Tobacco and Firearms lab in Rockville—one of the best in the country—and perhaps they can do more. But generally speaking, Van Gelder explains, the smudges on the pants and the samples from the store have the same class characteristics. They are very similar and yes, they could have come from the debris in that store. On the other hand, they could also have come from another fire scene in which the debris had a similar chemical composition.

A week after the cold depression of Durham Street, Pellegrini finds himself torn between elation and despair. Nine months into the Latonya Wallace investigation, the new lab report provides the first piece of substantive evidence in the file and the only piece of physical evidence to implicate the Fish Man. But if the lab analysts are willing to say only that the two samples are very similar, then that evidence still falls within the realm of reasonable doubt. It is a beginning, but unless the ATF lab can be more definitive, it is nothing more.

A few days after the lab report arrives on his desk, Pellegrini asks the captain to authorize a mainframe computer run of incident reports dating from January 1, 1978, to February 2, 1988. The information sought is the address for every fire or arson report in the area of Reservoir Hill bounded by North Avenue, Park Avenue, Druid Park Lake Drive and Madison Avenue.

The theory is simple enough: If the lab can't say for certain that those smudges come from Whitelock Street, then perhaps a detective, working backward, can prove that they couldn't have come from anywhere else.

The detective obsessed with the Latonya Wallace case may seem lost to everyone else in homicide, but to Pellegrini himself, the chaos of H88021 is slowly becoming order. After eight months, the file has fresh evidence, a viable suspect, a plausible theory.

Best of all, it has some direction.

FRIDAY, OCTOBER 7

"Well," says McLarney, admiring the board, "Worden's back." And back in black.

Three straight nights of midnight shift in late September brought three straight murders for the Big Man and Rick James. Two are down, and the chalkboard on the other side of the coffee room is adorned with the evidence of progress on the third case: "Any calls about a prostitute named Lenore who works Pennsylvania Avenue, call Worden or James at home re H88160."

Lenore, the mystery whore. By all accounts, she is the lone witness to the fatal stabbing of her ex-boyfriend, who was last seen arguing with Lenore's current beau in the 2200 block of the Avenue before falling to the ground with an unsightly hole in his upper right chest. Now, two weeks later, the current boyfriend is conveniently dead from cancer, and therefore, if the elusive businesswoman will be so kind as to come downtown and make a truthful statement, case number three will also be black. To that end, McLarney's squad has spent the last two weeks terrorizing the Avenue hookers, riding up to question every new face and scare away customers. It's gotten so bad that the girls are waving them off even as they open the car doors.

"I ain't Lenore," one shouted to Worden a week ago, even before the detective had a chance to speak.

"I know that, hon. But have you seen her?"

"She's not out tonight."

"Well, tell her if she'll just come in and talk to us, we'll stop bothering you and her both. Will you do that for us?"

"If I see her, I'll tell her."

"Thank you, dear."

Straight police work, the kind that keeps you out in the city streets. No oily politicians, no treacherous bosses, no scared young cops saying they don't know anything about the dead kid in the alley. The street gives you nothing worse than lying, thieving criminals and, hey, Worden has no complaints with that. It's their job. And his, too.

The return to routine has allowed Worden a measure of satisfaction, not that the last three cases were exactly brimming with challenge and complexity. The first was pretty much an accidental: three teenage drug dealers in a west side rowhouse, marveling over their host's new Saturday Night Special when it goes off with the barrel pointed at the youngest kid's chest. The second was a Highlandtown beating, a manslaughter with a billy boy laid out in an alley behind Lakewood Avenue, dead after he fell back from a punch and hit his head on the cement. The third was the Pennsylvania Avenue stabbing, still waiting for Miss Lenore's reappearance.

No, it wasn't the quality of the cases that announced Worden's return so much as the volume. Whether or not the case went down, the quality was always there with the Big Man; Monroe Street, in fact, was probably his best work in a long while. But a year ago, Worden had been nothing less than a machine, and McLarney remembered that time like an athlete remembers a championship season. Back then, the squad pretty much operated on the same principle as that cereal commercial: Give it to Worden. He'll eat anything. Go ahead, give him this one, give him another, and then put him on the file that Dave Brown and Waltemeyer are still struggling with. See? He likes it.

This year has been very different. Monroe Street, the Larry Young business, the open murders from March and April—the year had unfolded as an agonizing exercise in frustration, and by summer there was nothing to suggest that Worden's losing streak had an end.

In late August and early September, the cold, hard slap of reality was a fourteen-year-old shotgun victim by the name of Craig Rideout, stretched out in the early morning light on a Pimlico lawn, dead for hours before anyone found the body or called a cop. Worden labored for days to trace the shooting back to a crew doing shotgun robberies in the Northwest using a red Mazda. Talking to informants in his old district and checking other shotgun robbery reports eventually turned up one badass in particular, a non-taxpayer with a Cherry Hill address and a sheet that included arrests for armed robbery. Not only did Worden tie the kid to a red Mazda that had been seen all over the Northwest, but he learned that the boy was spending a lot of time with people around lower Park Heights near the murder scene.

For a couple of nights, Worden sat on the kid's house, waiting for anything that looked like a robbery crew to assemble near that Mazda. With no physical evidence, Worden could only hope that his man would go back out on the street with the shotgun to try another robbery. But then an inexplicable act by another detective blew the case apart: Two weeks after the Rideout murder, Worden came into work on a four-to-twelve shift and learned that Dave Hollingsworth, the detective on Stanton's shift handling another shotgun murder in the Northwest, had gone out to Cherry Hill and interviewed his suspect. Immediately the shotgun robberies in the Northwest came to an abrupt halt. No more red Mazdas, no more sightings of his suspect up around Park Heights.

Only several months later would Worden hear from his best suspect once more. On that occasion, the boy from Cherry Hill is on the other end of a 24-hour report. On that occasion, he's the body on the pavement, shot down by persons unknown on a street off the Martin Luther King Boulevard. The Rideout murder stayed red, and in Worden's mind it became a metaphor. Like everything else he touched, it was good police work with a bad ending, and like everything else in his year, it was unresolved.

But the Rideout case was only one jab in a left-right combination. In mid-September, the sucker punch landed in a crowded Central District courtroom, where state senator Larry Young went to trial for his well-publicized misdemeanor.

Trial is perhaps the wrong word for what actually happened. It was more of a spectacle, really, a public display by prosecutors and detectives who had no real interest in seeing the case pursued aggressively. Instead, Tim Doory of the state's attorney's office tried the case personally and with just enough vigor to lose by a judge's verdict. In laying out the scenario by which the senator had falsely reported his own abduction, Doory made a point of not calling the politician's aide as a witness, intentionally depriving the state's case of any motive for the false report and thereby avoiding any on-the-stand revelations about the senator's private life.

It was a gracious, honorable act and one that Worden understood and accepted. What he didn't accept was that this public demonstration was even necessary; it infuriated him that the prosecutors' office and police department were so eager to appear earnest in their pursuit of public misdeed that Larry Young had to be charged and tried and acquitted of a meaningless stupidity. Even so, when it came to his testimony, Worden fell on his sword with seeming indifference. Asked by the senator's attorney about the key conversation in which Young admitted that no crime had occurred, the detective didn't hesitate to punch the biggest possible hole in the prosecution's case.

"So let me understand, detective, you told the senator that he would not be charged if he admitted to you that no crime had occurred?"

"I told him he would not be charged by me."

"But he has been charged."

"Not by me."

Worden then acknowledged that the senator only admitted to the false report after being told that no investigation would proceed if he did just that. Worden also accurately described the conclusion of his conversation with Young, in which the senator declared that no crime had occurred and that he would look into the matter privately.

The senator's attorney finished his cross-examination with a tight smile of satisfaction. "Thank you, Detective Worden."

Thank you, indeed. With the senator's admission portrayed as a coerced act and with the prosecutor reluctant to pursue the motive behind the false report, the District Court judge needed little time to arrive at the expected verdict.

Leaving the courtroom, Larry Young approached Donald Worden and offered his hand. "Thank you for not lying," the senator said.

Worden looked up, surprised. "Why would I lie?"

In context, it was an extraordinary insult. After all, why would a detective lie? Why would he perjure himself? Why would he risk his own integrity, not to mention his job and his pension, to win a case like this? To nail some politician's pelt to a wall? To earn the undying respect of Larry Young's political enemies?

Like every cop, Worden had his cynical streak, but he wasn't really much of a stoic. Open murders and open deceit—the two operant themes of this godforsaken year—still seemed to bother him more than many younger detectives. It didn't often show, but there had always been a core of insistent anger inside Worden, a quiet rebellion against the inertia and politics of his own police department. Rarely were those emotions allowed to surface; instead, they festered deep inside, feeding his elevated and insubordinate hypertension. Only once, in fact, did Worden vent his rage during the Larry Young business, and that was a brief exchange in the coffee room, when Rick James tried to lighten his partner's mood.

"Hey, it's out of your hands," said James. "What the fuck are you gonna do?"

"I'll tell you what I'm ready to do," growled Worden. "I'm ready to stick my gun inside somebody's mouth, and that somebody is inside this headquarters building."

James left it alone after that. What, after all, remained to be said?

At the same time, Terry McLarney went into a clinical depression after hearing a rumor that Worden had expressed interest in an open posting for an investigator with the medical examiner's office. Worden's gone, he told others in the squad. We're losing him to this fucked-up year of his.

"Right now he just looks tired," McLarney told others in the squad. "I've never seen Donald looking so tired."

McLarney held tight to a slim thread of hope: Get Worden back out on the street with new murders. Good murders, good calls. McLarney believed that if anything could wipe the slate clean for a guy like Worden, it would be real police work.

But Monroe Street had been real police work; the Rideout case, too. They had just ended poorly. Even Worden himself wasn't really sure what was wrong, and he had no idea where this tunnel was taking him, or whether it even had a light at its end. The best that could be said was that Donald Worden had gotten used to traveling in the dark.

Then, suddenly, a little light began to show. Late September brought that three-for-a-quarter performance on the midnight shift, when Worden worked every body that fell within his field of vision. And one week after those clearances he picked up yet another whodunit on daywork. The case was a loser: a nude woman found carved up behind an elementary school on Greenspring Avenue, discovered by the post officer a good twelve hours after the murder. No identification, no match to any missing persons report.

The beauty of Worden's performance on that case would not come with its solution, although incredibly, he would come up with a suspect after staying with the file for more than a year. The beauty was that he refused to allow this woman to remain a Jane Doe—"a member of the deer family," as he liked to put it—to be buried for $200 by the state without the knowledge of friends or family.

For six days Worden was out in the street, looking for a name. The television stations and newspapers wouldn't run a photograph of the woman's face: she was too obviously dead. Her fingerprints didn't match up with anything in either the local computer or the federal data base available to the FBI. And though the body looked pretty clean—an indication that the woman had been living somewhere—no one ever came into a police district to say that their mother or sister or daughter had not come home. Worden checked the group home for homeless women on nearby Cottage Avenue. He checked with the detox and drug treatment centers, because the victim's liver looked a little gray at autopsy. He canvassed the streets around the elementary school and along the nearest city bus route.

The break had come last night, when he paraded the photograph through every bar and carryout in Pimlico. Finally someone at the Preakness Bar remembered that the dead woman had a boyfriend named Leon Sykes who used to live over on Moreland Avenue. That address was vacant, but a neighbor told him to try 1710 Bentalou. There, a young girl listened to Worden's story and took him to 1802 Longwood, where Leon Sykes looked at the photo and identified the dead woman as Barbara.

"What's her last name?"

"I never knew."

But Leon remembered where the dead woman's daughter lived. And thus, by pure police work, did Jane Doe—a black female, late twenties—become Barbara Womble, thirty-nine years, of 1633 Moreland Avenue.

Those six circuitous days and nights in Pimlico left no one with any doubt: Worden was back, having outlasted his worst year.

The Big Man's triumphant return was also marked by his renewed and unceasing torment of Dave Brown, whose abandonment of the Carol Wright case had not exactly gone unnoticed by the older detective. For at least a part of September, Brown's excuse was the Nina Perry investigation, which began when a couple of dopers were arrested in the car of a woman reported missing from her Stricker Street rowhouse a week earlier. Working with McLarney, Brown put that case together in fine fashion, pressuring one of the suspects to confess fully to the murder and then lead detectives to the victim's badly decomposed remains, which he had dumped in a Carroll County backwoods.

Worden watched the Nina Perry case unfold and thought that maybe, just maybe, a detective lurked somewhere within David John Brown. The Perry case was fine work, the kind that teaches a cop something about his craft. But Worden's generosity went no further.

"Clayvon Jones and Carol Wright," Worden declared in late September. "Let's see him do something with one of those."

But Clayvon Jones would not be the true test, not after Eddie Brown came strutting into the coffee room four days ago with a letter from the Baltimore City Jail in his right hand.

"Speak to yo' daddy," said the older detective, dropping the letter onto the desk with a flourish. Dave Brown read about three lines before turning in prayer to the green bulkhead wall.

"Thank you, Jesus. Thank you, Jesus. Thank you, Jesus. Thank you. Thank you. Thank you."

"Do I take care of you?" asked Eddie Brown.

"You do. You mah daddy."

The letter had arrived in the admin office that afternoon, a hastily scrawled missive from a prisoner who had witnessed the murder of Clayvon Jones in that east side courtyard back in June. Three months later, this witness needed to barter out from beneath a drug charge. Addressed to the homicide unit, his letter included details about the crime scene that only a bona fide witness could know.

No, the Clayvon Jones killing would not be much of an education. In Worden's considered opinion, its easy solution became simply another laurel beneath the weight of Brown's ass. That left Carol Wright, the woman run down on the South Baltimore parking lot. For a few weeks, Brown had at least talked about picking up the Carol Wright file again and sorting through the old leads. But as far as the board was concerned, the Carol Wright case still wasn't a murder and therefore it didn't exist.

These days, he wasn't even mentioning the case and, as Brown's sergeant, McLarney wasn't making much of a stink about it either. Indeed, with Nina Perry and Clayvon Jones both safely in the black, McLarney had a new appreciation for Dave Brown's talents.

In McLarney's mind, the Perry case in particular counted for a lot. Brown had worked hard and a tough case involving a genuine victim had gone down. That arrest had elevated Brown to hero-of-the-week status, and he was therefore entitled to a beer or two at Kavanaugh's with his loving and devoted sergeant. In fact, McLarney was so pleased with the Perry case that he stayed with Brown through its aftermath, sharing the remaining paperwork and evidentiary details. He only balked when it came time to pick up the victim's maggot-infested clothing at the ME's office.

"Fuck this, Dave. I'll give you a hand with this tomorrow," McLarney said after getting a quick whiff of the stench. "Let's come back for this stuff in the morning."

Dave Brown readily agreed and drove back to headquarters a contented man, at least until he realized McLarney wasn't scheduled to work the next day.

"Wait a second," he said, parking the Cavalier in the garage. "You're off tomorrow."

McLarney giggled.

"You little Irish potatohead."

"Potatohead?"

"You did me, you goddamn mick." That was the new and improved Dave Brown talking, a far cry from the detective who had penned that please-keep-me-in-homicide missive the month before. A man has to feel fairly secure before he's willing to call his immediate supervisor an Irish potatohead, even in the casual environment of a homicide office. And of course McLarney loved it. Sitting at an admin office typewriter that same evening, he immortalized the deed in a memo to the lieutenant:

To: Lt. Gary D'Addario, Homicide unit
From: Sgt. Terry McLarney, Homicide unit
Subject: Ethnic/Slurs Comments made by Det. David John Brown

Sir:

It is with sorrow and disappointment that I call to your attention the flagrant and wanton infliction of emotional distress which was wrought upon this supervisor on this date. It is something which I have never faced in this enlightened department, and hoped that I never would. However, you should know that on this date Det. David John Brown twice made vicious verbal attacks on my ancestry, once referring to me as "a little Irish potato head" and later calling me "a little mick head."

You, being of negligible ancestry yourself, can certainly understand my shame and chagrin. As you know, my dear mother was born and raised in Ireland and my father is the issue of fine people who were forced to flee that sainted isle during the terrible potato famine, which made the potato head remark particularly painful.

Sir, I would prefer that this matter be handled in-house by you as I would like to avoid the anguish and shame that my family would endure as a result of publicity generated by trial boards and civil action. Thus, I have decided not to make a complaint with the department's civil rights advisory board, though I reserve the right to file with the National Labor Relations Board should in-house remedies prove insufficient. Brown used to walk foot in the Inner Harbor; he knows the area. In fact, he knows most of Edmondson Avenue, also . . .

Funny stuff. A little too funny, thought Worden, reading a copy of the memo. McLarney's obvious delight in Dave Brown was helping to turn Carol Wright into nothing worse than a vague and distant memory. If the Nina Perry case meant anything at all, Worden thought, then now was the time for Brown to show it. Did he really want to work murders? Did he even know exactly what that meant? Or was he up here to submit overtime slips and close Kavanaugh's every other night? If McLarney wasn't going to stick a finger in Dave Brown's eye, then the Big Man would take that responsibility upon himself. For three weeks running, in fact, Worden had been knee deep in the younger detective's shit, waiting to see some movement on a case that Brown would like to see disappear. It's been the full Worden treatment—cold, demanding and a little bit vicious. For Dave Brown, a man who wants nothing more than to bask in the latest success, there is no joy, no mercy, and absolutely no chance of escape.

Now, on today's quiet eight-to-four shift, the younger detective is actually foolish enough to be caught reading the new issue of *Rolling Stone* in the coffee room, an act of utter indolence. Worden needs only to enter the room and ascertain that the Carol Wright file is not visible on Dave Brown's desk.

"De-*tec*-tive Brown," says Worden, imbuing each syllable with contempt.

"What?"

"Detective Brown . . ."

"What do you want?"

"I'll bet you like the sound of that, don't you?"

"The sound of what?"

"Detective Brown. Detective David John Brown."

"Go fuck yourself, Worden." Worden stares at the younger detective intently and for so long that Brown can no longer concentrate on the magazine.

"Quit staring at me, you old bastard."

"I'm not staring at you."

"The fuck you aren't."

"It's your conscience." Brown looks at him, uncomprehending.

"Where's the Carol Wright case?" says Worden.

"Hey, I've got to type the prosecution report for Nina Perry . . ."

"That was last month."

". . . and I got a warrant out this week on my boy Clayvon, so gimme a fucking break already."

"My heart pumps purple piss for you," says Worden.

"I didn't ask you about Clayvon Jones, did I? What's new with Carol Wright?"

"Nothing. I got my dick in my hands on that."

"De-*tec*-tive Brown . . ."

Dave Brown pulls open his top right drawer and grabs the .38, pulling the gun halfway out of the holster. Worden doesn't laugh.

"Gimme a quarter," says the older detective.

"What the hell for?"

"Gimme a quarter."

"If I give you a quarter, will you shut the fuck up and leave me alone?"

"Maybe," says Worden. Dave Brown stands up and fishes a coin from his trouser pocket. He throws the quarter at Worden, then sits again, burying his face behind the magazine. Worden gives him a good ten seconds.

"De-*tec*-tive Brown . . ."

NINE

Thursday, October 13

At its core, the crime is the same.

This time she is shot, not stabbed or garroted. This time the small frame is just a bit heavier and the hair is down, not pulled back in braids with a brightly colored beret. This time the vaginal swabs will provide proof of the rape in the form of seminal fluid. This time she did not disappear while walking to a library but to a bus stop. And this time the dead girl will be a year older, twelve instead of eleven. But in every important way, it is the same.

Nine months after Latonya Kim Wallace was discovered behind a Reservoir Hill rowhouse, Harry Edgerton is once again staring at an act of unequivocal evil in a Baltimore alley. The body, fully clothed, is crumpled at the edge of an old brick garage foundation behind a vacant rowhouse in the 1800 block of West Baltimore Street. The single bullet wound is to the back of the skull—a .32 or .38 from the look of it—fired at close range.

Her name was Andrea Perry.

And her mother knows when she watches the evening news and catches a glimpse of the ME's attendants carrying the gurney out of an alley a block away from her Fayette Street home. Andrea has only been missing since last night, and the unidentified victim on television is initially believed to be an older girl, possibly a young woman. But her mother knows.

The identification process at Penn Street is achingly painful, hard even for the ME's attendants, who can do this sort of thing four or five times a day. Later that day in the homicide office, Roger Nolan has barely started to interview the mother when she breaks down uncontrollably.

"Go home," he tells her. "We'll talk tomorrow."

At about the same moment, Edgerton stands in the autopsy room and watches another postmortem of another murdered child. This time, however, Edgerton is the primary detective. In fact, he's the only detective. And this time, he tells himself, it's all going to end differently.

But if the Andrea Perry case is now the exclusive property of the homicide unit's consummate loner, it is also a contradiction in terms: behold, the one-man red ball.

The Andrea Perry murder has all the earmarks of a major case—a dead child, a brutal rape and murder, a lead story on the six o'clock news—yet this time there are no special details, no herd of detectives at the crime scene, no second-day cadet searches. This time the brass is nowhere to be seen.

It might have gone this way even if someone other than Edgerton had taken the call. Because once already this year, D'Addario's men had spent themselves in a communal fight, gathering the entire shift for an absolutely essential case. For one little girl, they had called in extra troops from the districts. For one righteous cause, they had pursued their best suspects for weeks and then months, sacrificing other cases in the campaign for a single, small life. And none of it had mattered. The Latonya Wallace case had gone sour, reminding every man on the shift that all the time and money and effort mean nothing when the evidence isn't there. In the end, it was an open file like any other—a special tragedy, to be sure—but an open murder now in the care of one solitary detective.

Success is its own catalyst; failure, too. Without any arrest in the death of one child, the same shift of detectives had very little to deliver in the death of another. For Andrea Perry, there will be no general mobilization, no declaration of war. It is October; the arsenal is empty.

That it is Edgerton's case simply makes all of this easier. Of all the men on D'Addario's shift, he is the only one who would never think to ask for more troops. Nolan is with him, of course; Nolan is always with him. But beyond the sergeant, everyone else in the squad holds to his own cases. Even if Edgerton wants their help, he wouldn't know how to ask. From the crime scene forward, he is on his own: So be it.

From those first moments at the scene, Edgerton tells himself he will not make the same mistakes that he believes are buried in the Latonya Wallace file, and if he does, they will be his alone to deal with. He has watched Tom Pellegrini waste most of a year kicking himself for investigative flaws, real and imagined. Much of that is the kind of second-guessing that accompanies any unsolved case, but some of it, Edgerton knows, has to do with Pellegrini's feeling that the red-ball treatment had taken away control of the case. Landsman, Edgerton, Eddie Brown, the detail officers—every one of them had become a force for Tom to reckon with, particularly the veteran detectives who had so much more time than Pellegrini and, as a result, tended to influence the case to a greater degree. Well, thinks Edgerton, that was Tom. I won't have that problem.

For one thing, he has a crime scene—not just a site where the child's body has been dumped, but a bona fide murder scene. Edgerton and Nolan had taken the call alone, and for once they had taken their goddamn time with the body. They made sure to do everything in the proper order, to let the little girl be until they were absolutely ready to move her. They bagged the hands at the scene and carefully chronicled the exact array of clothing, noting that while she was fully dressed, her jacket and blouse seemed to have been improperly buttoned.

Working closely with the lab tech at the scene, Edgerton managed to pull several hairs from the victim's blouse, and he carefully noted even the smallest scars and injuries. Walking the length of the alley, he found a single .22 casing, though the head wound appeared to be the result of a larger caliber. With a wound to a fleshy part of the body, a detective can't really tell, because the skin expands at the point of contact and then returns to its shape after the bullet passes, leaving a smaller hole. But a head wound retains an accurate circumference; chances are good that the .22 casing had nothing to do with the murder.

There was no blood trail whatsoever. Edgerton carefully examined the victim's head and neck at the scene, satisfying himself that she had done all of her bleeding right there against the low brick foundation. In all probability, she had been led into the alley, forced to kneel down, and then shot, execution style, in the back of the head. Nor was there an exit wound, and a clean, remarkably unmutilated .32 round is subsequently recovered at the autopsy. In addition, the vaginal swabs will later come back positive with the seminal fluid of a secreter—a male whose ejaculate contained sufficient blood to type or DNA-test against any potential suspect. In contrast to the Latonya Wallace case, the killer of Andrea Perry has left behind a wealth of physical evidence.

But the interviews with two young men brought downtown by the first uniforms provide little. Apparently, neither one was the first to discover the body. One tells detectives that he learned about it from the other; the second says only that he had been walking on Baltimore Street when an old woman told him that there was a body in the alley. He had not gone to investigate, he tells Edgerton, but had simply told the second man, who flagged down a cop. Who was the old woman? The first young man has no idea.

As the case develops, Edgerton works deliberately and at his own pace. The initial canvass by Western officers was carefully done, but Edgerton spends days creating his own schematic diagram of the surrounding blocks, listing residents at each rowhouse and matching them with criminal histories and alibis. It is a rough little neighborhood, hard by the Western District's lower boundary with the Southern, and the Vine Street drug market a block away brought all kinds of trash into the area, greatly adding to any list of potential suspects. This is the kind of investigation that brings out the best in Edgerton, playing as it does to his strengths: More than any other detective in the unit, he can work a neighborhood until every other pedestrian is feeding him information.

Part of it is his appearance—black, reedy thin, and well groomed, with salt-and-pepper hair and thick mustache, Edgerton is attractive in a decidedly laid-back way. At crime scenes, the neighborhood girls actually line up on the other side of the police tape and giggle. Detective Edge, they call him. Unlike most of his colleagues, Edgerton maintains his own string of informants, and more often than not they are eighteen-year-old yoettes whose boyfriends are out in the streets shooting one another for drugs and gold chains. Time and again, some corner boy would be on his way to the Hopkins ER with holes in his torso and Edgerton's beeper would go off before the ambo could even arrive, the digital readout displaying the number of an east side pay phone.

Edgerton is at ease in the ghetto in a way that even the best white detectives are not. And more than most of the black investigators, too, Edgerton can somehow talk his way past the fact that he's a cop. Only Edgerton would have bothered to clean the blood from a wounded girl's hands in a University Hospital emergency room. Only Edgerton could share a smoke with a drug dealer in the back of a radio car on Hollins Street and emerge with a complete statement. In corner carryouts, in hospital waiting rooms, in rowhouse vestibules, Edgerton makes sudden and lasting connections with people who have no reason ever to trust a homicide detective. And now, in the case of Andrea Perry, a true victim, those connections come even easier.

The family and the neighborhood tell him that the child was last seen at eight the night before, walking her eighteen-year-old sister to the bus stop on West Baltimore Street. The sister says that as she boarded her bus, she saw Andrea walking north toward the 1800 block of Fayette and home. When the sister returned home at eleven and found that her mother was already asleep, she too went to bed. Not until the following morning did the family realize that the child had never arrived home. They filed their missing person's report and held out some hope until that evening news broadcast from just a block away.

But days after the murder, the media coverage has all faded away. The Andrea Perry murder isn't getting anything like a red-ball treatment from the city, and as the days wear on, Edgerton has to wonder about that. Perhaps it is because the victim was a year older, perhaps because her neighborhood was less stable and less central to the city than Reservoir Hill. For whatever reason, the newspapers and TV crews don't stay with this one and, as a result, there is no deluge of calls and anonymous tips such as those that accompanied the death of Latonya Wallace.

In fact, the only anonymous call on the case came a few hours after the body's discovery: a high-pitched male voice gave the name of a West Baltimore woman, claiming that he had seen her running out of the alley after hearing shots. Edgerton immediately decided the story was bullshit. This wasn't a woman's crime; the semen tells them that much. As with Latonya Wallace, this was a crime of one man, acting alone and for a motive that he could never share with other men, much less a woman.

Was this mystery woman then a witness? More bullshit, Edgerton reasoned. The killer chose the alley and the remains of that garage for an anonymous murder. He killed that little girl to prevent her from identifying him as a rapist, so why the hell would he fire that shot with anyone else in the alley? Edgerton was absolutely convinced that his suspect walked the little girl around those back alleys until he was sure they were alone. Only then did he pull the girl down against the brick wall. Only then did he bring out the gun.

Gary Dunnigan, who took the anonymous phone call, wrote out an office report and gave it to Edgerton for the file. Edgerton absorbed the information and checked the woman's name on the computer to assure himself that she wasn't a serious suspect. He even interviewed the woman's neighbors and relatives, learning enough about her to satisfy his curiosity, but in the first week of the investigation he does not pick the woman up.

After all, the story makes no sense, and besides, he's getting better information from his neighborhood canvass. One story has the little girl's murder as an act of retaliation against one of her relatives, the other as a predatory act by a dealer who simply wanted to show the neighborhood how hard he could be. There is talk about two drug traffickers in the area, and neither man seems to have much of an alibi.

For once, and to the amusement of the other detectives, Edgerton arrives in the homicide office early each day, grabbing the keys to a Cavalier and then disappearing into West Baltimore. Most afternoons, Edgerton works through the shift change, not returning until well into the evening. Some days Nolan is with him, other days he works alone, his whereabouts a mystery to the rest of the squad. Alone on the street, Edgerton can be more effective than any man who ever had a partner. Out on the street, he understands the special benefits of isolation; his critics do not. There are detectives in the homicide unit who never go anywhere in the ghetto alone, who always double up on any investigative trip to West Baltimore.

"You want company?" detectives routinely ask each other. And on those rare occasions when one investigator sets out for the slums alone, he is invariably cautioned: "Careful, bunk, don't get yourself captured."

From the outside looking in, Edgerton understands that the camaraderie of the unit can be a crutch. More often than not, Edgerton ventures into the high-rise projects alone and finds witnesses; more often than not, other detectives march through neighborhoods in twos and threes and find nothing. Edgerton learned long ago that even the best and most cooperative witnesses are more likely to talk to one detective than to a pair. And three detectives working a case are nothing short of a police riot in the eyes of a reluctant or untrusting witness. In truth, when all is said and done, the surest way for a cop to solve a murder is to get his ass out on the street and find a witness.

The better detectives all understand this: Worden often does some of his best work alone in a Cavalier, riding back out to a neighborhood to talk quietly with people who recoiled when it was Worden and James and Brown camped on their doorstep. But there are detectives in the unit who are genuinely fearful of riding alone.

Edgerton has no such fears; he wears his attitude like a shield. Two months ago, he was out at Edmondson and Payson working a drug murder and, without thinking twice, he wandered away from his crime scene and down the worst stretch of Edmondson Avenue alone, parting a block of corner boys as if he were Charlton Heston on the Universal Studio lot. He was looking for witnesses or, at the very least, for someone willing to whisper into a cop's ear some truth about what happened on Payson

Street an hour earlier. Instead, he got surly looks and silent rage from fifty black faces.

And yet he moved on, seemingly oblivious of the hostility until, at the corner of Edmondson and Brice, he watched a young kid, fourteen or fifteen years old, pass a paper bag to an older boy who ran around the block. For Edgerton, it was opportunity knocking. With the rest of the street watching coldly, he grabbed the kid by a shoulder and dragged him to a Cavalier around the corner, pressing the boy for details about the murder.

A Western uniform, watching from the crime scene two blocks away, later cautioned the detective.

"You shouldn't have gone down there alone," he told Edgerton. "What if some shit had started?"

To which Edgerton could only shake his head.

"I'm serious, man," the uniform said. "You only got six bullets."

"I don't even have that." Edgerton laughed. "I forgot my gun."

"YOU WHAT?"

"Yeah. I left my gun in my desk."

A cop at Edmondson and Brice with no gun. The Western uniforms were stunned; Edgerton was indifferent: "This job," he told them, "is ninety percent attitude."

Now, working the Andrea Perry murder, Edgerton is back in another West Baltimore neighborhood, mixing with the locals as few police can. He talks to the occupants of every rowhouse that backs up to his alley, he chats up the hangers-on at the carryouts and bars. Working from the bus stop toward his victim's home on Fayette Street, he checks every address for a witness who may have seen the child walking with someone. When nothing comes from that effort, he begins checking other sexual assault reports from the Southern and Western districts.

In fact, Edgerton makes a point early on in the investigation of calling the operations unit officers from the Southern, Southwestern and Western districts downtown and briefing them on the case. He tells them to be looking for anyone involved in anything sexual with underage girls, or any report involving an abduction or a .32-caliber weapon. Edgerton urges the ops unit officers in all three districts to call him with information that seems even remotely related. That, too, differs from the approach taken in the Latonya Wallace case, where district officers had been detailed downtown to help with the investigation. For this little girl, Edgerton decides, the districts will not come to CID; CID will go into the districts.

Only once, on the day after the body's discovery, is there any hint of the communal effort that normally accompanies a red-ball case, and it is prompted by Nolan, who for the sake of appearances asks McAllister, Kincaid and Bowman to give them a day's help to expand the canvass.

Looking through the case file that day, the other detectives in the squad wonder aloud why Edgerton hadn't immediately followed up on the anonymous call. At the very least, they argue, he should go out and grab the woman whom the male caller allegedly saw running from the alley.

"That's the last thing I want to do," says Edgerton, explaining his strategy to Nolan. "If I get her down here, what am I going to do? I have one question to ask her, and after that I've got nothing."

To Edgerton's way of thinking, it is another mistake that too many detectives make too often—the same mistake that they had made with the Fish Man in the Latonya Wallace case. You bring someone down and go at them in the interrogation room with no real ammunition. They walk out an hour later, more confident than before, and if you ever do get any leverage on them, you've only made it harder to come back and break them the second time.

"I ask her why she was running out of the alley, and she tells me she doesn't know what I'm talking about," Edgerton explains to Nolan. "And she's right. I don't know what I'm talking about."

He still doesn't believe that the woman named by the caller actually ran from the alley after the murder. But even if he did believe it, he would not risk an interrogation until it had at least a chance of success.

"If all else fails, then I bring her down here and ask my one question," the detective says, "and not before."

Nolan agrees. "It's your case," he tells Edgerton. "Do it your way."

Beyond his squad's limited help with the expanded canvass, Edgerton's isolation on the case is complete. Even D'Addario keeps his distance: He asks Nolan for regular progress reports and offers help if help is needed, but otherwise he is content to let Edgerton and his sergeant set their own pace.

The contrast with D'Addario's response to the Latonya Wallace investigation is striking. Edgerton hopes that the lieutenant's hands-off approach is, at least in part, a display of confidence in his investigator. More likely, the detective reasons, D'Addario has himself soured on the full-blown red-ball treatment. Throwing troops and money at a case had accomplished so little in Reservoir Hill that maybe the lieutenant is reluctant to travel the same road a second time. Or maybe, like everyone else on the shift, LTD is just too damn tired for another all-out campaign.

But Edgerton also knows that nothing happens in a vacuum. He is being left alone to work his case largely because D'Addario can afford to leave him alone. On the day that Andrea Perry was discovered, the clearance rate stood at a fat 74 percent, with five outstanding murder warrants still on the street—a rate that compares favorably to both the previous year's totals and the national average. As a result, D'Addario can once again make decisions without worrying about public consumption or the perceptions of the command staff. From talking with Pellegrini, Edgerton knows that the lieutenant has already expressed some dissatisfaction with the tidal wave of investigation that followed Latonya Wallace's death. At various stages in that probe, D'Addario had listened to Landsman and Pellegrini both argue that less could be more, and the lieutenant seemed to agree. If the clearance rate had been higher, if the department hadn't also been publicly sweating the murders of all those women in the Northwest, then the case might have gone differently. Now, with the board showing more black than red, the homicide unit's political equilibrium has been fully restored. Thanks to some hard work, some skillful maneuvering and not a little luck, D'Addario's reign has survived the threat and been returned to its rightful glory. And if the rise in the clearance rate and D'Addario's true feelings about the red-ball treatment aren't reasons enough for Edgerton to be granted his distance, then Edgerton also understands that he is alone on this case simply because the murder has fallen to Nolan's squad.

Not only does Nolan have absolute confidence in Edgerton's methods, but he is the sergeant least likely to ask for help from the rest of the shift and from D'Addario in particular. Of the three sergeants, only McLarney and Landsman are now counted among LTD's true disciples; Nolan had stayed on the fence during D'Addario's year-long conflict with the captain. Lately, the lieutenant has taken some pleasure in bringing that out.

Two nights ago, all three squad sergeants were in the coffee room as D'Addario prepared to leave at the end of a four-to-twelve shift.

"I note by my watch that it's nigh on twelve o'clock," he declared dramatically. "And I know that before the cock crows thrice, one of you shall betray me . . ."

The sergeants laughed nervously.

"... but it's okay, Roger, I understand. You gotta do what you gotta do."

As Nolan's man, Edgerton couldn't really be sure exactly why he was being isolated on the Andrea Perry case. It may well be Dee's faith in him, or it may be the lieutenant's new philosophy about leaving red balls to the primary investigator. Then again, it may just be that Roger Nolan is the one sergeant who is not about to ask his lieutenant for anything. Maybe, Edgerton thinks, it's a little of all three. For an outsider like himself, it's always harder to get a handle on the office politics.

But whatever the reasons for D'Addario's distance from the investigation, Edgerton understands that the effect is the same: He is on the longest possible leash. As a result, Andrea Perry will not become Latonya Wallace, just as Edgerton will not become another Pellegrini. Good-bye to the detail officers, to the FBI psych profiles, to the aerial photographs of the crime scene, to a hundred endless debates among a full squad of homicide detectives. Instead, this child's murder will be one man out in the street, with time enough and room enough to solve his murder. Or, perhaps, hang himself.

Whichever comes first.

It is a beautiful courthouse, truly impressive in its classical form. The bronze doors, the varied Italian marbles, the deep redwoods and gilded ceilings—the Clarence M. Mitchell Jr. Courthouse on North Calvert Street is a work of great architecture, as fine and glorious as any structure ever built in the city of Baltimore.

If justice itself were measured by the grandeur of its house, then a Baltimore detective would have little to fear. If well-cut stone and hand-carved woods could guarantee a righteous vengeance, then the Mitchell Courthouse and its companion across the street—the old post office building now known as Courthouse East—might be places of sanctuary for a Baltimore law officer.

The city fathers spared little when they created these two exquisite buildings in the heart of downtown, and in the last several years their descendants have been equally generous in their ongoing effort to renovate and preserve the beauty of both structures. From the arraignment courts to the jury rooms, from front lobbies to back corridors, the courthouse complex exists so that generations of law officers and lawyers could walk the halls of justice and feel their spirits soar. Stepping lightly down the restored portico of the post office building, or walking into the elegance of

Judge Hammerman's paneled palace, a detective has every reason to hold his head high in the knowledge that he has arrived at a place where society can exact its price. Justice will be done here; all the hard, dirty work performed in the city's rotten core will no doubt be gracefully shaped into a clean and solemn judgment of guilty. A jury of twelve respectable, thoughtful men and women will rise as one to render that verdict, imposing the law of a good and valiant people on an evil man.

So how is it that every Baltimore detective of this epoch enters his courthouse with his head down, his badge drawn with practiced boredom for the sheriff's deputies who man the metal detector in the first-floor lobby? How can those detectives step so heavily toward the elevators, oblivious of the beauty all around them? How can they crush their cigarette butts into the stone with such seeming indifference, then knock on a prosecutor's office door as if it were the very gate of purgatory? How can a homicide detective bring his best work to this, his final destination, wearing a look of utter resignation?

Well, for one thing, he's probably been up all night working two fresh shootings and a cutting on the midnight shift. No doubt the same detective scheduled to testify in Bothe's court this afternoon just finished his overnight paperwork in time to listen to a dayshift's roll call. No doubt he then spent another hour downing four cups of black coffee and an Egg McMuffin. Now he's probably lugging paper evidence bags from the ECU to some lawyer's cubbyhole on the third floor, where he will be informed that his best witness hasn't yet shown up for court and isn't answering a sheriff deputy's phone calls. Beyond those worldly concerns, this same detective—if he knows his business—is obligated to arrive in the legal arena with a mind clouded by something other than transcendent visions of moral victory. In his heart of hearts, a veteran detective is inspired not by the glories of the courthouse, but by Rule Number Nine in the lexicon, to wit:

9A. To a jury, any doubt is reasonable.
9B. The better the case, the worse the jury.

And, in addition to rules 9A and 9B:

9C. A good man is hard to find, but twelve of them, gathered together in one place, is a miracle.

A detective who ventures into the corridors of justice with anything less than a firm and familiar skepticism for the American legal process is a man leaning into the punches. It's one thing, after all, to see some of your best work torn to shreds by twelve of Baltimore's finest citizens, but it's another thing entirely to watch it happen from a state of naive incredulity. Better to check your expectations at the courthouse doors and enter its glistening corridors in full, willful anticipation of the debacle to follow.

The rock—and it's a fine, honorable rock—upon which our legal system is built states that a defendant is innocent until found guilty by the unanimous vote of a dozen peers. Better that a hundred guilty men should walk free before one innocent man is punished. Well, by that standard, the Baltimore court system is pretty much working to code.

Consider: In this particular year in the life of Baltimore's criminal justice system, the names of 200 perpetrators will be brought to the state's attorney's office in connection with 170 solved homicides.

Of those 200 suspects:

- Five cases will still be pending trial two years later. (In two of those instances, suspects were charged in warrants but never apprehended by detectives.)
- Five will die before trial or in the course of arrest. (Three of these are suicides, one the victim of a fire she set to kill someone else, one the victim in a police shootout.)
- Six will not be tried when prosecutors determine the killings to be justifiable by self-defense or a result of accidental causes.
- Two defendants will be declared not criminally responsible and sent to a state mental hospital.
- Three defendants age sixteen and younger will have their homicide charges remanded to juvenile court.
- Sixteen will have their charges dismissed prior to indictment due to lack of evidence. (On occasion, an aggressive homicide detective with insufficient evidence to prove a case will play a long shot and nonetheless charge his best suspect in the hope that the incarceration will provide sufficient leverage to provoke a confession in subsequent interrogations.)
- Twenty-four defendants will have their charges nol prossed or stetted by prosecutors after indictment. (A nol prosse represents the unequivocal dismissal of a grand jury indictment; a stet places the case on an

inactive docket, though the prosecution can be revived within a year if additional evidence is forthcoming. In time, most stet cases become dismissals.)

- Three defendants will have their charges dismissed or stetted when it becomes clear that they are, in fact, innocent of the crimes for which they have been accused. (The innocent-until-proven-guilty standard does indeed have some real meaning in Maryland's largest city, where it's not uncommon for the wrong man to be charged or even indicted for a violent crime. It happened, for example, in the shooting of Gene Cassidy, and it happened again in three separate murders handled by detectives on Stanton's shift. In those cases, the wrong man was charged as a result of faulty witness identifications—one from the dying victim, the other two from bystanders—and the defendants were subsequently cleared through additional investigation. Charging the wrong man on mediocre evidence is not difficult, and getting a grand jury to indict him is only a little harder. But after that, the chances of putting the wrong man into prison become minimal. It is, after all, hard enough for prosecutors in Baltimore to convict the guilty; the only scenario by which an innocent man could be successfully prosecuted on weak evidence would be one in which a defense attorney failed to evaluate the case and force-fed a plea to a client.)

Guilty or innocent, living or dead, deranged or competent—the winnowing process removes 64 of the original 200 defendants, or nearly 30 percent, before a single case is ever brought to court. And of the 136 men and women remaining:

- Eighty-one will accept plea agreements prior to trial. (Eleven of those defendants will plead to premeditated, first-degree murder, 35 to second-degree murder, 32 to manslaughter, and 3 to lesser charges.)
- Fifty-five homicide defendants will risk trial before a judge or jury. (Of that number, 25 defendants will be acquitted in jury trials. Twenty of the remaining 30 defendants will be found guilty of first-degree murder, 6 of second-degree murder, and 4 of manslaughter.)

Add 30 trial convictions to 81 pleas and the cumulative deterrent to murder in Baltimore is evident: 111 citizens have been convicted for committing an act of homicide.

By the reckoning of this particular year, the chance of actually being convicted of a crime after being identified by authorities is about 60 percent. And if you factor in those unsolved homicides in which there are no arrests, the chance of being caught and convicted for taking a life in Baltimore is just over 40 percent.

All of which is not to say that this unlucky minority then suffers punishment commensurate with their crime. Of the 111 defendants convicted in this year's homicides, 22 men and women—20 percent of the total—will be sentenced to less than five years' incarceration. Another 16 defendants—14 percent of the total—will receive sentences of less than ten years in prison. Given that Maryland's parole guidelines generally call for prisoners to serve about a third of their sentences, it can be said that three years after they committed their crimes, fewer than 30 percent of the Baltimore homicide unit's Class of 1988 is still behind prison walls.

Prosecutors and detectives understand the statistics. They know that even with the best cases—those that a state's attorney is willing to bring before a jury—the chance of success is only three in five. As a result, those prosecutions that are marginal, those in which there is any indication of justifiable self-defense, those in which the witnesses are unreliable or the physical evidence is ambiguous—all these cases soon fall by the side of the road, becoming dismissals or weak pleas.

But not every case that goes to plea is necessarily weak. In Baltimore, plea bargains can be had on reasonably strong cases—cases that no defendant and his attorney would dare risk taking to trial in the suburbs of Anne Arundel or Howard or Baltimore County. Yet in the city, prosecutors know that such cases, when brought to trial, are likely to result in acquittals.

The difference is, quite simply, Rule Number Nine.

The operant logic of a Baltimore city jury is as fantastical a process as any other of our universe's mysteries. This one is innocent because he seemed so polite and well spoken on the stand, that one because there were no fingerprints on the weapon to corroborate the testimony of four witnesses. And this one over here is telling the truth when he says he was beaten into a confession; we know that, of course, because why else would anyone willingly confess to a crime if he wasn't beaten?

In one particularly notable decision, a Baltimore jury found a defendant innocent of murder charges but guilty of assault with intent to murder. They believed the testimony of the eyewitness, who saw the defendant stab the victim in the back on a well-lit street, then run away to save himself. But they also believed the medical examiner, who explained that of all the stab wounds, a thrust to the chest had ultimately killed the victim. The jurors reasoned that they couldn't be absolutely sure that the defendant stabbed the victim more than once. Presumably, some other enraged assailant could have wandered by afterward, picked up the knife and finished the job.

Juries do not like to argue. They do not like to think. They do not like to sit for hours at a time, wading through evidence and testimony and lawyers' arguments. And in a homicide detective's view, a criminal jury resists its obligation to judge another human being. It's an ugly, painful business, after all, this process of labeling people murderers and criminals. Juries want to go home, to escape, to sleep it off. Our legal system prohibits a guilty verdict when there is reasonable doubt about a defendant's culpability, but in truth, juries want to doubt, and in the stress of the jury room, all doubts become reasonable justification for acquittal.

Reasonable doubt is the weak link in every prosecutor's chain and, with a complex case, the doubts multiply. Consequently, most of the battle-scarred veterans in the state's attorney's office prefer a straightforward, one- or two-witness homicide: It's an easier argument to present and an easier argument for a jury to accept. They believe your witnesses or they don't, but either way, you haven't asked them to think very hard or to pay attention for very long. But the more developed case file—the one that a detective built over weeks and months, the one that presents a mountain of not-so-glaringly-obvious evidence, the one that requires the prosecutor to subtly piece the case together like a puzzle—it's that kind of case on which a criminal jury can wreak real havoc.

Because in Baltimore, at least, the average juror doesn't want to spend time contemplating the inconsistencies in a defendant's statement, or the complex web of testimony that systematically destroys an alibi, or the discrepancies between a medical examiner's testimony and a defendant's self-defense claim. It's too complicated, too abstract. The average juror wants three upstanding citizens to say that they were eyeball witnesses to the crime and another two who can assure them of the killer's motivation. Throw in a recovered murder weapon, a few print hits and a positive DNA match and then, by God, you've got a jury ready to mete out some punishment.

To a detective, however, it's the circumstantial prosecutions that often represent the best police work, and for that reason Rule 9B has profound meaning. In theory, the dunkers take care of themselves in court. But the best cases—the kind a cop takes pride in—always do seem to get the worst juries.

As with every other part of the criminal justice machine, racial issues permeate the jury system in Baltimore. Given that the vast majority of urban violence is black-on-black crime, and given that the pool of possible jurors is 60 to 70 percent black, Baltimore prosecutors take almost every case into court with the knowledge that the crime will be seen through the lens of the black community's historical suspicion of a white-controlled police department and court system. The testimony of a black officer or detective is therefore considered necessary in many cases, a counterweight to the young defendant who, following his attorney's advice, is wearing his Sunday best and carrying the family Bible to and from court. That the victims are also black matters less; after all, they're not around to set such a good example in front of the jurors.

The effect of race on the judicial system is freely acknowledged by prosecutors and defense attorneys—black and white alike—although the issue is rarely raised directly in court. The better lawyers, whatever their color, refuse to manipulate jurors through racial distinctions; the others can do so with even the most indirect suggestions. Race is instead a tacit presence that accompanies almost every panel of twelve into a Baltimore jury room. Once, in a rare display, a black defense attorney actually pointed to her own forearm while giving closing arguments to an all-black panel: "Brothers and sisters," she said, as two white detectives went out of their minds in the back row of the gallery, "I think we all know what this case is about."

Still, it would be wrong to suggest that Baltimore's juries have become more lenient simply because they have become more black. Suspicion of the legal system within the black community is a real phenomenon, but veteran prosecutors can tell you that some of the best panels they've ever had have been all-black, whereas some of the worst and most indifferent have had a white majority. More than color, what has crippled the jury system in Baltimore is a factor that crosses all racial boundaries: television.

Pick any twelve people from Baltimore—from the black sections of Ashburton and Cherry Hill, from all-white Highlandtown or Hamilton—and chances are, you will come up with a few intelligent, discerning citizens. Some may have finished high school, one or two may have been to college. Most will be working folk, only a few will be skilled professionals. Baltimore is a blue-collar town, a stretch of the East Coast rust belt that never recovered when American steel and shipping began their downward spirals. Its population is underemployed, and it remains one of

America's most undereducated cities. Taxpayer flight has continued for more than two decades, and the vast majority of Baltimore's white and black middle and upper classes now reside outside the city proper. They are, in essence, the stuff from which county juries are made.

As a result, most city folk go into a jury room with no greater sophistication about crime and punishment than can be gleaned from a 19-inch television screen. More than anything else, it's the cathode-ray tube—not the prosecutor, not the defense attorney, certainly not the evidence—that gives a Baltimore juror his mind-set. Television ensures that criminal juries are empaneled with ridiculous expectations. Jurors want to see the murder—see it played out in front of their eyes on videotape in slow motion or, at the very least, see the guilty party fall to his knees at the witness stand, begging for mercy. Never mind that fingerprints are recovered in less than 10 percent of criminal cases, the average juror wants fingerprints on the gun, fingerprints on the knife, fingerprints on every door handle, window and house key. Never mind that the trace lab rarely makes a case, a juror nonetheless wants to see hairs and fibers and shoe prints and every other shard of science gleaned from *Hawaii Five-O* reruns. When a case does come complete with an excess of witnesses and physical evidence, then jurors demand a motive, a reason, a meaning to a murder that has otherwise been proven. And on those rare occasions when jurors are satisfied that the right man has actually been locked up for the right murder, they want to be assured that the defendant is truly a bad person and that they themselves are not bad people for doing this terrible thing to him.

To provide, in real life, the utter certainty about crime and culpability that pervades television is impossible. Nor is it easy to rid a juror of such expectations, although veteran prosecutors never lack for trying. In Baltimore, state's attorneys routinely call fingerprint experts to the stand in those cases in which no fingerprint evidence exists:

If you would, please explain to the jury how often fingerprints are recovered at crime scenes and how often they are not recovered. Explain how it is that many people, depending on their biochemistry at the time of the incident, do not leave detectable fingerprints. Explain how fingerprints can be obliterated and smudged. Explain how atmospheric conditions affect fingerprints. Explain just how rare it is to pull a fingerprint off a knife hilt or gun butt.

Similarly, the detectives themselves come to the stand to fight a losing battle with the last six episodes of *L.A. Law* and other network fare in which the lawyers—better-looking lawyers than we have in court today, mind you—always parade before the jury with guns and knives bagged and tagged and labeled Exhibit 1A.

A good defense attorney can blow ten minutes of smoke by glaring at a detective who tries to explain that weapons have a nasty habit of leaving the crime scene before the police arrive.

You mean you never recovered the murder weapon? This jury is supposed to convict my client without a murder weapon? What do you mean, it could be anywhere? Are you trying to tell us that after committing an act of murder, the defendant might have actually run away? And taken the gun with him? And then hidden it? Or thrown it from the Curtis Bay bridge?

On *Columbo*, the gun is always in the liquor cabinet behind the vermouth. But you didn't check behind the defendant's vermouth, did you, detective? No, you don't have the murder weapon. Your honor, I move that we unshackle this poor innocent waif and send him back to his loving family.

In the minds of Baltimore's prosecutors and detectives, at least, television has utterly shattered the notion of a thinking jury, strangled it with plot lines in which all ambiguity is obliterated and all questions answered. As a result, those charged with punishing the act of murder in Baltimore no longer believe in all that Norman Rockwell business about twelve angry men in shirtsleeves, arguing in sticky heat over the essential evidence. In the real world, it's more like a dozen brain-deads telling each other that the defendant seems like a nice, quiet young man, then laughing at the prosecutor's choice of tie. Defense attorneys are quick to call such thinking sour grapes, but in truth, the faithlessness that veteran prosecutors and detectives feel for the jury system goes deeper than that. The argument isn't that the government should win every murder trial; the system isn't built that way. But does anyone really believe that 45 percent of the homicide defendants brought to a court trial—the last stretch of the legal system's long, thinning bottleneck—are in fact innocent?

As a consequence, city juries have become a deterrent of sorts to prosecutors, who are willing to accept weaker pleas or tolerate dismissals rather than waste the city's time and money on cases involving defendants who are clearly guilty, but who have been charged on evidence that is anything less than overwhelming. Naturally, a competent defense attorney or public defender understands that in most cases, a jury trial is the last thing a city prosecutor wants, and he uses this leverage when he bargains for his client.

For the detectives, the decision to plea or dismiss a case is the flashpoint in their ongoing love-hate relationship with the state's attorney's office. True, thinks a detective, these people are on our side. True, they're working to put bad guys in prison at half the salary they might get at an outside firm. True, they're looking for the same justice we are. But brotherly feelings are out the window when a young assistant state's attorney, two years out of the University of Baltimore School of Law, gives up on a drug murder that took three weeks to develop. When that happens, the chip goes right back on the shoulder: I busted my ass to get reluctant witnesses into the grand jury, and what for? Just so this goof with pinstripes and a power tie could dump it on the stet docket? Hell, he didn't even have balls enough to pick up a phone and call me, much less ask how the damn file might be salvaged.

Some of the cases are weak and should be dumped, no doubt about that. Some of them arrived at the courthouse as viable prosecutions, only to self-destruct once the witnesses started backing up. Any homicide detective knows that most basic truth: Shit happens. But he also believes that too many borderline cases, and even a few that are healthy, manage to slip through the cracks, particularly with less experienced attorneys.

A good detective will excuse some of it as understandable and inevitable. As is true elsewhere, the Baltimore state's attorney's office is chronically understaffed and underfunded; its trial division is manned by a core of competent veterans and a slew of recent arrivals—younger lawyers who have worked their way up to felony violence after a few years in the district courts. Some will be good trial lawyers, some could go either way, and a few are genuinely dangerous in a courtroom. A detective hopes for a competent prosecutor, but he understands that the system runs by triage. The homicides are parceled out with an eye toward keeping the major cases—those involving true victims or those in which the defendant is suspected or charged with multiple crimes—in the hands of veteran attorneys. The hope is that in the most critical cases, the prosecutor will not be outclassed or intimidated by the coterie of experienced defense attorneys who by private retainer or court appointment always gravitate to city homicide cases.

Every detective also understands the need to take pleas on at least two-thirds or more of the viable murder prosecutions. Although most everyone outside the legal system regards "plea bargain" as a dirty word, those who make their living at the courthouse recognize it as a structural necessity. Without plea agreements, the system would lurch to a halt, with cases waiting for courtrooms the way commuter flights wait for runways in Atlanta. Even with the current ratio of pleas to trials, the delay between a murder indictment and the court trial averages between six and nine months.

But in a detective's mind, there is a vast difference between a good plea and a bad one. Second-degree and thirty is always a respectable plea, except for truly evil acts such as, say, child abuse cases or robbery murders. If the case is borderline, second-degree and twenty isn't too shabby, although it's not exactly the iron fist of justice when you consider that the parole board puts most of them back on the street after about seven to ten. In a true manslaughter case—a domestic murder that was the act of fear or impulse, though it could in no way be called an accident—anything from two to ten is reasonable. But what's hardest for a detective to swallow is a prosecutor allowing a particularly bad murder to go as second-degree, or calling a murder a manslaughter, or a manslaughter an accidental. Even in those instances, most detectives won't speak their piece unless they're asked, and the prosecutors don't usually ask. In the homicide unit, the time-worn philosophy is that it's on the prosecutor; you did your job, fuck him if he won't do his. Occasionally, however, a detective will cross the emotional boundary.

Worden, for instance, has been known to say something to a young prosecutor who's giving up on a file too quickly, or seems afraid to take a decent case into court. Landsman will sometimes do the same, and Edgerton, if you give him a chance, will tell a prosecutor how to try the case and then write out the closing argument. A lot of men in homicide carry around a case or two that still burns them. Garvey, for one, still isn't saying much to the ASA who turned the Myeisha Jenkins murder into a second-degree plea—Myeisha, who was all of nine when her mother let her boyfriend beat the child to death and dump her on the shoulder of the Baltimore-Washington Parkway. Garvey told the lawyer he was a piece of shit for taking that plea, told it to him in such a way that the man didn't even try to argue.

If he cares enough about a case, a detective can lobby or even argue for a particular strategy. But in the end, decisions about the legal approach to a case are not his to make. From crime scene to conviction, the courthouse is the only part of the process in which the detective becomes a passive participant, a player wholly dependent on the decisions of others. A detective is there to testify and otherwise serve the lawyers in any way he can. The lawyers, meanwhile, regard that service with varying amounts of appreciation. Some prosecutors consult the investigators on evidence and presentation, asking the opinions of veteran detectives who have been through the process more often than the attorneys. Others view the detectives as little more than props and gofers, responsible for showing up on time with the right evidence and the right witnesses.

Homicide detectives are further distanced from their cases because, as witnesses, they are sequestered and therefore prohibited from attending court and listening to other witnesses. Detectives in Baltimore spend 90 percent of their court time sitting on hard wooden benches in corridors, or running bags of evidence between the courtroom and the prosecutor's office, or chasing down a witness who's supposed to testify in the afternoon session but hasn't shown up, or maybe bullshitting with the secretaries upstairs in the Violent Crimes Unit. Court time for a detective is a strange limbo, a period of nonexistence that is only briefly interrupted when he is called to testify.

The stand is the last point in the process in which a detective's expertise counts for something. In most cases, the testimony of civilian witnesses—primed and prepared by the prosecutor before trial—will produce the most critical evidence. But in every case, the testimony of the detective, concerning the crime scene, the discovery of witnesses, the statements made by the defendant, lays the groundwork for the prosecution's case. Among prosecutors, there is a theory that says a detective's performance on the stand can rarely win a case, but it can be enough to wreck a prosecution.

Before taking the oath, a detective who knows his business makes a point of reading through the case file. After all, it's been six months and a lot of bodies between the arrest and trial. In 1987, a city detective—no longer in the homicide unit—responded to a prosecutor's question with an elaborate description of the crime scene and subsequent investigation. After a minute or two, he saw that the prosecutor was making strange faces. Even the defendant looked a little curious.

"Um, wait one second," said the detective, coming to grips with the disaster. "Your honor, I think I'm remembering the wrong murder . . ."

That spells mistrial with a capital M.

Many detectives prefer to take the file onto the stand, but with some judges that can be dangerous. A typical case file contains notes and reports on potential suspects and blind alleys that were eventually discarded, and a few judges will allow a defense attorney, on cross-examination, to take hold of the file and go fishing. Given an alternate suspect from a police file and a tolerant judge, a defense attorney can run for miles in front of a jury.

One detective, Mark Tomlin, makes a point of copying his trial notes onto the back of the defendant's computerized arrest sheet. Once, when Tomlin was testifying, a defense attorney asked to see his notes and began to suggest that they be admitted into evidence. He then turned the sheet over, looked at his client's priors, and returned it without another word.

Veteran detectives also go into court knowing the strengths and weaknesses of their cases; they can anticipate a defense attorney's line of questioning and answer accordingly. This doesn't mean responding with answers that are grandly deceptive, but tailoring answers so that they do the least damage. If, for example, the defense counsel knows that your witness picked his client from a lineup but failed to do so in a photo array the previous day, he's almost certainly going to ask about that. Anticipating, a good detective will, in the course of his answer, manage to work in the fact that the array used a picture of the suspect that was six years old, that the suspect's hair was different, that he had no mustache and whatever else can be said before the lawyer stops him from talking. Defense attorneys have now endured untold generations of slick, manipulative police witnesses; one consequence is the just-answer-yes-or-no style of cross-examination, which requires a detective to wait for the prosecutor's redirect to fully shape his answers.

On the other hand, if a detective is on the stand and not sure just where a defense attorney is going, his answers will become cautious and a little less specific, though not inaccurate in any detectable sense. A professional witness doesn't needlessly back himself into corners with blanket declarations and assurances, because a good attorney will then manage to produce an exception.

"Detective, you say that after Mr. Robinson was arrested for this crime, the robberies in the area of North and Longwood ceased."

"Yes, sir."

"Detective, may I call your attention to a police report dated . . ."

Experienced detectives take one other rule to the stand with them: They don't lie. The good ones don't, anyway, not about anything that could ever be directly contradicted in open court. Perjury can destroy a career, steal a pension, and maybe, if the lie is big enough and stupid enough, lead to some jail time. For a detective to falsify evidentiary material, to wrongly attribute statements to suspects and witnesses, carries a risk far greater than the reward. How much does it matter—really matter—to the detective if any one suspect charged with any one murder goes to prison? He does fourteen of these guys a year, a couple hundred in a career. For what reason is he going to start believing that the world ends when he doesn't win a case? If it's a police shooting, or if it's someone the cop knows, then some corners might be cut, but not for something that happened in the 1900 block of Etting Street on a Saturday night last summer.

The one notable exception to the marked honesty of a good police witness, the only point in the legal process where law officers can be expected to lie routinely or, at the very least, exaggerate, is probable cause.

For narcotics or vice detectives in particular it's become a ridiculous game, this business of establishing the correct legal prerequisites for a search or arrest. Not surprisingly, it isn't enough to say that the suspect was a squirrel who'd been out on that corner about ten minutes too long. No, the law of the land requires that the arresting officer had the opportunity to observe the defendant operating in a suspicious manner on a corner known for drug trafficking and that upon closer inspection, the officer noticed a glassine envelope sticking out of a sweatshirt pocket as well as a bulge in the front waistband indicative of a weapon.

Yeah. Right.

Probable cause on a street search is and always will be a cosmic joke, a systemic deceit. In some parts of Baltimore, PC means looking at a passing radio car for two seconds longer than an innocent man would. The courts can't acknowledge it, but in the real world you watch a guy until you're sure he's dirty, then you jack him up, find the dope or the gun and then create a legal justification for the arrest.

In homicide, where the name of the game is search-and-seizure, with affidavits written in advance for specific addresses, the PC generally has to be straight up. After all, you need the judge's signature on the warrant just to get you inside. A detective with a talent for the written word may be able to get some weak or exaggerated PC past a duty judge, but at least he's required to put something in the affidavit.

For the homicide detective, the only real moment of equivocation on the stand occurs not over the issue of probable cause, but when a defense attorney asks whether his defendant's statements were coerced, or whether his client asked for a lawyer before making those statements. In his heart of hearts, a good detective knows that every statement is, to some degree, the result of coercion if not outright fraud. But, holding to a strict legal definition, he can answer in the negative and call his testimony something other than perjury. After all, the defendant got his rights, he signed his Form 69. He had his chance.

"But did he want a lawyer?"

Well, a detective could ask, how do you define want? Probably half of all suspects get into an interrogation room and say they want a lawyer, or they might need a lawyer, or maybe they should talk to a lawyer. If they stick to it, if they really want that lawyer and they don't want to talk, then the interrogation is over. But any detective worth his salt tries—for a time, at least—to convince them otherwise, content in the knowledge that there isn't a Supreme Court justice standing outside the interrogation room door.

"Did my client ask for a lawyer?"

"No, he did not."

On the stand, the last rule for a homicide detective is that nothing is personal—nothing between the detective and the defendant, nothing between the detective and the lawyers. On the stand, demeanor counts. A cop who loses his cool long enough to display contempt or malice for the defendant or his counsel provides the jury with the image of a malevolent system, of a crusade rather than a prosecution. The defense attorney calls you a liar, you impassively deny that. He declares your investigation to be incompetent, you deny that, too. His client eyefucks you from the trial table, you ignore it.

For a veteran detective, there is nothing hard in any of that. After all, if it's the ordinary homicide case, the indifference is probably genuine. But even when the case matters, a veteran doesn't do anything to make the defendant believe that he cares, or that the outcome of this case has any relevance in any world that rates. In its way, it's an attitude that offers the defendant even less than anger or contempt. In court, a detective's message to the defendant is clear and unmistakable: Win or lose, you're still a piece of shit living on the margins. If the jury comes back guilty, you're down for some years; if the jury doesn't do the job, you still don't count. Six months from now, you'll be back in city jail on another charge, says the attitude. Either that or someone on my shift will be out there one night chalking your ass off.

Strangely, the defendants rarely take it personally. They come into the courtroom from the heat of the basement lockup; shackled and cuffed, they look around and catch the eye of the detective. More often than not, they nod or acknowledge the loyal opposition in some small way. In the course of a long trial, a few actually reach out and shake the detective's hand or mutter a senseless thank-you for no reason that can be discerned, as if the detective was doing them some kind of favor by showing up.

But on rare occasion, when a defendant is talking shit—performing in the courtroom, signifying, passing wolf tickets to the judge and prosecutor—a detective will step through the psychological barrier. Only then will the defendant be acknowledged in any real way; only then does a detective let anyone suspect that he may actually care about the legal outcome.

Earlier in the year, Dave Brown happened to be in a courtroom for the jury's verdict on two of his defendants—west-siders, age twenty-two and fourteen, charged with murdering an elderly minister in a street robbery near University Hospital the previous spring. Brown remained silent as the jury forewoman read out first-degree verdicts, but the older defendant suddenly lost his chill.

"You happy now, bitch?" he shouted, turning to glare at the detective.

The gallery fell into silence.

"Yes," said Brown quietly. "I'm pleased."

Inside a courtroom, it's as much as a detective allows himself.

WEDNESDAY, OCTOBER 19

At his cluttered desk on the fourth floor of Courthouse West, Lawrence C. Doan rearranges a stack of legal pads and runs one finger along the bottom of his dark bangs and then back over the top, carefully reassuring himself that all is in place. No cowlicks today. No antigravitational shift in the tie's Windsor. No lint on the lapels. No problem whatsoever, save for the fact that today he's going to try to prosecute a murder in the city of Baltimore, which is a little like trying to drive a Winnebago through the eye of a needle.

And now, when Doan wishes only to be left alone to review notes and prepare his opening, a homicide detective bounds through the door to yank his prosecutor's chain over matters large and small—a deliberate act of sadism, born of the same impulse that causes small children to pull the wings off flies.

"Are we ready?" asks Garvey.

"Are we ready," says Doan. "You come in here ten minutes before court and ask me that?"

"Just don't fuck up my case, Larry."

"How can I?" asks Doan. "It came to me prefucked."

Garvey ignores him. "The photos come in with me, right?" he asks, wondering about evidentiary order.

"No," says Doan, trying to think bigger thoughts, "I'll get those in with Wilson. Where's Wilson? Did you call the crime lab?"

"And the bullets?" asks Garvey, ignoring him. "Do you need the bullets today?"

"Which bullets? Where's Wilson, does he—"

"The bullets from the trunk of the car."

"Um, no. Not today. You can take those back to evidence control," says Doan, preoccupied. "Does Wilson know he's on this afternoon?"

"I think so."

"You think so?" says Doan. "You think so? What about Kopera?"

"What about him?"

Doan begins to change colors.

"You're not going to get to Kopera this afternoon, right?" asks Garvey.

Doan buries his head in his hands, contemplating the known realities. The federal budget deficit is out of control, the ozone layer is being depleted, twenty pissant countries have nuclear weapons and I, Lawrence Doan, am trapped in a small room with Rich Garvey, ten minutes away from opening arguments.

"No, I don't need Kopera," says Doan, regaining his calm. "I'll need Wilson probably."

"You want me to call him?" asks Garvey, now playful.

"Yes," says Doan. "Yes. Please. Call him."

"Well, Larry, if it'll help you relax . . ."

Doan shoots Garvey a look.

"Don't you look at me that way, motherfucker," says the detective, pushing back the suit jacket to reach his waist holster and grab the butt of his gun. "I'll shoot you full of holes right here and now and everyone in this courthouse will rule it justifiable."

The prosecutor responds with his middle finger, and the detective lifts the gun a few inches from the holster, then laughs.

"F. Lee Doan," says Garvey, smiling. "You better not lose this case, motherfucker."

"Well, if you'd do your fucking job and get me some witnesses . . ."

The standard prosecutorial lament, heard a thousand times a day by a thousand police officers in a thousand distant courthouses.

"You've got witnesses," counters Garvey. "Romaine Jackson, Sharon Henson, Vincent Booker . . ."

At the mention of Booker's name, Doan gives the detective another look.

"Well," says Garvey, shrugging, "he's definitely a witness . . ."

"We've been through this, goddammit," says Doan, growing irritated. "I do not want to put Vincent Booker on the witness stand. That's the last thing I want to do."

"Okay," says Garvey, shrugging. "But I think you're making a mistake."

"Yeah," says Doan, "I know you do. And I'm sure when we lose this case you'll be the first one to say I told you so."

"I sure as shit will be," says Garvey.

The prosecutor rubs his temples, then looks down at the pile of paper on his desk that represents the state's case against Robert Frazier in the murder of Lena Lucas. For the sake of giving Garvey grief, he has overstated the matter just a bit: The case against Frazier is solid and he does indeed have witnesses. But it is nonetheless a circumstantial prosecution, and therefore—as prosecutors enjoy pointing out—it is subject to circumstances beyond control. Without an eyeball witness or the murder weapon, without a full confession or an obvious motive, the web that connects Frazier to the death of his lover will be thin. To Garvey, who has built the case, Vincent Booker is part of that web; to avoid his testimony as a trial tactic is to weaken the case. But to Doan, Vincent Booker is a loose cannon rolling around on the deck of the ship, a witness who might be seen as an alternate suspect by the jurors.

After all, Vincent did sell Frazier's cocaine. He knew Lena Lucas and already admitted to his knowledge of the events that preceded his father's murder. Garvey himself believed that Vincent was probably present when Frazier demanded that old man Booker return the drugs he had taken from his son's room. Vincent probably stood there dumbstruck as Frazier used that knife to cut his father repeatedly in the face, demanding to know where the package was. He could still have been standing there when Frazier finally used the gun. Given those probable truths, no one could say where Vincent's trial testimony might lead.

No, thinks Doan again, the risks of Vincent Booker's testimony are greater than the benefits, though trying to argue the point with Garvey is futile. The detective is convinced that Frazier's attorney, Paul Polansky, will use Vincent Booker as an alternate suspect in any event. In Garvey's view, keeping Booker in the background will only play into the opposition's strategy.

That difference of opinion, coupled with the usual concerns about all the logistics involving evidence and witnesses, is enough to ruin whatever quiet reflection Doan had hoped for before this morning's arguments. Instead, a detective and his prosecutor begin the day in each other's faces.

Doan smiles, then waves his tormentor out of the cubicle for a few moments of silence. A veteran of the Baltimore courthouse, Larry Doan is short and stocky, with dark hair, pale skin, wire-rims, and an eye that wanders just enough to deny his face symmetry. In the courtroom, Doan's appearance and demeanor often suggest a near-permanent state of woe; at times he seems to embody every stereotype about the underpaid, overworked big-city prosecutor, his briefcase crammed with motions, answers to motions and stipulations, his values crowded by the rising tide of human despair. If the Baltimore state's attorney's office ever needed a poster boy, Doan would be the odds-on favorite.

Among the other lawyers in the trial division, Doan's reputation is reasonably good. He is said to be fair, reasoned and methodical with both evidence and witnesses. He preps hard for trials and his closing arguments are always competent, often skillful, though sometimes not nearly as strong or emotional as some think they could be. But in one respect, he is a rare prize for any homicide detective who happens to care about a case: Doan will fight. Assured that a defendant is guilty and that no reasonable plea can be taken, Doan isn't afraid to take a borderline or marginal case to a jury. Like any trial lawyer, he hates to lose, but he is willing to lose if the only alternative is a stet or dismissal.

Garvey is counting on this: He knows Doan will fight, just as he knows that the evidence against Robert Frazier is sufficient but not overwhelming. Kidding aside, he's glad to have Doan for this one.

Leaving the prosecutor's cubicle, the detective walks down the side stairwell to the third-floor hallway outside Cliff Gordy's courtroom. There are two benches in the hall and a third in the carpeted anteroom just outside Gordy's court. Because he is a sequestered witness, Garvey will make the three benches his office for the next week, as a prosecution that he worked hard to prepare unfolds without him.

For Garvey, the relegation to prosecutor's assistant is always hard to accept. Doan isn't one of those lawyers who wants a cop to be seen and not heard; he's willing to take advice. On the other hand, he's going to listen to that advice, evaluate it, and then try the case his way. Garvey, who knows the Lena Lucas case better than any man, is not exactly known for his abundant tact; in fact, he's never met an opinion he'd be unwilling to venture. Yet Doan must walk through Judge Gordy's double doors and try the case on the merits; Garvey must sit outside and play shepherd to the state's evidence and witnesses. The morning banter in Doan's office suggests the change in status: In February, it was Garvey who was sweating this case, scratching for every available piece of evidence. Now Garvey has the time to joke and tease. Now he can pretend not to know whether Wilson from the crime lab is going to show up for trial. Now he can criticize the trial strategy and demand victory. Now it's Larry Doan's turn to carry the weight.

Yet Garvey wants very much to win this case. For one thing, he has never lost a case that has gone to a jury trial and he'd like to keep that admirable record intact. For another, he would like to see Lena Lucas avenged. She was using cocaine and helping Frazier to deal; still, she was a good enough mother to her daughters and she never hurt anyone but herself. Both of Lena's daughters and her sister are scheduled as state's witnesses, and all three are waiting with Garvey. The rest of the family is already inside the court, but earlier that morning, they greeted Garvey in the corridor as if he were Moses down from Sinai. Good people, thinks Garvey, settling in on the bench. They deserve to win this.

The man of the hour, Robert Frazier, is already inside the courtroom and behind the defense table, sitting next to his lawyer with a hardbound copy of the New Testament in front of him, a cardboard marker pressed inside the Book of Luke. Frazier is wearing a well-tailored dark suit and a crisp white shirt, but somehow there's no mistaking his line of work. Just before the jury files in, Frazier stretches his tall frame, pushes his chair back and yawns like a man at ease in courtrooms. He turns to look at the members of the Lucas family in the back row, stares for a moment, then turns away.

The motions hearings were yesterday morning, with Doan successfully fighting off some routine efforts by Paul Polansky, who tried to have the identification of his client by Romaine Jackson—the young girl who saw Frazier enter Lena's building from her third-floor window—ruled inadmissible. Polansky argued that Frazier's photo had been given greater prominence in the photo array shown to the girl because it was in the upper left corner and because the other men seemed younger and less thin. Gordy denied the motion, as well as one that challenged a search warrant that Garvey and Donald Kincaid had written for Frazier's Chrysler after the arrest. Live .38 ammunition had been found in the trunk.

The rest of the day was spent on the selection of a jury—voir dire—the elaborate process by which potential jurors are screened for bias by the court. Voir dire is, in itself, an essential part of the trial strategy, with prosecutors using their limited number of "strikes" to keep out those potential jurors who have been beaten by police, have relatives in the prison system, or generally regard the criminal courts of the United States as a sham perpetrated by running dog capitalist jackals. At the same time, the defense attorney endeavors to use his strikes to remove all who are related to a law enforcement officer, who were ever the victims of a crime, or who truly believe that if the man seated at the defense table is accused of the crime, he must be guilty. Because the population of Baltimore generally holds membership in one or more categories, voir dire in the Lucas case took quite a while—at least until the lawyers exhausted the allowable strikes.

From his seat at the trial table, Doan now watches the product of yesterday's effort walk in from the jury room. A typical Baltimore jury—predominantly black, predominantly female. Polansky didn't exactly go out of his way to find white jurors willing to sit in judgment on his black client; nor, for that matter, did Larry Doan strike any white strays from the jury box. Still, watching the jurors file in, Doan is generally satisfied. Most are working people, but with the sole exception of the girl in the front row, all seem sharp and attentive, which matters for a case such as this one. The girl in the front row, however, is trouble. Doan watches her slump into her seat, arms crossed, staring at the floor. She's bored already; God knows what she'll be like after four days of testimony.

Judge Clifton Gordy calls the court to order and begins his preamble, explaining the legal arena to the jurors. Tall, quiet, serious, Gordy cuts quite a figure on the bench. His language is precise, his humor is sharp, and his manner often seems, to lawyers at least, well suited to tyranny. Attorneys who fail to rise when stating their objections in Gordy's court generally find themselves ignored. Gordy knows his law and he knows his lawyers; Doan, for example, worked for Gordy when the judge was heading the trial division. One other thing about the judge suits Doan in this case: Cliff Gordy is black, and that takes some of the edge off the fact that two white Jewish guys will be arguing the question of a black man's freedom. It will certainly help the black jurors to believe that the criminal justice system actually represents them.

As Gordy finishes his introduction and Doan rises to begin his opening, Garvey sits in the anteroom, struggling with the morning *Sun* crossword.

"British gun," says Garvey. "Four letters."

"S-T-E-N," says Dave Brown from the other end of the bench, where he waits in case the trial testimony turns to the Purnell Booker case. "A British gun is always Sten in crosswords."

"You're right," says Garvey.

Lost to them is Doan's greeting to the jury, his warning that this is a murder case, a nasty, ugly, gruesome murder case that involves the willful taking of human life. That accomplished, Doan begins the long, labored process by which jurors are shorn of preconceptions.

"This is not television," he assures the jury. "Unlike TV shows, motive is not an element of the crime of first-degree murder. You don't know exactly why it happened. It's something you would like to know, it's something the person trying the case would like to know, but it's not necessary to know it to prove the crime."

And then, following a standard script, Doan pulls out the jigsaw puzzle, the courtroom metaphor used by nearly every American prosecutor to earn his pay. You see, Doan tells the jury, this case is like a jigsaw puzzle. And like a puzzle that's been around the house for a while, some of the pieces might be missing. "But, ladies and gentlemen, even with the missing pieces, when you assemble that jigsaw puzzle, you can still determine what the puzzle is about and what it shows."

Doan launches into the story of Charlene Lucas. He touches all of the essentials: her relationship with Robert Frazier, her involvement in drugs, the crime scene itself and the investigation that followed. Doan tells the jurors about Romaine Jackson, who identified Frazier as the man who came home with Lena the night of the murder; he talks about Frazier's initial interview with Garvey in which the defendant offered an alibi and promised to come in with his own .38; he tells them about Sharon Denise Henson, "Nee-Cee," who failed to corroborate Frazier's alibi. He tells them about the nested clothes and the victim's nudity and the lack of forced entry—indications that Lena was murdered by someone she knew intimately.

"Give Mr. Frazier his fair day in court," Doan tells the jury. "Give him his trial and give Charlene Lucas her fair day in court and her family, who are here today, their day in court. And after you put it all together and you finish the puzzle, you are going to see a picture and that picture is going to be the defendant killing Charlene Lucas. Thank you."

The prosecutor does not mention the murder of Purnell Booker and that the ballistics report links that murder to the Lucas killing. He does not mention Vincent Booker, who admitted to supplying Frazier with .38 wadcutter reloads before both murders and told the detectives that his father was killed for taking Frazier's drugs. By the court's ruling on a pretrial motion, the Booker murder is prejudicial and not to be mentioned in the jury's presence—a ruling that appeals to both attorneys. Because just as Doan knows that Vincent Booker is a risk, so does Polansky. A good lawyer never asks any question without knowing the answer, and with Vincent Booker, Polansky can't be sure what the answers might be. As Frazier's attorney, he needs to raise the specter of Vincent Booker just enough to suggest an alternate suspect to the jury. But he, too, has decided not to risk calling Booker as a court witness. Loose cannons roll both ways.

During his opening, Polansky assures the jurors that Robert Frazier "has been fighting in the Baltimore City Jail for the last eight months to come here and tell you his story of Lena's death, to tell you that because of perhaps a poorly run police investigation they have the wrong man, to tell you that he is in no way, no shape, no form, guilty of this crime."

My client is not a saint, Polansky tells the jury. Drugs? Yes, he sold drugs. A .38-caliber handgun. Yes, he had a gun. You will hear good things and bad things about Robert Frazier, Polansky declares, but does any of that make him guilty of the murder?

"On a number of occasions in this case," says Polansky, "there is a man named Vincent Booker who is involved with Charlene Lucas and has access to her apartment . . . Well, this is not *Perry Mason* and people will not jump up in court and confess to murder. But the story that Robert Frazier is here to tell you will indicate that Vincent Booker committed this crime."

Polansky continues his rebuttal, explaining that Frazier cooperated in the police investigation, that he voluntarily came forward, but that it soon became clear that the detectives were focusing on him as a suspect to the exclusion of everything else. He didn't bring in the weapon, true; he was fearful of a handgun charge and these detectives were obviously trying to put the murder on him. And they were doing this after he tried to help them find Lena's killer.

"Mr. Doan told you about a puzzle and he is right," says Polansky, finding common ground. "You can tell a picture without seeing all of the pieces, if you're missing three, or four, or five pieces. But if you're missing too many pieces . . ."

In the anteroom, Garvey is vexed by puzzles of a different sort. When the court breaks for lunch, he is deep into the *Evening Sun* crossword, having battled the morning paper's puzzle to a draw. Dave Brown is asleep sitting up, the Booker case file in his lap.

Justice pauses for lunch. The detectives leave, they eat, they return to the bench to watch a steady parade of state's witnesses going in and out of the afternoon session: Lena Lucas's older daughter, to testify about Frazier's relationship with her mother and to shoot down the notion that Vincent Booker had access to the apartment; the upstairs neighbor at 17 North Gilmor, to testify to his discovery of the body and place the time of death; the first officer from the Western District, to testify to the preservation of the scene and the recovery of evidence; Wilson, from the crime lab, to bring the scene photos and testify to the attempt to lift fingerprints; Purvis, from the trace section, to testify about the comparison of latent prints and the inability to match any of the lifts from Gilmor Street to anyone other than Charlene Lucas.

When the bailiff finally comes for Garvey, he's just about done with the *Evening Sun*, having been stumped by some five-letter French river. Leaving the paper on the bench, Garvey moves toward the witness stand clothed in dark blue pinstripes, the power suit according him the required confidence. The Republican tie, the eyeglasses—ladies and gentlemen of the jury, meet the police department's vice president for sales and marketing.

"Good afternoon," says Doan in a stage voice. "How long have you been with the Baltimore City Police Department?"

"Over thirteen years," says Garvey, straightening his tie.

"Of that thirteen years, how long have you been with the homicide unit?"

"The last three and a half."

"And would you care to tell the ladies and gentlemen of the jury how many murder cases you've handled during that period of time."

"I've been assigned personally to slightly over fifty cases."

"And," says Doan, leading, "I assume you have been involved in one way or another in parts of other cases."

"Numerous investigations," says Garvey.

Slowly, Doan begins to take the detective through the crime scene at 17 North Gilmor. Garvey describes the apartment, giving special attention to the security features, including the burglar alarm that had been turned off. He provides a detailed description of the scene, and the jury again hears about the lack of forced entry, the nested pile of clothes, the scratches on the headboard suggesting that she was stabbed while lying in bed. Then, at Doan's direction, Garvey walks over to the jury box, where Doan takes him through the crime scene photos already admitted to evidence.

The photos themselves are always the source of considerable courtroom conflict, with defense attorneys arguing that the depiction of the bloodied victim is unnecessarily prejudicial and prosecutors arguing that the photos have probative value for a jury. Prosecutors usually win the argument, as Doan has in this case. Thus Lena Lucas and her wounds are displayed for the jurors in glossy splendor from a variety of camera angles over Polansky's continuing objection. The jurors seem impressed.

Garvey is at the jury box for ten minutes before returning to the witness stand, where Doan takes him through the search of the crime scene and the interviews with neighbors. The prosecutor makes a point of asking about street lighting outside the Gilmor Street rowhouse and Garvey describes the sodium vapor light in the middle of the block—an essential foundation for the coming testimony from Romaine Jackson.

"At this time, I have no further questions of Detective Garvey," says Doan after twenty-five minutes of testimony. "However, I wish to recall him later."

"You may," says Gordy. "Cross-examination, Mr. Polansky."

"For the same reasons, I will restrict my cross-examination to the testimony elicited on direct."

Fine with me, thinks Garvey, calm and collected on the stand. With just the boilerplate of the crime scene to worry about, he reasons, there won't be much in the way of controversy this afternoon.

Polansky goes into some detail on the pattern of wounds, prompting the detective to agree that the stab wounds came before the gunshot wound to the head; the defense wounds to the hands prove as much. The defense attorney also spends some time dealing with the empty purse, the broken bag of rice and the empty gelatin capsules on the bedroom floor. "So it would appear, would it not, sir, that whatever assailants attacked and killed Ms. Lucas probably took whatever drugs she had in that pocketbook?"

"Objection," says Doan.

The judge agrees that the defense attorney's question is too speculative, but the image of Vincent Booker hovers over the courtroom. Why, after all, would Frazier murder someone to take drugs that were already his? No reason unless, of course, he wanted to make the killing seem like a drug robbery.

Polansky moves forward, chronicling the drug paraphernalia scattered around the crime scene in an effort to make his point another way. He brings Garvey back to the nested clothes. The apartment was very tidy, was it not? Very neat, Garvey agrees.

"The kind of individual who would not take off her clothes and throw them on the floor but would take them off, fold them up and put them away. Would you agree?"

Oh my, thinks Garvey, you tricky bastard, you. "No," says the detective. "I would not agree."

Polansky leaves that seeming contradiction with the jury and moves on to state's exhibit 2U, a photograph of the bedroom floor after the bed had been lifted. The defense attorney points out a soft pack of Newport cigarettes visible on the floor.

"And there is an ashtray?" he adds.

"Yes, sir," says Garvey.

"Did you ever determine Ms. Lucas was a smoker?"

Aw shit, thinks Garvey. He's going to run wild with this crap. "I can't recall if I did or not."

"Do you think that might have been of some significance?"

"I'm sure the question came up during the investigation," says Garvey, trying to tiptoe around the minefield. "Obviously, the answer didn't have any significance."

"Did you ask her daughters or anyone close to her whether she was a smoker?"

"I don't recall specifically doing that."

"If she wasn't a smoker, do you agree that finding a pack of cigarettes would have been worth looking into?"

"I would agree the cigarette pack would have been," says Garvey, his voice clipped.

"To find out who was close to her and was a smoker," Polansky continues. "Because you assumed someone close to her was in there because there was no forced entry, correct?"

"That is correct," says Garvey.

"So it might be significant to find out if anyone close to her or any of the possible suspects which we'll talk about at some later time may have been a smoker and specifically a smoker of Newports."

"Objection," says Doan, trying for a broken field tackle. "Is there a question?"

"Yes," says Polansky. "Would you agree it is significant?"

"No," says Garvey, regrouping. "Because we don't know when the cigarette pack was placed there. It was beneath the bed. It certainly would have been something to look into, but it would have been something I wouldn't base an investigation on."

"Well," says Polansky, "except for the fact, sir, wouldn't you agree that Ms. Lucas was a very neat person and not likely to have left a pack of cigarettes on the floor for some long period of time?"

"Objection," says Doan.

"Isn't it much more likely the pack was left there the night of the murder?"

"Objection."

Gordy intervenes. "Can you answer that question to a reasonable degree of certainty? Yes or no?"

From the prosecution table, Doan is staring at the detective, his head moving back and forth in a slight, barely discernible shaking motion. Take the out, he wants to say. Take the out.

"I can answer," says Garvey.

"Overruled," says Gordy.

"Underneath the bed there appeared to be a fair amount of debris. The overall visible areas in the house were neat and tidy, but underneath the bed I would not characterize it as being neat and tidy."

"Was the phone under the bed?" asks Polansky.

"Yes," says Garvey, looking at the photo. "We moved that back to take the photograph."

"It is fair to say the phone wasn't lying there a long period of time?"

"I don't know when the phone was placed there," says Garvey.

A partial save by a veteran detective. Polansky counts his winnings and moves on, asking about the human hairs that were recovered from the sheet by the lab tech and sent to the trace section. Were they ever compared to anyone?

"You can't tell from a hair who it belongs to," says Garvey, now on his guard.

"They can't tell you anything more than that about hair. There is no scientific test that is at all helpful in a homicide investigation?"

"There is no way they can tell you that a particular hair can come from a particular person."

"Can they narrow it down to a white man's or black man's?" asks Polansky.

Garvey grants the point: "But they can't go too much farther."

The detective and defense attorney circle each other for several more questions until Polansky's point is clear: The hair recovered at the scene was never compared to anyone else's hair. Even though such a comparison would be pointless, Polansky leaves the impression that Garvey's investigation was less than thorough.

So far Polansky has earned his money. Garvey proves as much at the end of the cross-examination, when the defense attorney asks him about time-of-death.

"Rigor mortis had been fully set and she was coming out of rigor mortis," says the detective. "Also, with the dried bloodstains underneath her head—the blood was thick and coagulated and the outer edges of the blood were dried into the carpet—it seemed to me she had been there probably for twenty-four hours."

Polansky and Doan both look up. Twenty-four hours would put time of death at late afternoon the previous day.

"She had been dead for twenty-four hours?" asks Polansky.

"That's correct," says Garvey.

Doan looks hard at the witness, trying to make Garvey think the answer through.

"So it would have been your conclusion she had to have been killed at least at five P.M. on the twenty-first?" says Polansky.

Garvey realizes. "I take that back. No, I'm sorry. I got confused. I meant at least twelve hours."

"I thought that's what you meant," says Polansky. "Thank you. No further questions."

On redirect, Doan goes back to the recovered hairs, but that only allows Polansky, in his follow-up questions, to suggest again that the detective was not interested in pursuing all the evidence: "If you checked those hairs, you would have been able to determine whether they belonged to Mr. Frazier or Ms. Lucas or someone else. Is that not true?"

"If we did a comparison between their hairs we can tell if they were similar," repeats Garvey wearily.

"Which you had the ability to do, but you didn't do it," says Polansky.

"I felt no need to do it," says Garvey.

"That's a pity, sir. Thank you."

The last comment gets to Doan, who turns in his chair to look at Polansky. "Come on," he says sarcastically. Then Doan looks up at the judge. "I have no further questions."

"You may step down, sir," says Gordy.

The first day ends. In the corridor five minutes later, Garvey encounters Polansky and feigns anger, cocking a fist as if ready to throw a punch. "You miserable shyster," he says, smiling.

"Hey, now," says Polansky, a little defensive. "Nothing personal, Rich. I'm just doing the job."

"Oh, I know it," says Garvey, hitting the defense attorney's shoulder. "I got no complaint."

But Doan is not so easily mollified. Walking back to his office with Garvey, he issues a few choice epithets for his worthy adversary.

The hairs, the Newports—that was smoke, the raw material of any good defense attorney. Smoke is the theory that says: When you don't want to argue the state's evidence, create your own. No doubt Robert Frazier is ready to take the stand and declare that Vincent Booker buys Newports.

Garvey knows the cigarette pack could be a problem and he apologizes to Doan. "I'm sure I dealt with it out at the scene. I just couldn't remember the specifics, though."

"Don't worry about it," says Doan charitably. "But can we—"

"I'll check with Jackie or Henrietta right away," says Garvey, ahead of him. "Larry, I'm sure it was Lena's cigarettes, but I just don't remember who told me."

"Okay," says Doan. "The bullshit about the hair, I could care less, but he made some points on the cigarettes. We've got to shoot that down."

THURSDAY, OCTOBER 20

On the second day of the trial, Larry Doan moves quickly to make up for lost ground.

"Your honor," says Doan, as court comes to order. "The state at this time will recall Henrietta Lucas for two questions."

Polansky can see what is coming.

"Miss Lucas," asks the prosecutor, "were you aware at the time of the death of your mother whether she smoked?"

"Yes," says Lena's older daughter.

"Do you know, approximately, when she started smoking?"

"Around the beginning of this year."

"And," asks Doan, "what brand of cigarettes did she smoke, if you know?"

"Newports."

Polansky, sitting at the defense table, shakes his head. But he is not quite ready to give in. On the cross, he works hard to suggest that Robert Frazier spent more time with his lover than her grown daughter did and that he would be in a better position to know whether Lena was smoking or not. He tries to suggest that it was oddly coincidental that a forty-year-old woman would start smoking two months before her death. He asks the daughter whether she had discussed her testimony in detail with the prosecutor, suggesting to the jury that she may have been led to her answers. It is a good effort; once again, Polansky earns his money. Still, when Henrietta Lucas leaves the stand after five minutes' testimony, the cigarette pack is no longer a real threat.

Doan follows her with John Smialek, who describes the autopsy and the nature of the wounds and brings in as evidence a series of black-and-white photos depicting the injuries in detail. More than the scene photos, the antiseptic shots from the overhead camera on Penn Street catch the excess of violence: three gunshot wounds—one with thick powder burns to the left side of the face, one to the chest, one to the left arm; eleven stab wounds to the back, plus superficial cuts to the neck and lower jaw; defense wounds to the palm of the right hand. In the form of ten graphic pictures, admitted over the continuing objection of Robert Frazier's attorney, Lena Lucas is allowed her day in court.

But the morning's testimony is merely prelude to the real battle—a war of credibility that begins later in the day when a seventeen-year-old schoolgirl, obviously terrified, walks past Robert Frazier and takes the stand.

Romaine Jackson is literally shaking as she takes the oath; the jurors can see that. She sits demurely, hands in her lap, face locked on Doan, eyes unwilling to acknowledge the tall, dark man at the defendant's table. In Doan's worst nightmare, he sees this witness—this essential witness—collapsing from fear. He sees her unable to answer, unable to tell the truth about what she saw from her window on Gilmor Street that night, unable to recall the things that they had talked about in the pretrial interviews. All of which would be understandable, even forgivable: The state of Maryland will not allow her to cast a vote or buy a beer, but the state's attorney will nonetheless ask her to identify a murder suspect in open court.

"My name is Romaine Jackson," she says softly, responding to the clerk's questions. "I live at Sixteen-o-six West Pratt Street."

"Miss Jackson," says Doan soothingly, "try to keep your voice up so the ladies and gentlemen of the jury can hear you."

"Yes, sir."

As slowly, as calmly as possible, Doan takes her through the foundation questions and back to that night on Gilmor Street, back to the moment when she happened to be looking out of that third-floor window before falling off to sleep. The girl's answers are close to monosyllabic; the court clerk reminds her once again to speak into the microphone.

"At some point, did you have an occasion to see your neighbor Charlene Lucas outside of your apartment?" asks Doan.

"Yes."

"Would you tell the ladies and gentlemen of the jury approximately what time it was when you saw her?"

"Eleven o'clock going onto twelve."

"Was she by herself or with someone else?"

"Yes," says the girl. "A man."

"Do you see that individual in court today?"

"Yes, sir," says the girl.

"Would you point that individual out?"

Romaine Jackson's eyes break from the prosecutor for half a second, just long enough to follow her right hand in the direction of Robert Frazier.

"Him," she says quietly, her eyes once again riveted on Doan.

The prosecutor moves forward slowly. "Would you describe what the defendant looked like on that evening?"

"Tall, dark and slim," she says.

"What was he wearing that evening?"

"A black coat. A black jacket like this one."

"Was he wearing anything on his head?"

"A hat."

"What color was it?"

"A white hat," she says, a hand to her forehead, "with a snap on it."

She is crying now, just enough for it to show, not enough for Doan to think of stopping. Following the prosecutor's lead, she tells the court about how Lena and the tall man walked toward Lena's rowhouse next door and then disappeared from her view, how she fell asleep to the sound of an argument coming from a lower floor of the adjacent house, how she later heard about the murder.

"Miss Jackson," asks Doan, "after you discovered or learned that Charlene Lucas had been murdered, did you go to the police with the information you had?"

"No," she says, crying again.

"Why was that, ma'am?"

Polansky objects.

"Overruled," says Gordy.

"Scared," the girl says. "I didn't want to get involved."

"Are you still scared?"

"Yes," she says, her voice little more than a whisper.

Frightened but firm, Romaine Jackson holds to her testimony throughout Polansky's cross. The defense attorney works the edges of her story: the lighting on the street that night; the time that she was looking out the window; her reasons for looking out the window; her ability to hear the argument in the house next door. Polansky can't run roughshod over this young girl; even if harsh tactics could rattle her story, the jury would resent such treatment. Instead, he can only suggest that she is mistaken, that perhaps she cannot be sure she saw Robert Frazier when she says she saw him. Polansky works the corners of the girl's testimony for half an hour, prolonging her agony but doing little to change the essentials of her story. By the time she leaves the stand in the late afternoon, Romaine Jackson's quiet embrace of the truth is a powerful force.

"Whoa . . . Romaine, honey," says Garvey, catching her as she races out the rear doors of the courtroom. "Hey, now, tell the truth. That wasn't all that bad now, was it?"

"Yes," she says, now crying and laughing in the same breath. "It was."

"Oh, come on," says the detective, wrapping an arm around her. "I'll bet you got to like it a little at the end, didn't you?"

"No," she says, laughing. "No, I did not."

Half an hour later, when Doan emerges from the courtroom, Garvey buttonholes him in the third-floor corridor: "How'd my girl do in there?"

"She was great," says Doan without exaggeration. "Scared, but great."

But it is far from over. The next day's testimony brings the end of the state's case, with both attorneys skirmishing over the ballistic evidence and the .38 ammunition recovered in the case. With Dave Brown on the witness stand, Doan tries to limit the testimony to the .38 bullets recovered from Frazier's car after his arrest; Polansky, laboring hard not to violate the pretrial motions prohibiting any mention of the Purnell Booker slaying, probes Brown on cross about the issue of the earlier search warrant, when the detectives recovered the .38 wadcutter ammo and knives from beneath Vincent Booker's bed. It is a sensitive issue—neither attorney wants to cross the line that brings the Booker murder into testimony—and it requires four bench conferences with Gordy before Brown's testimony is successfully negotiated. On redirect, Doan makes sure to have Brown testify that the knives recovered from Vincent Booker were tested and found to be free of blood, but still Polansky has managed once again, with a few questions, to raise the specter of an alternate suspect.

He does so yet again when Joe Kopera, from the firearms unit, follows Brown to the stand. Doan leads Kopera through the examination of bullets used to kill the victim, as well as the .38 cartridges found in Frazier's car after his arrest. The bullets are all of the same caliber, Kopera agrees. But that testimony, although limited, opens the door to Polansky, who follows up by noting that the bullets that killed Lena Lucas are .38

wadcutters, and the bullets recovered from his client's car are .38 round-noses.

"So what you are saying," says Polansky, "is that while the bullets that came from Robert Frazier's car are indeed thirty-eights, they weren't the same kind of thirty-eights that were recovered from the crime scene."

"Yes, sir, that is correct."

"And some of the bullets—twelve of the bullets recovered from Vincent Booker's residence—were not only thirty-eight caliber but were also wadcutter. Is that correct?"

"Yes," says Kopera.

If Rich Garvey could hear this, if he could hear Polansky propping up the shadowy figure of Vincent Booker in front of the jury, he might be inclined to wring Doan's neck. The only way to counter Polansky is to make the link between the bullets taken from Vincent Booker and Robert Frazier, and the only way to do that is to put Vincent Booker on the stand. Booker himself could testify that he gave the wadcutters to Frazier on the night of the murder; that Frazier had told him they were going to get the drugs back from his father and had asked him for ammunition. But that kind of testimony might raise more questions than it would answer; in Doan's mind, the only reasoned alternative is to cut bait.

As the state nears the end of its presentation, the courtroom observers are divided in their opinion about which side is winning. Doan has laid his foundation and guided Romaine Jackson successfully through her precious testimony. But Polansky has done well at points, too, and his deft use of Vincent Booker may be enough to sway the jury. But Doan isn't quite finished. He surprises Polansky with one last witness, a witness the defense attorney did not expect to see used against his client.

"Your honor," says Doan, after the jurors have been dismissed for the day's lunch hour, "I would request that Sharon Denise Henson, once she is called, be called as a court's witness."

"Objection!" says Polansky, almost shouting.

"Your reasons for saying, Mr. Doan," asks Gordy, "in light of the objection?"

The prosecutor recounts Robert Frazier's attempt to use his second girlfriend as an alibi in the murder of his first, as well as the detectives' subsequent interrogation of Nee-Cee Henson, in which she admitted that Frazier had left her dinner party early and then failed to return until morning. Henson signed a written statement to that effect and then gave similar testimony to the grand jury; now, with Frazier looking at the possibility of life without parole, she is backing up, telling Doan that she remembers the dinner party more clearly now. Frazier, she says, left for only a few moments early in the evening and then stayed with her until morning.

The woman began backing away from her testimony weeks ago, when she first signed a written statement for a private investigator employed by Polansky. Her behavior does not surprise Doan, who has learned that she has repeatedly visited Frazier at the city jail. Now he asks Gordy to call her to the stand as a hostile witness. To the prosecutor, Sharon Henson is valuable precisely because her testimony will not be credible.

"It would be an injustice for this jury to be deprived of seeing her and hearing from her," says Doan, "and it would put the state in an impossible position to actually call her as its own witness."

"Mr. Polansky?" asks Gordy.

"Your honor, would it be possible to respond . . . to respond to Mr. Doan's argument after the break so I can have an opportunity to absorb this?"

"Denied."

"Can I have a minute to look at this?" he says, scanning a copy of the state's motion.

"You may," says Gordy, the very picture of bored irritation. "While Mr. Polansky is looking at that, I will note for the record this issue has been anticipated in this trial, according to conversations between counsel and the court, since the beginning of this trial."

Polansky takes a few more minutes, then attempts a response, arguing that Miss Henson's current version of events doesn't differ dramatically from her earlier testimony. It doesn't seem, Polansky argues, that the statements are so inconsistent as to justify calling her as a court's witness.

"Do you intend to call her as a witness in the defense case?"

"Well, I don't know," says Polansky. "I can't make that commitment at this point, your honor."

"Because if you were, these questions would be moot."

"I agree," says the defense attorney. "I think the likelihood is I will not call her."

Gordy then announces his decision: Although she is lying to save her man, Sharon Henson will testify against him. The woman takes the stand after the lunch break and begins an ordeal that lasts well over an hour. If a man's freedom wasn't at issue, if a family wasn't seated in the gallery, praying for vengeance, Henson's performance in service of her boyfriend might count as comedy. Black velvet evening dress, pillbox hat, fur wrap—her appearance alone makes it difficult to take her testimony seriously. Conscious of her big moment in this drama, she takes the oath and crosses her legs in the witness box as if to mimic the femme fatales of every Grade B film noir. Even the jury begins to giggle.

"How old are you, ma'am?" asks Doan.

"Twenty-five."

"Do you know an individual by the name of Robert Frazier?"

"Yes, I do."

"Do you see that individual in the courtroom today?"

"Yes."

"Point him out, please."

The woman points to the defense table, then, for just a moment, smiles softly at the defendant. Frazier looks back impassively.

Doan establishes Sharon Henson's relationship with Frazier for the jury's benefit, then takes her back to the night of her party and the murder. In her statements to Garvey and the grand jury, Henson acknowledged that she had been drinking and using drugs, but she had unequivocally stated that Frazier had left the party late that evening and not returned until morning. Now, she is remembering something altogether different.

"Do you still consider yourself Mr. Frazier's girlfriend today?" asks Doan.

"Do I really have to answer that?"

"Yes," says Gordy. "Answer the question."

"Yes, I do."

"And during the time that Mr. Frazier has been incarcerated you have visited him at the jail, have you not?"

"Yes, I have."

"Now, how many times have you visited him there?"

"Three times."

Doan heaps it on, asking Henson to list the Valentine's Day gifts she received from Frazier before the murder. Then he turns abruptly to the issue of the .38 revolver that Frazier had given her to hold after the killing, the weapon that Frazier had taken back from her four days before Garvey and Kincaid showed up to interview her.

"And when he asked you for the weapon," says Doan, his voice even, "did he tell you why he wanted it?"

"Yes, he did."

"What did he say, ma'am?"

"That the police would be coming to talk to me, and he told them that I had the gun for him, but he didn't ask me for it."

"And?" asks Doan, looking up from his notes.

Sharon Henson glowers at the prosecutor before answering. "Not to give it to them," she says, then glances apologetically toward her boyfriend.

"He told you that the police would be coming looking for it. He didn't want you to give it to them?" asks Doan.

"I remember that, yeah."

So far, so good. Doan pushes on to the night of the party. He has the woman recite the guest list and the menu, and when she claims poor memory, Doan reminds her that they spoke only ten days earlier in his office.

"At that time, did you tell me that you had ham and cheese, collard greens, corn on the cob, lobster and wine?"

"Yes," she says, unperturbed.

Doan leads her into the events of the party: Frazier's arrival, his departure to pick up the lobster, his wardrobe on the night of the party.

"What was Mr. Frazier wearing?"

"Beige."

"Beige?"

"Beige," she repeats.

"He had beige slacks on?"

"Uh-huh."

"Beige shirt?"

"Uh-huh."

"Did he have a jacket that he was wearing?"

"Coat," she says.

"What kind of coat?" asks Doan.

"Beige," she says.

"Was he wearing anything else beige?"

The jury laughs. Henson glares at them.

"His hat?" asks Doan.

"It's like a golf cap."

"The kind with a brim around the front?" asks Doan.

"Snaps on it," she says, nodding in agreement.

Suddenly, Larry Doan turns the corner on Sharon Henson. He brings out her statement to the detectives as well as her grand jury statement.

"When you spoke to police, didn't you tell them he was wearing a black waist-length jacket?"

"I spoke to the police," she says, the change in Doan's voice making her wary.

"Ma'am, is the answer yes or no?"

"I don't remember."

"You don't remember?"

"No."

"Do you remember telling the grand jury what he was wearing?"

"Objection, your honor," says Polansky.

Gordy overrules him. "Yes or no?" says the judge.

"They might have asked me," she says bitterly. "I don't remember."

And so it goes for half an hour, with Doan reading from the transcripts and Sharon Henson claiming to remember nothing.

"Isn't it true, ma'am, that during the course of the party you had an argument with Mr. Frazier?"

"Yes."

"And after the argument he left your apartment?"

"No."

"He never left your apartment?"

"He left for about twenty minutes, yes."

"And when he came back, what did he do?"

"He continued to mingle with the guests."

"And he stayed the whole night. This is what you are telling the ladies and gentlemen of the jury?"

"Yeah," she says.

"And you want them to believe that, right?"

Polansky is on his feet with the objection.

"Overruled," says Gordy.

At which point Sharon Henson looks across the courtroom at Larry Doan and smiles sweetly. It's as if she actually believes she's destroying the state's case; in fact, she is turning all of Paul Polansky's lawyering to dust.

"Is that right, ma'am?" asks Doan. "You want them to believe that he stayed the whole night with you. Is that right?"

"Well he did."

"Is your memory of the events of the twenty-second of February clearer today than it would have been on March seventeenth or March tenth of this year?"

"March? No. Yes."

"Is it clearer today?" says Doan, showing his irritation.

"I mean, I have talked it over with the people that was at the party."

Doan looks at the jury, giving them an honest-to-God double take. "Okay," he says, shaking his head. "You talked to some people at the party, and that made your recollections clearer?"

"It made me see a few more things about that night that I didn't see that night or whatever."

"You mean like how long your boyfriend stayed at your apartment? You needed someone else to tell you how long your boyfriend stayed at your apartment?"

"Excuse me, sir," hisses the woman. "I was under the influence of drugs and alcohol that night."

"So how," asks Doan, saying each word slowly, "do you remember it now?"

At the defense table, Polansky sits with his hand to his forehead, presumably thinking about the case that might have been. Subtle strategies have suddenly been rendered obsolete by simple vaudeville. The Newport cigarettes, the unchecked hairs and the ghost of Vincent Booker—all of that is out the window now that Doan is blowing holes in Sharon Henson for the courtroom's amusement. At times, the jurors laugh so loudly that Gordy uses the gavel.

Outside the courtroom, Rich Garvey fidgets as Henson's time on the stand lengthens. Only when Doan emerges is the true scope of the victory made clear to him.

"What happened with Nee-Cee?" he asks the prosecutor as they walk down the third-floor corridor. "How'd she go over?"

Doan smiles as if he had a dorsal fin sticking through the back of his pinstripes. "I killed her. I destroyed her," he tells the detective. "There's blood all over the floor in there."

"She was terrible?"

"She was a fucking joke. The jury was laughing at her," says Doan, unable to conceal his delight. "I'm serious. I fucking murdered her."

From here forward, it is a downhill ride. If Sharon Henson had held to the truth, if she had been willing to give the state what she gave them in March, she could have counted herself as nothing worse than one piece of the circumstantial puzzle. Instead, she chose to perjure herself and as a result, she exists in every juror's mind as evidence of Robert Frazier's desperation.

On Monday, the testimony begins again with Rich Garvey's return to the stand and the blow-by-blow of the investigative steps that led to Frazier's arrest. On the cross-examination, Polansky works hard to emphasize his client's early cooperation in the probe, Frazier's willingness to come downtown and be interviewed without a lawyer. At one particularly telling moment, Polansky asks about the wounds from both knife and gun, suggesting that the use of two weapons indicates that two suspects are involved.

"How many years have you been a police officer?" he asks Garvey.

"Thirteen."

"And you've investigated many, many homicide cases either directly or—"

"That's right," says Garvey.

"Have you ever had a case where the victim died by a stab wound and gun wound and there was only one perpetrator?" asks Polansky.

"Yes," says Garvey calmly.

"How many cases? What case? Name it."

"We had indications in the case of Purnell Booker that there was one perpetrator."

Take that, thinks Garvey. With one sweet little answer, the same jury that has been asked to worry about the mysterious Vincent Booker can now wonder about the fact that somewhere in this case another Booker exists as a victim. Polansky asks to approach the bench.

"I am not even sure what to do, whether to ask for a mistrial or not," he tells Gordy.

The judge smiles, shaking his head. "You're not going to do anything since you asked him."

"I didn't ask him," Polansky protests.

"He answered your question," says Gordy. "What is your request? What do you want me to do? Why did you come up here?"

"I don't know," says Polansky. "Now I'm wondering whether I should open the whole thing."

"I'm not going to let him open up the whole can of worms based on that answer."

"Thank you," says Polansky, still a little dazed. "I am not . . . I have no requests then."

Garvey's second trip to the stand is a carefully crafted piece of work and a redemption of sorts for his performance on the first day of the trial, but it is almost beside the point. So, too, is the testimony of Robert Frazier, who takes the stand the following day to explain himself to the jury and declare that he had no reason or desire to kill Charlene Lucas. Frazier's day in court has already been clouded by Sharon Henson; she has colored everything to which the jury is subsequently exposed. More than that, Henson's testimony provided a stark contrast to the other essential testimony in the case: Romaine Jackson was young and frightened and reluctant when she identified Robert Frazier as the man she saw with Lena on the night of the murder; Sharon Henson was hard and bitter and contemptuous when she took the same stand to deny her own words.

That is precisely the comparison that Doan makes in his closing argument to the jury. Rich Garvey, now permitted in the courtroom as an observer, watches several jurors nod in agreement as Doan paints a vivid picture of each woman—one is an innocent truth-teller, the other, a corrupt prevaricator. Once again he returns to Henson's testimony about her boyfriend's clothing. He gives special attention to one small piece of testimony, one tiny fragment gleaned from a week of legal argument. When Romaine Jackson testified, she was asked to describe the defendant's hat. A cap, she says, a white cap.

"She's got her hands up here and she says it has a snap on it," recalls Doan, hands to his head. "Has a snap on it . . . And when did that become significant?"

Sharon Henson, he tells the jury. A day later, Sharon Henson is on the stand trying to help her boyfriend. Oh, says Doan, in imitation, he was wearing all beige. Beige trench coat. Beige slacks. Beige shoes. Probably beige underwear and a beige golf cap . . .

The prosecutor pauses.

". . . with a snap on it."

By now, even the juror in the front row—the one who had Doan worried at the beginning of the trial—is nodding in agreement.

"Ladies and gentlemen, after seeing and listening to Romaine Jackson and then hearing that description from a woman who is doing her very best to help this defendant, can there be any question that the person that Romaine Jackson says she saw is the defendant?"

A helluva connect, thinks Garvey, as Doan moves on through the rest of the evidence, urging the jury to use common sense. "When you put it all together, that jigsaw puzzle we talked about will be clear. You will clearly see that this man—"

Doan wheels and points at the defense table.

"—despite all his protestations to the contrary is the man who brutally murdered Charlene Lucas in the early morning hours of February 22, 1988."

Polansky responds with his strongest stuff, listing the state's evidence on a nearby drawing board and then crossing off each item as he tries to explain away the circumstances. He does his best to knock down Romaine Jackson and to resurrect Vincent Booker as the logical alternative. He steers clear, however, of Sharon Henson.

In his final response to the jury, Larry Doan actually has the temerity to go to Polansky's drawing board and begin writing his own comments above his opponent's visual aid.

"Objection, your honor," says Polansky, tired and angry. "I would appreciate it if Mr. Doan wrote on his own board."

Doan shrugs with feigned embarrassment. The jury laughs.

"Overruled," says Gordy.

Polansky shakes his head; he knows the game is up. And no one is surprised when, only two hours after arguments, the courtroom is reconvened and the jurors file back into the box.

"Mr. Foreman, please stand," says the clerk. "How do you find the defendant Robert Frazier in indictment number 18809625 as to murder in the first degree, not guilty or guilty?"

"Guilty," says the foreman.

In the gallery, only the Lucas family reacts. Garvey stares blankly as the jury is polled. Doan shoots a look at Polansky, but the defense attorney continues to take notes. Robert Frazier stares straight ahead.

In the third-floor corridor ten minutes later, Jackie Lucas, the younger daughter, finds Garvey and wraps her arm around his shoulder.

Garvey is momentarily surprised. There are occasions like this, moments when the survivors and the detectives share whatever kind of belated victory comes from a courtroom. Too often, however, the family doesn't even show for court, or if they do, they regard the defendant and the authorities with equal shares of contempt.

"We did it," says Jackie Lucas, kissing Garvey lightly on the cheek.

"Yes, we did," says Garvey, laughing.

"He's going to the Pen, right?"

"Oh yeah," he says. "Gordy'll hammer him."

Doan follows the family out of the court, and Garvey and Dave Brown both congratulate him again on the closing argument. Writing on Polansky's board, he tells Doan, that was a nice touch.

"You liked that?" says Doan.

"Oh yeah," says Garvey, laughing. "That was real class."

Their voices rattle down the corridor as the highlights are told and retold. For the first time, Garvey and Brown are given a full account of the disaster that befell Sharon Henson. They are laughing loudly when Robert Frazier enters the corridor, his hands cuffed behind him, two sheriff's deputies trailing behind.

"Shhhhh," says Brown. "The man of the hour."

"Are we ready for the ceremonial eyefuck?" asks Garvey. "I definitely think we've earned it."

Brown nods in agreement.

Larry Doan shakes his head, then walks quietly to the stairwell and up to his office. The detectives wait a few more seconds as Frazier and the deputies approach. Slowly, silently, the defendant passes them with his head down, his hands gripping a stack of rolled-up court papers behind him. There is no eye contact. There are no angry words.

"Fuck it," says Garvey, grabbing his briefcase from the hallway bench. "He was no fun at all."

FRIDAY, OCTOBER 21

Once more across the same stale ground, once more into the breach. Once more into the gaping maw of that alley, that hellacious piece of pavement that had never done right by him in the past.

Tom Pellegrini parks the car on Newington, then walks down a cross alley cluttered with garbage and dead leaves. Fall has changed the rear of Newington Avenue again, making it seem a little more as it should be. To Pellegrini, the alley only looks right in colder weather—the bleak and pale vision to which he had grown accustomed months ago. The seasons shouldn't change in this alley, he thinks. Nothing should change until I know what happened here.

Pellegrini walks down the common alley and through the gate at the rear of 718 Newington. He stands where the body had been, looking yet again at the back of the house, at the kitchen door and the window frame and the metal fire stair running down from the roof.

Red-orange. Red-orange.

The colors of the day. Pellegrini checks the wood trim on the rear of the house carefully, looking for something, anything, that can be called red-orange.

Nothing.

Looking over the chain-link fence, Pellegrini scans the house next door. The yard of 716 Newington is empty now; Andrew and his shit-brown Lincoln are both long gone, the latter permanently repossessed by the finance company, the former tossed out of the house by his long-suffering churchwoman of a wife.

Red-orange. Red-orange.

The back door of 716 is painted red, about the right shade, too.

Pellegrini crosses over to the adjacent yard for a closer look. Yes, indeed. Red paint is the outer coat, with orange paint underneath.

Sonofabitch, thinks Pellegrini, scraping a sample off the door. The combination of the red and orange together is distinctive enough for the detective to believe he's found a match. Eight months after his original interrogation, Andrew is suddenly back in the running, and no one is more surprised than Pellegrini.

If not for the paint on the back door of 716 Newington, the detective wouldn't believe it. Andrew is a piece of work, to be sure, and Jay Landsman's original theory about the Lincoln being used to store the body had its merits. But there is nothing on Andrew's sheet that screams sex offender, nor had their lengthy interrogation of the man produced any doubts. For his part, Pellegrini had gone soft on Andrew as soon as the trunk of the Lincoln had come up clean. And later, when Andrew passed a state police polygraph on his statement, Pellegrini had all but put the man out of his mind. But the red-orange chip was physical evidence and somehow had to be explained. On that basis alone, Andrew was back onstage.

The paint chip was new, a belated bit of evidence that might have seemed comical to Pellegrini if the circumstances hadn't been so utterly aggravating. The damn thing had been down there in the evidence control unit since day one of the investigation, and it would still be down there if he and Landsman hadn't gone down to look over the collection of evidence one last time.

The trip downstairs had been routine. For weeks, Pellegrini had been reviewing the Latonya Wallace case file and the existing evidence, trying to come up with something new. Initially, Pellegrini hoped to find something that would lead to a fresh suspect, something that had been overlooked the first and second times through the file. Then, after the chemical analysis of the smudges on the little girl's pants had been tenuously linked to the Fish Man's burned-out store, Pellegrini had returned to the existing evidence in the more concrete hope that something else would link the store owner to the murder.

Instead, he got the paint chip. He and Landsman had discovered it yesterday afternoon after the little girl's clothes had gone to the trace lab for another examination. Van Gelder from the lab was with them and, in fact, it was he who first noticed the colored flake clinging to the inside of the yellow tights.

It seemed to be a semigloss paint in separate coats, with the red layered over the orange. A single color would have been harder to track, but how many objects in Reservoir Hill had been painted orange and then red? And what was the paint chip doing inside the dead girl's hose? And how the hell had they failed to notice it the first couple of times around?

Even as Pellegrini was elated to have a new piece of evidence, he was angry that it had not been discovered at the outset. Van Gelder offered no explanation, nor did Pellegrini want one. The Latonya Wallace murder was the year's most important investigation; how could the trace analysis have been anything but flawless?

Now, standing in the rear of Newington Avenue, Pellegrini's frustration is complete. Because from every outward indication the paint chip leads nowhere near the Fish Man—and it is toward the Fish Man that Pellegrini wants to go. It is the Fish Man who failed the polygraph, it is the Fish Man who knew Latonya and had paid her to work in his store, and it is the Fish Man who never managed any kind of alibi for the night of the child's disappearance. The Fish Man: Who else could the killer be?

For months, Pellegrini had spent every available moment delving into the old store owner's life, preparing himself for one last confrontation with his best suspect. In a way that was almost amusing, the Fish Man had long ago become inured to the pursuit. At every corner of his life, there stood an obsessed police detective—learning, gathering, waiting. In every crevice of the man's quiet little existence, there hovered Tom Pellegrini, rooting around for information.

They knew each other now. Pellegrini knew more about the Fish Man than he cared to remember, more about this wretched old guy than anyone outside his family. The Fish Man knew his pursuer by name; he knew Pellegrini's voice and manner, knew the ways in which the detective began a conversation or framed a question. Most of all, he knew—he had to know—exactly what Pellegrini was after.

Any other man would have raised some hell. Any other man would have called a lawyer who would have called the police department with a harassment complaint. Any other man, Pellegrini reasoned, would have eventually looked him in the eye and delivered the expected message: You and that badge can go fuck yourselves if you think I kill little girls. But none of that had ever happened.

Since that second interrogation at the homicide office, the two men had gone through a series of strange conversations, each more amiable than the last, each predicated on the Fish Man's initial assertion that he knew nothing about the murder. Pellegrini ended each discussion by reminding the store owner that the investigation was continuing and that detectives would probably need to speak with him again. Without fail, the Fish Man would assure him of continued cooperation. Earlier this month, Pellegrini had broached the idea of another visit to the homicide office in the near future. The suspect was obviously less than thrilled with the idea, but he didn't try to decline.

The more the detective learned about the Fish Man, the more the old man seemed capable of a child's murder. There was nothing definitive in his history, nothing you could point a finger to as evidence that the man was dangerous, if not psychotic. Instead, the old man's past revealed a fairly ordinary pattern of failed relationships with women. Over weeks, the detective had located and interviewed relatives and old girlfriends and the Fish Man's former wife—all of whom agreed that the man had problems relating with women. A few even suggested that he had a thing for younger girls, but the stories were short on specifics. Pellegrini also interviewed Latonya Wallace's playmates again, as well as the children who had worked for the Fish Man or ventured into his shop after school. Sure enough, they had all talked about the Fish Man's roving eye. He was fresh, they told the detective, you have to be careful around him.

The one woman whom Pellegrini had not been able to find was the alleged victim from the Fish Man's old rape charge in the 1950s. Pellegrini had pulled those reports off the microfilm and digested every page, but the teenage girl who had supposedly been attacked had never testified in court, and the charges had apparently been dropped. Using everything from the telephone book to social service records, Pellegrini mounted a feverish search to locate the woman, who would now be in her late forties and, if she still lived in Baltimore, probably listed under something other than her maiden name. But his search went nowhere, and finally Pellegrini allowed himself to be interviewed on a local television show so that he could mention the woman's name and last known address and ask anyone with information about her to come forward or call the homicide unit.

During the broadcast, Pellegrini was careful not to explain the woman's relationship to the case, nor did he mention the Fish Man by name. But he did acknowledge to the host of the show that he had developed a suspect in the case. Pellegrini immediately realized his mistake when the host turned to the television camera and declared, "City homicide detectives believe they now know who killed little Latonya Wallace . . ." That brief sortie into the public eye kept Pellegrini writing explanatory memos for days, and the police department was forced to issue a one-paragraph press release noting that while Detective Pellegrini had identified one possible suspect in the murder, other investigators were working on other leads. Worst of all, the long-lost rape victim never did come forward.

Beyond everything else Pellegrini had learned about his best suspect, one item in particular stood out in his mind. It was a coincidence perhaps, but a chilling one, and he had stumbled across it while checking back through a decade of open missing persons reports for young girls. In February, the investigators compared the Latonya Wallace case to other open child murders, but only recently did it occur to Pellegrini that missing persons cases should probably be examined as well. Checking the reports from one 1979 case, he found that a nine-year-old girl had disappeared from her parents' home on Montpelier Street, never to be seen alive again. And Montpelier Street rang a bell: Pellegrini had just been out to interview a man whose family had once been partners with the Fish Man in an earlier grocery store. The family had lived on Montpelier Street for the last twenty years; the Fish Man had visited them often.

The old missing persons file contained no photographs, but a couple of days later Pellegrini drove over to the Baltimore Sun building and asked permission to check the newspaper's photo morgue. The paper still had two pictures of the missing child, both black-and-white copies of her grade school portraits. Standing in the newspaper's library, Pellegrini looked down at the photographs and felt the strangest sensation. From every angle, the child was a dead ringer for Latonya Wallace.

Maybe that uncanny resemblance was coincidence; maybe each apparently insignificant detail stood alone, unrelated to anything else. But the prolonged research into the Fish Man's background was enough to convince Pellegrini that he needed to challenge the man one last time. After all, the old man had been given every opportunity to make himself less of a suspect, yet he had failed to do so. Pellegrini reasoned that he owed himself one more crack at the guy. Even as Pellegrini prepared himself for that last interrogation, a tiny paint chip materialized on the dead girl's stocking, taunting him with another suspect and another direction.

The taunt grows louder when Pellegrini returns from Reservoir Hill and visits the trace evidence lab with fresh samples from the rear door of 716 Newington. Sure enough, Van Gelder has no trouble matching them to the chip found inside the hose. Suddenly, Andrew elbows the Fish Man aside.

A short talk that same afternoon with Andrew's former wife yields the information that his suspect is still working with the city's Bureau of Highways, so Pellegrini visits the Fallsway garage, arriving just as the suspect's shift is ending. Asked if he would mind coming down to the homicide office for further questioning, Andrew becomes visibly upset, almost hostile.

No, he tells Pellegrini. I want a lawyer.

Later that same week, the detective returns to Reservoir Hill with a lab technician for a three-hour search of 716 Newington, concentrating on the basement room where Andrew had his bar and his television and spent most of his free time. Nine months is a long time for evidence to stay put; in the end, Pellegrini leaves with nothing more than a carpet sample that may or may not have something resembling a bloodstain.

Still, Andrew has suddenly started behaving like a suspect with things to hide, and that paint chip seems to Pellegrini like a tiny shard of irrevocable truth: Somewhere along the line, Latonya Wallace got a little portion of Andrew's back door wedged between her leg and her stocking.

For a brief time, it is hard not to be a little cheered by the developments. But less than a week later Pellegrini makes another trip to Newington Avenue and, as he once again walks that alley, he notices that there are red-orange paint chips from Andrew's back door all over the adjacent yards. On the last visit, he had noticed right away that the paint on the door had been peeling badly, but now, looking carefully at the pavement behind 716 and 718 and 720 Newington, he sees red-orange chips scattered everywhere by the rain and wind, flashing up at him like fool's gold. The chip from the tights must have already been on the ground when the little girl's body was dumped behind 718 Newington. But Pellegrini isn't quite ready to let go. How, he asks himself, did the chip get inside the stockings? How could it be between the leg and the hose unless it got there after the child had been undressed?

Van Gelder soon provides the answer. Checking the evidence yet again, the lab analyst notes that the stockings are now insideout, as they surely were during the recent examination by Landsman and Pellegrini. Chances are, the tights were rolled off the little girl's body at the autopsy and had remained inside-out ever since. Though it seemed for a time otherwise, the paint chip had been on the outside of the hose all along.

Given Van Gelder's explanation, Pellegrini immediately sees the rest of the story for what it is: Andrew became nervous, but who wouldn't be nervous when questioned yet again by a homicide detective? As for the carpet sample, Pellegrini knows that it doesn't have a prayer of a chance of coming back positive for human blood. To hell with Andrew, he thinks. He isn't a suspect, he's a wasted week.

The Fish Man, as durable a murder suspect as ever existed, once again returns to center stage.

Friday, October 28

Donald Waltemeyer grabs the dead girl by both arms, feeling for any tension in the hands and fingers. The girl's hands follow his freely, giving the appearance of a bizarre, horizontal dance.

"She's wet," he says.

Milton, the junkie on the sofa, nods.

"What'd you do? Put her in cold water?"

Milton nods again.

"Where? In the bath?"

"No. I just splashed her with water."

"From where? That bathtub?"

"Yeah."

Waltemeyer walks into the bathroom, where he satisfies himself that the tub is still covered with droplets. It is an old wives' tale among the junkies: Overdoses can be brought back by putting them in cold water, as if a bath can somehow rid them of whatever they've put in their veins.

"Lemme ask you this, Milton," says Waltemeyer. "Did you and her use the same works or did you fire your shit using something else?"

Milton gets up and moves toward the closet.

"Don't fucking show it to me," says Waltemeyer. "If you show it to me, I gotta lock you up."

"Oh."

"Just answer the question. Did you use the same needle?"

"No. I got my own."

"Okay then. Sit down and tell me again what happened."

Milton runs down the tale again, leaving nothing out. Waltemeyer hears again about how the white girl came by to fire up, about how she often came up here to shoot because her husband didn't like her using.

"Like I said, she brought me that box of noodles 'cause she used some last time she was here."

"This macaroni here?"

"Yeah. She brought that with her."

"She had her own dope?"

"Yeah. I had mine and then she came with hers."

"Where was she sitting when she fired?"

"This chair here. She fired up and then fell asleep. I looked over after a while and she wasn't breathing."

Waltemeyer nods. The call is straight up, and for that reason alone he feels good. After three months of tracking Geraldine Parrish and her missing relatives, even a simple overdose can be something of a reprieve. Waltemeyer had told himself that if he didn't get back into the rotation on this midnight shift, he would lose his mind. McLarney had agreed.

"Your run sheets have been getting messier and messier," the sergeant told him a week ago. "It's like a cry for help."

Maybe so. Waltemeyer had taken the Parrish case as far as he could, though there would be more work to come as trial preparation got under way. And he still hadn't figured out exactly what had happened to Geraldine's last husband, the aged Reverend Rayfield Gilliard, who died after a few weeks of marriage. A relative was now telling them that Miss Geraldine had ground two dozen Valium into the Reverend Gilliard's tuna salad, then watched as the old man slowly succumbed to a seizure. The story was solid enough that Doc Smialek and Marc Cohen, the assistant state's attorney handling the case, were willing to try for an exhumation order. Some days, Waltemeyer truly believed that the case had no end.

All of which makes this little overdose quite pleasing. One body, one witness, one page of a 24-hour report on the admin lieutenant's desk—police work as Waltemeyer remembers it. The lab tech is hard at work and the ME is on the way. The witness is even cooperative and apparently truthful. All is flowing gracefully toward a resolution until the first officer appears in the doorway to say that the dead girl's husband is downstairs.

"Do we need him for an ID?" asks the uniform.

"Yeah," says Waltemeyer, "but not if he's going to come up here and lose it. I don't want that."

"I'll warn him about that."

The husband comes to the bottom of the stairs, wearing an expression of incredible grief. He is a good-looking man, thirty or so, tall with long sandy brown hair.

"If you're going to go up there, you have to be calm," says the officer.

"I understand."

Hearing footsteps on the stairs, Waltemeyer turns back toward the young woman and notices that the left bra strap and part of the cup are exposed, with the sweater pulled back down the arm in the search for the fresh track. Leaning over at the last second, he pulls the sweater gently over her shoulder.

For a detective, it is a small but extraordinary act—extraordinary because the notion of privacy loses most of its meaning after a few months of working murders. What, after all, could be less private than a stranger, an interloper, evaluating a human being's last moments on earth? What could be less private than a body taken apart at autopsy, or a bedroom emptied of its contents by a search warrant, or a suicide note read and Xeroxed and stapled to the face sheet of a police incident report? After a year or two in the trenches, privacy is something that every detective learns to mock. More than compassion or sincerity or empathy, it is the first casualty of police work.

Two months ago, Mark Tomlin caught the year's first and only autoerotic death. It was an engineer in his late thirties, trussed up on his bed in leather underwear, suffocated by a plastic bag that the victim had placed on his own head. There were pulleys and levers that controlled the cords by which the victim was bound, and by moving an arm in a certain direction, the man could have freed himself. But long before he could do that, he passed out from lack of oxygen—a consequence of the plastic bag, which he had used to induce hypoxia, an ethereal, oxygen-deprived state in which masturbation supposedly becomes more erotic. That bedroom was a strange sight, and Tomlin, of course, couldn't help but show Polaroids to a few thousand other cops. After all, the poor guy looked damned silly decomposing in his leather shorts, arms trussed up over his head, toes clamped together by thumbcuffs, bondage magazines scattered across the dresser. Bizarre stuff, and no one would have believed it without the photographs. Neither privacy nor dignity had much of a chance on that one.

Almost every detective has encountered two or three scenes where some relative tried, for reasons of propriety more than deception, to dress a dead body. Likewise, almost every detective has handled a dozen overdoses in which mothers and fathers had felt compelled to hide the needle and cooker before the ambulance arrived. One suicide prompted a parent to painstakingly rewrite the victim's note in the desire to exclude one especially embarrassing admission. The world never stops insisting on values and standards, although such things no longer matter to the dead. The world never stops calling for a little dignity, a little propriety, but the cops never stop calling for the morgue wagon; between the two lies an abyss that can never be bridged.

In the Baltimore homicide office, privacy is a stillborn idea. The unit, after all, is a locker room of sorts, a male-dominated purgatory in which thirty-six detectives and detective sergeants wander in and out of each other's lives, cracking jokes as this detective's marriage implodes and that detective shows the unmistakable signs of alcohol addiction.

A homicide detective isn't any more or less degenerate than any other middle-aged American male, but since he spends his life prying up other men's secrets, he has little regard for his own. And in a world where the act of premeditated murder becomes routine, any more subtle sin has trouble competing. Any man can drink too much and wreck his station wagon on an upcounty road, but a homicide detective can tell the rest of his squad the story in a voice that betrays equal shares of bravado and embarrassment. Any man can pick up a woman in a downtown bar, but a homicide detective will later entertain his partner with a comedic soliloquy that describes in detail all the later action at the motel. Any man can lie to his wife, but a homicide detective will sit in the middle of the coffee room yelling into a phone extension that he has to work late on a case and if she doesn't believe that, she can go to hell. And then, after convincing her, he will slam down the receiver and stalk over to the coat rack.

"I'm down at the Market Bar," he will tell five other detectives, all of whom are fighting back laughter. "But if she calls back, I'm on the street."

A detective understands that another world is out there, another universe in which discretion and privacy still have meaning. Somewhere far from Baltimore, he knows, there are taxpayers who hold dear the idea of a good and secret death—a well-lived life, becalmed at its end, extinguished in some private, comfortable place with equal measures of grace and solitude. They've heard a lot about that kind of death, but they rarely see it. To them, death is violence and miscalculation, mindlessness and cruelty. And what, a detective can ask, does privacy matter amid that kind of carnage?

Several months ago, Danny Shea from Stanton's shift drove to a high-rise apartment house near the Hopkins campus for an unattended death. She was an elderly music teacher, fully rigored on her daybed, with the score of a Mozart concerto still open on the piano. The FM radio was playing quietly in the living room, tuned to a classical station at the end of the dial. Shea recognized the piece.

"You know what that is?" he asked a uniform, a young man writing his report at the kitchen table.

"What's what?"

"The piece on the radio."

"Uh-uh."

"Ravel," said Shea. " 'Pavane to a Dead Princess.' "

It was a beautiful, natural death, quite startling in its perfection. Shea suddenly felt himself an intruder in the old woman's apartment, a violator of a genuinely private act.

A similar feeling now comes over Donald Waltemeyer when he looks at a dead addict and listens to her husband walking up the stairs. There is nothing beautiful or poignant in the death of Lisa Turner: Waltemeyer knows that she was twenty-eight years old, that she was from North Carolina and that she was married. And for reasons beyond his comprehension, she came up to this second-floor shithole to fire heroin until it killed her. End of story.

And still, something clicks for just a moment, some long-lost switch in Waltemeyer's brain is suddenly thrown to overload. Perhaps it's because she was young, perhaps because she looks pretty in the light blue sweater. Perhaps it's because a price must be paid for all this privacy, because you can only be a bystander for so long without paying some of the cost yourself.

Waltemeyer looks down at the girl, listens to the husband struggle up the stairs, and suddenly, almost without thinking, reaches for the falling shoulder of a dead woman's sweater.

When the husband appears at the door, Waltemeyer asks the question immediately: "Is that her?"

"Oh God," the man says. "Oh my God."

"Okay, that's it," says Waltemeyer, motioning to the uniform. "Thank you, sir."

"Who the hell is he?" says the husband, glaring at Milton. "What the hell is he doing here?"

"Get him out of here," says Waltemeyer, blocking the husband's view. "Take him downstairs now."

"Just tell me who he is, goddammit."

Both uniforms grab the husband and begin pushing him out of the apartment. Easy, they tell him. Take it easy.

"I'm okay. I'm all right," he tells them in the hallway. "I'm okay."

They guide him to the other end of the hall, standing with him as he leans into the plasterboard and catches his breath.

"I just want to know what that guy was doing in there with her."

"It's his apartment," says one of the uniforms.

The husband shows his pain, and the uniform volunteers the obvious information: "She just went in there to fire up. She wasn't fucking the guy or anything like that."

Another small act of charity, but the husband shakes it off.

"I know that," says the husband quickly. "I just wanted to know if he was the guy that got her the drugs, that's all."

"No. She brought hers with her."

The husband nods. "I couldn't get her to stop," he tells the cop. "I loved her, but I couldn't get her to stop it. She wouldn't listen. She told me where she was going tonight because she knew I couldn't stop her . . ."

"Yeah," says the cop, uncomfortable.

"She was such a beautiful girl."

The cop says nothing.

"I loved her."

"Uh-huh," says the cop.

Waltemeyer finishes the scene and drives back to the office in silence, the entire event now confined to a page and a half of his notebook. He catches every light on St. Paul Street.

"What did you get?" asks McLarney.

"Nothing much. An OD."

"Junkie?"

"It was a young girl."

"Oh yeah?"

"Pretty."

Very pretty, thinks Waltemeyer. You could see how, if she had cleaned herself up, she would have been special. Long dark hair. Big traffic-light eyes.

"How old?" asks McLarney.

"Twenty-eight. She was married. I thought she was a lot younger at first."

Waltemeyer walks to a typewriter. In five minutes, it will all be just another 24-hour report. In five minutes, you can ask him about that loose sweater and he won't know what you're talking about. But now, right now, it's real.

"You know," he tells his sergeant. "The other day my boy comes home from school, and he's sitting there in the living room with me and he says, 'Hey, Dad, someone offered me coke in school today . . .' "

McLarney nods.

"And I'm thinking, aw shit, here it comes. And then he just smiles and tells me, 'But I asked for Pepsi instead.' "

McLarney laughs softly.

"Some nights you go out and see shit that's no good for you," says Waltemeyer suddenly. "You know what I mean? No fucking good at all."

Tuesday, November 1

Roger Nolan picks up the phone and begins shuffling through the admin office card file for Joe Kopera's home number. The department's best ballistics man will be working late tonight.

From the hallway comes the sound of loud banging on the large interrogation room door.

"Hey, Rog," says one of Stanton's detectives, "is that your man making all that noise?"

"Yeah. I'll be there in a second."

Nolan finds the number and reaches Kopera, explaining the situation quickly. He finishes the call to even louder banging.

"Hey, Rog, shut this motherfucker up, will you?"

Nolan walks through the fishbowl and out into the hallway. The devil himself has his face pressed against the window in the door, hands cupped around his eyes, trying to peer through the one-way glass.

"What's your problem?"

"I gotta go to the bathroom."

"The bathroom, huh? I bet you want a drink of water too."

The devil needs to take a leak. Evil incarnate wants a drink of water. Nolan shakes his head and opens the metal door. "I'll be damned," he tells the suspect. "Every time you put one of these motherfuckers in the box, they lose control of their bladder and start getting dizzy from thirst . . . Okay, c'mon, let's get it over with . . ."

The suspect steps slowly from the room, a thirty-one-year-old black man, thinly built, with receding, close-cropped hair and deep brown eyes. His face is rounded, his wide mouth marked by gap teeth and a long overbite. His sweatsuit is a size too big, his high-top tennis shoes well worn. Nothing in his appearance gives truth to his abominable deed: There is nothing in the face to inspire fear, nothing in the eyes to call extraordinary. He is altogether ordinary, and for that reason, too, he inspires contempt.

His name is Eugene Dale, and the computer sheet on Harry Edgerton's desk provides enough history for two murderers. Most of the arrests involve rape, attempted rape and handgun violations; in fact, Dale is now on parole, having just been released by the state corrections department after serving nine years for sexual assault.

"If you're not out here in three minutes," Nolan tells him at the men's room door, "I gotta come in there after you. Understand?"

Eugene Dale walks out of the men's room two minutes later, looking sheepish. Nolan points him back down the hallway.

"My drink," says the suspect.

"So?" says Nolan. "Drink."

Dale stops at the water cooler, then wipes the wetness from his face with his sleeve. The suspect is returned to his cubicle, where he waits for Edgerton, who is at this moment in another interview room, talking with the people who know Dale best, absorbing all of the available background for the coming interrogation.

It would have been a better piece of drama if an act of rare investigative genius had produced Eugene Dale. For the detectives who suffered through Latonya Wallace, it would have been a perfectly righteous moment if some subtle connection in the Andrea Perry case file had caused this man to materialize in an interrogation room. And for Harry Edgerton, it would have been pure vindication if some brilliant discovery during his lonely and methodical pursuit had given them the name.

But, as usual, poetic justice has no place here. Edgerton did everything possible to find his suspect, but in the end, the suspect found him. Wanted for the cold-blooded murder of one child, the man fidgeting in the large interrogation room waited all of two weeks before he went out and raped another.

Still, when the second rape report came in, everyone in the unit knew immediately what it meant. Edgerton had laid the groundwork for that, meeting with the operations people in three districts and warning them to be looking for anything sexual or anything involving a .32-caliber firearm. So when the second rape report was copied to the Southern District's operations unit, a female officer there, Rita Cohen, knew exactly what was what. The second victim was a thirteen-year-old who had been lured by Dale to a vacant rowhouse on South Mount Street, then threatened with a "silver-looking" handgun and raped. Dale let this girl live, though he warned her that if she told anyone about the attack he would find her again and shoot her in the back of the head. The young victim promised not to tell, but did precisely the opposite when she returned home to her mother. As it happened, she knew her attacker by name and address both—her best friend was the young daughter of Dale's girlfriend.

The crime was as stupid as it was evil. The girlfriend's daughter had even seen Dale walking the victim home just before the assault, which may have been why he did not murder the thirteen-year-old after raping her. He knew there was a witness, yet he abandoned all caution to satisfy his compulsion with another child.

After calling homicide and taking the rape victim's statement, the Southern plainclothes officers wrote a warrant for Dale's address on Gilmor Street, no more than a few blocks from the alley in which Andrea Perry had been murdered. The raid had been set for today, and though Edgerton was scheduled to be off, Nolan accompanied the Southern officers to the house and assured Edgerton that if the warrant produced any evidence or a viable suspect, he was back on the clock.

Less than half an hour after arriving at the Gilmor Street address, Nolan was on the phone to his detective, telling him, as he would tell Kopera later, to come back downtown. Eugene Dale wasn't home when the raiding party came through his front door, but in an upstairs closet the Southern officer found a .32-caliber revolver loaded with automatic shells. That was all Nolan needed to know: Not only was Andrea Perry murdered with a .32, but the ballistics report showed light rifling marks on the bullet, suggesting automatic ammo fired through a revolver. And when Nolan spoke with the other occupants of the Gilmor Street home, they, too, matched with the case file.

Dale's girlfriend, Rosalind, was strangely cooperative when questioned by Nolan, as was her girlfriend, Michelle, who happened to be dating Rosalind's ex-boyfriend. Both expressed some initial surprise at the possibility of Eugene being connected to either the rape or the murder; eventually, however, in a later interview with Edgerton, they would agree that Dale just might be the kind of guy who would do something like that. And once the detective learned a little more about Rosalind, they were convinced they were on the right track. Recalling the anonymous call that came into the homicide office right after Andrea Perry's murder—the call in which a male voice had claimed to see a woman run from the murder scene at the sound of gunshots—Edgerton mentioned the mystery woman's name to Michelle and Rosalind.

"Loretta?" said Rosalind. "She's my ex-boyfriend's sister. We're good friends."

But Loretta Langley was not good friends with Eugene Dale; they had disliked each other from the very start, Rosalind explained. At that moment, Edgerton had little doubt that the unidentified caller was none other than Eugene Dale, attempting in the clumsiest fashion to blame his girl's best friend for a rapemurder.

Days later, to satisfy himself that he had been right not to pick up

Loretta Langley for questioning on the strength of the anonymous call, Edgerton will interview Langley and tell her, for the first time, of the allegation that they had received in the earliest hours of the investigation. Asked if she would have thought of her best friend's boyfriend if told about the male caller, she will say no. If he'd talked to her three weeks ago, Loretta Langley would have been nothing more than another dead end; now she is yet another link between Eugene Dale and a child's murder.

Edgerton arrived at the homicide unit well before Nolan and began to go through the Southern district's paperwork on the rape report. Later that afternoon, well after Nolan had returned to the office from the raid, Eugene Dale sauntered up to the Gilmor Street address. Before he was grabbed by a waiting district operations unit, he had time to learn of the search-and-seizure warrant and to ask his girlfriend one very telling question: "Did they find the gun?"

He came to rest in the large interrogation room and remained there, ignored for hours, as Edgerton proceeded to interview Michelle and Rosalind. He stayed there long after Kopera arrived and took the revolver—an H&R .32, serial number AB 18407, a weapon now caked in fingerprint dust—downstairs to his lab.

Long after Roger Nolan escorts him to the bathroom, Eugene Dale is still sitting in the box, bored and irritated. Enough time passes so that when Edgerton finally enters the room, his suspect—true to the rule—is on the verge of sleep. As the interrogation begins just after 10:00 P.M., there is no banter and salesmanship; indeed, Edgerton treats his suspect with undisguised contempt.

"You want to talk to me, I'll listen," the detective says, pushing the rights form toward Dale. "You don't want to say anything, I just charge you with the murder and go home. I don't really care."

"What do you mean?" says Dale.

Edgerton blows cigarette smoke across the table. With any other murder, all this stupidity might be amusing. With Andrea Perry, it sticks in his throat.

"Look at me," says Edgerton, raising his voice. "You know that gun in your linen closet, right?"

Dale nods slowly.

"Where do you think that gun is right now?"

Dale says nothing.

"Where is it? Think hard, Eugene."

"You all got it."

"We got it," says Edgerton. "That's right. And right now, even as I'm talking to you, there are experts downstairs who are matching up that gun to the bullet we took out of that girl's head."

Eugene Dale shakes his head at the logic. Suddenly, both men feel a loud thump. A floor below, almost immediately beneath them, Joe Kopera is firing the .32 into a deep canister of water to produce the necessary slugs for comparison.

"That's your gun right there," says Edgerton. "Hear it? They're testing it right now."

"It's not my gun."

"It's in your fucking closet. Whose gun is it? Rosalind's? If we show that gun to the other little girl you messed with, she's going to say it was your gun, isn't she?"

"It's not my gun."

Edgerton stands up, his patience entirely leveled by five minutes in a room with this man. Dale looks up at the detective, his face a mixture of fright and sincerity.

"You're wasting my fucking time, Eugene."

"I didn't—"

"Who do you think you're fucking dealing with here?" asks Edgerton, his voice rising. "I don't have the time to listen to your stupid bullshit."

"Why are you yelling at me?"

Why am I yelling at you? Edgerton is tempted to tell the man the truth, to explain a little of the civilized world to a man living off its fringe. But that would be wasted breath.

"You don't like people yelling at you?"

Dale says nothing.

Edgerton walks out of the interrogation room with a small kernel of rage growing inside him, a heat that few murderers ever manage to spark inside a detective. Part of it is the stupidity of Dale's first attempt at a statement, part of it his childlike denial, but in the end what angers Harry Edgerton most is simply the magnitude of the crime. He sees Andrea Perry's school picture inside the binder and it stokes the rage; how could such a life be destroyed by the likes of Eugene Dale?

Edgerton's usual response toward a guilty man was a mild contempt bordering on indifference. In most instances, he didn't go out of his way to hassle his suspects; hell, they had enough problems. Like most detectives, Edgerton believed that you can talk to a murderer. You can share your cigarettes with him and walk him to the bathroom and laugh at his jokes when they're funny. You can even buy him a can of Pepsi if he's willing to initial each page of the statement.

But this is different. This time Edgerton didn't want to breathe the same air as his suspect. In truth, his anger ran deep enough to be called hate, a feeling that on this case could only come from a black detective. Edgerton was black, and Eugene Dale was black, and Andrea Perry, too: the usual barriers of race had been removed. Given that truth, it made sense that Edgerton could talk to people on the street and learn things, that he could go into the West Baltimore projects and come out knowing things that a white detective might never know. Even the best white cop feels the distance when he works with black victims and black suspects; to him they are otherworldly, as if their tragedy is the result of a ghetto pathology against which he is fully immunized. Working in a city where nearly 90 percent of all murder is black-on-black, a white detective might understand the nature of a black victim's tragedy, he might carefully differentiate between good people to be avenged and bad people to be pursued. But, ultimately, he never responds with the same intensity; his most innocent victims bring empathy, not anguish; his most ruthless suspects bring contempt, not rage. Edgerton, however, was not encumbered by such distinctions. Eugene Dale could be utterly real for him, just as Andrea Perry could be real; his rage at the crime could be personal.

Edgerton's response to Dale set him apart from the rest of his squad, but this time there was nothing unique about it: to be a black detective in homicide required a special sense of balance, a willingness to tolerate the excesses of many white colleagues, to ignore the cynical assessments and barbed humor of men for whom black-on-black violence represented a natural order. To them, the black middle class was simply a myth. They had heard about it, they had read about it, but damned if they could find it in the city of Baltimore. Edgerton, Requer, Eddie Brown—they were black, they were essentially middle class—but they proved nothing. They were cops and therefore, whether they knew it or not, they were all honorary Irishmen. That logic allowed the same detective who could comfortably partner with Eddie Brown to watch a black family move into the house next door, then go to the police computer the next day and run his new neighbors.

The prejudice ran deep. A man had only to stand in the coffee room and listen to a veteran white detective's scientific analysis of homeboy head shapes: ". . . Now your bullet head, he's a stone killer, he's dangerous. But your peanut heads, they're just dope dealers and sneak thieves. Now your swayback, he's generally a . . ."

Black detectives lived and worked around those limitations, tacitly offering themselves as contradictions to the ghetto scenes that greeted their white colleagues every night. If a white guy still insisted on missing the point, then fuck him. What was a black police going to do? Call the NAACP? For Edgerton and the other black detectives, there was no way to win the argument, and consequently, no argument.

But Edgerton does have an argument with Eugene Dale, one that he knows he can win. And when he walks out of the interrogation room the first time, he is as eager to give himself a break as to let Dale stew before going after a second, full statement.

Downstairs in the ballistics lab, Joe "No Compare 'em" Kopera, the dean of Baltimore's firearms examiners, has both bullets under the microscope and is slowly turning each slug in the positioning clay, lining up the rifling marks and striations in the split screen viewer. From the most obvious gouges on each bullet, Kopera determines almost immediately that they are both from .32-caliber projectiles from the same class of weapon, in this case a six with a left twist. This means that the rifling grooves on the inside of the barrel—which differ for each mode of firearm—carve a total of six deep channels around the back end of the projectile, each channel twisting to the left.

Knowing that much, Kopera can say that the bullet that killed Andrea Perry was fired from the same or similar make of .32 revolver seized in that afternoon's raid on Dale's house. But to say that the bullet was fired from that gun requires more; the striation marks—thin scrapings caused by imperfections and debris inside the gun barrel—also have to be matched. Leaving the microscope on, Kopera walks upstairs for coffee and a conference with the detectives.

"What's the verdict?" asks Nolan.

"Same type of weapon, same ammo. But it's going to take me a little while to be sure."

"Would it help if we tell you he's guilty?"

Kopera smiles and wanders into the coffee room. Edgerton is already back inside the large box, suffering through Dale's second statement. This time Edgerton mentions the possibility of fingerprints on the weapon, though in fact the lab tech couldn't lift any latents before the gun went downstairs to Kopera.

"If it's not your gun, then what will you say when we find your fingerprints all over it?"

"It is my gun," says Dale.

"It is your gun."

"Uh-huh."

Edgerton can almost hear the sound of Dale's brain lurching around in the dark. The Out. The Out. Where's my Out? Edgerton already knows which window his suspect will reach for.

"I mean it's my gun. But I didn't kill anyone."

"It's your gun but you didn't kill anyone."

"No. I let a couple guys borrow it that night. They said they needed it to scare someone."

"You let a couple guys borrow it. I had a feeling you were going to say that."

"I didn't know what they needed it for . . ."

"And these guys went out and raped this little girl," says Edgerton, glaring at the suspect, "and then they took her down the alley and shot her in the head, right?"

Dale shrugs. "I don't know what they did with it."

Edgerton looks at him coldly. "What's your friends' names?"

"Names?"

"Yeah. They've got names, right? You lent them your gun, so you had to at least know who they were."

"If I tell you that, then they're in trouble."

"Fuck yeah, they're in trouble. They're going to be charged with the murder, aren't they? But it's either them or you, Eugene, so what's the names?"

"I can't tell you."

Edgerton's had enough. "You're about to be charged in a death penalty murder case," he says in a voice rising with anger, "but you're not going to tell me the names of the mysterious friends who borrowed your gun 'cause it might get them in trouble. That's your story?"

"I can't tell."

"Because they don't exist."

"No."

"You don't have any friends. You don't have a friend in the fucking world."

"If I tell you, he'll kill me."

"If you don't tell me," shouts Edgerton, "I'm going to put you on Death Row. Your choice . . ."

Eugene Dale looks down at the table, then back at the detective. He shakes his head and raises his arms, a gesture of surrender, a plaintive appeal.

"Fuck it," says Edgerton, getting up again. "I don't even know why I'm bothering with you."

Edgerton slams the door to the large interrogation room, then greets his sergeant with a half-smile. "He's innocent."

"Oh yeah?"

"Yeah. Some friends borrowed the gun and then forgot to tell him they'd raped and killed a girl."

Nolan laughs. "Don't you just hate when that happens?"

"I swear I'm ready to hit this guy."

"That bad, huh?"

Edgerton wanders into the coffee room for a fresh cup, but after five minutes, Eugene Dale has something more to say. He bangs loudly on the door, but Edgerton ignores him. Eventually, Jay Landsman comes out of his office to check on the racket.

"Detective, sir, can I have a word with you?"

"With me?"

"Yes, sir. That other officer won't listen to me and I . . ."

Landsman shakes his head. "You don't want to talk to me," he says. "The only thing I want to do is kick the living shit out of you for what you did to that girl. You don't—"

"But I didn't—"

"Hey," says Landsman. "If you want to talk to me you're gonna do it without teeth, you understand that? You're better off with the other detective."

Dale retreats into the interrogation room as Landsman slams the door and walks back to his office, his day now considerably brighter than it had been.

Five minutes later, Edgerton returns to the hallway outside the interrogation room, now cool enough for one more sortie. As he opens the metal door, Kopera brushes past him on his way from the stairwell.

"It's a winner, Harry."

"Way to be, Dr. K."

"The striation is a little light, but I don't have any real problem."

"Okay. Thanks."

Edgerton slams the door behind him and lays it down for Eugene

Dale one last time: A living rape victim who will identify him as well as the gun. A ballistics match to the murder weapon. And, oh yeah, those fingerprints all over the gun . . .

"I'd like to tell you my friend's name."

"Okay," says Edgerton. "Tell me."

"But I don't know his name."

"You don't know his name."

"No. He told me but I forgot. But his nickname is Lips. He lives in West Baltimore."

"You don't know his name, but you let him borrow your gun."

"Uh-huh."

"Lips, from West Baltimore."

"That's what they call him."

"What's the other guy's name."

Dale shrugs.

"Eugene, do you know what I think?"

Dale looks at him, the picture of earnest cooperation.

"I think you're going back to prison."

Nonetheless, Edgerton works through the nonsensical story, emerging in the early morning hours with an eleven-page statement in which Dale, in a near-final version of events, lends the murder weapon to Lips and another east side man whom Dale actually names. Presumably, the second man is someone who has done wrong by Eugene Dale somewhere in his past. Dale admits to seeing Andrea Perry playing with his cousin, and he admits to being out on the street and hearing the gunshot from the alley. He even goes so far as to suggest that although his friends returned the gun with one shell spent, and although he believed that they had raped and killed the girl, he didn't go to the police because he couldn't get involved.

"I'm on parole," he reminds Edgerton.

As dawn arrives in the homicide office, Edgerton is at an admin office typewriter, working up the two-page charging documents for his suspect. But when he takes the papers into the interrogation room to show Dale, the suspect reads them quickly and then tears them to pieces, further endearing himself to Edgerton, whose typing skills are less than stellar.

"You don't need this," Dale says, "because I'm going to tell you the truth. I didn't kill that girl. In fact, I don't know who it was that killed her."

Edgerton listens to version number three.

"I don't know who really killed her. The reason I told you the other things was to protect my girlfriend and her family. I work every day while her relatives are always in and out of the apartment all hours. All of her sisters and brothers use the apartment while I'm sleeping in the bedroom."

Edgerton says nothing. At this point, why bother to say anything at all?

"One of them must have kept the gun in the linen closet. One of them must have killed that girl."

"Did you know the gun was kept in your linen closet?" asks Edgerton, almost bored.

"No I didn't. I know you can get five years for having a gun. I don't know who had that gun in the house. I really don't."

Edgerton nods, then walks out of the interrogation room and back to the admin office typewriter.

"Hey, Roger, look at what this asshole did," he says, holding up the shreds of the charging papers. "This took me forty minutes."

"He did that?"

"Yeah," says Edgerton, laughing. "He said I didn't need them 'cause he was going to tell me the truth."

Nolan shakes his head. "That's what you get for letting him hold on to the paperwork."

"Maybe I can tape it together," says Edgerton, more tired than hopeful.

The last statement by Eugene Dale concludes as the dayshift detectives are taking roll call in the main office, and many of those men are out on the street before Edgerton can retype the arrest sheets.

The Southern District wagon arrives an hour or so later, and Dale is cuffed for the ride back to the district bail hearing. Walking down the corridor, he asks again for Edgerton and the chance to make another statement. This time he is ignored.

But there will be one last encounter. A week or so after the arrest, Edgerton checks his gun at the Eager Street entrance of the Baltimore City Jail and follows a guard to the second-floor hellhole that prison administrators call an infirmary. It is a long walk up a set of metal stairs and down a hall cluttered with human failure. The inmates fall silent, staring as Edgerton passes through to the medical unit's administrative area.

A heavyset nurse waves him down. "He's on the way up from the tier."

Edgerton shows her the warrant, but she barely bothers to look at it. "Head hairs, chest hairs, pubic hairs and blood," he says. "I guess you've done this before."

"Mmm-hmmm."

Eugene Dale rounds the corner slowly, then stops at the sight of Edgerton. As the nurse waves the inmate toward an examination room, Dale moves close enough for Edgerton to notice the bruises and contusions, obvious signs of a bad beating. Even inside the city jail, the man's crimes merit special attention.

Edgerton follows his suspect into the examination room and watches as the nurse prepares a needle.

Dale looks at the syringe, then back at Edgerton. "What's this for?"

"A search-and-seizure warrant for your person," says Edgerton. "We're going to match your blood and hairs to semen and hairs we got from the girl."

"I already gave them blood."

"This is different. This is a court order for evidence."

"I don't want to."

"You don't have a choice."

"I want to talk to a lawyer."

Edgerton shoves the paper into Dale's hands, then points to the judge's signature at the bottom of the page. "You don't get to talk to a lawyer for this. It's signed by a judge—see that? We have a right to your blood and your hair."

Eugene Dale shakes his head. "Why do you need my blood?"

"For DNA testing. We're going to match it to the girl," says Edgerton.

"I want to talk to a lawyer."

Edgerton moves closer to his suspect, his voice low. "Either you let her take some blood and some hairs the easy way or I'm going to take it myself, because that warrant says I can. And I can tell you that you'd definitely rather have her do it."

Eugene Dale sits silently, almost in tears as the nurse brings the needle up to his right arm. Edgerton watches from the opposite wall as blood is drawn and then hairs plucked from his suspect's head and body. The detective is on the way out the door, samples in hand, when Eugene Dale speaks again.

"Don't you want to talk to me again?" he asks. "I want to tell the truth."

Edgerton ignores him.

"You want to hear the truth?"

"No," says Edgerton. "Not from you."

Wednesday, November 9

Rich Garvey stands shivering in the predawn emptiness of Fremont Avenue, staring at a pile of blood-soaked clothing, two spent .38 casings and a blue plastic lunch pail containing two submarine sandwiches wrapped in tin foil. So much for physical evidence.

Robert McAllister stands shivering next to Garvey, scanning the length of Fremont Avenue and its tributaries for any trace of human endeavor. It's not bad enough that the streets are empty, there aren't even any lights in the rowhouse windows. So much for witnesses.

In the few seconds before anyone speaks, Garvey looks at McAllister and McAllister looks at Garvey, each of them wordlessly communicating the same thought:

Hell of a case you got, Mac.

Whoa, you caught a tough one here, Garv.

And yet before anything unseemly can pass between two partners, the first officer—a kid by the name of Miranda, an earnest young soldier still basking in the wonder of it all—approaches them to offer up one little detail: "He was talking when we got here."

"He was talking?"

"Oh yeah."

"What did he say?"

"Well, he told us who shot him . . ."

If this universe is truly balanced, if there is a negative and positive to the order of things, then somewhere exists a yin to balance Rich Garvey's yang. Somewhere there exists another career cop, an Irishman no doubt, with wire-rim glasses and a dark mustache and a back problem. He is standing over his eleventh straight drug murder in silent suffering, bargaining with an indifferent God for one shred of physical evidence, for one ignorant, evasive witness. The anti-Garvey is a good cop, a good detective, but lately he has entertained a few doubts about his abilities, as has his sergeant. He is drinking a little too much and he is yelling at his kids. He knows nothing of balance and order, of Tao logic, of his alter ego in the city of Baltimore who is wantonly solving homicides with the good fortune of two men.

"Oh do tell," says Garvey.

"He said Warren Waddell shot him."

"Warren Waddell?"

"Yeah, he said his buddy Warren shot him in the back for no reason. He kept saying, 'I can't believe he shot me. I can't believe it.' "

"You heard all this?"

"I was standing right over him. Me and my side partner heard it all. He said this guy Warren works with him at a place called Precision Concrete."

Way to go, my man, way to go. Everything was going from gray to black in the rear of Medic 15, but you got it done, you said what had to be said. You left a little something behind for a homicide detective to remember you by, and for that Rich Garvey thanks you.

A dying declaration, the lawyers call it—admissible evidence in a Maryland courtroom if the victim is informed by competent medical personnel that he is dying or otherwise indicates that he believes himself to be dying. And while it's not uncommon for homicide victims to make dying declarations, it is a rare and special moment when those utterances are at all helpful to a detective, not to mention relevant.

Every homicide detective has a favorite story involving a murdered man's last words. Many of these tales center on the code of the street and its observance even at life's end. One involves the last moments of a West Baltimore doper, who was still talking when officers arrived.

"Who shot you?"

"I'll tell you in a minute," the victim declared, presumably unaware that he had about forty seconds left to live.

Having suffered deep stab wounds to the chest and face, one dying man claimed to have cut himself shaving. Another victim, shot five times in the chest and back, assured officers with his last breath that he would take care of the problem himself.

But perhaps the most classic dying declaration story belongs to Bob McAllister. Back in '82, during his first weeks as a homicide detective, Mac had worked a long detail case with other detectives and had been a secondary on a few calls, but otherwise he was pretty green. In the hope that he'd learn from a veteran, they paired him with Jake "the Snake" Coleman, alias the Polyester Prince, a gravel-voiced, bantamweight detective of legendary proportions. And so, when the call came in for a shooting on Pennsylvania Avenue, Jake Coleman was out the door with McAllister in tow.

The dead man at Pennsie and Gold was named Frank Gupton. McAllister can remember the name without hesitation; he also remembers that the case is still as open as the day is long.

"He was alive when we got here," said the first officer at the scene.

"Oh yeah?" said Coleman, encouraged.

"Yeah. We asked him who shot him."

"And?"

"He said, 'Fuck you.' "

Coleman slapped McAllister on the back. "Well, brother," he growled, imparting an early lesson to the younger detective, "looks like you got your first murder."

Now, standing out on Fremont Avenue, Garvey and McAllister both know enough about their victim, one Carlton Robinson, to say that whatever else he was, he wasn't cut from the same cloth as Frank Gupton. He wanted to be avenged.

An hour after clearing the scene, both detectives are in a west side rowhouse, talking with Carlton's girlfriend, who had packed the victim's lunch pail and kissed him good-bye as he left to catch an early morning ride to work.

The interview is hard. The girlfriend is pregnant with Carlton's child, and he was supporting her and talking about marriage. She knows that he usually caught his ride to work at Pennsylvania and North and she knows the name Warren Waddell as a co-worker who sometimes caught the same ride. But Garvey and McAllister have only a few minutes to talk with her before the sound of a ringing telephone fills the small apartment. The hospital, thinks Garvey, already aware of what the news will be.

"No," she wails, dropping the receiver on the floor and falling into a girlfriend's arms. "No, goddammit. No . . ."

Garvey stands up first.

"Why is this happening to me?"

Then McAllister.

"Why . . ."

Both detectives leave their cards in the kitchen and find their own way to the door. Everything so far—from the lunch pail to Carlton's willingness to name his killer to his girlfriend's tears—tells them they have a real victim here.

A few hours later, at a doughnut shop off Philadelphia Road in eastern Baltimore County, the site manager of Precision Concrete confirms as much: "Carlton was just a great guy, a really great guy. He was one of my best guys."

"And Waddell?" asks Garvey.

The manager rolls his eyes. "I mean, I'm amazed he actually killed him. I'm amazed he did it, but I'm not surprised he did it, you know?"

Warren was crazy, the manager says. He came to work every other day with a semiautomatic pistol tucked into his jeans, showing off his flash money and telling everyone about how good his drug connections were.

"Did he have drug connections?"

"Oh yeah."

It was hard getting Waddell to do work out at a site, the manager says. He'd rather spend time telling everyone else on the crew how dangerous he was and how he had killed people before.

Well, thought Garvey, listening to the manager ramble on, that much was true anyway. Back at the office an hour ago, the detectives had run Waddell's name and come up with an impressive sheet that culminated in a second-degree murder conviction twelve years ago. In fact, Waddell had just made parole.

"He's a mental case," says the manager, a sawed-off billy with dirty blond hair. "You know, I'd be scared to deal with him sometimes . . . I can't believe he killed Carlton."

For the regulars in the morning rush at the Dunkin' Donuts counter, the conversation is a startling diversion. The manager chose the spot because it was near the day's construction site; now, the businessmen at the counter are ordering refills and staring over their newspapers at the spectacle of two plainclothes detectives working a murder.

"What was Carlton like?"

"Carlton was a real good worker," says the manager. "I'm not sure, but I think it was Carlton who got Waddell his job with us. I know they came to work together all the time."

"Tell me what happened yesterday at work," says Garvey.

"Yesterday," says the manager, shaking his head. "Yesterday was just a joke. They were joking around, you know, teasing Warren."

"What about?"

"Different stuff, you know. The way he acted and how he didn't do any work."

"Was Carlton teasing him?"

"They all were. They called him a dickhead and he didn't like that."

"Why'd they call him a dickhead?"

"Because, you know," says the manager, shrugging off the question, "he's a dickhead."

Garvey laughs.

At one point, the manager tells them, Waddell flashed his semiauto and declared cryptically that tomorrow was election day and people always get killed on election day. Garvey has heard the summer heat wave theory and the full moon theory of inner-city mortality, but never the election day postulate. This is a new one.

"Tell me about this gun."

The manager describes the weapon as a 9mm semiauto with a clip of eighteen rounds. The casings at the scene were .38, but both Garvey and McAllister know that most people can't tell a .38 from a 9mm on first sight. Warren was proud of the gun, the manager says, recalling that Waddell had explained that he always mixed hollow-point and roundnose ammunition together in the clip, alternating between the two. "That's the way to kill a man," Waddell told anyone willing to listen.

That, too, matches up when both detectives return to the city to watch an assistant medical examiner pull bullets out of Carlton Robinson's body. It is a slow morning on Penn Street—a double suicide or murder-suicide from Montgomery County, another suicide from Anne Arundel, two probable overdoses, an unexplained collapse, and a ten-year-old girl run down by a truck. The detectives don't have to wait more than an hour to confirm that half the recovered slugs are hollow-point, the rest, standard roundnosed ammo.

The ballistic evidence is tinged with irony. Not only is November 9 election day in Maryland, it also happens to be the same day the state's vaunted Saturday Night Special law takes effect. Passed by the state legislature in the spring despite a $6.7 million lobbying effort backed by the National Rifle Association, the law set up a review board to identify and prohibit the sale of cheap handguns in Maryland. Touted as a victory over gun control opponents and a counterweight to handgun violence, the law is in truth a largely meaningless exercise. Not since the 1970s have cheap handguns been responsible for more than a handful of the city's homicides; nowadays even teenagers are walking around with semiautomatics tucked into their sweatpants. Smith & Wesson, Glock, Baretta, Sig Sauer—even the dickheads of the world, Warren Waddell included, are carrying quality weapons. And though Maryland's landmark gun control law is the pride of its political leaders, it has arrived about fifteen years too late.

On the day after Carlton Robinson's murder, Warren Waddell calls the manager to say he won't be coming to work. He also asks if his employer can pick up tomorrow's paycheck and meet him across town. Anticipating such a request, the detectives told supervisors at the construction company to explain to Waddell that he has to come to the office in Essex and sign for the check in person. The manager gives him that story and then asks if he really killed Carlton.

"I can't talk right now," Waddell says.

Then, to the amazement of all concerned, Waddell shows up the next morning to claim his paycheck, eyes the secretaries suspiciously, then leaves abruptly. He and the friend who drove him are arrested at a county police roadblock a mile or two away. Searched by the county officers, Waddell is found to be carrying a large amount of cash, an American Express card and a U.S. passport. Upon his arrest, he makes no statement, then further endears himself to Garvey and McAllister by faking a stomach ailment on the trip downtown, wasting two hours of the detectives' time at Sinai Hospital.

Everything about the case puts Waddell's signature on the murder—the victim's dying words, the fight and threats at work the previous day, the mixture of hollow-point and standard ammo, the suspect's behavior after the murder. Yet when Garvey brings the case into the state's attorney's office, he's told that it's an easy indictment but a loser in court.

The centerpiece of the case—Carlton Robinson's dying words—may prove inadmissible simply because the officers at the scene did not inform the victim that he was dying. Nor did Robinson specifically tell the officers that he believed his life was ending. Instead, the officers did the natural thing. They called for the ambo and leaned close to the victim, telling Robinson to hang on, assuring him that if he remained conscious he would make it.

Without an acknowledgment of imminent death by either the victim or his attendants, Robinson's accusation could well be knocked down by a defense attorney who knows his Maryland code.

And without the dying declaration, they have weak circumstance and little more. Having been through the murder mill once before, Waddell shows no interest in the interrogation process, nor does a subsequent search warrant produce the murder weapon.

Garvey, of course, has no choice but to charge the murder. For one thing, he knows that Warren Waddell murdered Carlton Robinson. For another, he owes it to himself to close the case in this Perfect Year. But even as Waddell is trundled off to city jail for pretrial detention, the detective knows that this is one case for the lawyers to salvage.

Frustrated by the initial reaction from the state's attorney's office, Garvey asks Don Giblin, his golfing buddy in the violent crimes unit, to shop around for a veteran prosecutor. Garvey has seen enough of the trial division to know that half the ASAs in the office will look at a file like this and immediately pronounce the legal problem insurmountable. As with the Lena Lucas murder, he needs a fighter.

"Get me a good one, Don," he tells Giblin over the telephone. "That's all I'm asking."

TEN

Deck the halls with boughs of holly,
Fa-la-la-la-la-la-la-la-la!
Throw that stiff up on the dolly,
Fa-la-la-la-la-la-la-la-la!
Talk to us and if you're willing,
Fa-la-la-la-la-la-la-la-la!
Tell us who did all this killing,
Fa-la-la-la-la-la-la-la-la!
Tell us how you want forgiveness,
Fa-la-la-la-la-la-la-la-la!
You don't know we've got a witness,
Fa-la-la-la-la-la-la-la-la,
Talk to us, you've nothing to lose,
Fa-la-la-la-la-la-la-la-la!
Why is blood upon your gym shoes?
Fa-la-la-la-la-la-la-la-la!
Want to make a good impression?
Fa-la-la-la-la-la-la-la-la!
Make yourself a fast confession,
Fa-la-la-la-la-la-la-la-la!

—Homicide unit Christmas song

Friday, December 2

Mostly for his own amusement, Donald Waltemeyer watches Mark Cohen watching the hole get deeper. The process—such as it is—consists of two distinct stages and Cohen's disposition changes noticeably between the two. The first four feet with the backhoe are quick and painless, and Cohen barely squirms; the next eighteen inches require hand shovels, and Waltemeyer sees the lawyer's face crease with something morc than expectation.

Pale and wire-thin, with spectacles and curly blond locks, Cohen looks like an innocent straight man standing next to the side of beef that is Waltemeyer, a professorial, three-piece Hardy propped up beside a muscular, working-class Laurel. Cohen is a good man, among the best of the city prosecutors, and Waltemeyer can't think of a better trial attorney for the sprawling colossus that began as the Geraldine Parrish murder-for-hire case. But Cohen is a lawyer, not a cop, and as the shovels work deeper into clay, he begins to look less and less comfortable. Mercifully, Waltemeyer gives him his out.

"Kinda cold out here," the detective says.

"Sure is," agrees Cohen, his collar turned up to the winter wind. "I'm going back to the car awhile."

"You want the keys for the heater?"

"No, I'll be okay."

Waltemeyer watches Cohen negotiate his way across the muddy field, made worse by an inch or two of recently melted snow. The lawyer steps lightly in his L. L. Bean duck boots, both hands hiking up the seams of his slacks an extra couple of inches. Waltemeyer knows the cold isn't the only thing the man is feeling: The stench—faint but foul in the frigid air—was there from about four feet down. Cohen couldn't help but get a whiff of it.

At the sound of something solid, the detective turns back toward the hole, taking a step forward to peer down over the edge. "What was that?"

"That's the top," says the cemetery manager. "You got the top of the box right there."

The two men in the hole concentrated their shovels on the edges of the wood, trying to free the top of the casket from the surrounding dirt. But at the first real stress, the pressed wood cracks and collapses.

"Just pull that shit up," says the manager. "Don't even mess with it."

"Not much of a casket," says Waltemeyer.

"I'm telling you," agrees the manager, a gravel-voiced, pear-shaped man. "She buried the man cheap as she could."

I'll bet she did, thinks Waltemeyer. Miss Geraldine wasn't about to be spending hard-won money on funerals, what with all the dearly departed she had to contend with. Even now, from inside the city jail, Geraldine Parrish was fighting hard to remain the sole heir of the Reverend Rayfield Gilliard's money and property, with a civil suit by the reverend's family still to be decided by a circuit court judge.

As for the good reverend himself, he is somewhere under this godforsaken mud slope, this potter's field just below the city's southern edge. Mount Zion, they called it. A consecrated cemetery; hallowed ground.

Bullshit, thinks Waltemeyer. The place is a small stretch of barren wetness running down off Hollins Ferry Road, owned and operated by one of the larger inner-city funeral homes, a volume business that can still scratch profit from even the cheapest burials. To the south is a low-income housing project, to the north, the Lansdowne Senior High School. At the top of the hill, near the cemetery entrance, is a convenience store; at the bottom, a polluted creek. Two hundred and fifty dollars gets the customer a plain pressed-wood box and a six-foot sliver of mud. If the body is unclaimed, if the state of Maryland has to serve as the sponsor, the price drops to a mere $200. Hell, thinks Waltemeyer, Mount Zion doesn't even look like a cemetery—only a few headstones mark what had to be the graves of thousands.

No, Geraldine hadn't exactly gone all out for her last husband, but then again, she had two more like him living with her over on Kennedy Street. The Black Widow's last conquest got a cheap coffin, no vault and no headstone. Still, the cemetery manager seemed to have no problem finding the spot a half an hour ago, walking across the barren plain with an air of practiced certainty.

"Right here," he said.

Row 78, grave 17.

"You sure it's him?" asked Waltemeyer.

"It oughta be," said the manager, surprised at the question. "Once you put 'em down there, they supposed to stay put."

If, in fact, the grave held the remains of the right Reverend Rayfield Gilliard, age seventy-eight, then the doctors on Penn Street could still do something with this case. Even with a body that had been in the ground for ten months, an adulterant could still be detectable. Twenty prescription Valium, ground into a last meal of tunafish—yes indeed, Smialek told Waltemeyer as they agreed to get the exhumation order, if that's what we're looking for, that's what we'll find.

Still, the Reverend Gilliard had been in the ground since February and Waltemeyer has to wonder what's even left down there. The cemetery manager said the winter burials would freeze in the ground, then decomp slower than those buried in warmer weather. It made some sense to the detective, but who even thinks about such things? Not Waltemeyer if he can help it. However much he enjoyed watching Mark Cohen squirm, he had to admit a private truth: This bothered him.

You find a body in the street and it's a murder. You sketch him, take his picture, check his pockets, roll him over. In that instant and for a few hours afterward, he's all yours, so much so that after a couple of years you don't think about it anymore. But once he's in the ground, once a preacher says some words and the dirt is on top of him, it's just different. Never mind that this is nothing more than a muddy field, never mind that the exhumation is a necessary investigative act—for Waltemeyer, it's still hard to believe that he has any right messing with a body in its final repose.

Naturally, his colleagues reacted to such doubts with all the warm sincerity for which Baltimore cops are known and admired. All the way through roll call this morning they had piled it on: Christ, Waltemeyer, what the fuck kind of asshole are you? We don't have enough murders to deal with in this fucking town, you got to go prancing around the goddamn cemeteries like Bela fucking Lugosi, digging up skeletons?

And Waltemeyer knew they had a point: In terms of criminal culpability, the exhumation seemed a bit redundant. They had Geraldine and her contract killer, Edwin, on three homicides and the repeated attempts on Dollie Brown. They had Geraldine and another triggerman charged with a fourth murder in the death of Albert Robinson, the old drunk from New Jersey found by the Clifton Park railbed back in '86. Waltemeyer had driven Corey Belt and Mark Cohen up to Bergen County for a few days to interview witnesses and nail down that charge. Four murders, five murders—at what point does another charge no longer matter?

Watching the gravediggers pry at the broken pieces of the casket top, Waltemeyer wonders whether it's worth it. Miss Geraldine will be going to prison in any case, and what happens today certainly isn't going to give Gilliard's family any peace of mind. On the other hand, the detective has to concede that, like the doctors on Penn Street, he, too, is a little curious.

Tossing the curled, rotting wood out of the hole, the gravediggers stand against the edges of the box. Waltemeyer leans over and looks down.

"Well?" says the manager.

Waltemeyer looks at the photograph of Gilliard, then down at the coffin. The dead man looks pretty good, considering the circumstances.

"He's a little small," says the detective. "The photo looks like a bigger man."

"They thin out when they in the ground," says the manager, impatient. "You know the motherfuckers don't stay too fat down there."

No, thinks Waltemeyer. I guess they don't.

It's hell trying to lift the bottom of the box out of the mud, and after ten minutes, the gravediggers give up, deferring instead to the ME's attendants, who simply lift the remains up and out using a plastic tarp.

"Way to go, Waltemeyer," the attendant says as he climbs from the grave, covered in mud. "You just went to the top of my list."

The body claimed, Waltemeyer and the gravediggers begin the slow, muddy trek back to the dirt road that divides Mount Zion. Stepping carefully toward the Cavalier, the detective watches the attendants load the black van, then looks through the car windshield at Mark Cohen. The prosecutor is looking down, seemingly preoccupied.

"You see him?" he asks Cohen in the car.

Cohen barely looks up, his face buried deep inside his briefcase, his hands working through the files inside.

"Mark, did you see him?"

"Yeah," says Cohen. "I saw him."

"Pretty ghoulish, huh?" says Waltemeyer. "I feel like I'm in a horror movie or something."

"Let's get downtown," says Cohen. "I've got to get back to the office."

Oh yeah, thinks Waltemeyer. He saw him.

The detective chooses to skip the actual autopsy, but it goes without a hitch—the cutters gathering tissue and organ samples for the toxicology, then checking the remains for any other overt signs of trauma. A perfectly straightforward piece of medical work, the examination could be a case study for the forensic pathology tests. At least it seems that way until an attendant is sewing up the chest cavity and notices the hospital identification bracelet on the cadaver's wrist. The ink is faded, but the name, clearly legible, is not Rayfield Gilliard.

Twenty minutes later, the telephone in the homicide unit bleats. A detective answers and then yells into the coffee room: "Waltemeyer, medical examiner on line one."

Sitting at Dave Brown's desk, Waltemeyer picks up the receiver and leans forward. After a second or two, his hand goes to his head and his fingers pinch the skin at the bridge of his nose.

"You're not kidding me, are you?" He leans back in the chair and stares up at the yellowing ceiling tile. His face is contorted, comical in its cartoon-like approximation of woe. He pulls a pencil from Brown's desk and begins writing on the back of a pawn shop card, sounding each word as he writes: "Hospital bracelet . . . Eugene . . . Dale . . . black, male . . ."

Great.

"No one noticed it until after the autopsy?" asks the detective.

Just great.

Waltemeyer hangs up the phone and gives himself half a minute before punching the intercom button on the phone extension.

"Captain?"

"Yes," says the voice on the phone.

"This is Waltemeyer, sir," says the detective, still holding the bridge of his nose. "Captain, are you sitting down?"

"Why?"

"Captain, I got goods news and bad news."

"Good news first."

"The autopsy went well."

"And the bad news?"

"We dug up the wrong guy."

"You're not serious."

"Oh, I'm serious."

"Jesus."

Eugene Dale. Some poor soul who had the misfortune to be chucked into the same potter's field at about the same time as the Reverend Gilliard. Now he's down on a gurney on Penn Street, looking a little worse for the day's events. Not much in this world can truly upset a homicide detective, but for Waltemeyer, disturbing the slumber of the innocent dead comes damn close. Waltemeyer wonders whether this Dale has relatives. And that name: Why does it sound familiar?

"You got the wrong guy?" asks a detective from Stanton's shift, working overtime on a court appearance. "Who'd you get?"

"Some poor bastard named Eugene Dale."

"Eugene Dale?"

"Yeah."

"D-A-L-E?"

Waltemeyer nods.

The other detective points at the board and the last couple of names under Rodger Nolan's section. "That's the same name as Edgerton's suspect."

"Who?"

"Eugene Dale."

"Who is?" asks Waltemeyer, still confused.

"The guy that Edgerton locked up for killing the little girl," says the detective. "He's got the same name as the guy you just dug up."

Waltemeyer looks at the board. "Eugene Dale," he says, reading the black ink. "I'll be damned."

"Where's Edgerton now?" asks the other detective.

"Off today," says Waltemeyer, absorbed in thought. What the hell does it matter who they dug up? It isn't Rayfield Gilliard; they know that much. Waltemeyer listens impassively as the other detective gets Edgerton on the phone and then runs through the preamble.

"Harry, was your guy a junior? Was his name Eugene Dale, Jr., or Eugene Dale the third, or something like that?"

The other detective nods, listening to the answer. Without hearing a word, Waltemeyer can imagine Edgerton's confusion.

"And did Dale's father die recently . . . Yeah, like February or so . . . Yeah, right . . . Well guess what, Harry, you're not gonna believe this, but Waltemeyer just dug up your suspect's father and had the guys at the morgue cut him open . . . Yeah, I'm serious."

Enough, thinks Waltemeyer, walking out of the coffee room. I'm not about to sit around here all day listening to this crap. Never mind that Edgerton is on the other end of the phone line absorbing this bizarre coincidence and fantasizing about a fresh trip to the city jail. Never mind that Edgerton imagines himself confronting the younger Dale with the information that the Baltimore Police Department dug up his father and played with him for no reason other than his son killed a little girl and lied about it. Never mind that Stanton's detective will be running over to Mark Tomlin's desk at the shift change, telling Tomlin about Waltemeyer's morning so Tomlin can draw one of his cartoons that every so often grace the coffee room wall. Never mind all that.

This, to Waltemeyer, is not funny.

Leaving the other detective on the phone with Edgerton, Waltemeyer borrows a Cavalier and takes another ride to Mount Zion.

"You back?" asks a gravedigger at the Hollins Ferry entrance.

"I'm back," says Waltemeyer. "Where's Mr. Brown right now?"

"He's in the office."

Waltemeyer walks across the driveway toward a small, one-room caretaker's shack. The cemetery manager, on his way out the door, meets him halfway.

"Mr. Brown, you and me got some talking to do," says Waltemeyer, looking at the ground.

"Why's that?"

"Because that body you dug up and gave us this morning . . ."

"What about it?"

"That was the wrong man."

The manager doesn't miss a beat. "Wrong man?" he says. "How could they tell?"

Waltemeyer hears that and thinks about grabbing the old man by his throat. How could they tell? Obviously, the manager figures that after lying in the ground ten months, one corpse looks a lot like another. Just so long as you pull the lid off and it ain't wearing a dress, right?

"He had an ID bracelet from the hospital," says Waltemeyer, fighting his temper. "It says he's Eugene Dale, not Rayfield Gilliard."

"Jesus," says the manager, shaking his head.

"Let's go inside and have a look at whatever records you got."

Waltemeyer follows the old man into the shack, then watches as he pulls three sets of 3-by-5 cards from a metal file drawer—January, February and March burials—and begins thumbing through them.

"What you say the name was?"

"Dale. D-A-L-E."

"Not in February," says the manager. He begins checking the March burials, stopping at the fourth card in the pile. Eugene Dale. Died March 10. Buried March 14. Section DD, Row 83, Grave 11. Waltemeyer picks up the February cards and finds Rayfield Gilliard. Died February 2. Buried February 8. Section DD, Row 78, Grave 17.

Not even close. Waltemeyer gives the manager a hard stare.

"You were five rows away."

"Well, he ain't in the right place."

"I know that," says Waltemeyer, his voice rising.

"I mean, we was at the right place, but he wasn't where he was supposed to be."

Waltemeyer looks at the floor.

"I didn't work that day," says the old man. "Someone else messed up."

"Someone else?"

"Yeah."

"You think if we dig where Eugene Dale is supposed to be, we're gonna find Gilliard?"

"Maybe."

"Why? They're buried a month apart."

"Maybe not," the manager agrees.

Waltemeyer picks up the burial cards and begins sorting through the lot, looking for burials on or near the eighth of February. To his amazement, the names are strangely familiar. Every other card seems to correspond to a 24-hour report.

Here is James Brown, Gilbert's murder, that kid who got stabbed to death on New Year's. And Barney Erely, the old drunk Pellegrini found bludgeoned in the alley off Clay Street a few weeks after Latonya Wallace, the derelict killed when he chose the wrong place to defecate. And Orlando Felton, that decomp from North Calvert Street, the overdose that McAllister and McLarney handled back in January. And Keller's drug killing from March, that homeboy with the unlikely last name of Ireland who made a bucket of money selling east side dope. Christ, all that cash and his family just dumps him in a potter's field. Dunnigan's drug murder from the Lafayette Court projects . . . the three little babies killed in Steinhice's arson case . . . Eddie Brown's fatal shooting from Vine Street. Waltemeyer reads on, both awed and amused. This one was Dave Brown's, this one was Shea's. Tomlin handled this one . . .

"You really don't know where he is," says Waltemeyer, putting down the cards, "do you, Mr. Brown?"

"No. Not exactly. Not right now."

"I didn't think so."

At that moment, Waltemeyer is ready to cut his losses and give up on Rayfield Gilliard; the medical examiners, however, are still insistent. They have a probable homicide and an exhumation order signed by a Baltimore County judge, and therefore Mount Zion is obligated to find the body.

Three weeks later they try again, digging down into the mud a full six rows from the spot where the state reburied Eugene Dale, Sr., in a better box than the one it tore apart. This time Waltemeyer does not ask for the logic behind the manager's insistence on the new location, in part for fear that there is no logic. They use the same backhoe, the same gravediggers, the same ME's attendants, who haul the second, heavier corpse to the surface, then check the wrists carefully for any identification.

"This one looks more like him," Waltemeyer says with hope, checking the photograph.

"Told you so," the manager says proudly.

Then the ME's man pulls a sock from the left foot to reveal half of a hospital toe tag. W-I-L are the only visible letters. Wilson? Williams? Wilmer? Who knows and who the hell cares if it isn't Rayfield Gilliard?

"Mr. Brown," Waltemeyer says to the manager, shaking his head in genuine amazement, "you are a piece of work."

The manager shrugs, saying that it looks like the right man to him. "Maybe the tag is wrong," he adds.

"Jesus Christ," says Waltemeyer. "Get me away from here before I lose my mind."

Leaving the cemetery grounds, Waltemeyer finds himself walking with a gravedigger. The workman quietly confirms his worst fears, explaining that back in February, when the ground was frozen and the snow deep, the manager had them dig a mass grave down by the creek; they could get the backhoe down there without getting it stuck. Then they dumped eight or nine coffins into that same hole. Easier this way, the manager told them.

Waltemeyer squints in the morning sunlight as the gravedigger finishes his story, his eyes narrowing across the bleak landscape. From the cemetery entrance at the top of the hill, a good part of the city skyline can be seen: the trade center, the USF&G building, the Maryland bank tower. The spires of mobtown, the harbor city, the land of pleasant living. The natives like to tell one another that if you can't live in Bawlmer, you can't live anywhere.

So where does that leave Barney Erely? And Orlando Felton? And Maurice Ireland? What was so wrong, so irrelevant, about them that they could end here beneath this wretched patch of county mud, wasted souls, with their city's gleaming skyscrapers just close enough to mock them? Drunks, addicts, dope peddlers, numbers men, children born to the wrong parents, battered wives, hated husbands, robbery victims, an innocent bystander or two, sons of Cain, victims of Cain—these were the lives lost by the city in a single year, the men and women who cluttered crime scenes and filled Penn Street freezers, leaving little more than red or black ink on a police department tally board. Birth, poverty, violent death, then an anonymous burial in the mud of Mount Zion. In life, the city could muster no purpose for these wasted souls; in death, the city had lost them entirely.

Gilliard and Dale and Erely and Ireland—they were all beyond reach. Even if someone wanted to rescue a loved one and preserve the memory with a real headstone, in a real cemetery, it was no longer possible. The unmarked graves and the manager's pathetic card file had seen to that. By rights, the city ought to build some kind of monument to its own indifference—Tomb of the Unknown Victim, it could be called. Set it up at Gold and Etting with a police honor guard. Drop a few shell casings in front of it and then chalk off a fresh human silhouette every half hour. Get the Edmondson High School band to play taps and charge the tourists a buck and a quarter.

Lost in life, lost in death. The brain-deads running Mount Zion had pretty much seen to that, thinks Waltemeyer, giving the muddy slope a last look. For $200 a pop, this alleged manager was willing to use any hole he could find, because what the hell, it was ridiculous to think that anyone was ever going to ask for one of them back. Waltemeyer thinks of their first encounter with the cemetery manager. The poor bastard probably shit blue when we showed up with that exhumation order.

After the second attempt, there will be no further excavations for the lost Reverend Gilliard. With a spate of murder charges already filed under Miss Geraldine's name, this one will have to slip away. The pathologists, the lawyers, the cops—no one has the stomach to risk disturbing any more graves. For Waltemeyer, however, such sentiments come too late. True, the Geraldine Parrish investigation has been his career case, and his unstinting pursuit of it has secured his reputation as one of the homicide unit's seasoned veterans. Nonetheless, his adventures in Mount Zion mark him with repute of an altogether different kind.

As if disinterring the odd, innocent body isn't hard enough for a Catholic conscience, he will return to the office one day in January to find a new nameplate on his desk, the kind of thing you can order from any office supply store.

"Det. Digger Waltemeyer," it reads.

MONDAY, DECEMBER 5

"I don't like the way he's laying," says Donald Worden, leaning over the bed. "Up on his side like that . . . like somebody rolled him."

Waltemeyer nods in agreement.

"I think," adds Worden, looking over the rest of the room, "that this one's gonna come back from the medical examiner as a murder."

"I think you're right," says Waltemeyer.

There is no overt trauma to the body, no bulletholes, no knife wounds, no bruises or contusions. A little bit of dried blood is visible around the mouth, but that could be the result of decomp. There is also no sign of struggle or ransacking in the motel room. But the old man is on his right side beneath the sheets, his back arched at an awkward angle, as if someone had pushed him into that strange position to check for signs of life.

He was sixty-five and white, a Southern Maryland man well known to the employees at the Eastgate Motel, a $25-a-night collection of double beds and bad wall prints on old Route 40 in East Baltimore. Once a week, Robert Wallace Yergin would drive to Baltimore from his home in Leonardtown, check into the Eastgate for a night, then spend the evening bringing young boys to and from the room.

For that purpose, at least, the Eastgate was situated perfectly. A few blocks from where Pulaski dead-ends into East Fayette Street, the motel is only blocks from the edges of Patterson Park, where $20 will pay for the services of a blond-haired billy kid anywhere from twelve to eighteen years old. The pedophile trade along Eastern Avenue is an old phenomenon, known to men up and down the East Coast. A few years back, when the vice squad wrote a warrant on a child pornography ring, they actually recovered some guidebooks to homosexual prostitution in major American cities. In Baltimore, the guides noted, the most promising locales were Wilkens near Monroe Street and Patterson Park along Eastern Avenue.

Not only is Robert Yergin's affinity for boys under the age of majority known to the desk men and cleaning crew at the Eastgate, but the employees are able to identify and describe the sixteen-year-old who has been Yergin's constant companion for the last several months. The kid is a Baltimore boy, the employees tell Worden, a street waif who for a pound or two of flesh had found a home with the old pervert down in the country. When Yergin came to Baltimore to troll for teenagers, he'd bring the kid, who would spend his time visiting friends from the old neighborhood.

"Maybe the boy is the one who took the car," says the twenty-five-year-old employee from housecleaning who found the body. "He might have just borrowed it or something."

"Maybe," says Worden.

"When you came in here and found him," asks Waltemeyer, "did you touch him or roll him over or anything to see if he was okay?"

"No way," says the employee. "I saw he was dead right away and just left him be."

"Did you touch anything in the room?" asks Worden. "Anything at all?"

"No, sir."

Worden gestures to the young man, drawing him across the room for a private conversation. Quietly, and in a way that the employee immediately recognizes as truthful, Worden explains that this death is going to be a murder. Worden tries to reassure him: We only care about the murder.

"Don't be offended," the detective says, "but if you touched anything from the room, if you took anything from the room, tell us now and it won't go any further . . ."

The employee understands. "No," he says. "I didn't steal nothin'."

"Okay, then," says Worden.

Waltemeyer waits for the young man to leave, then looks at Worden. "Well, if he didn't get the wallet," says Waltemeyer, "then someone else must've."

That's what it's beginning to look like: Man meets boy, man gets undressed, boy strangles man, steals cash, credit cards and Ford Thunderbird and drives off into the Baltimore sunset. Unless, of course, the kid who lived with him did it. Then it's man meets boy, man lives with boy, boy finally gets sick of playing grabass and chokes the living shit out of the landlord. That would play, too, thinks Worden.

The lab tech on call is Bernie Magsamen—good man, Bernie is, one of the best—and so they take their time with the scene, pulling fingerprints off the nightstand and the used drinking glasses near the bed and in the bathroom sink. They get a good sketch and several photographs of the body in that bizarre position. They go through the old man's belongings carefully, looking for what is missing, what may be missing, or what is there that shouldn't be.

They do this because they know they've caught a murder; they know it and act on it with the same resolve by which other men would declare the scene to be a motel room or its occupant to be dead. To Worden and Waltemeyer, the death of Robert Yergin is a murder even though the victim is sixty-five and overweight, fully primed for a heart attack, a stroke or some other natural death. To them it's a murder, though there isn't a suggestion of any struggle or any trauma to the body; it's a murder, though there isn't a hint of petechial hemorrhaging in the whites of the eyes—the postmortem telltale that so often occasions strangulation. To them it's a murder even after Worden finds the victim's wallet still fat with cash and credit cards in a jacket pocket, suggesting that anyone who killed the old man did a lousy job of robbing him. It's a murder because Robert Yergin, who takes to bed young boys he barely knows, is lying there in a weird position without his 1988 Ford Thunderbird. What else does a good detective need to know?

Little more than three hours later, Donald Worden is standing next to Donald Kincaid on the opposite side of town, staring at a thirty-foot smear of drying blood that ends in a red-purple lake after traveling the full length of a vacant West Lexington Street rowhouse. And although the man whose carotid artery painted this picture is still clinging to life at Bon Secours, this, too, will come back a murder. Worden knows it, not only because so much blood has been sprayed across the dirty hallway tile, but also because he has no viable suspect.

Two whodunits in one night—the new standard by which a Baltimore detective can be judged. Any professional can work a series of mysteries on successive nights or handle dunkers in tandem on a rough midnight shift. But what prompts a man who inherits one open case file to then answer the telephone three hours later, grab a fresh pair of plastic gloves and a flashlight, and leave out for a West Baltimore shooting call?

"Well, well," muses McLarney the morning after, as he stares at the fresh names on the board, "I guess it's finally reached that point where Donald won't trust anyone else with a murder."

This is the Donald Worden around whom Terry McLarney built a squad, the Worden that Dave Brown can never please, the Worden that Rick James loves to call his partner. Two crime scenes, two autopsies, two family notifications, two sets of interviews, two batches of paperwork, two trips to the police computer for sheets on two separate sets of players—and not a word of complaint from the Big Man. Not even the barest suggestion that Waltemeyer may want to go it alone on the Eastgate murder, or that Kincaid will have to make do without a secondary for Lexington Street.

No, sir, Worden's got himself a fresh pack of cigars, a full pot of coffee and McLarney's signature on the bottom of a departmental overtime slip. He hasn't slept in twenty-four hours and if he gets a break in either case, he won't get near a bed for twelve more. It's a hard road, a long haul—a ridiculous way for a grown man to earn a living. It's also about as close to a feeling of immortality as a career cop ever gets.

In the end, he resurrected himself. In the end, he simply waited his anger out, waited for that phone line to light up with the cure that was bound to come. Straight murders, one after another, each one a unique variation of that same eternal evil; just crime and punishment, meted out to a working cop in roughly equal shares. God knows Worden had talked enough about quitting; in this job, he liked to tell colleagues, you eat the bear until the bear eats you, and I'm going to walk before that bad boy gets hungry.

Tough-guy talk. But no one really believed that Donald Worden would loosen his grip on that silver shield. It would have to be the other way around.

Three days after Worden picks up two murders on a single shift, both cases are in the black. The break in the Yergin case comes as a direct result of Worden's prolonged interrogation of the victim's teenage companion, a conversation that makes it clear enough that in the absence of any other suspect, the old man's housemate will remain at the top of Worden's list. Two days later the kid—still frightened—calls the homicide unit to say he's heard that some white boys are driving the dead man's Thunderbird around Pigtown and Carroll Park.

Worden and Waltemeyer drive down to the upper end of the Southern District, where Waltemeyer talks to a few of the older hands with whom he served for so long. The Southern troops are already known for reading homicide teletypes, but for their old bunky Waltemeyer they'll go so far as to tow every T-bird in the district down to headquarters. An hour after the detectives' visit, two Southern men stop the right car at Pratt and Carey and take the driver, a seventeen-year-old male prostitute, into custody. Worden and Waltemeyer tag-team the suspect in the large interrogation room until he admits to being in the motel room; unaware that the autopsy proved the death to be suffocation, he claims the old man died of a seizure. When the two detectives complete the statement and leave the room, the kid stands up and uses the two-way window in the door as a mirror, breaking pimples and fretting over his complexion as if he's still an ordinary teenager, contemplating a Friday night date.

The Lexington Street murder, a dispute over a small narcotics sale, is solved on a recanvass of the shooting scene, when Worden's photographic memory matches the face of an old man who answers a door in the 1500 block with the face of a bystander he saw hanging out on a corner the night of the murder. Sure enough, the old man admits to being a witness and identifies the shooter from a photo array. But it's still a weak, one-witness case until the suspect arrives downtown, whereupon Worden lets loose with the full blue-eyed, white-haired father-figure treatment and persuades the shooter to give up everything. So effective is Worden's method that the suspect actually calls the detective from the city jail two weeks later with secondhand gossip about an unrelated murder.

"Detective Worden, I also just wanted to call and wish you a Merry Christmas," he tells the man who has jailed him. "For you and your family both."

"Thank you very much, Timmy," says Worden, a little touched. "My best to you and yours for the holidays."

Two up and two down. For Worden, the last weeks of a year that was so utterly frustrating now roll effortlessly onward, as if scripted for some cops-and-robbers television show in which all the crimes will be solved and explained before the last commercial break.

Three days before Christmas, the Big Man and Rick James go out on an East Baltimore shooting call, driving away from headquarters on a December night so unseasonably humid that the city is layered in thick, blinding fog. As the Cavalier lurches up Fayette Street, both detectives squint through the mist at the vaguest outline of rowhouses on either side of the street.

"This is fucking soup," says James.

"I always wanted to work a murder in fog," says Worden, almost wistful. "Like Sherlock Holmes."

"Yeah," agrees James. "That guy was always finding bodies in this shit . . ."

" 'Cause it was London," says Worden, pulling slowly through the light at Broadway.

"And it was always some motherfucker named Murray who did it. Murray something . . ."

"Murray?" says Worden, confused.

"Yeah, the killer was always named Murray."

"Moriarty, you mean. Professor Moriarty."

"Yeah," says James. "That's it. Moriarty. If we get a murder tonight, we gotta try and find a yo boy named Moriarty."

They do get a murder, a street shooting that stays a whodunit for only as long as it takes Worden to wade into a sea of black faces, a pale wanderer waiting for the crowd's natural hostility to dissipate, a patient, civil cop listening for the anonymous mention of a criminal's name.

Just before dawn on that same midnight shift, when the paperwork is complete and the office television offers nothing better than a test pattern, Donald Worden, strangely wired, wanders through the quiet looking for something else to occupy his time. James is asleep in the coffee room; Waltemeyer, pecking away at a 24-hour report in the admin office.

While making a fresh pot of coffee, the Big Man pries the plastic top from an unopened coffee can. Then, with the look of raw science filling his face, he sends the disk spinning through the stagnant air of the main office.

"Watch this," he says, walking over to pick up his new toy. He sends it back across the room, this time with a perfect ricochet off the tile floor.

"For my next trick," he says, preparing another launch, "we go off the ceiling."

Worden sends the plastic soaring. From the admin office, Waltemeyer looks up from the typewriter, momentarily distracted by what appears in the corner of his eye as a sort of thin, airborne blur. He looks over at Worden curiously, then back down at his report, as if dismissing the illusion.

"C'mon, Donald," yells Worden. "Get your ass out here . . ."

Waltemeyer looks up.

"C'mon, Donald. C'mon out and play."

Waltemeyer continues typing.

"Hey, Mrs. Waltemayer, can Donald come out and play today?"

Worden sends the disk soaring toward the plate glass that separates the two offices just as the admin lieutenant, an hour early for the coming dayshift, walks through the fishbowl toward his office. The plastic glances off the outer glass and sails gracefully past a wall column and into the open door of Nolan's office. The lieutenant stops in the doorway, marveling at the rare and extraordinary sight of Donald Worden, happy.

"Well?" asks the lieutenant, mystified.

"It's in the wrists, lieutenant," says Worden, smiling. "It's all in the wrists."

FRIDAY, DECEMBER 9

Rule Ten in the homicide handbook: There is too such a thing as a perfect murder. Always has been, and whoever tries to claim otherwise merely proves himself naive and romantic, a fool who is ignorant of rules one through nine.

A case in point: Here lies a black male by the name of Anthony Morris, twenty-one years of age, shot dead in the western half of Baltimore, Maryland. A young man of suddenly declining status in the local drug trade, Mr. Morris is found by Western uniforms in an empty courtyard of the Gilmor Homes, where a person or persons repeatedly compressed the trigger of a .38-caliber weapon and thus caused several small pieces of metal alloy to rip holes in Mr. Morris's body.

When removed from the corpse tomorrow morning, every one of these metal pieces will be splintered and mutilated, rendering them useless for comparison purposes. And because the weapon is a revolver, there aren't any spent casings lying around either. Even then, without a recovered weapon or a bullet or casing from a related crime—anything to which ballistic evidence might be compared—these problems are academic. Moreover, the crime scene is an asphalt courtyard in dead winter, barren of fingerprints, hairs, synthetic fibers, footprints, or anything else that could be mistaken as physical evidence. Nor is there anything in the pockets of the victim that constitutes a clue. Nor did Mr. Morris have anything illuminating to say to the first officers and paramedics—hardly surprising given that he was dead upon discovery.

Witnesses? On this midnight shift, in fact, there are no human beings whatsoever in this section of the Gilmor Homes projects. Emptied of its inhabitants for a pending renewal project, the courtyard into which Anthony Morris wandered is dark, cold and utterly devoid of human endeavor. No lights on the street, no lights in the boarded-up units, no pedestrians, no neighbors, no corner groceries or bars.

A helluva place to kill someone, thinks Rich Garvey, staring up and down the deserted courtyard. A perfect place, in fact. Anthony Morris is gunned down in a city of 730,000 and for all practical purposes, the crime scene could be the Nevada desert or the Arctic tundra or some other uncharted wilderness.

The original, anonymous call was for shots fired. Not even the report of a shooting or a body, not even a chance to talk to some people who found the victim. No passersby, no grieving relatives, no homeboys signifying from the corners. With McAllister working the crime scene, Garvey stands there shivering in the early hours of a winter morning, waiting, for any remote suggestion of life from the surrounding city—any warm, lighted place where a detective's first question could be asked.

Nothing. The silence is complete; the scene, vacant. There is only Garvey and his partner and the usual Western District faces in a swirl of blue-top emergency lights, alone with a corpse in a sleeping city. Garvey tells himself that it doesn't matter, that someone, somewhere, is ready and waiting to talk to him, to tell him about Anthony Morris and his enemies. Maybe the family, or a girlfriend, or some childhood buddy from the other end of the projects. Maybe an anonymous call to the homicide office, or a letter from some informant locked up on some pissant charge.

Because when you're the man with the perfect year, no scene can be too bleak. After all, what would he have been left with on Winchester Street if Biemiller hadn't grabbed the girlfriend at the scene? Or with the Fairfield bar robbery if the kid on the parking lot hadn't remembered the tag on that getaway car? Or the Langley murder up in Pimlico, the one where the uniforms made a drug arrest a half-block away and the guy turned out to be an eyeball witness?

Yeah, Garney tells himself, I don't have shit on this one. So what else is new? Except for the simplest kind of dunkers, they all look like weak sisters when you first get to the scene.

"Maybe you'll get a call on this one," says a Western uniform.

"Maybe," says Garvey, agreeable.

True to that hope, he and McAllister are in a rowhouse living room an hour later, a room brimming with survivors. The victim's mother, sisters, brothers and cousins are all arrayed at the edges of the room while the detectives stand in the center, exerting a certain centripetal force.

In the dry heat of the crowded room, Garvey watches McAllister launch into his standard exposition on what the grieving family should and shouldn't do in this, Their Time of Loss. Garvey never stops marveling at Mac's artistry with the families: Head tilted slightly, hands folded together at the waist, he's a parish priest, expressing his most heartfelt sorrow in slow, measured tones. Mac's even got a slight, endearing stutter that kicks in during moments of stress and adds a hint of vulnerability. At the scene an hour earlier, standing over the dead man, McAllister was as quick with a joke as any of them. Now, with the dead man's mother, he's Mr. Sharing and Caring. Phil fucking Donahue in a trenchcoat.

"Now there's absolutely no need for you to go down to the medical examiner's office. In fact, even if you wanted to go down there, they wouldn't let you in . . ."

"Where's that?" says the mother.

"At the medical examiner's," says McAllister slowly. "But you don't need to worry about that. All you have to do is contact the funeral home of your choice and tell them that the body is at the medical examiner's office at Penn and Lombard streets. They'll know exactly what to do. Okay?"

The mother nods.

"Now, we're going to try to find out who did this, but we're going to need the family's help . . . That's what we've come here to ask for . . ."

The sales pitch. McAllister gives it his best shot, his you-can't-bring-him-back-but-you-can-avenge-him soliloquy that leaves the mother nodding in agreement. Garvey looks around the room for some sign from the multitude, some small discomfort exhibited by a family member carrying a little bit of knowledge. The younger men and women seem distant, detached, but a few take the business cards, assuring the detectives that they know nothing but will call if there is so much as a rumor in the neighborhood.

"Again," says McAllister at the door, "let us express our condolences for your loss . . ."

Garvey looks at a room full of blank faces. Mother, brothers, sisters, cousins, friends—all of them seem to be ignorant of any reason for the murder. The phone in the homicide office won't exactly be lighting up on this one, he concedes.

"Again, don't hesitate to call us if you have any questions or any information at all," says McAllister, winding up.

Garvey moves toward the front door, leading the way out of the rowhouse. As the two detectives step outside, Garvey turns to his partner and prepares to explain why McAllister ought to become the primary investigator in this lost campaign. But he says nothing; instead, he looks over Mac's shoulder at a young man, a cousin of the victim, who has furtively pursued them out the door.

"Excuse me, officer . . ."

McAllister turns as well, increasing the cousin's apparent discomfort. The young man has something to say and he will not be denied.

"Excuse me," he says, his voice a whisper.

"Yes?" says Garvey.

"Can I . . . um . . ."

Here it comes, thinks Garvey. Here comes the moment when a grieving relative steps away from the rest of the family and bravely imparts a little truth. The cousin extends his hand and McAllister takes it first. Garvey follows suit, warming to the knowledge that he is truly golden, that he has somehow transcended reality and become the Midas of ghetto homicides.

"Can I . . ."

Yes, thinks Garvey, you can. You most certainly can tell us everything, every last little thing you know about your cousin Anthony. Tell us about the drugs he was firing, or the drugs he was dealing, or the beef he had with a customer last night. Tell us about some money problem that left a supplier handing out wolf tickets, swearing to get even. Tell us about the girls he was fooling with or the other boyfriends who threatened to light him up. Tell us what you heard on the street after the murder, or maybe even the name of the guy you heard bragging about the murder in some bar. You can tell us everything.

"Can I . . . um . . . ask a question?"

A question? Of course you can. I'll bet you want to remain anonymous. Hell, unless you're an eyewitness or something, you can even stay monogamous if you really want. We're your friends. We like you. We'll take you downtown for free coffee and doughnuts. We're cops. Trust us. Tell us everything.

"What is it?" asks McAllister.

"Is what you tryin' to tell me . . ."

"Yes?"

"Is what you tryin' to tell me that my cousin Anthony is dead?"

Garvey looks at McAllister, and McAllister looks at his shoes to keep from laughing aloud.

"Um, yes," says McAllister. "I'm afraid he's been fatally wounded. That's what we were talking about inside . . ."

"Damn," says the cousin, truly amazed.

"Anything else you wanted to tell us?"

"No," says the cousin. "Not really."

"Well, sorry again."

"Okay."

"We'll be in touch."

"Okay."

It's over. It's history. It was a helluva run—ten cases in a row beginning with Lena Lucas and old man Booker back in February. But now, with every fiber of his being, Garvey understands that the rocket scientist on the porch is nothing if not a messenger—a walking, talking presignification of all that is true to a murder police.

The words from the wayward cousin's mouth were all thickness and incoherence, but to Garvey they confirm every rule in the book. He didn't have a suspect, so of course his victim didn't survive. And with no suspect, there isn't likely to be any lab evidence or any chance of the victim surviving his wounds. And if Garvey ever does locate a witness to this crime, the witness will lie because everyone lies. And if he ever does get his hands on a suspect, that man will undoubtedly sleep in the interrogation room. And if this weak case ever manages to get within arm's length of a jury panel, every doubt will seem reasonable. And most especially: It's good to be good, but it's better to be lucky.

The brain-dead on the porch is an unmistakable divination, a reminder that the rules still apply—even for the likes of Rich Garvey. Never mind that ten days from now he'll be working a fresh drug murder on the east side, charging through a rowhouse door to grab the shooter beneath the colored lights of a decorated Christmas tree. Never mind that next year will be a crusade as successful as any other. Now, at this moment, Garvey can watch Anthony Morris's cousin slip back indoors and know, with the faith and certainty of a religion, that there is nothing coming back on this one—no telephone calls to the homicide office, no snitching from the city jail, no talk on the streets of the Western. The case will never go black; it will be open long after Garvey is soaking in his pension.

"Mac, did I imagine that conversation?" he asks, laughing, on the return trip to the office. "Or did it really happen?"

"No, no," says McAllister. "You must've imagined it. Put it out of your mind."

"Dee-tective," says Garvey, in bad imitation. "Is what you tryin' to say is that my cousin is dead?"

McAllister laughs.

"Next case," says Garvey.

In any man's work, perfection is an elusive, ethereal goal, an idea that does constant battle with the daily grind. But to a homicide detective, perfection is not even a possibility. On the streets of a city, the Perfect Year is a mere wisp of a thing, a dying fragment of hope, pale and starved and weak.

The Perfect Murder will kick its ass every time.

SUNDAY, DECEMBER 11

"Look," says Terry McLarney, watching the Bloom Street corners with mock innocence. "There's a criminal."

Half a block ahead of them, the kid on the corner seems to hear him say it. He turns abruptly from the Cavalier's headlights, moving down the street, one hand reaching back to pull a rolled newspaper from his pants pocket. McLarney and Dave Brown can both see the newspaper fall softly into the gutter.

"Patrol was so easy," says McLarney wistfully. "You know?"

Dave Brown knows. If the unmarked Chevy were a radio car, if they were wearing uniforms, if Bloom and Division was in their sector, they'd have a lockup just that easy. Throw the weasel against a wall, cuff him up good, then walk his ass back to that little stick of newsprint, that homemade sheath wrapped around a knife or a syringe or both.

"There used to be these two guys in my squad when I was in the Western," says McLarney, nostalgic. "They had this running bet over who could go out and get a lockup in the shortest time possible."

"In the Western," says Brown, "five minutes."

"Less," says McLarney. "After a while, I told them that they ought to make it more challenging. You know, something better than a Part Two arrest. But they didn't like that . . . too much work."

Brown turns onto Bloom and then turns again at Etting. They watch more corner boys drop glassine packets or run into rowhouses.

"See that house there," says McLarney, pointing to a two-story pile of painted brick. "I got thumped in there. Right in the hallway . . . Did I ever tell you that story?"

"I don't think so," says Brown, polite.

"It was a call for a man with a knife, and when I pulled up this guy just takes one look at me and runs into the house . . ."

"PC in my book," says Brown, turning right and cruising back toward Pennsylvania Avenue.

"So I run in after him and there's this convention of healthy black males in the living room. It was bizarre; we all just kinda looked at each other for a second."

Dave Brown laughs.

"So then I grab hold of my guy and they're all over me. Like five or six of 'em."

"What'd you do?"

"I got hit," says McLarney, laughing. "But I didn't let go of my guy either. By the time my bunkies answered the thirteen, everyone had run out the back except for my guy, who ended up getting beat for all his missing friends. I kinda felt sorry for him."

"What about you?" asks Brown.

"Stitches in my head."

"Was this before or after you got shot?"

"Before," says McLarney. "This was when I was in the Central."

One story after another spills from Terry McLarney's brain, his mood lightened by a night on the West Baltimore streets. A car ride through the west side never fails to have that effect on McLarney, who can roll through the ghetto remembering a strange thing that happened on this corner, a funny comment overheard down that street. On the surface, it all resembles a nightmare, but dig a little deeper and McLarney can show you the perverse eloquence of the thing, the unending inner-city comedy of crime and punishment.

That corner there, for instance, the one where Snot Boogie got shot.

"Snot Boogie?" asks Brown, disbelieving.

"Yeah," says McLarney. "And that's what his friends called him."

"Nice."

McLarney laughs, then leaps into the parable of Snot Boogie, who joined the neighborhood crap game, waited for the pot to thicken, then grabbed the cash and bolted down the street only to be shot dead by one of the irate players.

"So we're interviewing the witnesses down at the office and they're saying how Snot Boogie would always join the crap game, then run away with the pot, and that they'd finally gotten sick of it . . ."

Dave Brown drives in silence, barely tracking this historical digression.

"And I asked one of them, you know, I asked him why they even let Snot Boogie into the game if he always tried to run away with the money."

McLarney pauses for effect.

"And?" asks Brown.

"He just looked at me real bizarre," says McLarney. "And then he says, 'You gotta let him play . . . This is America.' "

Brown laughs loudly.

"I love that," says McLarney.

"Great story. Did it really happen?"

"Fuck yes."

Brown laughs again. McLarney's mood is contagious, even if the reason for tonight's jaunt was wearing thin.

"I don't think she's out tonight," says Brown, coasting up Pennsylvania Avenue for the fifth or sixth time.

"She's never out," says McLarney.

"Fuck this cocksucking bitch," says Brown, slamming a hand on the steering wheel. "I'm tired of this fucking shit."

McLarney looks at his detective with newfound delight, as if to encourage this sudden rant.

"I mean, we're the homicide unit, the murder police, the highly trained investigative elite who always get their man . . ."

"Careful," says McLarney. "You're giving me an erection."

"And who the fuck is she? She's a disease-ridden twenty-dollar-a-fuck junkie from Pennsylvania Avenue who's managed to elude us for three goddamn months. It's fucking embarrassing is what it is . . ."

Lenore, the Mystery Whore. The lone witness to Worden's September stabbing on Pennsylvania Avenue; the woman who can close the file by declaring that her now-dead boyfriend killed her then-dead boyfriend in a dispute over her affections. To Brown and Worden and everyone else in the squad, it is getting a bit embarrassing, this charging up and down the Avenue every other night, jacking up whores and addicts and coming nowhere near the elusive Miss Nore, who is always just beyond a detective's reach. By now, they've heard every line:

"She was out walking last night . . ."

"Nore? She down on Division Street not a while ago . . ."

"She came out the carryout and went that way . . ."

Christ, thinks Brown. It isn't bad enough that this junkie bitch doesn't have a permanent address. No, she's gotta move like the fucking wind. How in the hell do her customers find her?

"Maybe she's not real," says McLarney. "Maybe it's a hoax and all the derelicts out here made her up. It's a test to see how long we'll ride around looking."

McLarney smiles, warm with the thought of a $20 cockhound defying every law of metaphysics. A translucent wraith, she walks the streets of West Baltimore immune to the forces of authority. Some paid their $20 and swear her to be real, but to generations of homicide detectives, she is but the stuff of dreams, destined to be Baltimore's contribution to the treasure chest of American folklore: Paul Bunyan, the Headless Horseman of Tarrytown, the ghost ship *Mary Celeste*; Lenore, the Mystery Whore.

"So why does James have her sheet in the file?" counters Brown. "And why do I have her B of I photo in my pocket?"

"Whoa," says McLarney. "A clever hoax at that."

"Fuck this bitch," says Brown, still irritated. "She's not out here."

"What the hell," says McLarney. "Let's go 'round once more and then call it a night."

They don't have a prayer of finding her, of course. But McLarney loves being out on the street, out in the Western working a case that doesn't matter to anyone. Not to Worden or James or Brown. Not to the dead man and, in this case, not to the killer either. Not even to McLarney. Tonight is police work with neither pain nor pressure, conducted at no emotional cost by men who have no real stake in the outcome.

For McLarney especially, the hunt for Lenore is a pleasing distraction, just as the murder he worked last month with Waltemeyer was pleasing. What could matter less than a drug robbery in a Pimlico alley, with the victim a doper and the witness talking bullshit? And then a young suspect, Fat Danny by name, claiming total innocence, crying for justice in his grandparents' living room as detectives stalked through the house in search of the murder weapon?

"C'mon, stop crying," McLarney told the suspect, a bruiser of a kid with at least six inches on him. "Calm down—"

"I DIDN'T KILL NO ONE!" screams Fat Danny, sliding away until McLarney backs him against the kitchen sink, one hand wrapped around the kid's throat.

"C'mon, already," McLarney said. "You're gonna make it so we have to hurt you."

"I DIDN'T—"

"Look at me," said McLarney, glaring. "You're under arrest. Do you want us to hurt you?"

And then a Northwestern DEU officer, one of the raiders, silenced the frantic, struggling suspect with an offhand remark: "For Chrissakes, kid, you did a man's crime. Now act like a man."

Later that night, after McLarney brought a Coke and candy bar into the interrogation room and made friends with the fat kid, he sat at his desk and thought about how simple and strangely enjoyable it all was. When nothing mattered, McLarney told himself, he could actually love this job.

Same thing tonight, he muses. If we never find Lenore, if she stays a mystery, then we live forever, rolling across West Baltimore in a four-cylinder go-cart, telling stories and cracking jokes and watching brain-dead homeboys drop their dope. But if we somehow find her, we gotta go back. We gotta go back and pick up the phone on something else, something that might just be real: a woman raped and carved up, an infant beaten, a cop you worked with and called a friend shot twice in the head.

That one was anything but pleasing. That one was real and brutal and unforgiving. The Cassidy shooting had stayed with McLarney as no other case could, bleeding him a little more every time he thought about it. All of his effort had been repaid with the proper result; Butchie Frazier at a sentencing hearing in Judge Bothe's courtroom a couple of months ago, cuffed and sneering for the last time at life plus twenty, parole in no less than twenty-five. The verdict and sentence counted for something in McLarney's mind; God knows where he would be now if the outcome had been different. But life and twenty was a courtroom victory, one that seemed sufficient for only as long as Gene Cassidy was in the courtroom.

No, in the end it was simply not enough—not for McLarney, certainly not for Gene. After learning to handle his guide dog at a school in New Jersey, Cassidy had returned to his alma mater, enrolling at York College in a graduate teaching program. These were the first sure steps on a long road back, and yet the recovery had been repeatedly, almost routinely, hampered by a city that somehow found it possible to treat a blind police officer as if he were just one among hundreds. Bills for specialists and physical therapy went unpaid for months at a time, with doctors complaining to Cassidy and Cassidy unable to do anything more than refer them to the city. Requests for special equipment—such as a sight-reading computer to aid with Cassidy's studies—moved through the bureaucracy at an arthritic crawl. At one point, a friend of Patti Cassidy's actually called a radio talk show to confront the visiting mayor, asking whether or not the computer was going to be purchased before the next semester of classes.

It took more than a year, in fact, before there was an award ceremony for Cassidy, something that McLarney thought should have happened within weeks of his return from the hospital. A dead cop would have received the splendor of full honors at the funeral—the color guard, the twenty-one-gun salute, the folded flag offered to the widow by the commissioner of police. But a wounded cop seemed to paralyze the department; the brass had a hard time deciding what to say, much less cutting through its own red tape.

To McLarney, the departmental response to Cassidy's ordeal was a little bit obscene, and in the months that followed the shooting, he made himself a promise. If I ever get killed line-of-duty, McLarney told several other detectives, there shouldn't be anyone above the rank of sergeant at the funeral—except maybe D'Addario, who was a friend. Yeah, Dee could be there. But no color guard, no bagpipes, no command staff, no delegations from a dozen other departments. Just Jay Landsman calling the men to attention by shouting "Present arms," after which a hundred Baltimore cops would produce cold cans of Miller Lite and simultaneously pull the poptops.

Gene Cassidy's ceremony, when it finally occurs, is only a bit more formal. On the night after the latest search for the missing Lenore, McLarney once again finds himself back in the Western District, this time in the roll call room at the Riggs Avenue station house, watching from the edge of the room as the four-to-twelve shift collects in front of two dozen evenly spaced chairs. Gene himself asked that the ceremony be held here at the district, just as his old shift prepared to go out on the street. McLarney scans the uniforms and realizes that most of the men Cassidy worked with are now gone—some to other shifts and other districts, others to better-paying police departments in the surrounding counties. Still, there is some power to the moment when the shift lieutenant barks attention and the entire shift snaps rigid; Cassidy, sitting in a front-row seat with Patti beside him, rises too.

McLarney watches the brass and the television reporters crowd around the edge of the room as the police commissioner says some words and steps from the podium to give Cassidy the Medal of Valor and the Medal of Honor, the department's highest honors.

Then the majors and colonels drift away until Gene is alone in the recreation room with his family and his friends from the Western. McLarney, Belt, Biemiller, Tuggle, Wilhelm, Bowen, Lieutenant Bennett, maybe a dozen others hovering around two trays of cold cuts, listening to old rock 'n' roll on a tape player. Jokes are told and stories exchanged and soon Cassidy and his dog are wandering from the party, leading a young niece on an impromptu tour of the station house that ends, strangely enough, in the holding cells.

"Hey, Gene," says the turnkey, opening the front cage, "how you doing?"

"I'm all right. You busy tonight?"

"Not really."

Cassidy stands with his dog just inside the lockup while the turnkey fingerprints his niece and shows her an empty cell. The demonstration is interrupted by a rattle from the last row of cages.

"Yo, somebody take mah handcuffs off!"

"Who's that?" yells Cassidy, turning his head toward the sound.

"Why the fuck I need to be cuffed if I'm in the fuckin' cell?"

"Who's talking?"

"I'm talking, yo."

"Who are you?"

"I'm a fucking prisoner."

"What'd you do?" asks Cassidy, amused.

"I ain't done shit. Who are you?"

"I'm Gene Cassidy. I used to work here."

"Fuck you then."

And Gene Cassidy laughs loudly. For one last moment, he is home.

Thursday, December 15

They ring the tiled room in crisp blue uniforms, their faces still smooth and unmarked. They are nineteen, twenty, maybe twenty-two years old at the outside. Their devotion is complete, their virginity, uncompromised. Protect and Serve still rattles around in the uncluttered expanse of their minds. They are cadets, a class from nearby Anne Arundel County. Twenty-five police-to-bes, primed and polished for this morning's field trip from an academy classroom to hell's innermost circle.

"You all like what you see?" says Rick James, acknowledging the gallery. The cadets laugh nervously from the edges of the autopsy room—some watching, others trying not to watch, a few watching but not believing.

"You a detective?" asks a kid in the front row.

James nods.

"Homicide?"

"Yep. Baltimore city."

"Do you have a case down here?"

No, thinks James, I spend every morning in the autopsy room. The sights, the sounds, the ambiance—I love it all. James is tempted to have some fun with the class, but lets it drop.

"Yep," he says. "One of 'em's mine."

"Which one?" asks the kid.

"He's out in the hall."

An attendant, finishing with one cadaver, looks up. "Who you here for, Rick?"

"The little one."

The attendant looks out into the corridor, then turns his attention back to the work at hand. "We get to him next. Okay?"

"Hey, no problem."

James walks between two open bodies to say hello to Ann Dixon, the deputy ME and a hero to working detectives everywhere. Dixie comes complete with a clipped British accent and an American detective's view of the world. Not only that, she can hold her own at Cher's or Kavanaugh's. You got a body that needs cutting in the state of Maryland, you can't do any better than Dixie.

"Dr. Dixon, how are you this fine morning?"

"Fine, thank you," she says from the vivisection table.

"What's up with you?"

Dixie turns around holding a long-blade knife in one hand and a metal sharpening roll in the other. "You know me," she says, scraping one against the other. "I'm just looking for Mr. Right."

James smiles and wanders back to a rear office for coffee. He returns to find his victim's gurney in the center of the autopsy room, the body naked and stiff on the center tray.

"I'll tell you one thing," says the attendant, putting scalpel to skin. "I'd like to take a knife to the motherfucker that did this."

James looks over at the cadet class to see two dozen stunned, silent faces. After a half-hour or so in the autopsy room, they probably thought that they were ready, that they were slowly acclimating to the sights and sounds and smells of Penn Street. Then the cutters wheel this one out of the freezer, and they realize they aren't even close. From the center of the room, James can see some of the kids trying hard not to look, others trying to watch and then failing to contain their horror. In the corner of the room, a female cadet hides her face in the back of a taller companion, unwilling to look out for even a moment.

And no wonder. The body is little more than a small, brown island floating on a sea of stainless steel, a child's form with tiny hands reaching up, fingers curled. A two-year-old, beaten to death by a mother's boyfriend, who found it in himself to dress the swollen, lifeless body and then carry it to the ER at Bon Secours.

"What happened?" the hospital doctors asked the boyfriend.

"He was playing in the bathtub and fell."

He said it with a calm that bordered on bravado, and he kept on saying it when James and Eddie Brown arrived at the hospital. All that night, he repeated it like a mantra in the interrogation room. Michael was in the tub. Michael fell.

"Why did you dress him? Why didn't you rush him to the hospital?"

I didn't want him to be cold.

"If he was taking a bath, how come there was no water in the tub?"

I let it out.

"You let it out? The baby is unconscious, but you stop to let the water out of the tub?"

Yes.

"You beat him to death."

No. Michael fell.

But the doctors at Bon Secours weren't fooled; Michael Shaw's tiny body was more black and blue than brown, his injuries equivalent to those that a child might sustain if struck by an automobile traveling at thirty miles per hour. Nor do the examiners on Penn Street have any doubt: death by repeated blunt force trauma. The child literally had the life punched out of him.

Yet only when the pathologists begin their external examination of the child is Rick James completely revulsed.

"Did you see this?" asks the doctor, lifting the tiny legs. "He's split wide."

A true horror. The two-year-old boy had bled internally, his anus ripped apart by his twenty-year-old babysitter, his mother's lover.

Mouths open, eyes glazed, the Anne Arundel cadets are trapped, forced to watch the child disassembled from the corner of the autopsy room. A day's lesson.

On the ride back to headquarters, James says nothing; what in God's name is there to say? It ain't my kid, he tries to tell himself. It ain't where I live. It ain't nothing to me.

The standard defense, a homicide detective's established refuge. Only this time it isn't quite enough. This time, there is no dark hole in which to bury the anger.

Returning to the homicide office, James walks down the long blue hall away from the elevators, then peers through the wire mesh window in the door of the large interrogation room. The boyfriend is alone in there, leaning back in the middle chair, his sneakers up against the edge of the table.

"Look at him," James says to a nearby uniform, called downtown for prisoner transport. "Just look at him."

The boyfriend is whistling softly, replacing one tennis shoe after the other with elaborate precision, his reach limited by silver bracelets. He works with new laces—yellow and green—two for each high-top, inner-city style. Two hours from now, the turnkey at the Southwest lockup will pull out the same laces as a suicide precaution, but at the moment they are the sole focus of the boyfriend's shrinking universe.

"Look at him," says James. "Don't it just make you want to kick his ass?"

"Hey," says the uniform. "I'm with you."

James looks at the patrolman, then peers back into the interrogation room. The boyfriend notices the shadow on the one-way glass and turns in the chair.

"Eh mon," he says in a West Indian lilt. "I need gon to d'bathroom, yah know."

"Look at him," says James again.

He could beat him. He could beat this piece of shit until he was raw and bloody and no one in the office would say a damn thing. The uniforms would stay with their paperwork, the other detectives would block the hallway or maybe take a few shots themselves. And if the colonel came down the corridor to check on the commotion, he would only need to be told about little Michael Shaw, alone and silent on that long expanse of steel.

And could anyone really call it wrong? Could anyone believe that retribution so simple and swift could be less than just? Honor to a cop means that you don't hit a man who's wearing cuffs or is unable to fight back, you don't hit a man to obtain a statement, and you don't hit a man who doesn't deserve it. Police brutality? To hell with that. Police work has always been brutal; good police work, discreetly so.

A year ago in this same interrogation room, Jay Landsman was the supervisor working an assault-on-police case from Fells Point, a drunken brawl in which several suspects had used a length of lead pipe to bludgeon an intervening Southeast patrolman to within an inch of his life.

"Now," said Landsman, leading the main assailant into the box, "while you're in here I'm going to take your handcuffs off because, you know, I'm not a tough guy or anything, but I know you're a chickenshit asshole so it's not going to be a problem, right?"

Landsman unlocked the cuffs and the suspect rubbed his wrists.

"See, I knew you were chickenshit—"

The guy came up out of the chair with a wild roundhouse that clipped the side of the sergeant's head, after which Landsman stomped him so thoroughly that he would later keep a Polaroid of the bloodied suspect in his top desk drawer as a keepsake. Landsman walked out of the interrogation room just as the duty officer came down the hall.

"What the hell is going on?"

"Hey," Landsman told the captain, shrugging, "the motherfucker swung on me."

James could say the same thing now: This bastard sodomized and murdered a two-year-old child, then he swung on me and I fucked him up good. End of report.

"Go ahead," says the uniform, thinking the same thought. "I'll cover your back, man. I'd fucking love to see it."

James turns, looks at the uniform strangely, then lets go with an awkward, embarrassed smile. It would feel good to take the cuffs off this kid and make him feel some pain. Hell, with the cuffs off the guy would have a better opportunity than he gave that child. Simple justice would argue for something more than the life sentence awaiting Alvin Clement Richardson; simple justice argued for the bastard to be helpless, immobile, unable to ward off the blows.

And then what? After one sadist had been reduced to a bloody pulp in one interrogation room, where would that leave Rick James? The kid was dead. Nothing was going to bring him back. The mother? Judging from her behavior in the early morning interviews, she could've cared less. It was a murder, they told her. He beat your baby so bad the doctors are saying he could've been hit by a car. He killed your child.

"I don't think he'd do that," she replied. "He loves Michael."

James could beat him, but what the hell for? For peace of mind? For satisfaction? Alvin Richardson is just one sadistic bastard in a city full of sadistic bastards, and his crime is similarly common. Keller and Crutchfield had worked the suffocation of a two-year-old girl back in August; that same month, Shea and Hagin caught a one-year-old scalded to death by a babysitter. In September, Hollingsworth had a nine-month-old infant, strangled by her mother.

No, thinks James. I could beat this prick half to death and then dump him in the city jail infirmary and it wouldn't mean shit. Come Monday, I'll be back at work, looking through the wire mesh window at some other sociopath. James smiles again at the uniform, shakes his head and walks back into the main office.

"Eddie Brown," he says, moving toward the coffee machine, "will you take this guy for a piss? If I do it I'm liable to fuck him up."

Brown nods, walks over to the mailboxes and pulls the interrogation room key off its nail.

Tuesday, December 20

Jay Landsman bounces back and forth across the homicide office, comparing three separate stories from three separate squirrels. He had hoped for a quiet night, maybe even a chance to hit a bar with Pellegrini after the shift change, but now he has a full house: one in the large interrogation box, one in the small box, one on the couch in the fishbowl waiting his turn. To Landsman's eye, each looks more guilt-ridden and culpable than the last.

Donald Kincaid steps out of the largest cubicle with a few pages of interview notes in his hand. He shuts the door before speaking to Landsman.

"He seems like he's being helpful," says Kincaid.

"You think so?"

"Yeah. So far."

"I think he's being too helpful," says Landsman. "I think this motherfucker's pissing all over us and callin' it rain."

Kincaid smiles. Good one, Jay.

"Well, his pal over there on the couch is the one trying to put him in, right?" says Kincaid. "And he's definitely the one that was interested in the girl, you know? I wonder if she just pissed him off."

Landsman nods.

The girl isn't saying. She's all cut up inside a men's room at the Lever Brothers detergent plant over on Broening Highway. Overkill on the wounds, too, which makes the murder look like something personal, like a domestic. But that would be too easy; besides, the victim's husband is soon accounted for—he was waiting down in the parking lot, listening to the car radio, waiting for his wife to come off her shift. The plant guards had to go down there and get him after they found the body.

So, figures Landsman, cross off the husband and go a little lower on the list. Boyfriend? Ex-boyfriend? Wanted-to-be-a-boyfriend? She's young enough and pretty enough, married a year or so, but that doesn't mean much; she could still be getting some on the side down at the plant. Maybe it got out of hand.

"I mean, what the fuck is she doing in the men's room anyway?" says Kincaid. "You know what I'm sayin'?"

"Yeah," says Landsman. "That's what I'm thinking too, Donald."

Landsman looks again into the large interrogation room to see Chris Graul sitting across the table from Squirrel No. 1, taking more notes, running through his weak shit one more time. Graul is new to Landsman's squad from the check and fraud unit, a replacement for Fahlteich, who has been over in the sex offense unit for a few months now. After a couple of years following kited checks around town, Graul wanted to see about homicide work; after six years in Landsman's squad, Dick Fahlteich had seen enough murders for one career. With its nine-to-five, Monday-to-Friday routine, the rape unit was, for Fahlteich, a little like retirement with a paycheck.

Landsman watches through the wire mesh window as his new detective works around the edges of the kid's story. Graul for Fahlteich, Vernon Holley for Fred Ceruti—it had been a year of changes for his squad, but Landsman wasn't complaining. With all that time in robbery to his credit, Holley hit the ground running and was now handling murders on his own. Graul was a good find, too, though Landsman understood that since Graul was tight with Lieutenant Stanton from their time together in narcotics, the new detective would probably jump to the other shift at the first opportunity. Still, if that happened after Graul had proved himself, Landsman would be able to ask Stanton for a good detective in trade.

Suspects, victims, detectives—the players kept changing, yet the machine still managed to sputter and lurch forward. In fact, D'Addario's troops had steadily improved their clearance rate and were now virtually even with the other shift. The unit as a whole was posting a rate of 72 percent, just above the national average for murder clearance. All the complaints about the rate earlier in the year, all that hysteria about the overtime cap and the Northwest murders and the Latonya Wallace case refusing to drop—all of it didn't mean much at year's end. Somehow, the numbers always manage to be there come December.

And Landsman is a big part of the story: His squad's rate is above 75 percent, the highest for D'Addario's shift. Nolan's squad and McLarney's men had both gone through hot streaks earlier in the fall; now Landsman's crew was finishing the year with one closed case after another.

Indeed, for two months they could do no wrong. Dunnigan began it by putting down that drug ambush from Johnston Square, and Pellegrini followed with a manslaughter case from up on the Alameda, an accidental shooting in which some idiot killed a fourteen-year-old while doing tricks with his new semiautomatic. Then Holley, Requer and Dunnigan tag-teamed a pair of domestics and a week later, Requer followed with a hard-fought clearance on a drug murder in the Gold and Etting marketplace. Over the next month, everyone in the squad put down at least one more case, clearing each file within a day or two. With that much luck following the squad around, a little of the stuff even rubbed off on Pellegrini, who picked up the phone one winter evening and was treated to a second consecutive accidental shooting death. Fate itself seemed to feel obliged to offer an apology.

Tonight, if he has time, Landsman can saunter over to his section of the board and stare contentedly at a thick block of black ink. Twelve closed cases in a row, and this one—this bizarre stabbing inside a Broening Highway factory while three hundred employees worked the evening shift—well, he isn't going to allow such a sillyass case to end his streak. A girl gets killed inside a factory during working hours and it comes up a whodunit? No fucking way, thinks Landsman. There's a dunker in here somewhere; all I have to do is find it.

Arriving at the Lever Brothers plant earlier that night, Graul and Kincaid were ushered to the second floor of the main building to find the body of Ernestine Haskins, the thirty-year-old cafeteria manager, lying dead in a nearby men's room. A series of wounds riddled the torso, but the most lethal cut had slashed the jugular. The blouse and brassiere were pulled up, suggesting sex as a motive, just as blood spatter on a bathroom stall partition and defense wounds to the hands suggested a brief struggle. The weapon, probably a long kitchen blade, was missing.

The cafeteria had closed after serving dinner, although the area wasn't locked and it was accessible to anyone in the building. Just before the discovery of the murder, Haskins and two male employees were cleaning up and preparing to leave; for that reason alone the cafeteria employees deserved some special attention. One had discovered the body, the other had been with Haskins in the kitchen only minutes earlier.

Waiting for the factory shift to end, the two detectives processed the scene, walked the length of the cafeteria and checked the rest of the second floor, looking for a blood trail or anything else out of the ordinary. At the shift change shortly before midnight, Kincaid walked down to the plant's outer gate to watch the entire workforce sign out at the security gate and parade past him. He looked every male employee directly in the face, then down at the worker's shoes and pants cuffs, hoping for a few telltale specks of reddish brown.

Meanwhile, Graul acted on a tip provided by one of the cafeteria employees in an initial interview at the scene. Asked if Ernestine Haskins had any boyfriends or suitors at the plant, the employee offered the name of one man who, sure enough, happened to be on shift at that moment. Summoned by security guards, the man appeared in the cafeteria and expressed no immediate surprise at being informed of the murder. That alone didn't mean much: word of the killing had raced through the plant even before the detectives' arrival. More intriguing, however, was his willingness to admit that he had been interested in Ernestine Haskins. He knew she was married; still, she had seemed a little more than friendly and he thought she might go for something.

Kincaid and Graul gave the man's clothes a close inspection but found no stains or tears. His hands were clean and uncut, his face unscratched. Even so, he would have had time to clean up before the body was found. A radio car was called; the suitor and both cafeteria employees were sent downtown.

After more than two hours at the crime scene, the two detectives drove back to the office. Landsman had deposited the three arrivals in separate rooms, where in Landsman's considered opinion they had all displayed rodent-like behavior.

Squirrel No. 1, the cafeteria employee who had given Graul the tip about the woman's suitor, remained solicitous of the investigators and continued to suggest all kinds of motives that could have inspired the man to murder. The second cafeteria worker, Squirrel No. 2, seemed to know damn little about the murder of his boss other than that it happened. And Squirrel No. 3, the plant employee who had lusted for Ernestine, was now strangely indifferent to her violent death, as if it were just something else that happened at work that day.

Having spent an hour or so traveling between the offices and interrogation rooms, balancing one story against another, Landsman has already formed some opinions. Squirrel No. 2 in the large interrogation room? Brain-dead, thinks Landsman. Maybe brain-dead and guilty. Squirrel No. 1 in the small interrogation room? Too fucking helpful. Color him helpful and guilty. And Squirrel No. 3, waiting in the fishbowl, is an asshole, probably a guilty asshole at that.

Now, three hours into the investigation, Landsman watches Kincaid return to the room where Graul is still listening patiently to lies. It's into early morning now, and Landsman has so far been the very picture of earnest patience. No shouting. No wild rant. No twisted homicide humor amid the chaos of criminal investigation.

Landsman's restraint comes in small part because this is Graul's second case and Landsman is trying hard not to crowd a new detective, and in larger part because Ernestine Haskins—like Latonya Wallace—appears to be a real victim. And whatever else two decades in the department have done to Landsman, they have at least taught him that difference between a killing and a murder. It's one thing, after all, for a detective to cut up with the uniforms when they're gathered around some dead yo; it's another entirely to behave that way when the case involves a young wife with her blouse pulled up, her throat slit open and her husband waiting in the company lot. Even for Landsman, certain things remain decidedly unfunny. Likewise, despite his reputation, he does understand that there are moments when a rant does more harm than good. For hours, he lets Graul and Kincaid lead the charge, waiting until they've run out of fresh questions before beginning his own pursuit. Only in the earliest hours of the morning, when the cafeteria company officials call the homicide unit to reveal that the day's receipts are missing from the kitchen strongbox—only then does Landsman revert to form.

"What the fuck is this bullshit I've been listening to?" he mutters, storming back down the hall.

Squirrel No. 1 looks up in dismay as Landsman bursts into the small interrogation room.

"Hey, what the hell are you telling us?"

"What?"

"This is a robbery."

"What is?"

"This fucking murder. The cashbox is missing."

The employee shakes his head. Not me, he assures Landsman, though you might want to talk to that other boy who works in the kitchen. He was always talking about stealing that money. He tried to talk me into it.

Landsman takes that in, pivots, then charges past the large interrogation room, where the dead girl's suitor—now suddenly forgotten—is banging on the door, asking to go to the bathroom.

"Hey officer . . ."

"One minute," yells Landsman, turning the corner into the fishbowl, where the second cafeteria employee has been sitting between interviews.

"You," he tells Squirrel No. 2. "Get up."

The man follows Landsman back down the corridor and into the small interrogation room, now vacant because Graul has returned the first employee to the fishbowl through the main office. Musical witnesses.

"What happened to the money?" says Landsman, full of menace.

"What money?"

Wrong question. Landsman jumps in the face of Squirrel No. 2, railing on about how much they know about the robbery, about how serious a crime this is, about how they've already heard about how he wanted to steal that strongbox, about how Ernestine Haskins discovered the theft and confronted the thief in the men's room and was killed for the trouble.

"I didn't take the money."

"That's not what your friend says."

The man looks around the room for comfort. Kincaid and Graul stare back, impassive.

"What are you, stupid?" asks Landsman. "He put you in."

"What?"

"He's telling us you killed her."

"I . . . what?"

What the fuck, thinks Landsman. Do we need some kind of visual aid in here? Slowly, painfully, Squirrel No. 2 catches on.

"He's telling you that?"

"Sure is," says Kincaid.

"He's the one did it," says the man angrily. "He's the one."

Fine, thinks Landsman, storming back down the hall. I can live with this. After all, a stone whodunit has just been reduced to a simple either-or proposition. Now there's nothing better for a detective to do than put Squirrels No. 1 and 2 into the same cage.

But turning the corner into the aquarium, Landsman comes up too quickly on the Number One Squirrel, arriving just as the man is stuffing wad after wad of greenbacks inside the lining of his fellow employee's winter jacket.

"WHAT . . . WHAT THE FUCK ARE YOU DOING?"

The young man freezes, his hand caught very deep inside one very big cookie jar.

"WHAT THE FUCK . . . GIMME THAT!" sputters Landsman, grabbing the guy by the arm and tossing him out into the corridor.

The jacket lining is fat with fives and tens and twenties; the rest of the money is still in the man's own jacket pockets. He looks at Landsman sheepishly as Graul and Kincaid come running, having heard the commotion.

Landsman shakes his head, amazed. "While we're in there talking to one guy, this goofy motherfucker is sitting here on the couch stuffing the money into the other guy's coat. I just walked in, and he's shoving the fucking money into the lining like this . . ."

"Just now?" says Kincaid.

"Yeah, I walk up and he's shoving bills into the lining."

"I'll be damned."

"Yeah," says Landsman, laughing for the first time all night. "Can you believe it?"

Hours later, after the guilty man has confessed to murder in his fashion ("I had the knife to her throat, but I didn't cut her. She must have moved or something"), Landsman sits in the main office and dissects the case as Graul types his warrant.

"All that bullshit he was telling us about this guy and that guy," Landsman tells Kincaid. "I should have jumped on that earlier."

Maybe so, and maybe there's a lesson in that. When you're working murders, preparation and patience and subtlety take you only so far; sometimes anything more than the usual amount of conscientious precision becomes its own crippling burden. Witness Tom Pellegrini, who spends the night of Ernestine Haskins's murder as he has spent so many others in the last two months—searching for a rational approach to that which is unapproachable, for scientific exactitude in places where nothing is ever exact. The method to Landsman's madness is a hard, tight logic formed in a crucible of impulse and sudden anger. Pellegrini's madness, on the other hand, takes the form of an obsessively rational pursuit of the Answer.

In the annex office, Pellegrini's desk is adorned with a dozen or so milestones from this lonely, quixotic campaign. Reading material on new interrogation techniques, résumés of professional interviewers and private companies that specialize in criminal interrogative planning, paperback books on subliminal messages and body language, even a few reports from a meeting with a psychic that Pellegrini arranged in the hope that extrasensory investigative techniques would yield more than the usual strategies—all of that has now joined the paper storm of the Latonya Wallace case file.

In Pellegrini's mind, the other side of the argument holds sway: Instinct is not enough; emotion defies precision. Twice they had the Fish Man closeted in one of these soundproof boxes, twice they chose to rely on their own talents and instincts, twice he went home in a Central District radio car. Yet without a confession, Pellegrini knows, there is nothing left for this murder investigation. The witnesses will never come forward, or they never existed to begin with. The crime scene will never be found. The physical evidence will never be recovered.

For his last chance at the Fish Man, the primary detective in the Latonya Wallace case places all hope in reason and science. Landsman can break twenty more suspects as he broke the killer of Ernestine Haskins and it won't matter to Pellegrini. He has read and he has studied and he has carefully reviewed the previous interrogations of his best suspect. And in his heart of hearts, he believes that there ought to be some certainty to the thing, some method by which the confession of a guilty man can be derived from an algebra that the Baltimore detectives have not yet learned.

And yet, a month ago, back when Pellegrini was chewing on the second of those two accidental shootings, Landsman proved again that cautious rationality was often useless to a detective. On that occasion, too, Landsman had held back for a time, waiting quietly in the wings while his detective listened to three witnesses offer separate explanations for a rowhouse shooting that left a Lumbee Indian teenager dead. They were drinking beer and playing video games in the living room, the witnesses claimed. All of a sudden there was a knock on the apartment door. And then a hand coming through the open door. And then a gun in the hand. And then a single, unexplained gunshot.

Pellegrini had the two teenagers repeat their stories over and over, watching each witness for subliminal indications of deceit, the way the interrogation manuals teach you. He noticed that one guy's eyes broke right when he answered; according to the textbook, he was probably lying. Another guy backed up when Pellegrini got close to him; by the book, an introvert, a witness who can't be pressured too quickly.

With his sergeant in tow, Pellegrini worked through the kids' stories for more than an hour, catching a few contradictions and pursuing them to a few obvious lies. It was patient and it was methodical. It was also getting them nowhere.

Sometime after midnight, Landsman finally decided he'd had enough. He dragged a fat, pimply-faced white kid into his office, slammed the door hard and wheeled around in a rage, knocking his desk lamp to the floor. The fluorescent bulb shattered against the linoleum and the kid covered himself, waiting for a rain of blows that never came.

"I'M DONE FUCKING AROUND WITH YOU!"

The kid looked at the wall, terrified.

"YOU HEAR ME? I'M DONE FUCKING AROUND. WHO SHOT HIM?"

"I don't know. We couldn't see—"

"YOU'RE LYING! DON'T LIE TO ME!"

"No . . ."

"GODDAMN YOU! I'M WARNING YOU!"

"Don't hit me."

In the aquarium, the fat boy's friend and the third witness, a black teenager from the Southeast projects, could hear everything. And when the Landsman blitzkrieg came rolling down the hall, the black kid's worst fear owned him. The detective grabbed the kid, tossed him into the admin lieutenant's office and began spitting out profanity. It was all over in thirty seconds.

Returning to his own office a few minutes later, Landsman confronted the fat kid again. "You're done lying. Your buddy just gave you up."

And the fat kid simply nodded, almost relieved. "I didn't mean to shoot Jimmy. The gun just went off in my hand. I swear, it just went off."

Landsman smiled grimly.

"You broke your lamp," said the fat kid.

"Yeah," said Landsman, leaving the room. "How 'bout that?"

Outside, in the annex office, Pellegrini greeted his sergeant with a smile and a look that suggested regret. "Thanks, Sarge."

Landsman shrugged and smiled.

"You know," said Pellegrini, "I'd still be talking to them if you hadn't done that."

"Fuck it, Tom, you'd have done the same thing eventually," Landsman told him. "You were getting there."

But Pellegrini said nothing, uncertain. Then and now, Landsman teaches a truth that is a contradiction, an unnerving counterweight to Pellegrini's methodical pursuit of empirical answers. Landsman's lesson says that science, deliberation and precision are not enough. Whether he likes it or not, a good detective eventually has to pull the trigger.

THURSDAY, DECEMBER 22

Season's greetings from the Baltimore homicide unit, where a Styrofoam Santa Claus is taped to the annex office door, its visage marred by a deep, bloody, close-range gunshot wound carved into the old saint's forehead. The wound track was created with a penknife, the blood with a red felt-tipped pen, but the message is clear: Yo, Santa. This is Baltimore. Watch your back.

Along the metal bulkhead walls of the main office, Kim and Linda and the other sixth-floor secretaries have applied a few lonely strips of red and gold trim, some cardboard reindeer and a few candy canes. In the northeast corner of the office stands the unit's tree, sparingly decorated this year but otherwise unmarked by the cynical displays of holidays past. A few years back, some of the detectives retrieved a few morgue photos from the files—mostly shots of dead drug dealers and contract killers, a few of whom had beat out murder charges of their own. With some careful cutting, the detectives liberated the bullet-riddled bodies from the photo background and, overcome by the Yule spirit, pasted hand-drawn wings on the shoulders of the dead. In a way it was touching: Hard-core players like Squeaky Jordan and Abraham Partlow looked positively angelic hanging from those polyurethane branches.

Even the decorations that began as sincere gestures seem small and defeated in this place, where phrases such as "peace on earth" and "goodwill toward men" have no apparent connection to the work at hand. On the anniversary of their savior's birth, the men who work homicides are decidedly unsaved, stuck as they are in the usual rotation of shootings and cuttings and overdose cases. Still, the holiday will be acknowledged if not celebrated by the squads working the four-to-twelve and overnight on Christmas Eve. What the hell, this much irony ought to be marked in some meaningful way.

A year ago, there wasn't much Christmas mayhem at all, a shooting or two on the west side. But two years ago, the phone lines were all lit up, and the year before that was also a hellacious piece of work, with two domestic homicides and a serious shooting that kept Nolan's squad running until the light of day. On that Christmas, the early relief arrived to find Nolan's men suffering from a strange holiday fever, acting out a series of holiday homicides in the main office.

"Bitch," yelled Nolan, pointing his finger at Hollingsworth. "You got me the same thing last year . . . BANG!"

"You bastard, I already got a toaster," said Hollingsworth, turning his finger on Requer. "POW!"

"Oh yeah?" says Requer, firing a round in Nolan's direction. "Well, you burned the stuffing again this year."

Their little dramas weren't all that farfetched, either: On a legendary Christmas shift back in the early 1970s, a father killed his son in a dark meat–light meat argument at the family dinner table, plunging the carving knife into the kid's chest to assure himself of the first crack at the serving plate.

True, the captain always remembers to have a respectable deli spread brought up for the night crew. True, also, that the Christmas shift is the one night of the year when a detective can pull a bottle out of his desk without worrying about being caught by a roving duty officer. Even so, the holiday shift in homicide remains the most depressing duty imaginable. And as luck would have it this year, the three-week shift change for D'Addario's men falls on the morning of December 25. Landsman and McLarney will work their squads on the Christmas Eve four-to-twelve shift, followed by Nolan's men on midnight, followed by McLarney's men again for the Christmas dayshift relief.

No one is happy about the schedule, but Dave Brown, for one, has found a way around its rigors. He always makes a point of putting in early for vacation on the holidays, and this year, with a one-year-old daughter and fervent dreams of domestic bliss, he plans to be nowhere near headquarters on Christmas morning. Naturally, this absurd notion of Brown's becomes yet another item on Donald Worden's list of things for which the younger detective requires abuse, to wit:

1. Brown hasn't done shit with the Carol Wright case, which is still nothing more than a questionable death by automobile.

2. He has just finished five weeks of medical for a leg operation at Hopkins, a procedure allegedly made necessary by some sort of mysteri-

ous nerve damage or muscle spasms that any real man would ignore after a second beer.

3. His abilities as a homicide detective have yet to be truly tested.

4. He won't be around to drive to Pikesville for garlic bagels on the Sunday dayshift, since that happens to be Christmas Day.

5. Worse, he now has the nerve to be off on holiday while the rest of his squad has to work both ends of a shift change.

6. He's a piece of shit to begin with.

Worden, with his remarkable memory, has no need to write down this healthy little list. Instead, he keeps it on the tip of his tongue, so as to better reacquaint the younger man with the essential facts of life.

"Brown, you are a piece of shit," Worden declared on the elevator one evening a week ago. "As long as I've been on, do you know how many days I missed on medical?"

"Yes, you miserable bastard, I know," answered Brown, his voice rising. "You've never missed one lousy, stinking day for medical. You only told me about a thousand times, you . . ."

"Not one day," said Worden, smiling.

"Not one day," said Brown in falsetto imitation. "Give me a fuckin' break already, will you?"

"But your leg hurt a little so you—"

"It was a serious medical condition," yelled Brown, losing all patience. "There was an operation—a dangerous, life-threatening operation . . ."

Worden only smiled. He had the poor boy right where he wanted him; in fact, he'd had him there for weeks. Worden had become so utterly insufferable that the day after the encounter on the elevator, the Carol Wright folder suddenly and magically returned from the oblivion of the file cabinets to occupy a more prominent place on David Brown's desk.

"It has nothing to do with Worden," Brown insisted at the time. "This case has bothered the shit out of me for months and I always planned to come back on it as soon as I came off medical."

Probably so. But now, from the other side of the coffee room, Worden watches with a measure of personal satisfaction as the younger detective spends another day reacquainting himself with the dead billy girl on the gravel lot.

Brown picks through the pieces of the file, reacclimating himself to the office reports, scene photos, follow-ups and BPI shots of a dozen suspects who never panned out. Once again he reads the witness statements from Helen's Hollywood Bar, the woozy statements of drunks who wanted to believe that the killer was driving a Lotus custom through the streets of Baltimore. Once again he glances through the reports from all those random car stops of black sports cars and compacts in the southern districts of the city.

There is nothing worse than a billy murder, thinks Brown, contradicting any earlier assessments. I hate billies: They talk when they're not supposed to, they fuck up your investigation, they waste your time by prattling on about everything they know. Fuck this case, he tells himself. Gimme a drug murder in the projects where nobody saw a thing, he muses. Gimme something I can work with.

Brown rereads the various descriptions of the suspect provided by bar patrons, the contradictory statements about hair length and style and eye color and everything else. He lines up the ident photos collected from every old lead and looks for anything that comes close to matching, but without better descriptions it's hopeless. Not only that, but the ident photos all seem disturbingly similar. Every billy boy seems to stare out at the camera with one of those oh-so-this-is-my-mug-shot expressions; every one seems to sport tattoos, bad teeth and a tanktop shirt so dirty it could stand up on its own.

Look at this piece of work, thinks Brown, pulling one photo from the pile—a billy if ever there was one. The kid is an obvious motorhead, his shag of jet black hair parted in the middle and running halfway down to his ass. He's got fucked-up teeth—big surprise there—and weird blond eyebrows. Christ, the kid's got an expression so vacant that it qualifies as probable cause for a drug warrant . . .

Whoa. He's got blond eyebrows. Blond as can be, thinks Brown, stunned.

The detective holds the ident photo close, his eyes bouncing back and forth between the kid's hair and eyebrows. Black, blond. Black, blond. Gimme a fucking break here; they're right there in the photograph, plain as day. How the hell did I miss that the first time? he wonders, searching for the report that was once stapled to the photo.

Sure enough, the kid's name came from a car stop over by Pigtown, a follow-up by a Southern District officer on that lookout they had teletyped to patrol back in August. Brown finds the report and remembers it immediately: The guy was driving a black Mustang with a sunroof. Not exactly a T-top, not exactly a Lotus. But it was in the ballpark. A Mustang could have those low-to-the-ground performance tires, just as the traffic man had described. But the first time Brown read the report he had discounted it. The district officer stated unequivocally that the driver of the car had dark hair, and the one thing every witness agreed on was that Carol Wright's companion was blond. Only a week ago, after reopening the file, did he bother to ask the ident section to send him photos of the long shots like this one. And only now was he noticing the mismatched eyebrows.

"Donald, look at this."

Worden steps over, expecting something lame.

"This photo is from an arrest a couple weeks after my murder. Check out his eyebrows."

The older detective scans the ident photo and raises an eyebrow of his own. Why in hell would a blond billy boy dye his hair black? You might go the other way, but blond to black? How often does a kid do that?

A good catch, Worden admits to himself. A helluva good catch.

Given the four-month delay, there isn't a lot of hope for recovering any physical evidence, and it will be after the holidays before Brown and Worden get back on the street to chase this one. But when they do pluck the kid from his girlfriend's house in Pigtown on a January morning, Jimmy Lee Shrout's hair will be dyed red and he will act as though he's been waiting for them since August. The battered Mustang, found in front of the girlfriend's house that same day, will be towed to the Fallsway garage, where Worden is waiting with a lab tech. With the car up on a jack, the detective and tech begin by pulling greasy debris from the bottom, and for the first ten minutes or so they find dirt and shards of paper and pieces of leaves, until the lab tech is scoffing at the idea that anything will be left on the undercarriage after all this time.

"Well," Worden replies, pulling at the edge of a thin strand, trying to pry it from the front crossbar, "what do we call this, then?"

"I'll be damned."

Worden gently unwraps the strand from the crossbar, traversing the metal three times. Finally, a long, reddish hair slides into his hand.

"What color hair did she have?" the tech asks.

"Red," says Worden. "She had red hair."

Later that day, Jimmy Lee Shrout will wait for the detectives in the large interrogation room, and when the wait gets a little long, he will go to sleep. Later still, he will be shown a picture of Carol Wright and he will tell Brown and Worden that he remembers picking her up as she hitchhiked on Hanover Street. He also remembers that she went to see someone at the

Southern District and afterward he took her to a bar in Fell's Point. Yeah, Helen's—that was the name. They drank a little, she danced. Then he offered to drive her home, but she took him instead to this parking lot in South Baltimore, where she smoked his dope. He wanted to go home and sleep and he told her so. She got mad and left the car, after which he fell asleep behind the wheel. He woke up a short time later and drove away.

"Jimmy, she was run over on that lot."

"I didn't do that."

"Jimmy, you ran her down."

"I'd been drinking. I can't remember."

Later, in a second interview, Jimmy Shrout admits to remembering that he hit a slight bump as he drove off the gravel lot. He tells the detectives that he thought he'd hit a curb or something.

"Jimmy, there's no curb on that lot."

"I don't remember," the kid insists.

Brown is especially curious about one particular detail: "Later on, did you ever find a single sandal anywhere in your car?"

"A sandal?"

"Like a woman's summer thong."

"Yeah, a few weeks later. I came across something like that. I thought it was my girlfried's and I threw it out."

In the end, it will be nothing better than manslaughter by auto, which is nothing better than two or three years of state time, tops. The problem with homicide by auto is the same as homicide by arson: Without witnesses, no jury can be made to believe that someone killed that way isn't the victim of an accident.

Both Worden and Brown understand that, but Sprout's story will make it clear to them what actually happened in that parking lot. It wasn't Shrout who wanted to go home, it was Carol Wright. She wanted to go and Shrout was upset. After all, she'd driven across Baltimore with him, she'd smoked his shit, and now she wasn't going for anything. They argued and she got angry or maybe scared; either way, Brown and Worden cannot imagine that Carol Wright left that car of her own volition and walked across that gravel lot with only one shoe. No question about it: She left that car in a hurry.

All that waits in the future, but today, at the moment that Dave Brown notices the bad dye job in Jimmy Lee Sprout's ident photo, the case is solved, and it's solved as a murder, not an accidental death by auto, not a case pended by the medical examiner. Dave Brown has every reason to be satisfied: Regardless of what any prosecutor or jury wants to say about it later, today the death of Carol Wright is going down as a crime. Black hair, blond eyebrows, case closed.

Another case closes as well. A few hours after Brown shows him the ident photo, telling him to check the hair color, Worden watches Brown pack up his desk and walk to the coffee room coat rack.

"Sergeant," says Brown to McLarney, who sits across the aisle from Worden, "unless you need me for anything, I'm going to start my holiday."

"No, go ahead, Dave," agrees McLarney.

"Donald," says Brown, acknowledging the older detective, "have a good one."

"You too, David," answers Worden. "Merry Christmas to you and yours."

Brown stops in his tracks. David? Not Brown? And merry Christmas? Not "Season's greetings, you piece of shit"? Or even "Happy holidays, you worthless fuck"?

"That's it?" Brown asks, turning back to Worden. " 'Merry Christmas, David'? You're not going to give me shit? Last month I walked out of here and it was 'Happy Thanksgiving, you piece of shit.' "

"Merry Christmas, David," says Worden again.

Brown shakes his head and McLarney begins to laugh.

"You want me to call you a piece of shit," says Worden, "I'll call you a piece of shit."

"No, hey. I'm just confused."

"Oh, you're confused," says Worden, now smiling. "In that case, give me a quarter."

"You're always giving him quarters," says McLarney. "Why is Worden always taking quarters from you?"

Dave Brown shrugs.

"You don't know?" asks Worden.

"I have no fucking idea," says Brown, fishing out a coin and tossing it to the older detective. "He's Donald Worden. If he wants a quarter, I give him a quarter."

Worden smiles strangely at this particular gap in Dave Brown's education.

"Well," asks Brown, looking at Worden, "is there a reason?"

Still smiling, Worden holds Brown's latest contribution between thumb and forefinger, his arm extended upward so that the coin catches a little shine from the fluorescent lights.

"Twenty-five cents," says Worden.

"Yeah. So?"

"How long have I been a poh-leece?" asks Worden, giving it the full Hampden drawl.

And at last Dave Brown understands. Twenty-five cents, twenty-five years. Worden's small, symbolic affirmation.

"Pretty soon," says Worden, smiling, "I'm gonna have to ask for a nickel too."

Brown smiles as the logic settles in his mind. He's learned something he never even wondered about, the answer to a question he never thought to ask. Worden wants a quarter, you give him a quarter. He's the Big Man, for Chrissakes, the last natural police detective in America.

"Here, Brown," offers Worden, tossing the quarter back to the younger detective. "Merry Christmas to you."

Brown stands in the center of the coffee room, holding the quarter in his right hand, his face creased by confusion.

"You need a quarter, Donald, take it," he says, throwing the coin back.

Worden catches it and tosses it back in one fluid motion. "I don't want your money. Not today."

"You can have it."

"David," Worden says, tiring, "keep your fucking quarter. A merry Christmas to you and yours and I'll see you after the holidays."

Brown looks at Worden oddly, as if the entire contents of his mind had suddenly been rearranged like furniture. He hesitates in the doorway, waiting for God knows what.

"What're you hanging around for?" asks Worden.

"Nothing," Brown answers finally. "Merry Christmas, Donald."

He leaves as a free man, debts canceled and dues paid.

FRIDAY, DECEMBER 23

Tom Pellegrini sits like Ahab himself at the corner of the colonel's sixth-floor conference table, staring hard at the white whale of his own making.

Across the table is, in his opinion, Latonya Wallace's murderer, but the Fish Man doesn't look like a child-killer; he never has, really. The aging store owner is an everyman for West Baltimore, his dull, dark jacket, baggy trousers and work boots a statement of quiet surrender understood by any working man. Less typical is the smoking pipe he carries in a jacket pocket, an item that never made much sense to Pellegrini. For a Whitelock Street denizen, it seemed something of an affectation, a small island of rebellion speckling this sea of human conformity. On several occasions over the past year, Pellegrini had been tempted to grab the stinking, smoldering thing and send it soaring.

Today, he has done as much.

Amid so many greater issues to be decided, it is a small point, but to Pellegrini even the small points matter now. The Fish Man likes his pipe, and for that reason alone he cannot have it. During previous interrogations, the store owner had, at critical moments, drawn on his pipe as if it were its own answer, and Pellegrini had come to associate the smell of the Fish Man's weed with the man's unflappable calm and indifference. And so, when the Fish Man reaches for his pouch not five minutes after taking his seat at the table, Pellegrini tells him to put the pipe away.

This time, everything has to be different. This time, the old store owner has to be made to believe that he is truly beaten, that they know his darkest secret even before he reveals it. He has to be made to forget about those other trips downtown; he has to be denied the comfort of that history, and to the extent that the pipe was part of that history, he has to be denied that as well.

And other things, Pellegrini tells himself, will be different. The man sitting on the other side of the table, across from the Fish Man, is proof enough of that.

During the months of preparation for this final confrontation, the idea of interrogation as a clinical science has become a religion for Pellegrini, and the firm of Interrotec Associates Inc., in particular, a priestly class. Pellegrini has digested the firm's written material as well as its history of successful interviews in a variety of military and government security probes as well as criminal investigations. The company was good; the police departments who had worked with its interrogators said as much when he called them for references. The officers of the firm described themselves as "interrogational specialists, consultants and publishers dedicated to the research, development and enhancement of the art of interview." A mouthful, to be sure, but Pellegrini argued that in the Latonya Wallace case, as in no other, the quality and precision of this last interrogation was paramount.

Pellegrini had crafted his memo requesting the interrogator with that argument at its center, and he was careful to dwell on the reputation of the firm rather than the suggestion that the Baltimore unit lacked any necessary expertise. The use of the company's interviewers for one weekend would cost about a thousand dollars, and for a department as impoverished as the Baltimore force—where no real money is budgeted to pay street informants, much less contract out for investigative talent—Pellegrini's request was an extraordinary one.

Landsman backed him, of course. Not out of any great belief in the science of the thing, but simply because Pellegrini was the primary investigator. It was his murder, and this was a suspect he had pursued and developed for ten months. In Landsman's mind, the issue was clear: His detective had a right to see this thing through in whatever way he saw fit.

The captain also gave the proposal support, and as Pellegrini's memo traveled from gold braid to gold braid on the eighth floor, it met with surprisingly little resistance. More than anything else that year, the Latonya Wallace case had been a true crusade for the department as a whole, and in this rare instance, the bosses seemed to feel as their detectives did.

The money was allocated. The Interrotec people were contacted and the date set. A week ago, and then yesterday as well, Pellegrini had visited Whitelock Street and the Fish Man, reminding his suspect that he would probably need to talk with him again on Friday and suggesting that the store owner's cooperation was in every way required.

And now they begin.

"You understand why you're here," says the man on the other side of the table. The words are quiet but hard, and the voice speaking them somehow manages to impart conflicting emotions in every syllable—behind the voice is anger and empathy, unyielding patience and raging impulse.

To Pellegrini's eye, Glenn Foster has a real talent for interrogation, and the detective is satisfied to let the man lead this last charge. As the vice president of Interrotec and an acknowledged expert in the craft of criminal interrogation, Foster was sold to Pellegrini as something of a magic bullet—an interrogator who had been used by police agencies in eighteen criminal investigations and who had emerged with results every time. The Pentagon had used Foster for sensitive security interviews; veteran prosecutors and detectives who had worked with the Interrotec people swore by him.

In addition to his hired gun, Pellegrini can also count on the leverage being different than in the past. This time, he has the tar and burned wood samples—the virtual match between the smudges on the dead girl's pants and the debris from the Fish Man's gutted Whitelock Street store. That is evidence, to be sure, and more of it than they had for the first two interrogations of the store owner.

On the other hand, Pellegrini's attempt to isolate the store as the only logical source of the burned material had proved futile. The computer run he requested two months ago for Reservoir Hill arson and fire calls over the last several years has turned up a hundred or more separate addresses that had been damaged by fire. Now, months after the murder, there was no conceivable way for Pellegrini to eliminate many of those locations from consideration, or for him even to be sure which burned buildings were actually gutted back in February. Some had since been repaired; others had been vacant for years; still others—small structures or parts of structures that burned in small, unreported fires—might not even be on the computer list. No, the chemical analysis was leverage for this interrogation and nothing more. Still, leverage used properly could mean everything.

Granted his request for interrogative expertise, Pellegrini had told himself that if this last confrontation failed, he could close the file knowing that he had done everything conceivable. He told himself that there would be no more recrimination, that he would leave this bastard of a case in a file drawer and go back into the rotation—really go back this time—and work the murders hard. No more Theodore Johnsons. No more Barney Erelys. He told that to himself and to Landsman as well, but Pellegrini was more confident than he let on; in fact, he had a hard time imagining that this final assault on the Fish Man would fail. They had a quality interrogator lined up, a man who had taught criminology at universities and lectured at police academies nationwide. They had the chemical match. And still, after all these months, they had a suspect who knew the victim, who had blown his lie detector, who had no alibi, who matched the FBI's psychological profile of the killer, who had a history of sex offenses, whose willingness to subject himself to harsh, prolonged investigation was proven. This time, Pellegrini believed, they could win. He could win.

From the other side of the conference room table, Pellegrini listens to Foster circling like some calculating predator, probing for every weakness.

"Listen to me," says Foster.

"Hmmm," says the Fish Man, looking up.

"You understand why you're here."

"You brought me here."

"But you know why, don't you?"

The Fish Man says nothing.

"Why are you here?" asks Foster.

"It's about the girl," says the Fish Man, uncomfortable.

"The girl," says Foster.

"Yeah," says the Fish Man after a pause.

"Say her name," says Foster.

The Fish Man looks across the table.

"Say her name."

"Her name?" says the Fish Man, visibly upset.

"You know her name."

"Latonya." The store owner lets go of the name as though it's the very confession itself. With each answer, Pellegrini can feel the Fish Man losing a little bit of control. Foster is good, thinks Pellegrini. Damn good. Making the Fish Man say the little girl's name, for example: What better technique to bring an introvert like the old store owner out of his shell.

Born and bred deep in the Bible Belt, Foster had come to law enforcement after a stint as a Baptist minister, an experience that marked the pattern and delivery of his speech. His voice could be at one moment a blunt instrument, heavy with accusation, and at the next a faint whisper, hinting at broken secrets.

"Let me tell you why I'm here," Foster says to the Fish Man. "I'm here because I've seen your kind before. I know about your kind . . ."

The Fish Man looks up, curious.

"I've seen a thousand like you."

Pellegrini watches his suspect, trying to gauge his body language. The Fish Man's downward gaze at the table or at the floor is a sure sign of deception, according to the Kinesic Interviewing texts, just as the folded arms and backward lean in the chair suggest an introvert unwilling to accept control. To Pellegrini, all of the reading and preparation of the last three months now seems relevant to the moment—all of the science would now be put to the test.

". . . and you've never met anyone like me," Foster tells the Fish Man. "No, you haven't. You may have had people talk to you before, but not the way I'm going to talk to you. I know you, mister . . ."

Pellegrini listens as the lead interrogator begins an unyielding monologue, an endless rant in which Foster transforms himself from a merely mortal form into a towering figure of omnipotent authority. It is the standard prelude to any prolonged interrogation, the beginning of the soliloquy in which a detective establishes his own myth of expertise. For the Baltimore detectives, the speech usually consists of assuring a suspect that he's dealing with the reincarnation of Eliot Ness and that everyone who was ever foolish enough to sit in this box and talk shit to God's own detective is now marking time on Death Row. But to Pellegrini, Foster seems to be giving the standard lecture a little more dramatic intensity.

". . . I know all about you . . ."

Foster is good, all right, but he's only one weapon in the arsenal. Looking around the conference room, Pellegrini can take additional satisfaction, knowing that for this last interrogation, he is firing every gun.

As with the second interrogation of the Fish Man—the February encounter staged in the captain's office—this confrontation has also been choreographed. Once again, photographs of the dead girl have been placed directly in front of the suspect. This time, however, Pellegrini is using everything in the case file—not only the color photographs from the crime scene but also the larger black-and-white shots from the overhead camera at Penn Street. Every last insult to Latonya Wallace—the ligature across the neck; the thin, deep puncture wounds; the long, jagged tear of the final evisceration—is arrayed in front of the man that Pellegrini believes to be the killer. The photographs have been selected for maximum effect, yet Pellegrini knows that such a brutal psychological ploy can itself damage any confession.

It is a risk that every detective runs when he gives up too much of his case in the interrogation room, and in the case at hand, the risk is doubled. Not only could a defense attorney later claim that the Fish Man had confessed only after being shocked and awed by the horror of the photographs, but that same lawyer could argue that the confession itself included no independent corroboration. After all, even those facts that the detectives kept secret back in February—the ligature strangulation, the vaginal tearing—are now tacked to the conference room wall. Even if the Fish Man does break down and recount his murder of the child, no one can prove beyond a reasonable doubt that such a confession is genuine—unless the Fish Man's statement contains some additional details that can be independently corroborated.

Pellegrini knows all that; still, the photographs have been tacked to the bulletin boards, one glossy obscenity after another, each staring back at the store owner, each a terrifying appeal to conscience. There will be no interrogation after this one, the detective reasons, no other opportunity for which the last secrets of the murder need be preserved.

At the center of one bulletin board, Pellegrini has placed his trump cards. First there is the chemical analysis of the burned tar and wood chips from both the little girl's pants and the Fish Man's store. Each sample is represented by a long bar graph and the two graphs are remarkably similar. Prepared by the trace laboratory of the Bureau of Alcohol, Tobacco and Firearms, the analysis of the samples was an exacting piece of work, and the lab added a veteran analyst to its report. If Pellegrini needs some instant expertise, the man is outside the room now, ready and willing. So, too, are Jay Landsman and Tim Doory, the lead prosecutor in the Violent Crimes Unit, who would evaluate the results of the interrogation and make the ultimate decision of whether to charge the murder.

Above the cross-tab charts on the bulletin board, Pellegrini has fixed a blue line zoning map of the Reservoir Hill area, with between eighty and one hundred structures highlighted in yellow—each noting the location of a fire call within the past five years. The Fish Man's store on Whitelock Street, however, is marked in darker orange. The map is in every real sense a lie—a deception that Pellegrini can use without any fear of discovery. In truth, he has been unable to eliminate the vast majority of those yellow marks on the map; any one of them can theoretically have been the site at which the little girl's pants had been smudged. And yet, for the purpose of this interrogation, nothing like that can possibly be true. For this interrogation, Pellegrini will tell the Fish Man that the chemical analysis has left no doubt: The black smudges on the dead girl's pants came from the darker orange square at the elbow of Whitelock Street.

The chemical analysis—the linchpin of this interrogation—gave them real leverage, but it also gave them the Out. Maybe you didn't kill her, Foster can tell him. Maybe you didn't touch her and violate her and then choke the life from her. Maybe you weren't the one who took a kitchen knife to her afterward, emptying her until you were sure she was dead. But, Foster can say, you know who did do it. You know because she was killed on that Tuesday night and then left in your burned-out fish store all day Wednesday. She was left there to wait for the rainy darkness of early Thursday morning. She was in that store and the soot and burned wood on her pants proves it. If you didn't kill her, maybe someone else—someone you know, or someone whose name you don't remember—hid the little girl inside your store.

Beyond the snare of the chemical analysis, Pellegrini has little else: the failed polygraph, the acknowledged prior relationship with the dead girl, the absence of any verifiable alibi. The case is motive, opportunity and apparent deception, coupled with one lonely piece of physical evidence. A final trump card to be played at a key moment lies deep in Pellegrini's jacket pocket, where he carries one last photograph. But that old picture can't be called evidence; it is, the detective knows, no better than a hunch.

Foster meanders through the opening monologue. After spending half an hour establishing his own expertise, the veteran interrogator proceeds to lionize Pellegrini as well. Foster acknowledges that the Fish Man and his principal pursuer have met in the past, but, he explains, Pellegrini did not give up on this case after those earlier confrontations. No, Foster says, he continued to work on you. He continued to gather evidence.

The Fish Man remains impassive.

"What's going to happen here today is different from what happened when you talked to Detective Pellegrini before," says Foster.

The store owner nods slightly. A strange gesture, thinks Pellegrini.

"You've been here before, but you didn't tell the truth," says Foster, turning the corner and launching into the first confrontation. "We know that."

The Fish Man shakes his head.

"I'm telling you we know that."

"I don't know anything."

"Yes," says Foster quietly. "You do."

Very slowly and very deliberately, Foster begins to explain the chemical comparison of the dead girl's pants and the samples from the Whitelock Street store. At the appropriate moment, Pellegrini reaches down and pulls the soiled pants from a brown evidence bag, then lays the garment on the table, pointing to the black smudges near the knees.

The Fish Man doesn't react.

Foster presses on, pointing to a photograph of the dead girl behind Newington Avenue, showing the store owner that the black smudges were there on the pants when they found her.

"Now look at this," he says, pointing to the ATF report. "These lines here show what these stains are made of, and these over here, they show what it is that Detective Pellegrini took from your store."

Nothing. No reaction.

"See this map," says Pellegrini, pointing to the bulletin board. "We checked every building in Reservoir Hill where there has ever been a fire and none of them match these stains."

"None of them except yours," adds Foster.

The Fish Man shakes his head. He is not angry. He is not even defensive. To Pellegrini, his lack of response is unnerving.

"She was in your store and she got that stuff on her pants," says Foster.

"Either just before or just after she was killed, she got that stuff on her pants in your store."

"I don't know nothing about that," says the Fish Man.

"Yes, you do," says Foster.

The Fish Man shakes his head.

"Well, then what is this stuff from your store doing on her pants?"

"It can't be. I don't know how that can be."

Somehow they're not getting through. The interrogators return to their visual aids, covering the same ground a second time. Foster leads the store owner through it slowly enough so that there can be no mistaking the logic.

"Look at these lines here," says Foster, pointing to the ATF report. "It's exactly the same. How do you explain that?"

"I can't . . . I don't know."

"You do know," says Foster. "Don't lie to me."

"I'm not lying."

"Well then how do you explain it?"

The Fish Man shrugs.

"Maybe," suggests Foster, "maybe you didn't kill her. But maybe you know who did. Maybe you let someone else hide her in your store. Is that what you're hiding?"

The Fish Man looks up from the floor.

"Maybe someone else asked to put something in your store and you didn't even know what it was," says Foster, probing. "There's got to be some explanation because Latonya was in your store."

The Fish Man shakes his head, a little at first, then firmly. He backs up in his chair, folding his arms. He isn't buying. "She couldn't be in my store."

"But she was. Did someone else put her there?"

The Fish Man hesitates.

"What's his name?"

"No. No one put her there."

"Well, she was there. This report says that."

"No," says the Fish Man.

A dead end. Instinctively, Foster veers away from the confrontation and the two detectives begin leading their suspect through a complete statement. Pellegrini, in particular, probes for even the faintest suggestion of an alibi and asks all the requisite background questions once again. Slowly, painfully, the same answers—about his relationship with Latonya, his vague alibi, his feeling about women—come back across the table, and for the first time in ten months the Fish Man begins to show some impatience. And his answer to one question changes.

"When did you last see Latonya?" asks Pellegrini for perhaps the tenth time.

"When did I last see her?"

"Before she was killed."

"On Sunday. She came by the store."

"Sunday?" asks Pellegrini, startled.

The Fish Man nods.

"The Sunday before she disappeared?"

The Fish Man nods again.

It is a crack in the wall. In the earlier interrogations, the store owner swore that he hadn't seen the little girl for two weeks before the murder and Pellegrini had found no witness who could refute the claim definitively. Now, on his own, the Fish Man is putting the little girl in his store two days before the murder and only days after the fire that gutted the Whitelock Street shop.

"What did she come to the store about?"

"She came to see if she could help after the fire."

Pellegrini wonders. Is he lying to compensate for the chemical evidence, thinking that an earlier visit to the burned-out store could explain the stains on the pants? Or was he lying in the earlier interviews, when he was trying to distance himself from any contact with the dead girl? Is he telling the truth now with no memory of his earlier answers? Is he confused? Is he remembering this for the first time?

"When we talked to you before, you said you hadn't seen Latonya for two weeks before she disappeared," says Pellegrini. "Now you say you saw her the Sunday before."

"Two weeks?"

"You said you hadn't seen her for two weeks."

The Fish Man shakes his head.

"That's what you told us every other time. We wrote it down."

"I don't remember."

Something is happening here. Slowly, carefully, Foster leads the store owner back to the edge of the cliff, back to the ATF report and the insistent logic of the chemical samples.

"If you didn't have her in the store," asks the interrogator, "then who did?"

The Fish Man shakes his head. Pellegrini looks at his watch and realizes that they've been going at it for five full hours. Time matters here: A confession obtained within six or seven hours is of far greater evidentiary value than one produced in ten or twelve hours of interrogation.

Now or never, thinks Pellegrini as he pulls the last trick from his sleeve. From a jacket pocket comes the photograph of the little girl from Montpelier Street, the look-alike to Latonya who disappeared in the late 1970s. He has saved a copy of the photo he found in the newspaper library months earlier; he has saved it for just this moment.

"Tell me," says Pellegrini, handing the old picture to his suspect, "do you know who this is?"

Already in some distress from Foster's challenges, the Fish Man looks down at the photograph and suddenly seems to crumble. Pellegrini watches him pitch forward; his head drops, his hands grip the edges of the conference table.

"You know this girl?"

"Yes," says the Fish Man quietly, "I know her." He nods, his pain visible. He is falling apart in front of them, this man who had been nothing more than stone in every prior encounter. Now he is at the cliff's edge, looking over, ready to leap.

"How do you know this girl?"

The Fish Man hesitates for a moment, his hands still gripping the edges of the table.

"How do you know her?"

Then, just as suddenly, the moment passes. Whatever shock comes from that old photograph is abruptly gone. The Fish Man sits back in his chair and crosses his arms, and for just a moment he meets Pellegrini's eyes with a look of unmistakable menace. If you want me, the look seems to say, you're going to need more. If you want me, you're going to have to take me all the way.

"I thought," says the Fish Man, "you were showing me a picture of Latonya."

Like hell you did, thinks Pellegrini. Both interrogators share a look and Foster launches into another assault, this one delivered in nothing more than a whisper, his face only inches from the store owner.

"Listen to me. Are you listening to me?" says Foster. "I'm going to tell you the truth now. I'm going to tell you what I know . . ."

The Fish Man stares back intently.

"I've seen your kind before—many, many times before. I know what you're about; we all know what you're about. Tom over here knows you. Every one of us knows you because we've seen your kind before. You like the young girls and they like you, don't they? And that's fine as far as it goes, and as long as they can keep quiet about things, then you don't have any problem . . ."

Pellegrini looks at his suspect, stunned. The Fish Man is slowly nodding his head in seeming agreement.

"But you've got this one rule, don't you? You've got this one rule that you have to follow, this one rule that has to be obeyed, and we both know what that rule is, don't we?"

Again, the Fish Man nods his head.

"If you cry, you die," says Foster. "If you cry, you die."

The Fish Man is silent.

"That's the one rule you have, isn't it? If they cry out, then they've got to die. You like them a lot and you like it when they like you, but if they cry, they die. That's what happened with Latonya, and that's what happened with this girl right here," says Foster, pointing to the old photograph. "She cried and she died."

To Pellegrini, it seems an eternity before the suspect regains his composure, before he manages to stop nodding his head and respond. When at last he does, it is definitive, unshakable.

"No," says the man firmly. "I didn't hurt Latonya."

The steel in the Fish Man's voice forces Pellegrini to make his own confession: It's gone. They've lost him. They had come close; Pellegrini knew that. Foster's methods and talents and secrets were powerful and their plan had been carefully drawn and executed, but in the end, the case file is what it is. There exists, Pellegrini now knows, no magic bullet, no hidden science yet to be learned. Ultimately, the Answer is always evidence, plain and simple.

Before the interrogation began, in fact, Foster had tried to get Tim Doory to charge the murder on the basis of the ATF report alone, arguing that with the charge already on him, the Fish Man would be more inclined to confess. Possibly, but what if he didn't confess? What would they do with the charge then? Dismiss it prior to indictment? Issue a stet? This was a high-profile case, the kind that no prosecutor wants to lose. No, Doory told him, we charge when the evidence is there. Foster accepted the decision, but the question itself had unnerved both Pellegrini and Landsman; it was the first suggestion that their interrogator couldn't walk on water. Now, Doory paces in the hall outside the conference room with Landsman, periodically checking his watch. Six hours and counting.

"Hey, Jay," says the prosecutor. "It's been more than six. I'll hang around for another hour or so, but after that I don't know what we can do with it even if he does break."

Landsman nods, then walks to the conference room to listen for voices. He can tell by the long silences that things are no longer going well.

After seven straight hours of interrogation, Pellegrini and Foster slide out for a cigarette and a twenty-minute break. Doory grabs his overcoat and walks Pellegrini toward the elevator, telling the detective to call him at home if anything develops.

Landsman and the ATF analyst replace the two primary interrogators in the conference room, trying hard to pick up the thread.

"Let me ask you something," says Landsman.

"What's that?"

"Do you believe in God?"

"Do I believe in God?" asks the Fish Man.

"Yeah. I don't mean are you religious. I mean do you believe there's a God?"

"Oh yeah. I believe there's a God."

"Yeah," says Landsman. "Me, too."

The Fish Man nods in agreement.

"What do you think God might do to the person who killed Latonya?"

A shot in the dark from Landsman, but the Fish Man is now a veteran of the interrogation room and the ploy seems thin and transparent.

"I don't know," says the Fish Man.

"Do you think he feels like God will punish him for what he did to that girl?"

"I don't know," says the Fish Man coldly. "You'd have to ask him."

When Pellegrini and Foster return to the conference room, Landsman is still firing random salvos. But whatever tension had been created in the first six hours is now completely dissipated. Pellegrini is chagrined to see that Landsman is dragging on a cigarette; worse, the Fish Man is smoking his pipe.

Still, they give it the rest of the afternoon and early evening—fourteen hours in all—pressing their suspect longer and harder than most judges would permit. They know this, but in frustration, in anger, in certainty that there will be no further chance, they do it nonetheless. When the interrogation finally grinds to a halt, the Fish Man is sent at first to the fishbowl, then to a desk in the homicide office, where he watches the television screen blankly while waiting for a Central District radio car to return him to Whitelock Street.

"Are you watching this?" he asks Howard Corbin, who looks up to see a sitcom.

"No, I'm not," says Corbin.

"Is it all right if I change the channel then?" says the store owner.

"Sure," says Corbin. "Go 'head."

Corbin is comfortable with the man; he always was. Through the long months of working on the Latonya Wallace file, the aging detective never believed that the Fish Man had anything to do with the murder. Neither did Eddie Brown, and even Landsman had for a time shared their doubts. In the end, the Fish Man was Pellegrini's obsession alone.

"Is it all right if I smoke my pipe?" the store owner asks.

"I don't mind," says Corbin, turning to Jack Barrick across the room. "Sergeant, do you mind if he smokes?"

"Naw," says Barrick. "I don't give a damn."

There is no final scene for Tom Pellegrini and the Fish Man, no last words, no parting shots. In victory, a detective can be amusing and gracious, even generous; in defeat, he will try his damnedest to make believe you're no longer there. The long day ends as separate scenes in separate rooms. In one, a man celebrates freedom by changing channels on a television set and stuffing a pipe with cheap tobacco. In another, a detective clears his desk of a bloated, dog-eared file, gathers up his gun, briefcase and overcoat, and steps heavily into a corridor that leads only to an elevator and a dark city street.

SATURDAY, DECEMBER 31

They own you.

From the moment you thought the thought, you were their property. You don't believe it; hell, you didn't even imagine it. You were sure they'd never catch you, sure you could draw heart's blood twice and just walk away. But you should have saved yourself some trouble, called 911 yourself. Right from the start, you were a gift.

But hey, it looked like a good move when you made it, didn't it now? You got Ronnie in the back bedroom, stuck him good in a dozen places with that kitchen blade before he knew what was what. Ronnie did some screaming, but his brother didn't hear a thing with that box beat going so loud in the other bedroom. Yeah, you had Ronnie all to yourself, and when you came down the hallway toward the other bedroom, you figured Ronnie's brother deserved more of the same. The boy was still in bed when you walked in on him, looking up at the blade like he didn't know what it was for.

So you got them both. You got Ronnie and Ronnie's brother and getting them meant getting the package. Yeah, you got that shit the old-fashioned way, yo, you killed for it, and right now you should be out the door and halfway across Pimlico and smoking some of that hard-won product.

But no, you're still right here, staring at your killing hand. You fucked it up, cut the hand bad when Ronnie was oozing life and your knife got wet and slippery. You were sticking it to him when your hand just rode up over the hilt and the blade went deep into your palm. So now, when you should be across town practicing your don't-know-nothin' speech, you're sitting here in a house full of dead men, waiting for your hand to stop bleeding.

You try cleaning up in the bathroom, running cold water in the wound. But that doesn't really help, just makes you bleed a little slower is all. You try wrapping your hand in a bath towel, but the towel becomes a wet crimson mess on the bathroom floor. You walk down to the living room, your hand smearing red on the stairway wall, the banister and the downstairs light switch. Then you wrap your right hand in the sleeve of your sweatshirt, shrug on your winter coat and run.

All the way to your girlfriend's place, the throbbing in your hand tells you that there's no choice, that you're just going to keep bleeding unless you take the risk. You stash the package and even change your clothes, but the blood still keeps coming. When you hit West Belvedere just before daylight, you start running toward the hospital, trying to think your story through.

But it doesn't matter. They own you, bunk.

You don't know it, but you were theirs when they came in early to relieve the Friday overnight shift as daylight broke on the last day of this godforsaken year. They hadn't changed the coffeepot when the phone rang, and it was the older one, the white-haired police, who scrawled out the particulars on a used pawn shop card. A double, the dispatcher told them, so all three decided to ride up to Pimlico to look over your handiwork.

To the pale, dark-haired Italian, the younger one, you're a blessing. He works your crime scene the way he wishes he had worked another: He follows every blood trail and pulls samples from every room; he takes his time with the bodies before having each wrapped in sheets, preserving the trace evidence. He works that scene like it's the last one on earth, like these aren't the Fullard brothers but two victims who matter. He's hungry again, bunk, and he needs a clearance the same way you needed that cocaine.

You're about to become the property of that other one, too, the bear of a police with the white hair and the blue eyes. He hires on as a secondary, helps with the crime scene before wandering off to work the crowd. He's glad to be working murders, content to be back in the Northwest on a case. The Big Man began this year in a hole and then clawed his way out, so it's your bad luck to be on the wrong side of the curve.

And don't forget that sergeant, the joker in the leather jacket, who's been riding a streak since late October. He stalks all over your murder scene, sizing up your deeds and fitting together the first pieces of your sad little puzzle. He takes it personal, declaring that there is no way in hell his squad will end the year with an open double.

Here's the morning line, bunk: The three of them have their hooks into you deep and they haven't even met you yet. By now, they've marked your blood trail out of the bathroom and down the second-floor stairs. They're already on a Northwest patrolman's radio, asking citywide to have area hospital admissions checked for stabbing and cutting victims. They're working back on the Fullard brothers, learning who they hang with and who hangs with them. They got your number good.

If you understood that, if you understood anything about how they work, you might have caught a cab and gone to a hospital out in the county. At the very least, you might have come up with some story a little better than that garbage you gave the admitting nurse. Cut your hand climbing a fence, you told her. One of those chain-link jobs over by the middle school off Park Heights. Yeah, right: You slipped.

But anyone can see that the cut didn't come from no fence. Not when it's that deep and that straight. You think that'll play? You think the police who has just walked up to the nurses station is going to believe such weak shit?

"Landsman, from homicide," the cop tells the charge nurse, looking your way. "Is this the one?"

You're not about to panic or anything. They still don't know shit: You made sure both those bad boys were dead. You ditched the knife. You didn't leave witnesses. You're good to go.

"Lemme see your hand," says the cop in the leather jacket.

"Cut it on a fence."

He checks your palm for a good ten seconds. Then he looks at the blood on your coat sleeve.

"The fuck you did."

"I ain't lyin'."

"You cut it on a fence?"

"Yeah."

"What fence?"

You tell him what fence. Motherfucker, you think, he don't believe I got brains enough to think of a fence.

"Yeah," he says, looking right at you. "I know where that is. Let's go there and see."

See? See what?

"You're bleeding like a stuck pig," he tells you. "There better be some blood around the fence, right?"

Blood around the fence? You didn't think of that and he knows you didn't think of it.

"No," you hear yourself say. "Wait."

Yeah, he's waiting. He's standing there in the Sinai emergency room listening to your little world crumble. Now he's calling you a lying motherfucker, telling you that it won't take but a couple hours before they match the blood stains on that stairwell to the blood staining the new bandage on your hand. You didn't think of that either, did you?

"Okay, I was there," you say. "But I didn't kill them."

"Oh yeah?" says the cop. "Who did?"

"A Jamaican."

"What's his name?"

Think it through, bunk. Think it through. "I don't know his name. But he cut me, too. He said he'd kill me too if I said anything about him."

"He told you that. When did he tell you that?"

"He drove me to the hospital."

"He drove you here?" he asks. "He kills them, but he only cuts you and then gives you a lift to the hospital."

"Yeah. I ran away at first, but . . ."

He looks away, asking the resident if he's ready to discharge you. The cop looks back at you, smiling strangely. If you knew him, if you knew anything, then you'd know that he's already laughing at you. He's made you for a murdering little shitbird, tossing you into this year's pile with about a hundred others. The Fullard brothers, crimson and rigored in the morning light of their bedrooms, are already black names on Jay Landsman's section of the board.

You ride downtown to headquarters in a cage car, clinging to that story of yours, thinking that you can still pull this off. You're thinking—if it can be called thinking—that you can somehow get them to believe in a mystery Jake who cut your hand and drove you to Sinai.

"Tell me about this Jamaican," says the older, white-haired detective after dumping you in one of the lockboxes. "What's his name?"

He sits across the table from you, staring at you with those blue eyes like some kind of walrus.

"I only know his street name."

"So? What is it?"

And you give it up. A real street name for a real Jake, a homeboy in his late twenties who you know lives maybe a block or so from the Fullards. Yeah, you're thinking now, bunk. You're giving them just enough to be real, not enough for them to work with.

"Hey, Tom," says the white-haired detective, talking to the younger cop who came into the box with him. "Let me get with you for a second."

You can see their shadows on the other side of the one-way window in the interrogation room, watch them talking in the corridor outside. The old walrus walks away. The doorknob turns and the younger police, the Italian, comes back with pen and paper.

"I'm going to take your statement," he says. "But first, I need to advise you of these rights . . ."

The cop talks and writes slowly, giving you time to get the story straight. You were over there getting high with Ronnie and his brother, you tell him. Then they invited the Jamaican in, and a little later there was an argument. No one saw the Jake go into the kitchen and come out with a knife. But you saw him use that knife to kill Ronnie, then Ronnie's brother. You tried to grab the knife but got cut and ran away. Later, when you were walking home, the Jamaican drove up and told you to get in his car. He told you his beef was with the other two, that he wouldn't mess with you as long as you kept your mouth shut.

"That's why I lied about the fence at first," you tell him, looking at the floor.

"Hmmm," the young cop says, still writing.

And then the white-haired walrus is back in the room, carrying a black-and-white mug shot—a photograph of the Jamaican kid whose street name you gave up not ten minutes earlier.

"Is this the guy?" he asks you.

Christ. Goddamn. You can't believe it.

"That's him, ain't it?"

"No."

"You're a lying piece of shit," says the walrus. "That's the guy you described and he lives right at the corner house you described. You're pissing up my leg here."

"No, that's not him. It's another guy looks like him . . ."

"You thought we wouldn't even know who you were talking about, didn't you?" he says. "But I used to work that area. I've known the family you're talking about for years."

The man gets a street name and comes back ten minutes later with a fucking photograph. You can't believe it, but you don't know about the walrus, about the memory he carries around like a weapon. You don't know or you wouldn't have said a word.

Months from now, when an assistant state's attorney gets her hands on this case, she'll be told by the head of her trial team that it's a sure loser, that it's a circumstantial prospect. Which might give you a little hope if the names on the prosecution report were anything other than Worden and Landsman and Pellegrini. Because Worden will pull rank to make a direct appeal to the head of the trial division, and Pellegrini will brief the ASA on just how this case can be won. And in the end it will be Landsman on the stand in Bothe's court, sliding everything but the kitchen sink past your public defender, packing every answer with so much background and speculation and hearsay that at one point you'll actually turn and look at your own lawyer in dismay. In the end, it won't matter that the trace lab let every blood sample putrefy before the trial, and it won't matter that the prosecutors argued against taking the case, and it won't matter when you take the stand to tell the jury that horseshit about your murdering Jamaican. It won't matter, because from the very moment you picked up that kitchen knife, they owned you. And if you don't know that now, then you'll know it when your lawyer snaps his briefcase shut and tells you to stand and swallow double-life consecutive from an irritated Elsbeth Bothe.

But now, right now, you're still fighting it; you're working hard to remain the very picture of tormented innocence in that lockbox. You didn't kill them, you plead when the wagon man comes with the cuffs, the Jamaican did it. He killed them both; he cut your hand. On the way to the elevators, you scan the hallway and the office inside, staring at the men who are doing this to you: the white-haired cop; the younger, dark-haired one; the sergeant who leaned on you at the hospital—all three of them now certain and sure. You're still shaking your head, pleading, trying hard to look like a victim. But what could you possibly know about being a victim?

In four months, you'll be a trivia question to these men. In four months, when the carbon-sheet court notices show up in their mailboxes, the men who took your freedom will look down at your name in computer-embossed type and wonder who the hell you are: Wilson, David. Jury trial in part six. Christ, they'll think, which one is Wilson? Oh yeah, the double from Pimlico. Yeah, that brain-dead with the story about the Jake.

In time, your tragedy will be consigned to an admin office file drawer, and later to a strip of microfilm somewhere in the bowels of the headquarters building. In time, you will be nothing more than a 3-by-5 index card in the suspect name file, packed into the T-Z drawer with about ten thousand others. In time, you will mean nothing.

But today, as the wagon man checks your cuffs and checks his paperwork, you are the precious spoils of one day's war, the Holy Grail of one more ghetto crusade. To the detectives watching you leave, you are living, breathing testimony to a devotion that the world never sees. To them, you are validation for honorable lives spent in service of a lost cause. On this fading December afternoon, you are pride itself.

If the shift had been quiet, they might have gone straight home, eaten a little supper and slept until morning. But now it won't be an early night; you've killed two people and lied about it, proving to Donald Worden that he was born into this life to be nothing more or less than a homicide detective. You're the first step in Tom Pellegrini's long road back, the first opportunity for a young detective's redemption. You've become two black names beneath Jay Landsman's nameplate, the last entries of the year for a veteran sergeant who once again has the best rate on his shift.

And now, with the paperwork done, they might just head for Kavanaugh's or the Market Bar or some other hole where a cop can drink a murder down. It's New Year's Eve and they might raise a glass or two and toast themselves, or each other, or whatever remains of the one true brotherhood. But they won't raise a glass for you tonight. You're a murdering piece of shit; why would they want to drink to that? And yet they will think of you. They'll think about how perfectly they read the crime scene, how they had you backing up on your story at the hospital, how they even came up with the photo of the Jake you tried to put it on and how they made you eat that story too. They'll think of you and know, as only a detective can, that police work done well can be a fine and beautiful thing. They'll think of you and drink a little more, maybe laugh a little louder when Landsman tells the stories about his oatmeal box radar gun or Phyllis Pellegrini on Riker's Island.

Hell, they might even close Kavanaugh's and spend the rest of the night out on the parking lot, matching war stories, trying to sober themselves before daybreak and the drive home to a wife already up and putting on her makeup, to the sound of kids already bouncing around the house. Home to the smell of breakfast in the kitchen, to a bedroom with the shades pulled tight and the sheets disturbed by someone else's night. Another morning when the world spins along without them, another day of another year, measured for those who walk in light and deal with the living.

They sleep until dark.

EPILOGUE

The boundaries of this narrative—January 1, 1988, and December 31, 1988—are necessarily arbitrary, an artificial grid of days, weeks and months imposed on the long and true arc of men's lives. The homicide detectives of Gary D'Addario's shift were traveling their collective arc when this account began; they are traveling it still. The names, the faces, the scenes, the case files, the verdicts—these change. Yet the daily violence in any large American city provides a constant background against which a homicide detective seems to labor with timeless defiance. A few men transfer, a few retire, a few latch on to an extended investigation, but the homicide unit remains essentially the same.

The bodies still fall. The phone still bleats. The boys in the back office fill out the daily run sheets and argue about overtime. The admin lieutenant still calculates the clearance rate daily. The board still oozes red and black names. Long after the cases blur or fade entirely from a detective's memory, the job itself somehow retains a special luster.

Every year, the Baltimore homicide unit stages an alumni dinner at the firefighters' union hall in Canton, where a hundred or more current and former homicide detectives eat, drink and carouse with one another in celebration and remembrance of everything seen and done and said by men who spend the best part of their lives working murders. Jimmy Oz, Howard Corbin, Rod Brandner, Jake Coleman—every year the auditorium is filled with men who cling to memories of the hardest job they'll ever have. Not that all of those gathered were great detectives; in fact, some were pretty mediocre in their day. But even the worst of them belongs to a special brotherhood, has a special standing for having lived for a time in the darkest corner of the American experience.

Strangely, they don't talk much about the cases, and when they do, the murders themselves are little more than scenery. Instead, the stories they tell are about each other—about jokes cracked at crime scenes and things seen through the windshields of unmarked cars; about this asinine colonel, or that legendary, never-say-die prosecutor, or some long-legged blonde nursing supervisor at Hopkins, the young one who had this thing for police. What the hell ever happened to her anyway?

At the homicide reunion of 1988, the stories were about Joe Segretti, who at a crime scene in the east side projects of Waddy Court once pulled a bloody rag from a victim's head and, noticing an impression of the dead man's face, declared it the Shroud of Waddy: "A miracle for Baltimore," he assured his partner. "We gotta call the pope."

There were stories about Ed Halligan, once Terry McLarney's partner, who on one occasion got so drunk he dropped a pending case file into a rain-soaked gutter while walking home. When McLarney went to rescue him the following morning, he found the entire file laid out in perfect order on Halligan's living room floor, each page drying slowly. And everybody remembered the legendary Jimmy Ozazewski—"Jimmy Oz"—a true character, who once solved a red-ball case and proceeded to give television interviews from his own den while wearing a smoking jacket and puffing on an imported pipe.

And they remembered, too, the men no longer there, like John Kurinij, the mad Ukrainian who never did learn to curse properly, calling his suspects "sons-of-bitch-bitch" and bemoaning his "fuck-fuck" job. It was Jay Landsman and Gary D'Addario who got the call to go to Kurinij's house in the county, where they found his badge and holster arranged neatly on the table. Kurinij was in the bathroom, kneeling over the tub with the bath mat doubled beneath him, his blood seeping into the drain. A detective's suicide, clean and methodical: Landsman needed only to turn the spigot for the water to wash away the blood, leaving the bullet.

"Fuck him," said D'Addario, when Landsman began to lose control. "He knew when he did it that we'd find him like this."

Tales from the sanctum of the station house, back pages from a Book of Mayhem that has no beginning or end. In 1988, thirty detectives, six sergeants and two lieutenants wrote a few fresh stories of their own—comedy, tragedy, melodrama, satire—stories to be heard at many a reunion to come.

The jump in the clearance rate ended any substantive threat to Gary D'Addario's tenure as a homicide shift lieutenant, but the political intrigue in 1988 still took a toll. To save himself and his men from any real damage, he swallowed just enough to please the bosses. He squeezed out a little overtime, he pressed a few detectives to work more cases, he wrote some memos calling for follow-ups in several files. Most of that could be classified under the heading of necessary and normal evil.

True, D'Addario's relationship with the captain had never been close, but the events of 1988 left both men with few illusions. To D'Addario, it seemed that the captain was looking for unequivocal loyalty in his subordinates while offering little of the same. He hinted at an unwillingness to protect Donald Worden during the Larry Young mess, and he was unwilling to protect D'Addario when every fresh murder was coming in open. In the lieutenant's mind, the pattern had become all too familiar.

D'Addario survived it: Eight years as a homicide commander makes any man a connoisseur of survival. Along the way, he managed to get good and sometimes superb police work from his men. But D'Addario was a proud man, and the cost of remaining in homicide was finally too high. One night in 1989, when D'Addario was called downtown in the early morning hours for a police shooting, he heard about an opening for a lieutenant in vice enforcement, and the longer he thought about the idea, the better he liked it. Vice would give him nine-to-five hours, his own car, his own command. He went to the colonel that same week and the transfer was immediately approved. A month later, the homicide unit had a new shift lieutenant—a decent guy, too, fair and sympathetic to the men. But he had a tough act to follow. As one detective put it succinctly, "He ain't no Dee."

At this writing, D'Addario is the commander of the BPD's vice enforcement section. One of his best detectives there is Fred Ceruti, who still harbors some resentment about the events of 1988, but promises that he will be returning to homicide. "Hey," he says, smiling. "I'm still young."

Technically, Harry Edgerton remains a homicide detective, although the last two years might suggest otherwise.

Ed Burns, the only detective Edgerton was ever willing to call a partner, briefly returned to the homicide unit in early 1989 after completing his two-year FBI probe of the Warren Boardley drug organization in the Lexington Terrace projects. As chief protagonists in a bloody 1986 turf war in the projects, Boardley and his lieutenants were believed responsible for seven unsolved homicides and fourteen shootings. The federal probe eventually sent the key players to prison for terms ranging from double life to eighteen years without the possibility of parole. Edgerton, who had been removed from the probe because of a budget dispute between federal and local agencies, marked the November 1988 arrest of Boardley and his men by joining Burns and other agents in the raiding parties.

Almost immediately after the Boardley case was closed, Burns and Edgerton were both detailed to the Drug Enforcement Administration for a probe of yet another violent narcotics trafficker. Linwood "Rudy" Williams had already beaten two murder charges, a machine-gun possession charge and two drug charges in state courts, when the DEA began its investigation in mid-1989; he was also suspected in four Baltimore-area homicides in 1989 and 1990 alone. In March 1991, Williams and six codefendants were convicted in U.S. District Court as part of a federal drug conspiracy indictment. The primary investigator in the yearlong probe was Ed Burns; Edgerton was one of two chief prosecution witnesses.

The success of the Williams investigation, which involved wiretaps, room mikes, assets probes and the extensive use of a federal grand jury, was such that even Harry Edgerton's critics in the homicide unit had to sit up and take notice. The general opinion was that with Rudy Williams in federal detention, city homicide detectives were being spared three or four case files a year. But within the Baltimore department, a debate over the value of protracted investigation continues; both Edgerton and Burns have been told that after the Williams trial, they are to return to the homicide unit and the regular rotation.

Edgerton did get some satisfaction from the Andrea Perry case. His suspect in the rape-murder, Eugene Dale, became the only one of two hundred homicide defendants in 1988 to be tried under the death penalty statute in Baltimore. (Prosecutors made the decision to pursue capital punishment when the results of DNA testing on Dale's blood confirmed that the semen found inside the twelve-year-old's body was his own.) Although the effort to pursue the death penalty failed, Dale was convicted of first-degree murder and second-degree rape, and he has been sentenced to life without the possibility of parole.

If and when Edgerton does return to the homicide unit, his assignment is uncertain; the squad he left in 1989—Roger Nolan's—no longer exists.

The squad began to dissolve in early 1989, beginning with the loss of Edgerton to the Williams probe. Soon afterward, Donald Kincaid departed in a four-squad trade that brought two of Stanton's men to Nolan's crew. Kincaid then went to work for Jay Landsman, and for a time, at least, he was content—and Landsman was pleased enough to have acquired an experienced detective. But within months Kincaid had a fresh argument going—this time with the new lieutenant, who tried to hold some of the unit's veterans, Kincaid included, to a shorter leash. Kincaid's anger finally won out, and in the summer of 1990 he took his pension and retired after twenty-four years with the department.

His war with Edgerton, and then with the lieutenant, points to one of the real truths about life in any police department. For a detective or street police, the only real satisfaction is the work itself; when a cop spends more and more time getting aggravated with the details, he's finished. The attitude of co-workers, the indifference of superiors, the poor quality of the equipment—all of it pales if you still love the job; all of it matters if you don't.

The murder of Latonya Kim Wallace—the Angel of Reservoir Hill, as she became known in Baltimore—remains unsolved. The case folders have been returned to a file drawer; detectives in Landsman's squad are no longer actively investigating the death, though they continue to pursue any fresh information that comes in.

For Tom Pellegrini, the case left a legacy of frustration and doubt that took another year to overcome. Well into 1989, he continued to work around the edges of the file at the expense of other cases. In the end, he found little solace in the fact that the investigation had been pursued with greater diligence and perseverance than any other in recent memory; the greater the effort, in fact, the greater his frustration.

Months after his last interrogation of the Fish Man, Pellegrini came back to the file once more, scanning the existing evidence, compiling information, then typing an elaborate memorandum to the state's attorney's office. In it he argued that a circumstantial case existed against the old store owner—a case strong enough to put before a grand jury. But it didn't surprise Pellegrini when Tim Doory declined to prosecute the case. The little girl's murder was far too prominent, far too newsworthy, to risk a court trial on a thin web of evidence, or to bluff by charging a suspect in the hope of provoking a confession. And several detectives who had also worked on the case still didn't believe the old man was the killer. If he was truly guilty, they reasoned, three long interrogations would have, at the very least, punched some larger holes in his story.

Pellegrini learned to live with the ambiguity. Two years after walking into that rear yard on Newington Avenue, he could finally say that he had put the worst part of the Latonya Wallace case behind him—and it didn't hurt. He began 1990 with eight straight clearances.

Early this year, he undertook a small but telling task. Slowly, methodically, he began organizing the contents of the Latonya Wallace files, making them more accessible and understandable to any detective who may later have use for them. It was a quiet but necessary acknowledgment that Tom Pellegrini might be years gone before the truth is known, if indeed it is ever known.

Rich Garvey remains Rich Garvey, a detective for whom one year is much the same as the last. His 1989 campaign was as successful as his 1988 effort, and his clearance rate in 1990 was top-of-the-line.

But a look back at the 1988 case files reveals that the Perfect Year was an illusion in more ways than one. For example, the summer murder of the bartender in Fairfield, the robbery case that began when one patron remembered the license tag of the getaway car, ended disastrously. Despite the testimony of two codefendants, who confessed and accepted pleas of twenty and thirty years, the remaining two defendants were acquitted by a jury after two mistrials. The accused shooter, Westley Branch, was acquitted even though his fingerprint had been recovered from a Colt 45 can near the register. Garvey wasn't in the courtroom the day the jury verdict was read, which was just as well: The acquitted defendants marked the occasion with cheers and high-fives.

It was Garvey's first loss to a trial verdict, and other frustrations followed. Another murder case that he had worked with Bob Bowman in December 1988 suddenly collapsed in court when a member of the victim's own family took the stand to exonerate the killer; Garvey later learned that the family had been in contact with the defendant before the trial and some money had changed hands. Likewise, the death of Cornelius Langley, the victim of the daylight drug shooting on Woodland Avenue in August, was also unavenged. That case was dropped after Michael Langley, the state's chief witness and brother of the victim, was himself killed in an unrelated 1989 drug murder.

But there were victories, too. The conviction of Robert Frazier for the murder of Lena Lucas resulted in a life-without-parole sentence; so did the prosecution of Jerry Jackson, the east-sider who murdered Henry Plumer, then left the body in his basement. Perhaps the most gratifying outcome came in the case of Carlton Robinson, the young construction worker gunned down as he left the house to go to work on an icy November morning, killed because his friend and co-worker, Warren Waddell, had been called a dickhead at work the day before. The centerpiece of that prosecution was Robinson's dying words to the first officers at the scene, his final declaration in which he named Waddell as the shooter. And yet it was unclear whether Robinson believed that he was dying or whether the officers or paramedics had told him so—throwing the legal validity of the declaration into doubt.

Garvey had asked for a quality prosecutor in that case and he got one. Bill McCollum, an experienced attorney with the career criminals unit of the state's attorney's office, reinterviewed the paramedics who handled the call and learned that Carlton Robinson, on the way to the hospital, had openly acknowledged that he was dying. Months later, the paramedics remembered the November 9 shooting call because of the date—they, too, noted that it occurred on the day that the state's vaunted handgun law took effect.

In the end, a jury in Judge Bothe's court found Warren Waddell guilty of first-degree murder, a verdict that resulted in a life-without-parole term predicated on the fact that Waddell had only recently been paroled on a charge of homicide. At this writing, however, the verdict has been overturned by a Maryland appeals court because of prejudicial comments made by Judge Bothe in the presence of the jury; a new trial date has yet to be scheduled.

Still, the case against Waddell remains a viable prosecution, a victory snatched from the jaws of defeat by good legal work, and Garvey, for one, allowed himself some measure of satisfaction at the end of the first trial.

As a sheriff's deputy led Warren Waddell down the marble stairs to the basement lockup, the defendant stared sullenly at the detective for a second too long. Garvey responded by leaning over the railing and calling to the convicted man in a stage whisper: "See you later, dickhead."

McCollum, who was talking to another attorney a few feet away, suddenly made the connection. "You didn't just say what I thought you said?"

"Fuck yes," said Garvey. "Somebody had to."

Alone among the three squads of D'Addario's 1988 command, Terry McLarney's crew is still intact.

Eddie Brown moves steadily from case to case, seemingly impervious to the passage of time. Rick James, who worked hard and long on the March murder of cab driver Karen Renee Smith, has now moved far enough from Worden's shadow to be called a veteran. In fact, James's 1988 campaign was nearly as successful as Rich Garvey's: Alvin Richardson, who raped and murdered that two-year-old boy in November, was convicted in a jury trial and sentenced to life in prison, and Dennis

Wahls, who led police to the stolen jewelry and implicated himself in the cab driver's murder, pleaded guilty to first-degree murder and accepted a life sentence. Clinton Butler, the man whom Wahls named as the man who actually beat Karen Smith to death, was tried twice in Baltimore courtrooms. Despite Wahls's testimony and other corroborating evidence, the first jury was hung, the second found Butler innocent.

Donald Waltemeyer's career case went to trial in 1989, as prosecutors brought Geraldine Parrish into Judge Bothe's court for the murder of Albert Robinson, the alcoholic from Plainfield, New Jersey, found dead by the railbed in Clifton Park in 1986. Geraldine knew Albert Robinson from her storefront church in Plainfield, and years earlier she had convinced him to sign a life insurance policy that named her as the beneficiary. Of the four murders with which she was charged, the slaying of Robinson proved to have the most corroborative evidence. A trio of prosecutors told jurors an incredible, at times almost comical, tale in which Geraldine and a handful of other conspirators drove to New Jersey and lured Robinson into a car with promises of alcohol. Hours later, they shot him and left him for dead in a copse near Atlantic City. Robinson survived with only superficial wounds, but he was so drunk that he remembered nothing of the incident. A few months later, the gang returned to New Jersey, lured the drunk into the car once again, and this time drove him to Baltimore, where a teenage friend of one of Geraldine's nieces finished the job on the B&O railbed, leaving Rick James with a stone whodunit.

Geraldine disappointed no one at the trial. At one point, she threw a conniption in the jury's presence, flailing in her chair and spitting foam from the corners of her mouth. A bored Elsbeth Bothe ordered her to behave, ending the demonstration. Later, on the witness stand, Geraldine claimed she was duped by men who made her turn over the insurance policies and identify the prospective victims for them.

She wasn't convincing, and in this instance a jury had little problem agreeing on a verdict. Geraldine Parrish was sentenced to life in prison, after which she pleaded guilty to the remaining three murders and received concurrent life sentences. No one was more relieved to see the case end than Donald Waltemeyer, who returned to the rotation full time immediately after the trial.

Waltemeyer's partner, Dave Brown, no longer lives in a state of perpetual torment. For the last two years, Donald Worden has granted the younger detective a certain grudging acceptance, if not respect. It is true, however, that in the summer of 1989 the Big Man began charging Brown twenty-five cents apiece for his phone messages.

As for Terry McLarney himself, he continues to cling to the brotherhood. In 1989, he ignored a persistent cough until he could barely stand, then spent months recuperating from a bacterial infection around his heart. He was not expected to return to homicide, which is to say he was back in four months, looking leaner and healthier than he had in years.

At twenty-eight years of service and counting, Donald Worden is still a Baltimore police officer, still the center of McLarney's squad. And he is now a married man. The wedding was in the summer of 1989 and most of the shift was there. Toast followed toast, and the entire wedding party concluded the festivities at Kavanaugh's, with Diane gracing a barstool in her wedding dress and the Big Man holding court in a well-tailored tuxedo.

Marriage meant that Worden had to put in at least one more year to qualify his bride for full benefits, but that milestone came and went, and he is still working murders. He has stayed close to the Monroe Street case file and followed up on the few leads that have come into the unit in the last two years. Still, the death of John Randolph Scott in an alley off Monroe Street remains an open investigation—the only unsolved police-involved shooting in department history. The officers concerned remain, for the most part, on the street, although some, including Sergeant John Wiley, were subsequently reassigned to administrative duties within the department.

But other outcomes are more gratifying. Once last year, Worden was driving out to a shooting scene in the early morning hours when he passed the downtown bus station and noticed a clean-cut U.S. Navy seaman walking with a ragged-looking man on West Fayette Street. The combination seemed strange to Worden; he filed it away in that memory of his, and when the sailor turned up dead later that morning, beaten to death during a robbery in a nearby parking garage, Worden walked over to Kevin Davis, the primary on the case. Worden gave Davis a full description of the suspect; the two men got back in a Cavalier and found their man within hours.

The newspapers said the crime was solved by sheer luck, proving once again how little this world understands about what it means to be a detective.

* * *

A final postscript: In 1988, 234 men and women died violent deaths in the city of Baltimore. In 1989, 262 people were murdered. Last year, the murder rate jumped again, leaving 305 dead—the city's worst toll in almost twenty years.

In the first month of 1991, the city is averaging one murder a day.

AUTHOR'S NOTE

This book is a work of journalism. The names of the detectives, defendants, victims, prosecutors, police officers, pathologists and others identified in the text are, in fact, their real names. The events described in the book occurred in the manner described.

My research began in January 1988, when I joined the Baltimore Police Department's homicide unit with the unlikely rank of "police intern." As often happens when journalists hang around one place long enough, I became a piece of furniture in the unit, a benign part of the detectives' daily scenery. Within weeks they were acting as if allowing a reporter to gawk at the chaos of criminal investigation was entirely natural.

So that my presence would not interfere with the investigations, I agreed to look and dress the part. That meant cutting my hair, purchasing several sport coats, ties and slacks and removing a diamond-stud earring that had done little to endear me to the detectives themselves. Throughout my year in the unit, I never identified myself to anyone as a law officer. But my appearance, coupled with the presence of other police, often led civilians and even other police to assume that I was, in fact, a detective. To journalists trained to identify themselves while reporting, this may be perceived as a crime of omission. But to declare myself at crime scenes, during interviews or inside hospital emergency rooms would have dramatically impaired the investigations. In brief, there was no other way to research this book.

Still, the ethical ambiguity was there every time I quoted a witness, an emergency room doctor, a prison guard, or a victim's relative who assumed I was a law officer. For that reason, I have tried to accord these people as much anonymity as possible, balancing questions of fairness and privacy with the need for accuracy.

All of the detectives on Lieutenant D'Addario's shift signed release forms before seeing any portion of the manuscript. Other characters central to the book also gave approval for their names to be used. In order to obtain these releases, I promised the detectives and others that they would be allowed to review relevant portions of the manuscript and suggest changes for purposes of accuracy. I also told the detectives that if there was something in the manuscript that was not essential to the story but that could nonetheless harm their careers or personal lives, they could ask that it be deleted and I would consider the request. In the end, the detectives requested remarkably few changes, and the handful to which I agreed involved mundane items, such as one detective's comment about a woman in a bar or another's criticism of a specific superior. I allowed no changes that involved the handling of a case or in any way altered or muted the book's message.

In addition to the individual detectives, the police department itself had a limited right to review the manuscript—but only to ensure that undisclosed evidentiary material in pending cases (bullet calibers, manner of death, clothing of victim) was not being released in instances where such facts, if kept secret, might later help identify a suspect. No changes or deletions resulted from the department's review.

Representatives of the Baltimore state's attorney's office and the state Office of the Chief Medical Examiner also reviewed relevant portions of the manuscript for purposes of accuracy only. Like the detectives, they could suggest, but not insist on, changes.

Most of the dialogue in this narrative—perhaps 90 percent—comes from the scenes and conversations that I personally witnessed. In a few instances, however, important events occurred on shifts when I was not working or when I was busy reporting on the activities of other detectives. In those instances, I was careful not to use direct quotes for long portions of text, and I have tried to use only those quotes that were specifically recalled by the detectives. And when a character is shown to be thinking something, it is not mere presumption: In every case, subsequent actions made those thoughts apparent or I discussed the matter with that person afterward. And by reviewing the material with the detectives, I have tried to ensure that their thoughts have been portrayed as accurately as possible.

For the unprecedented and unparalleled cooperation of the Baltimore Police Department, I am indebted to the late Police Commissioner Edward J. Tilghman as well as the current commissioner, Edward V. Woods. I am also grateful to Deputy Commissioner for Operations Ronald J.

Mullen; retired Colonel Richard A. Lanham and Deputy Commissioner Joseph W. Nixon, both of whom headed the Criminal Investigations Division for portions of 1988; Captain John J. MacGillivary, commander of the Crimes Against Persons section; Lieutenant Stewart Oliver, administrative lieutenant for the persons section; as well as the multitude of BPD commanders, line officers and technicians who went out of their way to assist me.

This project would also not have been possible without the invaluable assistance of Director Dennis S. Hill, chief public information officer for the Baltimore department, and Lieutenant Rick Puller and Sergeant Michael A. Fry of the department's legal affairs unit.

I would also like to thank Chief Medical Examiner Dr. John E. Smialek and others in the medical examiner's office for advice and assistance; and Dr. Smialek and Michael Golden, spokesman for the state health department, for providing access to the OCME. In the city prosecutor's office, I am indebted to State's Attorney Stuart O. Simms, Chief of the Violent Crimes Unit Timothy V. Doory, and Chief of the Trial Division Ara Crowe.

On the editorial side, this book comes into the world only through the determined and devoted efforts of John Sterling, editor in chief at Houghton Mifflin, who saw the possibilities from the outset and simply refused to let any of them slip away. His patience, talent and expertise are responsible for much of what may be called good writing in these pages; I plead guilty to the rest. This book also benefited immensely from the efforts of Luise M. Erdmann, who proved that manuscript editing, when done well, is more art than craft. My thanks also to Rebecca Saikia-Wilson and everyone else at Houghton Mifflin who gave this project such strong support.

I am also grateful to my editors at the *Baltimore Sun*, who granted me leave to complete the work and were unswervingly supportive of the project, even after I blew a deadline or three. My thanks to James I. Houck, managing editor; Tom Linthicum, metropolitan desk editor; Anthony F. Barbieri, city editor; and writing coach Rebecca Corbett, who has been a source of advice and encouragement ever since I began making nightshift police rounds at the *Sun* eight years ago.

I would like to thank Bernard and Dorothy Simon, my parents, whose help over the last three years was essential, as well as Kayle Tucker, whose love and unstinting support was of equal value.

Most important, this book could not exist without the assistance of homicide shift lieutenants Gary D'Addario and Robert Stanton and the forty detectives and detective sergeants who served in their 1988 commands. They took the real risk here, and I hope they feel now that it was in some way worth it.

Finally, a note on one last ethical dilemma. Over a period of time, familiarity and even friendship can sometimes tangle the relationship between a journalist and his subjects. Knowing that, I began my tenure in the homicide unit committed to a policy of complete nonintervention. If the phone in the main office rang and there was no one but me to answer, then it was not meant to be answered. But the detectives themselves helped to corrupt me. It began with phone messages, then grew to spelling corrections and proofreading. ("You're a writer. Take a look at this affidavit.") And I shared with the detectives a year's worth of fast-food runs, bar arguments and station house humor: Even for a trained observer, it was hard to remain aloof.

In retrospect, it's good that the year ended when it did, before one of the detectives provoked me to intervene in some truly harmful way. Once, in December, I found myself crossing that line—"going native," as journalists say. I was in the back seat of an unmarked car cruising Pennsylvania Avenue, accompanying Terry McLarney and Dave Brown in their search for a witness. At one point, the detectives suddenly pulled over to the curb to confront a woman who matched the description. She was walking with two young men. McLarney jumped from the car and grabbed one man, but Brown's trenchcoat belt became caught in the car's shoulder harness and he fell back into the driver's seat. "Go," he yelled at me, still struggling with the harness. "Help Terry."

Armed with my ball-point pen, I followed McLarney, who was struggling to get one man up against a parked car while the second eyed him angrily.

"DO HIM!" McLarney yelled at me, gesturing toward the second man.

And so, in a moment of weakness, a newspaper reporter shoved a citizen of his city against a parked car and performed one of the most pathetic and incompetent body searches on record. When I got down to the guy's ankles, I looked up over my shoulder at McLarney.

He was, of course, laughing hard.

David Simon
Baltimore
March 1991

POST MORTEM

To properly credit the idea for this book, we journey back twenty years to a Christmas Eve I spent with Roger Nolan, Russ Carney, Donald Kincaid and Bill Lansey, observing some routine mayhem and preparing to write a brief feature article on the holiday observances of those charged with working murders. I, for one, enjoy the perversity of a silent, holy night punctuated by a double-cutting in Pimlico, and I thought there might be a few readers of the *Baltimore Sun* who might also be willing to appreciate the small wit of the thing.

So I brought a bottle up to headquarters, slipped past the security desk, and joined the homicide squad working overnight as they handled a street shooting, a drug overdose and the aforementioned knife fight. Later, with much of the work done and an early morning choral concert of holiday music playing on the office television, I sat with the detectives as Carney poured cheer.

The elevator doors rang and Kincaid appeared, back from the last shooting of the shift—a desultory affair that landed the victim in an emergency room bed with a gunshot wound to an upper leg. He would live to see New Year's.

"Most people are getting up right now, going under the tree and finding some kinda gift. A tie, or a new wallet or something," mused Kincaid. "This poor bastard gets a bullet for Christmas."

We laughed. And then—I will never forget the moment—Bill Lansey said:

"The shit that goes on up here. If someone just wrote down what happens in this place for one year, they'd have a goddamn book."

Two years later, Bill Lansey, bless him, was dead of a heart attack and I wasn't feeling all that good about things myself. Despite record profits, my newspaper was challenging its labor union with a contract of givebacks in medical coverage and provoking a strike—an economic stance that was to become thematic in journalism over the next couple decades. I hated my bosses just then, and being one to nurse a grudge I sensed it might be good to conjure a leave of absence, something that would hold my job at a daily newspaper but avoid the newsroom for a time.

Remembering Lansey's remark, I wrote to the Baltimore police commissioner, Edward J. Tilghman. Would it be possible, I asked with feigned innocence, to observe his detectives for a year?

Yes, he replied, it would.

To this day, I have no direct explanation for his decision. The captain in charge of the homicide unit was opposed to the idea, as was the deputy commissioner for operations, the number two in the department. And a straw poll of detectives in the unit quickly revealed most thought it a terrible notion to allow a reporter into the unit. My good fortune was that a police department is a paramilitary organization with a rigid chain of command. It is not, in any sense, a democracy.

I never managed to ask Tilghman about his decision. He died before the book was published—indeed, before I'd finished my research. "You need to ask why he let you in?" Rich Garvey later offered. "The man had a brain tumor. What other explanation do you need?"

Maybe so. But years later the CID commander, Dick Lanham, told me there was something more subtle in play. In response to questions about my status, Tilghman said his own years as a homicide detective were the most enjoyable and gratifying of his career. I suppose I'd like to believe his motivation for letting me inside was as pure as that, though Garvey was probably onto something as well.

In any event, I entered the unit in January 1988 with the improbable rank of police intern, working New Year's Day with the men—and all nineteen detectives and supervisors were male—of Lieutenant Gary D'Addario's shift.

The rules were fairly straightforward. I could not communicate what I witnessed to my newspaper and I had to obey the orders of the supervisors and investigators I followed. I could not quote anyone by name unless they agreed to be so quoted. And when my manuscript was complete, it would be reviewed by the department's legal affairs division—not to censor my work for general content but to assure that I did not reveal key pieces of evidence in cases still pending. As it turned out, no changes resulted from this review.

Shift after shift, with detectives looking on warily, I filled notepads with what seems to me now a frantic stream of quotes, case details, biographical data and general impressions. I read through all the detectives' case files from the previous year, as well as the H-files on some of the biggest cases I had chased as a police reporter: the Warren House shootings, the Bronstein murders, the Barksdale warfare in the Murphy Homes back in '82, the Harlem Park jacket slaying from '83. I couldn't believe I could just walk to the admin office and pull entire case files, then sit at a desk and read them at leisure. I couldn't believe I wasn't thrown off crime scenes, or out of interrogation rooms. I couldn't believe the department brass wasn't going to change its collective mind, confiscate my ID card and toss me onto Frederick Street.

But days became weeks and the detectives—even those cautious souls who would change their very tone when I walked up on their conversations—soon lost the will to perform, to pretend to be someone other than who they were.

I learned to drink. I dropped my Amex card now and then, whereupon the detectives more than matched me round for round, showing me I still had a lot to learn. Staggering from the Market Bar at closing one night, Donald Worden—who had allowed me to follow him on calls and through cases, but always with a certain veiled contempt—glared at me as if for the first time and drawled, "All right, Simon. What the hell do you wanna see? What the fuck do you think we're gonna show you?"

I had no answer. Notepads were stacked on my desk, a dog-eared tower of random detail that confused and intimidated me. I tried to work six days a week, but my marriage was ending and sometimes I worked seven. If the detectives went drinking after work, I was often in tow.

On night shifts, I would work doubles, coming in at four and staying through the midnight shift until early morning. Sometimes, coming off midnight, we drank at dawn, and I would stagger home to sleep until night. I learned to my amazement that if you forced yourself to drink the morning after a bad drunk, it somehow felt better.

On one February morning, I was hungover and late for morning roll call when Worden phoned to wake me with the news that a dead girl had been found in a Reservoir Hill alley. I was at the crime scene ten minutes later, staring at the eviscerated body of Latonya Wallace and the beginning of an investigation that would become the spine of the book.

I began to focus on that case. On Pellegrini, the new man. On Edgerton, the lone-wolf secondary on the case, and on Worden, the gruff conscience of the unit. I talked less, listened more and learned to pull out the pen and notepad discreetly, so as not to upset the delicate moments of ordinary squadroom life.

In time, because I read the casework voraciously and sat through multiple shifts to note the comings and goings of detectives, I became in some small way a clearinghouse of basic information:

"Where's Barlow?"

"He's in court. Part eighteen."

"Is Kevin with him?"

"No, he's at the bar."

"With who?"

"Rick James and Linda. And Garvey went, too."

"Who caught the one on Payson last night?"

"Edgerton. He went home after the morgue and he's coming back at six."

But mostly, I was comic to these men, an amusing twenty-something distraction—"a mouse tossed into a room full of cats," by Terry McLarney's description. "You're lucky we're so bored with each other."

If I went to a morning autopsy, Donald Steinhice would throw his voice and watch me eye the cadavers warily, just as Dave Brown would drag me to the Penn Restaurant to eat that nasty chorizo-and-egg platter so as to measure the fortitude of a novice. If I sat through a successful interrogation, Rich Garvey would turn to me at the end to ask if I had questions of my own, then laugh at whatever reportorial impulse resulted. And if I feel asleep on midnight shift, I would wake to find Polaroid photos of myself, head back in a chair, mouth open, flanked by smiling detectives imitating fellatio, their thumbs stuck through open zippers.

McLarney wrote my green sheet, the semi-annual evaluation so detested by working police in Baltimore. "Professional kibbitzer," he wrote in summation of my standing. "It's unclear what Intern Simon's actual responsibilities are, however his hygiene is satisfactory and he seems to know a good deal about our activities. His sexual appetites remain suspect, however."

At home, with a mattress on the bedroom floor and most of the furnishings in the possession of my ex-wife, I spent hours filling a computer with stream-of-consciousness rambling, emptying the notepads, trying to organize what I was witnessing into separate casefiles, biographies and chronologies.

The Latonya Wallace murder stayed open. I was mortified by this—and not because a killer roamed free and the destruction of a child was unavenged. No, I was too overawed by the manuscript I would soon have to write to waste a moment thinking in moral terms. Instead, I worried that the book would have no climax, that its conclusion would be open and empty and flawed.

I drank some more, though by summer the detectives, feeling sorry for me perhaps, were buying as many rounds as they put to my credit card. To avoid the heart of the matter—actually writing—I wasted a week or two interviewing the detectives at length with a tape recorder, producing the kind of interviews in which people who have for months been candid and open suddenly talk into a microphone with the certain knowledge that posterity is at stake.

Edgerton caught a second child-murder and solved it, and, without knowing it, I met in the mother of the dead girl one of the central characters of my next book, *The Corner*. Ella Thompson began for me at the door of her Fayette Street rowhouse, a mother's face contorted in grief. Four years later, I would wander into the recreation center on Vincent Street and encounter her again—by accident—as I began reporting a different narrative, one that even the best detectives can only glimpse.

During that year in the homicide unit, I never actually felt I'd gone native. Not in any way that seemed to matter. Not in my own mind, anyway. I dressed the part, and at crime scenes and in courtrooms I did what the supervisors and investigators told me to do. Ultimately, I enjoyed myself and the company of the detectives immensely. For four years I had written city murders in a cramped, two-dimensional way—filling the back columns of the metro section with the kind of journalism that reduces all human tragedy, especially those with black or brown victims, to bland, bite-sized morsels:

> A 22-year-old West Baltimore man was gunned down yesterday at an intersection near his home in an apparent drug-related incident. Detectives have no motive or suspects in the case, police said.
>
> Antwon Thompson, of the 1400 block of Stricker Street, was found by patrol officers called to the scene of . . .

Suddenly, I had been granted access to a world hidden, if not willfully ignored, by all of that dispassionate journalism. These weren't murders as benchmarks of a day's events. Nor were they the stuff of pristine, perfectly rendered morality plays. By summer, with the body count rising in the Baltimore heat, I came to realize that I was standing on the factory floor. This was death investigation as an assembly-line process, a growth industry for a rust-belt America that had long ceased to mass manufacture much of anything, save for heartbreak itself. Perhaps, I told myself, it was the ordinariness of it all that made it, well, extraordinary.

They went after the Fish Man for the last time in December. He didn't break. Latonya Wallace would not be avenged. But by then I had seen enough to know that the empty, ambiguous ending was the correct one. I called John Sterling, my editor in New York, and told him it was better this way.

"It's real," I said. "It's how the world works, or doesn't."

He agreed. In fact, he'd seen it before I did. He told me to start writing, and after staring at the computer screen for a couple weeks, wondering how you type the first fucking sentence of a fucking book, I found myself back at the Market Bar with McLarney, who swayed to the rhythm of a ninth Miller Lite and eyed me, much amused at my predicament.

"Isn't this what you actually do for a living?"

Sort of. Except not something so big as a book.

"I know what you're gonna write."

Do tell.

"It's not about the cases. The murders. I mean, you'll write about the murders so you have stuff to write about. But that's all just the bullshit."

I listened. Carefully.

"You're gonna write about us. About the guys. About how we act and the shit we say to each other, about how pissed off we get and how funny we are sometimes and the shit that goes on in that office."

I nodded. As if I'd known it all along.

"I've seen you taking notes when we were just bullshitting, when we're just sitting around with nothing to do but jerk each other around. We piss and moan and there you are writing. We tell a dirty joke and you're writing. We say anything or do anything and you're there with your pen and your notepad and a weird look on your face. And fuck if we didn't let you do it."

And then he laughed. At me, or with me—I've never quite been sure.

The book sold some copies. Not enough to make any bestseller lists, but enough that Sterling was willing to pay me if I could manage another idea for another tome. Roger Nolan confiscated my police intern ID and I went back to the *Sun*. The detectives went back to having their world unexamined. And save for an immediate, panicked reaction by the department brass in which there were threats to charge the entire unit with conduct unbecoming an officer—the raw wit and rampant profanity of their underlings left colonels and deputy commissioners shocked, shocked, I tell you—the general response to *Homicide: A Year on the Killing Streets* seemed to be no less muted than that which greets most narrative nonfiction.

Certainly, it didn't help that the tale came from Baltimore. The editor of the *New York Times Book Review* declined initially to review the work, declaring it to be a regional book. A few police reporters at other newspapers said nice things. One evening, when I was working rewrite, plugging out-of-town temperatures into the weather chart, William Friedkin called from Los Angeles to say how much he enjoyed the book.

"William who?"

"Friedkin. I directed the *French Connection*? *To Live and Die in L.A.*?

"Alvarez, stop fucking with me. I'm late with the goddam weather table."

A few more deep breaths like that one and the hardbacks copies were off the display shelves and consigned to the true-crime section. I nestled back into the *Sun*, took up my old beat and began encountering the detectives from the other side of the crime-scene tape. Once, at a triple murder in North Baltimore, I lost my temper at Terry McLarney when he wouldn't come out of an indoor crime scene to debrief me even as the home-final deadline passed. In the squadroom the next day, as I was ranting with probably a bit too much indignation, Donald Waltemeyer suddenly exploded out of his chair like a .45 round.

"Jesus fucking Christ, Simon. Listen to you. You're like one of these fuckin' defense lawyers who get you on the stand and start asking if it's true, Detective Waltemeyer, that you fucked some broad in 1929. Who gives a fuck? McLarney was on a scene and he didn't give a fuck about your fuckin' deadlines. So just go fuck yourself and tell your newspaper to go fuck itself and stop bein' a fuckin' lawyer with us."

I looked over to see McLarney giggling, hiding his face in his sportcoat.

"A whole year up here," Waltemeyer concluded, "and you're still nothing but a prissy bitch."

Ah, normalcy.

And it might've stayed that way had not Barry Levinson bought the book and metastasized the thing into an NBC drama, turning our small, self-contained world upside down. Suddenly, Edgerton was some proud, fully intellectualized peacock of a detective named Pembleton. And McLarney was bald with a funny mustache, and obsessed with the Lincoln assassination. And Worden was that actor—whatshisname—the one that got fucked in the ass in *Deliverance.* And Garvey? Damned if they didn't give Rich Garvey red hair and tits. He was a woman, for Chrissake.

For me, *Homicide: Life on the Street* was a strange stepchild at first. I admired the drama and the craft of it—and to the detectives themselves, I actually defended the show's willingness to fictionalize their world as a necessary license for long-form storytelling. I was certainly happy to have the book rediscovered; well before the NBC show ended its run, a quarter of a million copies were sold. But, in truth, I was ambivalent.

After reading the first three scripts, I wrote a long memo to Barry Levinson and Tom Fontana in which I explicated the intricacies of various investigative techniques and legal requirements. No, you cannot search a suspect's domicile for a weapon because a detective dreamed that the gun was there. Probable cause is a required element for any affiant to obtain a search-and-seizure warrant signed by a circuit court, and so forth and so on and furthermore, et cetera, et cetera . . .

Nonfiction boy, Fontana called me after that, and not with any particular fondness.

I went to the set a couple times during filming, standing around like any other tourist. The detectives themselves would occasionally show up, usually with wives or girlfriends who wanted to meet Danny Baldwin or Kyle Secor. A few took the gig of technical advisor, sitting by the video monitors and offering advice when asked, and sometimes, to the chagrin of the film company, when not.

A special moment in this regard belongs to Harry Edgerton, who, upon witnessing Frank Pembleton—his television alter ego—order a Scotch and a milk at a bar, shouted, "Cut."

Barry Levinson turned to look at his technical advisor as if to examine a new species. Assistant directors and junior producers scurried to immediately right the wrong.

"But there's no way I would drink something like that," Edgerton said to me later. "Scotch and milk? Seriously, Dave, people I know are gonna see that and what are they gonna think?"

Eventually, Gary D'Addario—a man of demonstrated tact and

discretion—became the solitary advisor and, in time, played the role of a tactical commander in the cast. And, as the novelty of filming wore thin, the other detectives drifted away. So did I, feeling, as all authors probably do on a film set, entirely beside the point.

To be fair, one of the producers, Gail Mutrux, had asked if I wanted to try my hand at writing the pilot for the show. Ridiculously ignorant of the money involved, I had declined, telling Gail—who first read *Homicide* and brought it to Levinson's attention as possible television fare—that she should get someone who knew what he was doing, if only to give the project a fighting chance. I would, if they wanted, take a later script, writing only when a template for the show was established.

Fontana and Levinson obliged. And that later script, which I co-wrote with David Mills, a friend from college newspaper days, proved so relentlessly dark and unsparing that NBC executives declined to allow it to be shot during that first season of the drama. It was only a year later, during the truncated, four-episode run of season two, that it was filmed, and then only because Robin Williams had agreed to star in the guest role.

I still have my first draft of that script—replete with Tom Fontana's notes in thick red ink. Our scenes were long and the speeches longer, and the descriptive sections were marred with the kind of camera direction that denotes an amateur effort. Once Tom and Jim Yoshimura got done adding additional scenes for the guest star—and cutting dialogue for other characters—maybe half of the script could be credited to Mills and me.

I thought this a personal failure—even after the episode won the Writer's Guild of America writing award—and I took the opportunity to remind myself where it was I actually belonged. Back at the *Sun*, working my beat, I began planning that second book, a year in the life of a West Baltimore drug corner. Mills, however, left his gig at the *Washington Post* for Hollywood, and after hiring on at *NYPD Blue* called back to assure me that any freelancer who, on a first script, manages to get half his words into an episode, is doing fine.

So after a second *Homicide* script—this one filmed with few changes—I jumped. It helped that my newspaper—once a good, gray lady of venerable, if somewhat hidebound traditions—had become the playground of a couple carpetbaggers from Philadelphia, two tone-deaf hacks for whom the apogee of all journalism was a five-part series that declared "The *Baltimore Sun* has learned" in the second paragraph, then offered a couple overreported pages of simplistic outrages and even more simplistic solutions.

There was a Pulitzer fever to the place, and a carefully crafted mythology in which no one knew how to do their job until the present regime brought tablets down from Sinai. I returned from my research on *The Corner* to a depressed and depressing newsroom, moreso after a series of buyouts began driving talented veterans to other newspapers. Eventually, cost-cutting and out-of-town ownership would all but destroy the place, but even by the mid-nineties, there was enough intellectual fraud and prize lust at the *Sun* for me to realize that whatever I had loved about the *Sun* was disappearing, and that, in the end, the artifice of television drama was, in comparison to the artifice of a crafted Pulitzer campaign, no longer a notable sin.

I hired on with the stepchild, and Tom Fontana and his crew taught me how to write television to a point where I was proud to work for the man. And when *The Corner* was published, I was ready, with Mills, to tell that story on HBO.

As for the detectives, most accepted *The Corner* as a legitimate story, fairly told. Following a shooting one day at Monroe and Fayette, Frank Barlow actually came across the yellow crime-scene tape to chat with me about old times and ask how the new project was going—an act of fraternization for which I had to explain myself for days afterward to touts and dealers and dope fiends. But other detectives regarded the second book as something of a betrayal—a narrative written not from the point of view of stalwart Baltimore police but in the voice of those they were chasing.

By the early nineties, that chase had turned brutal and unforgiving. Five years after I reported *Homicide*, the cocaine epidemic had overheated Baltimore's drug economy and transformed the inner city. Where once there were a couple dozen drug markets, now there more than a hundred corners. And where once the city's homicide unit had to work 240 slayings a year, suddenly they were contending with more than 300. The clearance rate slipped a bit, the bosses got nervous and, eventually, they panicked.

Since the reign of Donald Pomerleau, the homegrown management of the Baltimore department had devolved to mediocrity, but it was only amid the cocaine wars that the cost of such was revealed. It was one thing to have a half-senile commissioner caretaking a viable department in

1981, when crackhouses and speedballs were just a rumor in Baltimore. A decade later, actual leadership was a fundamental need and, for the first time since 1966, the city hired a commissioner from the outside, giving him a mandate to clean house.

He did. But in the worst way, because Thomas Frazier, arriving with an air of supreme confidence from San Jose, almost singlehandedly managed to destroy the Baltimore Police Department's homicide unit in the process.

For one thing, Frazier proved indifferent to the fact that inside every police agency in America there are two hierarchies. The first is the chain of command, where rank itself is the chief determinant; sergeants learn to supplicate before lieutenants, who prostrate themselves before majors, who genuflect before colonels, who kiss the haunches of deputy commissioners. That hierarchy is necessary to the form and it can never be wholly disregarded.

But the alternate hierarchy—equally essential—is one of expertise, and it exists for the department's technicians, those whose skill at a specific job requires due deference.

This defines a homicide detective.

Yet incredibly, Frazier came to Baltimore and immediately declared that the rotation of police officers from one assignment to the next would constitute his plan for revitalizing the city department. No officer, he declared, should remain in the same assignment for more than three years.

Never mind that it takes a homicide detective—not to mention other departmental investigators and technicians—at least that long to fully learn his craft and become effective. And never mind that rotation threatened the professional standing of every man in the homicide unit. Frazier cited his own career as a justification, declaring that he had, after three years in any assignment, become bored and desirous of new challenges.

Rotation chased some of the best men from the city, as they departed to investigative jobs with the federal government and the surrounding counties. When, for example, Gary Childs and Kevin Davis decided to leave before submitting to the policy, I interviewed Frazier and asked him how he felt about such losses.

"These are guys who can carry a squad," I said.

"Why does anyone need to be carried? Why can't every man in homicide be the best?"

As hyperbole, it sounds great. But the truth about the Baltimore homicide unit—even when it was at its best in the 1970s and 1980s, when clearance rates were well above the national averages—is that some detectives were brilliant, some were competent and some were notably ineffective.

Yet in every squad there seemed to be a Worden, a Childs, a Davis or a Garvey to center the half dozen men and keep watch over weaker colleagues. With thirty detectives and six sergeants, it was possible for squad supervisors to monitor the struggling detectives, to pair them with proven veterans, to ensure that cases didn't so easily slip between the cracks.

Frazier's other strategy—apart from simply chasing talent from the department—was to assign more detectives to the sixth floor. More squads. More new detectives. Eventually, the violent crimes task force was co-mingled with homicide on the sixth floor and another thirty bodies wandered to and fro amid the casework.

More detectives, less responsibility. And now, when a detective took a phone call on a murder, more likely than not he didn't know which squad was working the case or what the capabilities of a new detective actually were. There had always been rookies—one or two a squad—and the veterans would look out for them, nurture them, making sure they weren't given whodunits until they had gone out on a dozen calls as secondaries, or maybe even handled a dunker or two on their own. Now, whole squads were comprised of first-year men, and with the continuing departure of veterans the clearance rate fell dramatically.

A few years later, it was well below 50 percent, with the actual conviction rate hovering at about half that. And as in any institutional enterprise, once the expertise goes, it does not come back.

"They ruined us," Garvey told me before putting in his papers. "This was a great unit and it was like they had a plan to ruin it."

For my part, I had come to feel much the same in my own world, having seen some of the best reporters at my newspaper depart for the *New York Times*, the *Washington Post* and other papers—chased by an institutional arrogance that was every bit equal to that of the police department.

Struck, Wooten, Alvarez, Zorzi, Littwin, Thompson, Lippman, Hyman—some of the best reporters the *Baltimore Sun* had were marginalized, then bought out, shipped out and replaced with twenty-four-year-old acolytes, who, if they did nothing else, would never make the mistake of having an honest argument with newsroom management. In a time of growth, when the chance to truly enhance the institution was at hand, the new regime at the *Sun* hired about as much talent as they dispatched. And in the end, when the carpetbaggers finally departed, their mythology of heroic renewal intact, they had managed to achieve three Pulitzers in about a dozen years. During the previous dozen, the newspaper's morning and evening editions achieved exactly the same number.

Listening to Garvey over drinks that day, I came to realize that there was something emblematic here: that in postmodern America, whatever institution you serve or are served by—a police department or a newspaper, a political party or a church, Enron or Worldcom—you will eventually be betrayed.

It seemed very Greek the more I thought about it. The stuff of Aeschylus and Sophocles, except the gods were not Olympian but corporate and institutional. In every sense, ours seems a world in which individual human beings—be they trained detectives or knowledgeable reporters, hardened corner boys or third-generation longshoremen or smuggled eastern European sex workers—are destined to matter less and less.

After watching what was done to my newspaper, and to the Baltimore homicide unit, I began to write the pilot for a new HBO drama. *The Wire*, for better or for worse, has occupied my time since.

Just after reading the manuscript for *Homicide*, Terry McLarney mailed me a single sheet of white bond paper. Atop that solitary page:

"The Book. Volume II."

And then the sentence, "My God. They've all been transferred. I think I see now what it is they were trying to tell me."

That was the only shot fired across my bow before publication, the only warning—however lighthearted—that the book might prove problematic for those it characterized.

And in the wake of Frazier's rotation policy, as well as other departures of veteran detectives unrelated to that policy, McLarney's dry, comic lament might certainly seem prophetic.

But there is a corresponding truth, and one that also bears noting: In 1998, looking back a decade to the year when I followed these men with pen and notepad akimbo, it was accurate to say that more than three-quarters of them were no longer in the Baltimore city homicide unit. But, looking back ten years from my moment as a police intern, it is also true that three-quarters of the detectives who had manned the unit in

1978 were also gone. And they departed, of course, without any book having been written about them.

Time itself is a means of attrition.

And, in time, Baltimore became comfortable with its depiction in both *Homicide: A Year on the Killing Streets* and the television drama that followed. The mayor appeared on the show; Maryland's governor as well. The actors themselves came to be regarded as resident Baltimoreans, or Baltimorons as some of us like to call ourselves. Over the last decade and a half, I've signed copies of the book for the city's politicians, for its civic leaders, for its lawyers, its cops, its criminals.

In some quarters, though, my welcome has worn thin, perhaps because both *The Corner* and *The Wire* offer a much darker vision of the problems that confront the city. There is consternation about the net effect of all this murderous narrative on Baltimore's image and its viability as a tourist destination, to be sure. Conversely, there is also a peculiar pride at being part of a city that endures despite such an appalling and persistent rate of violence.

I know that sounds ridiculous—a hoary citing of lemons and lemonade—but there is something to it. From the first, *Homicide* was, I think, a blunt and clear-eyed response to the national neglect of urban problems, demonstrating if not our civic ability to solve those problems, then at least our honesty and wit in confronting them.

The Natty Boh beer ads used to declare Maryland to be "The Land of Pleasant Living," just as a standard credo of local pride claims of Baltimore that "If you can't live here, you can't live anywhere."

Such sentiments might seem grandly mocked by the contents of *Homicide* or *The Corner* or certainly, given its angry, political tone, *The Wire*. But no such sarcasm is intended, and among residents of this city I don't sense that many feel particularly abused. If you live here, you know the good, and you still sense the civic ideal that has somehow managed to survive so much poverty, violence and waste, so much mismanagement and indifference.

Recently, the city paid a half million dollars to a consultant seeking a new slogan for itself:

"Baltimore—Get In On It"

I like it. An implied secret. As if you need to walk these streets for a while before you're entitled to know for certain what is at stake in this city's survival and why so many people still care.

But I confess that my favorite slogan came from a short contest sponsored on the daily newspaper's website, where readers offered their own free suggestions to the highly paid image consultants, and one local resident, tongue in cheek, wrote:

"It's Baltimore, hon . . . duck!"

The detectives would have recognized the humor, and, more than that, the temperment that gives rise to such humor. Hell, if they could buy the bumper sticker, they'd probably have it on the back of every unmarked unit.

These men lived and worked without illusion, and late at night, when I was rewriting sections of the book for the third and fourth time, I realized that I was trying to achieve a voice, a statement even, that they would recognize as true.

Never mind the demographics of bookbuyers, or the sensibilities of other journalists, or, God forbid, whoever might be judging some book award somewhere. Fifteen years ago, when I was trapped at my computer, the only judgments that mattered to me were those of the detectives. If they read the book and pronounced it honest, I would not feel the shame that comes from snatching pieces of human lives and putting them on display for all to see.

This is not to say that everything I wrote was complimentary or ennobling. There are pages of the book on which these men appear to be racist or racially insensitive, sexist or homophobic, where their humor derives from the poverty and tragedy of others. And yet with a body on the ground—black, brown, or, on rare occasion, white—they did their job regardless. In this graceless age of ours, any sense of duty is remarkable enough to excuse any number of lesser sins. And so readers learned to forgive, just as the writer learned to forgive, and six hundred pages later the very candor of the detectives was a quality, rather than an embarrassment.

In the preface to *Let Us Now Praise Famous Men*, James Agee asked absolution for his journalistic trespass, declaring that "these I will write of are human beings, living in this world, innocent of such twistings as these which are taking place over their heads; and that they were dwelt among, investigated, spied on, revered and loved by other quite monstrous human beings, in the employment of others still more alien; and that they are now being looked into by still others, who have picked up their living as casually as if it were a book."

There are many journalists who believe that their craft must burden itself with a nodding, analytic tone, that they must report and write with feigned, practiced objectivity and the presumption of omniscient expertise. Many are consumed by the pursuit of scandal and human flaw, and believe it insufficient to look at human beings with a skeptical yet affectionate eye. Their work is, of course, accurate and justifiable—and no closer to the actual truth of things than any other form of storytelling.

Years ago, I read an interview with Richard Ben Cramer in which he was accused by a fellow journalist of engaging in a love that dares not speak its name—at least not in newsrooms. Regarding the candidates he followed for *What It Takes*, his masterful narrative of presidential politics, Cramer was asked if he actually liked the men he was covering.

"Like them?" he replied. "I love them."

How could he write a nine-hundred-page tome in their voices if he didn't love every last one of them, warts and all? And what kind of journalist follows human beings for years on end, recording their best moments and their worst, without acquiring some basic regard for their individuality, their dignity, their value?

I admit it. I love these guys.

At this writing, Richard Fahlteich—a detective in Landsman's squad in 1988—is a major and the commander of the homicide unit, though he is planning to retire after more than thirty years service within the month.

Lieutenant Terrence Patrick McLarney, who commanded a squad on D'Addario's shift fifteen years ago, is a shift commander, having fought his way back to the unit after years of exile in the Western and Central Districts, where he was banished after his shift commander politely declined an invitation to fisticuffs in the headquarters garage.

The reason McLarney felt the need to extend such an invitation was simply that his shift commander was no longer Gary D'Addario, who had been promoted first to captain, and, later, to major and command of the Northeastern District. The man who replaced D'Addario did not understand the homicide unit, in the opinion of many. He certainly didn't understand McLarney, who, despite his protestations, his calculated appearance and his general demeanor, happens to be one of the smartest, funniest and most honest souls I ever had the privilege to know.

For his part, D'Addario thrived not only as a district commander but as the technical advisor to *Homicide* and ensuing productions. His portrayal of Lieutenant Jasper, the tactical commander on the drama, brought, if not widespread acclaim, then an opportunity for many subordinate commanders to advise him on the value of his day job.

He was forced to resign abruptly three years ago by a police commissioner who never offered a reason, simply summoning D'Addario to his office and issuing the demand.

That this came a couple days after D'Addario first appeared in a brief scene of *The Wire*, playing the part of a grand jury prosecutor, may be relevant. The current city administration is known to dislike the HBO drama, and though D'Addario wasn't the only department veteran to appear in episodes, he was the only ranking commander to do so at the time. I wrote a letter to the mayor, noting that the part was a neutral one and that D'Addario's dialogue brought no discredit on the department. I suggested that if displeasure with the major stemmed from his appearance on the show, then the decision should be reconsidered, and, further, that the administration should inform us one way or another if it had concerns about officers appearing on the drama.

No response was forthcoming.

In 1995, Donald Worden retired on his own terms after more than three decades service. Kevin Davis—the Worden of Stanton's shift—called it quits the same day. I made it a point to go out with the two veterans on their last shift, when they picked up a suspect from the city jail and tried unsuccessfully to get him to roll on an old murder. That story of their last day on the job was my last staff byline for the *Sun*—a personal metaphor of sorts, not that anyone was going to notice.

Within a year, as the murder toll jumped and clearance rates fell, the department hired Worden back as a civilian contractor to help clear cold homicide cases. He is clearing them still, along with his cold case supervisor, Sergeant Roger Nolan, putting blue names on The Board even though he carries neither badge nor gun.

When I see Worden on occasion, usually for a pint or two at that Irish dive on O'Donnell Street, I always offer him a quarter. He politely declines, though he can't help but point out that it would now be forty-five cents.

Along with Fahlteich and McLarney, Worden and Nolan are the only remaining members of D'Addario's shift still on duty. Much of the remainder of that shift is scattered throughout mid-Atlantic law enforcement, most having put in their retirement papers to take better-paying investigative positions in other agencies.

Worden's partner, Rick James, went to work for the U.S. Defense Intelligence Agency. Rich Garvey and Bob McAllister took positions as investigators with the federal public defenders office, with Garvey working out of the Harrisburg, Pennsylvania, branch and McAllister employed in Baltimore.

Gary Childs became an investigator for the Carroll County State's Attorney's Office, and later a homicide detective in Baltimore County. He was joined in Baltimore County by Jay Landsman, who was, in turn, joined by his son. And with two generations of Landsmans working the same precinct, some hilarity naturally ensued.

Recently, on a surveillance, Jay got on the radio to ask if his son, who ranks him, had the eyeball on a car they were following.

"Got him, Dad," came the laconic radio response, followed by delighted laughter from the rest of the surveillance detail.

Without Roger Nolan to protect him, Harry Edgerton soon ran afoul of a department with little tolerance for iconoclasts.

In 1990, his longtime partner, Ed Burns, had returned from the successful joint FBI–Baltimore city prosecution of Warren Boardley's drug organization and immediately wrote a proposal for a specialized unit that could conduct long-term proactive investigations of violent drug crews. When that proposal disappeared on the eighth floor without so much as a response, Burns chose to cash in his chips, retiring in 1992 to begin a teaching career in the Baltimore city schools—a career that I shortstopped by a year or two, convincing Ed to go with me to West Baltimore to report and write *The Corner*. That partnership continues—Ed is currently a writer and producer on *The Wire*.

On his own, Edgerton left the shelter of Nolan's squad—where his sergeant always had his back, and where the complaints of co-workers were always received with some salt. He transferred from homicide to a fledgling investigative squad—the violent crimes task force—which Edgerton believed could become the major case squad that he and Burns had long imagined.

The VCU, however, proved to be nothing of the sort, and, as it began concentrating on meaningless street rips and corner raids, Edgerton began a singular rebellion, going his own way, ignoring the orders of supervisors and alienating fellow detectives as only Harry Edgerton can.

A deputy commissioner then assigned him the quixotic, existential task of recovering the gun of a patrol officer who had been wounded in East Baltimore. Within weeks Edgerton was in negotiations with an east-side dealer to do precisely that. His bargaining chip was a series of home-made porn videos, all packed in a leather case seized during a drug raid. Acknowledging to the dealer that the tapes were of a personal nature,

Edgerton was offering to exchange them for the officer's gun. But in the interim, as negotiations progressed, a supervisor charged him with failing to inventory both the tapes and the leather case with evidence control, and, pending a trial board, Edgerton was suspended with pay. Then, before that case could be heard, he was found in West Baltimore, armed with his service revolver though suspended, meeting with a man Edgerton described as an informant.

Donald Worden, a sage among murder police, is fond of pointing to the massive binder that is the Baltimore City Police Department's Code of Conduct and declaring: "If they want you, they got you."

The department wanted Edgerton, having tired of his indifference to chain of command and his willful disregard of anything other than casework. He was convinced, before any trial board could convene, to wait out his twenty-year anniversary and then retire with his pension intact. He now does security work with several companies.

Edgerton's partner in the Latonya Wallace case, Tom Pellegrini, continued to pick at the dead girl's case for years afterward, but to little avail. He finally visited the Fish Man one last time and encouraged his best suspect to write down on a slip of paper whether he was guilty or innocent, then hide the document.

"That way, if you ever die," Pellegrini explained, "I'll find the paper and at least I'll know."

When the Fish Man did indeed depart this vale, several years ago, no such document was recovered from his effects. Sometimes the magic works, sometimes not.

After retiring from the Baltimore department, Pellegrini did a tour of duty with the United Nations in Kosovo, teaching death investigation to fledgling detectives there. He currently operates a private investigation firm in Maryland.

Among others, Gary Dunnigan is now an insurance investigator. Downtown Eddie Brown went to work security for the Baltimore Ravens, as did Bertina Silver of Stanton's shift. Rick "The Bunk" Requer left to man the department's retirement services bureau, though his homicide incarnation lives on in Wendell Pierce's portrayal of the legendary Bunk Moreland on *The Wire*, right down to the ubiquitous cigar. The remaining detectives of D'Addario's shift—Donald Kincaid, Bob Bowman and David John Brown—have retired as well, though Dave Brown went out in a frustrating way, having sustaining a severe leg injury during the search of a vacant house.

Danny Shea died of cancer in 1991. I didn't follow him on many cases, as he was a veteran of Stanton's shift, but I have the distinct memory of standing with him at the most natural of deaths, in a Charles Village apartment where an elderly piano teacher expired in bed with her radio playing softly.

Ravel's "Pavanne for a Dead Princess" was broadcast at that moment, and Shea, being a man of deep and varied knowledge, knew this as I did not.

"A quiet, perfect death," he said, nodding at the cadaver and granting me a moment I always remember when thinking about Danny Shea.

Donald Waltemeyer, too, died of cancer last year, having retired from Baltimore city to become an investigator with the Aberdeen Police Department in northeast Maryland.

When McLarney and the other members of his old squad got together with Aberdeen veterans at the wake, they quickly realized that Digger Waltemeyer had managed to infuriate and endear himself to both departments in exactly the same manner. At the funeral, men in different dress uniforms assured each other that they were privileged to know and work with both a consummate investigator and a renowned pain in the ass.

Meanwhile, the police intern from that long-ago year is still at large, his whereabouts subject to rumor and the crude conjecture of certain unit veterans. He is seen occasionally on Baltimore film sets and glimpsed in cluttered production offices and writing rooms. Sometimes, he attends the Baltimore homicide reunions out in Parkville, where retired detectives never fail to talk the same shit and ask, with a wink and nod, when NBC is gonna get those bigass checks in the mail.

No comment to that. But the intern and his credit card stand ready, knowing that for many reasons, if not for his entire career, he owes these guys—every last one of them—more than a few rounds.

David Simon
Baltimore
May 2006

Case Closed

In the decade and a half since David Simon finished writing this book he has transformed himself from a T-shirt wearing, wet-behind-his diamond-studded-ear, notebook-toting journalist of questionable prowess into an award-winning author, acclaimed screenwriter and accomplished television producer. During that same fifteen years, I have advanced exactly one rank.

The years passed by and I had not seen much of Dave, save for a couple homicide reunions and the retirement parties of Gary D'Addario and Eugene Cassidy. Then one day my son called from North Carolina, "Dad, there is a show on HBO all about your police department." I replied that I was familiar with *The Wire* and asked Brian whether he actually watched the show. His response seemed almost reverential, "Dad, everyone in the Marine Corps watches *The Wire.*"

Simon had done it again.

Back in 1988, when a confused command staff allowed Dave to spend a year with us, my cronies and I smirked and played with him like infants who had found a new toy in their cribs. To our delight, Dave, a youthful teetotaler, would get noticeably intoxicated after only a few measly beers. He would join us after work, perhaps hoping to glimpse homicide's Holy Grail, but eventually he realized that we merely wanted to marvel at the spectacle of someone getting drunk on three little cans of liquid.

Dave took the good-natured ribbing and soon was operating unnoticed in our midst. He became the proverbial roach on the wall, soaking it all in while we were too busy fending off murders to calculate our behavior in his presence. At first we were wary of what transpired in front of Dave. We would check ourselves, our language, even our methodology. But, after a time, we were too busy to care; the busier we got, the more he scribbled. Though we allowed him to be present during routine interviews, legal concerns sometimes precluded his being physically in the room for certain interrogations. Back then we didn't have the viewing portals and microphones now common in every police department's interview rooms. We learned to open the door slowly, to avoid smashing Dave in the face. He would listen through cracks in the door frame, and he had excellent hearing, judging by how accurately he would later chronicle entire interrogations. When *Homicide: A Year on the Killing Streets* came out, we were gratified by how clearly Dave had captured the controlled chaos that permeates every urban homicide unit: the roller-coaster tempo of some investigations, the frustrations, the triumphs, the steady stream of unfathomable violence.

The now-sobered command staff reacted to the groundbreaking work by inquiring of the department's legal adviser whether we could be charged with conduct unbecoming an officer. Cooler heads prevailed and no charges were brought, though many of us watched our performance evaluations drop like lead weights in a polluted pond. But then came the NBC series based on the book and Dave's time with us was seen in a more positive, Hollywood-enhanced light.

We police are obsessed with describing our fellow man: Hispanic male, black male, white male, everyone categorically defined. We sit on the witness stand and say, "The black male entered through the front door, then the black male exited through the rear door," as if the black male would suddenly morph into a white or purple male if we didn't keep a close eye on things. With that acknowledged limitation, here is how I remember David Simon, as he was fifteen years ago.

He was a white guy. When he first showed up you knew, from just one glance, that no one would ever, ever, ask to substitute his urine for theirs. Though he claimed to have been a newspaper reporter before his internship with us, I couldn't verify that. I didn't remember seeing him around before, though he might have been around, and I might have looked directly at him but not remembered. He was easy not to notice. Of average height, his physique was not remarkable. Actually, it was not really a physique. There was a body there, to be sure, but it was devoid of things one normally associates with a body, like muscles. Those that did exist were cleverly hidden between bones and flesh. I never understood how a guy could carry a notepad in one hand and a pen in the other, all day long, and not have thicker arms. He had hair then, though of the wispy, not-long-for-this-world variety. It has since departed, revealing a gleaming dome, the closest hair now being eyebrows. Beneath those brows are eyes of an undetermined color, maybe green or brown. It all comes down to this:

"White male, six foot, 170, bald, poorly dressed, puzzled expression, reeking of beer, tattered notebook in possession, last seen . . ."

For me, one of the more poignant passages from *Homicide* was Donald Waltemeyer straightening the clothing of an overdosed junkie to make her more presentable just before her husband arrived to identify her remains. Dave called it a "small act of charity" and it was vintage Waltemeyer. I was Donald's sergeant for a long time and never fully understood him, but I respected him immensely.

Waltemeyer and I traveled twice to a rural corner of Indiana. An arsonist had set a fire there, killing his girlfriend and her two young children. He then made his way to Baltimore, set another fire, got caught, and felt compelled to confess his earlier crime to his transvestite cell mate, who immediately called us. We flew out for the preliminary hearing, but when the actual trial came around, Donald, a noted claustrophobic, argued for a road trip. The pink Cadillac he rented was wine colored, he claimed.

One morning, as we ate in a diner, several locals stopped to ask whether we were the detectives from Baltimore and to thank us. We were happy to be appreciated and Donald, beaming, related his surprise that people knew who we were. As the Cadillac loomed just beyond the plateglass window I reminded Donald that we were in a tiny, conservative town, hanging out with a transvestite and cruising around in a pink Cadillac. He chewed thoughtfully and replied, "I told you, it's wine colored."

Donald's passing saddened us all.

The job has changed some over the past fifteen years. The so-called *CSI* effect has raised juror expectations to unreasonable levels and become the bane of prosecutors everywhere. There is more witness intimidation, and, not surprisingly, a corresponding reduction in citizen cooperation. Gangs have discovered Baltimore. The drug problem has not abated. There are fewer dunkers and more whodunits. On the positive side, there are epithelial cells. (I love to say that word.) They exploded onto the scene just a few years back, like some wonder drug, spurred by advances in collection methods and the general march of DNA analysis. You can mask your face, wash your hands and throw your gun in the harbor, but you can't keep your skin from shedding DNA. Yet, in the overall scheme of things, those changes are minor and the job remains much as it was when captured by David Simon. It is all about crime scenes, interviews, and interrogations, played out against a backdrop of flawed humanity.

It always will be.

Terry McLarney
Lieutenant, Homicide
Baltimore
May 2006